Praise for *The Odyssey of Phillis Wheatley*

"Biographies of poets can veer into dry territory. Waldstreicher's text feels like a series of narrative enjambments: Each page bleeds into the next with a tantalizing sense of discovery as the author pulls into better focus a short, brilliant life lived in an era of opaque conflict."

—Andrew Dansby, *Houston Chronicle*

"[An] expansive new biography . . . *The Odyssey of Phillis Wheatley* is a rich and necessary book." —Farah Jasmine Griffin, *Oprah Daily*

"A fascinating and provocative account of [Wheatley's] life and work."

—Glenn Altschuler, *Florida Courier*

"[Waldstreicher] places Wheatley squarely in her times and shows how she navigated them . . . Waldstreicher vividly re-creates Wheatley's Boston . . . His portrait of colonial-era slavery is chilling, and he makes expert use of documents to show its cruelty."

—Mary Ann Gwinn, *Star Tribune* (Minneapolis)

"Magisterial . . . Waldstreicher excels at teasing out the subtle political messages within Wheatley's poetry . . . The historical scholarship dazzles and the incisive analysis of Wheatley's poetry suggests she had a more 'liberatory political agenda' than she's often credited for. The result is an indispensable take on an essential early American poet."

—*Publishers Weekly* (starred review)

"Prodigy-poet Phillis Wheatley launched a complexly creative and courageous life of strategic dissent that has never before been so fully illuminated . . . Waldstreicher zestfully establishes an intricately detailed context for his in-depth analysis of Wheatley's experiences and writings . . . Waldstreicher's engrossing restorative biography makes one hope for a *Hamilton*-style celebration of Wheatley's profound quest." —Donna Seaman, *Booklist*

Paula Vlodkowsky

DAVID WALDSTREICHER

THE ODYSSEY OF PHILLIS WHEATLEY

David Waldstreicher teaches history at the Graduate Center of the City University of New York and is the author of *Slavery's Constitution: From Revolution to Ratification* and *Runaway America: Benjamin Franklin, Slavery, and the American Revolution*. He has written for *The New York Times Book Review*, the *Boston Review*, and *The Atlantic*, among other publications.

THE ODYSSEY OF
PHILLIS WHEATLEY

THE ODYSSEY OF
PHILLIS
WHEATLEY

A POET'S JOURNEYS
⇜ THROUGH ⇝
AMERICAN SLAVERY AND INDEPENDENCE

DAVID WALDSTREICHER

PICADOR / FARRAR, STRAUS AND GIROUX

New York

Picador
120 Broadway, New York 10271

Printed in the United States of America
Originally published in 2023 by Farrar, Straus and Giroux
First paperback edition, 2024

The Library of Congress has cataloged the Farrar, Straus and Giroux
hardcover edition as follows:
Title: The odyssey of Phillis Wheatley : a poet's journeys through American
  slavery and independence / David Waldstreicher.
Description: First edition. | New York : Farrar, Straus and Giroux, 2023. |
  Includes bibliographical references and index.
Identifiers: LCCN 2022053331 | ISBN 9780809098248 (hardcover)
Subjects: LCSH: Wheatley, Phillis, 1753-1784. | African American women
  poets—Biography. | Poets, American—Colonial period, ca. 1600-1775—
  Biography. | Slaves—United States—Biography. | African American
  poets—Biography. | LCGFT: Biographies.
Classification: LCC PS866.W5 Z88 2023 | DDC 811/.1 [B]—dc23/eng/20221110
LC record available at https://lccn.loc.gov/2022053331

Paperback ISBN: 978-1-250-32173-2

Our books may be purchased in bulk for promotional, educational, or
business use. Please contact your local bookseller or the Macmillan
Corporate and Premium Sales Department at 1-800-221-7945, extension 5442,
or by email at MacmillanSpecialMarkets@macmillan.com.

For book club information, please email marketing@picadorusa.com.

picadorusa.com • Follow us on social media at @picador or @picadorusa

1   3   5   7   9   10   8   6   4   2

To Maya Robinson Waldstreicher,
Moses Henry Waldstreicher,
and their new world

CONTENTS

Eight pages of images follow page 230.

AUTHOR'S NOTE

The term "black" was used relatively infrequently in late eighteenth-century Anglo-America. "Negro," which is no longer used in contemporary English, was used at least as often. Neither term was capitalized, even though many nouns and adjectives were (inconsistently) capitalized.

In her poems and letters, Phillis Wheatley employed neither of these terms, both of which had negative and stereotypical implications when used by those who increasingly called themselves "white." She regularly used "African" in referring to herself and others, and sometimes the less common word "sable" to refer to skin color, as a modifier for "race," which she used to refer to nations more often than phenotypes. Wheatley preferred "African" and "sable" for political reasons: their use over and against "black" or "negro" pushed back against a rising tide of racism in her lifetime. In other words, she used "African" for some of the reasons that many today value and capitalize the term "Black."

In deference to Wheatley, and to call attention to the changing and politicized signifiers of identity to which Wheatley responded, I use "black" sparingly, in reference to how Wheatley's white contemporaries described Africans and their descendants or when it is clear I mean those people for whom we now use "black" or "Black" retrospectively, and do not capitalize. But when I am referring to nineteenth-, twentieth-, and twenty-first-century persons who identified as Black and used the term when referring to themselves and/or to Wheatley, as in the last chapter of the book, I then capitalize.

THE ODYSSEY OF
PHILLIS WHEATLEY

THE BEGINNINGS, THE TABLE, THE TALE

Everyone around Boston knew about the storm at the end of August 1767. They knew what could happen in gales "on the back of Cape Cod." Still, even after years in the coastal trade, the Nantucket merchants Hussey and Coffin had rarely felt such winds. By the grace of God, their schooner and their whale oil had made it safely to a Boston wharf, and they had returned to the fine house of their fellow trader John Wheatley.

The girl came with bowls, with bread. She did not sit at the table, but she listened.

The Wheatleys already knew about her ear. The girl had some sort of gift. John's wife, Susanna, and their daughter, eighteen-year-old Mary, who had a twin brother but no living sisters, had taught her to read English. It wasn't hard. Soon after they purchased her off the slave ship *Phillis* in 1761, they had noticed her "endeavoring to make letters upon the wall with a piece of chalk or charcoal." Four years later the twelve-year-old penned an impressive letter to a Mohegan missionary who had stayed in their home. She had also written elegies about the deaths of respected men and verse appeals to lapsed Christians that the Wheatleys showed to their friends and neighbors.

The poem Phillis began to write soon after that dinner, the first she published, addressed the near wreck and the Nantucket merchants. The occasion was standard stuff, especially in Massachusetts. Almost half a century earlier an even younger Bostonian, the twelve-year-old apprentice named Benjamin Franklin, had published a ballad broadside about a capsized rowboat and the drowning of a family and their enslaved man. Less conventionally, Phillis addressed Hussey and Coffin directly in her poem. She asks rhetorical questions about their peril: "Did Fear and Danger so perplex your Mind, / As made you fearful of the Whistling Wind?" It's not a dialogue: she doesn't quote their answers. She speaks of them, about them, to some larger purpose. They may be the subjects, along with the awesome elements, but the voice is clearly hers.

It isn't hard to imagine why the survivor of a slave ship could identify with another terrifying voyage, with voyagers who wondered whether the punishing winds were themselves alive ("Was it not Boreas knit his angry Brow / Against you?") and whether the stormy emotions of gods would doom or deliver, save or destroy. But enslaved girls were not encouraged to speak of those voyages. She begins riskily, then, as well as suddenly, in the gales and the waves, throwing us into the action aboard the boat: How did these older men, these merchants, *feel*? She invokes fear twice. Did they fear so much that even the wind seemed alive? Or, as experienced shippers, did their "Consideration," a double entendre meaning both thought and money, enable them to stay calm, to rationalize how the winds, like God, give as well as take?

Apparently not. Or it isn't for her to speculate on merchantmen's considerations. She returns to the trope of threatening deities: another wind god, Aeolus, was angry, haughty, frowning. She backs off: she depersonalizes, in a classical idiom that to modern readers has seemed so off-putting, so scholastic, so *white*. She reaches back to maritime cultures of the Greeks and Romans and the most popular of the neoclassical texts translated by the most ambitious English poets of the previous two generations.

Her first readers in print, in *The Newport Mercury* of December 21, 1767, and *The Boston Post-Boy* three weeks later, would have understood instantly. These lines are literally evocative of Homer's *Odyssey* and Virgil's *Aeneid* in their popular English versions. *The Odyssey* begins with a call to the muses to sing of Odysseus's "unnumber'd toils" on "stormy seas." In Alexander Pope's translation, the ghost of Agamemnon asks similar questions to the ghost of Amphimedon, one of the suitors slain by Odysseus: "What cause compell'd so many, and so gay, / To tread the downward, melancholy way? . . . did the rage of stormy Neptune sweep / Your lives at once, and whelm beneath the deep?" The storm-tossed voyages in Homer are also accompanied by questions about the gods' intentions.

Greeks, Romans, Britons, Africans. Can they be similar? What might this mean? Did she mean it literally—did she believe in these gods of the sea, like a pagan, an ancient? Phillis Wheatley could be talking about herself, imagining herself into the world of the poem—as storm-tossed victim or hero, as voice of the dead, as vessel of the gods. More important, she takes control of the references, the presence of the ancient, for the reader of the newspaper who could not have missed that the poem had been written by a "Negro Girl." The preface stresses her race. The poem itself places Africa, and her, in a shared ancient world that is at once past and present, a place where even she can speak with authority.

The boldness of address, the claim to share the ancient world on equal terms, is hidden by the seeming imitation, the classical references. But not enough—not nearly. Having established her classical propers, Phillis switches registers. The pagan deities are a metaphor: "Regard them not." A Christian salvation is at stake. If Hussey and Coffin had perished in the sea, "where wou'd they go? where wou'd be their Abode? / With the supreme and independent God, / Or made their Beds down in the Shades below"? Christians and Africans, like ancient Mediterraneans, believed in another world where the dead reside. They also equally believed in revelations. The poetic narrative returns to another tradition, at once classical and Christian, and especially important in early modern Western Christendom: the good death, to be preferred to the godless life full of fear. Are they saved? Are they going down—or up?

All depends on their faith, and who does the asking and the telling. Presented as the pious effort of a precocious slave and published in a newspaper, it's a Christian exhortation that demonstrates spiritual equality. Yet the salvation project presumes a Greek, Roman, and African world of shipwrecks, slaving, and women, a set of experiences analogous to the world she had known, the stories she couldn't tell to the enslavers who provided the pen and the paper on which she wrote. The classical revival provided her with a way of talking about her experience as an enslaved woman without talking about it directly. In Homer, the traffic in women is perfectly ordinary and yet akin to the original sin: a rupture that makes and unmakes the world. It is the job of the poet to knit the world back together, and maybe free herself in the process, like the singer at the end of *The Odyssey* who receives a pardon, perhaps because, in the end, he is as indispensable as the hero.

This story of Phillis Wheatley's odyssey takes its cues from what she brought to the table, including the books and newspapers she rewrote into overt and controversial arguments for freedom. It traces her remarkable journey from West Africa to Boston to London and back to America on the eve of the American Revolution. She published the first book in English by a person of African descent and the third book of poetry by a North American woman. The book's existence became an antislavery argument, and so did some of her poems. Despite being only nineteen years old at the time, Wheatley shaped her book's publication and reception. She gained her freedom as a direct result of that project. She was the only black person to elicit personal responses from the likes of Lord Dartmouth, Benjamin Franklin, George Washington, and Thomas Jefferson. Their public responses mattered because of how the problem of slavery had already come to be part of the imperial controversy. She became, in other words, a political actor as well as an artist and a celebrity. She was an inspired participant in the new movement against slavery and the most famous African in North America and Europe during the era of the American Revolution.

This book started to take shape when I began to wonder what it might mean to take Wheatley's interest in classical poets like Homer and Horace and their descendants in the neoclassical literature of the seventeenth and eighteenth centuries seriously. First I had to get past some of my own preconceptions and be able to read those old books, to see them as oddly familiar stories and as poems—to experience them as both wild and formulaic. Despite (or because of) my background in the study of U.S. history and culture, for me this was something like a conversion experience.

But the fundamental leap that has guided my writing of her story happened years before, when I asked my skeptical Temple University students to consider the possibility that she was one of them: a product of profound, complex historical forces who did not give in to an oppressive culture merely to win prizes as a poster child for literacy. In the classroom, sometimes this can be done just with a shift of tone, of presumption: When we read the lines "Remember, *Christians*, *Negros*, black as *Cain*, / May be refin'd, and join th' angelic train" in a mocking or satirical instead of a beseeching voice, Wheatley can suddenly become the organic intellectual of the enslaved—at least a "distant relative" if not a "soul sister." To sustain that perspective, though, it helps to know more about what she had to work with as well as what she was up against. We have to recover the drama of her life and times so that her poems can appear as what they were: actions in that drama.

The epic poets Wheatley loved, like John Milton and Alexander Pope, sometimes prefaced chapters of their book-length verses with statements of "The Argument," by which they meant, fascinatingly, not a theological or political disquisition but rather nothing more or less than the main, broadest lines of the story that might otherwise get lost in all the characters and allusions and subplots. So here's mine. Wheatley used what was available and gave (what seemed to later generations to be) rather unpromising materials subversive *and* productive meanings. In the process she became a political actor and an artist of quality and note. She channeled and redirected as well as created. To put it another way: she's Homer and Odysseus *and* the slaves and the women they knew or imagined. She aimed for the universal without forgetting who was suffering most and why: a message surely for our times as well as for all times.

She's also, distinctively, of the eighteenth-century Atlantic world and its obsessions, of a culture and politics shaped by profound neoclassical, Christian, and wartime British nationalist revivals. Literate people in Phillis Wheatley's world—the vast majority of the New Englanders she knew, and some if not most of the Africans—knew that the battles of the present, including the political struggles over Britain's empire that eventually turned some Britons into Americans, were undertaken in the idioms of the secular (Mediterranean and Anglo) and sacred (Jewish and Christian) pasts. All three revivals—Greco-Roman, Protestant, British American—could, and did, challenge, and also justify, African slavery. All three subcultures—religious, political, and literary—could welcome her or shut her out. And indeed, all three did both, before and after her emancipation. That's what cultures do in the harsh but clarifying light of politics. The arc of this history bends both toward and away from justice.

Like the American Revolution, which led in both proslavery and antislavery directions, her story has tragic dimensions. Patrons solicited her and failed her. She didn't earn a living and she died young. Politics and war victimized Phillis Wheatley, and may have disillusioned her. But there is little reason to imagine that she had illusions of lasting fame, glory, long life, or wealth. Both representative and one of a kind—like any life, but especially the lives of artists and activists who fascinate and become lightning rods—her story tells us much about slavery, about race, and about how both were made and remade with the American Revolution. Her own history demonstrates that the

American Revolution both strengthened and limited black slavery: she helped make it so.

The subtlety and the magnitude of her poetic interventions require a contextual approach. Her biography must be literary, but because she lived in revolutionary times and did not avoid controversy, it can only make sense if it is broadly cultural and political. She didn't leave the volume of documents that biographers of American revolutionaries usually rely upon. But her fame is the historian's untapped opportunity. She left not only words that were chosen with special care—clues hiding in plain sight, as poets do—but also faint footprints in the recorded lives of others. These clues require interpretation. All biographers interpret, even speculate; some admit it along the way, as I will, I hope not to the point of vitiating the importance of what we can learn about—and, just as important, from—the facts of Wheatley's odyssey. Modern scholarship about slaveries (ancient and modern, African and American), and studies of the books she read, the places she lived, and the history of the imperial controversy, have helped me to explain what she made, and remade, of her journeys "from Africa to America" and from freedom to slavery to freedom. To that extent, this is a joint exercise in history and literary criticism. Recent criticism especially has illuminated her artistry and suggested the liberatory political agenda buried in some of her poems—not just manifest, as it used to be thought, in her firstness as a black female author who regrettably chose stultifying neoclassical forms that make modern readers run from the library stacks.

But biography and history demand that we ask what she felt and experienced. Since the 1930s, writers of plays and of books for children and young adults have imagined the drama of her short life. So have, more recently, Black American poets who claim her, rightly, as an amazing and inspiring forebearer and a fellow sufferer from the sins of racism. Like the poets, I ask many questions in the pages that follow while trying to signal the evidentiary grounds on which my answers rely. We need to be open to questions we may not be able to answer with accustomed biographical certainty. We need to listen sympathetically and comparatively to several entangled cultural traditions in order to understand the life, the art, and the politics of this central, generative figure of the African diaspora and the American Revolution.

Wheatley asked, and forced others to ask, a key question of an age that thought of itself as modern and consistently measured itself against the ancient. Should hereditary, racial slavery exist in an era of enlightenment, salvation, and revolution? What could justify it? If Americans called for their British freedoms or their natural rights, what did that mean for their own slaves?

Each chapter here is about an encounter: a place or event, its facts, its personae, and her response. In each chapter memory does battle with harsh realities, especially those of war and enslavement. Each chapter is titled with a noun or nouns that eighteenth-century people modified. Wherever possible, I recur to her poetic or other written responses, because that's the best evidence we have and it's where she did her critical and fabulous work. This is a biography, and I wish it to be one that will last by being true to its quite distinctive subject. But I also write as a historian with half a lifetime's questions about the American Revolution, about slavery, and about how both have informed politics and culture in the United States. Part of Wheatley's attraction for me is in the questions she asked—even more than the answers she gave.

Wheatley's first published poem begins with five questions. These queries move from the merchants' experience to the mythical gods: they combine the practical, the spiritual, and the mysteriously allusive. A question can be a veiled statement. It can also be an invitation to begin a conversation. Given the right questions, in the right places in a revolutionary America, poems could be actions. As she wrote in an unfinished epic titled *America*, "Sometimes by Simile, a victory's won."

She tells us to begin at sea . . .

2

THE SHIP, THE TRADE, THE WARS

Before the *Phillis* landed and the seven-year-old was sold, she had at least one other name that we will never know. She would not have been the only one. There were many stories she could have told, but the New Englanders, the British people she was learning to call white, did not want to hear them.

Enslavement, the slave trade, traumatized. All the words we have for the extended process of turning people into products—"trade," "ship," "Middle Passage"—euphemized horror, and do so still. The slave trade had an effect on individuals of the sort we associate with modern wars: veterans often do not like to talk about the experience directly, especially to people who do not share it or admit their complicity.

Others, shipmates and those who had been shipped before, might have listened and done more than listen. Some have speculated that Obour Tanner, Wheatley's friend in Newport, Rhode Island—where her first poem would be published six years later—was a fellow captive on the *Phillis*. It would explain their intimacy, the length of their friendship that extended to nearly the rest of her life even though they lived in different towns. Obour and Phillis must have shared stories of families, of voyages, even before what might have become shared memories as adults. Boyrereau Brinch, who was captured in the Niger valley, taken to Barbados, and arrived in Boston just the summer before Wheatley did, remembered that Africans there "asked me many questions about my native country." They were happy to give, as well as receive, stories.

Brinch became known as Jeffrey Brace. His story was not written down and put in type until half a century later, when he was a very old man. The first published life narrative in English by an African American, a story of shipwreck and captivity in the West Indies by the Afro-Yankee sailor Briton Hammon, appeared in Boston less than a year before the arrival of Phillis in July 1761. The first brief narrative about enslavement and the Middle Passage published in English by an African, James Albert Ukawsaw Gronniosaw, appeared in England in 1772—helped along by the same network of Christian women who would help get Wheatley's *Poems on Various Subjects, Religious and Moral* into print the following year. The first extended narrative in book form, by Olaudah Equiano, became a bestseller five years after Wheatley's death. The slave narrative, so crucial in exposing what New World slavery had become, did not yet exist: Wheatley's generation created it. Our ability to know or extrapolate Wheatley's African story through firsthand testimonies is bound by the chains of enslavement, much as our ability to understand the next generation of the enslaved is indebted to their struggle against what they began to attack as a peculiar institution.

Only one story she told of her African past was recorded. It's the only story that survives of Phillis before she was Phillis, passed down in the Wheatley family to Susanna Wheatley's grandniece, Margaretta Odell, and published in her *Memoir and Poems of Phillis Wheatley* in 1834. Odell had been told that "she does not seem to have preserved any remembrance of the place of her nativity, or of her parents, excepting the simple circumstance that her mother *poured out water before the sun at his rising*." Of course this was a "simple" pagan ritual, Odell commented: perhaps, she imagined, Phillis remembered this alone because the young girl had seen it every morning and later could be reminded by the sunrise every morning. The sun rises everywhere. Mothers are always remembered. By 1834, Boston abolitionists like Odell were willing to admit trauma and family separation in the slave trade, if only gingerly when it implicated their own families.

Still, it was Phillis's story, a story she chose to tell, striking enough to pass through seventy years of talk about their famous Phillis and a proper Bostonian sieve too. It's possible she told it to explain something she felt one morning or many mornings, something she or another woman had said or done. She might have told it when she was eight or eighteen or twenty-eight, or at any or many times between. Its brevity and seeming exception as a preserved memory may mean anything or everything or nothing. It could be an authentic oral history elicited by members of a family that included Thomas Wallcut, one of New England's first antiquarians. It could be Wheatley's own most cherished, most symbolic truth, standing in for country, for culture, for family.

The story connects an African woman to her daughter, across an ocean, to the poems her daughter read: poems that described a world of war and gods, displacement and slavery, and foreigners who ask for hospitality. If she wondered, in retrospect, why her mother had anointed the ground in the morning, or why her captors and owners did not, she could also wonder why Homer invoked dawn's rosy fingers, why Aurora appears as a goddess, why heroes thanked the gods by having their slaves pour libations. *The Odyssey* begins with the most important goddess, unpropitiated, determining the action: Odysseus's shipmates, shipwrecked, ate the sun god's cattle, which moved her to call on Poseidon's wrath. In Homer's world, if not Wheatley's, anyone who could sail or board a ship could become a slave. So suppliants, from kings to commoners, remember and offer thanks to the gods.

Maybe things had not changed so much. Offering thanks, after all, was what Hussey and Coffin were doing when telling their stormy story. By 1761, when the *Phillis* crossed the Atlantic and back, seafaring had become big business, epic business, multiple entangled businesses that in Africa incentivized warfare and enslavement in ways that a reader of Homer might find familiar. The scale, the geography, and the distances were modern and yielded different, less poetic shards. Apart from the obvious, legendary dangers involved in ocean transit, conflicts over trade routes and access to slaves and raw materials often involved violent conflict as well as profits that needed to be counted and recorded on paper to be negotiated, divided up, taxed, or defended in court. All that attached to the slave trade required planning and careful record keeping. This is how the archive yields for us something unusually descriptive about the Boston ship that in 1761 brought a West African girl just old enough to have lost her front teeth.

The *Phillis* was owned by a wealthy merchant, Timothy Fitch of Brattle Street, and captained by Peter Gwinn. By 1759, Fitch was an experienced slave trader, with several ships of different sizes making what came to be called the triangular run from North America to West Africa to the Caribbean and then back home. He had enough capital under his belt, experience in the African trade, and confidence in his ongoing operation to give his ships what had become typical, neoclassical slave names: the *Pompey*, the *Caesar*, the *Phillis*. When we say that Phillis was renamed after the ship that brought her, we get it only half right. The ship itself was named after its main cargo, who were commonly given Latin names. Later, Fitch added another to his small fleet, the *Neptune*.

The traditional notion of the trade as a lean West African–Caribbean–North American trilateral underrates the complexity and chance of the enterprise. Fitch's letters reveal calculations involving multiple ships, many ports of call, and a profusion of variables, from the weather to the prices current to politics on three continents and dozens of coastlines, shaping these months-long voyages. These factors are of great importance for the light they can shine on a seven-year-old captive's West African origins and her experience as a trafficked person. Although to know what ship she came on and a little about the voyage is to know far more than we can know about most of the individuals carried across the Atlantic Ocean during the eighteenth century, it is vexing nevertheless. Even with these rare letters between the owner and his captain we cannot place her African origins in time or place in the manner we can precisely date her arrival in Boston.

In a poem Wheatley later invoked "Gambia's pleasing shores" as her native country. Gambia was not a nation then: it was a river valley, associated with what Fitch called "Senegall," the coastal portion of the larger Senegambian region—the closest and thus often first stop on the West African coast for European ships. New England rum and Virginia tobacco, both of which were carried on Fitch's ship, gave British American traders an advantage, even in French ports. In 1758, during the nearly global conflict later known as the Seven Years' War, Senegambia became even more attractive for American slavers after British forces defeated the French, taking the island ports of Gorée and St. Louis. The latter remained a British colony, making part of the coastal trade securely British.

By 1760, Senegambians had long experience with the European trade but not, by any means, the same experiences, any more than today's Americans have all had the same experience of so-called globalization. Everyone in the region could be said to be affected by the fundamental facts of their economy: European trade, in which slaves played an important role, shaped lives to a similar degree that trade shaped the lives of colonists in Boston or indigenous people in Iroquoia or the Ohio River valley. In the interior of Africa and America, alliances and wars remade states and empires in response to the new European markets for exotic goods and enslaved labor. West Africans didn't usually sell their own slaves: they sold people who were kidnapped, captured in war, or convicted of crimes. But slaves, like land in North America, had become a very marketable commodity and the one most available to freelancing young men as well as powerful states. As the market ramped up, as it did at midcentury in response to famine, so did raids and outright wars.

Since Fitch explicitly directed the *Phillis* to Senegal in November

1760, it has become tempting to state that Wheatley came direct from that modern African country or from Gambia. But she could have been taken or retaken at a number of West African ports. Like many a manager then and now, Fitch gave complex, almost contradictory directions to his captain in the hopes of minimizing his risk and maximizing his return. An ideal voyage would allow the captain to stop first at the "factory" or fort and "sell the whole of your Cargo thare to a Good Proffett & take Slaves & cash & Cum Directly Home that would shorten the Voyage Much." Yet "this is not Very Likely to be the Case." Fitch had advertised previous captives as hailing from a farther distance, the Windward Coast. "Make the best Trade you Can from place to place," he bade his captain, hoping he'd dispose of all the barrels of rum and other goods in the hold first, then substitute slaves destined for one or another Caribbean port. What mattered was transporting a full cargo: "Young Slaves[,] Slaves which I sopose wil be about 70 or Eighty More or Less [in total]." Fitch wanted slaves healthy, he wanted "as fiew women & Girls as possible," but a full cargo was a full cargo, cruel yet efficient, so worth the wait—or the bargains made—to the owner. Smaller vessels would be dispatched upriver to make smaller sales, and maybe smaller slave purchases in exchange. Rice and water had to be bought too, for the ten-week voyage west. Everything depended upon supply and the terms of trade along the hundreds of miles of African coast, as well as in places like Jamaica, Antigua, and Barbados.

Phillis's age and sex make it likely that she was from a coastal region, where children were sometimes pawned by their own families— used as security for loans or fulfillment of some kind of deal. When the deal went wrong or had to be adjusted, as it often did, the security could be split or sold. Numerous members of elite families found themselves sold and transported in this way. Others were kidnapped outright. Despite being prized at home, women and children were increasingly enslaved as trade goods became more desired and trade itself became a way to make and preserve livelihoods and kin groups. The more traditional forms of enslavement in Africa and the newer, more market-oriented forms converged. Export and local markets for slaves ultimately reinforced each other, and children became more vulnerable because easier to capture, assimilate, and trade. Ultimately, women, girls, and boys outnumbered the grown men shipped to the Americas. During the time of Wheatley's enslavement, a full third of the captives from Senegambia were children according to their European buyers' definition. It is unlikely that the initial sale or sales of the little girl who became Phillis Wheatley were a result of primordial African traditions, much less a lack of concern for children's lives; it was more likely a response to harsh cycles of trade and war, the local instances of the globalizing trends of her lifetime.

Those in Britain and America who wanted to justify the slavery of dark-skinned people in the Americas as it expanded again in the 1750s did so by saying that Africans enslaved each other. This conflated the Atlantic economy's racial slavery with "African" traditions. It was always more complicated than that. A European observer in the 1730s had noted that while Africans would not sell their families' slaves, enslavement and sale were becoming the legal punishment for every crime. Africans kept Europeans literally at bay—and African land off the market—by selectively adapting their cultures and economies and polities to the imperial visitor-traders from the West. The Diola people in Senegambia and the Fante developed new rituals to propitiate the spirits of slave trade victims—the kin and countrymen and -women who would otherwise haunt them.

The Muslim societies in West Africa followed similar trajectories. Islamic revivalists in the Sahel and interior Senegambian region fought against other peoples known as slave raiders. At the same time, the newly popular yet embattled religion gave its adherents more reason to war and enslave others, not their off-limits fellow Muslims. In reaction, some Muslim reformers began to argue that slavery was always, always wrong—much as Quakers were doing in the northern Atlantic, energized in part by the all too apparent sins of a proliferating marketplace and another series of brutalizing wars.

Wheatley could have been born into a Muslim family, or traded into one, and as a result have been literate (in Arabic) before being taken from her first or subsequent home. That would certainly explain the marks she made on the Wheatleys' walls and her quick appreciation of the possibilities of learning. Her age, if not her sex, however, makes it less than likely, as does the contemporary refusal to sell fellow Muslims except for "exceptional wrongdoing." Mature men were the prime captives from the interior; they drew higher prices and were more likely to be sold off before the ship returned all the way to Boston. Children were most likely to end up in the northern British colonies after more stops: what perhaps began as a supply factor became, ultimately, something of a preference or bargain.

Yet if Phillis did not have an Islamic literacy and cosmopolitanism, she likely acquired other kinds of knowledge of the world from the trade. She may have traveled far from home even before arriving in a West African port, and then she could have also seen Caribbean ports. A significant portion of the seven-year-old's life may have been spent in temporary places—in transit, among peoples of many nations—before she arrived in Boston.

In 1760, fitting out the *Phillis* for a winter departure, Fitch told Captain Gwinn to avoid staying in West Africa beyond May 11. "Bad consequences" would follow: slaves and sailors would sicken; the hull would rot. Nevertheless, despite the persisting war in Europe, the Atlantic, and the colonies, which had raised ship insurance rates, the spring venture must have gone reasonably well. Word arrived that the market for slaves was booming. Fitch sent Gwinn in the *Phillis* again, in November, to be trailed by the schooner *Pompey*. This time he suggested that the captain sell the *Pompey* for even more "Prime Young Boy Slaves" in the seller's market; 100 to 110 could be bought with the rum at current prices and could fit, somehow, in the *Phillis*, he predicted. He expected even more trade in "town" after another important British victory. Once again it was hurry up, but buy "as few Girl Slaves as Possible." Prices were good enough on the North American mainland for Fitch to suggest a few new strategies: selling the longboat to buy a few more "Prime" men, or a stop in Philadelphia, New York, or New Jersey, "where I hear there is no Duty on Slaves."

There were other reasons not to tarry at Gorée. Senegambian voyages did not stay long in port at midcentury, if only because of a high ratio of shipboard revolts there. Fitch had registered this reality by telling Captain William Ellery in 1759 to make "good use" of his "Guns and men" if necessary and to keep the slaves "well Secured." "Keep good Watch," he wrote the next year, "that you May Not be Cutt of[f] by your Own Slaves" or a raid by locals via small boats, "which has often ben the Case."

Still this voyage did not culminate to Fitch's satisfaction. Ninety-six people from the continent left on the *Phillis*, including the girl who became Phillis Wheatley. Only between seventy and eighty survived to become Africans in the Americas, even though the ship was not as crowded as others. This surely had something to do with how long the slaving and trading took, as well as the embarking condition of the victims. For the next year's voyage, which netted 118, Fitch wrote to Gwinn contradicting himself more than ever, yet in the process he revealed something about the previous run and thus Phillis's imprisoned shipmates: "As you'll be very Earley upon the Coast you are not to take any Children & Especilley Girls, if you Can avoid it by any means, & as fiew Woman as Possible, & them Likely." His protest makes it clear that Fitch must have been disappointed when Captain Gwinn arrived in Boston with at least one sickly young girl: "Take no Slave on Board that has the [Least] defect, or Sickly as you will be Early & have a Choice well assorted & Good Cargo, make no Doubt you'l be able to Pick Your Slaves. I had Rather you would be Two Months Longer on the Coast then to Bring off Such a Cargo as Your Last, which were very small & the meanest Cargo I Ever had Come." The possibly disproportionate number of women and children in this Middle Passage may also be suggested by the scolding Gwinn received the following year for not keeping his "small arms" in good working order during the last voyage. Girls and women, kept separate from the enslaved men, were usually not chained or considered likely to seize weapons and attack crewmen. New England's newspapers regularly reported such shipboard revolts wherever they occurred.

Fitch described war and slave revolts as exceptions to be avoided. But in referring to unusually rusty armaments, he gives away that organized violence was the shopworn rule of the trade. By the time Phillis arrived at Boston aboard a ship on which between ten and twenty-six Africans died, she would have seen death and privation on both sides of the Atlantic. The first stories she heard, and told, might well have been of mourning.

Hers was a world of war. She experienced what British people came to understand as a new kind of world war, one that was about access to colonies and trade. Lawrence Henry Gipson, the great historian of the British Empire during this period, referred to the misnamed Seven Years' War or French and Indian War as the Great War for the Empire because it ranged so far, including Africa and Asia. This war lasted longer than seven years, it started over North American colonies, it shook Europe, and it provided the timing for the largest and most successful slave rebellion that the British Empire had seen, in the crown jewel of Jamaica. The Brits were first battered in North America and western Europe but then victorious at sea. As disruptive as this Great War had been by 1761, it also stimulated the African trade and helped merchants further integrate and rationalize their economic activities in the Caribbean and Africa. It gave imperial overlords new colonies to manage and new ideas about how to govern their costly, increasingly profitable, yet controversial empire. The 1761 voyage of the *Phillis* probably disappointed its owner, but that seems to have led him to send the next ship out more quickly. Peter Gwinn was still sailing to Africa six years later when a different set of uncertainties about trade and empire exploded in Boston's streets.

Worlds continued to converge. African men with military training, often the products of expanding empires in Africa, spread a tradition of rebellion through the Atlantic. Women sometimes participated, but also created another, related tradition, in West Africa and the British Caribbean, as poets who represented, and often glorified, male authorities. Bardic women could be "key allies" of rulers, celebrating them publicly, explaining the social order, and exhorting warriors before battle. Women also sang, testified, and wailed—or what Europeans heard as wailing—to pour out their own grief or communicate to spirits. Death rituals became even more important in an age of war and slaving. Some aspects of the girl child's knowledge of how to be in the world, how to relate to others, how to survive and even thrive amid strangers, might, indeed, translate in an Atlantic world caught up in more trade, more profit, more war, and more slaving.

These facts of war, death, and slaving would have been more important to the girl who became Phillis Wheatley than any notion of Africa. Africa was a continent, not a country or a people, and only beginning to become an identity—in the slave trade and the Americas. Slavery thrived and expanded in West Africa and elsewhere—there because elsewhere—and she might not have initially understood slavery as the racializing, and exceptional, juggernaut it had become, most obviously in the Caribbean and the southern mainland of America, places she would hear more about, but later. It is more likely she and other captives aboard the *Phillis* perceived slavery, initially, as something closer to a widely shared worldly fate: a risk, if not a universal risk, in a world of war and traffic in persons.

It was America that was the question: it was what kinds of slavery the New World, and the different parts of it, knew. It remained to be seen, by the dozens of women, men, and children on a schooner in the Atlantic that dodged privateers and blustery winds, what kind of slavery they would know, and what kind of kin they might find, or make.

3

THE TOWN, THE FAMILIES, THE YOUTH

She arrived "slender" and "frail," "suffering from change of climate," shivering in "a quantity of dirty carpet." These physical descriptions are all we have. Neither version of the legend of Phillis's arrival written down by Susanna Wheatley's descendants pauses to wonder what it might have been like emotionally for a seven-year-old girl who probably didn't know much English to be bought on a wharf and brought to the center of bustling Boston.

Boston was small, an eighteenth-century walking city, more than half-ringed by wharves. It housed about fifteen thousand and five hundred souls: small for England, but crowded for the colonies. It was large enough, busy enough, important enough to its hinterland to support four newspapers. In 1761 the real news not only came in ships; that news was *of* ships: battles fought by sea in the Seven Years' War; vessels, departing and arriving with the goods that would make their way into ubiquitous shops and into the advertisements that, more than subscriptions, kept the printers' weekly four-page ventures afloat. One regular feature was a list of ships arrived, "cleared," departed. Often half of those ships were headed for Caribbean islands, New Englanders' most reliable and most important trading partners. Some ventured to other mainland colonial ports, some to England, a few to Europe. Occasionally, more often after the wartime capture of Gorée, they left for or returned from West Africa.

The arrival of the *Phillis* was expected, but a slaver direct from Africa did not put in every week or every month (though two more did that month, eight in all that year). Whether she heard by word of mouth or responded to the ads that appeared in the Boston papers by July 13, Susanna Wheatley wasn't wasting time. She was fifty-three, a woman with twin eighteen-year-olds, Mary and Nathaniel. She had buried three other children—a seven-year-old younger daughter most recently, and her own and her husband's namesakes before that. So she not only went to the pier where the *Phillis* had docked but "went on board herself." She wanted "a domestic," one she would train herself "by gentle usage" to take care of her in her old age. Something about the frail one "crouched down upon the ships deck" got her attention, "enlisted her sympathies." Her "interesting features," her "humble and modest demeanor," made Phillis special despite her dubious physical condition. Not a lark, but rather a bargain: "Owing to the frailty of the child, she procured her for a trifle, as the Captain had fears of her drop[p]ing off his hands, without Emolument by death."

It took weeks to sell so many young Africans. There had been another large shipment three weeks before, along with an ad for the "parcel of likely NEGRO Slaves," to be had at the Long Wharf, still advertised in the same newspapers that announced the enslaved cargo of the *Phillis*. There would be another ship from Africa the following week. After two weeks, some or all of those left aboard after Phillis's departure with Susanna Wheatley were advertised for sale at John Avery's house and distillery "near the South Market," on the third-of-a-mile-long wharf. Gwinn and Fitch offered their "parcel of Likely Negroes, imported from Africa, cheap for cash, or short Credit" (clarified, in another paper, as "Credit with Interest"). They were willing to exchange "small Negroes"—women and children—for "any Negro Man strong and hearty, tho not of the best moral character, which are proper subjects of transportation," meaning of greater value in the plantation zones where Gwinn's boat, or another trader's, would venture sooner or later. With this ad, readers were reminded that whatever their pretensions to form "moral character," citizens of the commonwealth had long participated in far-flung markets for Native and African war captives. Bostonians were far from the most active traders, but they were as discriminating about the people they bought and sold as they were famously so regarding other marketed items.

Buying and selling: that is some of what Phillis would have seen in her ride from dockside. Mrs. Wheatley did not require a bargain, at least not for the sake of funds, in her purchase of the sick-looking yet charming child. John Wheatley was a successful merchant and tailor for gentlefolk with a shop in King Street, one of the widest streets in town, a "central corridor" with brick structures leading to the Old Colony or State House and, on the other side, to Queen Street. On its water end King Street met the Long Wharf, a man-made structure with warehouses that, on all the maps, extended farther out into the bay than King Street did into town.

Brick houses adorned this prestigious, "fashionable" address in a city still built mostly of wood. Location meant much. Even the businesses on King Street took on grander names, like the Royal Exchange Tavern, which had a well-known namesake in London. In the Great Boston Fire of March 20, 1760, which obliterated 10 percent of the city households, the Wheatleys had suffered enough property damage to receive a £300 payment. A century later their house was remembered as a "hospitable mansion" staffed by "a few slaves who had grown old in service." Wheatley's shop sold, among other things, tea, rice, fish, turpentine, wine from Portugal, and candles made from whale oil: quintessential goods of a British seaborne empire that had as much to do with crossings by sea as with fertile North American land. The house and the goods within were not their only property either. John Wheatley had title to warehouses and real estate in Union Street. He owned a sloop, the *London Packet*, and ventured in whaling supplies with Joseph Rotch of the prominent Nantucket whaling family.

Then there was the carriage in which Phillis rode home, making a spectacle for her and perhaps of her, too. Six years later, only twenty carriages were counted in town for tax purposes. Thirteen of these belonged to suburbanites, so the carriage ride that went down in family lore might have been a smaller "chaise" not mentioned in tax lists, but that still had its luxuries in a walking town. At a time when many of their peers were leaving for cheaper, less congested locales outside town limits, the Wheatleys were lifers. They were aging, but they lived where they made their money, at the center of things, and at their age they expected to be driven around town. Life on the ocean meant attention to the minutiae of trade, of prices and ships, of local supply and demand. When the fire had raged in 1760, it consumed as many shops, like that of John Wheatley, as it did homes. Even the governor of Massachusetts complained: "At present every merchant is a shopkeeper and every shopkeeper a merchant." That made slave traders of many, amid a boom-and-bust economy that could shift, literally, with the winds and with the tides.

Historians used to debate the economy of Boston in the 1750s and 1760s, the distress felt by its inhabitants, and its impact on the coming of the American Revolution. The long-term trends suggest that the rich got richer, the poor poorer in the eighteenth century—especially by the 1750s. Bostonians had reason to put their hopes for better times in another imperial war, and they also had reason to resent the results during the extended postwar depression. But Phillis arrived and was purchased during an unparalleled wartime boom. Prime Minister William Pitt had decided to fund the North American war, to fight it vigorously on the waters, and to reimburse American expenses. As in earlier imperial wars, Massachusetts contributed not only ships but men—more than any other colony. The ensuing labor shortages and public spending led to higher expectations and, after an initial lull, a mini-spike in slave imports, including voyages direct from Africa. There were some signs of a coming downturn during the summer of 1761, but not enough to dissuade the three African voyagers from putting into port.

The casual reader of one of the four Boston newspapers would have noticed the profusion of goods for sale. These goods included slaves, sometimes in the same advertisement. In the issue of the *Boston Post-Boy* that carried the ad for the slave shipment that preceded the *Phillis*, the provincial lawyer Benjamin Prat, just appointed to an ill-fated judgeship in New York, offered "A Convenient Pew in King's Chappel, and a likely Negro Man." The African enslaved population of Boston had risen significantly with the expanded Caribbean trade, especially during the second and third decades of the eighteenth century—the youth of Benjamin Franklin. Connections of trade floated Boston's distinctive political economy. Yet trade also made them more British during these years as they produced, consumed, and played middlemen for more and more of the goods that empire brought and bought, including enslaved people.

Bostonians were as flexible, even canny, in their use of slave labor as in their other market activities. They adapted to what Atlantic war and trade made possible because they had had a hand in creating and re-creating that world. The advertisements that marketed young men and women testify to the range of work these people did. Slaves appear in the weekly papers as "Fit for town or country work," to be sold for "no fault" except "want of employ" or "want of a larger Negro," or a woman instead of a man. The active labor market was run conveniently through printers—no names, please! "Enquire of the Printer"—who passed on information through advertisements that did not mention the names of the enslaved either, shielding buyers and sellers from the possibility that literate slaves or their friends might try to affect the price or conditions of their sale.

The ads functioned as surveillance. Runaway and slave-for-sale ads were the first printed slave narratives, told by the masters. The story they tell is not one of the "carriage trade" or footmen gone saucy but rather one of thinking decisions to employ slaves' labor in many ways, creatively and profitably, while making it easier to dispose of them when their value no longer exceeded a market price. Sometimes they advertised to give away small children who got in the way of their mothers' work. Just as often, they expected hard cash, even for young children. Propertied people like Susanna Wheatley used slaves as movable property as well as a hedge for their old age. By midcentury, they appeared in one-fourth of the wills on record.

Phillis arrived in Boston at precisely the age at which some slave children in Massachusetts towns tended to be given away. This did not mean that children had no economic value. It meant that someone else decided to invest the cost of their keeping in them, in a cash-scarce economy built to conserve household labor. Bostonians knew how to size up talent and encourage it. New Englanders had relied on children and young adults for essential unpaid labor throughout the rapid development of the colony, often separating them from parents and siblings and children for the purpose. Productive households, under the oversight of patriarchs, trumped biological kinship. The New England town way proved as adaptable to slavery as it had to wartime.

The population of enslaved domestic workers developed a full range of skills that showed up in the ads when these people got put up for sale. Boston blacks worked as blacksmiths. Cooks. Shipwrights. Wig makers. Butchers. Gardeners. Tallow chandlers, who dipped candles. Glaziers, who fashioned glass. At least two young African men, Prince Demah Barnes and Scipio Moorhead, painted portraits for sale during the 1760s. Peter Fleet printed and delivered the *Boston Evening-Post*. He also cut wood engravings for Thomas Fleet's printing press. The sixteen-year-old "of an ingenious Turn, very capable of learning any Trade," placed on the market in 1762 might have ended up in any number of occupations. A "very likely Negro boy" of thirteen or fourteen "in the country about 3 or four months," as likely as not a shipmate of Wheatley's, already had "a great genius for a tradesman."

Nothing could have looked or sounded more like a particularly Boston-baked slavery. These other slave worker geniuses, driven we know not how hard, were incentivized at least as subtly and as violently as white boys at a time when young people were beaten, and beat up each other, both to build up and to break down their sense of independence. This servitude, racial but especially tough on youth, and probably tough *through* youth, dwarfed the more often remembered, sentimentalized, conspicuous forms of slavery consumption—the slave as pampered "footman." As with the imperious judge Peter Oliver, who kept "only" two slaves, one of whom, Quassia, "entertain[ed] guests with his wit." Or John Hancock, who returned from London in 1761 with a French horn for his uncle's slave, Cato.

Call it peculiarly northern or call it the common sense of the urban Americas in 1761, the mixed labor system—free, indentured, and enslaved—was in no jeopardy. By the 1750s the black population in Boston had risen above 10 percent, and quite possibly as high as the ratio in New York and Newport. The sudden influx of ships from Africa in 1760 and 1761 drove it still higher. The numbers are evident in the weekly and cumulative annual lists of mortalities the *Boston Gazette* and other papers published, always enumerated by race: in 1760, 508 whites, 68 blacks; in 1761, 448 whites, 83 blacks; in 1762, 390 whites, 66 blacks; in 1763, 344 whites, 63 blacks; in 1764, 471 whites, 77 blacks.

These rising numbers convey something that would have been extremely important to Phillis Wheatley, something that might have been at least as important as the virtues and quirks of the Wheatley family or the place of their house at the center of trade and town. She had a cohort. They were all over town. And despite the gradually emerging or sudden desire of Susanna Wheatley to develop Phillis into a great exception or experiment, the other Africans were not at all beneath her in abilities, skills, and accomplishments.

The existence of the thirteen-year-old "genius" tradesman suggests that other members of the "African wave" that came to New England during the 1750s assimilated as quickly as Phillis did. This was in part because there were many of them. One twelve-year-old boy, in the country "about a month," could already "speak English tolerably well." Who could teach him so fast? Black New Englanders lived in their masters' houses, often slept in attic spaces, and were treated as "perpetual children." But they also had each other.

Regulations tried to limit their movements, socializing, use of alcohol and public spaces with a curfew. Some were sold away, like the woman they called "ungovernable in a town family." For the enslaved, the undeniable odds against forming and keeping their own families made other kinds of relationships that much more important. The chances for manumission or self-purchase remained small. The opportunities they had in the city, the skills they could learn, made life a struggle. Not a struggle for freedom, literal or abstract, so much as for the chances to shape their everyday work and their relations with others.

Boyrereau Brinch recalled the welcome and fellowship of Boston's Africans in 1760. Others could compare notes about the ways of their masters, of the streets and wharves and meetinghouses. They were apart, yet never apart: in the household, yet never allowed to forget that they were foreign and different, in a culture that put other orphans and single people into families to work, that never mentioned their names in the newspaper without attaching a racial designation (black or negro), that more often mentioned *only* the racial designation and not even their names, even in news articles about crimes and accidents. Close, but distanced. Distanced, because close.

The results varied. What didn't vary was that they could be beaten, could be sold, could be treated as badly as any slave in the Americas. If they were not treated brutally as often, or as systematically, since like children they did have some rights to bodily safety enforceable in court and did not labor in mines or cane fields, it was still racial slavery, and nobody at the time thought otherwise even if they preferred the technically correct euphemism "servants." Chloe Spear, captured by Europeans at twelve and growing up in Boston at the same time as Wheatley, noticed the segregated seating in church and wondered how she could be expected to take an interest in the words of the Bible. Yet after she heard her master say that literacy "made negroes saucy," she took an interest anyway. Chloe paid a schoolmaster "five copper" to teach her in secret. When her master realized she could read, he took her to get baptized. Eventually, she felt a "family-like attachment."

Like a family member. In the family, but not of it. Like a daughter, but better: one who would never grow up, never leave, and might be replaced if she died.

Hannah Mather Crocker, who knew Phillis Wheatley personally, asserted that Susanna "set as much by her as if she had been her own," and that Phillis "had none but light duties put upon her." Margaretta Odell, speaking for the Wheatleys in 1834, insisted that Phillis "was not devoted to menial occupations, as was first intended; nor was she allowed to associate with the other domestics of the family, who were of her own color and condition, but was kept constantly about the person of her mistress." She "had a child's place in their house and in their hearts," Odell testified. For antislavery Bostonians of that later age, rapidly forgetting their own slaving pasts and focusing on southerly sins, real slavery meant two things: menial labor and the perversion of family bonds.

Still, there was a genuine overlap between being a slave, which we have come to understand (perhaps less than helpfully) in terms of "social death," or commodification, or non-personhood, and what became, in modern times, its polar opposite, "a child's place." The eighteenth century lies squarely in between the modern uplifting of childhood innocence and potential as the very essence of what it means to be human and to be loved and an earlier European ethos in which children were inferior, less valued people: at best, small adults; at worst, the prototypical original sinners. Moreover, servitude and apprenticeship remained fundamental institutions in eighteenth-century North America, especially for young people. In New England towns, everyone was placed in a household and expected to labor. Puritans fashioned their entire society to be familial to the point, or well past the point, of what we would call exploitation of children. This was the New

England that Benjamin Franklin ran away from. Despite their xeno-phobia, warring New Englanders had ready-made places for captives, especially young ones.

For a few generations, New England household slavery fit all too well with trends elsewhere in North America. Much more often than in the West Indies, slaves *were* children. In Virginia and the Carolinas, Anglo-American slavery became more familial and patriarchal in its very nature as more slaves survived and reproduced, as white Creole colonists began to inherit slaves and imagine themselves as the benev-olent wards of their plantation "people," whom they also called their "family." Even as imports from Africa spiked and settlers broke land for new plantations, many enslavers and enslaved entered second and third generations in the colonies. African slavery in America wasn't going to be temporary except for a very fortunate few. It was hered-itary, and it wasn't getting better. Slavery's myths evolved in the face of these twin realities. Both the myths and the realities would shape Wheatley's life despite what might seem to be the relatively good luck of landing in Boston with the Wheatleys.

In the wake of the extreme exploitation in the plantation zones and the trend toward biological reproduction that was specific to main-land slavery, doubts about American-style racialized and heritable slavery began to spread in the metropole as well as the middle and northern colonies by the 1750s. In response, some white Caribbeans and southerners began to justify slavery more explicitly as a benign patriarchy: a school for savages. These years also saw new efforts to convert indigenes, including schools to teach them literacy and Prot-estant Christianity—a project in which the Wheatleys and their kin would play a role. No one could say exactly what it meant to teach an Indian or an African to read and pray as a Christian.

While these sorts of ameliorating activities proceeded, violent or intractable slaves were sold south, like the men of supposed bad char-acter who were solicited in exchange for some of Wheatley's little and female shipmates in 1761. It was as difficult for the enslaved to have or keep a family in Boston households, where the average master had one to three slaves, as anywhere. Enslavers sold or gave away children and routinely broke up families. The desire to claim Phillis as a member of the Wheatley family presumed that she had and would have no other family that mattered. Phillis's desires took shape with an awareness of these limits.

4

THE TEACHERS

The family's legends differ on who taught Phillis Wheatley to read. John Wheatley testified in 1773 to Phillis's quickness: "Without any Assistance from School Education, and by only what she was taught in the Family, she, in sixteen Months Time from her arrival, attained the English Language, to which she was an utter Stranger before, to such a Degree, as to read any, the most difficult Parts of the Sacred Writings, to the great Astonishment of all who heard her." A grandnephew, Charles Stratford, insisted that Susanna, a "Lady of Education," could not resist: "They became at once, Teacher and Pupil." Others credited Mary Wheatley. Probably it was a family project led by the women.

While girls increasingly learned to write as well as read in New England, it remained standard to teach reading to young children well before writing. Nevertheless, Stratford wrote, "as soon as she could read well, she began to make Rhymes," probably without writing them down. "Seeing others write made me esteem it a valuable art," she said years later, in the closest thing we have to an interview with Wheatley. When asked "what put you upon writing Poetry," she responded, "Reading Rosamond, a play which was in verse Sir."

Joseph Addison's *Rosamond* (1707) was actually an experimental musical and an exercise in patriotism: Addison and others deemed the English overly enthusiastic about Italian operas. This short play reworked a legend of King Henry, his jealous queen, Eleanor, and the quite young object of his desire. It's ribald, with subsidiary section plots concerning men conned into doing their "duty" to their wives—hardly children's fare, we might think, but apparently our sense of that is still filtered through Victorian-era censorship of folk traditions. Contemporaries praised Addison for basing *Rosamond* on old English ballads and incorporating something of their style.

What's shocking or surprising to us in forgotten Augustan-age plays might not have been to a worldly, if young, Phillis. Slaves stayed up late hours, making everyone comfortable before themselves, keeping fires going, fetching and emptying vessels. They saw and heard everything. Nighttime was *their* time, an "alternative reality" for servants. In the course of explaining the Wheatleyan muse and her family's role in encouraging it, Odell noted that Phillis was quite active at night, so much so that Susanna eventually encouraged her to keep a candle burning and even a fire in winter.

Phillis would have understood why the plot of *Rosamond* resolves only when the "nymph" fakes taking a drug, which allows for the king and queen to address their jealousies and decide that they can pack Rosamond off to a convent instead of killing her. This then inspires the comic counterpart characters, Grideline and Sir Trusty, to behave themselves: "I'll too my plighted Vows renew, / Since 'tis so courtly to be true. / *Since conjugal Passion / Is come into Fashion, / And Marriage so blest on the Throne is, / Like a* Venus *I'll shine / Be fond and be fine, And Sir Trusty shall be my* Adonis." Despite or because of all the elders chasing youthful bodies, *Rosamond* is fundamentally about chastity and its preservation. Its importance to Wheatley—to the point of surfacing in an interview conducted by a minister who was so concerned with her faith that it reads more like a catechism—testifies to the variety of worldly experiences and influences upon her art from the beginning. It also suggests knowingness of her world and her audience, including the teachers whose desires would drive her days. Judging the motives and conflicts of men and women in their domestic spaces might be the difference between life and death—and certainly between one kind of life and others. In *Rosamond*, it's an open question between men and women, old and young, who really teaches whom.

One of Phillis Wheatley's earliest "rhymes" survives: a few lines that the young minister Jeremy Belknap scribbled in an almanac as dating from 1765, when Phillis was eleven or twelve. He called them her "first effort": this was in 1773, at the height of her fame.

> *Unto Salvation*
> *Mrs. Thacher's Son is gone ^ her Daughter too*
> * so I conclude*
> *They are both gone to be renewed*

Belknap wrote it down twice, struggling to figure out how to render the line breaks (see illustration in the photo section). In his second version it becomes a pair of couplets and begins to appear as what we would recognize as a quintessential child's or nursery rhyme (a Victorian-era term). More precisely, it resembles a great many contemporary trimeter or tetrameter hymn or ballad stanzas. When rendered as such, as below, the poem comes to seem more patterned and deliberate:

> *Mrs. Thacher's son is gone*
> *Unto Salvation*
> *Her Daughter too:*
> *So I conclude*
> *They are both gone*
> *To be renewed*

When Belknap scribbled, this was the fascinating juvenilia of a now nineteen-year-old prodigy on the verge of international fame: too ballad-like, over-reliant on rhyme to the point of seeming, to modern ears, almost joking (as well as repetitive) about the most serious of subjects.

But "Mrs. Thacher's Son" also follows conventions. It sets a stage Bostonians would have recognized. It directs us to the neighborhood as well as celestial realms. The Thachers lived a few blocks away from the Wheatleys but were members of Old South, the church down King Street that Phillis would join in 1771. Oxenbridge Thacher Jr., scion of ministers, had trained to be one but had a low voice and frail health. Well liked, he found success as a lawyer and member of the House of Representatives, arguing alongside James Otis in court against the Writs of Assistance and publishing *The Sentiments of a British American* (1764), an influential early patriot pamphlet. Calling a forty-five-year-old member of the legislature "Mrs. Thacher's son" suggests how much Phillis's world was shaped by women and their familial and neighboring relationships.

From her vantage point, it wasn't necessarily the matriarch who mattered most. Oxenbridge Thacher died of smallpox, despite being inoculated against the disease, in July 1765, a year after his wife, Sarah, succumbed. A disproportionate number of Africans died, as many as a third of those who perished in the outbreak of 1764–65. This was only the latest of a series of epidemics that had periodically taken away hundreds of people, including the children of leading ministers and merchants. In 1721–22, the controversy over smallpox inoculation as a risk to public health had actually politicized Africans' knowledge of that practice. The leading proponent of inoculation, Cotton Mather, cited his bondsman Onesimus's testimony to his immunity because of his prior inoculation in Africa, while skeptics responded with angry mockery of the "negro remedy." Giving people potentially fatal disease organisms raised questions about God's plan and the authority of ministers, at least after some of the most prominent ones in town supported inoculation. Between a succession of colonial wars and epidemics, Bostonians continued to live with sudden death despite the region having as high a life expectancy as anywhere in Europe.

As in "On Messrs. Hussey and Coffin," Wheatley inserted herself into the King Street neighborhood by seizing upon death and deliverance as common themes that linked rich and poor, women as well as men, children and adults. Perhaps the "first effort" is more representative of a series of early efforts, invocations really, applied to other mortal events. Whether taken seriously or as an attempt to lighten the mood (and Bostonians were accustomed to ballads that did both in turn), its concerns are immediate: life, death, and afterlife, while tragedy in the family could be a metaphor for church or nation.

West African women claimed distinct roles in mourning. Students of African and European deathways in eighteenth-century colonies find both a persistence and a convergence of cultures, as one might expect from people living and dying together, yet apart. When Wheatley began to compose in the elegiac mode, she could be both assimilating to post-Puritan New England and bending what was available to fit what she knew. She could even be making kin. Even if she did not imagine kinship to be possible with these neighbors, these efforts could have helped her establish something of her own by joining in communal mourning, on something more like her terms.

In church, Africans sat in a separate pew, above. In "Mrs. Thacher's Son," Phillis gets to "conclude," as she puts it in the first-person singular, that salvation has occurred. Judge Samuel Sewall, writing seventy years earlier against "the Selling of Joseph," in Boston, had buttressed his moral and religious argument against the new influx of African slaves by citing the dangers of "extravasat blood," meaning foreign peoples, in the polity. By contrast, southern masters were beginning to describe their slaves' performances of grief when masters died as prima facie evidence for the familial, domestic nature of slavery in North America. Phillis had indeed learned, quickly, more than her letters. As John Wheatley put it, she was already conversant with the knottier byways of the King James Version. She demonstrated a deep understanding of New England, of colonial culture, and of the needs of the Wheatleys, but perhaps most of all how to make them fit together with some of her own needs and desires. To be praised, cherished, made safe, she needed to praise, cherish. She needed to at least perform care, if not love.

Elegies—poems on death—would build her a public reputation within a few years. They take the central place in her *Poems on Various Subjects, Religious and Moral* (1773). Elegy is a capacious genre to which Wheatley would always return. Yet it is striking that by 1766 at the latest she was already doing much more than that. "On Virtue," the poem she identified as having written earliest of those that appear in her book, suggests an astonishingly quick maturation, even with the likelihood of revision over seven years.

From the quick end-stops of balladry or mere "rhymes," however elegiac, Wheatley had already graduated to blank verse—the form of Shakespeare and of Milton, the most popular and admired author of the era, the one who had most successfully and famously adapted classical forms and motifs to contemporary Christian ends. Even Isaac Watts, who composed the most popular hymns of the eighteenth century, lauded Milton's "Adventurous Muse," which "Shook off the chains, and built the verse sublime / A monument too high for coupled sounds to clime." An unrhymed form, blank verse might seem easier than going on and on in rhymed ballad stanzas, as Addison did, much less in iambic pentameter couplets like Alexander Pope, but it was actually less popular, associated with ambitious, lengthy, philosophical works. It was high-end, for poetry.

She begins with an admission of her immaturity: "O Thou bright jewel in my aim I strive / To comprehend thee. Thine own words declare / Wisdom is higher than a fool can reach." Self-debasement becomes a path to virtue as she reaches for the skies figuratively as well as literally. Virtue is an abstraction that can be imagined as an angel, a guiding spirit "with gentle hand" who "hovers o'er thine head," with height imagined, immediately, as both a metaphor for achievement and a heaven above. Virtue also has an assistant named Chastity, especially relevant for a thirteen-year-old girl who is in effect asking for closer assistance on earth "thro' my youthful years!"

No sooner has the poet asked Virtue to "guide my steps" in life and beyond, however, than she asks for literary help not merely in comprehending or understanding but in naming, describing Virtue. A Mosaic "what I shall call thee" returns again to poetic ambition: "Teach me a better strain, a nobler lay." The overall effect is to align piety with feminine purity, but both with artistic ends—under the light of a heavenly "queen." She's been saved, she experiences grace from above, but she's also learning how to be a poet, or a better one. The poem couldn't be holier, but it has a plotline. A "fool" is growing up, getting saved, staying chaste, and becoming a writer who may epitomize salvation, virtue, and art.

Where, how could Phillis have learned so quickly to enact the role of the heaven-inspired, Miltonic, but feminine poetic genius, beyond the oversight of enslavers? The presence of two feminine guides—wise Virtue personified and a younger (cherubic) Chastity—could have been understood, made permissible, as allegories of Susanna Wheatley's piety and Mary Wheatley's virgin purity. Either way, "On Virtue" insists upon a kind of ambition that could only have derived from an awareness of the range of possibilities that literacy in general—but poetry in particular—allowed.

These possibilities did not have to be a part of Susanna and Mary's lesson plans. Before the Romantics secularized the devotional strains and made the poet an isolated if not alienated seeker of the ineffable, poetry "invaded all forms of discourse" in the eighteenth century. Poems were "as accessible as prose" and even "drove, as well as responded to, most public conversations," even on topics like the place of servants. As Paula Backscheider writes, "Few of us would read poetry as a means of social advancement, as a source of news, or as mass entertainment, but eighteenth-century people increasingly did." During the era when Alexander Pope became a literary rock star and produced his notably profitable versions of *The Iliad* and *The Odyssey* (which came complete with plot summaries and explanatory footnotes aimed at the general reader), poetry in print—didactic, satirical, sacred, or secular— became more and more popular with a broader range of people.

By midcentury, that broader audience had turned into producers as well as consumers. These writer-readers included servants and women as well as gentlemen and would-be professionals. The number of women publishing books of poems in English doubled each decade during Wheatley's lifetime, but that does not begin to count the growing opportunities to circulate poems in manuscript and in newspapers and monthly magazines, where they would usually be presented anonymously. Some English servants and laborers managed to become known poets. The thresher Stephen Duck, the author of *Poems on Several Occasions* (1736), found patrons, went to school, and settled in a parsonage. The washerwoman Mary Collier replied to Duck's neglect of women workers—and not least their night work—with *The Woman's Labour* (1739), revised and expanded as her own *Poems on Several Occasions* in 1762. We sometimes think of this as the age of the rise of the novel and of Grub Street journalism, and it was, but many of those professionalizing authors, like the Irish outsider Oliver Goldsmith, made their London reputations with poems.

So did the characters of sentimental fiction. The dispossessed protagonist of *Pamela; or, Virtue Rewarded* (1740), Samuel Richardson's genre-defining novel, just turned fifteen and subject to a predatory master, writes a religious poem when she is denied permission to attend church. She dates letters to her parents in the time of her "bondage." Pamela's poems as well as letters to her parents demonstrate her worth to the gentleman-rake who imprisons and attempts to seduce her, but falls so in love that he turns poet too, apparently an apt symbol of his reformation.

If print, as it is said now, was the internet of the eighteenth century, it may not be too much to say that couplets were the tweets of the time, "highly transferrable," easy to read out and copy, with an "aphoristic tendency." They reflected and embodied a conversational quality, a doubleness of calls and responses, of copying and sharing, "a mobile, not to say restless mode of writing." Rather than appealing solely to the private, to the highly educated, or to committed individualists, poems punctuated the most public literatures. They showed up everywhere, from sermons to novels to political treatises. Couplets coupled with other commodities, on the same ships, in the same newspapers. Moreover, after 1750, the colonies experienced a remarkable proliferation of reading material, including spelling books. These were part and parcel of the overall expansion of consumer goods, but a set of them was received especially enthusiastically in Boston. The ads for new books in Boston newspapers of the early 1760s are almost as extensive, and impressive, as the textiles listed for sale. Or the inbound and outbound ship lists that registered the *Phillis*, five times for and five times from Africa.

Many of the books Wheatley especially admired appear in these ads, but she wouldn't have been dependent on new shipments. Ministers kept libraries and lent books. Of the seven ministers who attested to her authorship of the *Poems* in 1773, the Reverend Mather Byles has been considered most likely to have served as a literary mentor to Wheatley. This is not least because he retained and updated a collection of at least a fourth and probably more of his grandfather Increase Mather's and uncle Cotton Mather's famous library: several thousand books, which included translations of Horace and eventually Wheatley's own *Poems on Various Subjects*. Long before he became known as a well-regarded preacher and oft-quoted punster, Byles had been a prodigy who entered Harvard at fourteen, exchanged satires and mock elegies with the upstart Franklin brothers, edited the literary paper that succeeded their weekly, placed poems in London magazines and miscellanies, and cultivated a reputation as the "principal poet," even "state oracle" of his generation. He wrote fan letters to Isaac Watts and

Alexander Pope and received approving replies and gifts in kind, including Pope's translation of *The Odyssey*.

Byles liked to "battle wits" with women and also showed an interest in educating them. In 1730 he published Sarah Parsons Moorhead's poems, and after a woman wrote in to his magazine complaining of her father's hostility to learned women, Byles composed an essay of his own arguing that women's reason, memory, and judgment were as strong as those of men. Precisely because women's roles were domestic, he argued, they might have the leisure that permitted "greater liberty for speculation," a notion that befit an enlightened man in a society with slaves and servants. His daughter Elizabeth would be eulogized in 1765 as a remarkable conversationalist.

After his first wife's death in 1744, Byles published his best poems in a volume, declared himself finished with the genre, then remarried and promptly started another family that included two daughters, Mary and Catherine (Katy), who were just one and four years older than Phillis. Mary exchanged verses with her doting older half brother Mather Jr., who praised her for teaching their younger sister: he included a note for four-year-old Katy: "Don't cry because you cannot read this letter." Eight years later, twelve-year-old Katy was curating her own "COLLECTION OF POETRY taken from Various Authors." She grew up to be known as a reader and writer of verses.

Mary and Katy Byles's slightly younger cousin Hannah Mather remembered knowing Wheatley well. Her father, Samuel Mather, was another one of the eminent men who would attest to Phillis's accomplishment in the front matter of her 1773 *Poems*. Fifty years later, as a pathbreaking author herself, Hannah Mather Crocker still possessed a manuscript copy of "On Imagination," a poem Phillis had inscribed for her. She highlighted Wheatley and other women writers of earlier days in her memoir of Boston. She also jealously guarded her inherited portion of the Mather library and later donated it to the Boston Athenæum in exchange for access to other books that a scion of the

Puritan elite, if a woman, could still not take for granted, even as she was writing her *Observations on the Real Rights of Woman* (1818).

A surviving notebook begun with a "List of scholars in King Street," probably belonging to a student at a small school there sometime between 1766 and 1774, includes a girl's name along with that of five boys. Tantalizingly, the notebook includes a poem by Addison, an anonymous one taken from a Boston newspaper, and one by Phillis Wheatley, thanking an "S. P. Gallowy" for "correcting" some other poems she had shown him. Gallowy could have been a teacher, a friend or relative of one of the King Street students, or just another aspiring writer. There was no shortage of ministers and men of letters to teach, mentor, or publicize the enslaved prodigy who lived on King Street. One or more of them might have been especially important to Phillis. But they built on the foundations laid by women, and maybe girls as well. A lively, literate, poetry-loving group of children and adolescents passed in and near King Street during the 1760s. These young people, too, were Wheatley's cohort. Some of them may have taught her, shared books, or showed her how to get them. They and their teachers became her first readers.

5

THE PREACHERS

Hannah Mather, Katy Byles, and Mary Byles had something else in common that made it more likely that they would know and appreciate Phillis. They were the daughters, and granddaughters, of ministers.

Boston may have been the most literate city in the Western world. Yankee Protestants, men and women, had to be able to read the Bible. They also had to attend church (until recently, by law). In the mid-eighteenth century, admission to church membership meant writing a relation of religious experience, usually with the help of a clergyman. All this meant jobs for ministers, a college to train them, and a sacred vocation for the women who usually taught children to read. If only to make Christians, women had to have letters enough to teach letters. Mary, Katy, and Hannah had access to the thousands of books in the Mather family's collection. Old South Church, a few blocks from the Wheatleys, also had a well-stocked library of its own. Other Congregationalist ministers bought books with the specific intention of sharing them, the better to guide their charges toward the "various subjects, moral and religious," that Phillis would claim in the title of her own volume.

Of the seventeen men besides John Wheatley who signed a paper "Attestation" on the eve of publication in 1773 testifying that Phillis had written her *Poems*, seven were preachers. Figures like Mather Byles and Samuel Mather kept Congregational traditions alive even as Boston became a more open, Atlantic city and other strains of Protestantism competed more and more vigorously for congregants. These ministers take up the right-hand column (underneath the capitalized names of Governor Thomas Hutchinson and Lieutenant-Governor Andrew Oliver), with their eminence and authority indicated by "The Rev." before and their "D.D." (doctorates of divinity) after their at least locally famous names. (The left-hand column holds "Hon[orable]" judges and "Esq[uires].") In 1773, ministers still held real authority in Boston, even if the extent of that authority lay in custom and the minds of congregants more than in law.

Preachers shaped her art and her ambition from the beginning. One of the first of her poems that circulated was about the imminent demise of the Reverend Joseph Sewall, a minister whom no one in Boston could easily forget. When proposing to collect her poems in a volume for the first time, in February 1772, Phillis listed poems in the order she had written them or first shown them, probably to signal her rapid development as a writer. Before "On Virtue" and "On two Friends, who were cast away," both dated 1766, she placed "On the Death of the Rev. Dr. *Sewell*, when sick, 1765."

The septuagenarian Sewall didn't meet his maker until 1769, but he'd been quite ill in 1765. Known as an effective pastor who stressed family piety, at some point Sewall picked up the nickname "the weeping prophet." Wheatley would have seen Sewall carried in a chair up to his pulpit, still holding forth in Old South after more than fifty years. While Sewall was clearly well-liked by the Wheatley family, John and Susanna were members of New South Church rather than the nearer Old South. Phillis would choose differently, joining the Old South Church formally at the usual age of eighteen, in 1771, after a two-year delay in the settlement of a replacement for Sewall had occurred. She would ratify that choice when she was baptized by the Reverend Samuel Cooper—a grandson of Samuel and nephew of Joseph Sewall—at

Brattle Street Church, where he had been pastor since 1744. To praise Boston's leading preachers but to make her own choices among them pushed the claims that a female slave could make on membership in the covenanted community.

She also pushed the role of a poet in that community. In elegizing preachers, she took the concern for neighbors and friends who die or skirt death—Hussey and Coffin, the Thachers—and applied it to the most literally *established* men of the city. Ordinarily, women couldn't preach: they couldn't even pray out loud in Congregational churches, though some revivalists had challenged that unwritten rule. Wheatley's elegy to Sewall prays, praises, and preaches. She begins by imagining the "happy Saint" swiftly ascending to heaven, "praising with the happy dead . . . on the Immortal Shore." She voices the loss felt by the entire public, not merely his congregation: "We hear thy warnings and advice no more." The image of Sewall's ascent should inspire pious emulation of "the prophet" who "wing'd his rapturous way."

But then, there is a telling slip: a "begging for the Spirit of the Gods," forgetting the first duty of the monotheistic, if trinitarian, exercise by the young writer who was already imbibing Greek and Roman texts in translation. She returns immediately to the singular deity: "Christs Image on our minds impressd / And plant a Saviour in each glowing breast." In a subsequent surviving manuscript version she corrected this non-trinitarian "Spirit of the Gods" to "the Spirit of his God," and ultimately in the published *Poems* to "the Spirit of our God." The heavenly abodes, too, recover their Christian singularity.

The slip in the Christian voice, in other words, was probably unintentional, temporary: it isn't repeated in Wheatley's oeuvre. Yet it is tellingly very much in the spirit and the style of John Milton, and as such it calls attention to what accompanies the piety. In Milton's *Paradise Lost*, angels and devils, the servants of God and Satan, substitute for the alighting, powerful goddesses in classical myth, like Homer's Pallas Athena. While there are some angels in scripture, the Miltonic overpopulation of the sacred realms is more than a little suspect from the perspective of the Old Testament stories he rewrites. This itself calls attention to the poet's famous ambition "to justify the ways of God to man," as he put it at the outset of *Paradise Lost*. The comings and goings of angels, devils, and saints elevate the role of the poet to that of religious seer. Wheatley similarly interrupts the praise of the Lord—twice—by prayerful but nevertheless self-referential gestures that put the poet on the plane of the saving graces as well as those who aspire to be saved. She places them with herself in otherworldly realms where "fame" and "the mountains" too speak: "Sewall is dead, Swift-pinioned fame thus cryd / Is Sewall dead my trembling heart replyd." Bereft only at the thought of Sewall's absence on earth, she asks for the Lord to "send a Pastor for thy Churches Good."

We have regained focus on the blessed community, the hearers—but only until the twelve- or thirteen-year-old elegist again calls attention to herself, telling the reader she'll close with "an epitaph" for "his tomb":

> *Here lies a man bought with Christs precious blood*
> *Once a Poor sinner now a saint with God*
> *Behold ye rich and poor and fools and wise*
> *Nor let this monitor your hearts surprize*
> *I'll tell you all what this great saint has done*
> *That makes him Brighter than the Glorious Sun*

This isn't an epitaph at all. Epitaphs don't properly invoke the first person. But preachers can. It's a funeral *sermon*, directed at God, the dead, and the congregation: perhaps especially those who "listen" from "the seats above," where the slaves sat in Old South:

> *Mourn him ye indigent whom he has fed*
> *Seek yet more earnest for the Living bread*
> *E'en Christ your bread descend from above*
> *Implore his pity and his grace and Love.*

Mourn him ye youth whom he has Often told
Gods bounteous mercy from the times of Old
I too, have cause this heavy loss to mourn:
Because my monitor will not return

Wheatley is urging the readers of her elegy to find "the Same graces"—to be saved—through the contemplation of Sewall's example: the imitation of a saint. There's more than a little hubris here. Can anyone tell such a story and not be among the elect already?

"On the Death of Rev. Dr. Sewell" enacts the classic New England Puritan dilemma of the strenuous effort to be saved when salvation could be by God's grace alone. How did one know who was saved or whether outward signs of piety were mere vanity? New Englanders had long traditions of both ministerial authority and lay activism that could empower women as the "primary sources of religious authority" within families while still returning them to their silent places in the pews. Women couldn't be ministers, but they made up the majority of church members at a time when one had to apply and testify publicly for full membership. They often played a key role in recruiting, evaluating, and retaining pastors. The story of New England churches has sometimes been told as one of a decline from power and piety into worldliness, or from ministerial authority to congregational rebellion, but such stories were themselves sources of periodic renewal and controversy, built into the culture of Congregationalism from one generation to the next.

Death rituals, especially, could be the spur for people to join churches, not least because both epidemics and the sudden passing of old and young were seen, as in Wheatley's poem, as God's special province. When Wheatley seized upon the death of a minister, described him as a saint, and explained his extraordinary pastoral monitoring even though she wasn't actually a member of his congregation, she assumed a kind of lay leadership.

There is a similar "sermonic quality" to another, seemingly less bold, but already more accomplished blank verse poem, "To the University of Cambridge," which she recorded twice as "wrote in 1767" but did not publish until her book in 1773. Lecturing the future ministers in the entering or graduating classes of Harvard was actually a "common evangelical trope" and a mocking secular one as well. The students were known for getting in trouble: possibly she was commenting on the famous Butter Rebellion of 1766, when a student berated a tutor about the quality of the food, received a punishment, and inspired a walkout. A generation earlier, the teenage Benjamin Franklin had cut his literary teeth on this sort of upside-down monitoring. He did it in the voice of a woman (Silence Dogood, a riff on Cotton Mather's *Essays to Do Good*), too. In her address to the Harvard students, like her poem to the nearly shipwrecked Quakers Hussey and Coffin the same year, Wheatley foregrounded her neoclassical poetic ambitions as well as her African identity and piety explicitly, right up front—probably in reaction to the surprise or even shock she was encountering among those who read or heard her increasingly accomplished work. What was she about?

> While an intrinsic ardor bids me write
> The muse doth promise to assist my pen
> 'Twas but e'en now I left me native Shore
> The sable Land of error's darkest night
> There, sacred Nine! For you no place was found,
> Parent of mercy, 'twas thy Powerfull hand
> Brought me in Safety from the dark abode.

The defensive quality to Wheatley's voice here is striking, especially in light of its absence in the earlier Sewall elegy. For the first time it seems as if she were pushing a boulder uphill, arguing explicitly against objections and skepticism about people from a "sable Land." This poem is even more publicly oriented than the Sewall elegy, and potentially controversial, though clearly meant to be shown around.

She throws her "native Shore" under the proverbial bus, trading sympathy and understanding for a merely recent migrant ("'Twas but e'en") for a confirmation of white suspicions: Africa as a land of error, a "dark abode" as opposed to the heavenly abodes she'd invoked as Sewall's homecoming.

What she proposes to gain by sacrificing a "dark" Africa to celestial light (which she later revised into a less stark, Old Testament–style "Egyptian gloom") is the synergy of her classical and sacred ambitions: a combination that is more than a match for the science they're teaching across the river in Cambridge. The "Sons of Science" gaze upward to both "the heights of Heav'n" and the "glorious Systems of revolving worlds." But are they remaining focused on what matters? They'd better listen to this preaching, which, with the other "messengers from heav'n" they've "received," conveys the word of Christ and his meaning. "The Saviour's blood, for your Redemption flows" as we "S[ee] him, with hands stretch'd out upon the Cross! . . . What Condescention in the Son of God! / When the whole human race, by Sin had fal'n; / He deign'd to Die, that they might rise again."

The address to the students of Cambridge is the most Christocentric poem Wheatley ever preserved. It comes off as more decorous and less preachy in the revision for *Poems* in 1773. Along with two other poems, "An Address to the Deist" and "An Address to the Atheist," that she also wrote in 1767 but never published, the Cambridge poem may also be the most sermonic and the most evangelical, in the sense of depicting conversion as an experience actively sought and inspired, regardless of the status of the preacher or the convert. The poems on deism and atheism are also decidedly theological and insistent on the moment of salvation at stake, even for young people. They couldn't be more different from another, secular and rakish tradition in English verse typified by the waggish cavalier Robert Herrick in a famous line to which Wheatley referred directly or indirectly through subsequent riffs. Where Herrick urged virgin girls, "Gather ye rosebuds while ye may," and John Gay, in *The Beggar's Opera* (1728), urged, "Let's be gay / While we may / Beauty's a flower, despised in decay," the students, Wheatley insists, must "Improve your privileges while they Stay."

Rather than sow their wild oats at school, or even be distracted by the new learning, the youth had better hurry to "suppress" their sins, "the sable monster." The girl from the "sable Land" becomes the expert. What could be their excuse if, as the poet emphasizes and the scriptures foretold, at least one "Ethiop tells you, tis your greatest foe"? Similarly, in "An Address to the Deist," she asks demandingly, even sarcastically, right at the outset, "Must Ethiopians be employ'd for you? / Much I rejoice if any good I do." If "an Ethiopian" could be a spiritual expert and lecture Harvard students on "eternal ruin," they had better heed the lesson. Maybe it was even worth it to depict Africa as ignorant and sin as a sable (black) monster (though again, in revising, she'd decide that she didn't need to concede nearly so much). She was learning what her audience would tolerate—and from whom.

The revivals called the Great Awakening, and the subsequent revival of 1762–65 in New England, had expanded the possibilities. Preachers moved about: their comings and goings lured people from their villages and even created some of the colonies' first media events as people clamored to read the sermons, the journals, the testimonies of the saved. The lore of the awakening stresses great evangelists like the Englishman George Whitefield, who preached in Boston to tens of thousands, as well as the breakaway congregants who denounced their ministers as unsaved wretches who would guide the unwary to hell. "Old Lights," some of them pillars of the establishment, denounced excesses of "enthusiasm" and its challenge to reason as well as ministerial authority. What might be missed by focusing on the spectacles and the scandals is how many of the established leaders, like Joseph Sewall, welcomed revival as the normal godly course of things. Later, to be sure, elite ministers like the Wheatley supporters Charles Chauncy and Mather Byles broke ranks at the disorders of enthusiasm—such as women and slaves falling out in spiritual ferment and even preaching out-of-doors.

During the revivals Old South experienced record numbers of new communicants, especially youth and "outsiders," the largest number of whom in Boston were Africans and their children. The enthusiastic converts of the early 1740s included black children declaiming from the pews in Plymouth. Guests at one Boston dinner party were surprised to learn that their host's slave could preach just like Whitefield himself. If the modal religious speaker in New England remained a trained minister, the modal convert under the "uncompromising conversionist theology" of the evangelical revivalists could only be the as yet unconverted or unchurched, such as adolescents who had moved or been moved from home, of which there were many in a society that bound children lacking sufficient support to new families as indentured servants; young indigenous people, who often experienced serial servitude for the same reasons; and enslaved Africans, also often young and separated from their parents.

The new evangelicals praised spontaneity over formal learning. Their preferred preachers began from a text but modeled godly, almost instantaneous inspiration. These were the very qualities that amazed and inspired contemporaries about Wheatley's elegies and other occasional poems: an undeniably learned, and practiced, yet heartfelt spontaneity. A teenage Wheatley didn't have to choose between evangelism and the Congregational establishment any more than she had to swear allegiance to one church or one minister. Boston was a densely packed peninsula with numerous churches: the revivals had further breached the limits of church or town boundaries and encouraged people to choose their own spiritual company. The intense new possibilities became physically dangerous during the first of George Whitefield's nine visits to New England in 1740. So many thousands packed into New South Church that a disturbance led to a stampede that killed five people.

A young Susanna Wheatley was probably there that day. She and John were wed at New South in 1741, at the height of the revival wave. What's certain is that Susanna maintained a lasting affection for

Whitefield and ministers friendly to him. She repeatedly housed "New Light" preachers as honored guests at their King Street home. "Please send my love to Reverend Mr. Whitefield," she wrote to one of these clergymen in 1765, when Whitefield had recently departed the colonies after a two-year stay. The Whitefieldarians also put a special emphasis on missions. Whitefield's much-reported travels were, in essence, missions in the far-flung colonies on the part of a Church of England minister, regardless of whether his hosts or his listeners were dissenters or not: perhaps all the better, to his English sponsors, if they were. To house missionaries was to participate in their spiritual calling, which explicitly included, for many of these men, preaching to natives and Africans. While accepting slavery as biblically permissible, from 1740, Whitefield and his followers insisted on special meetings with Africans and special efforts to convert natives, a long-standing desire of the New England establishment who were rather embarrassed about their spotty record of success.

Revivalism allowed for a new reckoning. How much evangelicals might change the order of things in New England is another matter. Nothing could have been as traditional as conversions, separations, and new churches, and for that very reason little had as much potential. The new piety simultaneously excused the racial orders of colonial New England while opening up new ways to address its hypocrisies and reform them.

Wheatley's education and creative writing were an evangelical project from the start: a collaboration between the Wheatley family, their friends, and Phillis herself, modeled on the audacity and humility of preachers and converts at a time when sermons as well as poetry remained popular literature. The Wheatleys were not the only ones to mix preacherly ambitions, literacy projects, and even poetry. The ecumenical Irish Presbyterian Reverend John Moorhead, a close friend of the Wheatleys who led the "strangers church" in Boston, also became a major supporter of the revivals. His wife, Sarah Moorhead, who had matched wits with Mather Byles, wrote widely read poems addressed to the flamboyant revivalists Gilbert Tennent and James Davenport asking them to tone down for the sake of the movement. All of her surviving poems from the 1740s and 1750s are addressed to ministers, including Whitefield. Their enslaved young man, Scipio Moorhead, later achieved notice as a painter and probably executed the portrait from which the frontispiece of Wheatley's *Poems* would be copied.

But the most important precedent, model, and possibly inspiration for Phillis herself was the Mohegan preacher and teacher Samson Occom. At sixteen Occom had been converted by James Davenport, Connecticut's leading revivalist; his mother too had joined a New London church. Davenport's brother-in-law Eleazar Wheelock took a particular interest in the young adept, whom he took to calling his "black son." Occom studied Latin, Greek, and Hebrew with Wheelock, who wrote of plans to send him to Yale for formal training. When that didn't work out, Occom served as a schoolmaster and missionary to Montauks on Long Island. Wheelock's success with Occom made Wheelock himself more ambitious. With Occom as a main draw for fundraisers and for students, he landed an impressive bequest from a merchant and opened Moor's Indian Charity School as a prospective training ground for Native missionaries.

For many natives in New England and New York, conversion meant affiliation with impressive English institutions and unprecedented access to educational resources that could help them in various ways. As natives of several tribes developed separate churches, Christianity had become another way of being Indian, not spiritual transformation on English terms. Occom was a tireless and sincere evangelist. He also carefully, laboriously leveraged his rising fame on behalf of several Native communities. By the early 1760s he had married a Montauk, Mary Fowler, had relatives in still other tribes, and "transform[ed] himself into a sachem and shaman rolled into one." Meanwhile, he remained, for white Christians, a walking and preaching advertisement for revivalism and missions, for better and worse. When Whitefield toured

Connecticut in 1764, the great evangelist, ever aware of publicity, had Occom ride one of the horses pulling his chariot.

Whitefield conceived the idea of Occom's traveling to England to raise money for Wheelock's Indian school. As word spread (a London paper reported that Whitefield was going to bring a "black" who could preach; the report appeared a few months later in Boston), most New England clergy turned hostile to the idea. At this time, Mohegan in Connecticut were pursuing a land dispute with imperial administrators, and every minister and magistrate knew, from generations back, that natives going to London meant going over their provincial heads. Only the Reverend John Moorhead supported Occom that year, opening his pulpit to him during the Mohegan's summer 1765 stay in Boston. Still, Occom had already become so famous, far beyond the places he had been seen and heard, that there was talk of fraud. "Some say I can't talk Indian," he complained. "Others say I can't read." On the eve of his departure for London, quite possibly while staying in the Wheatleys' house, Occom wrote and published an autobiography in the *Boston News-Letter* to answer these charges.

In London, more than in Boston, Occom became a sensation. Introduced at court and to crowds by Whitefield, he preached to thousands, more than three hundred times in all. Even as Wheatley in Boston owned and sought to leverage her unconverted African origins, Occom in London opened some talks by meeting his hearers' skepticism head-on—noting his own "Dareing Presumption" to preach given that he'd been rescued by God from the most "heathenish Darkness and Gross Idolatry." Nothing could epitomize the "new light" better than "dark" origins, even as the same transformation provoked suspicion and jealousy.

Over two years Occom raised the unheard-of sum of £12,000 for the failing Indian Charity School. But unknown to Occom, Wheelock was already planning to move the school and turn it into a college for missionaries named for Lord Dartmouth, farther north in New

Hampshire, where proximity to more natives—and a grand design of converting Iroquoia—would substitute for the ongoing dearth of Native students, who weren't flocking to Connecticut to study with him. Occom would complain bitterly to Wheelock and others at having been made a spectacle in the metropolis for the good of the movement while his own large family's well-being had been neglected by Wheelock. He eventually shamed his mentor for turning his alma mater into "Alba Mater," a white mother—a turn of phrase that bitterly flaunted his proficiency in Latin and his awareness of racial fetishism at the same time. But he rarely expressed regret for his transatlantic journey. He had represented his people at the seat of the empire, a worthy enterprise in a long tradition.

When Wheatley first proposed to publish a book, she promised to include, as her first notable writing, a letter she sent to Occom. In his attestation printed as a preface to *Poems on Various Subjects, Religious and Moral*, John Wheatley testified simultaneously to Phillis's ambition and Occom's influence: "As to her WRITING, her own Curiosity led her to it; and this she learnt in so short a Time, that in the Year 1765, she wrote a Letter to the Rev. Mr. OCCOM, the *Indian* Minister, while in *England*." Her master did not hesitate to suggest that writing a letter to Occom, and Occom's journey, set the stage for Wheatley's emergence as a published poet. Phillis understood that a "black son" turned preacher might mean new kinds of opportunities for him, for her, and for their peoples. Conversion, education, and ministering to men were within her ken, as they had been for Samson Occom, whose sponsored fame took him all the way to the center of the British Empire. Poems that preached might reach as far.

6

THE MONARCH, THE POETS, THE SUBJECTS, THE ENSLAVED

George Whitefield had little doubt that Samson Occom could play a very special role if he was willing to travel far and talk to staring multitudes. In recognition of what he was up against, the great itinerant called the Mohegan preacher "the Daniel of his Age." Whitefield steered the way by taking him to see the sights of London and to be seen seeing them, as so-called Indian Kings of North America had done periodically since Pocahontas.

Occom witnessed the king come to Parliament, "put on his royal robes and crown," and sign the repeal of the notorious Stamp Act. That piece of legislation had taxed paper products from newspapers to legal documents and spurred eloquent denunciations and raucous street theater in North American towns. Occom made special note of the cheers that met the king's act as "the acclamations of a joyous people." Londoners and colonists, he learned, were often on the same page, albeit with a time lag. Occom also shared a meal with the pious William Legge, Lord Dartmouth, who tried to get him an audience with the king himself. That might or might not have happened, but Occom could claim success anyway. George III subscribed £150 to the Indian college. By the time he got home, Samson Occom was one of the few

North Americans who had seen the king of England or been seen by him. The preacher had not quite been treated as another Indian king, but he was learning a lot about patronage and more than a little about lobbying. Occom also began to criticize "the enslaving [of] the poor negroes in a barbarous manner." Words like these played better the farther one got from the scene of the crimes, especially when their terms resonated with other criticisms of the white colonists who were more and more often being called "the Americans."

In 1766, the monarch of four British kingdoms and many more colonies did not rule by fiat. Yet he remained at the center of everything. Much of the monarch's appeal lay in tradition, or culture, but as much of it in the unsettled, transactional, negotiated politics of an expanding British empire. Parliament made law and policy, but with the king's approval; the king still made or unmade ministries, those coalitions of lords who ran the government and the floor debates about policy and law in Parliament. Establishment figures spoke of the British government as the "king-in-Parliament," a mystery of several-in-one akin to the Trinity and as rife with useful and controversial ambiguities. The extent of parliamentary power, as the site of ultimate legitimacy and as a check on royal power, at home or abroad, arose regularly as a matter of dispute in England. Policy for the empire remained the subject of repeated and intense controversy in an age of wars, colonial acquisitions, and taxes at home and abroad to pay for them.

At flash points in the struggles over colonial policy it was especially tempting for North American and Caribbean settlers to argue for their partial autonomy on the basis of royal charters, or the notion that the real relationship between the mother country and the Anglo colonists lay not in the House of Lords and the House of Commons, where they did not have representation, but instead directly through the monarch. At this very moment, in the wake of the American Duties (or Sugar) Act, the Currency Act, and the Stamp Act, colonists insisted upon their British rights of representation to make their own laws, including taxes, through their own provincial legislatures, or mini-parliaments. The rub was that when they did so, they still had to concede royal power and parliamentary supremacy over imperial regulation, a category that might be defined broadly or narrowly—leading to endless dispute about the nature of various customs duties, internal versus external taxes, and sovereignty.

Already in 1765 some colonists explored alternative arguments. One was to appeal to natural, God-given rights. Another led in a more forgotten direction: celebrating their prior connection to the king, who, when petitioned, would set things right. Especially when combined with the patriotic joys of winning the Seven Years' War, in which Massachusetts soldiers played an outsized role, the results were striking. What would soon, or once again, be known as truculent, localist, independence-seeking Yankeedom experienced an imperial and royalist revival that patriots never imagined they would repudiate a decade later. Only by being subjects of the king could they argue as strenuously as they did, without seeming disloyal, that their rights had to be recognized, that evil ministers were to blame, or that illegal resistance was justified.

In a practical sense, the importance of the king loomed especially large after Governor Francis Bernard repeatedly prorogued—or suspended—the Massachusetts assembly over its protests against the new taxes. Bernard portrayed himself as the king's direct representative in the colony and wrote a treatise explaining that Massachusetts would function in a much more British fashion if the king would grant some titles of nobility (no doubt starting with Bernard's handpicked friends). Bostonians really had little choice other than to play a more-loyal-than-thou game. Expressions of fealty and actual petitions to a king who could—and eventually did—recall the arrogant Governor Bernard grew louder, as in the town of Weymouth's protest, printed in the Boston papers: "The King our Father, whom we have always lov'd and honour'd, and the Parliament of Great Britain, which we have always esteem'd and reverenc'd, will forgive us if we do not consent to our ruin." Overall, the relationship between king and people in the colonies appeared stronger than ever in 1766, fueled by more frequent shipping and by everyday actions that made kingship and subjecthood a real relationship as well as a metaphor for all just and godly authority.

The quotidian reality of royalty began any hour that Phillis stepped out onto King Street, the broad, central passageway that stretched from the Long Wharf to the city's most impressive civic structure, the Town House. The site of the colony government at the intersection of King and Queen Streets made a figurative as well as literal point. The royal person could be seen in the chamber, in a larger-than-life oil painting, but his authority would be seen and heard outside as well. In Wheatley's time, a new young king had ascended to the throne. The provincial government in Boston sponsored impressive, and notably loud, anniversary celebrations for the dates of his birth and eleva-tion. These scripted processions had distinct places for elected officials and Crown-appointed ones like the governor and lieutenant governor and the council, as well as His Majesty's troops and local militia like Boston's Ancient and Honorable Artillery Company. They never failed to march through King Street, probably under the arch of the State House, and fire three volleys at the end of their parade, to be met with ubiquitous, vocal "Demonstrations of Loyalty" by onlookers. Royal ships in the harbor fired their big guns; wealthier houses, probably in-cluding the Wheatleys', sported "illuminations"—candles or lanterns in the windows. At night, fireworks presented enough of a danger to inspire the governor's council to plead for "care" to be taken. These weren't once-a-year affairs: Wheatley would have seen, and helped pre-pare for, celebrations of the anniversary of George II's coronation *and* his accession to the throne every September and October, as well as the king's birthday and occasional special efforts, such as a combined revel for the birthday of the Prince of Wales, the anniversary of the acces-sion of the House of Hanover, and the surrender of Havana to British forces in August 1762. Royal anniversaries had become so regular that almanacs began to feature lists as well as calendar reminders of these festival days.

Poets took notice. It was their job to do more than notice these royal and imperial occasions. Wheatley's early favorite versifier, Joseph Addison, got his literary start as an Oxford student first by rhymes praising John Dryden, the age's great court panegyrist (and the first real professional), and then with a longer poem lamenting the lack of a Homer or Virgil to commemorate King William III's victories over the French. Addison proceeded, of course, to narrate the glories in verse anyway. He soon received a royal grant to fund a grand tour of Europe, which not only inspired his art but also qualified him for suitable patronage positions like an undersecretaryship of state for the Southern (that is, Colonial) Department. In 1761, Harvard tutors and students put together an entire volume of verses—some in Latin—to mourn the death of George II and to celebrate the elevation of his son to the throne. Not coincidentally, this project had been Governor Bernard's idea. Boston papers also published locals versifying on Prime Minister William Pitt and on the taking of "Great Guns" at Havana, including one poem written by a woman: a new wartime development in the colonies even though women in England had published poems on political events.

"A Poem on the Accession of King George III," published in the *Boston News-Letter*, predicted a new kind of universal peace—an end to all slavery, even the most modern kind—with the British victory: "In Chains no more dejected Slav'ry sweat / Each exil'd AEthiop seek his native seat." Ethiopians stood in for any and all Africans, as they had for the ancient Greeks and Romans. Alexander Pope, James Thomson, and other poet-enthusiasts of greater Britain had made similar gestures, and they meant it. Somehow more empire would or could mean less slavery, if it went the (true) English way. The author might have realized he or she was spitting into the sails. Prior victories in wars against the French and Spanish, and the ensuing growth of the British oceanic empire in Africa, the Caribbean, and North America, had repeatedly expanded the slave trade to and by British colonies, an effect that could be perceived in Boston once again in 1763. Yet the occasional antislavery verse allowed, perhaps even encouraged, patriotic ambivalence of the sort that Pope had elaborated about Britain's growing empire a generation before.

Poets went with the flow, yet their formulaic neoclassicism provided some cover for dissenting, even idiosyncratic views. Even as the successful poets courted attention and patronage—often at court itself—their aspirations for genius, for godliness, and for rewards could lead them to a very public kind of adventurousness. Celebrating kings and patrons, they carved out a place for, and in a real sense celebrated, themselves, even while protesting, strenuously, that they weren't so self-referential—or bought off—as they might seem. As with the Greek and Roman classical poets they took as models, imperial themes (and Crown rewards) inspired considerable reflection about who and what poets might become if they hewed too close to power.

No one understood the uses of poetry in colonial Boston better than Wheatley's closest literary model, Mather Byles. Son of a saddler, adopted by his namesake uncle Cotton and grandfather Increase Mather, Byles was singled out early for greatness. Already in his twenties he was renowned all over Boston as a poet who mocked people, who delighted many, but who did not challenge authority. In some early newspaper writings he took the name of "Proteus Echo": a wry comment on the dilemma of neoclassicism's shape-shifting, persona-hiding range as well as its studious anxieties about proper imitations. His first acknowledged publication was *A Poem on the Death of His Late Majesty King George* (1727); he followed with another on the death of the queen in 1738, and with similar efforts on the arrival of new colony governors who literally carried royal seals of commission. Having cut his literary teeth on the royals, he turned to the doyens of verse. The famous hymnist Isaac Watts replied to his praise poem by advising him not to be too enthusiastic in praise of politicians, or about the classics, at the expense of "Moses or Christ." Byles got Alexander Pope's attention with flattering letters that did not just border on but actually were self-parody: "We look on your letter, as you would look upon the original Parchment of a Homer. We pay you a Deference and Veneration belonging to a Race of Superior Beings."

By his thirties Byles had settled in: the preacher as wit, often a kind mentor, sometimes a cruel snob. He could at best perform well and encourage the young. There was no getting out of the colonial relationship, any more than Byles himself could hope to do more than inherit the great mantle of the Mathers, do some good, and get some laughs. He took the burdens and the privileges in stride, distributing equally around town the celebrated puns that tended to give him the last word. That was another luxury Wheatley could not have.

Byles best represented his era in his "acute self-consciousness" about patronage, about power, about religion, and about poetry itself. The longest and most striking poems in his *Poems on Several Occasions* (1744) are about the ambitions of the poet and the need to keep them all (including "the baser arts of flattery") in proportion, since the poet's glory ultimately derives from the royal, the divine, and the "immortal Laurels" of the very few who lived up to the role, such as Milton, Watts, and Pope. Replying at length "To an ingenious young gentleman, on his dedicating a Poem" to him, Reverend Byles expressed pride in being a tutor but insisted that his influence actually paled next to that of his ideal poet and patron, who taught him all from afar: "Not I, but mighty POPE inspir'd thy Muse. / He, wondrous Bard! Whose Numbers reach our Shore, / Tho' Oceans roll between, and Tempests roar . . . From him I gather what you I give," insisted the poet-mentor as minister, who might as well be talking about the Lord. All the more reason to "Let sacred Subjects fill the Air around" and "Write for ETERNITY!"

Byles's royalism would prove almost as much his rock as his Congregational, anti-revivalist faith, his marriages into the governing families of the commonwealth, and his tenure at Hollis Street Church. His wives died, his sons moved away, his congregation ultimately disowned him in 1777 because of his strenuous loyalism. But his young daughters, Katy and Mary, Wheatley's contemporaries, remained devoted. They too "gloried" in their king and queen and even kept calling their neighbors "rebels" for another half a century.

Their father perhaps best expressed his sense of the value of the "lineage based hierarchies" in their lives when he watched the raucous funeral procession of the Afro-Native patriot martyr Crispus Attucks after the Boston Massacre, in 1770. "They call me a brainless Tory," he remarked, "but tell me, my young friend, which is better—to be ruled by one tyrant three thousand miles away, or by three thousand tyrants not a mile away." Some of this ethos was tradition, perhaps as much of it self-serving privilege, especially in the hands of professional scions like Byles. But most of all, monarch loving, like the poems that expressed it, was politics. What made it powerful and flexible also made it vulnerable.

Rumors swirled in 1764 about a tax on stamps. This would be a general tax, wider in its social and geographical impact than the previous American Duties Act, which had targeted smugglers and other New Englanders who made rum from French Caribbean molasses. That earlier law had been supported by the powerful lobby of British West Indies planters whose sugar products were undercut by illegal competition. Though even the Crown-appointed governor Bernard argued against it on economic and political grounds, pleas against the Sugar Act from Boston and Newport had fallen on deaf ears. By late 1764, it had become clear that narrowly regional economic appeals coming out of New England would not buck the trend toward regulation through taxation or gain much sympathy beyond Yankeedom.

Bostonians had their arguments ready, and they could reprint similar ones from other colonies in their newspapers. "Americans"—the term became a meme in 1764 and 1765, distinguishing mainlanders from Caribbean planters—possessed the same "love of liberty" as

Britons back home. Perhaps even more so, since many of them had "fled from the Oppression and Slavery of arbitrary Governments, have imbibed the Principle still more strongly being by the Experience of both, confirmed in a love of Freedom, and a detestation of Bondage."

Slavery wasn't an empty metaphor. It didn't mean just political oppression either. The early adopter Stephen Hopkins of Providence, Rhode Island, had a neat definition: "Those who are governed at the will of another, . . . and whose property may be taken from them by taxes, or otherwise, without their own consent, and against their will, are in the miserable condition of slaves." The New York and Boston papers batted the notion back and forth. After word of the actual Stamp Act reached both cities in May, the rhetoric intensified. "Its [*sic*] surely a matter of small import, what we are called if we are *compleat slaves*," a New Englander wrote in response to a long article in the New York paper on the Stamp Act. "We seem to be treated worse than the ancient Hebrews," responded another New Yorker: the English seemed to show "worse than Egyptian jealousy." One writer for the *Boston Evening-Post* thought the problem infected an equally traditional and resonant trope, the idea of Britain as the mother country of the colonies: "What wise parent ever treated an adult child like an infant, much less a slave?"

The two powerful political metaphors of parents and children, and of masters and slaves, melded when the controversy heated in Boston, as Wheatley would not fail to notice. Along with the four newspapers that carried reports of them, royal festivals provided an ideal means for demonstrating public opinion and the possibilities of loyal protest. Good British patriots sent petitions to the king and even demonstrated in the streets against the king's evil ministers when necessary. On August 14, the resistance leaders who would become known as the Loyal Nine and later the Sons of Liberty led a crowd who hung effigies of stamp distributors from trees in High Street, along with a boot with a "Green-vile sole" (a pun on Lord Bute and Lord Grenville, the high officials who had promoted the tax) with a "devil protruding from it," which they cut down and took to the courthouse. Proceeding loudly through King Street to Kilby, around the corner from the Wheatley store and house, to a building that they believed had been built for the stamp distributor, they leveled it and made a bonfire with the remains. The threatening spectacle inspired the resignation of the appointed distributor of the stamps. But it wasn't enough for Boston's artisan radicals, who connected economic hard times with the selfishness of elites in the pay of the Grenville administration. Twelve days later, after learning that Lieutenant Governor Thomas Hutchinson had actually opined to his superiors that some British "liberties" had been taken too far in the colonies and needed to be curtailed, a crowd made another bonfire in King Street and then made one of the Court of Admiralty. After defacing the dwelling of a customs officer, they proceeded to Hutchinson's mansion and tore it down symbolically and physically, piece by piece.

Some Bostonians were shocked. Those who called themselves Whigs and patriots regrouped. More peaceful means remained: Why not be more patient when "laying grievances" at "the feet of his most sacred Majesty, our dread Sovereign"? Yet radicals denounced a mere petitioning approach as "slavish." In case the point wasn't clear, this writer compared some mild petitioners of Marblehead to the real slaves at hand in New England, proposing another crowd action to target them: "For my own part I engage to furnish a sufficient quantity of black paint, to cover them with their proper colour, and would distinctly enjoin the operator to give them a double blackness, to distinguish them from their *superior slaves*, whose sable appearance is natural."

Rumors crisscrossed the ocean that Parliament might well repeal the Stamp Act, especially with a new ministry coming in—if only the resistance did not try to make their problem with the taxes too much an issue of principles and rights. Patriot leaders debated strategy. Some sought to channel the crowd's energy and anger into nonviolent royalist celebration, the safest form of protest. On November 1, the date the Stamp Act went into effect, the Sons of Liberty split the difference and staged the inverse of a royal birthday fete: a mock funeral for liberty. Instead of cannon salutes, bells tolled in mourning; ships lowered colors to half-mast. Effigies proceeded to the courthouse again, this time with mocking verses attached. All the "inhabitants"—meaning, white citizens—were warned "to keep their Negroes in." There would be no confusion about whose liberty was at stake. The gesture was repeated four days later when, instead of the traditional Pope's Day parade and melee, the rival North End and South End clubs united in protest, "nor was any Negro allowed to approach near the stages" where effigies burned.

King Street remained the center of protests: Wheatley would have seen most of these events. Africans began to be banned from the crowds by protest leaders in part because so many had participated in them. As Parliament debated, the opposition in London egged on the protesters across the water who had taken their name, Whigs. None other than William Pitt himself, the former prime minister, "rejoice[d] that America has resisted. Three million . . . of people, so dead to all feelings of liberty, as voluntarily to submit to be slaves, would have been fit instruments to make slaves of the rest" of the British Empire, he proclaimed in the widely reported debate over the repeal of the Stamp Act. When an issue of the *London Gazette* arrived on May 17 confirming repeal, the governor ordered the guns at Castle William and elsewhere to be fired and summoned the council to drink to the king's health. The selectmen of the town appointed the formal celebration for the next Monday. Debtors were set free from the prison, and everyone saw the best fireworks ever shot off in New England. Celebrations deliberately emphasized the king's assent to repeal. On Boston Common illuminated transparencies displayed the king and the queen and fourteen illustrious patriots with verses about how they had fought off slavery.

Precisely because the rhetoric likening colonists to slaves had been so successful, the implications grew harder to miss. The next week, the Boston town meeting endorsed a committee report directing its representatives to the legislature to support a bill against the importation of slaves, not as a temporary economic or public safety measure, but rather in order to advance "the total abolishing of slavery from among us." No other records besides the terse official ones reveal how far some Boston patriots felt constrained or compelled to make their slavery rhetoric mesh with their reality. There is no record of the votes. We know only that in 1765 there were already patriots who were willing to give up African slavery because, as James Otis had realized after the Sugar Act, accusations of hypocrisy could prevent their protests against taxes from being taken seriously.

Neither slavery nor Parliament would be easy to take on. During the coming years, Bostonians would celebrate the anniversary of the August 14 protest and the March repeal of the Stamp Act with processions and orations. They toasted their resistance to slavery and the wisdom of the king. Had their "British blood" and equal rights been recognized, or merely their persistence? Celebrating and publishing essays and poems kept the issues alive for rounds of protests-as-festivals and festivals-as-protests over the next ten years. The implications for African enslavement began to be noticed more often, but they were even less clear, and more dangerous, because already so entangled with the debate over the nature and extent of settlers' liberties.

Sometime during or after these controversies, Phillis weighed in with a poem, "To the King's Most Excellent Majesty on His Repealing the American Stamp Act." She did not publish in any newspaper: a strategy that might have derived from the fact that she hadn't yet published any of her poems, but may be even more comprehensible when we realize that her fellow Africans had been banned from celebrating repeal in the streets lest anyone confuse the meaning of the Whig protests against "slavery." (Their continued presence would become an issue at the 1768 anniversary as well.)

The first surviving draft, probably passed to friends of Susanna Wheatley's in Philadelphia who were expressing interest in her poems by 1767, is not dated but suggests 1766 or 1767 in its similarities to the worshipful and pious poems she wrote in honor of Sewall, and also because of its formal limitations. Cheating more than a bit on the end-of-line words and phrases for rhyme's sake, the couplets (as in several of her early poems that exist in manuscript) all too often form separable ideas that don't necessarily follow: "May your Sceptre many nations sway / Resent it on them that dislike Obey." She leans heavily on the king's awesome powers: not at all the standard patriot emphasis. She was composing in pieces, a line or couplet at a time, writing herself into the conversation on monarchs, poets, and subjects, with some difficulty in trying to inflate the king while making her own abjection somehow proof of his greatness: "But how shall we exalt the British king / Who ruleth France Possessing every thing / The sweet remembrance of whose favours past / The meanest peasants bless the great the last." No one could exalt the king higher. There is nothing risky or controversial in her approach, which makes the sovereign all powerful and the subjects ever grateful, even the "meanest peasants," which in America would be, or include, the enslaved.

As in the Sewall poem, she remembers to switch to a less classical, more Christian register, asking God's protection for the king: "May heaven protect and Guard him from on high / And at his presence every evil fly." Suddenly the freedom narrative enters, and it isn't clear what she means—except that she must mean to thank George especially for the most recent dispensation, the occasion for the poem, the repeal: "Thus every clime with equal gladness see / When kings do Smile it sets their Subjects free."

Writing in 1766 or 1767, in response to one of the repeal celebrations or anniversaries, Wheatley must be tentative. She's endorsing not the radical claims but rather the conservative Whig loyalism that relies on the traditional relationship, where subjects apologize to ask for royal dispensation in "every clime," even North America. Subjects are like the slave-like Marblehead petitioners mocked by the Boston critic: they beg only for amelioration in this world. In a closing couplet she returns to majesty and piety and the results of sin: "When wars came on the proudest rebel fled / God thunder'd fury on their guilty head."

Six or seven years later, for her volume aimed at an English as well as American audience, her political voice as well as her prosody would be more confident. She dates the poem to 1768—not the time of repeal at all. It's possible that she did revise for the next round, the Townshend Acts controversy in 1767–68. Either way, dating at 1768 served two purposes. It suggested the repeated, cyclical nature of the controversy over colonial liberties, and the king's role in it: colonial protest, royal dispensation. Moreover, presenting the much-improved version as five years old, and as the sixth poem in the book, contributed to the convincing argument the book would make for her rapidly maturing genius. Backdating the very effective revision to 1766 might have been less than believable. As an effort of 1768, it more plausibly documented her quick yet visible maturation.

In this version, she's more clearly a participant in the relationship between king and subjects, more able to present herself as the national poet praying to God for her sovereign. The horrors of war, mentioned twice in the original, perhaps still terrifying to the enslaved, ship-traumatized youngster, are gone. Subjects have more consequential roles. So does the poet, who more assertively claims to be a member of a community whose "meanest peasants" have political opinions. They don't cower before some godlike potentate. They obey "with love and readiness" the king of a better, more enlightened empire of "num'rous nations." They don't just "bless" but "admire" and "reward" the patriot king.

She ends this time with her best revised line: "A monarch's smile can set his subjects free!" It is their freedom, the we, the British subjects who are the real subject of the poem, even when it seems to be the king. Could all the subjects be free? Can those who are not free be freed eventually by sovereign authority? In other words, were the enslaved subjects too? Freedom from slavery could be a metaphor for political liberties, everyone knew. Repeal, argued patriots, proved that the king was a father, and colonists "are not slaves, or even servants." Between 1766 and 1773, Phillis Wheatley would begin to turn such turns of phrase back around, making imperial politics a catalyst for African emancipation.

7

THE NATIONS

From the first to the second versions of Phillis's Stamp Act poem, King George III devolves from terrifying potentate to "our father." Yet his power magnifies. Deference to the king as a loving father figure helped finesse the fact that Parliament, with the king's assent, made the laws and the imperial policies to which many Bostonians objected. Ideally, "royal benevolence" in this sort of family served the colonists well. It made every Englishman, at home and abroad, a monarch over his freely held home and property, compared "to the slavery of France" under a real tyrant like King Louis XV.

A few months later, those who raised their glasses at the anniversary of the August 14 stamp office destruction, an event held under the Liberty Tree that year, proclaimed their very first toast to "THE KING." Then they prayed that "an abhorrence of Slavery should ever remain the best Criterion of a true British Subject," called "None but Tories Slaves," and proclaimed "America" before closing with a wish: "May that Day which sees America submit to Slavery, be the last of her existence." Bolder, explicit calls for colonists to "unite," even across colony lines, "and never submit calmly to be chain'd in perpetual servitude" culminated in reminders of ultimate fealty: *Let us still be loyal to the best of Kings.*

This conditional royalism came from the same Cambridge enthusiast for liberty who had insisted that "pusillanimous" Marblehead petitioners should be painted black twice. Nevertheless, talk of slavery opened a Pandora's box. What was slavery, in America, after all? If slavery was taking people's property (themselves) and making them serve without their consent, then British Americans were the foremost slave drivers in the empire. *That* kind of slavery could be explained or excused by race, the Cambridge writer presumed. Blackness distinguished legitimate and illegitimate slaveries. This was so settled in Anglo-America that one could joke about it, presumably.

But blackness failed to explain too much. Too often the color line seemed to morph into geographical lines. Or was it vice versa? Did the remarkable growth of the British Empire establish more gradations of citizenship, of belonging, so that metropolitan English people saw not fellow Britons abroad so much as another Indies populated mainly by racially marked savages or barbarians? James Otis had seen the problem right away. Protesting the Sugar Act in his long essay *The Rights of the British Colonies Asserted and Proved*, the lawyer had expressed outrage that colonists could be treated like mere savages or slaves—as the colonized rather than as "freeborn British *white* subjects." He did not shirk from the implications of his views. Otis came right out and mocked African slavery as unnatural and race as a political fiction invented to justify it. He blamed the whole notion of racial slavery on the British West Indian slave drivers who were, not coincidentally, in favor of the new taxes on their trading partners, the New England distillers and shippers. Those fair-weather friends, Otis suggested, would enslave anybody to keep their special privileges. The slave trade itself tended to "diminish the idea of the inestimable value of liberty."

Most patriots did not follow Otis's antiracist turn, preferring to improve instead on his blame of the British West Indians. The Otis admirer John Adams scribbled angrily that Caribbean colonists "deserve to be made slaves to their own Negroes." Stamps coming on a ship from Jamaica bore "marks of Creole slavery." Some leading New

Englanders, in other words, when they considered a geopolitical limit to their freedoms that threatened to become racialized and "enslave" them, projected the problem onto the Caribbean Creoles. This moment has been forgotten in part because Jamaican planters soon won back their New England friends by refusing the hated stamps. During these years they too were having a controversy about governors and legislative privileges. But not Barbados, the much older English colony. In 1766, a New Englander blasted colonists on Barbados who accepted the Stamp Act as "content to become Slaves (which they richly deserve for their inhumanity to those whom they have made so)."

The ease with which Otis, Adams, and others blasted West Indian whites as tainted by slavery hints at a forgotten origin of the American Revolution. At the first stirrings of the imperial controversy, both slavery and race were politicized. British writers who supported the stamp tax and more thoroughgoing imperial regulation leaned on the presence of Africans and indigenous people to justify distinctions between the treatment of settler colonies and "home" lands. Distinctions between North America and Jamaica didn't seem important in London, except for the fact that the West Indies appeared to bring more wealth to the metropole. No wonder Otis made it a point to call himself white, in italics, even while proceeding to denounce all kinds of slavery and racial restrictions. The contradictions were there for all to see and to use. Otis's family shipped fish and lumber to the West Indies for molasses. Only weeks after the Bostonian critic hotly denounced a Barbadian writer as a *slavish Creole*," a townsman advertised "four young likely negro men and one young girl, from Barbados," along with "good Barbados Rum & sugar, & wine by cash," in the same newspaper.

Most of those who called themselves patriots or Whigs chose to dodge the implications. Some others, especially of the younger generation, did not. Timothy Pickering of Salem wrote to the *Boston Gazette* about "how contrary is *our slavery* to the spirit of the gospel, from the beginning to the end of it; for in the first place, our Africans are torn from their tender parents the most of them when little children." In light of colonial child stealing, who were the patriots to compare bad imperial parenting to, of all things, slavery? Nathaniel Appleton Jr., a Boston merchant and the son of a minister, directly compared the colonists' rights to those of their slaves: "Oh! ye sons of Liberty, pause a moment, give me your ear. Is your conduct consistent? can you review our late struggles for liberty, and think of the slave-trade at the same time, and not blush?" Like Otis, Appleton also mocked racial justifications for slavery: "Methinks were you an African, I could see you blush." Most Africans in America had been taken from a land of innocence to the West Indies, a land of wickedness. Few were Christianized there, which obviated that excuse for the slave trade. Only ending slavery would "shew all the world, that we are true sons of Liberty." He closed by urging the Massachusetts legislature to action. But the provincial assembly took up the question, debated it, and tabled it.

Meanwhile, invocations of tyrannical "slavery" and the mother country as "unnatural Parent" amplified with the passage of the Townshend Acts, the suspension of the New York Assembly for its resistance to the quartering of troops, and the prorogue of the Massachusetts House by the governor for its refusal to rescind its resolution approving New York's action. The recurring, intersecting tropes of imperial parents, colonial children, and slaves gave the enslaved African poet, only emerging from childhood herself, much to think about. So did the invocations of an incipient American identity, and a need for colonial unity, that seemed to rely on a familial, emotional, yet uneasy relation to Britain. If political debate in newspapers, pamphlets, and sermons trucked in such metaphors, certainly poets could join the conversation.

Sometime in 1768, Phillis drafted a mini-epic she titled, simply, "America." It survives only in a version she or the Wheatleys sent, in 1769, to friends, probably in or near Philadelphia, where a group of women, including the poets Hannah Griffitts and Annis Boudinot Stockton, circulated manuscripts during these years. This standard piece of foolscap is folded like a letter, but opens as a three-poem chapbook, with "America" written ornately at the top.

All three of these poems are among those listed in her first published proposal for a volume, in 1772; none of them appeared in the actual London edition of *Poems on Various Subjects, Religious and Moral* a year later. Yet this is not a draft. It's semipublic, part of a world of formal manuscript circulation among women readers and writers of poetry. The second piece included in the folded booklet is a much-revised version of "Atheism," one of her first efforts from 1765 or 1766. The third is the newest, an occasional poem praising Commodore Samuel Hood, then in Boston Harbor, for pardoning a deserter in February 1769. Together the three works suggest her emerging range and ambition, from political allegory to religious verse to panegyric. So does her first-name signature with flourish, one of the most ornate that survive from her pen. If Phillis does not yet claim a surname, she's already cultivating a readership, as well as a topic, that goes beyond those whom she knows in Boston. Most strikingly, in "America" she takes the patriot movement as her own.

"America" begins as conventionally as its title, by 1768, would have led readers to expect. Poems and narratives about the New World and its settlement—especially the northeastern portion of it—had long since developed settled conventions. The first two couplets gallop over the conquest of New England in order to set the stage for a newer, contemporary drama:

> New England first a wilderness was found
> Till for a continent 'twas destin'd round.

As in the closing couplet of "To the King's Most Excellent Majesty," she throws out some gory battle imagery, perhaps to justify the epic ambition in this secular story of a nation born, tested, or made, as in *The Iliad* and *The Aeneid*:

> From feild to feild the savage monsters run
> E'er yet Brittania had her work begun.

Yet New England glorification isn't where Wheatley is going—at least not in the traditional Puritan sense that would remain tethered to the refuge and the covenant. The New World epic framing seems to allow Wheatley to escape, for a moment, any explicitly religious theme. This is the first extant poem of hers with no direct reference to God or salvation. Freed from that burden, the poem instead bursts out of history with the metaphors of the political moment. New Englanders, once weak before natives, now faced with conflict from home, are really the vanguard of British liberty, which is not a force of imperial tyranny but rather one of redemption:

> *Thy Power, O Liberty, makes strong the weak*
> *And (wond'rous instinct) Ethiopians speak.*

The New Englanders' efforts to colonize the continent and the patriot struggle for British liberties can be compared to, leads to, the liberty she was taking by writing. All three are inspired underdogs. She too, an "Ethiopian," speaks by an instinct that is universal, like liberty.

Apostrophizing Liberty as something like a Homeric female goddess, she begins the next couplet with the subtle yet unmistakable bombshell that explains exactly what she is doing:

> *Sometimes by Simile, a victory's won.*

It's a one-liner so modest yet so powerful, and so trippingly seductive with assonance and internal rhyme, that it gets away with introducing a complex, almost counterintuitive idea, at least for a white Anglo audience. If Ethiopians speak—if they enter the conversation about liberty, Britannia, and America—it is going to be through comparison, revealing explicitly, as similes do, "an unexpected likeness between two seemingly disparate things." The things here are Africans and British Americans. They are also another pair: fighting for political rights and struggling against enslavement and racial presumptions. Given the previous stanzas' focus on the New Englanders' battles, the implication is clear: the speech of Ethiopians in America is itself a simile for a political struggle. Speaking may be instinctual, a natural liberty, but poesis, or poetic making, with similes, is a battle. Writing is fighting by other means.

I'm drawing back the curtain, she announces. I will use figures of speech to compare oppressions, to defamiliarize, and to politicize. And not just any figure of speech. Eighteenth-century readers knew simile as the particular favorite of the ancients, and sometimes denigrated it as vulgar and primitive. Pope had argued, in favor of the "ancients" against the "moderns" in the preface to his translation of *The Iliad of Homer*, that the "wild paradise" of Homer's world was true to nature as well as inspired by a kind of genius that was best seen in his similes. The descriptions and figures seen as "exuberant" and rude by decorous critics were actually the essence of his genius. When Wheatley invokes simile, she is invoking Homer—saying also, in effect, that sometimes by recourse to Greek classics, however primitive they may seem, meaning is made, a transformation can occur—a victory is won.

As if acknowledging the conventional yet potentially risky meanings of the line that compared the technique of simile to a military or political tactic, she turns immediately, even abruptly, to coy, yet familiar, narration—beginning with the safest, most sacred Marian trope to contain the possibly subversive implications of a frontal assault via simile that might lead to an Ethiopian, as well an American, victory:

> *Sometimes by Simile, a victory's won.*
> *A certain lady had an only son.*

Victory always had a double meaning, as soul saving and as combat for Christians. The rest of the poem is an allegorical story about America, that only son of Britannia, during the second, Townshend Acts phase of imperial controversy, when the new duties on items less particular and politicized than sugar or paper, that is, paint and tea, had begun to seem piled on and punitive, deliberately designed not only to extract money or prevent smuggling but also to make the point of who was in charge. Wheatley's simile turns discreetly from Ethiopians being like patriots to Americans being like neglected, abused children. This directly mimics patriot protest while shadowing its potential reversal, or transformation, into antislavery. Having introduced "Ethiopians," in addition to signing her verses, she makes it hard for any reader, then or now, to forget who is speaking and what may be at stake.

Her narrative of America takes cues from the Whig writers, including Oxenbridge Thacher, who employed the maternal metaphor to question powerful Britons' motives and to criticize them for neglecting blood ties. It also fit the "narrative concentration" in which affairs of state were figured as domestic dramas. Britannia is an unfeeling, inconsistent mother. Her sympathy is only "seeming," as she "laid" taxes on her son like "Scourges," or whippings:

> He grew up daily virtuous as he grew
> Fearing his Strength which she undoubted knew
> She laid some taxes on her darling son
> And would have laid another act there on
> Amend your manners I'll the task remove
> Was said with seeming Sympathy and Love
> By many Scourges she his goodness try'd
> Untill at length the Best of Infants cry'd
> He wept, Brittania turn'd a senseless ear.

There's not much attempt to rationalize the abusive authority figure about whom this Ethiopian is taking the liberty to speak. It softened only a bit to employ a symbolic queen in the place of the actual present-day king. The mother Britain's eventual remorse is treated skeptically. She claims maternity but seems not to feel it:

> *At last awaken'd by maternal fear*
> *Why weeps americus why weeps my Child*
> *Thus spake Brittania, thus benign and mild*
> *My dear mama said he, shall I repeat—*
> *Then prostrate fell, at her maternal feet*
> *What ails the rebel, great Brittania Cry'd*
> *Indeed said he, you have no Cause to Chide*
> *You see each day my fluent tears my food*
> *Without regard, what no more English blood?*
> *Has length of time drove from our English veins*
> *The kindred he to Great Brittania deigns?*

With "Brittain keeping down / New English force," young America "weeps afresh to feel the Iron chain." Wheatley is claiming American identity, a voice for herself, and at the same time asserting a particular understanding of slavery's "Iron chain," as useful political knowledge.

In this confusion of voices—America's, Wheatley's, Britannia's—the poem returns to its initial framing to restore a history of a particular kind: the epic of growth, or "increase," where America, now again New England, fulfills British destiny. Agenoria, the goddess of courage and industry, inspires Americans to "arise / Lest distant continents with vult'ring eyes / Should charge America with Negligence." Wheatley's gesture invokes the daunting, increasingly troubling *translatio imperii*—westward the course of empire takes its way, as an English enthusiast for New England, the poet and scholar Bishop George Berkeley, had put it in 1726, elaborating a Virgilian theme while echoing Milton's shift to prophecy in the last two books of *Paradise Lost*. The "distant continents," other nations with "vult'ring eyes," like Milton's Satan, will not get in the way of this industrious, fecund national family. Freed from burdensome taxes, America would naturally, inevitably, "increase like thee," adding to Britain's wealth rather than that of other nations. If not, then its demographic "profusion" would proceed anyway, to its own, if not England's, benefit.

Wheatley's loyalty to New England and American visions has sometimes been questioned as naive. Once she is given her due as a politically
aware person, and poetry is understood as a performance of possibilities rather than as solely an expression of feelings, it becomes easier to
understand why her boldness, including this early, initial seizure of an
opportunity to suggest the wrongs of slavery, is built upon stories of
nations and pursued through analogies to parents and children.

It isn't that she was insensitive to the harsh realities of racial slavery.
It's that she saw the magnitude of the task at hand, on both the political
and the personal levels, and the need to proceed carefully—even more
carefully than the colonial point men like Benjamin Franklin who also
spun the relationship of slavery and liberty for far-flung audiences.
For even as she perceived an opening in the trope of enslavement for
colony-metropole relations gone sour, heard the new cries of hypocrisy
close at hand, and proceeded to push the possible similes, another reality would have been apparent in the streets, in the houses, and in the
same newspapers that reported on politics near and far.

Her cohort was growing up. But they weren't being treated as members of a family. Despite postwar economic uncertainties, their value
in the labor market had increased, and their enslavers took advantage.
Increasing numbers of ads appeared for the sale of girls Phillis's age "for
no fault but want of employ." Having a "very good Temper," much like
Phillis in the eyes of the Wheatleys, could be a selling point for a "strong
and hearty" boy. So could having been "brought up from age 10" to
be an "excellent cook [who] can do every kind of work necessary for a
large family." In July 1768, one reader had had enough of the cruel jux-
taposition of complimenting people publicly in order to sell them. He
or she complained about an ad offering a sixteen-year-old, about Phillis's age: "The poor Boy is acknowledg'd to be guilty of no fault: Is it not
then a glaring Absurdity, that he should be Sold!" Some Bostonians still
thought that there was, or should be, more to servitude, however racial

it had become, than the marketplace. Yet the logic of profit trumped tradition or morality. The achievements of assimilated, hardworking Africans were put on display, turned against them in ads that helped pay the printers' bills, too. Good for the city, suitable for the country, part of estates or on their own, privately via the printers or by public auction: the market re-enslaved them, making slavery a living, thriving institution in Boston and its environs. This market for slaves also made it very, very difficult for Africans to keep their own families together.

Six years later, when Susanna Wheatley died, Phillis would write to her enslaved friend Obour Tanner that her owner had taken her in, treated her like a daughter. Nevertheless, Phillis lived under threat of sale. Even kinder enslavers consulted the bottom line. Their heirs divided their assets when they died, especially the marketable assets. What friends she made were as likely as not to be moved. Imagine how careful the enslaved had to be in a community where they could be "sold for no other Fault, but having too long a Tongue," or being "addicted to be Funny in his talking." Or liking to go out at night. Or for "inclin[ing] to the sea," in the case of one eighteen-year-old boy. Or for being the mother of two children who, according to her anxious proprietor, "breeds too fast."

Piety might inspire a New Englander to treat their slaves better. But then it might not. When a satirist under the name "Sophistes" chose to expose the logic relied on by opponents of the bill in the House against the slave trade, he singled out both the religious and the racial hypocrisy, how enslavers had made them mesh. It was odd to see New Englanders, being slave traders, always going on about their pious ancestors' search for liberty. This "snarling set of levelers" seemed hypocritically jealous of "plantation people" in the empire. After all, Africans were the sons of Ham, and thus the "property of anyone." Self-evidently, Sophistes wrote mockingly, "whiteness is the emblem of innocence, blackness the emblem of guilt and wickedness."

Like Wheatley's "America," the argument of Sophistes leads the reader from common, local, and British pride to embarrassing New

England contradictions. It bears repeating, because this wasn't the first time such views appeared in Boston newspapers: racism might have been common sense, but it was being satirized, too, in full view of anyone who could read. A year later another writer went so far as to argue that "the subject of enslaving the Africans has been properly refuted by the best writers in England and America, that I can't but blush for the supreme legislature, that Slavery is permitted in any of the British dominions, and especially in this province." Yet the slavers had evidently won the day in 1767, with an assist from a distinctly biblical racism in the form of the Hamitic curse, an old purported proof that positioned Africans as the accursed "Sons of Ham," who had shamed his father, Noah.

Given how closely her poems tracked public events and their discussion in newspapers, there is every reason to believe that Phillis Wheatley was completely aware of these defensive, racial excuses for slavery and the increasingly pointed attacks on them—perhaps just as aware as she was of the need to please. Both awareness and need shaped another poem she wrote in 1768, one she published for the first time in her book five years later. It's the opposite of an epic, and unlike "America" it is now famous, even infamous, the subject of a great deal of commentary. Yet we might think of it as the other side of the story Wheatley tells in "America," deliberately first person, seemingly direct, as chiseled and polished as "America" is rough or unfinished, yet just as allusive and still more elusive: a time bomb of poetic and political ambition. It has been described as "the most reviled poem in African American literature" for its seeming thankfulness for enslavement.

On Being Brought from Africa to America

'TWAS mercy brought me from my Pagan land,
Taught my benighted soul to understand
That there's a God, that there's a Saviour too:
Once I redemption neither sought nor knew.

The emphasis on God's mercy leading to individual salvation was the very marrow of "New Divinity" Calvinism. This is a religious testimony, the only sort (apart from criminal confessions) that Africans in Massachusetts could, as yet, publicly offer. It assimilates her journey from Africa to that of any sinner to God in order to secure for her a voice: the special, conditional authority of the convert. It panders to its white audience, lets them off the hook, by suggesting that the slave trade itself may save souls.

Or does it? Can we, should we, read these two couplets differently once we know that antislavery writers in Boston were already calling the notion of the salvation of Africans through the slave trade an "abominable hypocrisy"? That others were resorting to satire to make the point? Even if that is hard to do after two centuries of reading and quoting every founding father or mother or brother at face value, as if they expressed their literal if not simple beliefs whenever they put pen to paper or leaden type to press, it has of late become easier to see the artful whiteface mockery of pious racists in the second half of the poem, which pivots from Christian consensus to a debate over the future of dark-skinned people:

> Some view our sable race with scornful eye,
> "Their colour is a diabolic die."
> Remember, Christians, Negros, black as Cain,
> May be refin'd, and join th' angelic train.

These two couplets appear to be the real point, set up by the first four lines that seem to bathe enslavement in evangelical glory, something white folks might want to believe. "Some" then divides that white majority, who are quoted literally and disapprovingly, then ironically in italics. The voice in the poem educates by moving from simple first-person testimony ("Once I redemption neither sought nor knew") to skeptical quotation ("'Their colour is a diabolic die'") to second-person imperative ("Remember") and, in the end, double entendre ("black," "refin'd"). Try reading the last line out loud, straight, and then in a mocking or eye-rolling tone. It works both ways.

It's a stunning reversal, a mirror for racists presented like a gift of flowers, freely offered, ending softly with more metaphors, so softly that we might miss that "colour," blackness, has been relativized, refined out of its diabolism before our prejudicial eyes. In eight lines Phillis gives a seminar on race as a fiction, an ideology, a projection of sinfulness, a construct that is getting in the way of universal salvation.

Like any good rhetorician she begins on points of agreement, here the seeming facts of her own history. She was brought, she was taught, she was converted by "mercy": a blessed thing. But if conversion excused, even sanctified slavery, why should the progress from paganism to assimilation stop there? Turning immediately to the problem of racism, to unchristian scorn, undermines the putative uses of conversion as a proslavery talking point. Certain other Christians are in dire need of refinement with their alchemical, even medieval, talk of diabolism. The poet mocks racism's metaphors—mark of Cain, black magic, whiteness as purity—and instructs us to remember what they really are: choices among words, ways of thinking.

Wheatley calls attention to how we make race by how we use language. The commas and italics slow down the reader, making us linger over words, implicating us: Are we with the author, or are we allied with the "some" who play the race card with cute offhand remarks about color? If blackness is a metaphor for humanity's intrinsic, universal sin, is it fair to suggest that mere skin indicates its presence? If we say darker skin is "sable," as Wheatley does elsewhere and as Pope had in reference to indigenous peoples, it might evoke nature, or even royalty: these people can be, or have, kings. If we call it a "diabolic die," as "some" dubiously do, we might be evoking the black arts of devil worship, not to mention slave-produced indigo dye. "Refin'd" may even suggest slave-harvested cane made into molasses, rum, and white sugar.

By the fourth and final couplet Wheatley has turned the tables, much as in "America," through simile. Christians, like Britons, need to be shown their prejudices and complacencies. Less metaphorically and more directly, she also questions racial thinking by telling a story. If enslavement is a fortunate fall, a progress, it's a historical one, akin to the arc of history, from ancient Greece and Rome and Egypt, to Israel, to the new Israel: redeemed America. The historical arc might put Africa in the past, but then where does that place so-called Christians who speak regressively of diabolism, of witchcraft? Real Christians don't believe in the occult or in Old Testament curses, whether Cain or Ham (they were increasingly conflated in Wheatley's time). Reject the simile, "black as Cain," that visits slavery on sin from soon after Eden, calls it color, then forgets that it is just a language game. That stuff is "unrefin'd," its motives suspect.

Wheatley has claimed to be redeemed, but only to turn that line, the saved versus the damned, against those who look upon her with scorn: which is to say, unchristian masters. The would-be Christians in the poem are the ones not remembering and not moving forward in "th' angelic train." The poem seizes control of the meaning of Africa and America in time, to say that race is a static, ahistorical way of thinking about slavery, Christianity, and civilization.

The ambivalence about Africa with which the poem begins parallels contemporary ambivalence about the ancient worlds, both Hebrew and Mediterranean, to which people looked for answers as to whether slavery was morally justifiable and under what conditions. By 1767, Wheatley's invocations of Africa had already turned double-edged. They use presumptions of African pagan backwardness to challenge easy notions of progress. "Must Ethiopians be imploy'd for you / Greatly rejoice if any good I do," she had asked in "Deism," which went through a number of extant variants. That poem too might be seen as following a self-hating script—if it did not end in a prose encomium that sounds precisely like an adaptation of her African mother's morning sun rite, but simultaneously classicized and Christianized: "May I O eternal salute aurora to begin thy Praise, shall mortal dust do that which immortals scarcely can comprehend." References to the sun as Aurora fill contemporary translations from Homer and Ovid: in *The Metamorphoses*, Aurora mourns a son lost in war. In her poetic appeal to wayward Harvard students, Wheatley had referred to "the Sable land of error's darkest night / There, sacred Nine! For you no place was found, / Parent of mercy, 'twas thy Powerfull hand / Brought me in safety from the dark abode." Christianity saves, but it also allows her access to the "sacred" classical muses. If this is a refusal of Africa on behalf of Christianity, it is also a valorization of her authority to mediate between two ancient worlds—Africa and the Mediterranean—and this modern one, to show the way forward to salvation.

"On Being Brought from Africa to America" was a coming-out effort for Wheatley as an African, a Christian, and an American all at once. She joins the Latin poets like Horace who were, like Wheatley, the subjects of a far-flung slaving, assimilating empire. They too made exile their "primal scene" and constant theme, but Wheatley was beginning to Christianize and politicize their studied (and, in Horace, deftly ironic) reflections on aristocrats and slaves. If "On Being Brought from Africa to America" was read in 1768, it could also have been understood not as a celebration of slavery as salvation for Africans but rather as another heartfelt, and partly satirical, attack on evangelical and racial defenses of the slave trade. Drawing white readers in by offering the voice of experience, the poem puts up a mirror to their desires for assurance and forgiveness from those they oppressed. Instead of an epic narrative of enslavement and conversion, "On Being Brought from Africa to America" quotes secondhand racist nonsense to show that the favor of universal salvation is, too often, not returned by would-be Christians. It's her response to being urged, disingenuously, to testify. If Wheatley is willing to play with American slavery as a fortunate fall, it's mainly to debunk race as a proslavery language game.

Perhaps for this very reason, while she chose or was persuaded to circulate "America" in manuscript to some Pennsylvania women, some of whom were Quakers, there is no record of "On Being Brought from Africa to America" ever being shown to anyone before it appeared in the London edition of her book in 1773. It was too subversive, too risky, too early for her to showcase in town. Things were moving too fast. Before the year 1768 was out, the rhetoric had turned all too real. The imperial controversy would be conducted more intimately than ever. Americans would be treated like wayward children, even like slaves. Boston would be a "garrison'd town."

8

THE OCCUPATION

Seven men-of-war, including one named the *Senegal*, and several smaller vessels arrived at the end of September and surrounded Boston harbor, ringing the Long Wharf "as if intended for a formal Siege." A thousand men, then hundreds more, of the Fourteenth and Twenty-Ninth Regiments marched up the wharf onto King Street with drums and fifes playing, regimental colors flying, and bayonets fixed. Their presence caused a crisis over where the soldiers would sleep: the very issue that had brought matters to a head in New York and inspired Massachusetts's controversial statement of support. The issue of quartering soldiers had merged with the problem of taxation, of sovereignty, of government itself.

Why the astonishing display, with one regiment "camped in the commons" and the other using "the State-House and Faneuil Hall for barracks"? Bostonians' actions and Bostonian publicity had forced the issue. In response, the empire had chosen to make the city the center of customs enforcement for the entire coast of North America. The point of the troops was to force submission. The colony had come a long way from its position as the most willing and able supplier of warriors for Britain just a decade before. Townspeople had rioted, attacking the houses of the royally appointed lieutenant governor and the office of the customs commissioners. Now Boston would be "a spectacle to all North America." Boston's patriot leaders embraced the spectacle as they sought to spread their version of events, including the threat of "slavery" now embodied by a standing army.

Governor Bernard had wanted troops to quell riots in 1767. London and the military commanders resisted for many months. Commodore Samuel Hood in Halifax responded to officials' pleas for help by sending the HMS *Romney*, but the efforts of emboldened customs officers to enforce the Townshend duties had led to more violent incidents on ship and shore. Now the immediate rationale for moving the regiments to Boston, according to Lord Hillsborough, the new secretary of state for the colonies, was the embarrassing "disorders" of March 18, 1768, the anniversary of the Stamp Act repeal, when the newly arrived members of the American Board of Customs Commissioners, agents of the king who had been posted to Boston, had been hanged in effigy during a parade down King Street. Resistance leaders insisted that Governor Bernard and others had exaggerated. It had been just "disorderly boys" making trouble, not the citizens or even the people. The Loyal Nine had even cut down the effigies. But other reports cited eight hundred "young fellows and Negroes" threatening the customs office down the street from the Town House.

Phillis Wheatley recognized the importance of the troops' arrival. Her poem "On the Arrival of the Ships of War, and Landing of the Troops" was never published and has not survived. Yet two and a half years later, the effort seemed impressive enough to be included in her initial book proposal. The title suggests her awareness of the importance of the event, her status as an eyewitness at the center of the action on King Street, and a captive Bostonian's sensitivity to comings and goings and their reverberations. By chronicling the arrival of the ships and soldiers, she bid, again, to be a laureate of Boston, writing in response to public events and what they seemed to portend.

The fact that the poem wasn't published might make her ambition seem premature, her grasp beyond her reach. Or was it? Never had imperial affairs seemed so consequential and yet so intimate as during the occupation that could not be called such because, technically, it was a police action. Some patriots like Samuel Adams said it made Boston a garrison, but the term didn't catch on quite yet. It didn't really fit a town of more than fifteen thousand (suddenly, seventeen thousand, with the arrival of eight hundred more troops by December and as many more attached women and children) that remained a center of trade. Castle William, the actual fort, was off on an island in the harbor; troops shuttled back and forth, on and off the Long Wharf, according to the political temperature—not unlike Governor Bernard, who had himself rowed offshore when he felt intimidated by periodic demonstrations, also known as mobs. That fall, the governor himself began to seem less relevant. What more could he do after repeatedly shutting down the provincial assembly and denouncing the patriots in letters to London that leaked to newspapers and further damaged his reputation in Massachusetts?

Instead, soldiers themselves became the news that fall. How would they behave, whose side were they on when camped in a British city where they socialized with locals and competed with them for off-duty work? They were not nearly as strange as patriot radicals insisted in depicting this standing army as the advance guard of enslavement. On the other hand, their threatening presence could not be made to seem anywhere near as normal as officials proposed.

Wheatley's carefully neutral choice of words—the "arrival" of the vessels, the soldiers' "landing"—spoke to the strangeness but also the openness of the moment, the ambiguity of loyalties in the imperial crisis. As much as anything that had occurred since the Sugar Act, the military presence marked Boston as what it still was, after 140 years: a colony. It may be that her poem about the landing of troops, an imperial spectacle, seemed too neutral to please anyone as the leaves dropped during the fall of 1768 and even more regimentals—suddenly now constituting a third of the adult males in town—found lodgings where they could, all over the city. The housing situation made their comings and goings all the more conspicuous and provocative.

She wouldn't have written, certainly couldn't have published, an ode, an encomium, or on the other hand a lament. No one else did either. What classical, or religious, precedent or context might she have found that wouldn't rankle some readers? Even more, what could she have written that did not call too much attention to her own presence? The redcoats drilled on the Common with full music on Sundays, disrupting church, attracting "boys and negroes." A town that forbade theater had itself become a display, a proscenium of imperial power and its limits, as everyone interpreted the behavior of the troops and their officers for what it might mean. Even theater itself became an issue as officers planned to produce a play. The locals, who still enforced a Puritan ban on such performances, complained. Someone observed, provocatively, that in Britain, Parliament, not localities, licensed plays.

Five Boston newspapers began to differentiate themselves— sometimes subtly, often not—according to their attitudes toward the occupation and nonimportation. But the standard anonymity of political essays combined with editorial discretion did not allow for the full propaganda potential of what the *Boston Gazette* decried as these latest attempts to "subdue Americans to the yoke." So the patriots started what was in effect an organized occupation news bureau, called it the "Journal of the Times," and sent its sensational contents to be published in a New York newspaper, after which the same stories could be reprinted innocently in Boston papers. The city had become a theater of empire and resistance, and no one knew when or how the play would end.

Decades after the city was truly occupied territory in 1775, Bostonians still told a joke about the British army's forays there: that they came to capture Boston, only to become captives of Boston. The humor turned on the prevalence of captivity and slavery in the Atlantic world. It also revealed an essential truth about 1768–70. The soldiers both fraternized and clashed with the civilians with whom they shared much, much more than living spaces. Desertion quickly became a problem. So did harassment, theft, seduction, rape, and jurisdiction over crimes petty and capital.

Phillis wouldn't be the only African with an interest in civil-military relations. Other Africans were involved, on every side of every contest. His Majesty's Twenty-Ninth Regiment had at least half a dozen (formerly or currently enslaved) African drummers. They would have been among the first redcoats to be seen and heard parading off the Long Wharf. One of their other carefully chosen, very public jobs was to administer the lash to fellow soldiers, an event that first occurred within days of the troops' arrival—nine or ten of them, on the Common. The "Journal of the Times" registered shock: "To behold Britons scourged by Negro drummers, was a new and very disagreeable spectacle."

If the presence of so many troops and the sight of ships of war made some Bostonians feel enslaved, the presence of just as many (a thousand to fifteen hundred) Africans in town raised for some military men the possibility that a more forceful imposition of British rule might find useful support from slaves and former slaves. Perhaps Africans even held the balance of power.

Within weeks, an ostensibly drunken captain named John Wilson, already angered at the reception of his regiment by the locals, approached a group of blacks in the street and told them that "soldiers were come to procure their freedoms" and that together they would "drive all the Liberty Boys to the devil." Some witnesses accused Wilson of telling slaves to go home and "cut their Masters' Throats and promising them as a Reward, if they would appear at the Place of Parade, to make them free." Magistrates and selectmen "were in an uproar." In true English fashion they fell to disputing whether the prosecution of Captain Wilson should be governed by martial or com-

mon law. Frustrated in seeking to put Wilson to trial (varying accounts
have him still there months later or, alternately, reassigned elsewhere),
the Whigs kept trying to address the issue of civilian police authority.
In June 1769, Justice of the Peace Richard Dana advised juries not to
submit to the casual violence of soldiers, which he called a mark of
slavery.

On at least one occasion, when civil officials prosecuted and convicted a soldier for theft, they sold him as an indentured servant (or as
an outraged colonel Alexander Mackay put it, "as a slave"). A political
point was being made—local over "garrison" law. Skeptics countered
that the entire affair was a deserter's ruse, a collusion between a soldier
and his labor-starved, wage-paying new employers. That such an event
could be construed as a liberation or as yet another colonial fraud reveals the oddity of Boston during the late 1760s. The troops experienced both harassment and hospitality. If soldiers blended in, that was
one problem. If they didn't—if they policed—that was another.

No wonder attention turned repeatedly to the Africans, the young
people, and the women stopped by sentries as they went about their
business, who became the objects of scorn and desire to the bored
young men carrying bayonets. The presence of these people, people
like Phillis Wheatley, in patriot crowds could be disputed—or relied
on with plausible deniability. Their ability to spark incidents with soldiers would prove more difficult to contain.

The hopes of moderates could be kept alive by the professionalism and
probity of officers like Samuel Hood, the head of the naval squadron
in America. After he arrived from Halifax in November, the "Journal
of the Times" reported a rumor that Commodore Hood had written
directly to the Board of Customs Commissioners, asking them how
many ships of the line it would take to ensure the safe collection of His
Majesty's tax revenues. Hood, like other governors and high-ranking
officers, had written many letters that were scrutinized carefully in

London (his were actually published) and made the basis of policy decisions, including the crackdown. Meanwhile, the well-liked commodore tried hard to get along with colonists.

Within a few weeks of his arrival, though, Hood performed a different kind of spectacle in response to the ongoing crisis of desertion in his ranks. After a court-martial of absconding sailors held aboard the HMS *Mermaid*, two were flogged "from ship to ship," and another, presumably the ringleader, ordered to be hanged by his neck in public view of the harbor. Everyone knew this was serious. To the great dismay of locals, a deserter of the Fourteenth Regiment named Richard Ames had been executed by gunshot on Boston Common in October. This time, military theater supplied a different ending. At the appointed hour, with a crowd watching "on the wharfs," the man "was brought on Deck, and just going to be turn'd off when a pardon was read to him by Order of Commodore Hood." Even the "Journal of the Times" was impressed enough to finish its report with a grudging compliment: "*Commodore Hood, in this Act of Humanity and Mercy, has given no unfavourable Idea of his Prudence and Capacity as an Officer.*"

Wheatley seized upon this moment as one that might reduce the tensions that made Africans appear to be a potential fifth column on behalf of the redcoats. Her praise poem "To the Hon.ble Commodore Hood on his Pardoning a Deserter" picks up on the old, even ancient traditions that informed the spectacle in the harbor. Where the "Journal of the Times" portrayed an enlightened man of rank showing good judgment ("prudence" and "capacity"), Wheatley elaborated the aristocratic, even monarchical implications of Hood's display of mercy. She's so impressed—and can so take for granted that everyone else is—that she can uncharacteristically insert her own feelings in the first-person subjective: "It was thy noble soul and high desert / That caus'd these breathings of my grateful heart / You sav'd a soul from Pluto's dreary shore / You sav'd his body and he asks no more."

It's difficult now to credit such an unabashed turn of praise for a career naval officer upon whom history has bestowed something less than the "Immortal wreaths" Wheatley gives him. As so often in her oeuvre, most memorably in the poem to Hussey and Coffin the previous year, her classical framing pivots toward the pious. The fearful glance at the downward, deadly depths rises upward instead. Once again, Wheatley takes her vocation as herald of the transformation of death or near death into life, or better yet, eternal life. By the time she's halfway done, the genteel officer is turned into a man of feeling *and* divinity. She has to "Hail" him and invoke his rank just to keep him on the ground, or rather shipboard, as she imagines God's assent to his wise display of sovereign power.

The surviving copy of the Hood poem closes out the three in the folded page she sent to Philadelphia that includes "America" and "Atheism." In a sense it combines the themes of both these earlier poems while addressing, and even resolving, their real risks. "To the Hon.ble Commodore Hood" seeks reconciliation between the patriots and British officialdom. It takes the sting out of the celebration of New England virtue, and accusations of bad imperial mothering, that suffused "America." Instead, as in "Atheism" and the earlier poem on Hussey and Coffin's salvation, she reintroduces herself as the poet who can lead a classically informed audience from Pluto's underworld (also mentioned in "Atheism"), the dangerous ocean, to a renewed focus on God's sovereignty on earth (or water)—but without claiming to be more pious than the person she addresses, as "Atheism" did. Wheatley recognized Hood's ritual of benign sovereignty and answered with a performance of continued assimilation to the local and the imperial culture on the secular and sacred terms that she hoped, or prayed, could be owned.

As ads for runaway soldiers in the newspapers began to appear alongside the ones for fugitive and salable slaves, it became rather too obvious that Africans and newly arrived military men in Boston had a few things in common. Enslaved people and Britons in uniform alike were generally classified as strangers in Boston even while constituting a significant part or more of the current population and an even greater proportion of the workers. Both groups slept in the houses of intimate enemies. Both faced dire punishments for desertion. If the enslaved were often mocked for their color, referred to as black or negro, redcoat soldiers were called lobster backs, or worse, "bloody-backs," in reference to the shameful whippings they received.

The disturbing similarities cut another way as well, one that placed the enslaved squarely in the middle. Soldiers and civilians were subjecting each other to intense surveillance, episodes of violence, and an uncertain future. In other words, they were treating each other the way the children and the Africans of Boston had always been treated. Neither redcoats nor townspeople liked it. Young people and Africans stood in the middle, excited and fearful, wondering what it all meant.

The patriot movement tried to seize control of the situation, with its paradox of fraternizing and distancing, its extremes of abuse and desertion, by acceding to some understandings of permissible conduct by soldiers and civilians that had been negotiated with the more sympathetic, or sensitive, officers. Playing defense against the redcoats' abuses while maintaining the slower propaganda war over who were the perpetrators and who the victims, the organized patriots stepped up their harassment of the customs officials and their scrutiny of merchants and shopkeepers who failed to boycott imports in opposition to the Townshend duties. In the press, this meant exposés. On the streets, it meant a special role for "lads" about Wheatley's age (sixteen) and "boys" even younger.

Relying on minors to police transgressors—including, inevitably, the common soldiers who enforced curfews—created some plausible deniability for quasi-legal activity like sliming the doors of importers and insulting their customers. It also made everyday life into contests of spin waged in shouted curses, passing shoves, coats of tar, and letters to imperial authorities, any and all of which could be written up for the newspapers. During January 1769, for example, the "Journal of the Times" described how Governor Bernard's exposed letters to London had whined that boys in King's Alley tipped over the sentry box in front of the Custom House while failing to mention the insults civilians received from soldiers or "their practice with the Negroes."

General Thomas Gage and Commodore Hood continued to shuttle companies and regiments in and out of town depending on skirmishes in the streets and military needs elsewhere, but the on-the-ground situation seemed, to them at least, increasingly pointless. They wanted to leave. Governor Bernard, Lieutenant Governor Thomas Hutchinson, and the customs commissioners begged them to stay. In a kind of compromise, Hood left for Halifax and two of the regiments departed as well. Less than half of the soldiers, about eight hundred, remained in town. The verbal taunting and violent confrontations only increased—at least in part because both organized resistance and official repression had ebbed. One night in October, mobs brutally tarred and feathered the customs informant George Gailer and beat up a man mistaken for the Tory printer-editor John Mein.

The patriots might seem to have had the upper hand. They certainly had the crowds in the street and most of the press. But indebted merchants wavered. Patriots singled out Tories who refused to cooperate with nonimportation, but Mein exposed merchants who imported British goods even though they had pledged not to do so. These alleged hypocrites included Nathaniel Wheatley, who claimed that his "forty pieces of Russia duck" (nautical cloth excluded from the nonimportation resolves) had been somehow misidentified as "Irish linen." On January 1, 1770, the nonimportation agreement expired. Patriots turned to street demonstrations against shopkeepers who began importing taxed items. One of them, Theophilus Lillie, placed an essay in the newspapers that sounded what had become a Tory refrain against the unofficial, crowd-enforced "Laws I am sure I never gave my consent either in person or by my representative . . . I own I had rather be a slave under one Master; for if I know who he is, I may, perhaps, be able to please him, than a slave to a hundred or more, who I don't know where to find, nor what they will expect from me."

On Thursday, February 22, a morning when schools let out early, 150 "Boys and Children" raised effigies of the four most notorious shopkeepers in front of Lillie's shop. Ebenezer Richardson, a neighbor well known as a collaborator, started demanding that adults passing by help him take the effigies down. The crowd turned on him and pushed him into his house. More boys gathered, shouting at the "informer." Richardson yelled back, threatening them, telling them they had to disperse from "the King's highway." Kids made shaming noises and threw trash. Richardson got his gun and fired "swanshot" out his second story. More trash and sticks and stones came his way, breaking windows. His next spray of pellets hit the ten-year-old Christopher Seider fatally in the chest.

This now-forgotten accident (or child murder) less than two weeks before the Boston Massacre displays the intimacy of even Boston's major commercial streets and the tendency of political events to encompass young people. Seider, an indentured servant, lived with Grizzell Apthorp, a widow and pillar of the Anglican church who actually owned and rented out the large building that served as the customs office. It might seem an accident that a poor boy, son of German immigrants, got so tragically involved, even as an unlucky victim. Or was Seider enacting a rebellion against his Tory mistress, only to become the apt, because humble, symbol of the people who showed up for town meetings and did the real work of the resistance movement?

Why not both? If the bloody riot had political meanings, so could the aftermath. Bostonians knew how to do funerals to make a point. Seider's coffin bore three Latin inscriptions: "The serpent is lurking in the grass. The fatal dart is thrown. Innocence is nowhere safe." Five hundred schoolboys led the cortege from the Tree of Liberty (conveniently near Seider's parents' house) through King Street to the Town House, followed by between thirteen hundred and two thousand others mourning the "little hero and first martyr to a noble cause." The boy showed a "manly spirit" on his deathbed, insisted the *Boston Evening-Post*. The "several heroic pieces"—poems—"found in his pocket, particularly *Wolfe's Summit of human Glory*," an illustrated broadside song describing the siege of Quebec in 1759, "give reason to think he had a martial Genius, and would have made a clever man."

Before he'd been run out of town, the printer John Mein had complained about the patriot tendency to excuse mobs as the random actions of "boys and negroes." Colonel Alexander Mackay, one of the now departed officers who, like Samuel Hood, had earned the respect of many Bostonians, thought that the townspeople preferred "abuse, falsehoods and scribbling" to "powder and balls." He had a point, though he apparently underestimated the impression that rhymes about war could make on ordinary, and apparently literate, boys like Christopher Seider, not to mention the scribbling battle to define who were heroes and what was a mob. (Besides, Mackay had scribbled his own arch remark.)

Now that it had come to powder and shot, Wheatley, too, couldn't look away. She'd already claimed the elegiac and heroic modes as her own, and young people had been embraced, not disavowed, as the main actors of the drama. She leaped in, shifting completely to the arch-patriot point of view, echoing the very phrases of the newspaper accounts, but within an epic frame: "In heavens eternal court it was decreed / How the first martyr for the cause should bleed." A necessary prelude, and familiar sacrifice: the heavenly court derives from the beginning of *The Odyssey*. Only the gods could have insisted upon such a scene. But Seider's snuffed-out "martial Genius," and the human villainy of Richardson, fit *The Iliad* better than crafty and mature Odysseus's survival story, so Wheatley turns to the other Homeric epic:

> To clear the country of the hated brood
> He whet his courage for the common good
> Long hid before, a vile infernal here

Prevents Achilles in his mid career
Where'er this fury darts his Pois'nous breath
All are endanger'd to the shafts of death.

Wheatley is trying hard to bring the republican, patriot rhetoric of the "common good," and the mortal sins of Tory transgressors, to the original epic frame of Homer with its individual valor and bloody death scenes. Britons are again the unfeeling enemy. Where she had imagined Commodore Hood—a real warrior—as an inspired Christian, her Seider doesn't evoke salvation. "Gasping on the ground," he talks war.

Wheatley works with what the papers had printed about the contents of Seider's pockets and what she saw and heard on the street. The more ongoing drama, with far more backstory, involved the "wretch" Richardson, saved by authorities from an angry mob. He can't look upon his victim and flies like the fallen Miltonic archangel, "banish'd" from heaven, or rather Boston.

Having dispatched the murderer, Wheatley shifts to an explicit identification with a unified Boston populace at the funeral, speaking not only for, but to, the martyred boy: "We bring the body from the watry bower . . . Snider behold with what Majestic Love / The Illustrious retinue begins to move." It's the only instance in Wheatley's surviving oeuvre where she depicts herself as part of a crowd. That crowd, like the "cor[p]se" it carries, now has the properties of fame. Even "freedoms foes" can't help but see "Majesty in Death," and presumably in the spectacular train of mourners as well.

Wheatley and those who encouraged her didn't have much opportunity to publish or even circulate her effort. The customs-informer riot, the death of Seider, and his funeral were immediately overshadowed by the even more deadly and even better publicized "soldier riot" and "Massacre" of March 5, which took place one week after the funeral

Wheatley described, on the same day that accounts of the Seider funeral itself appeared in a newspaper.

While Wheatley performed her audacious merger with the patriot crowd, the status and the future of Africans in Boston had become less clear. The participation of Africans in protests for liberty suggested that their enslavement could and would continue to be challenged. The criticism and disavowal of their presence suggested the opposite.

We are accustomed to look, in retrospect, for signs that slavery was on its way out in New England—or on the other hand, that Boston was America, slavery deeply entrenched, and racial caste firmly in place. Wheatley would have seen, all around her, signs of both countervailing trends. The provincial legislature had declined to move on antislavery. But antislavery essays, shaming the patriots on their own behalf, continued to appear occasionally in Boston newspapers in 1769. Fewer Boston ships sailed for Africa, but Peter Gwinn still did voyage that year, eight years after he brought Phillis. Trade of all sorts had slowed, but the market for slaves in town didn't slow down at all, with ads in the papers and even an occasional auction to dispose of two, five, or seven at a time. The moral legitimacy and political wisdom of enslaving Africans remained subject to the questions of 1767, yet Bostonians, including Wheatley, didn't know that slavery in Massachusetts would end in their lifetimes any more than they knew that the province would be in revolt before then, or that the next time redcoat regiments came to Boston it would truly mean an occupation, and a war. Slavery remained both perfectly ordinary and distinctively American. Africans continued to assimilate and to be kept apart.

The path to the famous "riot in King Street" also tells this seemingly contradictory story of proslavery, antislavery, and the contribution of both to the coming of the American Revolution. Again it was boys setting off a chain of events, but this time not with the hated customs officers as the proximate political cause, but rather soldiers and Africans on both sides, as both perpetrators and victims. On March 2, an apprentice or servant (one Bostonian remembered him as black) who pressed a soldier of the Twenty-Ninth Regiment for payment on behalf of his master (either for charcoal or for a haircut) got struck down in response. According to another account, it all started when an off-duty soldier sought employment at a Boston ropewalk, only to be told by a worker that he could clean the privy. In either or both cases, a fight ensued. Thomas Walker, one of the Afro-Caribbean drummers of the Twenty-Ninth, led several dozen of his fellows from the barracks back to the ropewalk, seeking revenge. A justice of the peace shouted at the drummer, "What have you to do with white people's quarrels?" Walker was said to have replied cagily or ironically, perhaps in reference to his literally leading role in any and every parade or battle, "I suppose I may look on." The *Boston News-Letter*, which usually sought to be balanced with respect to Whigs, Tories, and soldiers, portrayed Walker as "intent on wounding or probably killing" and took pleasure in reporting him as "said to be much wounded."

Three days later, on the fifth, another altercation began after a bored soldier kept striking his sword while walking alongside a brick wall, causing dangerous sparks to fly. A "lad" admonished him. A sentry rifle butted another teenager who insulted him. This time, young people converged on King Street, knocked over the sentry shack once again, and threatened the Custom House, leading the troops to come out, and be pelted by snowballs. When Captain Thomas Preston's troops fired on the shouting crowd, three "lads" Phillis's age bled, dying, in the street, along with a ship's mate and forty-seven-year-old Crispus Attucks, a "molatto" man from Framingham, probably a sailor, who had mentioned being on his way from New Providence in the Bahamas to North Carolina.

When four were buried, in what some reckoned the largest public gathering ever on the continent, the processions converged on the deadly spot in King Street to begin the funeral march, again just yards from the Wheatley house. Phillis wrote another poem, most likely the only one published in newspapers on the event, though it did not appear with her name attached. The published poem has several of

Wheatley's favorite words ("Lo," "shades," "heaven," "freedom," and "friends": see Table 2). It reads as if part of a longer effort than the twelve lines squeezed into the end of the lengthy account of the massacre and the funeral in the *Evening-Post* on March 12. Whether as an excerpt or an attempt to capture the kinetic excitement of the events of March 5, it begins in the middle of the drama, with the "heaven-directed" gunshot, and ends imagining the "fame" and the epitaph the martyrs earned: "the letter'd *Stone* shall tell, / How *Caldwell*, *Attucks*, *Gray*, and *Mav'rick* fell . . ."

Invoking heaven and freedom, tending a classical funeral pyre, Phillis had made it into print in Boston for the second time, anonymously. It took the military occupation, a shattering, increasingly deadly controversy about the doings of young people, and her third try at marking the times. For the briefest of moments, she even had the last word, though few would have known it was hers. Several days later, the king's men retreated to their fort on the bay.

9

THE FRIENDS

Like many violent events in history, the Boston Massacre seemed to change everything and nothing. Patriots had made their point about troops in a political tinderbox, but the underlying issues of the imperial controversy remained. The events of early 1770 confirmed the effectiveness of protest but also the seeming necessity for the empire to draw a line that preserved the sovereignty of king and Parliament.

The nonimportation movement, which boys in Boston had fought to protect, gradually unraveled later in the year, difficult as it was to sustain across different port towns. Now events like the "massacre," and its villains, including the soldiers who would stand trial for murder, seemed the clearest proof of the ministerial plot to enslave. That, at least, was the argument of the radical Whigs like Samuel Adams and a young minister at the Second Church named John Lathrop. A onetime tutor at Moor's Indian Charity School, Lathrop preached a sermon the Sunday after the massacre titled "Innocent Blood Crying to God from the Streets of Boston" in which he described the "unparalleled barbarity" of the soldiers, who deserved to be punished by death. His sermon, quickly printed, would be praised and denounced in London, only to appear in a second edition in Boston and in an anniversary rendition the next year. At another extreme, Thomas Hutchinson, soon to be confirmed as colony governor, and his friend and fellow judge Peter Oliver saw the entire *province* as "sinking into perfect barbarism" thanks to radicals and their "black regiment" of clergymen.

In Boston and beyond, much seemed to hinge on the outcome of the soldier trials delayed until the fall, especially after Ebenezer Richardson was convicted but pardoned for the murder of Christopher Seider. Patriots gathered evidence and published accounts that cried murder, but also acknowledged that verdicts of murder for events at a riot might well backfire, leading to more drastic changes in policy from London.

Phillis Wheatley had participated in these events and the battle for their meaning with enthusiasm, or at least strategy. She showed an ability to respond quickly, like Crispus Attucks and other people of African descent who joined crowds and sometimes catalyzed confrontations. This alacrity of response appeared again, for all to see. During the spring and summer and into the fall, New Englanders had issued calls for a revival of the militia tradition. The departure of the regimental redcoats seemed to allow for citizen training without it becoming another direct challenge to authority. This led to copycat experiments by the very people who had, controversially, precipitated the events of the past winter.

On a Monday in late September, "a company of youths" numbering about thirty "mustered on the Common with firelocks." The novices made a few loud and frightening mistakes with their guns, but no one was hurt, and they all went home. But that same evening,

> a number of Negro *Grenadiers*, gathered up in the common and from thence, under commanders (flushed with a military spirit) took it upon them to patrol several streets in town, with a drum beating, fifes playing and other music, until some of the inhabitants, fearing the ill consequences from such un-

lawful assemblies, broke their drum, and quickly dispersed them, ordering them to go peaceably to their masters.

It wasn't clear which side of the imperial conflict the pop-up black militia meant to support—or whether that ambiguity was the point. The lesson, to the author of this account, should have been obvious but had to be made clear anyway: "This may serve to caution masters against allowing their servants too much liberty, in the execution of preconcerted schemes, which may be attended with consequences fatal to the inhabitants." Five months later, another newspaper noted that black "Companies" meeting regularly "for Entertainment" had "quarreled with each other, and now go about the Streets in the Evening with Clubs and other Weapons." Officially, the selectmen had restricted such activities before, authorizing constables to "take up" any slaves out at night without a lantern who couldn't show proof that they were out on an errand.

Such illicit and perhaps illegal activities might seem to be as far removed from Phillis's reading and praying, watching and scribbling, as a parade or a street brawl is from a poet or penitent's lamplight in the attic. But they might be more properly seen as a black version of Bostonians' well-known propensity to join together—and to divide the next day. Or as a male version of Phillis's own attempts to use the resources at hand to make friends and better her daily life. A younger generation of Africans were taking liberties, together as well as alone, whether it seemed like imitation or like initiative—though any doubts about the current status of enslaved persons would have been put to rest by a perusal of the same newspapers as they reported the drama of the massacre and the ensuing trials of the soldiers in court and in public opinion. If anything, an increasing number of the young men and women of Phillis's cohort seem to have been put up for sale—sometimes for "no fault," or "want of employ," in the sellers' jargon, but also for "lying and stealing" (despite being "genteel, strong, hearty," and "good-natured"). Estate sales and auctions still included people like "a Negro boy, about 14 Years of Age, who can be recommended for his Honesty," along with furniture and "a large Soap kettle which will contain two Barrels." Once again the loosening of credit and revival of trade breathed new life into the slave market. Peter Gwinn certainly noticed and sailed for Africa once again.

Fewer antislavery essays appeared in Boston newspapers during this phase of the imperial crisis. But supporters of the nascent movement did not give up so easily. The Reverend Samuel Cooke ended his prestigious annual Election Day sermon, pronounced before the legislators and the Harvard Corporation, with a direct appeal to the members to pass a bill against the slave trade. The renewed debate in the legislature brought Timothy Pickering to Isaiah Thomas's new patriot paper, to renew his earlier charges of patriot hypocrisy over slavery. Yet radical Whig stalwarts like James Warren, who were turning March 5 into a new annual holiday to keep the spirit of liberty alive, believed that a move against slavery would sap the intercolonial support that had made resistance in Boston so much more effective. "If passed into an act, it should have a bad effect on the union of the colonies," he told his friend John Adams. The General Court passed it anyway, only to see the measure vetoed by Governor Hutchinson, on the grounds that it contradicted the king's prerogative over the trade. The problem of slavery implicated, and sometimes confused, the key political issue of sovereignty, and vice versa.

While much of the credibility of the patriot resistance depended on the "murderers" of March 5 getting a fair trial, the radicals thought things were going too far when several Africans testified on behalf of the king's men. The defense relied on the especially impressive testimony of Andrew Wendell, praised by his owner Oliver Wendell, a selectman of the town, for his "character for truth" and "integrity." Andrew "has been well educated," Wendell added, and mentioned, as proof of his literacy, that Andrew "had wrote poetry." Most compellingly, Andrew Wendell insisted that Captain Preston had not, in fact, given the order to fire during the melee in King Street. It was also

Andrew Wendell who first suggested that the intimidatingly tall and muscular Crispus Attucks had been at the center of the crowd, rushing the soldiers and in effect causing the bullets to fly.

The defense attorney John Adams, a believer in law and order as well as a radical patriot, peppered his defense of Preston and the soldiers with repeated descriptions of the mob as a "motley rabble of saucy boys, negroes and molattoes, Irish teagues and out landish jack tarrs." Attucks, in his hands, became a one-man wrecking crew. But this was in response to Andrew Wendell's testimony and the unflattering light it shed on patriots. Adams wanted the soldiers acquitted—but the aggressive white patriot adults to appear as the peaceable, propertied, patient victims of bad policy. By race-baiting black participants as mere opportunists, like boys in the streets, Adams could support the rule of law, show how reasonable the colonists had been, and help keep the movement together. He had already doubled down on his what-about, both-sides strategy, however, when blacks turned out to be some of the best witnesses at the trial, once again showing their ubiquity in the streets of Boston and their ability to draw attention to their own position and to seize the opportunities of the imperial controversy.

John Adams's cousin Samuel Adams and other radicals took another tack. They went directly after Andrew for contributing to the acquittal of most of the redcoats. The prosecuting attorney Robert Treat Paine tried calling Andrew's testimony "flights of fancy" that "may be ornamental in a *Poet* (It was suggested in favour of Andrew's Understanding, that he had wrote poetry), but, will never establish the Credibility of an *Historian*." Even after the trials they refused to let it go—probably because the trials seemed to racialize the divisions between patriot and Tory in ways that might be politically useful. For Sam Adams, who had earlier shown sympathy to antislavery, Andrew, a "negro," had testified not so much in defense of Preston as against the people of Boston. He knew what side Africans were on. The enslaved of Boston, he wrote as "Vindex," had been "tamper'd with to cut their master's throats. I hope Andrew is not one of these. His character for integrity and even for *learning,* for he can both 'read and write,' has been an occasion wrought to so high a pitch, that I am loath even *to hint* anything that may tend to depreciate it," Adams continued with tongue firmly in cheek. Less subtly, he proceeded to disparage Andrew Wendell's testimony by equating it with the tall tales of romantic conquests that Andrew and his fellow bondsmen supposedly told when they gathered in kitchens. For Adams, the complication of political "slavery" that tended to accompany black participation clouded the true, original issue: that "to be called to account by a common soldier, or any soldier" on the streets of Boston was "a badge of slavery which none but a *slave* will wear."

Black participation and black testimony so threatened patriot radicals that it had to be refuted repeatedly—and creatively. Two acrostic poems mocked Andrew Wendell's veracity and literacy:

> *A NDREW a naughty black! O Strange!*
> *N o one would think a black would change!*
> *D iscipled in a tory's school!*
> *R eads, talks and reasons like a fool*
> *E xperienc'd here to lye for some!*
> *W ill do to send to lye at home!!!*

This first acrostic evokes a slave-for-sale advertisement ("will do to send"). It suggests that Andrew Wendell's reading and writing and speaking skills are a specifically Tory discipline. Black eloquence and literacy are, in other words, the inherent opposites of truth and reason, because of their miseducation in slavery.

The second poem, appearing five weeks later, the week of the March 5 anniversary of the massacre, depicts Africans as natural, as opposed to calculated and Tory-educated, liars:

> *A s Negroes and L——rs in judgment agree*
> *N o wonder that vice with her airs is so free*

D evice and low cunning do commonly stand!
R elated in friendship and join hand in hand!
E xperience doth teach that poor black and white!
W hen blended together, as one, will unite.

In a classic example of the progress of racism under the heat lamp of politics, the racial denigration grows more explicit, more up front in the very first line. The mixed mobs of March 5 were themselves the problem. Andrew Wendell's literacy could put him at center stage, make him an equal member of the community in a real sense. Such "blended" friendships could be a political threat even if some found them compatible with bondage. When threatened, patriots like Sam Adams reached for the color line already there in their pockets and their pages, like the ballads poor Christopher Seider had carried. They simultaneously relied on race and elaborated it in response to the friendships that politics had wrought.

Phillis had been thinking about whether friendship could transcend race or status. In a poem she titled "On Friendship" and signed on March 15, 1769, she imagined "Amicitia" (Latin for friendship) as a goddess, "divinely Bright" with "ample reign." Typical of Wheatley's early and later verse in its intensive combination of classical and religious evocations, it is also suggestive of the direct address in her other early verses like "Atheism," the poems directed at men like Hussey and Coffin, and the more abstract, group-directed poem to the Harvard students. She is expressing "gratitude" to a particular individual while praising feminine friendship in general. Friendship, personified and latinized, is akin to love: "Amor like me doth triumph at the sight." She imagines herself, like the angelic goddess, able to wish her friend to action as well as thought, or perhaps more specifically to visiting: "Now let my thoughts in Contemplation steer / The Footsteps of the Superlative fair."

Who was Phillis's "Superlative" friend? Given her use of poems to reach out to people, it could have been anyone—or rather, any woman. "Superlative" may suggest a person of some recognized social stature or reputation. The term "fair" usually equated femininity and light-colored skin. Perhaps the addressee was one of the other young female poets, or someone who had shown an interest, or encouraged her to use the language of friendship to describe their relationship.

By 1770 or 1771, when she was seventeen years old, friendship clearly had more than a literary or metaphorical meaning to Wheatley. By then she had bonded with Obour Tanner, an enslaved woman who lived in Newport, Rhode Island, where Susanna Wheatley may have had friends and spent time, bringing Phillis along. According to women of the famous Beecher family who knew Tanner in her old age and received seven of their letters as a gift, Tanner had recognized Wheatley as a fellow captive from on board the *Phillis*. Obour was probably a few years older, and the legend of their travel together aboard the slave ship can be seen as having figurative if not literal meaning for the two women.

They had a connection that transcended their different places of residence, a bond reinforced by the generationally specific surge of imported Africans during the late 1750s and early 1760s. They called each other sister as well as friend. In letters often carried by their fellow "servants," they had discussed the dilemmas of African evangelical Protestants:

> Dear Sister
> I rec'd your favour of February 6th [1772] for which I give you my sincere thanks. I greatly rejoice with you in that realizing view, and I hope experience, of the Saving change which you So emphatically describe. Happy were it for us if we could arrive to that evangelical Repentance, and the true holiness of heart which you mention.

Obour Tanner had joined the First Church in Newport in 1768 and participated in the revivals, and probably schooling, led by the lay preacher Sarah Osborn. These evangelicals spoke regularly of saving grace and God's love. Osborn also "equated religion with literacy" and gave women a "new vocabulary of individual experience to justify their authority and leadership." As it had for the Reverends Eleazar Wheelock and George Whitefield, the conversion of natives and Africans demonstrated God at work and justified revivalistic means.

In her letters to Tanner, Wheatley seems at least as comfortable with this specifically evangelical language of friendship as she had been with the Latin-quoting style of literary sensibility in "On Friendship." With Obour she emphasizes Christ much more than she does even in her poems about religion. Christ here is the key to God's love, which extends to Africans and allows a safe space for them to talk about what we would call issues of identity as well as intimacy:

> Inexpressibly happy Should we be could we have a due Sense of Beauties and excellence of the Crucified Saviour. In his Crucifixion may be seen marvelous displays of Grace and Love, Sufficient to draw and invite us to the rich and endless treasures of his mercy; let us rejoice in and adore the wonders of God's infinite Love in bringing us from a land Semblant of darkness itself, and where the divine light of revelation (being obscur'd) is as darkness. Here, the knowledge of the true God and eternal life are made manifest; But there, profound ignorance overshadows the Land. Your observation is true, namely, that there was nothing in us to recommend us to God. Many of our fellow creatures are pass'd by, when the bowels of divine love expanded towards us. May this goodness & long Suffering of God lead us to unfeign'd repentance.

The other side of their lament about unsaved black people in Africa and America was an optimism that if the two of them had come into Christian fellowship, and turned their abjection into the potential for saving grace, so could anyone: "It gives me very great pleasure to hear of so many of my Nation, Seeking with eagerness the way to true felicity." Phillis chose to end her letter on this note, an identification with Africans and a pledge of friendship to Obour, that could be continued and strengthened by writing to each other, even if illness intervened or letters took months to find their way:

> I hope the correspondence between us will continue, (my being much indispos'd this winter past was the reason of my not answering yours before now) which correspondence I hope may have the happy effect of improving our mutual friendship. Till we meet in the regions of consummate blessedness, let us endeavor by the assistance of divine grace, to live the life, and we Shall die the death of the Righteous. May this be our happy case and of those who are travelling to the region of Felicity, is the earnest request of your affectionate
> Friend & hum[ble]. Ser[van]t. Phillis Wheatley

Letters like this one, themselves carried by friends, traveled slowly, whether in New England or between new and old England. Yet for all the inefficiency by modern standards, they took on that much more importance for requiring the very care, and the relationships with third parties, that they advanced. According to John Wheatley, Phillis's first notable piece of writing had been this kind of letter, to Samson Occom, while he was in England. Evangelical correspondence modeled loving friendship. Occom too demonstrated his ability to navigate the distances between colonists and several Native nations with extremely careful yet heartfelt letters.

In this Occom took a cue from his mentor George Whitefield. The great revivalist had as sharp a sense of the power of the press as he did for extemporaneous preaching, but his letters especially linked the spoken and written word and allowed his mission to be all the more powerful and popular for being transatlantic. For the white Wheatleys, who had flocked to see him thirty years before and had hosted him in their house, George Whitefield was the ultimate friend: he kept coming back—with six trips to the colonies—and kept sending other traveling preachers. John Wesley, the founder of the Methodists, eulogized his mentor and sometimes rival as having "had a heart susceptible of the most generous and tender friendship . . . of all others, this was the most distinguished part of his character."

These Protestants understood friendship as something that could transcend hierarchies without necessarily challenging them. While he insisted in 1740 that slaves should be converted, and that "if born and bred up here, are equally capable of the same Improvement," Whitefield had modified his early focus on enslavers' sins. He embraced slave labor as the support of a favorite project, an orphanage in Georgia, and extended this turn in his thinking to the problem of slavery in general, a position that earned critical commentary in a Boston newspaper in 1770. By then, the great evangelist preferred to discuss slavery as a "metaphor for unredeemed sin." This was a traditional Pauline understanding of slavery, indebted to the Stoic notion of being enslaved to human vices through habit. It had helped make Christianity safe for Rome, pushing back against the new religion's egalitarian and emancipatory potential. Wheatley never once voiced this accommodationist perspective, even as she did play with the notion of saved Africans' fortunate fall into captivity.

Yet Whitefield also understood that friendship, like paternity and maternity, could be a potent political simile. While he remained in the Church of England, he struggled with ecclesiastical authorities in ways that reminded many people of the controversies between the colonies and the empire. He wrote sympathetically to New England Congregationalists about "a deep laid plot against your civil and religious liberties" just before he left America in April 1764. He spoke out against the Stamp Act in 1765. By the late 1760s he had linked his fight against the oversight of the Church of England with the patriot movement. Meanwhile, Boston radicals like Sam Adams and clerics like Charles Chauncy warned about High Church designs to send an Anglican bishop. Whitefield "found a voice that Americans wanted to hear" and planned a seventh trip to North America. In his farewell London sermon, he denounced the soldiers who had interrupted Sunday worship by drilling on Boston Common, much as the patriot firebrand John Lathrop had in his massacre sermon.

After he arrived in Boston on August 14, 1770, the anniversary of the Stamp Act protests, Whitefield preached several times a day, first in the pulpits of Old South, where Wheatley worshipped, and Old North, where Lathrop now presided. He probably stayed at the Wheatleys' house again as he proceeded to preach every day and ventured to neighboring towns despite his asthma attacks. Six weeks later, at the end of September, he collapsed, gasped, "I am going," and died. A committee from Old South went to Newburyport to retrieve his body for a spectacular Boston funeral, but the minister in whose house he died refused to part with the body. They held a funeral service in Boston anyway, at which John Lathrop preached. Within days mourners published elegies in the newspapers. One called the preacher "Our Father and Friend." Another called him America's "only friend."

Phillis Wheatley outdid her fellow mourners in a commemorative elegy she produced with the same speed she had shown in getting her Christopher Seider poem into print. With the backing of the Wheatleys, whose enthusiasms she ratified by composing this accomplished and lengthy work, the poem immediately made Phillis famous as the young enslaved girl who could out-elegize anyone in America. She parlayed the death of the great Whitefield into an event of her own, something that had never happened before: an equivalent to Samson Occom's preaching.

The Wheatleys did not publish her elegy in a newspaper, or anonymously. Instead, they advertised a separate publication, with her name, in all four Boston papers (in one case just below an ad to sell a "likely negro boy" of fourteen who wouldn't drink rum). This time there was no question of appropriateness and less likelihood of a backlash from those who thought that black participation in public life would embarrass the patriot or the pious cause. Everyone understood that a young, African female slave could serve as the ultimate example of Whitefield's message of salvation. The first broadside edition, put forth on October 11 for a mere "7 Coppers" with a bulk discount to "travelling traders, &c.," became the most popular poem of many on Whitefield. It was reprinted at least nine times, including twice in a different London version, and then included in a pamphlet with a sermon by the Reverend Ebenezer Pemberton Jr., which announced her authorship and identity as "PHILLIS, a Servant girl of 17 Years of Age, belonging to Mr. J. Wheatly, of Boston;—She has been but nine years in the Country, from AFRICA." It was later reprinted in a separate eight-page deluxe edition with generous margins, by Ezekiel Russell.

The black border of the broadside and the inclusion of Whitefield's coffin announces that this event is not dissimilar to the Boston Massacre and funeral, which had been heralded with similar sensational effects. This is a "lavish," custom-made woodcut, unusual for quick-profit prints like funeral elegies, which were usually rushed from the press as single sheets to be handed out at graveside or in church, like the funeral gloves and rings that evaded Puritans' distaste for conspicuous consumption. It was equally unusual to single out the author in any way, much less as "a Negro Girl, in Boston." Suddenly she was not only an author but an acknowledged one, at a time when most women who wrote for print did not sign their works. Phillis actually headlines her elegy, her name above the image of the corpse and the title of the poem in the pamphlet reprint. For an eighteenth-century author, this was star billing. Subsequently, Isaiah Thomas's pirated reprint needed only the title *Phillis's Poem on the Death of Mr. Whitefield*. Editions followed from printers in Philadelphia, New York, and Newport. A notice in a New Hampshire newspaper bragged on her behalf that the poem "would have done honor to a Pope or Shakespeare."

The printers saw the potential audience for whom Wheatley's authorship would reinforce the evangelical message and (perhaps even less expected in some quarters) a patriot Whig message. Phillis seized the moment for something especially ambitious. Her "ELEGIAC POEM, on the DEATH of that celebrated Divine" combined the themes of piety, politics, and race she had been working through since her patriotic and national "America" poems. Yet each theme emerged more daringly explicit under the rhetorical umbrella of the departed evangelist.

She begins by hailing the "happy Saint" in heaven, his "immortal throne." The contrast is to real-world kings: "To thee complaints of grievance are unknown." The imperial controversy still plagued the British king, but Whitefield is something of an opposite now whose most famous attributes—his carefully modulated voice, the even more impressive throngs that heard it—inspire not filial adulation but friendly "emulation." His "strains of eloquence refin'd / Inflame the soul, and captivate the mind." Wheatley is so in tune here with evangelical style that she isn't worried about the implications of souls on fire.

What's shocking is how little time she spends on Whitefield's works, his popularity, or even the accessible style that must have interested her as a writer as well as a Christian, before returning to the politics. Whitefield's sympathetic position in imperial politics becomes a reflection, an epitome, of his piety, made specific and personal by the image of the good reverend as friend. Whitefieldarian friendship extends across the Atlantic. It *visits* in person and in prayer, redeeming souls and, perhaps, even the imperial relationship in the wake of the Boston Massacre:

> *When his* AMERICANS *were burden'd sore,*
> *When streets were crimson'd with their guiltless gore!*
> *Unrival'd friendship in his breast now strove:*
> *The fruit thereof was charity and love.*
> *Towards* America—*couldst thou do more*
> *Than leave thy native home, the* British *shore,*
> *To cross the great Atlantic's wat'ry road,*
> *To see* America's *distress'd abode?*
> *Thy prayers, great Saint, and thy incessant cries,*
> *Have pierc'd the bosom of thy native skies!*

Wheatley's Whitefield is nothing if not active. She shifts into a narrative mode, and we are asked to imagine that most social and friendly of preachers in his night prayers, where America remained as important as Christ, since the evangelist's essential mission had been to bring young Americans to him:

> *He pray'd that grace in every heart might dwell:*
> *He long'd to see* America *excell;*
> *He charg'd its youth to let the grace divine*
> *Arise, and in their future actions shine;*
> *He offer'd* THAT *he did himself receive,*
> *A greater gift not* GOD *himself can give:*
> *He urg'd the need of* HIM *to every one;*
> *It was no less than* GOD's *co-equal* SON!

By the middle of this second, longer stanza, the elegy itself becomes a sermon. Wheatley ventriloquizes the master preacher. It isn't the first time she deliberately blended her voice with a minister, but this time, with a preacher so many had heard and read, she reproduces his cadences and emphases, his Calvinistic brinkmanship, and his oft-criticized preaching to the preachers, even quoting him addressing "my dear AMERICANS" to ensure that we understand that they were one of Whitefield's special concerns.

But not his only one. Wheatley's Whitefield, like the actual Anglos of the early 1770s, can't think of Americans without thinking of Africans:

> *Take* HIM *ye wretched for your only good;*
> *Take* HIM *ye starving souls to be your food.*
> *Ye thirsty, come to this life-giving stream:*
> *Ye Preachers, take him for your joyful theme:*
> *Take* HIM, *"my dear* AMERICANS," *he said,*
> *Be your complaints in his kind bosom laid:*

> Take HIM *ye* Africans, *he longs for you;*
> *Impartial* SAVIOUR, *is his title due.*

Wheatley expresses perfectly the egalitarian "impartial" potential of Whitefield's awakening. Africans might choose, alike yet separately, to join in: "If you will chuse to walk in grace's road, / You shall be sons, and kings, and priests to GOD."

Would that grace make Africans "kings" of their own—or is kingship here a metaphor for the rule of the spirit, for becoming a full-fledged member of God's kingdom? Would the equality be solely spiritual, in God's eyes? It's not clear, because for decades Whitefield and his followers hadn't been clear, often disagreeing on precisely these matters. What Wheatley has done here, though, is to raise and to implicate, once again, the African question in the American question, using a religious as well as imperial perspective to do so. That the question remained open is revealed in the alternate version the Wheatleys sent to London to be published there, in which the imagined preacher's final words shift, with only seeming clarity added, from "You shall be sons, and kings, and priests to GOD" to "He'll make you free, and Kings, and Priests to God."

The matter of salvation remained uppermost, and Wheatley closed out the elegy with a decorous third stanza addressed directly to Whitefield's patron, Selina Hastings, the Countess of Huntingdon, who had supported him as a clergyman in England while also sponsoring his American projects. This too is a direct address, and a flattering one to the "Great COUNTESS," who is told that "we *Americans* revere thy name," one of the most direct or explicit claims to American identity Wheatley had yet made (and right after she had distinguished "Americans" from "Africans"). She sympathizes and apologizes on behalf of New England that they won't be sending the great man home, as before, "to brighten these distressful days." In case Huntingdon failed to get the message—the hope that what the countess called her "connexion" would persist even after the traveling evangelist's death—

Wheatley wrote a letter enclosing a copy of the poem, on October 25. Huntingdon's loss was of course the heaven-bound saint's gain, though Wheatley manages to turn that into a compliment about the "filial imitation" the countess had shown to Whitefield and to the "Divine Benefactor" of all.

Who was Phillis to offer such a compliment? Could she "Apologize for my boldness" enough to declare once again, as she had in the poem, who most resembled the divine? The poem, in its direct address to Whitefield's patron (as noted in the title of the first broadside versions), surely spoke for itself. And yet it didn't—or, more could be said. There was a relationship, still to be pursued or underlined, between the aristocrat's patronage of the great evangelist, the countess's own powerful womanhood, and her interest in Americans, natives, and African converts. The point couldn't be made strongly enough, even to Hastings, a woman whose enthusiasm for the very sort of "staged literacy events" that the Wheatleys performed would propel her, the next year, into the position of patron extraordinaire as the underwriter of the first published slave narratives.

African literacy meant conversion. Conversion implied spiritual equality. And that might leave more up for grabs. When Wheatley self-consciously apologized to the aristocratic female builder of a trans-atlantic benevolent "connection" that "the Tongues of the Learned are insufficient, much less the pen of an untutor'd African, to paint in lively characters, the excellencies" of the late George Whitefield, now a "Citizen of Zion!" she was speaking the language of a powerful Englishwoman. The countess had the wherewithal to build her own chapels outside the purview of the Church of England. She was so well known that her own letter responding to condolences would appear in Boston newspapers, which almost never published women's writings by name. The poem was an obvious bid for friendship and patronage on Wheatley's part, and it would turn out to be a successful one.

10

THE WOMEN

During the year and a half after Wheatley became famous, she entered what would be considered, in conventional literary terms, her most productive phase. She began to write in more poetic genres. More elegies appeared as broadsides, with her name on them. There was talk of a book.

Samson Occom wrote to Susanna Wheatley suggesting that Phillis be freed so that she could travel to "her Native Country" to evangelize there. Quaker women had done similar things, after all. Given that Occom himself was about to set out on his own as a missionary and author—and with continued support from the Wheatleys—he could hardly have offered a greater compliment or sense of Phillis Wheatley's potential. To a significant extent, they identified with each other.

In 1771 the white Wheatleys reckoned Phillis to be about eighteen. But she remained enslaved. What did her dawning adulthood mean? How did her fame matter when that very renown included, was predicated in part upon, her servitude? Whitefield's doctrine of spiritual equality had potential, and it had limits. So did the role Phillis had come to play as a member of a particular household.

That household was changing. At the unusually late age of twenty-seven, on January 31, 1771, Mary Wheatley married the Reverend John

Lathrop. The young prelate of the Second (later Old North) Church would soon give another widely noted sermon reprising his Boston Massacre address of the year before. For the Wheatleys, he had impeccable credentials. Though from Connecticut, he traveled in some of the same pious circles. His forebears, including the famous dissenter John Lathropp, went back to the great migration of the 1630s. As a young graduate he'd taught at Reverend Wheelock's school. A ballad on Boston's ministers composed by Hannah Mather in 1774 gives a vivid sense of Lathrop as both mild in temperament and steadfast in his ideals: the young man as old pro, one of the neo-traditionalists who helped New England's churches to weather the aftermath of Whitefield's revivals and become a resource for revolutionary politics:

> *Lathrop is so clever, Old North Forever,—*
> *How pleasing both the sounds,*
> *Texts he explains, in pious strains*
> *confin'd to sober bounds.*
> *But when he treats of bloody streets*
> *And massacres so dire,*
> *When chous'd of rights by sinful whights*
> *How dreadful is his ire.*

Another versifier's tour of the pulpits also stressed Lathrop's integrity—insisting that he hadn't married into the wealthy Wheatley family for money: "And John Old North, tho' little worth / Won't sacrifice for gold."

At a moment when patriots turned up their screeds against greedy Tories who defied boycotts or did royal officials' bidding, the young preacher seemed the opposite: personally kind, yet uncompromising in general. Lathrop had flat out called the massacre a murder in the reputation-making oration that administration men would mock for years as "the bloody flag." Moderates, though, could not be much encouraged by his patient explanations of godly resistance to tyranny or his observation, in a December 1770 Thanksgiving sermon, that "however rich and powerful a kingdom may be, it is perfectly easy for g[o]d to humble & destroy it . . . he has a 1000d ways to overthrow & totally demolish ye proudest Empires." Anticipating the hopes of 1776, he even predicted that such a "general war" could be the cause of a "general reformation." It was a good sign, he preached, that Bostonians had not bent to the "yoke of slavery" in the form of a standing army. For Lathrop, as for Wheatley, absolute dominion belonged to God alone. On the anniversary of the massacre, he summarized the "dreadful" doctrine. All are "born with equal right to life, & ye common privileges of it. We are all brethren, ye descendants of one parent," all in God's family. All had "a natural right to life, to liberty, and to own property," even if "some think the bulk of mankind should be born to be beasts of burden."

Phillis would keep ties to the Lathrops, who expressed affection for her. John affirmed her "singular genius" and gave her books. She would live with their growing family for a time in 1776. Still, Mary Wheatley's departure from the house on King Street, her position as a well-known minister's wife, and her rapid succession of pregnancies must have changed the emotional equation between a more mature Phillis and an aging Susanna Wheatley. Susanna needed her more, grew even more invested in her enslaved confidante and surrogate daughter, at the very moment when she became widely known even beyond Boston.

Meanwhile, John Wheatley advertised his retirement and asked his townsmen to come settle all their debts. Nathaniel Wheatley had fully taken over the family business. A hint of the difference this made survives in the form of several business letters he dictated to Phillis beginning in 1770. It was the role a sister or a wife might have played. Nathaniel had neither of those at home. So it fell to the Wheatleys' extremely literate servant, an everyday example of Phillis's exceptional, yet ordinary and unchanged, status as neither child nor adult, as chattel yet special, as in and yet not of the family. She was surrounded by people she knew well, African and English, coming of age, yet the meaning of her own maturity, as a woman and as an artist, remained ambiguous.

On August 18, Phillis expressed both continuity and change by joining Old South Church. The biggest meetinghouse in Boston had the benefit of being closer to the Wheatleys' house than John and Susanna's New South. Old South seated more Africans in the upper floor's pews than other meetinghouses, and Africans had been baptized there for decades. Wheatley had memorialized the church's former minister Joseph Sewall and would eventually do the same for the current leader, the avuncular and well-liked patriot Samuel Cooper (a grandson of the Sewalls), who was there while a permanent replacement was sought and his own Brattle Street Church building underwent reconstruction.

There could be no more New Englandish way of showing belonging and independence at the same time than joining the church of one's choice. It also helped that Old South had just eliminated the test of relation, in which new members had to explain their religious experience. But this was no rejection of the Wheatley family. Lucy Tyler Marshall, the wife of Dr. Samuel Marshall, a relative of Susanna's, joined Old South on the same day. It is possible that Susanna herself had started worshipping at the closer building in light of her own declining health, though they had a carriage and driver.

On the other hand, Phillis hadn't chosen Old North, which might have kept her closer to the Lathrops. Nor had she gone the way of Nathaniel, who, perhaps shockingly, would soon be a regular at King's Chapel, the increasingly controversial Anglican bastion in Boston that had begun to attract more natives and strangers. The Wheatleys were all going their own way as John and Susanna passed into old age. For the family, Phillis's presence in their home smoothed several transitions, though there would be hints of tension, even jealousy, from Nathaniel and Mary.

Phillis Wheatley was neither native nor stranger, neither child nor adult, neither sister nor daughter to Bostonians, to the whites she sometimes called friends. Yet her writing and her other everyday

actions assumed aspects of all these roles. And she was newly interesting to, and possibly more in demand by, Boston friends and acquaintances since her unprecedented celebrity, after the Whitefield poem.
More than ever, because more was expected of her, she had to please.
She made the experience and its frustrations an overt and a subtle
theme of both her art and her self-presentation even as she honed both
in 1771 and 1772.

Boston's other enslaved experienced something similar. Increasing
numbers of the advertisements for their sale in newspapers stressed
the woman or man chattel's "Honesty and Good Temper," sunny disposition, and "very clever" mind as well as specific skills, in a way that
went far beyond lending support to the claim that these individuals
were being "sold for no fault." These people were valued—at times,
to the pound sterling—for their emotional as well as intellectual and
physical labor. More ads noted slaves' linguistic skills: as Phillis's cohort grew up and slave imports declined somewhat, more and more
Africans spoke "good English, and that very handsomely." As Andrew
Wendell testified in court but had his skills and honesty derided as
doubtful in the *Boston Gazette* for political reasons, the enslaved could
even be admitted to be "genteel" in the same paper when it was in their
owners' interests to do so—as it might be when they absconded with
themselves.

Wheatley family reminiscences suggest the increasing emotional
demands on Phillis and, less directly, the care she had to take to deal
with expectations. "Being an Educated Lady," Aunt Susanna Wheatley "appreciated her talent, and gave Phillis full scope for her Genius,"
Charles Stratford heard from his mother. "The result was that she
became a favourite, not only in the family, but of Literary Men and
Women of those times; Aunt clothed her in good apparel, and made
her an intimate of her Sitting-Room, yet she had the good sense to
always withdraw when company came, unless particularly desired to
remain, as they often came to have an interview with her." Margaretta

Odell stressed "the propriety of her behavior" as Susanna kept her always near, apart from other servants. Phillis was "modest, unassuming," very "gentle-tempered," yet "extremely affectionate." She didn't exhibit the slightest "literary vanity." Most of all, she "never indulged her muse in any fits of sullenness or caprice. She was at all times accessible."

At all times accessible. Not only that: *gentle, affectionate.* Being to Susanna "as a daughter," she "returned her affection with unbounded gratitude, and was so devoted to her interests as to have no will in opposition to that of her benefactress." What Odell described might be the ideal emotional features of women, even a fantasy of women held by women as much as men, features of any young woman, or child—but even more so of a slave in the family who was a child-woman. But here these ideal feminine-slave attributes, this emotional sensitivity and responsiveness, are epitomized by her literary abilities and practice: "If any one requested her to write upon any particular subject or event, she immediately set herself to the task, and produced something on the given theme." It was essential, in family lore, that "nothing was forced," that Phillis pleased by nature, that she had become artful without "vanity." Because of this fantasy and her fulfillment of it, which Odell summarized as not the "chains" of slavery but as "the golden links of love and the silken bands of gratitude," Phillis gained privileges and her special standing, which Odell illustrated by describing her taking up a dustrag or sewing needle only to drop either implement to pick up her pen or book at any time. Her primary labors had become emotional as well as literary. She demonstrated the good taste and good intentions of the Wheatleys by having a will of her own that never conflicted with theirs.

Other anecdotes from this time return to Phillis's table manners as the epitome of her care for whites' feelings, how she put them at ease. Sometimes New Englanders shocked English gentlemen and women by inviting their servants to sit and eat with them. But they regularly enforced racial distinctions by having enslaved Africans do the serving and sit elsewhere, as any reader of Phillis's first published poem, the preface for which described her waiting "at table," would have recognized. The first time Phillis came to tea at the Lathrops', the servants went into a tizzy. Would they have to serve an African, a slave? Eventually, though, after her return from London, Phillis did take tea at the same table with white women—but only when they insisted. Eunice Fitch—none other than the second wife of Timothy Fitch, owner of the *Phillis*, who had sent a slaver to Africa as recently as 1771—overruled her anxious daughters and stepdaughters, "who could not bear that they should sit down at table with a colored person" (as someone who had heard the story later put it using polite nineteenth-century language). Phillis should sit at their tea table when she herself was the guest of honor, the one who could describe famous lords and ladies and inform them about the latest styles in the metropolis. According to Odell, however—and this is most revealing of the family's design, and Wheatley's careful course—Phillis "always declined the seat offered her at the board, and, requesting that a side-table might be laid for her, dined modestly apart from the rest of the company." Tea was one thing, a meal something else. To Odell, this was "dignified and judicious," properly feminine emotional intelligence. To Wheatley, it was an everyday balancing act, always knowing her audience at least as well as they knew themselves.

Susanna compensated by emphasizing the special privileges. She saw and described Phillis more and more as a daughter or like one, a legacy she passed to other women in the family. One time, after one of these invitations to other women's houses, "the weather changed during the absence of Phillis," who had suffered a major health scare during the winter of 1771–72. Susanna "ordered Prince (also an African and a slave) to take the chaise, and bring home her protegee." When the small carriage approached the house, Susanna expressed outrage at what she saw: "Do look at that saucy varlet—if he hasn't the impudence to sit upon the same seat with my Phillis!" Whatever the nature of the "severe reprimand" she gave to Prince for wanting to socialize with Phillis, Susanna chose to vocally and memorably reinforce the message that Phillis could and should be an exception that proved the rules. The family slavery that the Wheatleys and other New Englanders practiced had room for both care and punishment, for treating servants as family, for keeping them at a close distance, and for returning them to market. If Phillis remained poised between child and adult, between daughter and servant, and had no family of her own, she could continue to be all those things. For Susanna Wheatley as she aged, Phillis had come to epitomize and to fulfill many aspects of her life as a mother, a sister, and a supporter of missionaries. The better Phillis, approaching adulthood, presented herself, the more Susanna's essential goodness must have been apparent—except, probably, to Prince, the other kind of slave (or child), the one she reprimanded without tenderness.

The poems that brought Phillis fame beyond Boston were about men and often directed to men. But like her ballad-like first rhyme about "Mrs. Thacher's Son" and "Her Daughter too," her elegies of 1771 and 1772 are addressed to women and children. Even when the deceased was a man, or when these poems console men, they do so through women. These elegies broadened her network of women much as some of her earlier-circulated manuscripts had, but in a newly intense way, radiating out from Susanna's large extended family and the Boston merchant community. They perform her "at all times accessible" femininity, youth, and enslavement while they refine her reputation for piety and insight. These poems admit Wheatley into families as well as public circles of mourning, confirming what she had done with Whitefield and the Countess of Huntingdon. They help others grieve and gently but firmly tell them to get over it. In doing so, they may hint

at her own sorrows, ones that Boston had made and, not coincidentally, did not wish to hear about.

Dr. Thomas Leonard, the son of a minister from Plymouth, married Thankful Hubbard, "an agreeable young lady," daughter of the
merchant, slave trader, and Old South deacon Thomas Hubbard, in
November 1770. Eight months later, after a "long languishment," the
well-liked young physician died. Leonard's death, like Whitefield's, was
a notable public event in Boston, given more than the usual sentence
in newspapers, and once again Wheatley had a special proximity to
the bereaved. She began her elegy in the neoclassical vein, denouncing
death as a "Grim Monarch" who demands all, regardless of "youth"
and "science" (two aspects of Dr. Leonard's public identity) or "the
charms of love." Here the address of the poem changes to "the friend,
the spouse," who "from his dark realm to save, / In vain we ask the
tyrant of the grave."

The poem's most revealing word may be the "we" that Wheatley
drops as she presents herself as the archetypal friend. She transitions
to a direct address to the "Fair mourner," Thankful Hubbard Leonard.
Those who knew Wheatley and the traditions she relies on here, of the
poet as minister, would have anticipated the preacherly, authoritative
tone that follows, first gesturing at the body on its bier, "undistin-
guish'd from the vulgar dead," then referring, in the kind of gesture
that had not yet been rendered all too familiar in graveyard poetry, to
the vivid image of a wife's "rolling tears" chasing "each other down the
alter'd face." The sentiment may pass muster because the theme is its
well-meaning excess. Thankful needs, rather, to be thankful, and to
consider that precisely because the doctor had been blessed and not
at all vulgar, he is now better off. Her job is to think elevated thoughts
about how she will join him above. Grief is a test that the poet, like the
chaplain, helps the mourners to pass. The broadside version acknowledges that an elegy from Phillis Wheatley is a literary event that raises
the question of her own role in the drama. Unlike most broadside elegies, this one is signed, in printed italics, with her full name, in a man-

ner that replicates the full signature that Wheatley had only recently begun to put on her circulating manuscripts.

One of her next elegies appeared in a newspaper without her signature but also circulated in manuscript under her name. This time she wrote even more intimately. Dr. Samuel Marshall also died young, just six weeks after Phillis and Lucy both joined Old South. Marshall was if anything even more beloved than his colleague Hubbard, a "universal friend," according to Wheatley, but perhaps because of the closer connection to Lucy and her family, Wheatley can merge the medical and the familial, again participating in the community of mourning: "The sire, the friend, in him we have oft found, / With gen'rous friendship did his soul abound." Naming Dr. Marshall twice as a "sire" as well as friend, Wheatley identifies with the doctor's young patients and Marshall's own children. In doing so, she is able audaciously to raise what must have been on everyone's mind: Lucy Marshall's pregnancy. The child itself "in dark confines is toss'd / And seems in anguish for its father lost." In the end Lucy is assured that Samuel awaits her "in the fields of light; / To thy embrace, his joyful spirit moves, / To thee the partner of his earthly loves."

It was a small step further from imagining captured, confined children, bereft of protective fathers as she herself had been, to focusing on the children themselves, and giving them voice, as Wheatley had begun to do in other elegies. In "On the Death of a Young Miss, Aged 5 Years," the "enraptur'd innocent" flies to the "unknown beatitude above." Nancy Robertson's parents needn't just take the usual advice. Through the medium of Phillis, they are invited to "imitate her language" in the form of the deceased's imagined speech about "songs of praise" to God's "Infinite love and majesty."

Wheatley gains authority by speaking in the voice of dead children. Assuring the parents that the child "looks down" in "bliss," she can ask plainly, "Why would you wish your daughter back again? No—bow resign'd. Let hope your grief control / And check the rising tumult of your soul." By this poem's conclusion, she can offer advice that is not only pious and emotional but even philosophical, comparing the journey of life to something else she had experienced, not long since, as a child—an ocean voyage.

To James and Mehitable Sullivan, who had suffered the triple loss of a sister, brother, and their infant daughter Avis, Wheatley admitted that while to the mother it would feel like "half her soul" to "Resign thy friends to that Almighty hand," she could and should nevertheless focus on the "heav'nly pleasure" that now belonged to Avis. In a "masterly performance" she titled "A Poem on the Death of Charles Eliot, Aged 12 Months," she gave the toddler a full eight couplets, in quotation marks, to speak his "Thanks to my God, who snatch'd me to the skies" before he had ever sinned: "New glories rush upon my expanding mind; A noble ardor now, my bosom fires, / To utter what the heav'nly muse inspires!" The more eloquent the babe, the stronger and more decisive becomes Phillis's own voice—perhaps because she knew a thing or two about children being snatched and the results being attributed to God.

The elegies are important. Almost a majority of the poems Wheatley published and wrote were elegies. But they are also just one part of her evolving repertoire, developed in dialogue with her Bostonian "friends," especially the older women who visited her and invited her to visit. As she continued to make the most of death in Boston, she also wrote poems that, like the one to Hussey and Coffin, celebrated the saving of life.

These poems also made friends, if not kin. Two efforts directly addressed ladies who contemplated or completed perilous voyages. Both follow women, seemingly alone, from southerly shores to safer places. Wheatley may hint at the higher number and proportion of slaves in these places, but she seems more compelled by the possibilities of knowing about other women who traveled the Atlantic. "To a Lady on Her Remarkable Preservation in a Hurricane in North-Carolina" was drafted after a particularly destructive storm of September 1769 or a survivor's description later. The framing here is wholly and explicitly classical, with Boreas and Aeolus playing their "stern" and "angry" roles. But here the Nereids, nymphs of the sea, rescue Maria, at God's design, to "Instruct thy mind / Things of eternal consequence to weigh." This is shipwreck from a woman's perspective: once saved, Maria's fears for her husband's life (which might have prompted her dangerous journey) "are all relieved." After landing, she is reunited with her "daughter blooming with superior grace" and able to "joyful show thy spouse his heir" and receive due credit for "the blessings of maternal care."

In "To a Lady on Coming to America for Her Health," with her child, Phillis asks the muse for inspiration to see her subject as like a goddess, and carried by the deities "from Jamaica's fervid shore." At a time when Phillis herself experienced recurring illness, she paints a woman who can call upon supernatural intervention. As her narrative of inspiration and imagination suggests, the subject of the poem is not only one woman's sympathy for another who turns out to be a mother. It is also Phillis's own imagination of travel as uplift:

> "Arise, ye winds, America explore,
> Waft me, ye gales, from this malignant shore;
> The Northern milder climes I long to greet,
> There hope that health will my arrival meet."
> Soon as she spoke in my ideal view
> The winds assented, and the vessel flew.

Meanwhile, back in Jamaica, even the luxuriant vegetation in "the grove's dark recesses" suffers with the "bereft" lonely husband.

For Wheatley "America" remains New England extended, a better northern place that even saves Jamaica from tragedy. (In her 1773 *Poems* she had to retitle this poem for clarity's sake, for English readers did not make fine distinctions between Jamaica and the mainland: the lady travels to "North America.") Still, the poem suggests and pursues Atlantic connections even while reinforcing differences that may not be reducible to climate. Understood as one of Wheatley's explorations of the possibilities, for *her*, of other women and their families, the moving force becomes Wheatley's own desire for connections as well as for flights of fancy or inspiration that might become, in different senses, real. As the perspective shifts from that of the goddess, to the lady, to Wheatley herself as the imaginative narrator of the story, she becomes an agent of the poem: a bearer, as well as narrator, of healing, feminine friendship.

> *From thence I turn, and leave the sultry plain,*
> *And swift pursue thy passage o'er the main:*
> *The ship arrives before the fav'ring wind,*
> *And make the* Philadelphian *port assign'd,*
> *Thence I attend you to* Bostonia's *arms,*
> *Where gen'rous friendship ev'ry bosom warms:*
> *Thrice welcome here! may health revive again,*
> *Bloom on thy cheek, and bound in ev'ry vein!*

Wheatley reunites the family to happy tears and hugs, and she even imagines a friendly, echoing community there: "With shouts of joy Jamaica's rocks resound, / With shouts of joy the country rings around." The edge is taken off the judgment of the climate. It is a friendly gesture and a necessary one. Read in light of Wheatley's other poems, though, it extends her intimate ambit all the way to Britain's most lucrative colony. One can also read it as a negotiation between women, where in exchange for a gift memorializing their feelings and experiences and the stories they told about it, Wheatley's acquaintances, in "gen'rous friendship," must admit her superior vision and ambition. In doing that, they sent both Wheatley and themselves to further meditation on her identity.

Two of those friends recognized as much on January 1, 1772, dur-

ing the winter when Wheatley was "much indispos'd." Using the initial
L., this person—possibly John Lathrop (Mary wouldn't have mistaken
the year when Phillis came to be enslaved in Boston)—sent a poem
and an account of its creation to the *London Magazine*:

> There is in this town a young *Negro* woman, who left *her* coun-
> try at ten years of age, and has been in *this* eight years. She is
> a compleat sempstress, an accomplished mistress of her pen,
> and discovers a most surprising genius. Some of her produc-
> tions have seen the light, among which is a poem on the death
> of Rev. Mr. George Whitefield.—The following was occasioned
> by her being in company with some young ladies of family,
> when one of them said she did not remember, among all the
> poetical pieces she had seen, ever to have met with a poem
> upon RECOLLECTION.

This is Wheatley's scene, with elite young women ("of family") at their
house or a friend's. They are also interested in poetry and attempting
to show how clever and how literary they can be. Could "one of them,"
the "A.M." to whom the poem is addressed (possibly Abigail May, who
was exactly Wheatley's age, or Agnes Moorhead, or Abigail Mather),
have been pointing to her own youth, self-consciously calling attention to the unlikelihood of a young woman being able to remember a
poem about remembering? Was there also a darker, perhaps less conscious, competitive motive: to see how an enslaved person, not allowed
to speak her own dark memories, might handle, might abstract, a forbidden subject?

   L. had no doubt to whom the remark was directed: "The *African*
(so let me call her, for so in fact she is) took the hint, went home to
her master's, and soon sent what follows." L. is fascinated, or imagines
London readers will be fascinated, not only by the poem that results
but at the genteel and kind fashion in which Phillis returned the provocation along with a fifty-five-line lyric "Recollection."

MADAM,

   Agreeable to your proposing *Recollection* as a subject proper
for me to write upon, I enclose these few thoughts upon it;
and, as you was the first person who mentioned it, I thought
that none more proper to dedicate it to; and, if it meets your
approbation, the poem is honoured, and the authoress satisfied. I am, Madam,

                              Your very humble servant,
                              PHILLIS.

The poem identifies Wheatley in the first couplet as it turns to
"MNEME," or Mnemosyne, goddess of memory and mother of the
nine Muses, as the glorious bestower of recollection to all, including
"Your vent'rous Afric." He (later corrected to she) comes at night with
inspiration for poets. The classical framing permits a global, deep-
historical portfolio for "[t]he Heavenly Phantom," who "points the actions done / In the past worlds, and tribes beneath the sun. / He, from
his throne in ev'ry human breast, / Has *vice* condemn'd, and every
virtue bless'd."

   As often in her religious poems, Wheatley shifts to the dangers
of ignoring heavenly warnings, but here in what seems a more political and collective vein. Sometimes a "race" forgets history and experiences God's "redoubled fury." At a time when patriots were urging
American Britons to remember the lessons of history, what lessons,
what "horrid crime," committed by what "race," could Wheatley have
had in mind? She turns from the ambiguity that could be read as either
a patriot blast or a muted antislavery hint back to herself and pious
soul-searching: "To recollect, inglorious I return; / 'Tis mine past fol-
lies and past crimes to mourn. / The *virtue*, ah! unequal to the *vice*, /
Will scarce afford small reason to rejoice."

   Memory should inspire humility, and repentance. By elaborating a
lesson that applied to each individual, Wheatley can explore her own
dilemma as an enslaved person seeking an audience, salvation, or even

freedom. At the same time, she allows that some who come to the table with her will likely ignore the challenge to moral and political complacency that occupies the six lines at the center of the poem. The women at the tea table found Phillis at once more audacious and, if they were the sort to notice, more subtle. No wonder they kept her close, and yet at a distance, inviting her to tea, expecting her to perform, but taking their refuge in the ruses of memory.

11

THE PROPOSAL

Wheatley continued to pen elegies that addressed a striking and enlarged range of eminent "friends." One, to the Reverend Timothy Pitkin, a Connecticut associate of the Reverend Samson Occom's, elaborated the device of the departed speaking directly to the survivor, urging piety and resignation—to a minister, no less—in anticipation of his own voyage to heaven. A later, equally ambitious one consoled the lieutenant governor, Andrew Oliver, when his wife died. Here she described her work as "heav'nly tidings" come direct "from the Afric muse."

During the winter of 1771–72, despite the illness she remarked upon in letters, she undertook two larger projects: a published proposal for a two-hundred-page volume of poems, and another epyllion or mini-epic, one of the two longest poems she wrote, that would help justify the book and lure subscribers to promise to buy a copy upon its publication. The book would not appear in 1772, and not in Boston. Yet the proposal itself was another publication event and a milestone. It advanced her opportunities and contributed to the sense of possibility she cultivated.

The proposal advertisement appeared three times, beginning on

February 29, 1772, in a new newspaper published by Ezekiel Russell, the ambitious young publisher who had printed one of the versions of Wheatley's Whitefield elegy. Russell specialized in ballads—some written by his wife, Sarah Russell—but also put out most of the antislavery pamphlets that appeared during these years. He had recently started printing a pro-government weekly. He had never published a book, though, and was hardly in a position to risk the capital investment represented by a volume "handsomely bound and lettered," which meant stamped on the spine of the leather cover with the author's name. He set the price somewhat high, at four shillings (three if merely "stitched in blue" paper like a pamphlet), and asked for subscribers in advance. If "Three Hundred Copies are subscribed for," the book would appear "with all Speed."

This publication strategy may have been somewhat unusual in the colonies, but less so for volumes of poetry. Given that poems were passed around in manuscript, sometimes sold in broadside form, and became salable mainly in response to major events like battles and deaths, it made sense to gauge the Wheatley network and the reach of her fame. Subscribers could come to Russell's office in Marlborough Street. Probably the Wheatleys also collected names and payments.

What is more unusual is the amount of space Russell could and did devote to the ad at a time when his newspaper, the *Censor*, struggled. Its unattractive name was no joke. Russell's paper—really, more of a magazine—was sponsored by, and partly written by, Governor Hutchinson and Lieutenant Governor Oliver. After more than three months of publication, the *Censor* had not run a single other advertisement. The February 29 issue in which the proposal appeared was actually the first time the *Censor* really looked like a newspaper (on its first two pages at least), before turning back to magazine mode. Read in columns after a deconstruction of Sam Adams's recent essays, a denunciation of the *Boston Gazette* for its "insatiable lust of scandal," or before a typically snobbish piece on an Irish member of the Sons of Liberty, the "Proposals for Printing by Subscription" a volume by Wheatley presented more like news than anything that had yet appeared there.

The proposal underlines how the poems had been "wrote at several times, and upon various occasions, by PHILLIS, a Negro Girl, from the Strength of her own Genius, it being but a few Years since she came to this Town an uncultivated Barbarian from *Africa*." Russell or the Wheatleys framed her authorship sensationally, emphasizing Phillis's youth and apparent transformation, attributable only to exceptional "genius"—a term increasingly associated with Wheatley and newly understood during the late eighteenth century as meaning the inherent, special capabilities of a rare individual. How precisely she had learned to write poetry and what the implications of her success might be seemed less immediately important in securing an audience for the book than addressing the matter of her origins and status to prove that the genius was in fact her own: a question that even the well-disposed Countess of Huntingdon would ask. "The Poems having been seen and read by the best Judges, who think them well worthy of the Publick View; and upon critical examination," the proposal continued, in language that has misled readers ever since into thinking that Wheatley actually sat through some kind of semiofficial "examination" or trial by "judges." No such staged event occurred because it wasn't necessary. The most eminent men in the province had already interacted with her. These informal judges "find that the declared Author was capable of writing them."

The advertisement, however, devoted even more space to the part that Wheatley herself must have shaped: a list of the poems that would appear in the volume. Here she broke convention by dating all twenty-eight poems—by presenting her table of contents as in effect a chronicle, a portrait of her history as an artist. She follows this scheme even to the point of including two versions of her poem "On the Death of Reverend Dr. Sewell," the first from 1765 "when [he was] sick" and the second in 1769, presumably one of the revisions that itself could show-case her ability to improve her timely and inspired efforts.

As a story of a poet's development the list showcases her ability to move from religion to politics and back, much as New England ministers did during these years. The first six poems include her faith-based missive to the students at Harvard and her addresses "to the Atheist" and "to the Deist," as well as "On Virtue." The next group commences with the challenging and, for the ambition suggested by the titles, eyebrow-raising "On America," "On the King" (the Stamp Act repeal poem), and "Thoughts on Being Brought from Africa to America." A middle group of verses includes the poems about Commodore Hood and the elegies to Seider, the Boston Massacre victims, and Whitefield. Here it becomes clear that any putative distinction between religious and political poetry—or between her particular concerns and those of a Boston public—have been rendered of as little significance to her as they were to most readers of the town's newspapers.

After the self-dating poems on the occupation and the massacre, the list proceeds to seven elegies and a panegyric, all from the past year: a testament to her range and continued productivity, complete with the names of the subjects who would have been known to locals. The twenty-seventh and penultimate poem is simply named "Golia[t]h of Gath," without any "On" or "To" or "Thoughts" to suggest ode, elegy, or any of the shorter poetic genres. Given the size of the protagonist of the Goliath story and its biblical origins, Wheatley is signaling epic, narrative ambitions. She hedged her bets, but just a bit, by rounding out the volume with the poem that many local readers would have seen most recently—the elegy "On the Death of Dr. Samuel Marshall." Russell or the Wheatleys added a one-sentence paragraph that heightened the notion of the book's publication as a special, even historic event that might itself exert a change for the author: "It is hoped Encouragement will be given to this Publication, as a reward to a very uncommon Genius, at present a Slave."

At present a slave. Did the Wheatleys, did Phillis, envision enough sales to fund Phillis's emancipation? Or was book authorship itself seen as incompatible with racial servitude, so much so that the contradiction had to be admitted? It's impossible to know, because we don't know for certain why Russell did not actually publish the book in 1772. The merchant John Andrews, an enthusiastic subscriber for the volume, provides a clue to the fate of the proposal. He wrote to his brother-in-law on May 29 that the volume had not yet appeared "for want of Spirit to carry on anything of the kind here." Later he would remark that Phillis had withheld her poems from the press with the prospect of a greater "emolument" by publishing them in London. Events likely had spoiled Russell's plans and required the Wheatleys to rethink their publishing strategy. As Andrews, a merchant, had been in a position to know, a major credit crisis that commenced with London bank failures led to a recession in Boston and across the British Atlantic. Ezekiel Russell folded the *Censor* after May 2—just three weeks after printing the advertisement for the third time.

Russell admitted that his political weekly had been bested by another up-and-coming printer. The more savvy and experienced Isaiah Thomas's attempt to create an elevated magazine of political debate, the *Massachusetts Spy*, at first appeared three times a week, but really took off when Thomas abandoned his attempts to be a neutral carrier and began to take the patriot side as stridently as the *Boston Gazette* but with even more original content. Wheatley's competing printers, it seems, formed another ambitious, parallel cohort, both excited by expanded possibilities in 1771–72 and yet limited by the fickle trade winds. In early 1772 there were, briefly, six newspapers in Boston: two old partisan standards, two that tried to be moderate (one of which tended to be cautious; the other of which claimed to publish all sides), and two experimental efforts by printers who proved relatively open to antislavery (Thomas and Russell). Not coincidentally this moment saw more poems of many kinds being published in those newspapers, more pamphlets (including sermons like those of John

Lathrop), and some other daring efforts by young writers. Their poetic, and not always politic, ambitions informed Wheatley's longest poem and her highest hopes for her book.

Just as Wheatley's volume was being advertised by Russell, a rich merchant's son named James Allen presented a commissioned poem for the anniversary of the Boston Massacre, only to have it censored as insufficiently supportive of the patriot program. Allen had shown around manuscript segments of *The Retrospect*, an ambitious narrative poem about the Seven Years' War that criticized "base-born faction" and described British arms as likely to subdue anyone in the world, including, it now seemed to some readers, the colonies. For this reason or others, Allen had a Tory reputation. While Allen had previously dropped out of Harvard and spent his days drinking and reciting poetry, his classmate Dr. Joseph Warren, the orator of the day, had seen an opportunity to reclaim Boston's most promising epic poet for the patriot side, to no avail it seemed. Yet after the committee in charge of the festivities refused to sponsor his massacre poem as a pamphlet, none other than Ezekiel Russell published it along with commentary on the controversy and extracts from Allen's epic in progress.

In seemingly very different poems about arms and men, Allen represented British soldiery as weak and craven for the anniversary of the massacre, but as glorious and invincible in his other, ongoing "Tory" effort about the war. The political and literary problem, in other words, didn't lie mainly with an arrogant inebriate who had changed his mind or just liked to show off his skill for any occasion. The great war for the empire, Allen's original subject, had forced a reckoning among the victors over what the armies had done, who deserved the laurels, and what the empire actually stood for. Russell or whoever edited Allen's poems for him saw no small "irony" in the controversy over how to read Allen's new poem and his dismissal over its content or his political reputation. To call it ironic was something of a concession: ironic style already had a Tory or at least moderate political reputation, going back to the great Tory satires of an earlier generation and, more currently, the mocking sensibility that Tories like Mather Byles increasingly adopted when exposing Whiggish hypocrisies.

Like young Christopher Seider with the ballad of General Wolfe in his pocket, the James Allen affair shows how Bostonians did politics by war and talk about war, and sometimes in verse. Adverse publicity had shaped the Boston Massacre and its aftermath; facing a public relations disaster, the troops had been removed. Newspaper writers displayed a striking self-consciousness about publicity after seeing how the successful effort to frame the deaths in Boston as a massacre had nevertheless failed to determine the course of justice in the case of the soldiers, who were acquitted. Despite the multiplication and effectiveness of patriot voices in venues like Thomas's *Spy* and the *Boston Gazette*, Samuel Adams was frustrated enough by Tory offensives dripping with satiric wit to propose, and to see through, a key innovation: the development of intercolonial committees of correspondence that retailed stories for the press as well as plans for resistance throughout the colonies. These improved networks of information and action successfully framed the news during the coming years. Their media effects began to make independence, in the countryside as well as in Boston, more than thinkable.

The press in Boston, in 1772, was both partisan and unpredictable. As often in British and U.S. history, especially when there was competition, it operated simultaneously as a tool of the powerful and as an insurgent, creative force. There had been an unanticipated loss, for Wheatley, in allying with a young printer like Russell who had so many irons in the fire and who was working with the embattled Hutchinson administration. On the other hand, her poems themselves had already displayed her patriot bona fides. And like others she had good reason to reach across political as well as religious divides.

Even more important, it remained unclear whether the Whigs would continue to stand against the slave trade, or if Governor

Hutchinson would continue to block such efforts. Fewer articles against slavery had appeared in the *Boston Gazette* and in the *Massachusetts Spy* from later 1770 to early 1772. But Ezekiel Russell showed persistent sympathy to antislavery—not so much by what he did in the *Censor*, for which he was mainly a hired technician, as by what else he published and proposed to publish.

James Swan, a young merchant and recent migrant, had written a biting attack on the slave trade. Isaiah Thomas took subscriptions for the work beginning in November 1771. Patriots, however, discouraged the publication, spreading rumors that the essay was a disguised Tory attack on New England hypocrisy by a "North Briton." Instead, Swan found his way to Russell, who advertised for subscriptions to Swan's seventy-page tract in March and April for a pistareen (a little more than a shilling, or a proportional price to the unbound three-shilling version of Wheatley's two hundred pages). While the ad more than hinted at the controversial content, the pamphlet did not actually appear until later, in November 1772.

Swan introduced his argument against the slave trade by dealing with its relationship to the patriot controversy. He insisted there was no real conflict: "I am a most sincere well-wisher to the common cause of Liberty, both *personal* and *constitutional*." All Britons, everyone in the empire, should be enemies of slavery, because "no country can be called free when there is one slave." Swan returned later to the grave implications of patriot hypocrisy if they "deprive the poor Black people of their Freedom, when there is as little reason for it as there is for making Slaves of British Subjects." He also incorporated recent arguments by the Pennsylvania Quaker Anthony Benezet (in *A Caution and Warning to Great Britain and Her Colonies* [1766] and in *Some Historical Account of Guinea* [1771]) on the decidedly un-civilizing nature of the African trade, using, as Benezet did, testimonies of Europeans who had been to Africa and who participated in the slave trade to demonstrate its violent, destructive, and even commercially inefficient nature. But Swan spent more of his time constructing his arguments in "the form of a Sermon," the "easiest" and "plainest" way, to demonstrate the "barbarity" of Euro-American slaving.

As in a sermon, Swan grappled first with Old Testament bans and limits on the enslavement of fellow Hebrews. Some said Africans were not Hebrews, so Jewish law did not apply. But was it so clear that Africans, who might well have come out of Egypt, were not descendants of the Hebrews? he asked. And once out of Africa, how could the next generations of Africans, as Creoles born in America, not be considered brethren, subject to the emancipation law of the seventh year? Besides, the treatment of Africans in the West Indian and southern colonies (here Swan spared New England, or left its version of slavery open to discussion) clearly contravened biblical laws regarding the just treatment of either Hebrew or foreign slaves.

Swan capped his argument, however, with Bostonians especially in mind by twice quoting George Whitefield from the great preacher's early critical days. Not only had Whitefield written, in a public letter to southern mainland planters, that their cruel treatment of slaves offended God; he had also cited a verse from the beginning of the second book of Samuel, in which David asked God the cause of a famine. God answered that "it is for Saul, and his bloody house, because he slew the Gibeonites . . . These Gibeonites were only hewers of wood and drawers of water; or in other words, Slaves like yours." It was easier for Swan, in Boston, to invoke God's wrath against slavers, and even the likelihood that divine punishment would likely come "many years" after the deed, because Samuel and Whitefield had done it for him. Benezet, in his *Caution and Warning*, had quoted the same Whitefield passage at greater length.

A turn in antislavery toward scripture, and specifically toward Hebrew scriptures, can also be seen in the writings of the English activist Granville Sharp and in some Pennsylvania Quakers like Benezet who were beginning to build a transatlantic antislavery movement. The example of David, in the books of Samuel, provided Wheatley with a special opportunity as well. The bloody chronicles of Saul and

David—the kings in Israel whom God upraised and dethroned—are filled with unlikely heroes whose fates exemplify providence. They could be read as parallels to the Homeric epics, an alternate classicism suggesting secular as well as sacred truths. "I thank you for recommending the Bible to be my chief Study, I find and Acknowledge it the best of Books, it contains an endless treasure of wisdom and knowledge," Wheatley would write in April to John Thornton, the evangelist patron of Samson Occom and friend of the Countess of Huntingdon. Wheatley's phrasing exemplifies the reading of the Bible as history as well as moral teaching, a kind of reading that could reclaim the Old Testament from doubts about the relevance of Hebrew law for modern Christians. Or as Granville Sharp had put it, before he started to study English law in order to help fugitive slaves in court, he had never read any law books "except the Bible."

What Whitefield and others had observed, however, was that despite traditional uses of ancient slaveries to justify the modern kind, some, even many, Old Testament passages had special implications for the meaning of slavery in Israel and in any society, like Britain, that aspired to that legacy of chosenness and liberation. It remained more than possible to think of slaving as something that broke moral rules, that innovated and brought down God's wrath. Slavery could represent not modern, civilizing commerce, as it did for the African trade's leading defenders, but a return to what Swan and Benezet repeatedly called the "ignorance and barbarity of the darkest ages."

The story of David had been a popular reference in sermons in New England, especially in wartime. John Milton's friend Thomas Ellwood had published *Davideis: The Life of David, King of Israel* (1712), reprinted four times in the colonies, which began with the renowned Goliath scene. Mather Byles had included a shorter, mainly descriptive poem on Goliath, sketching the verses from the book of Samuel, in his 1744 collection. Still, in the wake of Swan and Benezet, the story had an untapped antislavery potential in Wheatley's hands. The parallels, for her, were almost too obvious. A youth of humble origins, small of stature, best known for playing his lyre and singing, takes on the largest of enemies and becomes famous for slaying him. Wheatley almost hides the bravado of her identification and her ambition by titling her poem not with David but with the would-be oppressor, "Goliath of Gath."

Wheatley's 111-couplet Bible story is far too long for a broadside or newspaper publication and much longer than the original narrative treatment of David and Goliath in the first book of Samuel. In writing it, she was clearly thinking of her own book. It elevates Wheatley to a different status as an author. So does the invocation of "YE martial pow'rs, and all ye tuneful nine" Muses to "Inspire my song and aid my high design." The identification of her high design with warriors and with "the poet and the sage" at the poem's outset called up Homer and Virgil (their beginning bids to "sing for our time, too" of the "rage" of "wars and the man") as well as Milton's deliberate, Christianizing echo: "Sing, heav'nly Muse." But by specifically mentioning the "sacred lyre," Wheatley also identifies with her subject, David, and his ability to move kings and destroy warriors, in God's name, with his song.

With the appearance of Goliath before the armies of Israel and his offer to fight a picked Hebrew champion, Wheatley raises the stakes of the confrontation. It is more than pride, or just another battle, where, as in the *Iliad*, a one-on-one fight may as well substitute for the clash of armies, because "he who wins in triumph may demand / Perpetual service from the vanquish'd land," the giant proclaims. Their armies mocked, threatened with slavery, "all *Israel*" is "trembling" and "affrighted" until David "in youthful bloom appears, / And warlike courage far beyond his years." As in Samuel (where the details of the challenge, Israel's response, and David's arrival are drawn out), David is rebuked by his elder brother for even daring to show up and ask about the victor's reward. Wheatley reverses the order of rewards from the King James Version, stressing first a more ambiguous, and meaningful, "Freedom in Israel for his house" to the combatant who could vanquish Goliath, as well as "wealth unknown" and the king's "royal daughter."

Hearing of this, King Saul calls "for the young hero," the "stripling" shepherd who thinks he can slay the Philistine. David tells him that God protected him against the lion and the bear, and will do the same before "this monster." To this point Wheatley has telescoped events but has not introduced new characters. But immediately after David's prophetic boast, "a radiant cherub," as in classical epics and other Bible stories (but not the books of Samuel), flies down to Goliath and lays it all out, as if in fairness, or to give even the pagan a chance at redemption. "[T]hou shalt perish by a beardless boy: / Such is the mandate from the realms above," the diminutive angel tells him: "And should I try the vengeance to remove, / Myself a rebel to my king would prove. / *Goliath* say, shall grace to him be shown, / Who dares heav'ns monarch, and insults his throne?"

Goliath condemns himself with the ultimate impious as well as antipoetic reply: "Your words are lost on me." Wheatley inflates the significance of words at every turn in the story of David and Goliath. When Goliath mocks David's appearance with a typically Homeric and secular insult—that the gods must have cursed this boy who will become food for dogs and vermin—David replies with the poem's longest speech, a sermonic blast that allies his powerful words with those of the Lord. After clarifying God's sovereignty and David's role, Wheatley has some more Homeric fun with "scenes of slaughter" and "seas of blood" and Goliath's dripping, lifeless head. "Israel's damsels" take over the singing of the victory. Unlike in Samuel, though, where the praise song of the women gives David a higher body count than King Saul ever had, distressing the monarch and hinting at problems to come, Wheatley's singing women herald only triumph, not trouble. The narrative ends with David presenting himself and Goliath's head before Saul, who is all grace while marveling again at the youth's obscurity and small size. The king "confer[s] riches and the royal bride" and brings the youth into an intimate alliance: "Knit to my soul for ever thou remain / With me, nor quit my regal roof again."

Speaking God's words, the little songster David slays the enslaver and inherits the kingdom. Wheatley's ancient Israel is a world of battles in which slavery and freedom are at stake. God intervenes; young people who ordinarily serve and sing make history. They find new homes, new families. There was more to Wheatley's book proposal than its table of contents could convey. She doesn't (yet) write explicitly, as James Swan did, that American slavery is ungodly, unbiblical, and wrong. It was more important for her and for the politics of the moment that slavery could get mixed up in any conflict of nations, and that consequently, for any individual or nation, it could end as well as begin.

12

THE MOVEMENT

While Phillis Wheatley built a network, considered the form of a book, and wrote elegies and an epyllion about a young singer's sacred triumph against a slaver, a fugitive named James Somerset, formerly of Boston and now of London, discovered a way to slay his own Goliath. His famous victory in *Somerset v. Steuart* at the Court of King's Bench in June 1772 prevented the North American customs commissioner Charles Steuart from re-enslaving him onto a Jamaica-bound ship. The six-month trial helped to focus, and launch, a transatlantic antislavery movement.

Wheatley and Somerset might seem to have had little in common. Somerset had been bought off a ship in Virginia in 1749, about four years before Phillis was born and twelve years before she arrived in Boston. On the other hand, each had been imprisoned and sent from Africa aboard a slave ship at about the same age. While James Somerset traversed the Atlantic coast serving a merchant and customs official, delivering messages and mail, Phillis Wheatley wrote poems praised by merchants and officials. After Somerset became famous in Boston because of what he did in London, Phillis Wheatley went to London to capitalize upon the fame she had earned in Boston. They might seem like people who reacted more than acted, subjects of categories and grand historical forces rather than makers of their own or others' destinies. They were not activists in a modern social movement. But their literal movements, and the publicity that their actions brought, freed them. Their examples helped make the controversy about slavery something that could be imagined and pursued across distances, something that could flourish precisely because it was publicized, part of the news that came on ships and made its way into print. As the imperial controversy entered a new phase of protest and publicity, it became more difficult to separate the problem of slavery from the problem of America.

Among the many Scottish merchants who plied the Atlantic and focused on Virginia tobacco, Charles Steuart might be considered especially canny, and lucky. The colonies would be his making. He set out as a teenager, apprenticed to a trader in his store, then gained more skills by spending a year in a Boston countinghouse owned by an uncle. A merchant himself by the time he bought Somerset in 1749, he also traded in captives from Barbados, St. Kitts, and Senegal. Like many of his clients, for his own purposes he preferred youngsters from Africa to experienced adult men from the West Indies who might have been "ship'd off for great Crimes." During the Seven Years' War, Steuart had an opportunity to show his loyalty to the empire when an angry mob in Norfolk, Virginia, tried to attack a grounded ship of Spanish prisoners who had earlier surrendered after the British capture of Havana. Steuart, who held a newly inked government contract to supply the ship and send it on its way, fended off the crowd and prevented what could have become an international incident. He distinguished himself as a man of parts who valued rules and order over the sovereignty of a local mob that might have included his customers. The British empire of trade functioned and even held together by cultivating people like him, even—or especially—when they had egregiously Scots Jacobite names like Charles Steuart.

Steuart's reward would be an audience with the king and, even better, the post of surveyor general of customs for the Eastern District of North America. Colleagues praised his efficiency. When the department was reorganized, he became cashier and paymaster for all the colonies: the man responsible for the money, the most desirable and highest-ranking customs post at a time when customs duties had been made more enforceable and more controversial than ever. He also knew when he couldn't win. During the Stamp Act crisis, in fear of violent crowds, he issued clearances to ships to leave harbor without stamps, apologizing to his superiors in London and pointing out just how extreme the losses would have been all along the coast and in the Caribbean had ships been left to rot in port. This was another way the empire worked.

Steuart apparently liked Somerset, or at least his service, enough to bring him along in his travels up and down the coast. They took longer postings in Philadelphia and, in 1767, Boston. Somerset must have been good at getting around, since a part of his forced labor involved acting as a courier for Steuart. It's no leap to imagine the well-dressed Somerset Steuart, as he was known then, delivering confidential messages from customs officials to governors and ship captains and in the process gaining first- or secondhand knowledge of political developments. James Murray, a merchant friend of Steuart's and the justice of the peace who controversially rented barracks to the troops in Boston, remembered Somerset from Steuart's visits at his country home in Milton. Steuart's assistant collector in Boston, the merchant Nathaniel Coffin, was sufficiently impressed with the twenty-six-year-old Somerset and his place in their lives to refer to him as an intimate: "[My] children with [Coffin's enslaved] Sapho and Tombo desire to be mentioned in terms of highest Friendship to able Mr. Somerset Stewart." A year and an ocean away he remained, for Coffin, "our friend Somersett."

Coffin liked to curry favor with his boss, but die-hard king's men like him needed their friends too, especially with customs officers being denounced as "bloodsuckers upon our trade" and a "curse more deplorable than Egyptian Darkness." Steuart, probably with Somerset, had to hide out at Castle William when he and the other feuding customs commissioners received violent threats. Luckily or not, he and Somerset had already left for England to take care of the estate of his deceased brother-in-law—he had a large extended family, and Steuart could continue to collect his salary while in England—when the Boston Massacre broke the stalemate over the actions of the collectors and their protection by troops.

What Somerset did in England, and even his presence there rather than Boston in 1771, had something, even much, to do with the imperial controversy. He probably sensed Steuart's overstretch, his vulnerability, even as he tasted the possibilities of anonymity as well as community in London. Somerset may have been less a lucky English fugitive who brought the right test case than a transatlantic Rosa Parks of the eighteenth century: a well-prepared actor in history who only appeared in retrospect to be a random, apolitical victim and thus an apt symbol for a movement. Somerset had spent at least a year with Steuart in Philadelphia, where he could have known of Anthony Benezet, John Woolman, and their successful efforts to turn Pennsylvania Quakers against not only the slave trade but slavery itself. In Boston during the "garrison" years he had a front seat to the imperial controversy and how it had begun to implicate actual Africans as well as "slavery." After his arrival in London he began to take advantage of urban opportunities, including the African community there, which numbered in the thousands. He traveled to Bristol, Edinburgh, and elsewhere with Steuart and on Steuart's behalf, much as he had in North America, testing, in effect, whether the kind of control of property over distance that Steuart managed for the empire and for himself could be effected as easily at "home" in the British Isles. He took the other kingly Stuart name of James when he was baptized in August 1771: two men and one woman sponsored him at St. Andrew's Church in Holborn Street. And some weeks later, in October, he "insulted" Charles Steuart and took off.

It took slave catchers eight weeks to find him, and when they did, twenty-three years of service notwithstanding, Charles Steuart had his right-hand man put in irons on a ship bound for Jamaica. Had it been up to Steuart, James Somerset would have endured a second Middle Passage and likely never would have passed a boundary line again.

But the Londoners who had served as James Somerset's baptismal godparents went to William Murray, Lord Mansfield, the chief justice of the King's Bench, to ask for a writ of habeas corpus, which he granted. Released but bound for appearance at trial, James Somerset went to see Granville Sharp, who was already known for teaching himself enough law to help fugitives in court. In his 1767 tract, Sharp had pointed out that colonial newspapers in places like New York revealed a severe and unbiblical kind of hereditary slavery that enforced the chattel principle for children as well as adults. Perhaps New York should be known as "New Barbary": a Mediterranean comparison that not only suggested American colonists' barbarism but also implicated Britons who complained about North African trafficking in European captives. Where earlier metropolitan commentators on "the African trade" had stressed its overall importance in the empire while proposing that its rough edges could be reformed, Sharp portrayed the slave trade and the rising numbers of West Africans in England as proof of imperial corruption. Colonial American slavery could be a threat to English liberty. It could also be a threat to revealed religion. Like his Quaker counterparts in North America, Sharp, who had earlier learned Hebrew and Greek so that he could parse both testaments in the original, had concluded that scripture did not support the kinds of enslavement that Britons practiced.

Beginning in 1766, Sharp secured counsel for fugitive slaves in several early test cases that had come before Mansfield's court. By 1772, however, he had changed course as far as the Americans were concerned, deciding that a better or more honest strategy at the imperial center was to blame British officialdom, not the colonists, for the slave trade. Himself a clerk in Britain's munitions supply department, he found the English radical Whig opposition's critique of imperial policy, and patriot colonists' defense of God-given, natural, and traditional English liberties, to be persuasive. Maybe the Protestant North American colonists were exactly what some of them said they were: creators of a newer, purer, even Hebraic or Anglo-Saxon republic, the bastion of original freedoms in an empire beginning to stink of (late) Rome. Sharp also began to notice the voices criticizing slavery in the northern colonies. The implications would not have been lost on him when the West Indies lobby took the *Somerset* case off Charles Steuart's hands, itching to gain a precedent for absolute property in slaves throughout the empire. Suddenly northern mainland America looked more English, a place to begin the broader work of emancipation. During the extended, six-month interval of Somerset's hearings and trial, Sharp began to correspond with Anthony Benezet. They had already excerpted and reprinted each other's pamphlets, and together they began to exchange ideas on how to grow a transatlantic antislavery movement. Benezet supplied information about the horrors of slavery in Africa but also optimistic reports about opposition to the slave trade from New England all the way to Virginia.

In stepped Benjamin Franklin, then residing in London as colony agent for Massachusetts, Pennsylvania, New Jersey, and Georgia. Very concerned about accusations of patriot hypocrisy, he had been spreading word of a fundamental difference in nature and outlook between powerful Caribbean planter interests and the continental Americans who were fighting for their liberties and who would actually curtail the slave trade through legislative action if only they were permitted to do so. Sharp seems to have been assured by Franklin's spin and his promise to Benezet to "work in concert" on the matter of slavery. Far from depicting all Americans as slave-driving nabobs and hypocrites as he had in 1767, he began to echo and even elaborate the Boston-to-Philadelphia patriot line amplified by Franklin. Americans were defenders of British liberties against the corruptions of empire, including slavery. Northern America, unlike the empire in the East or West

Indies, resembled an earlier, prelapsarian England: more Christian, more republican, less socially stratified. By early 1773, Sharp would be citing James Otis on natural rights and ancient English "northern country" liberties and their incompatibility with slavery—in a pamphlet he published first in New Jersey.

Chief Justice Mansfield, however, had a different take on the increasingly tangled problem of slavery and colonial relations, one that affected his initial attempts to get the parties in *Somerset v. Steuart* to settle out of court. Most of all, he anticipated the many possible complications of this suit—not only for English liberties, not only for African slavery, but also for parliamentary and royal authority, which he saw as inseparable. To the great jurist, the case, above all, was a conflict of laws. Slavery was positively established by law in the colonies, but no statute authorized the institution on English soil. In pronouncements from the King's Bench in one of Sharp's earlier test cases, Mansfield had made it clear that while jurisdiction always came first, such conflicts of law were always to be avoided when they could be, lest parties take unjust advantage of them. He even said that he'd prefer that slaves believed that they were lawfully bound and that masters did not, since both would "behave better"! Mansfield did not flinch from adapting common law, in the absence of statutes, to unanticipated new realities in order to preserve the system. African slavery was one relatively new reality in the long annals of English law. But so was the colonial controversy. Who decided and how were as important as what was decided.

The habeas writ on Somerset's behalf put English law above the statute law of slavery in the colonies. So had Mansfield outside his courtroom as a leader in the House of Lords, holder of a seat on the Privy Council for Plantation Affairs, and a cabinet member. He "articulated a key ideological plank of the New Toryism" when he stated that Parliament "represents the whole British empire, and has the authority to bind every part and every subject without the least distinction, whether such subjects have a right to vote or not, or whether the law binds places within the realm or without." At the first hearing and the last in *Somerset v. Steuart*, he suggested that the West Indians who were backing Steuart should proceed directly to Parliament if they wanted their property rights in England confirmed. If it came to a question between the colonies and Parliament, whether the issue was taxes or property in slaves, there was no question.

This was precisely why Mansfield had been denounced, repeatedly, in the *Boston Gazette*. While no one did more to establish the independence and weight of the judiciary in eighteenth-century England, Mansfield did so as a political actor: a Scottish provincial who had made good in the new, larger British nation, in which each realm had its particular traditions and place, but within an empire centered on London. No one thought more clearly about the place of colonies—as inferior to that of the British provinces—except perhaps Mansfield's own protégé, William Blackstone, whose *Commentaries on the Laws of England* had just been reprinted in Philadelphia and advertised in Boston in a revised edition. Blackstone made it all plain. Even recently conquered territories like Quebec had a right to retain their traditional laws that mere colonies did not—or as Mansfield had put it before voting against repeal of the Stamp Act, "Colonists . . . are more emphatically subjects of Great Britain than those within the realm."

In Lord Mansfield's hands, patriot rhetoric seemed to become reality. In one debate, he had gone so far as to say of the battle with the colonists, in the House of Lords, that "if you do not kill them, they will kill you." The fact that Mansfield could say something this aggressive and yet statesmanlike in the House of Lords, while the chief judge in the nation's highest court, for some colonists epitomized the plural office-holding and judicial appointments that they were blasting in Massachusetts. No wonder Thomas Hutchinson "adored" Mansfield, long before the lord chief justice shared Hutchinson's experience of having his house and manuscripts destroyed by an angry mob (during the Gordon Riots of 1780). But while Hutchinson's tactics of delay and constitutional fealty—expressed in actions like repeatedly proroguing the assembly and getting his salary paid through London—hit still another wall of opposition in Massachusetts, the widely admired and appreciated Mansfield could try the case with seeming distance from public opinion and Parliament in spite of his over-the-top habit of reading newspapers during oral arguments. He has gone down in history for making clear that some kind of law was higher than the law of slavery. He should also be remembered for how his actions reflected and accelerated the American crisis.

Unlike most trials at the King's Bench, this case would not be resolved in minutes or hours. As Somerset and Sharp's team added counsel, dug into precedents, and made long oral arguments, at first the lawyers asked for postponements; then the judges did as well so that other cases would not be knocked off the docket. These delays actually helped make *Somerset v. Steuart* a "media event." By February, a newspaper debate commenced, with most writers taking the side of Somerset. Final arguments from the defense did not occur until May 21, with increasing intimations, reported in the newspapers, that Mansfield and the other three judges would rule for freedom.

Mansfield tried to stave off the sense of an imminent radical departure in law. He reiterated his initial comment that "merchants" would be better off applying to Parliament for a resolution if they expected a precedent in favor of slave law, and even suggested that Steuart find a reason to "release" Somerset, presumably through some financial settlement. But the lawyers doubled down: the case had become about politics. Meanwhile, in June, Franklin weighed in anonymously in print with a curse of "pharisaical Britain" for freeing one slave and pronouncing English freedoms while doing nothing about the slave trade. The Barbados colony agent Samuel Estwick, in turn, played right into both Franklin's and Mansfield's geographies of virtue by insisting that people were property, that colonial law could not be repugnant to English law, and that Parliament needed to legislate with its most valuable colonies in mind.

Various versions of what Mansfield actually said when pronouncing judgment on June 22, 1772, can seem to conflict in emphasis or implications. Nevertheless, two features with particular implications for the colonies stand out. Most famously, he echoed Somerset's counsel in pronouncing English air "too free to breathe" for slaves—a comment taken immediately by Africans themselves, and by many ever since, as striking down slavery itself in England, even though it didn't.

The judge also said that Somerset's fugitivity—his movement—and the attempt of Steuart to counter it through sale had made his emancipating decision unavoidable. It wasn't that slavery was illegal. It was that moving anyone against their will to the West Indies, even a slave, constituted an "act of high dominion" unheard of under English law. Even though the state could do precisely that in the case of convicts and impressed seamen, "no master was ever allowed here to take a slave by force to be sold abroad because he deserted from his service, or for any reason whatever." In making slavery "odious" and a creature only of "positive" municipal law, Mansfield followed precedent and, to judge from London papers, public opinion. He hadn't freed a single slave besides James Somerset, but he did something that some would find more threatening and that would have particular implications for enslaved people, like Phillis Wheatley, who had a chance to travel. He reinforced the sense of slavery as a colonial vice, not an English one. Freedom for people in England, black and white, trumped not only race-based slavery but also property rights in the colonies.

In making the forced movement of slaves from England illegal, Mansfield confirmed what Somerset and Sharp had begun: a modern black politics that highlighted personhood as the right to move and to not be moved. Fugitives and their sustenance, more than rebels and their violence, became the symbol and practice of resistance, and alliances across boundaries came to seem the best way, short of war or legislation, to undermine the astonishing power of modern enslavers in a nautical age. Appropriately, Somerset's reward was to disappear into anonymity, though not before two hundred of his fellow black Londoners feted him at a celebration that earned a sympathetic notice in two London papers, along with a celebratory couplet: "Tyrants, no more the servile yoke prepare, / For breath of Slaves too pure in British air." He also lived on as a symbol, immediately to certain Africans in England and America who fled their servitude on the figurative advice of "Uncle Somerset." After the *Somerset* decision, some North American enslaved people invented England as the first North Star, a place in the British Empire where freedom reigned, if you could get there.

What made the *Somerset* case the true beginning of the antislavery movement was not just the precedent but the publicity. British West Indians, the most effective lobbyists of the mid-eighteenth century, immediately stepped it up with articles in the *Gentleman's Magazine* and a second edition of Estwick's pamphlet, pushing still harder their proslavery argument that the issue was really race: Africans had no rights because they were property, and they were property because they weren't equally human. Mainland southerners, south of Virginia, with not very many printing presses, did their best to ignore the issue, except for a few sotto voce warnings about the case as another not especially surprising power grab coming out of London. Only Boston hosted a full-on debate as the slavery issue roared back into the town's newspapers.

During the spring of 1772, in the wake of the Hutchinson administration's attempts to launch its own newspaper and to put the maverick editor Isaiah Thomas on trial for libel, patriot writers like Samuel Adams threw down their rhetorical gauntlets. They speculated that the crisis of government would lead to independence without a radical change such as the removal of Governor Hutchinson. In June, news arrived of the administration's plans to pay the Massachusetts

Superior Court out of London instead of the assembly. In October the radical patriots planned the new Committee of Correspondence to spread word of threats to liberty throughout the province, a strategy sanctioned by the Boston town meeting on November 2. The *Boston Gazette* and Richard Draper's *Massachusetts Gazette and the Boston Weekly News-Letter* continued to throw fire, accusing each other of traitorous behavior. Who printed what, and what it might mean in Boston and in London, had never been so controversial as when accounts of the *Somerset* case arrived in the harbor.

The first descriptions of the trial in process appeared in the *Boston Weekly News-Letter* on July 23, and in the Tory-leaning but "timid" *Post-Boy* as well as the self-declared open and neutral *Evening-Post* during the following week. They described the May 12 proceedings accurately and conveyed the logic of Mansfield's thinking as revealed in his questions to counsel. By way of a "correspondent," these reports also stressed how "pregnant with consequences" the trial seemed to slaveholders in the empire and went so far as to suggest that the metropole would soon be flooded with runaway Africans. Another report in the *Post-Boy* told the other, antislavery side: Somerset's lawyers, some in London had said, could be still bolder and argue that English law had never sanctioned slavery at all.

A month later, as reports of the decision of June 22 came in, the pro-administration press continued to take the lead in coverage, with the *News-Letter* in front again by putting out a special supplement with pages of detailed information. While the *Post-Boy* continued to highlight the practical worries of the planters, Draper's unrelentingly Tory paper seemed to revel in the glory of British liberty in the hands of Mansfield, at the expense of hypocritical provincials. The *Post-Boy* and *Evening-Post* reprinted some of this material a few days later, including the key Mansfieldian conclusion that removing an enslaved person constituted "so high an act of dominion" as to be incompatible with English liberty.

Meanwhile, the *Boston Gazette* remained uncharacteristically silent. Isaiah Thomas, in the *Spy*, avoided the trial and full verdict but, true to his earlier sympathetic gestures to Wheatley and other Africans, published the short account of the courtroom at the moment of the verdict, when blacks in the galleries bowed in respect to Lord Chief Justice Mansfield. Two weeks later, however, he inaugurated the local patriot pushback against the implications of *Somerset* with an original letter from "Ben Scotus" that, à la Benjamin Franklin, accused Mansfield of hypocrisy for freeing one slave and "hold[ing] millions in chains."

Revealingly, Ben Scotus explicitly distanced himself from another entry in the emerging debate: a long treatise by the pseudonymous "John Marsham" (a seventeenth-century Hebrew Bible scholar) who insisted upon divine sanction for the African slave trade, on the grounds of the curse of Ham and the license given in Leviticus 25 for Hebrews to hold other peoples in perpetual slavery. Writers in the *Evening-Post* and the *Spy* proceeded to carry on, for months, the most extensive and learned battle yet waged over the meaning of the Old and New Testaments for New World slavery, complete with references to Benezet and Sharp, outraged voices denouncing Markham for mediocre scholarship, and reactionary readings of history and the word of God. The *Post-Boy* continued to hedge, uncomfortable enough with the smug Mansfieldism of Draper's *News-Letter* to go out of their way to publish a prediction that the *Somerset* case would prove even more troublesome and controversial than the Stamp Act—especially in the West Indies. In October, the *Post-Boy* printed an excerpt from some proslavery "Reflections on the Negro Cause" by Edward Long, a Jamaica planter. And still the militant *Boston Gazette* remained silent—except for one short, understated London reprint, on September 21, suggesting that "as Blacks are now free in this country, gentlemen will not be so fond of bringing them here as they used to be."

During the coming weeks, the paper shifted to complaints about the independence of judges in Massachusetts instead of the boldness of a certain judge in London. On the all too relative matter of slavery, patriots had been exposed as hypocrites and checkmated, for the moment.

The coverage of the *Somerset* case in Boston was as extensive as anywhere but London, but it varied. Antislavery and proslavery positions exfoliated in the hothouse of colonial protest and metropolitan pushback. Because of the daring actions of James Somerset and Granville Sharp, in the forge of imperial politics, both antislavery and proslavery became movements—entangled at birth, much as in the sacred scriptures that seemed to presume, yet also criticized and limited, human bondage. Men and women who paid attention, like Phillis Wheatley, might well have wondered whether the path forward lay in embracing ancient wisdom or modern politics.

The pattern in Boston was nevertheless clear. For the hard-line patriots seeking autonomy in the empire, antislavery might not be consistency, the evasion of hypocrisy, or the arc of history bending toward justice, but rather a poison pill that threatened everything. In the principled, politically savvy, and hairsplitting hands of Mansfield, the oppression of the enslaved could eviscerate Whig points about process and obliterate their claims to virtue all at once. The case had not only made them look like hypocrites: it created another precedent for metropolitan decisions about colonial matters.

Simultaneously, to the loyal administration men, their colleague Charles Steuart notwithstanding, antislavery seemed suddenly, increasingly, useful. The *Somerset* case suggested to them that, just as they had known all along, men like Mansfield and Hutchinson, from on high and in the courts, rather than James Otis and Sam Adams in taverns and newspapers, knew best how to parse and distribute British freedoms.

Meanwhile, a credit crisis loomed. James Swan's antislavery pamphlet, and Phillis Wheatley's book, remained in manuscript at Russell's printing house, seeking subscribers. It was hard to know whether their moment had passed or not yet arrived.

13

THE MOMENT

The poem that got Phillis Wheatley to England and sped the publication of her book wasn't about James Somerset or Lord Mansfield, though it did link colonial protests to the future of slavery for Africans. It was about Lord Dartmouth.

After the usual transatlantic six-week delay, word arrived in late September 1772 of Dartmouth's appointment to the king's cabinet as head of the Board of Trade and secretary of state for the Southern Department (the colonies in the Americas, especially the lucrative ones, being south of most of Europe). He had held the former position before, in 1765–66. Speculations about a possible shift in American policy, along with the effects of bank failures in London, shoved debate about the future of slavery after *Somerset v. Steuart* to the back burner. Subsequent reports from London included optimistic statements that Dartmouth's American policy would be characterized by "lenient measures," even in response to recent provocations like the burning of the revenue-enforcing cutter ship, the *Gaspee*, in Rhode Island.

While cabinet members served at the pleasure of the prime minister and the king, the future of colonial policy might still be at stake in the appointment. The previous holder of the position, the Earl of Hillsborough, had become well known for the disdainful view of colonists revealed in his hard-line responses to protests and his attempts to block royal grants to the Ohio River valley lands supposedly opened up to settlement during the Seven Years' War but still home to indigenous peoples. Hillsborough found himself forced out of office in 1772 because too many fellow cabinet officers had invested in those speculative ventures. Moreover, having called for the revocation of charters in response to the smuggling and tumult in New England, Hillsborough was thoroughly disgusted by the *Gaspee* affair. Activists in Boston returned the revulsion. They had long since taken to calling the excrement they sometimes smeared on the houses of customs informers "Hillsborough paint."

Dartmouth, by contrast, was known as friendly to Americans. He had voted in the House of Lords for the repeal of the Stamp Act. Agents like Franklin lobbied for his reappointment. Dartmouth himself received word of Americans' "satisfaction" already in August, through the agents and merchants who circulated in London, the same week he kissed the king's ring and took the oath of office. Hopeful colonists conveniently ignored the earl's vote in 1766 for the Declaratory Act, which signaled his unwavering commitment to Parliament's sovereignty. In addition to wishful thinking, part of what may have distracted them was Dartmouth's sheer agreeability and willingness to listen to colonials. If Hillsborough's hard-line belligerence made manifest the dark side of empire and aristocracy, Dartmouth reminded many who knew him of another side, marked by moderation and what was then called, approvingly, "condescension."

William Legge, Earl of Dartmouth, saw no conflict in the task of just administration and holding a hundred thousand acres of land in recently conquered East Florida. In that he was typical, not much different from Hillsborough. But he had other distinctive qualities that loomed larger in Boston and especially for the Wheatleys. Legge had a well-earned reputation as an evangelical Christian and a pious reformer. He had been an early supporter and friend of George Whitefield's who had once hosted a revival at his summer home. When the

Countess of Huntingdon suffered an illness, there was talk of her friend Dartmouth assuming oversight of her dissenting chapels. Some colleagues actually mocked him as "the Psalm-Singer" for his connections to Methodists. He also oversaw the trust for Moor's Indian Charity School. When Eleazar Wheelock betrayed his protégé Samson Occom by taking funds raised for the school in order to start Dartmouth College—all without consulting the earl—Dartmouth chose not to be flattered but rather to see it from Occom's perspective: he never again responded to another of Wheelock's letters.

In the minds of people on both sides of the Atlantic who watched the political scene, Dartmouth's genteel reforming ethos could not easily be separated from his imperial responsibilities, any more than Mansfield's politics could be separated from his judgments—if only because the reformers wouldn't have it. On October 10, 1772, Granville Sharp didn't hesitate to initiate a correspondence with Legge about the troops that had just been sent from Boston to St. Vincent for a campaign against the native Caribs. The Caribs had begun to fight back against their dispossession in favor of new settlers, and there had been talk of deporting them to Africa, probably because, as Sharp noted, they were "descended of a mixt race, between African negroes and the ancient Caribee Indians." Sharp had never written to Dartmouth before, but he presumed upon their shared piety and made a national appeal for justice: "For God's sake, my Lord, if you really are the *conscientious* man that I believe you to be, inquire strictly and carefully into this matter." Dartmouth's response is even more revealing. He not only read Sharp's letter, he actually asked Sharp, fresh from his triumph in Somerset's case, to come see him the very next day. He assured Sharp that the current St. Vincent policy was none of his doing and that he would weigh in appropriately.

Sharp was not the only concerned person to be thinking about Dartmouth and the colonies and their implications on October 10, 1772. On the same day, across the sea in Boston, another imperial functionary sought to mobilize Dartmouth's power by appealing to his interest in evangelized natives and Africans. Thomas Wooldridge knocked on the Wheatleys' door in King Street, hoping for a story he could retail in exchange for attention, support, and a closer connection in the wake of Dartmouth's return to power.

Wooldridge was a London merchant with property in Staffordshire, the site of the Dartmouth manor. He bought land and moved to East Florida in 1767 with an appointment, probably through Dartmouth, as provost marshal and, later, receiver general for the new colony, as well as a subsidiary post as fort adjutant and barracks master of St. Marks. Sometime during the late 1760s he began to feud with the new governor and military commander, James Grant. By 1771, Wooldridge was doing mercantile business in New England, South Carolina, and the West Indies and traveling back to England. He tried to sell his Florida sinecure or resign while depending on Dartmouth to try to shore him up with the "tyrant" Grant or secure him a new position. He married Susannah Kelly, a business partner's daughter, and returned to North America, but stayed mainly in New York, where his new father-in-law had given him several thousand acres as a dowry. From there Wooldridge sent occasional reports back to Dartmouth.

Thomas Wooldridge was rude and presumptuous and had a knack for trouble. His letters show the habits of a courtier, or at least a lobbyist. At minimum he was another kind of character, like Charles Steuart, who made the empire work. In October 1772, above all he wanted an excuse to flatter and please his newly elevated patron and make it clear that he could become Dartmouth's main man in more colonies than East Florida. "I have lately travelled through all the New-England Provinces," he wrote, probably with some exaggeration, "where they rejoiced with me upon the Happy occasion" of Dartmouth's appointment. "Their fears are removed, and they seem to anticipate the full enjoyment of Civil & Religious Liberty." Wooldridge then didn't miss a beat in saying that he planned to spend the winter in the West Indies, "where I shall be happy to be honored by your commands," and then come home to London.

But by the time Wooldridge actually sent this letter, five more weeks had passed. Why the delay, when he was responding to the opportunities of the moment, to Dartmouth's ascent? By November 24, he had gained more information, made more plans to make himself useful to Dartmouth, and incorporated Phillis Wheatley into them. "While in Boston," he "heard of a very extraordinary female slave who had made some verses on our mutually dear deceased Friend," George Whitefield. "I visited her mistress, and found by conversing with the African, that she was no Impostor." Wooldridge asked to see, or was shown, a copy of Wheatley's letter to the Countess of Huntingdon that had covered her Whitefield poem. In his own letter Wooldridge almost gives away his calculation by admitting that Dartmouth himself probably had already seen Wheatley's letter to Huntingdon. She was already famous in Huntingdon's and Dartmouth's circles, he realized. He was just catching up.

So Wooldridge did something that we might ascribe to simple, outright racism but which, in light of his own desires, suggests how complicated racial politics could be in 1772 and how his visit became an opportunity not just for him but for Phillis Wheatley. He said, flatly, to the Wheatleys that it wasn't enough to see several of Phillis's manuscripts, even though he admits in the letter that he had already been convinced that she had written them. Like an autograph hunter out for an even better souvenir to keep or sell, he asked her to compose, or at least write out, something on the spot.

Phillis told her demanding visitor, in a distinctly ladylike fashion that nevertheless allowed for her youth and slave status, that "she was then busy and engaged for the Day," but he could "propose a Subject" and return for the results in the morning. Wooldridge suggested "the Earl of Dartmouth" and was more than satisfied to come back. When he did, Phillis took out some paper and rather theatrically began writing out a fifty-line praise poem, "To the Right Hon. William Earl of Dartmouth, His Majesty's Secretary of State for North America &.c &.c. &.c."

The first half of the poem describes New England's delight at Dartmouth's appointment. It is nothing less than a new day, when the sun of "Fair Freedom rose" again. The "northern clime" is "exulting" in the "Paternal Sway" and "Silken reins" of the earl's leadership. Wheatley signals identification with the patriot movement and with official Britain at once when she narrates the effects of Freedom shining: "Hated Faction dies, / Soon as he saw the triumph long desir'd / Sick at the view, he languish'd and expir'd." Freedom is feminine, faction masculine in this contest of the deities projected onto imperial and partisan politics.

The classical frame, with sun-freedom as goddess and faction as owlish demon, makes colonial satisfaction the measure of Dartmouth's greatness: "No more of grievance unredress'd complain / Or injur'd Rights, or groan beneath the chain, / Which Wanton Tyranny with lawless hand, Made to enslave, O Liberty! Thy Land." Wheatley doesn't hesitate to refer directly to politics or to use current Whig rhetoric. For the first time she compares restrictions on the colonies to the chains of slavery, participating in the long-standing debate about tyranny.

At the mention of liberty, though, she draws explicit attention to herself and to her own relation to the question of liberties, asserting, "My Soul rekindles at thy glorious name / Thy beams essential to the vital Flame." Liberty is life, Wheatley has stated outright; it is the light of her soul. And she has said so right after condemning tyranny as enslavement. In the next six-line stanza, which she would later edit out, she retreats a bit, back to Dartmouth as paternal hero, the Americans as grateful subjects:

> The Patriot's breast, what Heav'nly virtue warms!
> And adds new lustre to his mental charms;
> While in thy Speech, the Graces all combine;
> Apollos too, with Sons of Thunder Join,
> Then Shall the Race of Injur'd Freedom bless
> The Sire, the Friend, and messenger of Peace.

This redirection brings us back to the beginning, but it does not resolve the problem of identity and of voice that Wheatley has raised explicitly, and which, if Wooldridge is to be believed, informed the very scene of composition and transmission of the poem. Clearly the author identifies with the oppressed New England or American "Race of Injur'd Freedom," still hoping for benevolent "Paternal Sway" from the king or his lords. What about the other people with injured freedoms, the ones Wheatley never, ever called a "race"?

Wheatley knew very well, by 1772, that any performance of hers would be understood as an African one, with relevance for the question of American-style racialized slavery. The second half of the Dartmouth poem answers the question she imagines an enlightened Dartmouth asking in response to her self-assertion in the poem, her calling attention to her own rekindled soul. She turns Wooldridge's rude if commonplace question, the question Lady Huntingdon had already asked—can this slave, this African, have written such fine English verse?—into another set of questions entirely. Why had she chosen to write this particular "advent'rous Song"? Was it only because of Dartmouth's appointment, an administrative change New Englanders hoped would be epic? Or was it because the issues of colonial liberties and African slavery were truly, not just metaphorically, linked?

> *While you, my Lord, read o'er th' advent'rous Song*
> *And wonder whence Such daring boldness Sprung:*
> *Hence, flow my wishes for the common good*
> *By feeling hearts alone, best understood.*
>
> *From Native clime, when Seeming cruel fate*
> *Me snatch'd from Afric's fancy'd happy Seat,*
> *Impetuous.—Ah! what bitter pangs molest*
> *What Sorrows labor'd in the Parent-breast!*
> *That more than Stone, ne'er Soft compassion mov'd*
> *Who from its Father Seiz'd his much belov'd.*
> *Such once my case.—Thus I deplore the day*
> *When Britons weep beneath Tyrannic sway.*

Instead of political restrictions seeming akin to enslavement—instead of tyranny being like slavery—the equation is reversed. Slavery is wrong because it is like the tyranny that participants in the debates of 1772 have been hearing so much about.

And Wheatley no longer merely fashions herself an invisible member of a Boston chorus of praise. She becomes a colonial informant, a highly visible expert on tyranny, liberty, and slavery. From being suspect or a freak of nature, she becomes an exotic republican who wishes for the common good with a heart as feeling as any. The emphasis on feeling suggests a particularly feminine appeal, just as her performance for Wooldridge presumed the parlor dance of withdrawal and presentation when the gentleman returned to call again. She imagines Dartmouth's responding to the poem that is not yet finished: that act of imagination licenses her to tell Dartmouth how she feels, and how her father felt, about her enslavement.

Yet that presentation of feeling, and the freedom to speak it, begs the question of her subsequent and current oppression, her "Seeming cruel fate." Is it only seeming, because she's been saved? It isn't. She mocks "fancy'd" Anglo presumptions that Africans remember their homeland as a "happy seat" given that it is a place where fathers like hers lose daughters to the slave trade. She feels losses of liberty deeply not in spite of being a foreign enslaved woman but because of her father's African experience of having his daughter "snatch'd" away (not "brought," as in her earlier poem "On Being Brought from Africa to America"). She equates her father's grief with the anguish of the patriots faced with tyranny. Her history, as much as that of any British colonist, explains her good citizenship.

The invocation of her father is all the more effective because it is not the first reference to paternity in the poem. Dartmouth had been introduced as the "sire" as well as "friend" of peace and liberty. Her own African experience, then, also gives her insight into the paternal and maternal metaphors through which Anglos discussed imperial politics. The poem, in other words, is simultaneously about politics—

a characterization of what was happening in 1772—and about how people were talking about politics, the metaphors they used. It is essential that this double argument about realities and perceptions, what she feels and what her "song" actually does, comes after Wheatley's demonstration, in the first stanzas, of her ability to do colonial politics so expertly and so typically: that is, in going over the heads of local officials to praise distant powerful officials in the hope that they will change policy. These carefully ordered claims allow her new argument against slavery and her echo of the argument for colonial redress to work in tandem. They reinforce her adoption of a universal perspective as well as local knowledge. Awareness of chattel slavery's wrongs—her international as well as local experience—actually comes to support her own standing as a patriot poet and a political subject of Britain and New England.

The Dartmouth praise poem, then, is about validating an enslaved woman's perspective on political events in England and America. It introduces the slave persona into Anglo-American and African diaspora literature, and it does so through a formal political action (the settler appeal to a lord and administrator) that reverses the then-standard argument that specific political oppressions of the moment were like a generic slavery. Suddenly aspects of specific Africans' enslavement, like Somerset's attempted removal from England or Wheatley's from Africa, were to be seen in light of general political principles like Magna Carta, parliamentary supremacy, or the rights of British subjects.

What the poem isn't about may be as revealing as the number and weight of things it is about. By referring to race twice—but before mentioning herself—Wheatley ensures that the poem is not about hers. The initial mention of the word "race" refers to the inhabitants of the "northern clime," New England, while the next more ambiguously invokes "the Race of injur'd Freedom" who bless Dartmouth. Given the aggressive revival of the arguments that invoked blackness to defend a racialized, hereditary slavery in 1772, this too is a statement—an insistence that slavery was indeed a relative thing, a historical creation, not necessarily permanent, not simply biblically sanctioned, not a destiny ordained for certain races descended from Cain or from Ham and naturally suited to tropical climes. If slavery was relative and historical, so was "race." It was just another word, a metaphor for more complex realities, and maybe not a very good or important one.

The final lines take the edge off her boldness and the immense (and unrealistic) power that she grants the earl by wishing him "heav'nly grace." The final image is of Dartmouth saved, not just with the "Immortal Honours" that "grace the Patriots' name," but winging his way to heaven itself, "like the Prophet," to meet "thy Sire, the Everlasting God." This elevates the earl even further of course, but it also treats him like some of her earlier subjects: Reverend Sewall, or one of her dead infants who provide pious instruction to the living while validating the poet's participation in God's design. Just in case Dartmouth did not get the message, Wheatley summarized the argument in the cover letter she gave to Wooldridge. The occasion, the moment of Dartmouth's oath of office, excused the "freedom from an African" to write to him, since all of "the (now) happy America" rejoiced at the appointment of one of America's "greatest advocates." She wished him success, God's blessings, and signed her name no less or more humbly than any correspondent, "Your Lordship's Most Ob[edien]t. & devoted Humbl[e] Serv[an]t, Phillis Wheatley." She dated the letter October 10 but added a brief biographical sketch that was verified and augmented by Nathaniel Wheatley. Wooldridge waited for this document before sending his letter and Phillis's packet off to Dartmouth on November 24, on a ship from New York.

"To the Right Honl. William Earl of Dartmouth" and the letter that accompanied it emphasized distance and difference (New England, America, African enslavement) overcome by commonality (British and Christian). The poem also replays themes of Wheatley's previous efforts: an advertisement for herself and her project. At the most

propitious moment, when the politics of the empire intersected with
the politics of slavery like planets coming into alignment, it presents
Wheatley and what she meant to the most powerful person likely to
be sympathetic to her. No one so high in the government would have
been more interested in Phillis Wheatley.

Had she thought about Dartmouth, about writing to or about him,
earlier than the moment Wooldridge narrated? Word of Dartmouth's
selection for the secretaryship had not arrived in Boston until about
September 28. Still, given knowledge of Dartmouth's connections to
the Countess of Huntingdon, Whitefield, and Occom, Wheatley had
fully as much patronage at stake as Wooldridge did. The poem is so
long and polished that it seems likely she had already written it or anticipated such an opportunity. Some earlier link, or the prospect of one
through Occom, may have inspired her to anticipate writing to Dartmouth well before Thomas Wooldridge's arrival. She could have seen
him, or someone like him, coming, but she needed an excuse, a more
direct personal connection, to initiate a poetic correspondence with,
as well as about, Lord Dartmouth. It could have been Brook Watson,
a merchant and business associate of Wooldridge's father-in-law, William Kelly. Watson had spent his childhood in Boston, and he was one
of the people Wheatley would visit when she went to London less than
a year later. He understood her well enough to present her with a fancy
edition of Milton's *Paradise Lost*.

The key connection between Wheatley in Boston and Dartmouth
in England was probably not Brook Watson himself but rather Susannah Kelly Wooldridge. The story Thomas Wooldridge told of his visit
to the Wheatleys' invokes Phillis's "mistress," but most of the stories
we have about visits to and by Wheatley in Boston are about other
women, or facilitated by them. What if it was his American-born wife,
Susannah, who had wanted to meet Wheatley—or already had before
and made the connection that Thomas later reported as his own brilliant idea?

Phillis left a clue hiding in plain sight. In her book a year later she included a poem, "Ode to Neptune. *On Mrs. W——'s Voyage to En-gland*," placing it right after her revision of the Dartmouth poem. Un-like any other poem in the volume, it has a precise place and date after its last stanza: "*Boston, October* 10, 1772," the same date she gave to the Dartmouth poem. "Mrs. W——" is identified as "my Susannah," which has usually been assumed to be Susanna Wheatley. But Susanna Wheatley would not have even contemplated any six-week sea voyage at her age and state of health, there is no record of her ever traveling to England, and she spelled her name without an "h" at the end. This poem is about, and for, Susannah Kelly Wooldridge, and it carries, or invites, an intimacy that is utterly absent from Thomas Wooldridge's version of his coy and transactional encounter on October 10.

The women, Susanna and Susannah, cooked up the occasion for Phillis Wheatley to address Lord Dartmouth, leading Phillis to later join this second poem of thanks to her better-known bid for freedom:

> I.
> *WHILE raging tempests shake the shore,*
> *While AE'lus' thunders round us roar,*
> *And sweep impetuous o'er the plain*
> *Be still, O tyrant of the main;*
> *Nor let thy brow contracted frowns betray,*
> *While my* Susannah *skims the wat'ry way.*

Two words occur in both poems: "impetuous" and "tyrant" or "tyr-anny." In the Dartmouth poem "impetuous" refers to the actions of slave traders; in "Ode to Neptune" it is the dangerous winds of Aeolus. In "To the Right Honorable" tyranny is political oppression and slav-ery; in "Ode to Neptune" it is the potentially life-threatening storms of the sea god. Read together, as they would be in her book, the poems clarify the use of the ancient and the modern to illuminate each other, through the common fact of sea voyages in the Mediterranean and the Atlantic. Wheatley focuses on those similarities to comment on the relationship between personal situations associated with women and public events, the domain of men. The link, as ever, is the ocean and how its deep waters could mean either reward or danger, liberation or oppression.

As in *The Aeneid* and Wheatley's first published poem to the merchants Hussey and Coffin, Neptune calms the waters, making a return home to England possible for Susannah, or to those who sing for her. Instead of New England basking in the sun, here it is Britain that receives happy communications, in the form of a woman courted by "unnumber'd charms" and "welcome smiles":

> II.
>
> *The* Pow'r *propitious hears the lay,*
> *The blue-ey'd daughters of the sea*
> *With sweeter cadence glide along,*
> *And* Thames *responsive joins the song.*
> *Pleas'd with their notes* Sol *sheds benign his ray,*
> *And double radiance decks the face of day.*

> III.
>
> *To court thee to* Britannia's *arms*
> *Serene the climes and mild the sky,*
> *Her region boasts unnumber'd charms,*
> *Thy welcome smiles in ev'ry eye.*
> *Thy promise,* Neptune *keep, record my pray'r,*
> *Nor give my wishes to the empty air.*

Wheatley chose to memorialize this moment as significant in the story of her artistry in the making that her book tells. Where women are absent from the Dartmouth poem except for Wheatley herself and the feminine figure of freedom, "Ode to Neptune" combines her primal, repeated use of the sea and the voyage with her performance of personal connection to the white women who constituted both her network and, so often, her first audience. It is a shadow praise poem for them, a nod also to the other Susanna that epitomizes how the important moment of October 10, 1772, had actually been made. It is as seemingly apolitical and classical as the Dartmouth poem is explicitly political and religious, an ode to a god who concerns himself with women and their voyages, telling a story about women moving men that can be told only in allegory. In this moment, after the *Somerset* case, Wheatley sought a "serene," "mild," feminine Britannia that she could court and who, like the Wooldridges, courted her.

14

THE CAMPAIGN

Before Wooldridge sent his packet to Dartmouth, and possibly even before he came to their house, the Wheatleys began to buttonhole some of Phillis's supporters to make an "attestation"—to state in writing that she had actually written the poems. With the plan for Russell to publish her poems clearly dead, publishing in London seemed the next, possibly even better, option. But that required a strategic adjustment as well as a reconsideration of primary and secondary audiences for the book. First and foremost was the problem of proof. John Andrews referred to this sheet or two as "papers drawn up and signed."

As in a legal document, the length and even the details mattered less than the formality. Because it served as traveling papers—allowing her book manuscript, and eventually Phillis herself, to travel—we might think of the attestation as her passport (though England was no foreign country). Like the just recently invented passport, the attestation tracked her origins as well as her age and bore most prominently the signatures and titles of officialdom: Governor Hutchinson, Lieutenant Governor Oliver. Andrews exaggerated only a bit when he described the signatories as "most of ye people of Note in this place." All the signatories stood ready to "assure the World" beyond Boston "that the POEMS . . . were (as we verily believe) written by PHILLIS, a young

Negro Girl, who was but a few Years since, brought an uncultivated Barbarian from *Africa*, and has ever since been, and now is, under the Disadvantage of serving as a Slave in a Family in this Town."

As if anticipating how much this sounded like a distinctly colonial urban legend, the attestation concluded with another statement, one that has created confusion about who Phillis Wheatley was in 1773 and what she was doing: "She has been examined by some of the best Judges, and is thought qualified to write them." "Judges" conjures the image of a discrete event: a trial, or (worse?) a school entrance examination, before a select group of men. But Phillis Wheatley didn't need to sit before an examining board in Boston. While some who signed the attestation, like Hutchinson, actually sat on the bench in Massachusetts, and others, like Joseph Green, were respected and well-known Boston writers and critics, Phillis Wheatley didn't have to appear before a "Wheatley court" or examining board precisely because she knew these men and they knew her. Even people like the customs commissioner Henry Hulton, who had never met her and had been traveling extensively, had already been "told she has read most of the best English books and translations from the antients, and that she converses upon them with great propriety." The eighteen men are better described as a group of people Wheatley had written *for*, written *to*, and in some cases written *about*. Some of them had been talking her up for years.

The attestation was designed to show the breadth of her associations in Boston and to palliate the skepticism of outsiders. In addition to the governor and lieutenant governor, for whom she had just written an elegy, there were five "Hon[orable]" members of the governor's council; the merchants Green, Richard Carey, and John Hancock, listed as "Esq[uires]"; and seven ministers, who themselves ran a gamut from the Irish-born preacher to the poor and outsiders, John Moorhead, to the anti-revivalist "Old Brick" of the establishment and champion of reason and balance, the Reverend Charles Chauncy of the First Church of Boston.

Chauncy had blamed slaving for God's evident dissatisfaction with America in a published sermon during the imperial crisis. During the same week as the Wooldridge visit, Chauncy gave Wheatley a book, the English dissenting minister Thomas Amory's *Daily Devotion Assisted and Recommended in Four Sermons*, recently republished by Ezekiel Russell. The gift probably marked the occasion of a visit and his signing of the attestation. Phillis later gave the book to the Wheatleys' young nephew Thomas Wallcut, a student at Dartmouth College—an act that might seem callous, even passive-aggressive, if Wheatley had not *already* written her poem "To the Rev. Dr. Thomas Amory on Reading His Sermons on Daily Devotion, in Which That Duty Is Recommended and Assisted," that was included in the very manuscript Chauncy was attesting that he had examined. She must have had access to the book, as with the similar book by John Lathrop, *The Importance of Early Piety*, which she also gave to Wallcut. Chauncy and other ministers often acted as book distributors, as professional spreaders of the word at a time—before the existence of public libraries—when they themselves owned or curated the largest libraries in town. With his gift Chauncy acknowledged, sensibly enough, that someone on the verge of publishing a book filled with pious gestures to ministers, which even took a ministerial stance to its readers, ought to themselves own the sermons they wrote poems about, even if the person in question was owned. Wheatley repeated the pastoral gesture when she sent that copy or a duplicate to Wallcut, the missionary in training.

Next on the list came the friendly yet aloof Mather Byles, and then Ebenezer Pemberton, the divine who had given the Whitefield funeral sermon that the printer Isaiah Thomas published in pamphlet form with Wheatley's elegy attached. Pemberton was close enough to the Wheatleys to carry letters from Phillis to Newport for Obour Tanner and Samuel Hopkins. Andrew Elliot, her own pastor Samuel Cooper, and Samuel Mather rounded out the more typical Congregationalists, while Moorhead, the iconoclastic ecumenical, finished the ministers on the list before "Mr. John Wheatley, her Master." Half secular and half sacred, these men's titles alone suggested the broad approval that Wheatley had inspired as well as the thematic range of her work.

According to Andrews, the Wheatleys' great expectations had been temporarily set back by the demands for proof. If so, they didn't miss much of a beat. The Wheatleys' approach to getting the book published in London, as it developed in late 1772 and early 1773, has all the marks of a studied publicity campaign. They wrote to people. They collected signatures. They spread samples of her poems widely, through manuscripts and in print. At some point they began to plan for Phillis herself to go to London, they said repeatedly, for her health: the ocean air would do her good. It's true that she had been sick the previous winter, and doctors did sometimes suggest voyaging on the water as a palliative for chronic pulmonary diseases. But that was what we would now call the public transcript, a performance or simplification meant to distract attention from an unfeminine and un-slave-like seeking of fame. Really, the Wheatleys and their allies expected Phillis to serve, in London, as an advertisement for herself, increasing the chance of what they hoped would be a "large emolument" from the publication of the volume, as Andrews put it. They did not imagine Phillis making a Somerset-like run for freedom, because going to London and returning with greater fame and better literary prospects for having been there had become a viable course.

Andrews, who stressed the "emolument," had a merchant's focus on the bottom line. For the white Wheatleys, who did not lack means, the goals seem to have been different, higher, and subtle, requiring careful management because the stakes involved both their aspirations for Phillis and their own good name. They drew the ship captain Robert Calef, who sailed their *London Packet* several times a year, into the plan. During his November–December voyage, Calef went to see Archibald Bell, a printer with ties to Whitefield's patron Selina Hastings, the Countess of Huntingdon, in order to give him Wheatley's manuscript to consider for publication. Bell made a trip to the countess's estate with the sheaf of poems in hand. The London publication plan had launched. Bell would publish the poems if Huntingdon approved and promoted them.

Huntingdon was "greatly pleas'd with" Wheatley's poems, Bell wrote to Susanna—not even waiting for his own return voyage to relay the news. Turning the printer's visit into a literary salon, she "pray'd him to Read them; and would often break in upon him and Say, 'is this or that, very fine? do read another.'" Selina, an aristocrat who had developed an evangelical Christian fellowship that deliberately bridged classes and reached out to natives and Africans, declared to Bell in quintessential Methodist style that "she found her heart to knit with her." The countess's favor seemed urgent because it was much more than a willingness to subscribe for a few copies or provide the equivalent of a blurb. Huntingdon had been subsidizing evangelical publications for years. She was also friends with English "bluestocking" women of letters. She knew the market for poems, for religion, and for women authors.

Still, the more interested Selina the great patron became, the more she worried that she might be duped, or that people would think she had been and disbelieve the true story she was hearing and the feelings that Wheatley's poems inspired. She "questioned him [Bell] very much, whether she was Real without a deception? He then Convinc'd her by bringing my Name [Calef] in question. She is expected in Town in a Short time when we are both to wait upon her." The testimony of the ship captain who actually knew Wheatley sealed the deal.

Huntingdon agreed to the Wheatleys' proposal to dedicate the book to her—and thought ahead to the book's physical appearance and reception. She took a patron's liberty in asking for "one thing She desir'd which She Said She hardly thou't would be denied her, that was to have Phillis' picture in the frontispiece"—another kind of proof of authorship, which the countess turned artfully into a performance of gratitude. This gave Calef another reason to get a letter onto the next ship. A portrait needed to be taken, in time for Calef's next return journey from Boston to London, "so that if you would get it done it can be

Engrav'd here, I do imagine it can be Easily done, and think it would contribute greatly to the Sale of the Book."

On receiving Calef's letter, Susanna Wheatley did not allow her own illness, or that of her husband (who had suffered a bad fall), to prevent her from writing personally to Huntingdon. She reminded the countess of the evangelical ties they had in common and offered to open her house, apparently not for the first time, to any missionaries that her Methodist Connection should sponsor. Susanna also chose to exaggerate Samson Occom's recent visit and preaching in Boston as "universally admired," even though Occom himself complained that, as in 1765, only their mutual friend John Moorhead had opened his pulpit for him.

The Wheatleys also acted on the portrait request immediately, if they had not already anticipated it (some portrait of Phillis did hang in Mrs. Wheatley's rooms). There were a number of portraitists in Boston who could do the job, including two Africans. Prince Demah Barnes preceded Wheatley in traveling to London to improve his artistic prospects in 1771. A still more likely artist is Scipio Moorhead, the young man enslaved by John and Sarah Moorhead. In addition to being a poet herself and a friend of the Wheatleys', Sarah Moorhead taught drawing. Phillis had probably known Scipio for years. In words or not, Wheatley and Scipio Moorhead probably compared notes on their arts and what their pious mistresses permitted and encouraged. If he painted the frontispiece portrait, it must have been a collaboration in more ways than we can know.

Contemporaries would have recognized at once the pious and the literary conventions in the portrait, or at least the engraving based on it. The now famous image of Phillis Wheatley is the "portrait of a young bluestocking." Alexander Pope, as a literary superstar and key interlocutor for leading female poets, had often appeared similarly as in meditation, with one hand raised. The engraving also has much in common with portraits of the Countess of Huntingdon, who was also repeatedly depicted in a modest cap, with an index finger on her brain, inspired by the books around her. The portrait, then, sold the book in part by placing Wheatley directly among the transatlantic community of women who were readers and writers of religious verse like hers, down to the posture she held and the objects placed within her reach.

The image also conveys respect for Phillis's artistic as well as religious inspiration. The book on the desk lies closest to the viewer, linking us to the scene of writing. It is small: a quarto Bible, or possibly a book of hymns. It could also be a book of poems, to be imitated, as with all poems as well as prayers if they did anything worth doing. The page on which she writes, and even the quill, are larger still, and connected, right arm to left, to her attractive, contemplative face, looking slightly upward. The narrow black band around her neck may be a subtle variant on the metal collar that had been a convention in portraits of African slaves. Nevertheless, this is the portrait of a lady as a poet, a thinking person, who rests her arm and elbow on her own table, her own papers.

The occasion to sit for Scipio Moorhead in particular meant much more to Wheatley than joining the club of colonists with the means to have their likenesses taken. Some time after the book manuscript went to England with Calef, she wrote a poem, "To S. M. a Young *African* Painter, on Seeing his Works," which she would later place toward the end of the published book, just before poems written in March and April 1773. In "To S. M.," she's intent on describing Moorhead's portraits, possibly including the portrait of her later engraved as the frontispiece to her book, as revealing profound interior truths—as a godlike "new creation," akin to her poetry:

> TO show the lab'ring bosom's deep intent,
> And thought in living characters to paint,
> When first thy pencil did those beauties give,
> And breathing figures learnt from thee to live,
> How did those prospects give my soul delight,
> A new creation rushing on my sight?

For the first time or the only time we know of, when her book's appearance seemed imminent, and her audience continued to grow, Wheatley was able to praise another enslaved person in a poem, as an artist like her. S.M., too, is a "wond'rous youth." Encouraging him, she argues for what was possible when Africans received encouragement and credit.

The structure of her praise, moving on to call the subject of the poem to look up to salvation ("On deathless glories fix thine ardent view"), is familiar from her elegies. Yet Wheatley lingers, identifying strongly with the artist's process, perhaps enabled by the painter's choice of angelic subject matter: "Still may the painter's and the poet's fire / To aid thy pencil, and thy verse conspire!" Done right, in the path of virtue, such art can lead to "immortal fame!" The poem resolves in the familiar way, with an admonition to keep focused on the "everlasting day" of heaven, and not just fame—but with the poet and the painter together: "There shall thy tongue in heav'nly murmurs flow, / And there my muse with heav'nly transport glow." Definitely chaste, "To S. M." is also romantic in two important senses: its upraising of the artist's creative vision and its sacralization of the relationship between a man and a woman. She had broadened the meaning of her own path to fame. It might have implications for other Africans as well as Americans.

The years 1772 and 1773 signified more than her own coming of age. The campaign for Phillis and her book took place at a moment of remarkable optimism about the printed word and a sudden profusion of African and indigenous men as published authors. In December, James Albert Ukawsaw Gronniosaw published the first slave narrative by an African in England, transcribed by the bluestocking Hannah More, with a dedication to the Countess of Huntingdon. (When Wheatley's book appeared, the dedication would be almost identical.) In New England, Samson Occom's sermon on the execution of the penitent murderer Moses Paul became a bestseller, leading him to receive "continual calls to preach." This sermon became a "turning point" for Occom in his path away from Reverend Wheelock's orbit and into a freelance ministry that allowed him to work in less encumbered fashion as a Mohegan leader. Two years later he would publish his own collection of hymns as a fundraiser for his ministry. Everyone knew that the printed word could do the work of the Lord. For Occom and Wheatley, publication in pamphlet or book form had the potential to do still more.

They weren't the only ones asking the question of what miracles publicity could perform and for whom. Two other Boston publicity campaigns intersected with Wheatley's path to London. Frustrated by the strengthening of administrative power through the Crown payment of governors' and judges' salaries, Samuel Adams and a committee of twenty-one Bostonians, working with the town meeting, developed the Boston Committee of Correspondence. Building on efforts during the occupation and afterward to use newspapers to spread the patriots' way of looking at events, the committee sent appeals to towns all over Massachusetts, inviting them to reciprocate with expressions of their heartfelt sentiments about imperial and provincial political trends. These responses would be retailed by the dozen in the sympathetic Boston newspapers and then reprinted in other colonies. The Committees of Correspondence proved to be a brilliant innovation in organizing and networking that wed local institutions, like New England town meetings, to fluid, multidirectional means of dissemination in handwritten letters and in print. The committees, with their meetings and resolutions, made the resistance activity into a movement: more participatory, better networked, and unprecedentedly publicized. In other words, the patriot resistance movement worked around institutions of government even while relying upon certain of them (the colonial mail system), much as Phillis and the Wheatleys looked to London while still trying to use the printers and newspapers in Boston that remained open to them.

For even after the *Somerset* case, it still wasn't evident which faction—the patriots or loyalists—would be more attuned to the problem of slavery or to the appeals of Africans. Nine years after James Otis mocked racial and other nature-based justifications in order to undermine colonial inequality under the laws of Parliament, slavery wasn't an unquestioned, timeless "institution," as a later master class and still later historians would insist. It was acknowledged as a problem not because it was "peculiar" to a North American region, which it wasn't, but rather because it had grown by leaps and bounds during the eighteenth century and had already been politicized. No one needed to wait for a movement to start, or for natural rights ideas to surge to the fore as they eventually did when other arguments against colonial regulation proved insufficient. Slavery wasn't just a patriot, or a loyalist, talking point, because it already had been both these things. That created opportunities and uncertainties.

In January 1773, the enslaved Bostonians Felix Holbrook, Peter Bestes, Sambo Freeman, and Chester Joie began to write and distribute a series of petitions that asked not only for their own emancipation but for that of all the Africans in the province. With increasing boldness, they invoked biblical, geopolitical, and legal arguments against North American slavery. Their petitions placed increasing emphasis on the patriots' self-evident hypocrisy if they did not address the issue.

These Bostonians picked this moment, after the *Somerset* case, the Committees of Correspondence, and Wheatley's plans for her book, to publish a petition both in Thomas's *Spy* and as *The Appendix*—an afterword to a new edition of an antislavery essay published by Ezekiel Russell. Their next petition and publication, in April 1773, would be in the form of a printed circular addressed to representatives from each town in Massachusetts and as another "appendix," this time to a reprint of James Swan's antislavery treatise. Swan made a point of stating that his pamphlet was being reprinted with the circular from Holbrook and others "at the earnest desire of the Negroes in Boston." Holbrook and his friends, in other words, acted as representatives of black Massachusetts and as their own committee of correspondence. In May they teamed up with the newest popular patriot pamphleteer, the Baptist minister John Allen. According to Allen, these enslaved men could not get a new petition into any newspaper, so he decided to insert it along with his own elaborated statement about how "Real Slavery" would "ruin America" in the fourth edition of his *Oration upon the Beauties of Liberty* (for which Allen had to change publishers to reprint it with enhanced antislavery material).

During the winter and early spring of 1773 there were similar signs of a widened orbit, and political meaning, for Wheatley and her work. In February, the Philadelphia physician Benjamin Rush, inspired and pushed by Anthony Benezet, published *An Address to the Inhabitants of the British Settlements in America upon Slave-Keeping*. To answer the anti-*Somerset* proslavery diatribes that put increasing stress on race as an explanation for Africans' enslavement, Rush held up Phillis Wheatley as an example of African equality sufficient to resolve the dubious question of racial difference: "There is now in the town of Boston a Free Negro Girl, about 18 years of age, who has been but 9 years in the country, whose singular genius and accomplishments are such as not only do honor to her sex, but to human nature." Already Wheatley's actual name, unmentioned by Rush, didn't matter as much as the idea of her "genius" and fame, itself an antislavery argument: "Several of her poems have been printed, and read with pleasure by the public." The publication as well as the well-known quality of Wheatley's work made it easier for Rush to brush off "the vulgar notion of their being descended from Cain."

As occurred so often in Phillis Wheatley's life, women anticipated and provoked the actions of men. Before Rush's pamphlet appeared, on December 1, 1772, the young Bostonian Ruth Barrell Andrews, wife of Wheatley's fan John Andrews and certainly an acquaintance of the Wheatleys' (the Andrewses' marriage ceremony had been performed in 1771 by the Reverend John Lathrop, who had himself just married Mary Wheatley), wrote a poem called "Slavery." Using words like "dignity," "elegance," and, like Rush, "genius" to describe Phillis Wheatley, Andrews made it clear that her fellow Bostonian's accomplishment did more than leave her in awe as a reader and as a writer—itself no small thing for the daughter of a poet and niece of the well-known Boston wit and Wheatley supporter Joseph Green. In 1772, Phillis's verse also made Andrews certain that African slavery could never be compatible with her own values, including the value she placed on poetry.

> We've recent proof that dignity of mind
> Is not to color or to rank confin'd
> A youthful female of this sable tribe
> Enrich'd with wisdom unalay'd by pride
> Her elegance of thought must clearly prove,
> The rays of knowledge, brighten from above.
> Where can we boast a genious of our own
> Whose rare abilities have her's outshone?
> Her nat'ral graces yet unrival'd beam,
> And teach the value of a soul within:
> The merit Phillis may with justice claim
> Her comprehensive poems ascertain:
> They speak a soul beneficently great
> A soul whose magnitude surmounts her fate
> My pen shall not presume to paint her praise,
> I leave the Theme to far sublimer lays.
> I only dare, tho humbly to maintain
> No Earthly power can enslave the brain.

While Christian salvation, for evangelicals like Whitefield and Huntingdon, had not required opposition to slavery, African "genius" might be another matter. Genius called the categorical mark of Cain into question. It didn't seem compatible with slave status or with race as its justification. No wonder Rush, in Philadelphia, presumed that Wheatley wasn't any longer enslaved, just as the earlier proposal for Wheatley's book had jumped the gun to call her "at present" a slave. Ruthie Andrews attests to Phillis's brilliance from the standpoint of an eyewitness and insists, like Rush, that the antislavery implications of Wheatley's work and her fame should be obvious—*before* her book saw print.

Slavery could not have been a distant phenomenon for Ruth Barrell Andrews: her brother Joseph Barrell, a very successful merchant, had married Hannah Fitch, a daughter of Timothy Fitch, the owner of the slaving ship *Phillis*. (The closeness of these families also helps explain how Phillis could have found herself at the Fitches' house for tea after she returned from England.) Ruthie might have felt empowered as a poet, as well as emboldened to criticize slavery, by Wheatley's newly forthright example, just weeks before, in her poem to Lord Dartmouth. She also felt intimidated, even eclipsed, as an aspiring writer. When her nephew Charles Eliot had died in September, she had written an elegy for the parents, but Phillis had actually beaten her to the punch a day or two before. As a result, Ruth didn't send her own poem around the usual circuit of friends, leaving her husband to praise her verses wistfully without actually including them in a letter to her own brother William in Philadelphia. Still, there's not a bit of resentment or jealousy in "Slavery." Instead, there is admiration, inspiration, and a clear sense that much was at stake in how Phillis Wheatley's book would be received.

Wheatley had ascended beyond authorship. She was now a subject of poems herself, someone whose seeing and being seen had become public, political, even inspirational to some. A hint of what this attention meant to her appeared in the *Massachusetts Spy* on January 7, 1773, in an anonymous poem that has multiple markers of her style. (See Table 2 in the appendix.) It had appeared earlier, on October 11, 1771, in the New London *Connecticut Gazette*, the paper that sponsored more debate about slavery than any other in New England. The *Gazette* closely followed Samson Occom, had published Wheatley's Whitefield poem, and would later devote even more space to her writings and travels.

On Night and Sleep

Night spreads her sable curtains round
And all's in silent Darkness drown'd.
The Moon displays her borrow'd Light,
And twinkling Stars declare the Night.
Slumber, with all her Magic Pow'rs,
Enchants the Soul, and kills the Hours;
'Till kind Aurora's gentler Ray,
Darkness dispels, and brings on Day;
While Sol with his enlivening Beams,
Arouzes Nature from her Dreams.

The poem is in tetrameter couplets at a time when Wheatley was experimenting more often outside what had been her usual iambic pentameter and her occasional compositions in blank verse. But several internal indicators suggest her authorship. The imagery of the sun, the specific reference to "Aurora," the invocation of the soul, and the use of the adjective "sable" are all recognized signatures of Wheatley's poetry. In "An Hymn to the Evening," which would appear first in her volume that fall, she also invokes the "sable curtains of the night . . . till fair *Aurora* rise." Aurora appears more than any other classical god in Wheatley, most recently in "To S. M. a Young *African* Painter." That poem also ends with an invocation of night as the only thing that can eclipse thoughts of heaven or the afterimage left by heavenly art: "Cease, gentle muse! The solemn gloom of night / Now seals the fair creation from my sight." This poem could also be a study for what became "Thoughts on the Works of Providence" in her book, with its "sable veil, that *Night* in silence draws, / Conceals effects, but shews th' *Almighty Cause*; Night seals in sleep the wide creation fair, / And all is peaceful but the brow of care."

Wheatley had a particular interest in the nighttime—the slaves' and servants' time, when, according to some family lore, she wrote by candlelight. But perhaps she had more of a need now, when her poems were seeing the light of day and being seen as political. Hers is a similar yet somewhat lighter, less portentous take on night than Bostonians perused in Edward Young's "wildly popular" *The Complaint; or, Night-Thoughts* (1744–47), a book-length blank verse poem just advertised by a Boston bookseller in the same issue of the *Spy* in which "On Night and Sleep" appeared. While Young too invokes night as "sable" at the outset and "sable curtain" several times, for him night itself is a "sable goddess" who portends either eternal darkness or a time to "nurse the tender thought," to attend to the immortal soul. Night "opens upon the noblest scenes." Day is deceptive, worldly; night is "when heaven's most intimate with man." It is the time of doubt, and argument with doubters, as well as of fevered writing (Young, too, was a night writer), of fears of damnation assuaged only by tremendous self-control or divine inspiration of a kind that takes Young nine "books"—thousands of lines—to develop. This anonymous poet, by contrast, seems confident, in control, less awed, in tune with Aurora and her muse—more so than Ruth Barrell Andrews, who was following her work so avidly.

So what might Phillis Wheatley have been doing publishing anonymously and apolitically, but perhaps recognizably enough to her fans, in the *Massachusetts Spy* on January 7, 1773, during the same week when a new elegy of hers (on the death of Thankful Leonard) appeared as a signed broadside?

At this precise moment, when other Boston blacks were using the language of patriot protest in petitioning against slavery, when some patriots were coming around but others continued to keep their distance, Wheatley herself was beginning to hedge her bets. She had reached out to prominent Tories and to patriots who had signed the attestation that would preface her book of poems. That statement assured readers that yes, she, an African, had actually written them, which everyone in Boston already knew. Phillis Wheatley read the news. Phillis Wheatley was part of the news. Phillis Wheatley knew all too well that anything she did could be praised and doubted and mocked, in print and in the parlors of Boston.

At a time when she was being racialized anew as an example of African "genius," she claimed the right not only to represent or to pray but also to pass when she felt like it, and even, or also, to dream, without any gesture to prayer. Anonymously, she could try things out, as she did in the night, beyond the monitoring gaze of the Wheatleys and other "friends." If so, she's claiming the night, having a little fun, pulling back the curtain to provide her fans a glimpse into her nocturnal writing process in the attic room of her own. And maybe, just maybe, at a time when she was being celebrated, when she found it easier and easier to publish what she wrote, she was seeing what it might be like to again be unknown, to be mysterious, to be ambiguous, even while winking to those in the know: something like what we would call trolling.

The kind of self-consciousness as well as self-confidence that it would have taken, in the midst of her ascent to fame, when the fate of Africans was on the public agenda as never before, to publish something so secular and light and anonymous is also on display in a poem she did sign, an elegy about Mary Sanford Oliver, who died on March 17, addressed to her husband, Lieutenant Governor Andrew Oliver, which she dated March 24, 1773. The august standing of the Olivers and their notable sorrows—having lost three daughters "when just arrived to Womens Estate"—heightens the astonishing powers of "ALL-conquering Death" described in the poem's first nine couplets. Death's sovereignty is ultimately God's doing. Heaven is "virtue's reward," before which "all descriptive arts, and eloquence are faint." Yet the same certitude that marks Mary's ascent as God's evident command informs the role—the importance, however playfully introduced—of this poet: "Nor cans't thou, *Oliver*, assent refuse / To heav'nly tidings from the *Afric* muse."

This line almost mocks how seriously she is being taken by her fans. Wheatley takes a bit, but only a bit, off the self-laureating gesture in the last stanza, which as in earlier elegies asks the mourner to "Restrain the sorrow" and "Forgive the muse, forgive th' advent'rous lays, / That fain thy soul to heav'nly scenes would raise." She is as ambitious as ever, yet more aware of who is watching—no doubt because more and more people *were* watching.

By March, the Wheatleys had stepped up their publication campaign. To raise interest in London as well as Boston, they sent Phillis's parlor poem "On Recollection" to the *London Magazine*, prefaced by the story of its composition. They also placed it in the *Boston Post-Boy*. Soon afterward, Nathaniel Wheatley decided that he would sail in Calef's next passage to London. The family planned for Phillis to join him—for her health, they told people; to oversee the volume's production, ostensibly, as Huntingdon and Bell had agreed to proceed; but also to engage in a kind of celebrity book tour, to prove her authorship in the flesh and stimulate interest in *Poems on Various Subjects, Religious and Moral*. Susanna seems to have been all-in at this point, even though she would or could not accompany Phillis to London.

This put more of a burden on Nathaniel to manage her debut. A new subscription for the London volume appeared in the two Tory-sympathizing Boston papers on April 19, asking for partial payment of a shilling (half of the cost of the unbound book). The next week, the *Post-Boy* reported that "Mr. Nathaniel Wheatley of this town, Merchant," would sail on the *London Packet*. A week later the same paper announced the ship's departure along with "Phillis, Servant of Mr. Wheatley, the extraordinary Poetess." The politically middle-of-the-road *Evening-Post* called her "the ingenious Negro Poet." A few days later, the Tory *News-Letter* responded to being scooped by combining the phrases and calling her "the extraordinary Negro Poet." The editor tried to add something new by stating that Phillis's voyage to London came "at the Invitation of the Countess of Huntingdon," a rumor that he retracted, the next week, as "a mistake." The *Gazette* and the *Spy*, the patriot papers, took no notice.

The three Boston papers that participated in the Wheatleys' publicity campaign also published prominently the "Lines, written by PHILLIS (Mr. Wheatley's Negro Girl) just before she sailed for England" on May 1. It's the first and only poem we know of that Phillis addressed to Susanna Wheatley, who must have been delighted: she mailed a copy on the next ship to the *London Chronicle* with the tease that they had "no doubt heard of Phillis." Like all the publicity campaigns of 1773, the poem made a question—one that could not be answered definitively, one that could only be asked again and again—out of the distance between Boston and London.

In recognition of Susanna's piety, Wheatley composed her "farewell" in a hymn style: quatrains with alternating tetrameter and trimeter lines of the kind that Isaac Watts had made so popular. In the second stanza she counters the (true) rumor that she was voyaging to advance her poetic career "at the invitation of the Countess," with the response the Wheatleys had been spreading in Boston and even had given to Lady Huntingdon: a doctor had advised sea air for her health. Perhaps so, in May. (It had to be the sea: no one went to London for their health, and the poem itself described London fog as "misty Vapours crown'd / Which cloud Aurora's thousand Dyes, / And veil her Charms around.") But even more than the un-slave-like freedom of an author to travel, to reverse the Middle Passage, and to even write about it, this freedom to leave her mistress requires an apology and declaration of loyalty, which also serves as testimony to her collaboration with the aging matron whose queen-like "Reign" is "luxuriant":

> SUSANNA *mourns, nor can I bear*
>   *To see the Christal Show'r*
> *Fast falling.—the indulgent Tear,*
>   *In sad Departure's Hour!*

Not unregarding, lo! I see
  Thy Soul with Grief oppress'd:
Ah! curb the rising Groan for me,
  Nor sighs disturb thy Breast.

Susanna mourns for Phillis while Phillis mourns her own health . . .
and Susanna's mourning. Yet it's spring, the "garden blooms" with life.
Is the trip worth it—and for whom?

The poem is Wheatley's most public acknowledgment of her close
relationship with her first and most important patron: her purchaser,
her owner. Set in its public context of an "extraordinary Negro poet"
journeying to the seat of empire without the enslaver who was also her
friend, the poem also asks another question, beyond the one about the
meaning of distance in the empire, that it can't answer: What comes
next for the child-woman who was so like, yet unlike, James Somerset?
Lacking details that could be shared, Wheatley allegorizes the journey from an America figured as the countryside to Britain's "mantl'd
Town." It is a challenge, a "Temptation." The "Temptation . . . with all
thy hated Train" could be moral—the city, for a "country" woman. It
could be a journey, for a person of faith. Or it might be even more tangible: to not return at all.

15

THE METROPOLIS

Wheatley's frailty had become a regular theme in her letters as well as in some of her recent poems. Still, there was more than poetic justice in the cover story of Phillis Wheatley voyaging on the *London Packet* for her health. What she called asthma on one occasion had probably been caused or worsened by her previous trip across the Atlantic a dozen years before, the Middle Passage from Africa on the *Phillis*, from which she arrived, according to Wheatley family legend, a "poor, naked child (for she had no other covering than a quantity of dirty carpet about her, like a 'fillibeg' [kilt])."

That story she still wouldn't, or couldn't, tell—not in print at least, even as her poems reached more people and became more ambitious, more daring, enticingly personal, and sometimes even confrontational. Even the story of being torn away from her father that she had introduced in the poem to Lord Dartmouth left it ambiguous who had done that violent theft or whether she thought that mattered. She played with ironic, unintended consequences of her enslavement as a "mercy" in a way that sowed doubt about slaving voyages, yet without directly confronting the issue of blame.

For sojourners from Boston to London in 1773, it was no longer clear what direction history was going where it came to slavery. Ships occasionally departed Boston for Africa, returning to New England with enslaved people after one or more stops at southerly ports. Ads in the newspapers continued to sell slaves "for no fault." On the other hand, hardly anyone in Boston spoke up for the slave trade, except for the ever more unpopular Governor Hutchinson. Even while brushing off petitions and resolves of the legislature, he defended not slavery so much as the right of London to make the rules.

The *Somerset* case left a less ambiguous legacy where it came to travel. Enslaved people remained enslaved when they went to London. But they couldn't be forced to return to colonies. In other words, being British in England gave them rights at a moment when colonists were arguing that being British should protect settler liberties in America. Tories gleefully threw African slavery's evils in the face of patriot calls for liberty. For this very reason, more—not most, but more—patriots in northern North America found themselves willing to give up on black slavery, and some were willing to say so publicly, if it seemed that they couldn't have their British liberty and slave property too. Word got around. While Wheatley was in London, a Philadelphian could write to a friend in Boston "much pleased that the attention of your Towns is turned to the miserable state of the *Africans*, whom we hold as slaves among us. It is a *standing reproach*. I would it were held in general Abhorrence!!" Just as important and revealing as a gentleman in Quaker Philadelphia admitting that Massachusetts seemed about to take the lead in antislavery was the fact that the letter appeared in the rabidly antiadministration *Boston Gazette*, which had so carefully ignored and then mostly mocked the *Somerset* case. That same year, Harvard students debated the morality of slavery formally and publicly at commencement—something that could only have occurred if antislavery beliefs had become almost as respectable in local circles as owning and selling people had been for generations.

An anonymous self-identified member of the enslaved community sealed the arguments in the *Gazette* on August 23 when he maintained that while much had been said of "Liberty and Property," "the Rights of Mankind," and "Arbitrary Power," nevertheless "the most suffering Part of this State, those who have not only all the Miseries of Slavery to bear, but have the Rod of Oppression actually exercised over them; have hitherto been Silent, and the Reason is obvious: the want of Literature"—that is, illiteracy. Much as Wheatley had in her letter to Huntingdon and in the preface to her book, the writer modestly disparaged his own skills in order to call attention to the significance of his entry into the conversation, his representation of the voice of the enslaved, his saying what needed to be said in print. Slavery is "repugnant to the laws of a free Constitution" as well as the Golden Rule of "do unto others." Not only the Sons of Liberty but Boston's ministers too were complicit: "Behold our wives and Children taken from us, bought and sold like dumb Beasts, and often with less regard: Yet you were never heard to speak one word from the Pulpit against the unrighteous dealing." Illiteracy in an otherwise extremely literate New England epitomized the hypocrisy and the conspiracy to cover it up. Blaming Africans for the slave trade, the most traditional defense, wouldn't or shouldn't fly either: "We have neither sold nor forfeited our Liberty, and we have as good right to Freedom as any of the sons of Adam."

The stress this anonymous African put on literacy as providing an opening to antislavery suggests the implications of Wheatley's voyage to the metropolis at the moment her book was in press. Even before she arrived in England, the possible outcomes were at once personal (whether an emancipating exception would be made for her) and political (whether her "genius" had larger implications for the fate of Africans in Britain and America).

With Nathaniel, she spent more than five weeks on ship and six weeks in or near London. The first forty days, from May 8 to June 17, gave her much time to reflect on the meaning of the journey. She worked on some of the poems in her manuscript for the English audience, such that, for example, the revised version of her most recent poem, "A Farewell to America," more vividly evokes not only the ship "sweep[ing] the liquid plain" of the ocean but also that she had "with astonish'd eyes explore[d] / The wide-extended main." She also might have retooled a poem written earlier that year for Joseph Rotch Jr., "To a Gentleman on His Voyage to *Great-Britain* for the Recovery of His Health," where America's "bleak regions" are contrasted with the healthful "vast *Atlantic*." As a whole, the new book manuscript celebrated many things British while downplaying the very local details, like New Englanders' names, which had been so important to how she originally got attention in Boston. Like most if not all travelers at a time when London was the capital of America, Wheatley intended to please and hoped to make her mark.

To go to London, especially for a young person, was to *ascend*. The city had forty times the population of Boston. To an English squint Boston looked like a town, hardly a city—barely larger and less economically significant than Bridgetown, Barbados. Wheatley's fellow Bostonian Josiah Quincy II wrote that the crowds and opulence of London "far surpass all I had imagined." As in any true metropolis, the majority of London's denizens hailed from elsewhere, driven by aspiration and by necessity from all over England and its empire. A "galaxy of genius," a showplace of magnificence, a concentration of squalor: all these became apparent to the first-time visitor. All of these views might have been anticipated, too, by someone as literate as Wheatley, for Anglo culture teemed with celebrations and denunciations of metropolis and empire, of London as the epitome of what was right and what was wrong with the world.

Slavery had become one of those things taken for granted yet changing and sometimes denounced. Native Britons might see the colonies as the home of slave drivers and slaves, but such impressions at a distance intensified when more and more colonists brought slaves with them to the metropolis. More empire after the Seven Years' War meant more people leading transatlantic lives, like Benjamin Franklin and Charles Steuart, with black "servants" in tow. While there were a thousand or more wealthy Americans in the metropolis at any one time, there were by the 1770s ten to twenty thousand Africans in Britain, with about half these in London. In a London servant population of eighty thousand, they represented as many as 10 percent or more, "a significant portion of the servant class." From being prized exotic possessions pictured in paintings with silver collars around their necks, Africans, especially men, had become part of the London scene, a community that looked like Boston in this respect except for the fact that in London more of the Africans, like James Somerset, had become free adults. Little wonder that Americans complained that their slaves were corrupted by the London air—which really meant corrupted by their London fellows.

For six weeks Phillis would take much of it in. But first she attended to the evangelical literary connections that had paved her way—so important, and so obvious, that John Lathrop worried that she would come home a "flaming Methodist." Susanna Wheatley had written to the Countess of Huntingdon, after all, that "I tell Phillis to act wholly under the direction of your Ladiship," down to the clothes she should purchase, which should be as plain as possible, if only to match those in the portrait she carried with her.

She and Nathaniel Wheatley probably headed straight to the house of the wealthy philanthropist John Thornton, leader of the Methodist Connection in Clapham, the site of the private chapel where the Countess of Huntingdon would usually have been found. But Selina had been ill and returned to her South Wales estate that spring. The Wheatleys still stayed "about a week" with the Thorntons, surely discussing among other things their mutual friend Samson Occom (Thornton had taken Occom's side against the Reverend Wheelock and even secured him a small pension). At the Thorntons', Phillis met Hannah Wilberforce, Thornton's half sister and the aunt of the later antislavery leader William Wilberforce.

On June 27, from London, Wheatley wrote to Huntingdon, "Disap-

pointed by the absence of the honour of waiting upon your Ladyship."
With an arch gesture meant to remind the countess of their plans for
the book, she added, "I should think my self very happy in Seeing your
Ladyship, and if you was So desirous of the Image of the Author as to
propose it for a Frontispiece I flatter myself that you would accept the
Reality." The "patronage" of Selina, "not more eminent in the Station
of Life than in your exemplary Piety and Virtue," would guard Wheatley's "Juvenile productions" from criticism. She sealed the letter in wax
with her own "PW" ring, itself a sign of her rising status. Huntingdon replied with a request that Phillis and Nathaniel come visit her in
Wales.

By the time they received that invitation, they had made other
plans. The countess had previously taken the trouble to set up the
Wheatleys to meet several of her important and impressive friends in
London. But the story Wheatley told of her London experience suggests a whirlwind of visiting that quite exceeded the loving bonds of
the Methodist fellowship.

It was almost a fantasy of the American in London. On July 1, her
"Farewell to America" appeared in the *London Chronicle*, and soon she
hardly needed letters of introduction. "I can't say but my voyage to England has conduced to the recovery (in a great measure) of my Health,"
she would later concede to Obour, but it wasn't about the weather. "The
Friends I found there among the Nobility and the Gentry, Their Benevolent conduct towards me, the unexpected, and unmerited civil-
ity and Complaisance with which I was treated by all, fills me with
astonishment. I can scarcely Realize it," she still felt months after she
left. (Realizing how less than humble it might sound, she immediately
shifted gears: "This I humbly hope has the happy Effect of lessning me
in my own Esteem.")

In a letter to David Wooster, a Connecticut acquaintance related by
marriage to the recipient of one of her elegies, she described a plunge
into the secular world and into freedom. Lord Dartmouth himself
set the tone by conversing for half an hour with Wheatley and giving

her a gift of five guineas "to get the whole of Mr. Pope's Works, as the best he could recommend." Next she visited Lord Lincoln (Henry Fiennes Pelham-Clinton), a member of Parliament and nephew of the former prime ministers Newcastle and Pelham. This American-born former soldier in the wars for North America was so charmed that he returned the visit "at my own Lodgings" and took with him "the Famous" Dr. Daniel Solander, a naturalist and curator of the new British Museum who had recently returned from "his late expedition round the world" with Joseph Banks and Captain James Cook. Solander probably got her a special pass to the museum, which she mentioned having seen, along with other tourist highlights of the city: Westminster Abbey, Greenwich Hospital, the Royal Observatory at Greenwich, other museums and pleasure gardens, "&c. &c. too many things and Places to trouble you with in a Letter." These places were all around town, London city and Westminster, a kind of grand tour in miniature that included paintings and exhibits, plays and personages. There was even talk of a royal audience.

Wheatley fast collected political and scientific as well as religious friends—women as well as men, she hastened to add, including the sisters Lady Cavendish and Lady Carteret Webb, who had been converted at the Countess of Huntingdon's chapel, and Mary Palmer, "a Poetess and accomplished Lady," sister of the painter Joshua Reynolds. Her list continued with Israel Mauduit, a merchant in the American trade, well-known dissenting Protestant, political pamphleteer, holder of many sinecures, and agent for Massachusetts who had taken the side of Governor Hutchinson. Next came "Benjamin Franklin Esqr. F[ellow of the]. R[oyal]. S[ociety]," the most prestigious club of scientists in Britain.

Franklin was the most famous American in London or anywhere because of his scientific pursuits. He had been in London almost continuously since 1757, as agent for Pennsylvania and other colonies including Georgia and Massachusetts but also, not coincidentally given eighteenth-century English attitudes toward what we would see as conflicts of interest, as a Crown officeholder, the postmaster general for North America. His fame and his several appointments, in turn, help explain why he was also leading the propaganda effort against taxes and regulations while simultaneously beating back recurring criticisms from colonial radicals that he was not pushing hard enough. These critics, joined by old enemies in Pennsylvania, speculated that Franklin wasn't aggressive as a colonial agent because he himself hoped for a seat in Parliament or another lucrative plum like the governorship of New Jersey he had secured for his son, William. To prove his patriot bona fides, Franklin had recently forwarded some mysteriously acquired letters that the then Massachusetts Bay province lieutenant governor, Hutchinson, had written to the late undersecretary of state Thomas Whately after the Townshend Acts. In these letters, Hutchinson had supported a crackdown on protesting colonists, something he had not dared to do publicly in Boston.

Meanwhile, since the *Somerset* case, Franklin had been playing defense against Tory accusations of American Whig hypocrisy on slavery. He assured Anthony Benezet and Benjamin Rush that he would "act in concert" with them against slavery, but he wrote anonymous pieces for the press that blamed the English for the slave trade, mocking Mansfield's logic that upraised free English air over colonial liberties. Slavery, for Franklin in 1773, had to be seen as an example of British tyranny, not American provincialism or hypocrisy. For political reasons, he needed to deflect any new publicity, any sense of the timeliness or priority of the slavery issue, whatever his personal beliefs or his plans for King, the enslaved man he held in London, or Peter, the other enslaved man he and William had brought across the Atlantic, who had hired himself out and refused to return.

In the summer of 1773, Franklin's brilliant ways with people and with prose were not working so smoothly anymore. The contradictions in his strategies, which led his critics to call him names like "Dr. Doubleface," would soon blow up when patriots in the Massachusetts legislature, against his explicit instructions, published the Hutchinson

letters, leading to a search for who had purloined them in the first place
after Whately's death and who had then sent them back across the Atlantic. A round of accusations, followed by a near-fatal duel involving
two alleged leakers and then an admission by Franklin of his middle-
man role, would lead directly to his humiliation before the Privy Council and the loss of his position as postmaster general.

Franklin was also desperately seeking Lord Dartmouth's support
for policy changes at this time, with noncommittal results at best.
When Wheatley began to circulate, and confirmed Dartmouth's personal blessings, Franklin of all people had to take notice. It meant
something for him to be on the right side of the now famous African if she was being favored by Lord Dartmouth and if her poems—
with whatever message they might convey about America and about
slavery—were about to hit the London bookshops.

In her own later letter, Wheatley mentioned going *to* Benjamin
Franklin as one among many highlights of her trip. Franklin himself
told a different story in a July 7 letter to his relation the Boston merchant Jonathan Williams Sr. He had gone to see *her.* And, he insisted,
it hadn't gone well at all.

Apparently, it all started with a typical act by the white Wheatleys. They had implored Williams "to mention her" trip to London to
his wife's uncle Franklin. Franklin obliged with what he described less
as an endorsement than a polite social call: "Upon your Recommendation I went to see the black Poetess and offer'd her any Services I
could do her." But he made quick work of the visit—blaming Nathaniel
Wheatley: "Before I left the House, I understood her Master was there
and had sent her to me but did not come into the Room himself, and I
thought was not pleased with the Visit. I should perhaps have enquired
first for him; but I had heard nothing of him. And I have heard nothing since of her."

The focus on hearing, from a master of publicity, is telling. No
more than eighteen days had passed between Phillis's arrival in London, Franklin's social call, and his statement to Williams that since

he'd "heard nothing," the matter was closed. Why was he washing his hands (or ears) so quickly? (Williams certainly got the message, apologizing for having involved Franklin at all.)

With antislavery making the Americans look bad, Franklin had at least as much reason to tamp down the favorable publicity Wheatley had received as to try to get in on it. It was classic Franklin, managing people and appearances in person and by writing. By visiting, Franklin made a careful, possibly useful gesture in the direction of Dartmouth's patronage and increasingly fashionable antislavery. He avoided appearing to shun Wheatley. But at a time when he publicized much by speaking carefully in the halls of power and anonymously in the press, he did the opposite with Wheatley, saying nothing as far as we know, except in one private, family letter, while he claimed to have "heard nothing." The Wheatleys, he told Williams, were unheard of— silent, and private, as far as he was concerned. At best, Franklin had flirted. At worst, he had done damage control and run away as fast as he could. He certainly did nothing to help her get more attention.

At the same time, it's clear that the most famous and powerful of Americans had been put in a position of having to respond to an enslaved person, to another voyager who had come up from obscurity and become famous in London for being both accomplished and American. Phillis and Susanna did at least succeed in making Franklin not publicly contradict Dartmouth or the positive image that Wheatley projected. That was apparently the most Franklin would do. Instead, he chose to blame the "young master," who, he more than implied, had been the rude one who couldn't be bothered to pay his respects to him, the most famous American in London. He seems to be projecting his own ambivalence about visiting the genius African poet onto Nathaniel Wheatley, and in doing so dodging a bullet, or at least some complicated politics.

Franklin was as shrewd a judge of human motives and actions as Phillis Wheatley. He had already begun writing the famous *Autobiography* in which he prided himself on not being quick to take offense while sometimes being quick to take advantage (while detailing, decades after the fact, who else had done so to their own detriment). Franklin admitted that he hadn't really even tried to meet Nathaniel Wheatley. He instead capitalized on the indifference with which Nathaniel was being treated, which was exactly the kind of thing that the experienced diplomat Franklin would have perceived and made use of.

To be sure, Nathaniel might well have snubbed Franklin and been acting out his own frustrations at playing second fiddle to Phillis. The trip had originally been his own, not Phillis or Susanna's idea. He had his own business and his own agenda in London. He could reasonably or unreasonably have been less than thrilled with all the attention Phillis, his charge, received from lords and ladies. What might it have been like for a rising thirty-year-old merchant with his own connections to become less than an afterthought when accompanying his family's famous nineteen-year-old enslaved girl? To be identified, primarily, as *her master*, at a time when New Englanders were being derided as avaricious, as politically extremist, and sometimes as hypocritical slave drivers? The record is meager, but it is revealing that no one else who recorded meeting Phillis mentioned the young master, Nathaniel. Was he so unimpressive, so unheard of, or only relatively so? Or just choosing to keep his distance? There is no record of Nathaniel Wheatley ever showing personal resentment toward Phillis—or, on the other hand, of any particular kindness or concern for her prospects, either, *after* the London trip and the death of Susanna Wheatley.

He appears to have been with the family program as far as Phillis was concerned until this very moment. Earlier, she wrote some letters that he dictated. On one occasion he expressed admiration for the family friend Samson Occom, to whom he sent funds. What is clear is that these six weeks in London fundamentally changed Nathaniel's life and his relationship to his own family, just as much as or more than the voyage changed Phillis Wheatley's life. Family members expected Nathaniel back soon, if only to see his dying mother, but he did not return to Boston with Phillis on the next crossing of the *London Packet*. Or on next sailings after that. By November he was engaged to Mary Enderby. She was the daughter of the wealthy John Enderby, one of the merchants from whom Wheatley imported goods. The couple didn't go to Boston for another year.

Who, then, took Phillis to see the sights of London? Not Nathaniel Wheatley, not Benjamin Franklin, but Granville Sharp, the abolitionist. They went together to the famous Tower, actually a large complex, a "little town" unto itself where captive African lions and a bear from New York drew crowds. And that was just the beginning: Sharp attended her at "the Horse Armoury, Sma[ll] Armoury, the Crowns, Sceptres, Diadems, the Fount for christin[in]g the Royal Family." He also gave her at least one of his pamphlets (the one that survives with her signature of possession is not even one of his antislavery efforts). It is tempting still to wonder whether they discussed James Somerset, their likely mutual acquaintance, or the outcome and meaning of Somerset's case.

The larger truth is that they didn't need to discuss it. There was far more political punch to be had in being seen, together, in front of the Crown emblems and the wild animals from Africa and America. She expressed this in the decidedly secular and compressed travel account she wrote in October to Wooster. There, her narration of kindnesses bestowed, visits made and received, and travel around the metropolis culminates in the gift of money for books from Dartmouth ("I also got Hudibrass [Samuel Butler's *Hudibras*, a widely admired satiric romp about the English Civil War], Don Quixot[e], & [John] Gay's Fables") and something particularly special: "a Folio Edition of Milton's Paradise Lost" from Brook Watson. What could have been more appropriate mementos to give an aspiring poet? Yet, at the same time, could Phillis, herself property, actually own anything, even books? That legal conundrum hadn't reached the King's Bench yet, but even the most traditional among the lords and ladies could understand the implications. In Wheatley's case, the genteel rituals of the metropolis, the gifts and beneficence of aristocrats, raised the question of what happens when the empire comes home.

By July 17 she knew she was returning on Calef's next voyage, alone. She wrote to Huntingdon regretfully declining the invitation to come to Wales. "I long to see my friends there [in Boston]," she told the countess, while celebrating Selina's own friendship with another "African so worthy to be honour'd with your Ladiship's approbation," probably James Albert Ukawsaw Gronniosaw. She could not have yet heard that Susanna Wheatley had taken a turn for the worse and pined for her to come home. She had simply accomplished what she had sailed to accomplish, and her ride, and the tide, waited.

On the voyage home she did not lack for reading matter. She could dive and swim in the eighteen volumes of Pope's *Works* that Dartmouth had paid for, which included his translations of *The Iliad* and *The Odyssey*, along with the other great hits of English literature she had acquired. To the several other passengers and crew, perhaps her box of books appeared as leather-bound testimonies to her propertied freedom, a patrimony for having joined the ranks of authors. Musing on these books, by the end of the voyage, in early September, she returned to one of the great themes of both the Greek and Roman classics and the Restoration- and Augustan-era British poets, with an ode called, simply, "Ocean."

As in the earlier mini-epics and the poem on the ship captains that launched her career, Wheatley uses the sea's awesome power to speak to and about the people around her. She remains cautious about ocean-going, as she had been in "Ode to Neptune" for Susannah Wooldridge and in "A Farewell to America" for Susanna Wheatley. Nevertheless, she begins with a strikingly expansive, confident overture to what "the feast of Genius, and the play of Art" can accomplish under the "muse divine."

She then proceeds with a creation story. Chaos "Wav'd his dread Sceptre," creating not the world we know but "Confusion," until "the divine Command" created the earth and sun while taming "the new made seas." But Neptune, "the mighty Sire of Ocean frownd / 'His awful trident shook the solid Ground.'" Wheatley chooses here, for the first time in her extant verse, a direct quotation from another poet or poets—not an uncommon feature of eighteenth-century poetry, in which imitation was not only expected but recognized as a necessary accompaniment to both creativity and meaning. What's revealing is that the line comes directly from Pope's translation of *The Iliad*, which she had with her on the *London Packet*. It isn't an exact quotation, but rather a composite of several phrases and lines from at least three of the twenty-four books (five volumes) of Pope's *Iliad of Homer*. More than ever, Wheatley lays claim to the neoclassical tradition through the poet who, by translating the Greek into English heroic couplets, made Homer both familiar and new. On this occasion, though, Homer and Pope were newly hers in their multivolume plenitude. To quote becomes a performance of ownership, of mastery.

So this is another Neptune tale, as "The King of Tempests thunders o'er the plain," obeyed by the winds, who cause "waves on waves devolving without End." The fallen world is one of tempests contained, yet deadly. Fallen Man comes not in the form of Adam but rather Neptune's would-be rival, the daring ship captain, Robert Calef, a "proud Courser [who] paws the blue abode, / Impetuous bounds, and mocks the driver's rod." The captain refuses "bounds" and even "mocks" the implements of bondage. Wheatley chooses to depict him as literally the opposite of a slave. In the most tentative and drafty couplets of the one surviving manuscript of the poem, she uses a classical allegory to top, or at least justify, the imagery: the Greek myth of Europa, a violent creation and ur–abduction story Homer too had referenced in the fourteenth book of *The Iliad* (which also features Neptune in a prominent role).

In the original version, Zeus turns himself into a lovely bull to trick the maiden Europa, swims her to Crete, then transforms into an eagle in order to make love to (or in some versions, rape) her and, ultimately, create a dynasty and nation of men. Wheatley's version pacifies the story: "There too the Heifer fair as that which bore / Divine Europa to the Cretan shore. / With guileless mein the gentle Creature strays / Quaffs the pure stream, and crops ambrosial Grass." Allegory "softens and reconciles every thing," as Pope observed in his copious notes to the same chapter. As if admitting she had taken a confusing turn, or changed the subject, Wheatley returns in three couplets to the "finny sovereign" Neptune and his "vengeance."

The remaining thirty lines bring the reader to more allegory, but aboard the *London Packet* itself:

> Twas but e'er now an Eagle young and gay
> Pursu'd his passage thro' the aierial way
> He aim'd his piece, would C[ale]f's hand do more
> Yes, him he brought to pluto's dreary shore

Who is this bird, this "royal youth," who failed to "obey" his "Father's mandate" and then, dying after Calef shot him down, regrets his "rashness"? Neptune hears his cries and wants to know. The bird, "Iscarius," probably an amalgam of Icarus (who disobeyed his father, a fellow fugitive slave, and flew too near the sun) and Judas Iscariot, explains: Captain Robert Calef prevails over the winds and waves.

> Saw you not Sire, a tall and Gallant ship
> Which proudly skims the surface of the deep
> With pompous form from Boston's port she came
> She flies, and London her resounding name
> O'er the rough surge the dauntless Chief prevails
> For partial Aura fills his swelling sails
> His fatal musket shortens thus my day
> And thus the victor take my life away

This poem, which Wheatley earmarked for inclusion in a second collection of verse, makes the ocean a site of tragedy and triumph, danger and opportunity. For Londoners and Bostonians, ocean meant empire; it meant fate. Wheatley sounds as optimistic as ever. Yet the dangerous waves remain. Could gun-toting Massachusetts ship captains, who had once brought her in bondage to Boston, be trusted to act as friends of the enslaved? Were they agents of freedom or death? Was she a protected passenger or, like Europa, a privileged captive still? Was she a bird, an Icarus, disobeying a father figure—flying too high?

16

THE EMANCIPATION

From slavery to freedom. This is the traditional narrative of African American history, and insofar as we see the ubiquity of slavery, abolition, and race it has become the central narrative of U.S. history. It leads us to expect an event, a date, a proclamation. We want history to confirm the precision and moral clarity that was necessary to argue against, to fight against, the enslavement of our ancestors or of others. Yet if history tells us anything about slavery, it is that emancipation has usually been a drawn-out process, for both individuals and nations. It's rife with ambiguities about how it happened, not least because emancipation begs the question of what freedom will mean. In the biblical Exodus, the end of slavery becomes a story, a story that frames the history that will follow.

James Somerset, with an assist from Granville Sharp and the Court of King's Bench, had turned his master Charles Steuart's trip "home" to England into an emancipation. It took many months and led to speculation about what it might mean for others in Britain and its colonies. But it didn't take Somerset's case or even her parallel voyage to London with her "young master" to raise the issue of personal emancipation for Wheatley. Her achievement, her fame, and the ongoing prospect of book publication had done that repeatedly, even obviously, well before the summer of 1773. The February 1772 Boston advertisement for her volume had called her "a very uncommon Genius, at present a Slave," tantalizing the sympathetic reader not only with the possibility that she might soon be freed but also with a hint that recognizing her genius by buying the book might help to free her.

Wheatley's book was a signal early instance of philanthropic marketing, and like most consumer politics it could be seen as a path to change or a surface reform that confirmed rather than challenged the system. If Wheatley thought of Terence, the Carthage-born playwright, as an enslaved African, she would also have known that he had been freed because of his education, his talents, and his success, with no more antislavery implications than the ubiquity of both freed people and slaves in Rome already suggested.

There are no fewer than four possible concrete scenarios for how Phillis Wheatley became free by the autumn of 1773, three of which are supported by her few words on the subject.

The first possibility, one that Phillis Wheatley did not herself signal but which might have shaped her actions, is that it had been in the cards since February 1772 if not earlier, but delayed by the Wheatleys until her adulthood, or the publication of her book, or her return from England. John Andrews had explained the turn from Boston publication in favor of a London edition as a bid for a "large emolument." If he was correct, Phillis Wheatley and the white Wheatleys probably imagined that profits would pay for or at least subsidize Phillis's emancipation. New Englanders always worried about people outside households becoming public charges on the towns and required former owners, whether paid off in a deal with their enslaved or not, to post bond in case the freed person became a public charge on the town. This further limited the practice of negotiated and purchased freedom, which was already fraught with risk and fraud. Still, enslaved people, particularly men, sometimes purchased themselves and even their family members. For New Englanders who participated in man-umissions and self-funded emancipations, it posed little or no threat to slavery in general. If anything, it confirmed that the enslaved re-mained legal property with a price.

The voyage to London, subsidized with little up-front cost by the Wheatleys as owners of the ship, then could have amounted to what scholars once called, in reference to how slavery actually ended in the North, "philanthropy at bargain prices." The bargain here would be the leveraged proceeds from the book, which could serve as ei-ther the funds for self-purchase, a nest egg, the legally required bond, or even all three. The London trip might be a bargain for the white Wheatleys in another sense: not only freedom for Phillis but also, for Susanna, John, and Nathaniel, public recognition that they had done right by raising up a pious enslaved genius without directly challeng-ing slavery itself. From their perspective, they were doing what their friend George Whitefield had done, recognizing Africans' humanity while trying to make their enslavement, as well as one exceptional and pious slave's liberation, serve everyone's salvation.

Despite Nathaniel's accompaniment in London and the cover story that Phillis voyaged for her health, however, something about the Wheatleys' reach began to exceed their oceanwide grasp. Phillis's pub-lic acclaim, her ensuing trip to Britain, and the actual publication of her book made her status a public issue. The second possibility, then, is that she was emancipated after her trip because during the months before and during her well-publicized voyage public opinion beyond Boston increasingly demanded it, while the Wheatleys, for various reasons, sought to delay the day.

Public hints that her emancipation was expected actually came first from Philadelphia, then a hub of antislavery propagation. Ben-jamin Rush, in his antislavery pamphlet published in February 1773, assumed that she was a "Free Negro," in light of the fact that some of her poems had been "printed." Rush was arguing against racial justi-fications for slavery, so his error concerning her current status didn't affect his main point, but readers of Rush, and there were many, would have been surprised to learn later, upon encountering the publicity leading up to her voyage, that Wheatley was in fact still enslaved. Then, in a comment inserted in a digest of London news from June, while Wheatley was still traveling, in the August 23 *Pennsylvania Chronicle*, a writer quoted the advance publicity for her book, including John Wheatley's attestation of her identity as an enslaved African, and noted pointedly, "It is hoped (though it is not so expressed) that the profits of this publication will in the first place be applied to purchasing the freedom of the author; and, if, so, it is not doubted that every friend of the rights of humanity will liberally contribute to such an emancipation both of mind and body, always dreadful, but felt with double poignancy by genius and sensibility." This way of putting the matter had the very real effect of taking whatever plans the Wheatleys had or had not "expressed" out of the picture and even raising the possibility that the Wheatleys were less patrons than pious hypocrites.

Two British reviewers of her book also pointed to certain expectations and unavoidable questions. The American-style soft selling of her status as "Negro Servant to Mr. John Wheatley, of Boston" on the frontispiece portrait didn't deflect the question of her enslavement and current status—not least because the version of the attestation included in the front matter of the book stressed again her origins as "a few Years since, brought an uncultivated Barbarian from *Africa*" as well as "the Disadvantage of serving as a Slave in a Family in this Town." One of the first reviews to appear in September, in the *Gentleman's Magazine*, ended by objecting that "youth, innocence, and piety, united with genius, have not yet been able to restore her to the condition and character with which she was invested by the Great Author of her being. So powerful is custom in rendering the heart insensible to the rights of nature, and the claims of excellence." Three months later, the most critical review, by John Langhorne, extended the outrage over colonial cluelessness from the Wheatleys to their townsfolk and their liberty trees: "We are much concerned to find that this ingenious young woman is yet a slave. The people of Boston boast themselves chiefly on their principles of liberty. One such act as the purchase of her freedom, would, in our opinion, have done them more honour than hanging a thousand trees with ribbons and emblems."

These reviewers, like Rush, presumed that the book's existence and its quality spoke to the question of whether racial differences could justify the enslavement of Africans in Europe and the Americas. Langhorne raised the stakes further, by doing explicitly what Franklin had feared, because it had been such a prominent aspect of the debate over the *Somerset* case: he made another North American slave an embodiment of the imperial controversy and an embarrassment to Americans. Phillis had become fully politicized: this was why Granville Sharp treated her as the second coming of James Somerset, and in doing that, he made the benevolent Nathaniel Wheatley, the representative of a reforming merchant family, look like the equivalent of Charles Steuart. No wonder Nathaniel Wheatley had seemed so bothered and managed to wash his hands of responsibility for Phillis. We don't know whether he was inclined to Toryism—his decision to stay in London had other motives and can hardly be seen as unusual in 1773—but the gamut of responses to Wheatley there seemed to make both his family and his city look bad even as he was trying to trade on his reputation and prospects. It made the young slave of the man Franklin called a "young master" look like the quintessential victim, not only of racial slavery, but of American double-dealing.

The word on the street in Philadelphia and London, in other words, favored, even demanded, her emancipation, now not just because of a respect for genius but also for the same political reasons that increasingly undergirded rising antislavery in England. Here lies the third possibility, an adjunct of the second: Phillis took advantage of the moment and insisted that she be freed either immediately or, more likely, upon coming home. Her return trip without Nathaniel, though explicable in other ways, may also point to a deal that freed her if she agreed to leave London quietly as soon as possible. Nathaniel Wheatley, in this scenario, tired quickly of the embarrassment and wanted to get on with his life, which he did in part by committing himself to English mercantile and family ties. If Phillis had "the stronger hand" at that moment, if she forced the issue, it's important to remember how she got into that stronger negotiating position. Her quick pivot in London from the sponsorship of religious adepts like the Countess of Huntingdon and John Thornton and Lord Dartmouth to visits with the abolitionist Granville Sharp and the colonial agent Benjamin Franklin had supercharged the political force field that surrounded her.

According to Wheatley, though, her actual emancipation did not occur *in* London, though it did happen *because of* London. The fourth possibility, then, is that she insisted on it, made it happen, but *after* she returned, with assistance from people she met in England—something that is still compatible with her reaching an understanding with Nathaniel in London or even with a prior, original understanding from 1772 or earlier. This scenario seems the most likely because it hews closest to the greater part of the best evidence—her specific words—and it combines aspects of the others. Recalling the moment to David Wooster in October, she strongly emphasized the difference her trip had made: "Since my return to America my Master, has at the desire of my friends in England given me my Freedom." This remarkable statement makes the Wheatleys sound rather less than willing, and could point either to the embarrassing effects of publicity, of being shamed by entreaties by other elite English men or women, or to pointed personal messages Wheatley or Captain Calef brought back on the *London Packet*.

Either way, she hadn't taken any chances in the summer of 1773. She'd evidently received some good legal advice: "The instrument is drawn, so as to secure me and my property from the hands of Exectutrs administrators, &c. of my master, and secure whatsoever Should be given me as my Own. A Copy is Sent to Isra[el] Mauduit Esqr. F.R.S." Although she credited her master and her "English friends," and used the passive voice in describing how it became official ("The instrument is drawn"), here she has taken the initiative herself—being so bold as to confirm the lawyer and Massachusetts representative Mauduit as *her* transatlantic agent or "friend," giving herself the status of a merchant, a province, the proprietor of a book published in London. There's no Susanna or Nathaniel mentoring or guiding her path in this version. This suggests her own careful actions in the process, even if it was literally the case that new friends like the Tory colony agent had stepped in to assist her. Why not deposit the document with a lawyer in Boston? English friends are the decisive factor, and Wheatley seeks to maintain those ties, to associate them with her emancipation. Twice in this statement she chooses to identify her freedom with her trip—and with her property.

Phillis could not have seen any of her reviews in print before her departure from London, but she did not need to: she knew what they embodied and further publicized. People had intervened on her behalf. She had encouragement and prospects. Sold as a genius, given as gifts the classic books that for her constituted stock-in-trade, she could not long remain enslaved property herself. In practice, she had hardly even had a master while in London. She was more like a young woman traveling with older kinfolk and making more new friends than the Wheatleys could have anticipated. Now she held a copyright, a property. That changed something, if not everything.

So English air, or London reviews and friends, had freed Phillis as much as it had freed James Somerset and as much as Susanna and John Wheatley did formally emancipate her sometime between her return in September and her letter to Wooster in October.

On the other hand, back in Boston, a year later, she would walk it back, depicting her emancipation as an outright gift that came three months later. In an October 1774 letter to the pious John Thornton in which she lamented Susanna's death and described how, as Thornton had apparently foretold, some people "who seem'd to respect me while under my mistresses patronage . . . have already put on a reserve," she praised "my old master's generous behavior in granting me my freedom, and still so kind to me I delight to acknowledge my great obligations to him, this he did about 3 months before the death of my dear mistress [on March 2, 1774] & at her desire, as well as his own humanity, of wch I hope ever to retain a grateful Sense, and treat him with that respect which is ever due to a paternal friendship." Here the stress is on continuities, not a radical break into property-owning freedom. Besides, even "if this had not been the Case"—if she hadn't been freed at all—"I hope I should willingly Submit to Servitude to be free in Christ."

This is a very different situation than she had described to Wooster. Clearly John Thornton, however sympathetic in his own way, was not one of the "English friends" who had spoken up for her immediate emancipation. Or if he had been, he had made it very clear that she needed more than literary "patronage." She emphasized her continuing "paternal" ties to the Wheatleys and put the initiative later and all in their hands.

Had she changed her mind about London, about emancipation, about her situation, or about the Wheatleys between October 1773 and October 1774, in light of disappointments—the absence of the financial wherewithal she had hoped for but which had been withheld by those who declined to buy or help sell her book? Had other promises been exchanged that made a more gradual emancipation story more attractive, more useful? Was it about the difference between writing to Wooster—stressing her prospects and need for patronage and book distribution assistance from an elite Connecticut family—and writing to Thornton, a different kind of "friend," one who would expect and reward gratitude and loyalty as well as pious resignation?

The seeming contradiction or dissembling makes sense when we realize the ambiguous meaning of freedom for Wheatley as a single young black woman at a time when poets and other would-be writers needed (but usually didn't get) patrons, and all New England young people, legally as well as by custom, had to be settled in households.

The situation became still more complicated upon her return

because her enslaver, mentor, friend, and matron, Susanna, lay dying on King Street. The strategy of securing emancipation papers and sending them to Israel Mauduit in London, and her revelation of that fact to select individuals like Wooster, must have been affected by the fact that she was going to be without Susanna's protection very soon and Nathaniel had abdicated any responsibility. When she wrote that "the Instrument is drawn, so as to secure me and my property from the hands of Exectutrs administrators, &c. of my master," she had to have been thinking about what could happen when one or both of the failing Wheatleys died. She could become a beneficiary or could have become part of what the estate's beneficiaries, Nathaniel and Mary, received. When masters passed, as any reader of a Boston newspaper could tell, the chattel principle of slavery prevailed. Household properties were enumerated, distributed, advertised, sold. Like other enslaved New Englanders, Phillis Wheatley would have been thinking ahead even if she had not become famous, even if her precise status had not become a matter of published speculation in 1773. In emancipation as in slavery, the details mattered.

So did the story. It mattered so much that there was no point in being consistent. Flattery and thankfulness might gain her more freedom than a precise recounting of what, in reality, had already been a complex process. Phillis Wheatley took pains to get a legal document that must have been dated, to secure her emancipation. She not only sent it across the ocean to a man who epitomized transatlantic ties but also told a man in another colony that she had done so. Her enslavement ended officially on one day during the later months of 1773. Yet in telling the story, she obscured the dates, the causes, and the agents of her emancipation, including her own role in making it happen. She covered her tracks because the story of her liberation, like her authorship, had not concluded.

17

THE PATRONS

Wheatley had reason to be optimistic as she saw Boston Harbor from the water at the end of her second Atlantic crossing. Bell's initial pre-publication ads had stressed the Countess of Huntingdon's support. The actual announcement for the book appearing in the *London Chronicle* three months later in early September stressed that she had recently been

> conversed with by many of the principal Nobility and Gentry of this Country, who have been singularly distinguished for their learning and abilities, among whom was the Earl of Dartmouth and the late Lord Lyttelton, and others who unanimously expressed their approbation of her genius, and their amazement at the gifts with which infinite wisdom has furnished her.

A week later the testimonials and reviews spread over an entire page.

This high praise—it could hardly have been higher—was followed by very strong reviews in leading venues like the *Gentleman's Magazine*. (The one major dissenting review did not appear until December in the *Monthly Review*.) Her book, coming on the next ship, was her property, the tangible expression of her freedom, and the source of future security. How could she realize that property as a guarantee of what emancipation could mean? Even as the book demonstrated that she had patrons, it also had to serve as her calling card in a bid for future support.

In both of the letters in which she described her emancipation with rather different emphases, to Wooster and to Thornton, she was looking, explicitly, for help. Her literary patronage and her continued, if legally free, status in a patriarchal household could not be separated.

Patronage had multiple meanings for an enslaved, young, colonial female poet. It made for strange bedfellows and perhaps stranger rhetoric. But it always had, for colonists as well as for her favorite classical, and neoclassical, poets—some of whom, like Horace and Pope, had more than a little to say about slavery. In her book, in the revisions she made while in London, the search for patronage became more than a thread. It became the story—one we can understand if we read her *Poems on Various Subjects, Religious and Moral* in their stitched and bound order, as a story. The Horatian patronage tale, in turn, helped Phillis Wheatley to argue, and some readers to understand, that the book's publication was not really compatible with the continued enslavement of its author. By dealing both forthrightly and allegorically with patronage in a world of slaves and freed men and women, from the book's very first, introductory verse, Wheatley made her book that much more effective as an argument against both slavery in general and her own enslavement in particular.

Inserted by her excited publisher into the advertisement, the namedropping of the recently departed Lord Lyttelton at the head of those whom Wheatley had impressed spoke volumes because Lyttelton had bespoken volumes. Bell wanted more than financial backing: he wanted the endorsement of the foremost aristocratic patron of poets in mid-eighteenth-century Britain. Wheatley understood this strategy, and it shaped how she framed and edited her book. The fact that George Lyttelton died a few weeks after meeting Wheatley, before he could see more than her manuscript, should not obscure what this lordly patron tells us about Wheatley's prospects and hopes. Bell must have understood that she had actually imitated Lord Lyttelton in such a creative way, in the opening poem of her book, as to make a meeting imperative as soon as she arrived in London, much as she had gotten to London by writing to and about the Countess of Huntingdon and Lord Dartmouth.

Lyttelton was no afterthought. Though largely forgotten today, in some ways he was a bigger fish to land than Huntingdon or even Dartmouth because he was someone who had won real, material support for poets: the kinds of sinecures and outright grants of money from the royal treasury or his friends' pockets of which most poets could only dream. It's a measure of Wheatley's ambition and her needs that the first poem in her book can be read as an extended invitation to Lyttelton to consider her as another British genius to discover and support.

A patriot-poet in his youth who had been inspired and befriended by Alexander Pope, during the 1730s Lyttelton had gained favor as a literary "talent-spotter" for the Prince of Wales, who invested in the opposition to Prime Minister Robert Walpole. George Lyttelton mostly gave up writing poems when he turned evangelical and ascended to high political office, but he nurtured national treasures like James Thomson and Henry Fielding, continued to be anthologized, and stayed in the patronage game in very much the way that Bell's ad suggested. London magazines called him "Maecenas," after the Roman politician, poet, and patron of Virgil and Horace, so often that the nickname became "a source of embarrassment." He showed particular interest in female writers and even made exceptions to his turn from poetry to history for certain female friends, as when he co-wrote *Dialogues of the Dead* (1760) with the salonist Elizabeth Montagu, and some verses to preface Elizabeth Carter's *Poems on Several Occasions* (1762). Both Montagu and Carter were members of a literary coterie that sought to make merit, rather than sex or class, its guiding rationale. Lyttelton proposed support for English women writers, as opposed to French ones, as a patriotic duty. By 1770, aspiring writers like Wheatley went to Lyttelton to ask him to subscribe for their books. His name on a list could by itself help sell a book.

Supporting poets was a way to not only participate in literary life but also gain and retain a reputation for discernment and virtue. In the new style of midcentury England, patrons raised up brilliant commoners to show how much they themselves deserved their nobility and wealth. After the death of his neighbor the poet William Shenstone in 1763, Lyttelton had taken up the cause of their mutual friend "the poetical shoemaker" James Woodhouse. The shoemaker's first bid for recognition had been an elegy asking for access to Shenstone's famous gardens at his estate, the Leasowes, which Shenstone had festooned with verse epitaphs in an ultimate literalization of the pastoral tradition by which walking, reading, writing, and working become all the same thing. Shenstone himself had made a recurrent theme of poets' poverty and their need for patrons and a rural retreat: "Ye sons of Wealth! Protect the Muses' train; / From winds protect them, and with food supply." Woodhouse dedicated his revised *Poems on Several Occasions* (1766) to Lyttelton and filled it with his elegies to Shenstone, his own former "Maecenas."

These patronage relations did not always work out, at least in the sense of creating careers or livelihoods for the ordinary men and women celebrated as natural geniuses by aristocrats. But sometimes they functioned in the shorter term as genuine artistic collaborations. Patronage remained an important part of British literary culture not only because of the economics of publication but also because of how, in a deeply hierarchical society, the very existence of patronized "found" poets, who were fed books and friends as well as money in order to produce more neat little leather-bound volumes, helped readers and writers think about what poems and poets were and what they were for. Patronage as a kind of friendship itself became a common subject of poems. The same issue of the *Gentleman's Magazine* that reviewed Wheatley's book also carried an elegy on the great patron Lyttelton's sudden death on August 22: "To raise poor Merit from his lowly cell / And cheer his heart, from penury set free / Oh cans't thou blame, O Woodhouse, if I tell / That Lyttelton, kind friend, did this for thee?"

Patrons like Lyttelton sought to balance the genius in their found protégés with the demands of classical learning by making themselves the judges of when education or taste was sadly lacking and when talent triumphed over status. Late-eighteenth-century writers expressed the tensions in the patronage system through riffs on ancient Greek and Roman poets, ruminations on fame, odes to rustic retirement, and meditations on gratitude to the great and the generous. After all, the notion that the ancients had excelled, more than the moderns, at poetry was often attributed to the lordly cash bequests and sinecures that, it seemed, the increasingly professional, metropolitan, and often impoverished class of English authors had lost. So many London writers who hailed originally from the provinces, like Oliver Goldsmith and Samuel Johnson, made their reputation with poems but their living (or not) with prose that they themselves derided as hackwork. As he tried to make it in the marketplace, Johnson mocked Lyttelton's taste and pretensions, in part because he knew all too well that only a very few would gain lasting "preferment."

When Wheatley decided to begin her *Poems* with a direct address, "To Maecenas," precisely as Horace began his books of *Odes*, his *Epodes*, his *Satires*, and his *Epistles*, she didn't have to tell readers why she would imitate and elaborate on the most self-conscious and slave-conscious of poets, the one who addressed matters of patronage and literary ambition so artfully, so directly, and so often. She could be direct through indirection, *through* Horace:

To Maecenas

MAECENAS, *you, beneath the myrtle shade,*
Read o'er what poets sung, and shepherds play'd.
What felt those poets but you feel the same?

> *Does not your soul possess the sacred flame?*
> *Their noble strains your equal genius shares*
> *In softer language, and diviner airs.*

The link to ancients and possible patrons through previous genera-tions of admirers and imitators can be made another way, through an explicit imitation. Compare young George Lyttelton's appeal to Pope, from 1732, republished in 1758 in what became the most popular anthology of the eighteenth century, Robert Dodsley's *Collection of Poems in Six Volumes by Several Hands*:

> *POPE! to whose reed beneath the beachen shade,*
> *The nymphs of Thames a pleas'd attention paid;*
> *While yet thy Muse, content with humbler praise,*
> *Warbled in Windsor's Grove her sylvan lays;*
> *Though now sublimely born on Homer's wing,*
> *Of glorious wars, and godlike chiefs she sing;*
> *Wilt thou with me re-visit once again,*
> *The chrystal fountain, and the flow'ry plain?*
> *Wilt thou indulgent hear my verse relate,*
> *The various changes of a lover's state;*
> *And while each turn of passion I pursue,*
> *Ask thy own heart if what I tell be true?*

Lyttelton's exchange with Pope is clearly a model. Yet hers must be different, for Lyttelton was not only an aspiring poet but also Pope's social superior, and a man. He could joke about the London women who swooned for Homer's champion because he had actually walked and recited with him. Lyttelton hadn't needed a modern Maecenas so much as a literary mentor and friend.

Wheatley's imagined Maecenas is an "equal genius," but he isn't a poet: he's a lover of poets, a victor who might share his reward (myrtle and shade). Possibly, with "diviner airs," he's more religious. Any of

Wheatley's friends and most of her readers would believe themselves more pious than the ancients. Any of them might qualify as a person of great feeling. But it isn't necessarily Mather Byles; Selina, Countess of Huntingdon; Susanna Wheatley; or even Lyttelton himself to whom Wheatley appeals. It's all of them at once, and anyone who is willing to join in as a promoter or a sympathetic reader. It's any and all possible future patrons who, like Maecenas, might themselves be remembered by association with the memorable writers of their time. And it's any reader who has learned to expect a poet to abase herself, with earnest pledges and knowing winks, before a tradition she must imitate in order to demonstrate genius.

These dialogues about patrons, genius, and verse were often also a conversation with, and about, Alexander Pope, not coincidentally Wheatley's favorite. As he wrote and quipped his way to stardom and a gentleman's estate, mocking mere scribblers and court poets along the way, Pope had made a proper relation to the ancients and to patrons a theme of many of his poems. His creative translations of Homer's *Iliad* and *Odyssey* celebrated Homer's natural genius and his moral sense, especially in the extensive commentary and explanation aimed at those who (like himself, Woodhouse, and Wheatley) had limited or no Greek and Latin. One reason Pope defended Homer was that he worried, as Dryden had, that his Roman exemplars Horace and Virgil had been "well-mannered court slaves" who wrote to validate a decadent emperor and please the rich and powerful. Ironically, in waging these battles, he could draw on some of those same Roman poets who, in their own republic's fall and empire's rise, found risks and opportunities—and wrote about them. Pope had written "imitations" of Horace's satires and epistles, for example, that sought to demonstrate his own independence, moderation, and good taste. Two of them, in 1737 and 1738, praised his young friends George Lyttelton and William Murray (later Lord Mansfield) as epitomes of forthright, fearless political rectitude.

Horace became the most translated and revered of the Roman

poets in eighteenth-century Anglo-America, even more than Virgil, because of his winning combination of morality, sophistication, and in-group humor. Much of this derived from his self-consciousness about the dilemmas of the life-hardened author among patrons and in the marketplace. In one of the first of the ample notes to his ubiquitous midcentury translation of Horace, Philip Francis called Horace's "flattery" of his patron, Maecenas, "bold, yet delicate." Eighteenth-century translators also make clear how often Horace referred to slaves and frankly addressed relations of all kinds with people whom later, twentieth-century translators would euphemize as "servants" and "lads."

This was because slavery had been a major social question in Horace's world, not to mention a matter of personal interest to him. Horace's father had been a former slave, a fact his rivals or enemies apparently never let him forget. As the slaving Roman empire expanded, and vast lands were expropriated and given to soldiers for their service, freed persons came to constitute a high proportion of the populace in Rome. There they became a source of political instability. Neither citizens, landowners, nor slaves, freedmen were, in effect, the mainstay or even majority in the crowds that demagogues could use against the propertied senators who ran the republic. Horace himself had served as a soldier and a bureaucrat, and lost that status, but his patron, the sometime poet Maecenas, had prospered under Augustus. Maecenas eventually managed to secure a farm for Horace, from which he wrote ambivalently about his waning metropolitan relevance.

Whether in odes, satires, or verse epistles, a hallmark of Horace's writing is his ironic wit about the fate and feelings of people like himself: masters in a slave society where some slaves became free. In several of his poems that begin "To Maecenas," he praises his patron for overlooking his own origins in a "Race of Slaves." In one satire, Horace has his slave Davus completely mock his master's inability to be satisfied with what he has. Davus becomes the Stoic philosopher while the master and poet is reduced to a mere man of flesh, a slave in spirit.

Poems on Various Subjects, Religious and Moral (1773). The frontispiece, engraved from a painting possibly done by Scipio Moorhead, is the only known contemporary portrait of Wheatley. The original painting has never been found. *(Massachusetts Historical Society)*

Joseph Blackburn, *Timothy Fitch*, 1760. Fitch owned and directed the voyage of the *Phillis*, the slaving ship in which the girl later known as Phillis Wheatley was transported from West Africa in 1761. *(Peabody-Essex Museum)*

RIGHT: In a diary he kept in a 1773 almanac, Reverend Jeremy Belknap copied down "Phillis Wheatley's first effort" at a poem, on the 1765 death of Oxenbridge Thacher. *(Massachusetts Historical Society)*

BELOW: "To the King's Most Excellent Majesty." This poem, written sometime after the repeal of the Stamp Act in March 1766, shows Wheatley's early turn to political topics and her melding of the sacred and secular. *(Historical Society of Pennsylvania)*

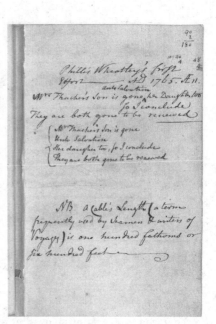

Joseph Sewall, by Nathanael Hurd, 1768 *(Museum of Fine Arts, Boston)*

Mather Byles, by John Singleton Copley, 1765–1767 *(American Antiquarian Society)*

Reverend Samuel Cooper, by John Singleton Copley *(Massachusetts Historical Society)*

Reverend Samson Occom *(Connecticut Historical Society)*

Ministers were key interlocutors for Wheatley. Sewall, Byles, and Cooper were among the Boston divines whom Wheatley knew well and who signed the attestation that she had written the poems in her 1773 book. Byles's verse directly influenced hers. She wrote one of her first poems about Sewall, and one of her last about Cooper. Reverend Samson Occom modeled her trip to England and was an important inspiration and correspondent. Countess Huntingdon (*next page*), the lay leader of a Methodist "Connexion" in England and the patron of the evangelist George Whitefield, materially supported the publication of Wheatley's book.

RIGHT: Selina Hastings, the Countess of Huntingdon (*Birdwell Library Special Collections, Southern Methodist University*)

BELOW: Wheatley included the epyllion "America" in this folded selection of three poems in her hand, which, like others, survived in the collections of women in Philadelphia who were writers and readers of poetry. It is mentioned in an early proposal for her book but did not fit the more conciliatory approach to the themes of tyranny and oppression and the imperial controversy in her 1773 book. (*Rush Family Papers, Library Company of Philadelphia*)

J. Huntingdon

SELINA, COUNTESS OF HUNTINGDON.

Boston Harbor, *Royal American Magazine*, January 1774. Boston's harbor and wharves dominated its landscape and made it a staging ground for imperial regulation. *(Courtesy of the American Antiquarian Society)*

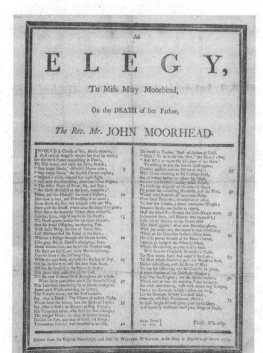

An ELEGY, to Miss Mary Moorhead, 1773 (Massachusetts Historical Society)

RIGHT: Letter to Obour Tanner, 1774 (*Massachusetts Historical Society*)

BELOW: Letter to Reverend Samuel Hopkins, 1774 (*Historical Society of Pennsylvania*)

Wheatley continued to publish and actively distribute her poems after her return from England. Several of her letters to Obour Tanner and to Samuel Hopkins in Newport, Rhode Island, discuss the distribution of and payments received for her book.

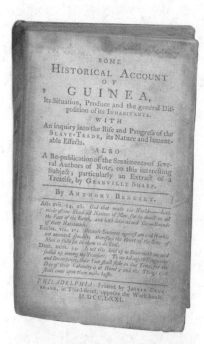

Anthony Benezet, *Some Historical Account of Guinea*, 1771. Phillis Wheatley signed her copy of Anthony Benezet's important antislavery book about West Africa. *(Special Collections, Swem Library, College of William and Mary)*

Bickerstaff's Boston Almanack for the year 1782, published by Ezekiel Russell *(American Antiquarian Society)*

to be caft afide with Contempt, as worthlefs and trifling Effufions.

As to the Difadvantages fhe has laboured under, with Regard to Learning, nothing needs to be of- fered, as her Mafter's Letter in the following Page will fufficiently fhew the Difficulties in this Refpect fhe had to encounter.

With all their Imperfections, the Poems are now humbly fubmitted to the Perufal of the Public.

Phillis Wheatley, the surprising African Poetess, arrived from England, at Boston, about a fortnight ago.

Rivington's Gazetteer September 23, 1773. N° 23. — 3:2.

Boston. September 20. 1773. In Captain Calef from London, came Passengers. Captain Hillhouse and Lady, Mr Aleing; also Phillis, the extraordinary poetical genius, negro Servant to Mr. John Wheatley, of this Town

Boston Evening Post. 28 Sept.r 1773.3: 2. 3:2.
23 Sept.

Thomas Jefferson's copy of *Poems on Various Subjects, Religious and Moral.* Wheatley's celebrity is well illustrated by her sometime publisher Ezekiel Russell's choice to put her image on the front of his 1782 almanac, and by the marginalia referring to her appearance in newspapers, in Jefferson's hand, in the copy of her book that is now in the Library of Congress, which purchased Jefferson's library in 1815. *(Library of Congress)*

Two odes somewhat creepily praise a slave named Phillis, describing an infatuation that seems neither mutual nor appropriate. In the first poem in his first book of *Epistles*, addressed like so many of them to Maecenas, he describes himself as like a liberated gladiator (gladiators were trained slaves). In the tenth epistle, he's a fugitive slave. The last describes his book itself as an aging object in the marketplace—like a manumitted, perhaps because no longer desirable, slave boy—flying to "Afric," then Spain, flung about only to end up teaching letters to schoolboys, yet testifying still to the moderate virtues of the author, "a Free-man's son" who, though he has slavery on the brain, is nevertheless clearly a master.

Horace is masterful, but as a writer he depicts himself as vulnerable, self-critical enough to compare himself to his own or anyone's slave. He plays with his own and his readers' feelings. When Wheatley begins by putting her Maecenas under Pope's "myrtle shade," where Lyttelton himself had got his start, she offers the kind of compliment she hoped to receive: "What felt those poets but you feel the same? / Does not your soul possess the sacred flame? / Their noble strains your equal genius shares / In softer language and diviner airs." Like Pope she immediately renews the link to the ancients and makes them over in modern, even fashionable language: in her generation, the language of feeling, more than faintly pious, generalized to apply even to distant, unknown readers.

The stress on feeling, and the bond between poets and readers, as opposed to the differences between slaves and masters or Africans and Europeans, informs the next stanza, on Homer, the "Great Sire of verse," and what it is like to read him. It's thrilling. The reaction is "deep-felt." The gods' emotions are heard, seen, felt in the body as severe weather. The still-roiling debate about the ancients versus the moderns had seized upon Homer as possibly an example of primitive virtues (and, to Pope, as the most inventive writer of all time, the epitome of "genius")—or, alternately to "modern" skeptics on the other side of the controversy, as limited artistically and morally by his archaic barbarisms. Wheatley admits that Homer appeals to emotions over reason, but suggests, like Homer's translator Pope, that what "moderns" decry as the ancient habits, overwrought similes, and sheer brutal violence in Homer also give way to "gentler strains" that may even approach the "diviner airs" of her Maecenas: "When gentler strains demand thy graceful song, / The length'ning line moves languishing along. / When great *Patroclus* courts *Achilles*' aid, / The grateful tribute of my tears is paid." There is plenty of crying in Homer, especially in *The Odyssey*, a testament to the ways poetry for Homer "belongs to the defeated and the dead" (or as Pope put it, *The Iliad* is for kings and heroes, but *The Odyssey* is for everybody). Describing her readerly response—tears—as "tribute" also directly compares the devoted, perhaps naive but deeply affected, "grateful" reader to the characters in Homer who regularly—on pain of retribution—offer ritual tributes to the gods and are deeply moved by their evident powers. Poetry itself becomes an epic game, and Wheatley's introductory verse epistle, it becomes clear, is a poem about epic poems' writers and readers: a recovery of the sacred flame, at once modern and ancient.

Moving on to the great Roman poet Virgil, though, not coincidentally the poet of imperial renewal who most glorified power and who said much less than Homer or Horace about the enslaved, she introduces a note of insecurity, appropriate for the first-time author: "O could I rival thine and *Virgil*'s page, / Or claim the *Muses* with the *Mantuan* Sage . . . But here I sit, and mourn a grov'ling mind / That fain would mount, and ride upon the wind." Maecenas, she says, isn't subject to these insecurities. This is a common self-deprecating gesture, one indulged in by Horace occasionally (but usually about his status or human failings, not his poems), and by Mather Byles explicitly in his *Poems on Several Occasions*, in contemplation of Milton. Wheatley takes the humility much further: "But I less happy, cannot raise the song, / The fault'ring music dies upon my tongue." Why would she be less happy? Because she is not quite yet a celebrated writer, at least not in the metropole. Or is there another reason that she'd have a "grov'ling," downbeaten, submissive mind?

No sooner has Wheatley introduced this counterpoint, a nod to skepticism about her abilities or achievement and a hint at her enslaved status, than she pivots to a later Roman poet-playwright: "The happier *Terence* all the choir inspir'd, / His soul replenish'd, and his bosom fir'd." In the poem, Terence's name is followed by an asterisk which leads to a footnote at the bottom of the page that makes the reference clear: "He was an *African* by birth."

> *But say,* ye Muses, *why this partial grace,*
> *To one alone of* Afric's *sable race;*
> *From age to age transmitting thus his name,*
> *With the first glory in the rolls of fame?*

Terence is happier because he is blessed by the muses, and renowned (his plays were especially popular assigned reading for students of Latin in the eighteenth century). So Wheatley does not have to be the first African. There is no color bar in the classical canon. She needn't falter—if she gets patronized.

There is still more to Wheatley's identification with Terence. The standard biographies and commentaries made it clear that Terence had been a captive and enslaved. Like Wheatley, he had also been suspected of not having actually authored his verse. But then he had been freed as a result of his success. Terence is a precedent for emancipation as well as literary "grace."

Perhaps even more important, Terence elaborated on the Greek, and later Roman, Plautine tradition of plays that revolve around slaves and masters, in which the slaves are often more clever and are sometimes rewarded with freedom. Much as Horace claimed to have revived Greek forms, and Pope to have rescued and reinvigorated Homer, Wheatley establishes herself as a worthy beneficiary of this Roman tradition of creative imitation and revival. She reminds readers that nothing could be more classical than poetry about slavery, than slaves making poetry, or slaves gaining freedom. Anyone claiming that African slaves couldn't write English neoclassical verse had to be, simply, ignorant as well as unfeeling.

Having performed this end run around Virgil and racist condescension through Terence, she can return to the praise of the patron and name her ambitions:

> *Thy virtues, great* Maecenas! *shall be sung*
> *In praise of him, from whom those virtues sprung:*
> *While blooming wreaths around thy temple spread,*
> *I'll snatch a laurel from thine honour'd head,*
> *While you indulgent smile upon the deed.*

Instead of Wheatley herself being "snatched" from her father's house, as she will describe later in the volume, or the infant Charles Eliot being "snatch'd" by God from his parents, she does the snatching herself. Byles, in his poem praising Milton as his muse, had imagined himself "boldly snatch[ing] / A spreading Branch from his immortal Laurels." The literati, however, would have recognized not Byles's provincial product from thirty years earlier but more likely a direct reference to a famous incident in which Elizabeth Carter, poet and translator, visited Alexander Pope's gardens at Twickenham on the river Thames in 1738 when the poet was absent and dared to take a laurel sprig for herself. Was Carter's bold symbolic gesture itself a riff on the famous "rape of the lock," the curl snipped from a woman that Pope had satirized as a mock-epic battle? Carter's twig led to a prolonged series of epigrammatic commentaries upon the deed by everyone from Samuel Johnson to Stephen Duck, and a very careful response by Carter, initiating a tradition of English women writers—and others like Woodhouse—addressing Pope, Shenstone, and other poet-patrons through meditations on their semipublic, proprietary gardens as metaphors for the literary public.

So in "To Maecenas" we again come full circle, to the occasion of publication: Wheatley's London visit, what it portended, and the role of the patrons in determining how she would be read and more, in a flurry of references that begin with London's great river Thames and proceed to link her favorite images to come in *Poems*—sun, water—to an idealized reader, listener, and defender. Her book may be called *Poems on Various Subjects, Religious and Moral*, but its first subject is Wheatley herself—Wheatley in transition from slavery to freedom, from attic scribbling to occasional publication and local fame to bookmaking and a name in the republic of letters. Coinciding with her long ship passage from Boston, when she likely wrote the poem, the ambiguous, allegorical identity of Maecenas seems deliberate and appropriate. She is traveling as much away from the pious Susanna as she is floating to any particular patron like Lady Huntingdon or Lord Lyttelton. She hopes to be heard and defended, but not just by one: by many.

18

THE BOOK

The "lays" that follow "To Maecenas" are as "religious and moral" as the volume's title promises. The emphasis is on the general, the universal, and the classical, but moderated and punctuated, at least every third poem, with piety. The poems, when read in the order Wheatley intended, also tell a story. They chart her development as a poet, her fulfillment of her early promise, and her development into a sophisticated adult worthy of patronage, capable of wisdom on "various" topics, Christian but literate in the classics, African and American but also decidedly British.

This pattern appears immediately: the second poem, the early effort "On Virtue," in the context of the volume, takes some of the edge off her ambition, and classical orientation, in "To Maecenas." Christian identifications could also balance Greco-Romanist snobberies. In her revision of the 1767 poem to the Harvard students, "my native Shore / The sable Land of error's darkest night / There, sacred Nine! For you no place was found" becomes "The land of errors, and *Egyptian* gloom," which focuses the fortunate fall on an ancient paganism while excising any implication that Africans can't own the muses, or that race defines worth. (The "sable monster" of sin also transforms into the more decidedly biblical "deadly serpent in its egg.") She is clarifying her relation to Africa and to blackness: they are neither the same, damned thing nor anything to excuse.

Wheatley does her utmost, too, to make the volume less distinctively New England bound. In the poem on Reverend Sewall's death, "the continent" is no longer "ruined" at the loss of a Boston minister. "The King's Most Excellent Majesty" is thanked, with a footnote that clarifies the occasion (repeal of the Stamp Act) instead of in its title, which has the effect of lessening the particular event that was so important to patriot Whig Bostonians while still magnifying the British king as deliverer. The Whitefield elegy is stripped of its earlier claim that "AMERICANS were burden'd sore, / When streets were crimson'd with their guiltless gore!" Whitefield no longer sympathizes especially with "New-England's much-distress'd Abode": now he simply "long'd to see America excel" in piety. And as she moves to a trio of elegies on lesser-known persons, she avoids anything that would make her seem narrow or provincial or even too religious, like her excised poems "Deism" and "Atheism" (present in her 1772 proposals) might have.

"America," her epyllion with its extended simile warning of the consequences of the parental neglect and abuse of colonies qua children, is disinvited from her London premiere. So are her poems on Commodore Hood "pardoning a deserter," a poem on "the landing of the Troops," the poem on the death of Christopher Seider, and her eyewitness lyric on the Boston Massacre. Instead, we have "On Being Brought from Africa to America," in which "sable," used here for the first time in the book, drips with irony. In the context of what contemporaries liked to call "enlarged views" of Britishness, Christianity, and humanity, especially the universal salvation to believers promised in the Sewall and Whitefield elegies that precede it, "On Being Brought from Africa to America" seems even more clear as an argument against race. Perhaps Wheatley saved it for the book for this reason, never intending for it to be read alone as an introduction to her work or her attitude toward her enslavement.

After the elegies, the book showcases more ambition, with the lengthy "Goliath of Gath," and then a 131-line ecumenical praise poem, "Thoughts on the WORKS of PROVIDENCE." This ode incorporates aspects of the earlier short poems on night and day, including the one published anonymously. God ordains the sun's miraculous movements, the sunrise and sunset; there is eternal goodness in both day and night's "sable veil":

> Creation smiles in various beauty gay,
> While day to night, and night succeeds to day:
> That Wisdom, which attends Jehovah's ways,
> Shines most conspicuous in the solar rays:
> Without them, destitute of heat and light,
> This world would be the reign of endless night:
> In their excess how would our race complain,
> Abhorring life! how hate its length'ned chain!

Wheatley does here exactly what she said her mother had done: praise the sun and the power that brings the day. Maybe Africans are favored by this life-giving force, but instead of depicting Africans as a race, she once again stresses the human race. She adds a hint that the moment of the sable veil, night's advance, is also an equally special time that "conceals effects, but shews th' *Almighty Cause*." God directs the day to be the time of reason, and yet we must also "trace him in the night's repose."

Following two especially accomplished but previously unpublished recent elegies, "To a Lady on the Death of Three Relations" and "To a Clergyman on the Death of his Lady," Wheatley returns to the themes of day and night in "An Hymn to the Morning" and "An Hymn to the Evening," for which "On Night and Sleep" also could have functioned as a study. The morning poem invokes Aurora—but this time playfully, as a bit too much, for while her song has been "demand[ed]" by the goddess, "I feel [the sun's] fervid beams too strong, / And scarce begun, concludes th' abortive song." In the evening poem, the sunset is even more beautiful, inspiring and worthy of "praise of him who gives the light, / And draws the sable curtains of the night."

These poems make repeated and new classical gestures, for example, to Calliope as well as Aurora, while reprising the lighter aspects as well as the specific references in "To Maecenas." Like Pope, Wheatley aims to please a broad audience looking for a middle way: religious but not doctrinaire, moral but not judgmental of any particular social stratum, playful but not fanciful, feminine but not easily dismissed as uneducated or unworldly. The different possible attitudes that may arise daily at dawn or dusk, or in the life course with the death of intimates, are suggested by the oscillation, every few poems, between epic ambition and forms like the elegy, with its repeated theme of resignation to God's will. The pairing of hymns to morning and evening, and of Reason and Fancy in "Thoughts on the Works of Providence," makes a similar point.

So does the pairing of "On Recollection" with a new poem, "On Imagination." The poet is not going to be contained in any easily dismissed argument such as the superiority of reason to revelation, the moderns over the ancients, or vice versa. Thematically, "Recollection" makes "Mneme," or memory, the creature of the night, who has the power to shame "virtue" into better behavior. The moral power that might result is humbling when turned upon the self, yet "[s]weeter than Maro's [Virgil's] entertaining strains." She demonstrates classical knowledge—and when to put it away. "Imagination," which is also "fancy," is nothing if not free. Like Horace, Wheatley suggests the possible relativity of slavery, that free people can be slaves to their own notions: fancy's "silken fetters all the senses bind / And soft captivity involves the mind." Yet she does not rest there. The literal flights of fancy in the poem come back down to earth when she makes it clear that the act of imagination and memory she is describing is typified by her thinking about the sun when it is absent:

Though Winter *frowns to* Fancy's *raptur'd eyes*
The fields may flourish, and gay scenes arise;
The frozen deeps may break the iron bands,
And bid their waters murmur o'er the sands.

. . . .

Winter *austere forbids me to aspire,*
And northern tempests damp the rising fire;
They chill the tides of Fancy's *flowing sea,*
Cease then, my song, cease the unequal lay.

Are these all too real northern tempests the storms of the North Atlantic, the cold of a Boston winter, or the "iron bands" that take Africans into slavery there?

She performs a different counterpoint with the Hebrew Bible and the New Testament by devoting so much space to "Goliath of Gath" after her most Christocentric poems (to the Harvard students and George Whitefield), then moving on, after the morning and evening poems, to a paraphrase and elaboration titled simply "Isaiah lxiii. 1–8." The book of Isaiah, with its prophecies and judgments of sinners, had special importance to antislavery writers during the late eighteenth century. Where the morning and evening poems stress God's love, in what was often understood to be the Christian way, "Isaiah" focuses on God's anger and vengeance, and again on a battle scene, here with the real Almighty rather than the gods of Greek myth. The passage describes the prophet's vision of another victory over the Edomite enslavers, the villains of the Goliath poem; this text was often interpreted by Christians as a portent of Christ's later victories.

After the elegy on the death of the infant Charles Eliot, which also reestablishes the Christian God's sovereignty, *Poems on Various Subjects* shifts again, back to British imperial subjects. A short and new or previously unpublished poem praises "Captain H——D of the 65th Regiment," probably John Handfield Jr. This officer was the son of Lieutenant Colonel John Handfield, who had served in Canada during the Seven Years' War, participated regretfully in the deportation of the Acadians from Nova Scotia (including his wife's relatives), and then resigned from service in 1760, spending the years from 1760 to early 1763 in Boston before retiring to Ireland. To reintroduce her loyalty to the British Empire, Wheatley chooses a noncontroversial figure who was almost certainly better liked in Boston (where he had been known as a boy) than some more recently arrived officers. His "valour" joins "the Christian, and the hero"—which is to say, resolves any seeming conflict between the classical and the religious subjects of the previous groups of poems. This is the imperial controversy from a rather English if not Tory perspective, according to which the fundamental facts of the colonial enterprise are not God's plan or the defeat of the natives (as in "America") but rather the imperial forces that protect it. The depiction of Handfield could not be more enthusiastic about the mission, which, with the explicit naming of the Sixty-Fifth Regiment (still in Boston), cannot be missed: "Go, hero brave, still grace the post of fame, / And add new glories to thine honour'd name, / Still to the field, and still to virtue true: *Britannia* glories in no son like you."

This valentine to the British establishment sets up Wheatley's revised version of her poem to Lord Dartmouth, the other possible patron besides Lord Lyttelton and the Countess of Huntingdon mentioned by name in Bell's advertisement for the book. This version is even more flattering to Dartmouth than the earlier one she had sent to him a year before. It needs to be, because the premise of "New England" as a place of "grievance unredress'd" is unavoidable in the poem. Here the "silken reins" of empire are held not by "fancy" but by the new secretary of state, and by implication by more benevolent Britons, who will allow "*Freedom's* charms unfold. / Long lost to realms beneath the northern skies." She also cut out a series of couplets that had ascribed hoped-for policy changes to a revival of "Liberty." That would have been too provincial and critical for a British readership that would surely include supporters of imperial policy. Instead, she proceeds directly to her Horatian self-reference, now a stand-alone stanza, that not only demonstrates her own ability to participate in the conversation about British liberties but also turns the tables by making her African father (rather than Dartmouth, the lord whose sway is "blissful" but no longer "paternal") the new center of the story. The real experts on "love of *Freedom*" are her *African* people. By choosing her father, now mentioned twice, rather than her mother to mention specifically, Wheatley may be testifying to her actual experience. She is certainly elevating her father to the heroic level of the classical figures and mourning parents who populate the rest of her book.

Once again, African American slavery and Greek or Roman slavery have much in common besides names like Phillis. But what does this imply about an American slavery in which so few seem to be emancipated? The insistence on slave catching as "snatching" in the Dartmouth poem serves to remind the reader of the poet who would snatch a laurel to join the progress of the arts since the ancients. Placing the slave's narrative in the middle of the Dartmouth poem also directly evokes books 14 and 15 of Pope's translation of *The Odyssey*, in which the disguised Odysseus, presenting himself as an aging fugitive, hears his own slave, Eumaeus, tell the story of his enslavement as a youth. As never before, thanks to the role-playing he is doing to infiltrate his own household, Odysseus identifies with his "divine swineherd": "thou (he cries) has felt / The spite of fortune too! Her cruel hand / Snatch'd thee an infant from thy native land! / Snatch'd from thy parent's arms." For Pope, in his notes, Eumaeus is the "monarch of the Swains," not only because he was originally of noble birth in a far-off land, but because he epitomizes the "vein of humanity" in Homer's poem, as opposed to the bloody *Iliad*: "Eumaeus tending his herds is more amiable than Achilles in all his destructive glory."

On the one hand, this theme allows Pope to embrace *The Odyssey*'s reconciliation of mastery, kingship, and slavery. As his Odysseus puts it, reflecting on Eumaeus's story, "one choice blessing (such is Jove's high will) / Has sweeten'd all thy bitter draught of ill: / Torn from thy country to no hapless end, / The Gods have, in a master, giv'n a friend." Mastery, at least in Odysseus's hands (or from his vantage point), is really a kind of friendship. Everyone is potentially a slave in *The Odyssey*. The disguised Odysseus is repeatedly called one, and his own slaves Eumaeus and Eurycleia (another "person of wisdom," Pope asserts) actually save the day from the evil suitors, whose greed and bad manners are epitomized by their abuse and corruption of slaves and their bad jokes about selling people who cross them.

On the other hand, Eumaeus is in the end rewarded with his freedom as well as our sympathy. Wheatley's neoclassical echoes might seem to relativize slavery as just another "seeming cruel fate," potentially God's will, like death. For Wheatley, though, there is another side to her references to ancient slaveries, when interspersed with songs about God and suffering. They introduce the possibility of emancipation. They raise the question of modern, British, and American slavery's true nature. They encourage readers to wonder what modern, British, or American empire is for if it is nothing but a pale imitation of ancient pagans. It may be even worse. If worthy slaves are not freed and if slavery has become hereditary, then clearly American slavery is *worse* than the ancient, or for that matter African, kinds of bondage. Complacent defenders of slavery come off quite badly by comparison with the brilliant, literate enslaved author.

Four other new poems join her most recent odes and elegies in rounding out the volume. "To a Gentleman on his Voyage to *Great-Britain* for the Recovery of his Health" pairs "Ode to Neptune" in describing the powerful sea as a possibly benign force. An ocean voyage, she acknowledges, does not inspire "chant of gay *Elysian* scenes" or "flow'ry plains," but then neither does New England, "these bleak regions and inclement skies, / Where chilling winds return the winter past, / And nature shudders at the furious blast." A "Hymn to Humanity" depicts an "S. P. G." ("S. P. Gallowy Esq. who corrected some poetic essays of the Authoress," according to the Boston schoolbook copyist) as a beneficent friend who encouraged her. Gallowy could have been a Boston patron, but the version in *Poems on Various Subjects* gives no hint besides the initials. Like Maecenas, S.P.G. provides friendship to "Afric's muse" and deserves "Immortal *Friendship* laurel-crown'd." The poem moves from an evangelical register, in which the subject is inspired by "the prince of heavn'ly birth," to a classical one, suggesting the necessity of Wheatley's turns toward the ancients and back.

The other new, ambitious, long poem, "Niobe in Distress for her Children slain by Apollo," makes a similarly bold but more allusive gesture, elaborating on a story "from *Ovid's* Metamorphoses, Book VI, and from a view of the painting of Mr. Richard Wilson," which she could have seen in London. Niobe tempts the gods by bragging about having more children than one of their favorites; Apollo slays all ten of her progeny in retribution. But Wheatley doesn't follow Ovid's interpretation—or at least not in most translations, where the focus is usually on Niobe's tragic pride. Instead, she follows the collaborative translation put together by Samuel Garth and the riff on the Niobe story in Alexander Pope's *Iliad*, book 24, as well as Wilson's painting and engravings of it, which highlight the severity of the gods' anger and Niobe's own pain and loss. Her Niobe is more vulnerable and has less power, but she claims the center of attention, as a mother, "beautiful in woe." It seems likely that this is her nod toward her own mother, safely classicized and universalized.

By the time the reader finishes with "Niobe," there can be no doubt that Wheatley is as much a neoclassical poet as she is a writer of religious hymns and elegies or occasional political verse. She also reinforces the elevation of painting and poetry together by Horace in his final epistle (later known as the "Ars Poetica") by referring directly in the poem's title to her visual inspiration by Richard Wilson—and then by following "Niobe" immediately with "To S. M. a young *African* Painter, on Seeing his Works." Here she has it more than both ways, showing that her imagination can be fired by artful visual images as much as by words, and by African boys as much as by Englishmen and mythical mothers. She urges young Scipio Moorhead to "nobler themes" while folding his canvas into her own play of "Aurora's eyes" and "the solemn gloom of night." At the same time, she is suggesting that these two black artists may "conspire" together.

These final pages suggest an effort to bring the reader decidedly up-to-date with the real subject of *Poems on Various Subjects*: Phillis herself. Unlike all the other poems in the volume, the last elegy, to Lieutenant Governor Oliver, is actually dated ("*March* 24, 1773"). It is followed by her "Farewel to America. To Mrs. S. W.," which careful readers of the advertisements or the physical book's prefaces would have understood for what it was: a poem written to mark the late summer trip to London that had been scheduled to promote the book itself.

Yet there is one more pair of pieces that actually close the *Poems*: the most playful and in a sense forward-looking verses in the book. It's a rebus: a poem in the form of a riddle, in this case with six clues, the answers to which form the letters of a word. The poem of clues is signed by "I. B.," probably James Bowdoin II, a published poet himself and one of her eighteen signees of the attestation at the front of the book. A well-connected lawyer, wealthy merchant, and member of the governor's council, he was a leader of the opposition, yet got along notably well with the British officers in town, including Commodore Hood. As such, he was the perfect model and foil for an attempt to end by looking ahead, and by bridging Boston and London, Whig and Tory, in 1773.

Bowdoin's rebus is concise, with six clues in five stanzas of three lines, ending with a big hint: "Th'initials show a vanquish'd town, / That adds fresh glory and renown / To old *Britannia's* fame." It's a giveaway: everyone in Boston would know that the answer could only be Quebec. The real challenge is for Wheatley to answer in kind, which she does in a rebus of her own in her preferred pentameter couplets: "THE poet asks, and Phillis can't refuse / To shew th'obedience of the Infant muse."

Why not be an infant as well as an African muse, if it means her "obedience" is to be mainly figurative or artistic, in a dialogue that gives her the last word? Wheatley is creating an identity after slavery before her readers' eyes, under the protection of possible patrons like Bowdoin. Her decodings in the rebus confirm her knowledge of things biblical, classical, and imperial, from "Israel's army" to "Menelaus" to Lord Camden "zealous to support our laws" and "Quebec now vanquished." If Quebec is the proof of British-American glory and harmony, there is promise yet in her American home:

> Boston's *a town, polite and debonair,*
> *To which the beaux and beauteous nymphs repair,*
> Each Helen *strikes the mind with sweet surprise,*
> *While living lightning flashes from her eyes.*

The portrait Wheatley paints of herself in her "Answer to the *Rebus*" is classically educated, aware of biblical referents, feminine, genteel, and politically literate. With "I.B.," she's still celebrating the Seven Years' War. Returning to 1763 would be better for both England and America. This is the British provincial on the eve of the Revolution, appreciative of peers like Camden who stand up for American rights, cheering (but not too hard) for her "debonair" town: one of the nymphs. Maybe, like Walt Whitman, she could be a poet and yet represent multitudes. She returns symbolically to Boston in possession of Britain and, more important, herself.

19

THE READERS

Eleven newspapers in the colonies announced Phillis Wheatley's return as a passenger on a ship laden with goods. In Thomas's *Massachusetts Spy* and in the *Boston Post-Boy*, she was "the celebrated young negro poetess, Phillis." Not to be outdone, in the *News-Letter*, the *Evening-Post*, and the *Boston Gazette* she appeared as "the extraordinary Poetical Genius, Negro Servant to Mr. John Wheatley." These reports were even more effusive than the advance notices and initial reviews of her book. She had herself become a kind of imported fashion: not anonymous and later to be named for the ship that carried her as in 1761, but given almost equal billing with the *London Packet* itself. Americans now echoed, and even amplified, metropolitan taste. One didn't have to have her book in hand to know that she had achieved a kind of fame usually reserved for the likes of Lord Lyttelton, Lord Dartmouth, the Countess of Huntingdon, or Benjamin Franklin.

Settled back in Boston, she remained a sight to see. Jabez Maud Fisher, the son of a Philadelphia Quaker merchant, toured the notable buildings of Boston, took in sermons by Samuel Cooper and a Baptist preacher, and then accompanied one of the Rotches to "see the celebrated Miss Phillis Wheatley who has been just returned from England—where she has been much caress'd." Wheatley showed her visitors "a Vol. of her Poetry which is shortly to appear in Print," probably a manuscript copy, "& a number of her Letters sensible."

The most recent British monthlies came to America with the London newspapers on every ship. In September, the *Gentleman's Magazine* had stressed her "youth, innocence, and piety, united with genius." By December there began to be some pushback to the hype. Reviews mattered because many people read them who would not have quick access to the book. Aware of the possibly antislavery implications of her genius, the *Critical Review* acknowledged her as a remarkable "literary phenomenon" given that "the Negroes of Africa are generally treated as a dull, ignorant, and ignoble race of men, fit only to be slaves, and incapable of any considerable attainment in the liberal arts and sciences." Bernard Romans, a surveyor and military man as well as an aspiring poet who had managed to place a paean to the American "asylum of mankind" in Isaiah Thomas's new *Royal American Magazine*, called Wheatley a mere "Phoenix of her race," an exception that actually proved a rule about "the contrary effect of education on this sable generation."

Racist attacks on Wheatley responded to *antislavery* readings of her and her work. The London *Monthly Review* led the attempted backlash. Its terms, nevertheless, are revealing. The reviewer John Langhorne read Wheatley carefully enough to notice her interest in solar imagery, but labored to deny that "genius is the offspring of the sun." That would have surely led to real instances of African achievement. Yet Wheatley claimed not just her African identity but also a direct relationship with Greeks and Romans. So he posited tropical "sloth" as the opposite of Mediterranean chill: "The country that gave birth to Alexander and Aristotle . . . was Macedonia, naturally a cold and ungenial region. Homer and Hesiod breathed the cool and temperate air of the Meles, and the poets and heroes of Greece and Rome had no very intimate connection with the sun" (something that Homer's ritualized invocations of "dawn's rosy fingers" obviously contradicted, in any translation). Besides, Wheatley's poems didn't even "bear [any]

endemial marks of solar fire or spirit." They were "merely imitative," he
insisted. Like most of "these people," Wheatley showed no "invention."
Few contemporaries would have failed to be puzzled by this dichotomy
between imitation and invention. (Not until the triumph of Romanticism and its modernist successors did writers or critics insist that
everything be made new.) Wheatley's more open-minded or careful
readers would have recognized a ruse—not least because Wheatley's
book took up the issue of models and influence and demonstrated
any absolute divide between imitation and inspiration to be as false a
choice as it had been for Milton and Pope.

Unable to sustain these contradictions, Langhorne admitted that
Wheatley "has written many good lines, and now and then one of
superior character has dropped from her pen," such as, revealingly,
her invocation of how "the sun slumbers in the ocean's arms" from
"Thoughts on the Works of Providence." He proceeded to give away
the game by not being able to resist Wheatley's actual invocation of
Africa, and her father's suffering, in the Dartmouth poem. The political opportunity to tweak the Americans for their hypocrisy on slavery
trumped his racial sneer, and Wheatley becomes, in the last paragraph
of the review, "an ingenious young woman," freeing whom would do
more for humanity than a thousand liberty trees.

A turn of phrase like this resonated far from the Liberty Tree in
Boston. Willing to put aside a racist agenda to score a point against
Americans, Langhorne was as much an exception that proved a rule as
Wheatley herself might seem to be, and perhaps more. People couldn't
read Wheatley without thinking of slavery, and they could no longer
think of slavery without thinking about the colonial resistance movement. With enemies like these, it's not hard to see why Wheatley continued to win friends.

In 1773, Wheatley could mean very different things to different
people, and even to the same people. Mercy Otis Warren, herself an
ambitious writer who had published patriot poems and plays anonymously in the *Massachusetts Spy*, replied to a friend who had sent

her excerpts from two new books—Wheatley's *Poems* and Hester Chapone's *Letters on the Improvement of the Mind* (1773)—that while the latter might be more accomplished, the most striking thing was the "flowing" quality of the verse of the "gentle African . . . barbarian girl, but lately taught either letters or language except the uncouth jargon of the Numidian shore. These circumstances justly weighed," Warren insisted, Wheatley "must bear away the palm of superior applause as best entitled to the claim of original genius." In other words, the more African she was imagined to be, the more impressive her genius. Or as a Latin teacher in Boston put it in the "Four Lines in Latin Verse to be put under the frontispiece of PHILLIS's performances" he published with an advertisement for his services in a Boston newspaper, "Determination, hard work, and skill made a poet out of Pindar, / And young love wrote the songs for Sappho; / Their wealth, their time, their place—all of these things favored them. / But divine inspiration alone creates Phillis's genius." As he angled for students with his own imitation of Horace in the wake of Wheatley's neoclassical triumph, Wheatley's example helped this ambitious pedagogue argue that his teaching served both God and Juno.

Stereotypes shaped Wheatley's reception at every turn. But images of Africanness didn't keep aspiring white women writers from continuing to identify with what she had been able to do without a formal (that is, male) education. A Leeds woman responded in verse to the excess of shock some people expressed and in doing so made her own way into London's *Sentimental Magazine*: "Why stand amaz'd at Afric's muse! / Why struck with sacred awe! / One God our genius did infuse / One colour's nature's law."

Similarly, when Mary Scott published a verse tribute to the women writers of England in 1774, she praised the "considerable merit" of Wheatley as a "Daughter of Shenstone" and included her as one of the most recent additions to the honor roll along with Hannah More and Hester Chapone. Shenstone was known to be antislavery: one of his elegies pivoted from the notion of being enslaved to love to an extended description of the horrors of the slave trade. (An American fan, Mary Eveleigh of South Carolina, ratified Scott's taste by gifting Wheatley with Shenstone's *Works* in exchange for *Poems on Various Subjects, Religious and Moral*.) The *Monthly Review* balked again, claiming that Scott had "impeached her own judgment" by praising Wheatley. On the other hand, Hannah More herself, just beginning a long career as a condescending crusader for reforms, including antislavery, only joked at being compared to "the black girl," without questioning Scott's aesthetic judgment. A few years later, a writer who wanted to mock the bluestockings in verse gave Wheatley a starring role with no reference to race or geography. There were many readers for whom Wheatley's sex mattered as much as or more than her enslavement or her color.

Readers' responses to Wheatley had become a Rorschach test for slavery, for race, and for sex all at once. The most striking testimony to just how affecting her achievement could be in 1773–74 comes from the diary of Philip Vickers Fithian, a recent graduate of the College of New Jersey at Princeton who served as a tutor for the children of Robert Carter III, owner of one of the largest plantations in Virginia. Fithian scribbled repeatedly of his shock at how white Virginians treated the enslaved. Still, he was happy to be stunned when his charge, fifteen-year-old Bob Carter Jr., usually an indifferent student, expressed "astonishment" at the *Monthly Review*'s account of Wheatley's work that Fithian read to him. For Bob, Langhorne's mostly negative review wasn't a takedown; it was a revelation. He just couldn't stop talking about it, "sometimes wanting to see her, then to know if She knew grammer, Latin, &c. [A]t last he expressed himself in a manner very unusual for a Boy of his turn. & suddenly exclaimed, Good God! I wish I was in Heaven!" As Robert Carter Sr.'s biographer puts it, "that was Baptist talk, and told anyone who had been listening" that young Bob had been spending time in the slave quarters, as Baptist preachers controversially did. If the young man had a rebellious streak, it could be expressed as sympathy with Phillis Wheatley.

This reaction led Fithian, a conscientious instructor, to scour the new issues of other magazines for more information. "Like Bob I am at once fill'd with pleasure & surprise, when I see the remarks of the reviewers confirmed as to the Writings of that ingenious *African Phillis Wheatly* of Boston; her verses seem to discover that She is tolerably well acquainted with Poetry, Learning & Religion." He proceeded to copy out the eight lines of "On Being Brought from Africa to America" from one of the reviews. Fithian did not stay long enough at Nomini Hall to see the senior Robert Carter convert to Methodism and begin praying and taking Communion with his slaves, all of whom he would, famously, emancipate in 1791. Nor did Phillis Wheatley convert the Carters to Jesus or to antislavery. Yet even readers of her most negative review, ensconced on a plantation, could see where her poems pushed people.

Meanwhile, Phillis found herself "very Busy ever since my arrival," she told her friend Obour Tanner, probably with visitors and tending to Susanna Wheatley. The sixty-five-year-old matriarch seemed on the verge of death. Her sister Elizabeth Wallcut had expressed alarm when Susanna was "near her end" without Phillis at her side. By late October she had been bedridden for a total of fourteen weeks—that is, since soon after Phillis's departure for London—but was doing somewhat better after her return. It's fairly certain that Mary Wheatley Lathrop was not taking care of her mother, or even attentive. Her third child arrived on December 27. Something else, though, had come between Susanna and Mary, who was known as Polly. Nephew Christopher Wallcut would later refer to Polly having "made up matter with aunt weatly before her Death." Susanna's attachment to Phillis might have had something to do with their breach. Polly never got to go to London! Such a grievance would mirror, suggestively, her twin brother Nathaniel's resentful behavior and his disinclination to return home, which Wallcut also noted drily in his letter.

In addition to intensive caretaking, Phillis had a new job: trying to sell her book, even as she waited for the ship with the bound volumes to come in. Like other colonists, she used opportunities provided by friends who traveled—in her case, enslaved men like Primus Babcock or ministers like Ebenezer Pemberton—to send letters to other friends, or friends of the Wheatleys', who could act as distributors. When she wrote to David Wooster in New Haven, Connecticut, she was able, thanks to Babcock, to express pleasure at the knowledge of the Woosters' good health before "taking the Freedom to transmit to you, a short Sketch of my voyage and return from London where I went for the recovery of my health as advised by my Physician." Like the trip itself, the narrative of the trip served as a polite bid for patronage. She informed Wooster of her legal freedom before launching into the more material purpose of the letter: she had "enclos'd Proposals" for her book, about to arrive, and asked him frankly to "use your interest with Gentlemen & Ladies of your acquaintance to subscribe also, for the more subscribers there are, the more it will be to my advantage as I am to have half the sale of the Books." She had to be bold in asking, "for I am now upon my own footing and whatever I get by this is entirely mine, & it is the Chief I have to depend upon."

She also had to ask for something more. In the absence of copyright protection that could extend effectively to the colonies, she wanted Wooster to use his influence to make sure that no pirated edition came from the printers in Connecticut, "as it will be a great hurt to me, preventing any further Benefit that I might receive from the Sale of my Copies from England." After telling Wooster the price (two shillings, six pence extra for a bound book), she revealed that she had already taken an unusual precaution before leaving England: personalizing the books by autographing them. "If any should be so ungenerous as to reprint them the Genuine Copy may be known" by her signature on the frontispiece. This probably had involved signing the first folded sheets of the initial printing of three hundred before the rest of the sheets were printed and bound. She wrote similar letters to Obour Tanner in Newport, who loyally distributed the books and collected the shillings.

So did Tanner's pastor, the Reverend Samuel Hopkins; the longtime family friend and model celebrity Samson Occom in New London; and several printers.

Wheatley showed tremendous business sense. She had returned confident. The worry about a pirated edition suggests real expectations for sales. Yet so much was changing at the end of 1773. The newspapers were filled with the resistance to the Tea Act, which delayed the landing of the *Dartmouth*, the ship owned by the Rotches that carried boxes of *Poems on Various Subjects, Religious and Moral* in addition to 114 controversial chests of tea. The *Dartmouth* sailed into the harbor on November 28, but angry crowds and a town committee did not allow it to unload anything. While the patriots decided to let Francis Rotch bring other cargo besides the tea into town after a tense several days, the ensuing Boston Tea Party postponed her book's initial distribution and newspaper advertisements, which finally appeared in January.

Meanwhile, in addition to Susanna's illness, the seventy-year-old Reverend John Moorhead suffered the last of a series of strokes and died in early December. The Moorheads and Wheatleys had remained very close. John Lathrop and Ebenezer Pemberton served as pallbearers; "a Great Concourse of People attended this Funeral." Wheatley penned an especially lengthy elegy, addressed to the Moorheads' daughter Mary, which appeared as a broadside after the funeral on December 15. The poem lingers longer on death's terrors and the feelings of loss than some of her earlier elegies before moving on to depict Moorhead as a prophet as well as an effective saver of souls. The printer reproduced Wheatley's dating of the manuscript and her signature below the verses, confirming her ownership of herself and her work.

The obituaries and the funeral sermon alike stressed Moorhead's "just abhorrence of all duplicity and deceit." The Reverend David MacGregor, his fellow Presbyterian, even chose as his text "That they are not all Israelites, which are of Israel." Occom, also a friend of Moorhead's, was an expert on this theme, and he thought on it a great deal in early 1774 as he depended on John Thornton, via Phillis and Susanna, for a contribution of £25 to keep a roof over his large family. Like Wheatley, Occom faced an uncertain future even as he experienced a renewed celebrity. His execution sermon for his fellow native Moses Paul became a quick bestseller in 1772, going through nineteen editions and helping to turn him into an intertribal figure who spoke for as well as to Native peoples. It may have enabled him to publish the hymnal he had been working on for some time. Yet like Wheatley he was still scrambling for economic, moral, and political support.

Sometime very early in the new year Occom wrote a now-missing letter to Phillis on matters of particular concern to both of them, including "the Negroes" and their "natural Rights." Occom probably had been trying out sermon material. Few of his unpublished efforts from these years survive, but during the 1780s he would pointedly criticize slaveholding ministers and call out the hypocrisy of those who "inslave the poor Negroes in such barbarous manner, as out do the savage Indians in North America, and these are called Christian Nations." It's also likely he was inspired by the revival of the antislavery petition campaign in Massachusetts, now extended in late 1773 to the direct lobbying of legislators. More antislavery essays appeared in newspapers: in this round, the patriot printers in New England found it harder to keep their distance in the wake of renewed accusations of hypocrisy, much as the *Boston Gazette* had recently found it harder to ignore Wheatley. Occom's local paper in Connecticut had run a poem by "A Negro" a year and a half before that complained "Of inconsistent men, who wish to find / A partial god to vindicate their cause, / And plead their freedom, while they break its laws" as well as an antislavery essay by "O.," possibly Occom himself. And the day before Phillis received Occom's letter, Thomas's *Spy* ran an essay by "A Son of AFRICA" that asked if the New Englanders' hearts were not as "hard" as "the Britains . . . when you hold them in slavery that are intitled to liberty, by the law of nature, as equal as yourselves." At least natives got missionaries, Son of Africa argued pointedly. Slavery wasn't reasonable; it wasn't biblical; it arguably wasn't even, post-*Somerset*, "the law of Great-Britain."

In her reply to Occom, which might have been meant only for his eyes, Wheatley lays out all these antislavery arguments in elegant and persuasive terms:

> Rev'd and honor'd Sir,
>
> I HAVE this Day received your obliging kind Epistle, and am greatly satisfied with your Reasons respecting the Negroes, and think highly reasonable what you offer in Vindication of their natural Rights: Those that invade them cannot be insensible that the divine Light is chasing away the thick Darkness which broods over the Land of Africa; and the Chaos which has reign'd so long, is converting into a beautiful Order, and reveals more and more clearly, the glorious Dispensation of civil and religious Liberty, which are so inseparably united, that there is little or no Enjoyment of the one without the other.

The "heathen" excuse for enslaving in order to save souls was no longer going to cut it in a world with Wheatleys and Occoms. Wheatley is talking to the person who was most like her in 1774—as a race man—about what their own fame means. Occom rehearsed an argument he would later make; Wheatley extended hers as well.

Wheatley hints for the first time at the kind of civil "Chaos" that she likely experienced as a victim of war and the slave trade, and why she valued an "order" in Boston that seemed to value her. The patriots like John Lathrop, who were insisting that politics did belong in the pulpit, had a point—one that applied to slavery as well, she continued:

> Otherwise, perhaps, the Israelites had been less solicitous for their Freedom from Egyptian Slavery; I do not say they would have been contented without it, by no Means, for in every

human Breast, God has implanted a Principle, which we call Love of Freedom; it is impatient of Oppression, and pants for Deliverance; and by leave of our modern Egyptians I will assert, that the same Principle lives in us. God grant Deliverance in his own Way and Time, and get him honour upon all those whose Avarice impels them to countenance and help forward the Calamities of their fellow Creatures. This I desire not for their Hurt, but to convince them of the strange Absurdity of their Conduct whose Words and Actions are so diametrically opposite. How well the cry for Liberty, and the reverse Disposition for the exercise of oppressive Power over others agree,—I humbly think it does not require the Penetration of a Philosopher to determine.

Occom's comments about slavery and true religion had invited Wheatley to be more expansive still, to treat slavery more directly than by simile and more pointedly in relation to faith. Old Testament precedents for slavery's limitation and emancipation were already part of the debate. Exodus, in particular, "swings between a religious and political symbol" since the English Revolution of the seventeenth century, when the phrase "civil and religious liberty," suggesting their inseparability, became commonplace. So was the notion of national punishments for national sins. If God punished the Egyptians and later the Hebrews for their disobedience, the Americans were likely to be punished for the sin of slavery.

Wheatley's remarks on patriot hypocrisy spoke especially to the New England moment of early 1774, in the wake of the violent and divisive Boston Tea Party (which Lord Mansfield would call "the last overt act of high treason"), the increased reliance upon natural rights arguments, and even overt calls for independence by the patriots there. The new, bolder version of Felix Holbrook's petition against African slavery had been read in the Massachusetts legislature on January 26. A watered-down bill focusing on the slave trade, advanced this time by the radical Samuel Adams among others, would pass on March 8, only to be left in limbo when Governor Hutchinson conveniently dissolved the General Court the next day. He would veto it, again, at the next opportunity. A similar measure, against the slave trade, was being considered in Connecticut. The religious argument predicting divine chastisement waxed stronger in the wake of political uncertainty.

If New England patriots were comparing themselves to the ancient Hebrews—possibly punished but praying to be saved—who were Wheatley's "modern Egyptians"? No one had used that explicit phrase before in print in the colonies. Joseph Warren had recently complained of the "Egyptian darkness" covering the General Court under threat of dismissal by Governor Hutchinson. Anthony Benezet had pronounced the enslavement of Africans to be "worse than Egyptian Bondage," with good reason. In the preface to a reprint of his poem "The Dying Negro," the English poet Thomas Day had very recently chided American "inconsistency" and called Americans worse than Spartans. Granville Sharp had picked up the Quaker theme of God's likely retribution and stressed the threat slavery posed to ancient liberties that had passed from the Hebrew republic to the English. In the first issue of Isaiah Thomas and Joseph Greenleaf's *Royal American Magazine* in January, "A Christian" wrote to support the antislavery bill, asserting that "unless we give that liberty to others, for which we contend, I cannot hope that the *righteous Lord who loveth righteousness*, will smile upon us, and give us the blessing of freedom—while we refuse to extend freedom to our fellow men, our principles are narrow and corrupt."

None of these, however, had explicitly called contemporary slavery "modern" as opposed to ancient—even though the same writer ("A Christian") would turn right around a few months later and use the phrase "modern Egyptians" to apply to the British in the wake of the oppressive Boston Port Act. Wheatley had something else in mind: the larger debate about ancient and modern learning, and poetry, that had made her use of classical forms so pregnant with implications. To refer to "our modern Egyptians" raised the question of American modernity, American progress, in a more profound, encompassing, and disturbing sense. She raised the distinct possibility that it was not the English but rather the Americans who were sending history backward and represented the worst, not the best, of ancient traditions—because of slavery. Africans and natives, more than white Americans, deserved divine deliverance from modern corruptions.

When we consider how radical and how direct Wheatley could sound in a private letter to Occom, leaving simile behind, it begins to appear tremendously important that Occom decided to publish this part of the letter in the *Connecticut Gazette*, and almost certainly without Wheatley's explicit permission—and that it was quickly reprinted in ten other newspapers, including Boston's *Spy*, *Post-Boy*, *Evening-Post*, and *News-Letter* (but not the arch-patriot *Gazette*). Could this have been what Wheatley intended? Occom did not claim responsibility explicitly, but the identification of the "Negro Girl of Mr. Wheatley's," at a time when she was twenty-one and no longer actually belonged to Mr. Wheatley, sounds like Occom or someone else who had known her at some distance for a long time, but not intimately. Occom himself had many children and had recently referred to Phillis, in a September letter to Susanna, as "the little Miss." Given that he had been asked to sell her books, ads for which had recently appeared in the same paper, perhaps he was thinking that by emphasizing her youth in publicizing this letter as "a Specimen of her Ingenuity," as the brief prefacing note claimed, he could do as he'd been asked while making their agreed-upon political points innocently enough. Another factor might have tempted him. There was no more risk of Susanna's disapproval: she had died the previous week, on March 2. The report of her death appeared in Boston papers before the local reprintings of the letter.

Still, for Phillis Wheatley, the widespread publication of this letter, coinciding with Susanna's death, was a striking instance of the difficulty of controlling how she appeared in the press after achieving

celebrity. (It was a lesson that Benjamin Franklin, as successful a ma-
nipulator of print and personae as had ever lived, was about to learn in
the worst of ways after his forwarding of Thomas Hutchinson's private
letters blew up in the scandal that led to his humiliation before the
Board of Trade and the loss of his Crown-appointed postmastership.)
There are indications that with Wheatley's book publication drawing
out into an extended process, her patronage issues unresolved at best,
and the colonial and slavery controversies heating each other to a boil,
she was already mulling when and under what circumstances publishing in newspapers under her name actually worked to her advantage
and when it did not.

Wheatley's fame and good reviews surely continued to open doors,
but they also meant more would be at stake in what she wrote and how
she circulated her poems. She was taking more control—as, for example, with "On Night and Sleep," the eight lines she published anonymously in the friendly confines of the *Connecticut Gazette* in October
1771, and again in the *Spy* in January 1773, before rewriting several of
its lines as part of a longer poem in her book. Her longtime fan John
Andrews registered her withholding of poems when he complained in
January 1774 that "after so long a time, have at last got Phillis's poems
in print," but "these dont seem to be near all her productions, She's an
artful jade, I believe, & intends to have ye benefit of another volume."

Andrews, a merchant, followed the money even when he thought
about poetry, and of course Phillis had to as well. But she also had other,
not unrelated motives for saving some poems, in addition to political
and personal reasons for keeping certain verses out of her London edition. Much as she had done with her English opportunities, she needed
to cultivate patrons and friendly printers in Boston and beyond all the
more carefully given Susanna's demise. The meaning of her emancipation remained under construction while she continued to live in the
Wheatley mansion and tried to collect her shilling per volume of *Poems*. Moreover, she must have felt as if under a microscope, as famous

people, enslaved people, and racially marked people do. Her field of play had grown immeasurably, as had her artistic range. Yet in some ways, her margin for error had shrunk.

During this period, between December 1773 and June 1774, for the first time, a series of unsigned poems appeared—in the *Boston Post-Boy*, Isaiah Thomas's *Spy*, his new *Royal American Magazine*, and the Thomas-affiliated *Essex Journal* in Newburyport—that have key characteristics of Wheatley's writing. These include the use of classical terms like "Aurora" and "Phoebus" that were rarely used by other poets publishing in North America. Other more common but still quintessentially Wheatleyan images, phrases, and stylistic signatures also appear in these poems (see Tables 1 and 2 in the appendix).

Three of these venues were distinguished by having a regular "Poet's Corner" (the *Spy*), a section for "Poetical Essays" (the *Royal American Magazine*), or a "Parnassian Packet" (*Essex Journal*) where unsigned or pseudonymous submissions appeared. In England, "magazines offered [to poets] a way of gaining exposure and building relationships with printers and booksellers." Other Boston printers had signaled receptivity, but she would have known by then that most publishers of books and broadsides struggled from year to year, as the most frequent printer of antislavery pamphlets, Ezekiel Russell, currently did (he had just moved to Salem). By sending new poems anonymously into the network of Isaiah Thomas, the most ambitious and successful young Boston printer, and working with his present and former partners who had also shown a willingness to publish material sympathetic to Africans and to antislavery, Wheatley could look to the future without making her still-new book seem dated or incomplete, as John Andrews charged. She also could experiment a bit without every effort having to be measured in the political cauldron she had stirred.

While publishing was "no longer suspect" for women, anonymous publication remained the norm rather than the exception during the eighteenth century, and especially for novelists, poets, and women.

The benefits of having one's name attached to one's verse varied. Anonymity could lend poems an "impersonal authority." Some famous authors—perhaps most notably and notoriously Swift and Pope—played with anonymity in order to satirize, for personal and political reasons. "Being guessed at might be a writer's ambition," as the literary historian John Mullan puts it, and "mischief and modesty could go together." Readers, in turn, came to relish the guessing as a literary parlor game.

Maybe Wheatley was also playing. She might have feared that some, even many people wouldn't understand how she could write at all while Susanna, the mistress of the house if no longer of her, lay dying. If so, she started as safely as possible. The first of these anonymous poems that suggest her authorship, an elegy for the merchant's daughter Elizabeth Inches "by a Friend," appeared with the death notice in the *Boston Post-Boy*, a very common way of publishing the traditional elegies that were sometimes passed around in manuscript (as in the case of the infant Charles Eliot) or in broadside form (as in the case of her elegies for the Hubbards and the Moorheads). Her earlier poem on Samuel Marshall had also first appeared without attribution in a newspaper.

"Betsey" Inches, as in other Wheatley elegies, "flies" to "Realms unknown" and "her Saviour's Arms," before the poet turns to her father and his mourning. Much less commonly in a New England funeral elegy, however, Inches appears not only as a "Daughter" and "Friend" but also as "Mistress" of "Servants." This other constituency, people Wheatley might have known better but had never written about specifically in verse as far as we know with the exception of Scipio Moorhead, appears as mourners: "Her Faithful Servants the sad Loss deplore, / Their lov'd young Mistress is to them no more. / The fair Companions of her tender Youth / Her fate lament with Sympathy and Truth." Did Phillis belong with the "Servants" (a term that both included and euphemized the enslaved), or with "the fair Companions" in December 1773, or with both? Or could she talk about servants explicitly because she was suddenly no longer one? Not everyone knew of the legal change, not yet. It still depended on who else was in the room, who was the audience. Knowing fans might have picked up on the lack of specificity here, but those who really knew her writing would have cinched the task of identifying the author when the second stanza invoked one of Wheatley's more frequently invoked abstractions, "Recollection," and ended with the invocation of "my daring Muse"—the kind of self-referential gesture that appeared more and more often in Wheatley's poems. In 1773, as we have seen, Wheatley regularly referred to her muse, an understandable result of being celebrated as a poet and continually quizzed about her method and her inspiration. Muse talk was itself another classical simile for sacred and for human motives.

A month later, the *Essex Journal* and the *Spy* both published a poem for the new year to "oblige a Customer." These verses too signaled Wheatley, with her favorite classical figures, signature pentameter, and, self-consciously as ever, her muse. In Boston that year, New Year's blessings had to recognize civil strife, not least because the Poet's Corner in Thomas's papers had been filled with patriot calls to defend liberty. So she prays that "No sound of war . . . Nor war-like drums, nor trumpet wake the spring, / Nor fatal battles, the ripe autumn bring." The poem ends with a clear endorsement of the Whig cause, but in the earlier, less bellicose terms of reciprocal obligations and British belonging, with no villains named but rather ample room to be read variously by those who might find blame on both sides for the affair of the tea.

Another poem, "The Triumph of the Redeemer," published January 24 in the *Post-Boy*, combined the themes of heavenly flight and poetic inspiration in the Betsey Inches and New Year's verses. The ostensible subject matter—Christ's rising—almost gets lost in the rapture of composition, equally joined by the angels. The poet sounds unmistakably happy, "transported"—delighted to be writing, and writing about being delighted:

> SOME seraph teach my daring song to rise,
> O! Let me catch the music of the skies;
> Illume my breast, exalt, refine the whole,
> And pour melodious numbers on my soul.
> What glories burst on my transported sight!
> What charms with more than mortal beauty bright!
> What anthems ring! What melting lays inspire!
> What god-like angels strike the sounding lyre!

For all the ways the angels inspire awe, there is less humility and more self-regard than in the earlier, signed religious poems. Wheatley strives for Christian humility and "a Soul united to Jesus" in the letters she wrote in late 1773 and early 1774 to John Thornton and Obour Tanner after her return from London, repeatedly anticipating their admonitions and asking to be remembered in their "closet" of private prayer. As in this poem, she expressed to Thornton a desire to "meditate continually" on Jesus's sacrifice for mankind's sins, "which Angels are continually exploring, yet not equal to the search." But freed from the gaze of her pious friends, with her name unattached to the effort, her religion seems concerned less with salvation and more with soulful expansiveness—even ecstasy—and the poet's "finer art." Poetic conventions, yes—but hers in particular. Wheatley's readers would have recognized her familiar godly call, angelic response, invocation of "soul," "heav'nly" replies, and references to her "daring song" and "lays," while Aurora, her favorite classical figure, once again shines.

Susanna's illness and death, also a theme of her surviving letters to Tanner and Thornton, amplified these themes of salvation and vocation, and surely provided some of the inspiration (and night thoughts). Only "through the goodness of God" had Mrs. Wheatley persisted "in a very weak & languishing Condition" for so long. "To alleviate our sorrows we had the satisfaction to se[e] her depart in inexpressible raptures, earnest longings & impatient thirstings for the *upper* Courts of the Lord," she wrote to Obour. Wheatley described the quintessential

Good Death, as confirmed by Christopher Wallcut, who wrote to his brother that "[Aunt Susanna] had her senses till the Last moment, and I may venter to say she die a penetant Christian." To Thornton too, Wheatley limned something more dramatic and moving:

> About a half hour before her Death, she spoke with more audible voice, than she had 3 months before. She called her friends and relations around her, and charged them not to leave their great work undone until *that* hour, but to fear God, and keep his Commandments, being ask'd if her faith faild her She answer'd, No. She Spr[ead] out her arms crying come! come quickly! come, come! O pray for an easy and quick Passage! She eagerly longed to depart to be with Christ . . . I sat the whole time by her bed Side, and Saw with Grief and Wonder, the Effects of Sin on the human race.

For months Susanna had prayed aloud for Nathaniel, still in England with his new bride, and for Phillis, at least according to Phillis. Except for the broadside elegy for Reverend Moorhead, Phillis didn't admit to writing or publishing anything new: there are no published poems or extant manuscripts from this period besides the ten letters that constitute more than half of those that survive in her hand. We know that Susanna was thinking enough of the matter to explicitly forbid that Phillis write anything about *her*. The female patron who had encouraged her elegies wanted no elegy. She knew Phillis well enough to know that if she had, Phillis would be rehearsing it in the nights, weeks, months before she met the Lord. This might have been the final act of humility of a pious woman who liked to erase her presence, or it might have been a way to retain her caretaker's full attention. It surely suggests the degree of control she exerted in the house on King Street and beyond.

If Phillis Wheatley had grown up, and grown outward, on her trip to London, and if her soul expanded upon being free and receiving money for her work, these deathbed months also reminded her of limits—to her health, to her patronage system, to her writerly practice, to her identity and prospects as an author. The moment of emancipation was also a moment of death, and everyone in Boston knew what the death of white people could mean for black people. Emancipation from Susanna Wheatley meant something astonishing and of course open-ended, something that could contribute to a new burst of creativity: as she affirmed to Samson Occom, enslaved people pant for deliverance. But this freedom also meant loss. "Let us imagine the loss of a Parent, Sister or Brother the tenderness of all these were united in her," she wrote to Obour, to whom she had little reason to dissemble about this. To someone else who had lost parents and siblings, she could speak from experience.

Susanna was her enslaver and yet something like kin by adoption. Phillis did feel in some measure chosen, rescued from a still worse fate: "I was a poor little outcast & a stranger when she took me in: not only into her house but I presently became a sharer in her most tender affections," perhaps even at the emotional if not material expense of Susanna's own surviving biological children and grandchildren. To Obour she could say it, without shame or fear of judgment, dropping for a moment the evangelical frame: "I was treated by her more like a child than her Servant; no opportunity was left unimprov'd, of giving me the best of advice," perhaps in ways that had not worked quite so well with Susanna Wheatley's actual, thirty-year-old twin children, but which Phillis now praised as "terms how tender! how engaging"— terms that, after all, were something like what she was aiming for in her recent poems, published anonymously at a moment when she couldn't be certain how she'd be judged or taken care of, or exactly who or where her audience, or future family, might be.

Two more poems on night appeared in the *Royal American Magazine* during the two months that followed, one in the first issue after Susanna's death. Where in "On Night and Sleep" "Night spreads her sable curtains round," the darkness in this later "sable night" poem is more uncertain and interior, even as she invokes two social types on constant display in Boston—the "chiefs of bloody battles" and the "sleeping virgins" who dream of "courtship." Now night is a time, most of all, of "*Contemplation*." Her "muse" can "begin the song! / The theme, his power, to whom these scenes belong, / Whose word omnisic form'd the beauteous earth, / And call'd the radiant sun and moon to birth!"

She could hope, as she contemplated the money that Obour remitted along with her "good advices[, to] be resigned to the afflicting hand of a Seemingly frowning Providence . . . that while he strikes one Comfort *dead* he raises up another." But her night poems express the uncertainties. The coming of "Solemn night," in "On Night" published in June, can "sooth each pain, and drive each care away . . . ease the anxious heart of thrilling fear, / While flattering hope deludes each starting tear." In night's silence, however, "wild Ambition plans each airy scheme, / But blasting Envy poisons ev'ry dream." A free, published Wheatley, not knowing what her readers or even what the living but possibly envious Wheatleys might mean for her own dreams, had more secrets than ever to keep, and more need for those hours before "fair Aurora reassumes her sphere."

20

THE BARBARIANS

Captain Calef returned from London in May, again without Nathaniel Wheatley, but with another three hundred copies of *Poems*, a second printing. Phillis wrote as soon as she could, via Ebenezer Pemberton, to Obour Tanner and to Samuel Hopkins in Newport to let them know she had more books. A third shipment would arrive in late June. In New London, Connecticut, books could be purchased from the local printer Timothy Green. Samson Occom also had "a few." The book was selling—modestly, but selling.

The enslaved and their allies in New England had cause for optimism as well. Wheatley's February 11 letter to Occom was not the only voice calling the patriots on their hypocrisy, which was one reason why it reverberated in ten more newspapers. Ezekiel Russell put out an edition of the attorney Francis Hargrave's argument on behalf of Somerset, advertising its relevance to a freedom case about to be tried in Massachusetts. In May and June, the new governor, Thomas Gage, received even more forceful petitions addressed to him as "Captain General and Governor in Chief in and over This Province," and secondarily to "the Honourable his Majestys Council and the Honourable House of Representatives," from "a Grate [Great] Number of Blackes of this Province." This mode of address covered all bases and also hedged their bets. For these Afro-Yankees, the power struggle in the empire remained an opportunity.

Though actual legislation stalled, antislavery activists were in a stronger position than ever in Boston for several reasons. Public opinion appeared to be shifting, though not because of any decline in the enslaved population or of the market for them: sale and fugitive ads continued to appear regularly. The patriots' responsiveness to antislavery reflected the political situation in the empire. Massachusetts, and particularly Boston, risked isolation after the Tea Party, as word reached London of Massachusetts's refusal to apologize or pay for the tea, and the administration considered its response. In a series of essays in a London paper, the former Boston printer John Mein resurfaced as "Sagittarius," an expert on the "barbarous" Boston mobbing and tarring and feathering that he had experienced himself. He repeated his claims from years earlier that Bostonian smugglers always blamed their selfish, economically motivated political violence on "Strangers, Boys, Negroes and [now] Mohawks." The Tea Party proved that it was actually local Tories, threatened with violence, who were "groaning under worse than Egyptian bondage." Bostonians talked and talked of government ministers "forging infernal chains" and "galling fetters," yet "notwithstanding the immutable laws of nature, and the public resolution of their own Town Meeting, they actually have in town two thousand Negroe slaves, who neither by themselves in person, nor by representatives of their own free election ever gave consent to their present state of bondage." Mein's mockery of patriot arguments for representation in light of the enslavement of what he estimated to be 13 percent of the population (two thousand out of about fifteen thousand) must have been especially galling to patriots. His tally of just three thousand men actually "able but not willing to fight" was positively chilling.

Not as chilling, though, as the Boston Port Act and the other measures together known as the Coercive Acts, which arrived with Governor-General Gage in early May 1774. "Imagine to yourself the horror painted in the faces of a string of slaves condemn'd by the In-

quisition to perpetual drudgery at the oar! Such is the dejection im-
printed on every countenance," reported John Andrews. The printer
John Boyle predicted "undistinguished Ruin" for "Thousands of our
Inhabitants," since trade would be disallowed and even transportation
of essential supplies severely restricted. Coasting ships would have to
be cleared in Marblehead; the government itself would be removed
to Salem. (When Nathaniel Wheatley finally returned in September,
Phillis wrote that his two-month passage had been made even more
"tedious" by having to proceed through Salem.) Parliament chose to
make an example of Boston by forbidding town meetings more than
once a year—but also punished Massachusetts as a whole by increasing
the executive and appointive powers of the governor while switching
appointments to the council to now be made by the king. The out-
voted opposition in Parliament didn't hesitate to accuse the ministry
of desiring to "enslave America." They added that Americans would be
"abject slaves" if they consented, so New Englanders didn't feel at all
provincial when they doubled down on their favorite metaphor that
was more than a metaphor. It was up to folks like Mein and Wheatley
to push the contradictions as radical Whigs like Samuel Adams increasingly conceded the justice of antislavery and even supported the
enslaved men's petitions and then moved on to business as usual in
their calls for intercolonial support.

The blockade of Boston, to be enforced by the navy, began officially
on June 1. British officialdom had responded to what Mein had called
Boston barbarism with a siege that Adams and the Committee of Correspondence called "barbarous" in turn. Over the course of the rest
of the year, thousands left the city for the countryside. Other Massachusetts towns then became the hotbeds of radicalism as rural people
detected threats to their political liberties if not their livelihoods. Ver-
bally and physically intimidated Tories in the towns began to flee to
Boston. Meanwhile, Boston began to experience a second occupation,
regiment by regiment in greater numbers than ever, marching once
again from the wharf up King Street and camping on the Common for

months despite a special Quartering Act passed to require the town to house them suitably. By November there were four thousand soldiers, outnumbering those whom Mein had called the able-bodied men of Boston. That was not all. The navy had been tasked with enforcement, which meant more ships and sailors as well.

"Like an African habituated to slavery I begin to be a bit more reconcil'd to the loss of business and an inactive state of life," the merchant Andrews wrote in August. While he blamed the radicals for letting things get out of hand, he was cheered by the support of the country people who sent supplies and resolutions of support: "It won't be for want of *their* endeavours if they [the British] don't make slaves of the whole continent." Meanwhile, the Reverend John Allen, author of the notable patriot *Oration upon the Beauties of Liberty* in 1772, published a revised version and a new fast day sermon in which he amplified the petitions of the Africans and argued that keeping slaves was a sin and a direct cause of the patriots' worsening troubles. In a footnote he praised several men who had emancipated their slaves. Tories grew more vocal and more adept at calling out the "prostitution of words" with which Americans talked of their enslavement. "No People ever so cruelly enslaved their Fellow-Creatures as the Americans; and even the Savages, use not their captive Enemies, with more Barbarity," insisted William Allen, a wealthy merchant and chief justice of the Supreme Court of Pennsylvania who had resigned and sailed for London.

Abigail Adams, writing to her husband, John, at the Continental Congress in Philadelphia, testified to a recurrence of the events of the first occupation, when certain British soldiers and Boston slaves had appeared to contemplate an alliance. "There has been in Town a conspiracy of the Negroes. At present it is kept pretty private and was discoverd by one who endeavourd to diswaid them from it—he being threatned with his life, applied to justice Quincy [Adams's cousin] for protection." This time, it appeared to Adams, British officialdom considered more seriously arming the enslaved because the idea had come from Africans themselves.

They conducted in this way—got an Irishman to draw up a petition ~~letting~~ to the Govener telling him they would fight for him provided he would arm them and engage to liberate them if he conquerd, and it is said that he attended so much to it as to consult Pircy [Earl Percy, Gage's second-in-command] upon it, and one [Lieut.?] Small has been very buisy and active. There is but little said, and what Steps they will take in consequence of it I know not.

In 1774, the solution of emancipation seemed to Abigail Adams not only logical and maybe even possible but worth underlining when writing to someone as politically connected as her husband. She added, "I wish most sincerely there was not a Slave in the province. It allways appeard a most iniquitious Scheme to me—fight ourselfs for what we are daily robbing and plundering from those who have as good a right to freedom as we have. You know my mind upon this Subject."

Wheatley, who had been called a former barbarian in the proposal for and preface to her own book, had been emancipated at least in part because of the debate over patriot hypocrisy and slavery. She had friends, possible patrons, and debts—what she called "gratitude"—on both sides of the increasingly heated Anglo-American conversation over who were the enslavers and who the barbarians. Though already emancipated, she had much invested in how this controversy about barbarism and American identity would develop. She also had as deep an understanding about its terms as anyone, because she had for years been participating and had even become a talking point in it. The debate's intensification spelled risk as well as opportunity.

No poems survive in her hand, or appeared under her name in print, from 1774 or early 1775, leading some scholars to infer that this was a period when she began to suffer neglect, even a fatal change of fortune. Margaretta Odell, the white Wheatleys' grandniece writing during the 1830s, insisted that Phillis was "utterly desolate" and alone after Susanna's death. Then again, Odell also had heard that even after

London Phillis remained "the same single-hearted, unsophisticated being." In October, Phillis told John Thornton of the "reserve" that had been "put on" by "those who seem'd to respect me while under my mistress's patronage." This is the most direct evidence of Susanna Wheatley's power and effectiveness in Boston that has survived, outstripping anything that the Wheatley descendants would venture to say or perhaps could even imagine about their eighteenth-century forebear. Yet even this statement of disappointment suggests that Phillis continued to actively promote herself and her book. What she posited to Thornton as an effect of the loss of Susanna and "patronage" was also an effect of her emancipation and the ambiguity of her status and prospects in the eyes of those who had known her as enslaved.

She certainly still had admirers who sought her out. Deborah Cushing enthusiastically sent a copy of *Poems* to her husband, Thomas, Speaker of the Massachusetts House and, in September 1774, a delegate to the Continental Congress in Philadelphia. To explain why she took the trouble, which her husband "may wonder about," she suggested that he might not want to be in select company in Philadelphia without knowing Wheatley's work: "Mrs. Dickerson & Mrs. Clymer Mrs. Bullock," all wives of delegates to Congress, "with some other Ladys were so pleased with phillis & her performances they bought her Books and got her to compose some pieces for them. I thought it would be very . . . agreeabel." Mary Norris Dickinson and Elizabeth Meredith Clymer were Philadelphians and intimates of some of the women, like Hannah Griffitts, who had circulated Wheatley's poems years before, but Mary DeVeaux Bulloch was from Savannah, Georgia. Did Thomas Cushing, pleading Massachusetts's case to the other colonies as they banned imports including slaves, find his wife's gift as agreeable as she thought he should? He didn't necessarily need his own copy: the Library Company of Philadelphia, which had opened its shelves to Congress, already had one.

Whether Deborah Cushing actually had helped distribute copies or was just keeping up with fashions, her enthusiasm and networking show that some things had not changed for Wheatley after her emancipation, in 1774. She was still in demand. She also still lived with the Wheatleys. Young Thomas Wallcut, the Dartmouth College student and nephew of the Wheatleys', wrote her affectionately with a request to be "recommended to all your"—not *my*—"Dear family." The Reverend John Lathrop signaled his continued appreciation and recognition of her ambitions and prospects, as well as their connection, with the gift of a three-volume set of books, *The Beauties of the English Stage* (1756). This collection of "the most Affecting and Sentimental Passages, Soliloquies, Similies, Descriptions, &c. in the English Plays, Ancient and Modern" was more than a tea-table tome and strikingly different from the devotionals and sermons she had been gifted by other ministers. In an age when plays were often still in verse, this was in effect a greatest hits poetry collection and reference work, organized by subjects from "Absence" and "Action" to "Youth" and "Zeal," perfect for reading aloud in company—or for writerly inspiration. This present, like Cushing's letter, suggests that at least some Bostonians tried to make a free Phillis Wheatley feel at home—even as the astute Abigail Adams identified Africans, and some Africans identified themselves, as political beings and potentially a fifth column.

The Reverend Samuel Hopkins had a different idea as to where Phillis might belong. Encouraged by the conversion of numerous Africans in his congregation during Sarah Osborn's revival, he had developed plans to send two of these men, John Quamine and Bristol Yamma, to the College of New Jersey and then to West Africa as missionaries. Once there they would assist the Afro-British Reverend Philip Quaque, who had been laboring in isolation as a chaplain at Cape Coast Castle for some years. Several years before, Samson Occom had advanced the notion of Phillis's going to Africa as an extension of the Huntingdon circle's missionary enterprises. For Occom, as for Hopkins and

John Thornton, Phillis in Africa would be just like Occom evangelizing in Indian country. Members of the evangelical network saw this as a duty and the true purpose of the exceptional education certain former "savages" had received.

When Wheatley corresponded with Hopkins during the winter of 1774 about her books, she mentioned his published proposal, a solicitation for funds to send Quamine and Yamma to college and then to Africa. She pleaded the return of her asthma and Susanna Wheatley's illness to explain why it was "impracticable for me to do anything at present with respect to that paper, but what I can do in influencing my Christian friends and acquaintance to promote this laudable design shall not be wanting." She went on to express "sympathetic Joy to see at distant time the thick cloud of ignorance dispersing from the face of my benighted Country." But much as in the letter to Occom she wrote two days later, the acknowledgment of African misery and spiritual inferiority comes with a pointed judgment: "Europe and America have long been fed with the heavenly provision" of "know[ing] the Lord . . . and I fear they loathe it, while Africa is perishing with a Spiritual Famine."

Hopkins must have been excited by Wheatley's eloquent validation of the missionary project. It was in his interest to ignore how her carefully qualified embrace of the notion created a deliberate distance. He clearly respected her: he not only distributed her book but also wrote on the back of one of her letters that she was "much accomplished." At the same time, whether he realized it consciously or not, he was offering patronage, engaging in an exchange with someone at least as famous as he was, seeking an endorsement (in 1776 he'd simply use some of her letter as a blurb), and being flattered in turn. Wheatley took as well as gave. When she described Africa as her country and prayed to Hopkins, "O that they could partake of the crumbs, which fall from the table, of these distinguished children of the Kingdome," she was praising John Quamine, whom she probably knew personally as a friend of Tanner's. When she depicted Africans as starving for

God's word, she posed them as innocents "unprejudiced against the truth therefore tis to be hoped they would receive it with their Whole heart." When she cited "the divine royal Psalmist" (King David) on how "Ethiopia Shall Soon Stretch forth her hands Unto God," she offered her friends "Obour Tanner and I trust many others within your knowledge" as "living witnesses" and managed an elegant segue to a quite specific request that Hopkins convey her message: "Please give my love to her & I intend to write her soon." Signing on to Hopkins's Africa project with words alone, she was building her real community at home.

Hopkins, though, chose to take her words literally. He wrote her back with more information, including a West African geography lesson (she noted laconically, "I Observe your Reference to the Maps of Guinea & Salmon's Gazetteer, and shall consult them") and a detailed rendering of Reverend Quaque's "little or no *apparent* Success in his mission." In her subsequent response, she seems sympathetic to the Oxford-educated Quaque, more so than to his critic Hopkins. She hoped that the stories Hopkins spread about Quaque's ineffectiveness might turn out to be "only a misrepresentation," devoting her sympathy, and trademark irony, to the pious African Christian who, like her, operated under a white microscope: "Let us not be discouraged, but still hope that God will bring about this great work, tho' Phillip may *not* be the Instrument in the Divine Hand to perform this work of wonder, turning the Africans *from darkness to light*." She also hinted at the emotional intelligence and care that went into her own successes when she wondered "if Phillip would introduce himself properly to them, (I don't know the reverse) he might be more Successful; and in setting a good example which is more powerfully winning than Instruction." At the beginning and the end of this reply she got back to what mattered most materially to her: the distribution of her books.

This was more than horse, or book, trading. By then, it seems, Hopkins had conceived a more detailed plan of Phillis's going to Africa with his missionaries, perhaps as a wife to Quamine (who was actually already married) or Yamma or, eventually, Quaque. It's not clear when or even if he told Wheatley this, but he certainly told John Thornton, the man with the money and connections in England. When Thornton wrote to Phillis on August 1, in a letter he sent along with Nathaniel Wheatley to Boston, he didn't even bother dancing around the matter— while also proposing that he himself could replace Susanna as Phillis's "instruct[or] . . . in the principles of the true Religion." Wheatley responded by observing that the rest of the Wheatley family remained kind and that he really could not offer mentorship "from the great distance of your residence." She wasn't going to be controlled, much less married off, so easily. She reminded him of her emancipation, while acknowledging that even if she hadn't received her freedom, it was of course more important to "be a *Servant of Christ* and that is the most perfect freedom."

If this was a concession, it didn't cost much, and she exacted her price in the rest of the letter by subtly mocking the entire missionary project as a fantasy. Hopkins and Thornton couldn't put themselves in the shoes of Africans—either the ones they knew or the ones they didn't—and not least because they couldn't stop lumping them all together:

> You propose my returning to Africa with Bristol yamma and John Quamine if either of them upon Strict enquiry is Such, as I dare give my heart and hand to, I believe either of them good enough if not too good for me, or they would not be fit for missionaries; but why do you hon'd Sir, wish those poor men so much trouble as to carry me So long a voyage? Upon my arrival, how like a Barbarian Should I look to the Natives; I can promise that my tongue shall be quiet for a strong reason indeed being an utter stranger to the Language of Anamaboe.

"Now to be Serious," she added, signaling that she is actually amused by the absurdity of Thornton's idea and only getting started on her

objections, "This undertaking appears too hazardous, and not sufficiently Eligible, to go—and leave my British and American Friends."

British and American. Friends. Her language. *She* knew what it was
like to not speak the language, the real root meaning of "barbarian" in
Roman times. She was reminding Thornton, who should have known,
that she had prospects, she had friends, that she was as American and
as British as she was African. All three were her "country."

Besides, while Hopkins had "repeatedly informd me by Letters of
their pro[gress] in Learning also an Account of John Quamine's family
and Kingdom [in Anomabu]," she insisted that she had never actually
met Quamine or Yamma. This might not have been true, since fifteen months later she could tell Obour Tanner about spending a "very
agre[e]abl[e]" evening with Quamine, and if she knew him, she surely
knew too that he was already married. She was hardly "resign[ing]
it all to God's wise governance," as she stated in closing the letter to
Thornton. She was blasting, politely and firmly and yet with tongue in
cheek, what Thornton at least considered a "generous Offer."

In doing so, she deliberately called attention to the relativity, and
the politics, in the accusations of barbarism being thrown about in the
now intertwined debates about the empire and slavery. From an Anglo, Christian perspective, Africans needed saving. But they had their
own vantage point on who were the barbarians.

By then still another contender had emerged for the most barbaric
group in Boston. Bored, ill-housed, and ill-fed troops, in greater numbers than in 1770, began to return the resentment they received from
civilians. Their officers realized they were sitting atop a tinderbox—
that's why they were there—but it became more and more difficult to
prevent incidents like an armed showdown and mutual arrest at night
between the town watch and an officer. (One lieutenant blamed the
cheapness of drink in the rum-distilling town.) For months, General
and Governor Thomas Gage toed an excruciatingly careful line, agree-

ing to forbid soldiers to carry arms in the streets, for example: a change from the last occupation that made some of his men feel angry and vulnerable, like the settlers they policed. "I am in continual apprehension we shall soon experience another *fifth* of *March*, which God forbid!" wrote Andrews. By September, Gage was once again throwing up his hands in letters home, asking for twenty thousand troops, and executing sorties to seize arms from depots in the countryside. Meanwhile, independent militia companies trained, a rump Massachusetts Provincial Assembly met without the governor's permission, and Boston and Massachusetts patriots issued public pronouncements about the "barbarous cruelties" of the occupation and the "more than savage barbarity of the soldiers, encouraged and often joined and headed by the officers."

People in the towns responded with an outpouring of support for Boston and hostility to the king's men. It seemed as if, having talked for a decade about their looming enslavement, New Englanders had seen it, or made it, come true. Boston men were outnumbered; they faced violence at home; their friends fled. The most striking echo of actual enslavement, though, lay on water and shore, in the vessels and persons of the great British navy, tasked with enforcing the closing of the port and all trade. The army had to get along, to some extent, to survive living among civilians. For every flashy redcoat rogue who denounced Yankees and waved a sword, there was another who was willing to trade, break other rules, or toy with desertion. General Gage himself was married to an American, and his own staff began to appear to him as "a domesticated core of aging officers who were themselves virtually American."

The navy, by contrast, seemed disturbingly impersonal: oppression made systematic, even brutal. In his *Oration on the Beauties of Liberty*, John Allen sought to take away the legitimacy of the fleet by referring to naval officers as "pirate[s], who took away property without their consent, by violence." John Lathrop concurred and would use the same language in late 1775. The navy's job was to intimidate, and they followed an increasingly strict code of professional conduct that trumped local authorities. At their head from 1772 until July 1774, Admiral John Montagu had been chosen precisely because he was expected to take a harder line than previous commanders. The admiral complied. He constantly referred to colonists as "rascals, smugglers and rebels." John Adams complained in his diary that despite Montagu's "genteel" upbringing, he had "brutal, hoggish manners."

At this extended moment, when the issue of the troops became the symbol and reality of the patriot cause and the fulcrum of the emerging American identity, Phillis chose to write poems about naval officers. Her first, which doesn't survive but is listed in her 1779 proposal for a new volume, was addressed to the hated admiral Montagu himself. To Wheatley, paeans to navalists were de rigueur, part of being a British poet since Addison and Young. Naval subjects also extended the oceanic themes that characterized so much of her verse, from the poem to Hussey and Coffin to the Captain Hood tribute of 1769, from "Ode to Neptune" in her book to "Ocean" on her return from London. It would have been a departure not to write about the leading or admirable British gentlemen in arms, on land or sea, and she wasn't quite that "American" yet.

On October 30, the same day she wrote to John Thornton declining to sail to Africa as a missionary, she committed an ambitious poem, "To Lieut. R—— of the Royal Navy," under her name to the *Royal American Magazine*, where, as suggested earlier, she had published several poems anonymously. The editor Joseph Greenleaf, apparently a careful reader of Wheatley, published her poem and Lieutenant John Rochfort's reply together. He prefaced the first poem as "*by Philis (a young African, of surprising genius)*" along with his own comment on "*the importance of education*," the relativity of barbarism, and the ironies of modern slavery: "*It is probable* Europe *and* Affrica *would be alike* savage *or polite in the same circumstances; though it may be questioned, whether men who have no* artificial *wants, are capable of being so ferocious as those, who by faring* sumptuously every day, *are reduced to a habit of thinking it necessary to* their *happiness, to plunder the whole human race.*" Given this kind of sympathetic (and antislavery) introduction, it becomes easier to understand why Wheatley remained somewhat optimistic about her ability to please patriots, neutrals, and royally commissioned Britons at once.

She begins by identifying the "wondrous theme" of selfless, second-generation elite officers like Lieutenants John Rochfort and John Greaves, ripe for fame, with the comparable ambitions of the self-effacing muse-awakened poet. These officers are modest and public-spirited. They couldn't be more different from what patriot complaints described. From there, she takes a new kind of Homeric turn, playful and even flirtatious, which turns attention to herself as bard: "Had you appear'd on the Achaian shore / Troy had now stood, and Helen charm'd no more." Are military and poetic reputations for real? It is as if she were playing with her own reputation as well as theirs, freed to laugh in a game that is rendered less dangerous through neoclassical resonances.

But there is a real subject here, a principle beneath the over-the-top flattery. It is "purer joys in friendship's sacred flame, / The noblest gift, and of immortal kind, / That brightens, dignifies the manly mind." Friendship, one of her constant themes, was especially important in 1774. She isn't so much snatching a laurel or even modeling patronage again as she is remodeling the reoccupation of Boston, trying to find her way back in time to what she had called, in her letter to Thornton that same day, her "British and American friends."

Had she ended the poem there, she would have accomplished something that she had been trying to accomplish. Yet the situation seemed to require more. After an elegant gesture of humility ("Calliope, half gracious to my prayer, / Grants but the half and scatters half in air"), she returns to the praise with an almost terrifying picture of the oceanic Britons as akin to the storied classical gods in flight, bending nature and mere mortals (indigenous peoples, including Africans?) to their will. "From ocean sprung," Greaves and Rochfort, "two chiefs of matchless grace," appear like Neptune, or Homeric mortals seeking glory. Why would Wheatley seek to portray the cream of the British navy from the vantage of "trembling natives of the peaceful plain"? Which side is she on? While she hints at British violence, and in doing so reminds us who's writing, her very authenticity in seeing the "native" perspective while still acknowledging British supremacy makes the case she's still a bard of the empire. The British Phillis had an investment in an empire that, no matter what the radical patriots were saying, remains "in virtue's cause."

Rochfort's "Answer," dated December 2, makes it clear why her own effort couldn't be anonymous or pseudonymous: he names her directly as "WH—TL—Y," because he has been challenged by her lines to reply in kind with a poem as much about her specifically as hers was about him. Rochfort is as flirtatious as can be while reciprocating her praise: "Behold with reverence, and with joy adore; / The lovely daughter of the Affric shore, / Where every grace, and every virtue join, / That kindles friendship, and makes love divine." He can't resist a reference to her "hue as diff'rent as the souls above," and moves on to a picture of a "torrid" yet verdant, idealized Africa, "where nature taught (tho' strange it is to tell,) / Her flowing pencil Europe to excell." Sir Isaac Newton might have revealed nature's art, he writes, but Wheatley *is* nature's art. He follows her lead by claiming greatness for Britain as "sovereign of the deep," but also by echoing her hint of the dark side of empire. With Wheatley claiming the laurel for Africa, Britain "No more can boast, but of the power to kill, / By force of arms, or diabolic skill. / For softer strains, we quickly must repair / To Wheatly's song, for Wheatly is the fair; / That has the art, which art could ne'er acquire; / To dress each sentence with seraphic fire."

High praise, but she wasn't satisfied. Rochfort had put her on a solely African pedestal. He offered friendship but ignored her Britishness.

Her "Reply to the Answer in our last by the Gentleman in the Navy" is dated only three days later, even though it did not appear until the next, January 1775 issue of the *Royal American Magazine*. Wheatley

praises his song and notes how its high quality belies the "vain conceit" she might indulge if she focused only on his praise of her skill.
Instead, she feels "a soft affection" for him, "while I each golden sentiment admire / In thee, the muse's bright celestial fire." She seizes upon
his description of her as "a muse untutored," while adding, modestly
and obviously falsely, to his description of her that she is "unknown to
fame." Insisting, facetiously, that actually Rochfort is the better writer
enables her to break down the separation he has, intentionally or unintentionally, posed between African and British genius by exoticizing
sun-drenched Africa and her natural muse: "My pen, least favour'd
by the tuneful nine, / Can never rival, never equal thine; / Then fix
the humble Afric muse's seat / At British Homer's and Sir Isaac's feet."
By humbly removing herself to Milton and Newton's feet, Wheatley
affirms her claim. Just as she'd asserted to Thornton, she was African
and British.

On those grounds, she proceeds to comment on Rochfort's vision
of Africa. There's more than a hint of irony, a verbal eye roll, in her
approach to his pastoral fantasy of Africa. Greaves might have been sta-
tioned at the mouth of the Gambia River a few years before, and maybe
they actually discussed that, but on the other hand maybe that's what
led his friend Rochfort to overreach in telling an African what Africa
looked like. She mocks his "fair description" of "artless grottos, and the
sylvan shade; / Charmed with thy painting, how my bosom burns!"

Still, she takes it over, owns it, extends it, even peoples it, at least for
a few couplets, if only to show that she can:

> And pleasing Gambia on my soul returns,
> With native grace in spring's luxuriant reign,
> Smiles the gay mead, and Eden blooms again.
> The various bower, the tuneful flowing stream,
> The soft retreats, the lovers golden dream,
> Her soil spontaneous, yields exhaustless stores;
> For phoebus revels on her verdant shores.

Whose flowery births, a fragrant train appear,
And crown the youth throughout the smiling year.

The idea of a fecund Africa was proving useful to abolitionists like Anthony Benezet, who in *Some Historical Account of Guinea*, the book
of his that Phillis owned, mined European travel narratives to suggest that the problem with Africa was not any inherent barbarism but
rather the violence that European slave traders cultivated for their own
purposes. No sooner does she indulge the notion of unspoiled Africa,
though, than she turns and relativizes it, reminding us that she knows
at least as much about England as she does about Senegal. She ends by
simile, reminding us that the same sun shines in Britain as in Africa:

There, as in Britain's favour'd isle, behold
The bending harvest ripen into gold!
Just are thy views of Afric's blissful plain,
On the warm limits of the land and main.

In case the reader doesn't get how imaginative, if not imaginary, this
is all getting, she says so: "Pleas'd with the theme, see sportive fancy
play, / In realms devoted to the God of day!" So she plays on, with
more musing on Newton as "Europa's bard," on "Rochford's matchless
pen" as a possible replacement for Newton and Milton (ha-ha), and
"the charms of friendship in the sprightly lay."

Why was Phillis Wheatley seeking or finding friendship, and play,
in the officers of the navy at a time of such publicly expressed tensions
between soldiers and civilians? With both sides seizing arms, and a
series of skirmishes over weapons that led finally to the "shot heard
round the world" at Lexington, there was a not-so-cold war going on
in eastern Massachusetts during late 1774 and early 1775. On the other
hand, Joseph Greenleaf, whose "royal" magazine leaned decidedly patriot, didn't hesitate to publish her praise, which testified both to her
own reputation and to the fact that no one could say what might hap-

pen next. Loyalty and royalty were still possible, even necessary, but increasingly as fraught politically as bold claims about the character of Americans—or Africans.

It's a measure of her state of mind, the state of public affairs, and her careful strategy that she did not publish other poems than these, besides the broadside elegy for John Moorhead, under her name between the appearance of her book in September 1773 and the beginning of the war nineteen months later. It's also impossible to imagine, as well as against the contemporary testimony of Deborah Cushing, that she wasn't writing any. Wheatley was being careful and may not have at first intended even this exchange with Rochfort for print. Her delicate tracking, after her return, between American, British, and African identities made practical and political sense. It responded to her various appreciative audiences, to her less than sufficient prospects in both Boston and London, and to the different meanings ascribed to Africa and Africans in the enmeshed debates over the empire and slavery. As patriot and Tory ideologies hardened, she typified the many who tried not to choose, which even in Boston was a larger number of people than historical hindsight tends to see. As in the letters that have survived, she was selling books, making friends, and hedging her bets. She needed to keep writing, and to show her writing, but had to minimize risk. She couldn't afford to offend, and her letter to Occom suggests her awareness that she could not trust either side.

She was writing, but the balance of opposing forces and audiences became more and more difficult. Two other ambitious, anonymous poems, which appeared during the weeks before Lexington and Concord in venues that had published her before, reviewed the stakes and hinted at her continued ambition to please, to find friends and patrons, and yet still, subtly, to push.

"Thoughts on Tyranny," for the February 1775 *Royal American Magazine* and signed by "W.," begins with nostalgia for ancient times that did not experience so much political controversy. (See appendix.) It reviews the ancient history and tries to find some optimism. "Social love," and "mutual friendship," of the sort expressed between Wheatley and Rochfort, are natural. The story is secular, though the hint of the biblical flood gives it a suggestion of sacred grounding. The subject of tyranny and resistance to it, in 1775, was being more and more often addressed in a secular, historical register, with examples from ancient Greece and Rome to modern Europe, including English history. Wheatley's version of this story rehearses cycles of history that both sides of the debate about British policy could embrace. Mainly, and plainly, Americans are invited to stay in a tradition of "freedom's cause" and "human grandeur" that stretches from Greece to Rome to England, emperors and bad kings notwithstanding, at a moment, after Paine's *Common Sense*, when monarchy itself had been publicly questioned and the king blamed for British tyranny, as opposed to being the guarantor of liberty against mistaken officials who threatened colonial liberties.

As the poem moves on to modern history, the absolutist Charles I is named only to be "scorn[ed]." The narrative stops there, however: it is too dangerous, too controversial in February 1775, to get beyond the English Civil War and describe more recent history. At the verge of the precipice, Wheatley hopes that anti-tyranny, the "patriotic fire," can still hold the empire together, can preserve the sense of a British past and American future that she had described years before in her own poems.

If "Thoughts on Tyranny" appealed to patriots to keep their place within the long story from ancient to modern liberty—to *not* rebel—a new rebus, in the *Boston Evening-Post*, made a more personal appeal, to understand the man who was trying, and failing, to hold it all together. Wheatley probably couldn't know that by March 13, General Thomas Gage anticipated war, as his later arriving orders from Lord Dartmouth did explicitly. "A Rebus" triangulates Wheatley's concerns about the rhetoric she could hear and read in a desperate, if neat, effort to salvage the governor and general's reputation to Bostonians, and perhaps to make up for what Bostonians had done to him. Acknowledging that Gage had stretched to control his "warlike Bands" with his dubiously "double-Delegated trusts" of governor and commander, the poem admits the patriot critique of the Coercive Acts and the troops that enforced them but in the end relies, as the empire so often relied, on praise and prudence, and "the conduct of a skillful friend" to keep it all together. (See appendix.)

The sympathetic answer to the rebus that appeared in the paper's very next issue made even clearer the equipoise she was trying so hard to maintain between Boston and Britain, Africa and America, classicism and Christianity. The clue answers that spelled out "Thomas Gage" establish this common cultural and political property in Troy, heaven, oysters, medicine, African coasts, the sun, and George III. It speaks to those who hoped that Gage and George could each remain benevolent and shows her again lightly correcting both sides, hedging ever so carefully, knowing that without leaders to praise, nations don't exist and poets would be out of fashion and out of work.

But the patriots weren't playing, weren't joining. Two weeks later, two other versifiers published bitter alternate responses to the rebus that invoked men selling out for gold, modern traitors, and strutting geese as answers to the clues. The radical patriot version of the present crisis portrayed a very different image of Governor Gage, a ministerial tool: "A Man, who I fear, has been led by the Nose; / A Man who, I'm certain, by loss or by gain, / In the Trade of Slave-making, no laurels can claim." In the contest to control whose dark vision of barbarism and slavery could be seen, the king's men weren't winning. Neither was Wheatley, but it wasn't for lack of trying.

21

THE AMERICANS

The "shot heard round the world" didn't come as much of a shock to people in New England. Bostonians had been worrying that civil war was on the horizon since at least February. *The Newport Mercury*, the newspaper in which Wheatley's first published poem had appeared eight years earlier, called the skirmish and retreat at Lexington and Concord the beginning of "the American Civil War." For the time being, the name stuck. Only victory could make this civil war the "American Revolution."

Patriots like Wheatley had been invoking an American identity for a decade. Insults flung across the Atlantic during the imperial controversy heightened a sense of difference between England and its North American colonies. Some argued that separation was inevitable, while others, when challenged, walked it back, pledging loyalty and their Britishness. As Wheatley understood, a growing sense of alienation or Americanness did not resolve either the pressing political or the new military questions of 1775.

In Virginia, a standoff similar to the one that stymied Governor Gage, about who would control stockpiles of arms, precipitated a crisis. As in Boston, some enslaved men offered assistance to the governor, Lord Dunmore. At first he rebuffed them, but word got around, and by

April Dunmore made threats to free and arm slaves rather than remit control over the stash of guns in Williamsburg. Virginia's governor-general soon found himself fleeing to the ship in harbor where he had moved the munitions, as the executive and customs officers in Boston had done five years before. Events in Virginia didn't change but rather confirmed the pattern of distinctively American civil war and revolution: a chess game to control weapons that spiraled into a "complex triangularity of events" in part because it involved the enslaved from the beginning.

Wars of any kind, but especially civil wars, created opportunities for enslaved people in the Americas, even without the Anglo rhetoric of liberty versus enslavement or the specific armed confrontations in Boston and Virginia that led to North American war in 1775. Before the year was out, similar fears of slave revolt, fanned or not by British officials, precipitated revolutionary action and regime change by the least likely revolutionaries—rich landowners—in North Carolina, South Carolina, and Maryland as well as Virginia.

Rhetoric in Massachusetts reverberated in London and became reality elsewhere. In March, Dr. Samuel Johnson, the veteran Tory poet, critic, lexicographer, and pamphleteer, had defended the Coercive Acts by asking, "How is it we hear the loudest yelps for liberty from the drivers of Negroes?" That's the still-famous part of *Taxation No Tyranny*, which sold out in four editions. But Johnson also asked whether slaves could be called out as soldiers to silence the outrageous claims to sovereignty in the colonies. Looking ahead to the possibility of civil war—or just trying to make the Mansfieldian point that sovereignty over its colonies had to be more important to the empire than slavery—Johnson asserted that the only justifiable revolution in the current situation would be one that would turn loyal African slaves into replacement colonial overlords: "They may be more grateful and honest than their masters."

This kind of anti-settler Toryism shocked many colonists. It certainly played into the hands of colonial radicals. Pro-American writers

replied, understandably enough, by accusing Johnson of identity politics, of simply disliking American Creoles and reversing the equation
by courting Africans. Johnson and those like him not only wanted to
turn the Americans into slaves, as patriots had hyperbolically warned
for a decade, but proposed "a Saturnalia of cruelty" where Africans
would "wreak a barbarous vengeance on their degraded masters."
Being accused of extreme hypocrisy and threatened with social revolution did little, in the short run, to make American rhetoric more
honest about American reality.

If the enslaved waited anxiously, choosing the side of freedom for
themselves, whichever that might be in their time and place, what did
that mean for a free African who had publicly identified with both
her British and her American friends? Had Wheatley already made
her "choice of identity" in 1773 when she returned home? Had it been
made for her by the onset of war? Wheatley knew enough about slavery in Africa and the ancient Mediterranean and Near East to know
that in most societies with slaves and even in the few slavery-based
societies, the enslaved as individuals sometimes won their freedom.
War enslaved, but it also liberated. Still, the possible futures of other
Africans and their descendants in revolutionary New England and
America had real implications for her own prospects. Wartime developments and black collective experiences shaped the choices she
could make.

Like three out of every four Bostonians, in 1775 Phillis Wheatley
became a refugee. She left town with John and Mary Lathrop, probably
by the first week of May, as it became apparent that while Gage com-
manded Boston city, patriots had the countryside, an American army
gathered in the suburbs, and the inhabitants were "Flocking out of
Town." When the governor gave ambiguous instructions about what
goods people would be allowed to bring out, and his soldiers began to
seize what they could, some left "everything" behind. John Andrews,
whose savings were invested in merchandise, hunkered in town even
after his wife, Ruth, left: "Its Said without Scruple that those who leave

the town, forfeit all the effects they leave behind—whether they hold it up as only a means to detain people or not I cant Say." The effects of this default confiscation doctrine revealed how much slavery still mattered in Boston as well as who in particular might find the occupation liberating, as Andrews added that "many" stayed in order to keep hold of their slaves "who would other ways have gone." John Wheatley remained, probably because of his age, but possibly also to protect the property he had accumulated over his lifetime and still hoped to pass on to his children. Nathaniel Wheatley decamped for a few months to Nantucket. His English and merchant connections served him well; he wrote of a ship full of goods ready to sail and wishing he had another to fill with barrels of oil.

Wheatley saw little advantage to staying in the depopulated city. The Lathrops intended to go to John's hometown of Norwich, Connecticut, at first but quickly settled in Providence, Rhode Island, where John had been invited to serve as a substitute pastor. By October, Nathaniel and his family had also moved there. In Providence, Wheatley had increased proximity to Obour Tanner, whose Newport friends John Quamine, Cato Coggeshall, and the stonemason Zingo Stevens passed time with her in town. In addition to having a critical mass of free and enslaved Africans, Providence seemed much like Boston in other ways. The town housed deeply committed patriots and loyalists, some who pushed for abolition and others who pushed against it, a divide typified by the brothers Moses and John Brown. The Providence town meeting had passed a resolution against keeping slaves in 1774. Yet only a year later, petitioned by Moses Brown and the assembly delegate Stephen Hopkins with a bill to ban the slave trade, both the town and the assembly weighed it down with riders and ultimately defeated it.

Meanwhile, Wheatley found an opportunity to renew her laureate dialogues with military leaders in the appointment of Virginia's George Washington as commander of the provincial armed forces. Washington was known to have military experience and seemed to impress everyone wherever he went—including the Continental Congress—with his gentlemanly bearing and equanimity. He also gained instant support from some New Englanders, like John Adams, who were eager to cement the patriot alliance by having a southerner command mostly Yankee troops in what was, for the time being, a northern military standoff.

Washington quickly decided that he needed to whip or cajole these New England volunteers, who in effect had answered the call like a militia, into something more like a standing army. This meant more professional standards for the officer corps, who should be chosen by their fellow gentlemen and Congress rather than elected by their companies. It also meant more careful modes of recruitment, mindful of the likelihood of a longer war with strenuous campaigns and pitched battles. During the nine-month stalemate, or siege, in and around Boston there was considerable time to consider and act on these matters, on which he and some others thought the success of the American resistance might rest. The general established headquarters in Cambridge and immediately expressed consternation about the youngsters and Africans who populated the ranks, directing that no more of the above should be enlisted.

Washington's enlistments directive followed a May 20 order from the Massachusetts Committee of Safety that slaves should not be admitted into the army of Massachusetts (though the legislature declined to approve or disapprove that resolution), and an order from General Horatio Gates not to enlist any "stroller, negro or vagabond." New Englanders hated standing armies more than ever after recent events, but precisely because they leaned heavily on the tradition of citizens in self-defense, they thought that enslaved men serving in arms—and perhaps also free blacks as well—might discourage enlistments and raise questions about their future status that neither the army nor the Continental Congress nor Massachusetts would or could answer. This didn't change the facts on the ground. At minimum, hundreds of free

Africans, enslaved men, and former slaves bore arms in New England. At least thirty-three had already fought, at Bunker Hill.

During the summer of 1775, patriot newspapers filled with rumors of British incitement of violence by Native Americans and enslaved people. General Gage had speculated about the strategic necessity of enlisting Africans in a letter to the secretary of war. These debates reached a crescendo on October 26, when William Henry Lyttelton, the younger brother of the late Lord George Lyttelton, former governor of both South Carolina and Jamaica, and now a member of the House of Commons, formally proposed arming slaves to put down the Americans.

On the same day Lyttelton stood up in Westminster, Wheatley sent a poem and a cover letter to General Washington, using a title—"your Excellency"—that Washington had accepted but that his already jealous second-in-command, General Charles Lee, called a "bauble" that made him "spew." She had clearly been contemplating how to switch her praises to American military leaders, to fall in line with their attempts to establish continental authority. She stressed in her cover letter how "your being appointed by the Continental Congress to be Generalissimo of the armies of North America, together with the fame of your virtues, excite sensations not easy to suppress." As in the poems sent with cover letters to the Countess of Huntingdon and Lord Dartmouth, the performance of refined yet deep emotion elevates Wheatley to the position she had been auditioning for: poet laureate, then of Boston, now of the American union headquartered militarily in Cambridge. In the poem itself, she puts herself on the plane of the military leader by placing Washington amid the deities, as the central actor in "Columbia's scenes of glorious toils," the new epic that is America.

The figure of Columbia, a classicized symbol for America, had been used recently by a few colonials like the poet Philip Freneau. Wheatley's version is a composite of Pallas Athena, the goddess associated with war, and Phoebus Apollo, the god of the Muses. Comparing the movement of her armies "through a thousand gates" to the motions of Aeolus (the wind) on the ocean and to autumn leaves descending, Wheatley elevates the American cause at a moment when the actual armies were doing everything but descending "in bright array" upon the enemy.

The raw New England troops had held steady at Bunker Hill, where they were on the defensive, but Washington himself was deeply frustrated by "indifferent" Yankee officers and even more by the ordinary soldiers, the "exceeding dirty and nasty people [who] had they been properly conducted at Bunker Hill (on the 17th of June) or those that were there properly supported, the [British] Regulars would have met with a shameful defeat; & a much more considerable loss than they did." By invoking the gods and the armies, though, Wheatley positions herself to speak not only to Washington but for the soldiers and the heavens about Washington. She addresses the evident risk of a breakdown among the bickering generals—or between the general and "the warrior's train."

At this point "To His Excellency General Washington" begins to rewrite and incorporate Wheatley's as yet unpublished epyllion "America," with its vision of a war-torn colonial history that culminates in a young America breaking free from a tired, cranky Britannia. From "New England first a wilderness was found / Till for a continent 'twas destin'd round" in "America," we get "One century scarce perform'd its destin'd round / When Gallic powers Columbia's fury found," which makes the Seven Years' War a sign of American, not British, glory. Now, as in much contemporary commentary, America possesses the world's hopes for liberty. It isn't pretty, with "rising hills of dead," but that's the way of epics and nations, and of politics, as Wheatley switches gears again, making it very clear what side she's on. Britain, blind to America's rise and its "heaven-defended race," will regret its "thirst of boundless power too late." She ends with a remarkably confident endorsement of Washington's leadership, to the point of anticipating his crowning as a new Caesar: "A crown, a mansion, and a throne that shine, / With gold unfading, WASHINGTON! be thine."

When Wheatley sent her letter, Washington had just concluded meetings with a committee from the Continental Congress about how to reform and reconstitute the army after the enlistments of 1775 expired at the end of the year. Thomas Lynch of South Carolina, Benjamin Harrison V of Virginia, and Benjamin Franklin agreed with Washington that no blacks should be recruited or admitted into the army. Congress made it official, and several colonies followed suit. If Wheatley was advertising her own loyalty and advocating for Africans, free or enslaved, as Americans, she had picked a key moment, but it wasn't clear who would listen.

The issue of black loyalties immediately became more important, and more complicated, on November 7, when Lord Dunmore issued his proclamation offering freedom to enslaved men who joined his army. The proclamation yielded Dunmore hundreds of men, but it also had a unifying effect on the patriots, who were well prepared for it and denounced it as self-interested and not even antislavery, for only fighting men would be freed. They also stated, cynically and without evidence, that once no longer of military use, any slaves who escaped to British lines would probably be resold in the West Indies.

At a time when desertions and enlistments were a grave concern in New England, Dunmore raised the stakes and reopened the question of policy—and a competition for black loyalties. As General Washington wrote to his military secretary (and Continental Congress member) Joseph Reed on December 15, exactly when he later said he received Wheatley's letter with her poem enclosed, "If the Virginians are wise, that Arch Traitor to the Rights of Humanity, Lord Dunmore, should be instantly crushd, if it takes the force of the whole Colony to do it. [O]therwise, like a snow Ball in rolling, his army will get size—some through Fear—some through promises—and some from Inclination joining his Standard—But that which renders the measure indispensably necessary, is, the Negros; for if he gets formidable, numbers of them will be tempted to join who will be affraid to do it without."

If he had not already been sensitized by Wheatley, a visit in camp from free black troops who objected to being discarded led the commander to worry that such men, who had knowledge of the terrain and his army, might switch sides. Washington didn't change his mind on arming enslaved people, which when done by the British remained both a real threat and a major propaganda point for the Americans. But on December 30 he decided to keep the already enlisted Africans, opening the door for future recruitments or reenlistments of those who were free or might be freed in order to serve.

The black soldiers who visited Washington asked or inspired him to make a distinction that Dunmore had obscured by offering places in his army to free "indented servants, Negroes, or others (appertaining to rebels)." Dunmore was offering what New England already had. Race didn't have to mean enslaved status, because it didn't always. For Washington and the patriots, accepting the American loyalty of free and indentured black soldiers might mean not only retaining their services but also avoiding a race to the bottom that would threaten both America and slavery. A writer for the *Virginia Gazette* who offered the most extensive commentary on Dunmore's proclamation anticipated Washington's logic (and Jefferson's in his draft of the Declaration of Independence). After proposing that enslaved people should not trust Dunmore's offer for a minute, he praised "the Americans" in general for "repeatedly pass[ing] acts, laying heavy duties upon imported negroes, by which they meant altogether to prevent the horrid traffick." This had been prevented by English merchants and the royal negative on colonial laws. In 1775, as Wheatley understood, many white Americans, south and north, still wanted, even expected, to have their slavery and their antislavery too—or at least found it useful, even necessary, to say so.

Washington received Wheatley's letter, he said, in "the middle of

December," at a low point in his own morale and at the height of the anxious strategizing about enlistments. When he finally wrote back to Wheatley on February 28, 1776, he did not acknowledge how the timing and the substance of her panegyric had spoken directly to the problems of that moment. Referring instead to the many cares and distractions of his office, he wrote that only in February did he rediscover her offering.

The publicity-conscious leader had other motives for the delay. He needed public praise but didn't want it to seem obvious that he had decided to accept the aid of the famous African. In a long letter of February 10 to his secretary General Joseph Reed, who managed communications, he had stated that he was not offended at what Reed had told him about the criticism he was getting in the press—that on the contrary he needed to know public opinion about the army and his leadership, "whether they be favourable, or otherwise." He ended the same letter by describing how Wheatley's letter had just happened to reappear when he was clearing his desk. Maybe Reed would be amused by it—a cover he immediately contradicted by suggesting that Wheatley and her poem meant more than that, but had to be managed correctly: "I brought it to light again—at first, with a view of doing justice to her great poetical Genius, I had a great Mind to publish the Poem, but not knowing whether it might not be considered rather as a mark of my own vanity than as a Compliment to her I laid it aside till I came across it again in the manner just mentioned." In other words, the timing was now just right to publish it, if Washington didn't seem to be doing it himself.

Washington knew very well the public value of patriotic poetry: a few months later, after receiving an ode from a young David Humphreys, he promoted him to a position on his staff. And his letter to Reed suggests that he knew exactly who Wheatley was and the possible implications of acknowledging receipt of, or publicizing, her letter. So he had thought of enlisting Wheatley immediately, in December, then paused, burying the letter but not throwing it away. Now that the issue of Wheatley's cohort of young free African Americans had been at least temporarily resolved, after word could spread of his decision of December 30, he sent her letter and poem to the officer who was managing his public relations. Only then did he write her back.

Washington was treating Wheatley as diplomatically as he maneuvered around his black soldiers: ignoring and then acknowledging them with a careful eye on public opinion, Congress, and the course of the war. His letter of February 28 to Wheatley returns her praise and affirms her value, reiterating his claim in the letter to General Reed that he would have had her excellent poem published himself if it would not have made him appear vain. He then offers to receive her, much as he had received the delegation of black soldiers:

> I thank you most sincerely for your polite notice of me, in the elegant Lines you enclosed; and however undeserving I may be of such encomium and panegyrick, the style and manner exhibit a striking proof of your great poetical Talents. In honour of which, and as a tribute justly due to you, I would have published the Poem, had I not been apprehensive, that, while I only meant to give the World this new instance of your genius, I might have incurred the imputation of Vanity. This, and nothing else, determined me not to give it place in the public Prints.
>
> If you should ever come to Cambridge, or near Head Quarters, I shall be happy to see a person so favoured by the Muses, and to whom nature has been so liberal and beneficent in her dispensations. I am, with great Respect, Your obed[ien]t humble servant,
>
> G. Washington

Timing was everything. Washington felt renewed optimism as his war council hit upon the new strategy of taking Dorchester Heights to force the British to depart Boston or face bombardment. The fortifications were being built as Washington wrote his letter to Wheatley; his troops began lobbing projectiles two days later. When he sent the poem and letter to Reed, he was preparing literary ammunition for when it would be most useful. The British left; Washington and his men marched back to town on March 7. By the end of the month, Joseph Reed sent the poem and Wheatley's cover letter to two key venues where he had connections, the *Virginia Gazette* and the *Pennsylvania Magazine*, where it was prefaced with an acknowledgment of her identity as "the famous Phillis Wheatley, the African poetess."

Washington's decision to not only acknowledge but also secure publication of "To His Excellency" and her letter to him may have encouraged Wheatley. Yet she had been waiting too long to be lulled into confidence that the African and American struggles had been rendered mutually supportive, much less identical. A few weeks before hearing back from Washington, she wrote to Obour Tanner, who had commiserated with her about wartime conditions. She continued their dialogue—and her sarcasm—about "the proceedings of nations that are fav[ore]d with the divine revelation of the Gospel." She described herself as "a mere spectator" who nevertheless felt "anxious suspense concerning the fortune of this unnatural civil Contest"—a far more moderate, and judgmental, stance than she had taken in her paean to Washington. As she had two years before in her letter to Occom, she made it devastatingly clear that to her, to Obour, and to God the clash of nations in 1776 was a three-way affair:

> Possibly the Ambition & thirst of dominion in some, is designed as the punishment of the national vices of others, tho' it bears the appearance of greater Barbarity than that of the unciviliz'd part of mankind. But Let us leave the Event to him whose wisdom alone can bring good out of Evil. & he is infinitely superior to all the Craftiness of the enemies of this seemingly devoted Country.

Wheatley's ambiguities are deliberate, and telling, as the similes extend. Whose thirst of dominion (over Americans? over slaves?) was being visited upon whose national vices (ambition for power? slaving?). The real absurdity in this context, to Wheatley, is the old notion that Africans had been punished with slavery for their barbarity. Barbarians, supposedly, were people who made war without rules or reason, attacking everyone, including women and children. Who, indeed, was a barbarian in an "unnatural contest," a civil war in which one hardly knew which side God might take? Granville Sharp would resign his job as a clerk at the ordnance department in the Tower of London out of concern that this British civil war might be divine punishment for slavery. Or perhaps the greater national punishment lay in store for the more profound hypocrites, the Americans, at a time when the "common cause" in the north and south was being built around the supposed "savage barbarities" of Dunmore and his allies. The "seemingly devoted" patriots might be in the right, or the crafty, domineering empire might be, but both "nations" showed hypocrisy.

In 1776, Wheatley embodied patriotism, talked freedom, even treated with the commander in chief, but she could not be an uncritical believer in the American cause. She retained her right to judge even as Washington embraced her words. This letter to Tanner had been "carried by Mr. Zingo" and referred to having "pass'd the last evening" with him and John Quamine "very agreeably." With her friends of color—Occom, Tanner, these Newport men—Wheatley expressed herself differently than she did in the poems she wrote for her largely white audiences. It wasn't an absolute difference, but there was a difference. There's no question that she meant what she wrote, that she expressed herself personally and politically in her poems. But they remained performances, crafted with a sense of time and place, when the times and her places were changing.

Certain attitudes hardened in the cauldron of civil war and revolution. John Lathrop's sermons were one measure of the changes that she would have seen and heard. Throughout the early 1770s, no one made the patriot case for America as a new Israel, preserving religious and civil liberty against the ever-present threat of corruption and enslavement, more eloquently or more consistently. Lathrop had anticipated the drift of patriot thinking and perhaps even influenced its language in defining the murder of Christopher Seider by troops shooting into a crowd as "unparalleled barbarity." In 1771 he stressed natural rights and did not qualify the implications of his remark that "some think the bulk of mankind should be born to be beasts of burden": he even cited Granville Sharp on the subject. In July 1775 he was reading and citing Sharp on representation in a republic and using the same language as Wheatley in describing an American "love of freedom, civil and religious."

The British asserted absolute control over property, and now life, Lathrop emphasized in his sermons. Blood had been shed. Resistance could not be more just, whether in Massachusetts or Virginia. Yet certain things changed with the war. In 1776 he repeatedly stressed the British "endeavours to engage the negro slaves to murder their masters," even recalling how "one Wilson a captain in the British forces at Boston was detected in this kind of villainy" in 1768, and how one of Gage's underlings had more recently promoted "the same black plan." New England, he noted in this vein, had much in common with events in South Carolina, which he had heard about from a gentleman in Providence. So Americans were one—against the English and their African minions.

After the Declaration of Independence, Lathrop followed its logic. King George was Pharaoh, ordering the murder of young children. He had brought the Native hosts down upon settlers. Now his servants "employed their sacred instruments, with sums of money, to tamper with domestics . . . not only to leave their master's service, but to kill the families on wh[ich] they depend, and join in the general conspiracy against the country. This discovers a degree of baseness and cruelty wh[ich] the ancient heathen would have been ashamed of." In his December 1776 thanksgiving sermon, "Negroes" counted among the "foreign Mercenaries, Savages, Canadians," and "disaffected Americans who have joined the Enemy" but may lurk unnoticed among the faithful. His battle stories featured stolen, not liberated or emancipated, slaves and black soldiers. For Lathrop, in the revolutionary moment, the white Americans were Israel, and the league of Britons, natives, and Africans reminded him of the wrong sorts of ancients. Lathrop and the Americans had inverted the terms of Wheatley's own criticism of the "modern Egyptians," published for her by Occom two years earlier. Phillis was free, and probably a member of John Lathrop's household. But as a former domestic, foreign-born person with English friends, she found herself implicated as a possible enemy in the American story he told.

In response to these loyalty scares Wheatley continued to seek the highest forms of patronage and patriotism. In December she wrote another epic fragment about the capture of General Charles Lee—a difficult subject, but also an appropriate one. Lee had been acclaimed as an experienced British soldier who chose the American side. He had been in Boston in August 1774 and later especially visible in Rhode Island shoring up defenses and intimidating Tories. Nicknamed Boiling Water by his Mohawk allies during the Seven Years' War, Lee "would say almost anything," but in his own way he understood the battle for hearts and minds as well as Washington. He had published a pamphlet on why American militia would fight better than British regulars, and he might have even believed it for a while based on his past experience. While Lee was in Providence, Wheatley could have seen him; he participated in public events, and locals like the future general Nathanael Greene were impressed by his "genius and learning." New England newspapers published his exchange of letters with his old friend General John Burgoyne, in which Lee predicted the fall of the British Empire.

During the first half of 1776, Lee's political activities were argu-

ably as important as his work on American defenses, and some—
including Lee himself and Joseph Reed, who egged him on—thought
him a logical replacement for Washington, who faced strong criticism
for seeming to be indecisive about strategy. When Lee delayed joining Washington's forces in retreat across New Jersey in late November
1776, he was attempting to rally the militia to raid dispersed British
parties in the northern parts of the state and to persuade Washington
to let him remain there. His detour to an inn at Basking Ridge and
capture by some redcoats who had served under him years before were
not only hurtful to the cause but also embarrassing, although initial
coverage in newspapers emphasized that Lee had been transacting important business when surprised and overtaken. Military historians
recognize this moment of retreat and loss as a "psychological crisis"
for Washington as well as his fellow officers and troops. On December
17, the Continental Congress fled Philadelphia; two days later Thomas
Paine began his *American Crisis* papers with the famously stark admission "These are the times that try men's souls."

Wheatley responded with an occasional poem that is also a Homeric portrait of war as a mind game played out in public. She sent her
seventy lines "On the Capture of General Lee" to James Bowdoin II,
president of the Executive Council and a longtime admirer of her work,
within days of reports of Lee's capture appearing in the newspapers.
Even more than "To His Excellency General Washington," it is in epic
style, to the point of echoing the beginning of *The Iliad*, identifying
Lee as a tragic hero: "The deed perfidious, and the Hero's fate, / In tender strains, celestial Muse! Relate." The fault is with a traitor who informed the British captors, a "latent foe to friendship," not Lee, whose
"boding sigh" seems to know and accept his fatal error even as he crit-
icizes himself for agreeing "to waste an hour in banquets or repose."
Like Agamemnon or Achilles, he has a fatal flaw, or flaws. Wheatley
paints him quite accurately: he talks too much. Like other Americans
in 1776, Wheatley was ready to simultaneously praise generals and
mock them in a minor key or at least bring them down to earth as all

too human. She had learned not only from Homer and Pope but also from her many interactions with military men.

Wheatley could also identify with the betrayal of friendship and hospitality that frames the tragic narrative of Lee's capture. She demonstrates her own patriotism, which side she is on, by describing the British commander's less than gentlemanly taunting of the captured Lee ("Say, art thou he, beneath whose vengeful hands / Our best of heroes grasp'd in death the sands . . . But Oh! How chang'd!"). This "boaster" of a general makes it easy—too easy—for Lee, the "hero of renown," to project his own "arrogance of tongue" and "wild ambition" back onto his comrades turned foes, and to explain the recent course of the war. This is a political contest, and the results foreordained if the Americans are truly the forces they have claimed to be: "For plunder you, and we for freedom fight." If Lee was an imperfect, if impressive, mouthpiece for fantasies of "brave troops innumerous as the sands," Wheatley repairs the prospects of the Continentals by invoking "Godlike Washington . . . in whom the virtues join, / And heaven-taught prudence speaks the man divine." However long Washington had made Wheatley wait, he was the one with more cards and the skill to hold them.

The poet had cast her lot. Like other Africans, she had skin in the game, and she knew that this war, for black people as much as anyone else, was politics by other means. James Bowdoin, though, held on to her ambitious manuscript permanently, probably because Lee's reputation had suddenly become as controversial, and subject to events, as that of black soldiers. Wheatley retained a copy, though, for her next book, as she considered a future in Boston and America. She remained "*the famous* Phillis Wheatley, *the African poetess*," even if the patriots wouldn't call her American.

22

THE FREE

Wheatley's opportunities changed during the Revolutionary War, but her fame did not. She remained newsworthy, fascinating, and sometimes irresistible to a regional, national, and international audience. Even those who could not get a copy of her book could read the widely available London reviews and the references of others to them. The French philosopher Voltaire, who was about as famous and widely read as it was possible to be during the eighteenth century, had already cited her in 1774 as an example of how "genius, which is rare everywhere, can be found in all parts of the earth." She proved that his predecessor Fontenelle, an important contributor to the debate about the ancients and the moderns, had been "wrong to say that there would never be poets among Negroes." These sorts of backhanded compliments allowed Voltaire to seem careful and reasonably enlightened in his skepticism about slavery and racism. Similarly, the secretary of the French delegation to the United States after the Treaty of Alliance, the Marquis de Barbé-Marbois, expressed pleasure as well as surprise at her "imagination, poetry, and zeal" even if he found her meter and choice of subjects to be lacking.

Wheatley was an American curiosity whose existence and nature spoke to Europe about both Africa and the new nation. As the revolutionaries continued to depict their opponents as "savage" attackers of towns and as allies of Natives and Africans, these relatively positive images of an African American had immediate as well as long-term political implications even when they were carefully measured and limited. Benjamin Franklin, in France negotiating and solidifying the alliance, did everything he could to reinforce the sense that the United States represented the future of a liberated mankind. The persistence of slavery and the position of free African Americans like Wheatley, who proved what was possible while suggesting what remained unaccomplished, especially concerned the more self-consciously enlightened, cosmopolitan, and engaged patriots in North America and abroad.

When Barbé-Marbois, in his semiofficial diplomatic capacity, circulated a set of queries to leaders of each new American state about its population, natural resources, laws, and institutions, he inspired Thomas Jefferson to gradually develop his *Notes on the State of Virginia* (1781–87), in which he tentatively took on Voltaire, Marbois, and all the others who had used the genius or lack of genius in Wheatley and other black authors as evidence to assess the futures of America and its inhabitants, including the enslaved. In part because they could be exploratory and indirect and avoid religious controversies, natural histories of the New World, like poetry and travel writings, had become a way of doing cultural politics. During this period especially, these learned scientific tomes refined proslavery and antislavery arguments out of studies of vegetation, climate, population, Native and settler and mammalian bodies, and achievements in the arts.

Where it came to supposedly less civilized peoples, natural historians and philosophers paid special attention to their arts as well as their laws, with comparisons to ancient peoples that Europeans knew the most about: Greeks and Romans. Another scientific fan of Wheatley, Johann Friedrich Blumenbach, began to collect a library of African authors as evidence of the unity of the human species and the equality and permeability of races. This helps explain why Thomas Jefferson commented on her in *Notes on the State of Virginia*, which he began writing in 1781, in a chapter on laws and their reform.

Jefferson agreed that slavery was wrong, and a cancer in Virginia, which is one reason why he was so eager to engage in this debate. But he wanted slavery to be dealt with on his Virginian terms, not those of Voltaire in Paris, of Wheatley in Massachusetts, or of anyone in London. Quite possibly in direct response to conversations with Barbé-Marbois, with the French audience especially in mind, Jefferson shaped the central "Laws" chapter of his book around his now-famous slam: "Religion, indeed, has produced a Phillis Whately; but it could not produce a poet. The compositions published under her name are below the dignity of criticism. The heroes of the Dunciad are to her as Hercules to the author of that poem [that is, Alexander Pope]."

Wheatley takes up only a few lines at the center of Jefferson's lengthy defense of the Americans at their weak point—as enslavers—but in a sense it is all about her, made necessary by her fame. She becomes key negative proof. If she is not a poet, if she is merely a pious parrot, if she is laughable, so is any depiction of Virginia or the United States as a weird tropical province unworthy of international engagement or support because of its barbarous slaving or its hypocrisy. The quickness of the dismissal is rhetorical, deliberatively over the top, and essential to the dubious argument. Her poetry becomes merely religious to Jefferson in order to say it has neither classical nor modern virtues. Its relationship to genius is that of those who populate the mock-epic (*The Dunciad*) to real heroic subjects. Her engagement with Pope and the poets Pope translated—Homer, Horace—is winked away. The short-guy joke on Pope (Wheatley is to the hacks that Pope mocked as the hunchback Pope is to Hercules) evokes Jefferson's lengthy attack, in earlier chapters, on the Comte de Buffon and Abbé Raynal's widely publicized notion, in their own natural histories, that the New World had led to a natural degeneration of mammalian life—shrinkages in size and population as well as human achievements in literature and science due to both climate and the immoral and wasteful practices of the settlers.

The degeneration thesis that Franklin and Jefferson were keen to debunk encompassed the shocking imperial revival of slavery, that ancient blight that Europeans had made modern in the maw of the sugar plantations. Buffon and Raynal's prediction that a Black Spartacus would arise to redress the wrongs of the New World acted like tinder upon Jefferson's fear of what it might imply for an enslaved American poet to have either an original or an appropriately imitative relationship to Greek and Roman classics. Jefferson clearly felt "threatened." So rather than present any evidence from her poems, he revises the classical context for both Wheatley and African slavery. He depicts her as the opposite of both Greeks and Romans. He compares Roman slaves' literary achievements to what he describes as minor, overrated scribblings by Wheatley and her English contemporary Ignatius Sancho. If Roman slavery was harsher, as he asserts, and Roman slaves artful nevertheless, that must say something about Africans. This reversed the comparison of ancient and modern slavery invoked by an earlier key French Enlightenment thinker, Montesquieu, whose 1748 denunciation of racial justifications for New World slavery in *The Spirit of the Laws* had become a touchstone of antislavery arguments, echoed, for example, in 1764 by James Otis, in 1766 by Anthony Benezet, and in 1772 by James Swan. As such, it also reversed Wheatley's contention that American slaveholders were akin to modern Egyptians who singled out one people for perpetual, hereditary bondage with little to no hope of manumission.

Jefferson's discussion of Wheatley and other black writers as merely imitative and thus inferior to creative Roman slaves had potentially devastating implications given his insistence that modern, American African slavery was kinder and gentler than the Roman variety, and only a temporary, washable stain on Virginian and American character, one that could be dispensed with, he implied hopefully, after American independence was secured with French aid. His refusal to even admit the neoclassical ambitions in what he archly called "the compositions published under her name" suggests the nature of the game here. Not only slavery but the meaning of the American Revolution could be at play in readers' responses to Phillis Wheatley, and it was certainly so in the response of Jefferson, who worked on his book between gigs as a member of the Continental Congress, governor of Virginia, and U.S. minister to France.

The most telling detail of all may be his handling of Terence and of Homer. Jefferson doesn't tell his readers that Wheatley had claimed the North African Roman and formerly enslaved poet Terence as a predecessor in "To Maecenas," at the very outset of her book. He couldn't, if only because he had already characterized Wheatley as a naive religious writer (Terence's verse plays are downright bawdy). Instead, he asserted that Terence did not prove anything about black slavery, since he was "of the race of whites": an unprovable contention about Terentius Afer that is still debated today. Homer did have his noble enslaved swineherd Eumaeus complain about the sheer waste of human bondage, Jefferson admits (quoting Pope's translation), but only to assert immediately that "the slaves of which Homer speaks were whites" too.

Jefferson also ignores another important dimension of Wheatley's identification with Terence as a slave and as "African by birth": that Terence, like Wheatley, had been suspected of getting help in writing, only later to be vindicated, celebrated, and emancipated. By reenacting Terence's Roman drama in her writing and her life, Wheatley had put herself directly, and increasingly during the Revolutionary War, into the position of emancipated writers with something to say about political men and about the relationships between slaves and masters. If she had been male, nothing could have been more neoclassical. But Jefferson denies the qualifications of a few male or female African slaves to participate in the republic of letters, as well as any precedent the ancients might suggest for emancipation, whether on the grounds of individual excellence or human equality.

Jefferson doubled down on race and a seemingly scientific inquiry before launching into his chain of suppositions about black and ancient bodies and minds because Wheatley had employed religion and neoclassical culture to dissolve race and to join in the transatlantic attack on slavery. While he drafted the *Notes* during the war, he waited until 1785, after her death, to publish the book. These writings were part of the ongoing public diplomacy of the American Revolution, in which no one knew exactly which way history was going for African slavery, for Virginia, or for the United States but everyone knew that perceptions shaped politics.

Much like the antislavery petitioners in Massachusetts and the black soldiers who chose different sides, other emerging black intellectuals recognized the debate over Wheatley's reputation as one front in their struggle. Jupiter Hammon had published pious verses in 1760, becoming the first African to do so in English. He was the enslaved steward of the Lloyd family's plantation on the North Shore of Long Island. Hammon attended school as a young person and was later encouraged by Mary Pemberton Lloyd, an author of homilies and the mother of one of Wheatley's attesters, the Reverend Ebenezer Pemberton. By 1778, when he was sixty-seven years old, Hammon could be said to be a voice of an older generation. But as part of the wartime reckoning, he entered the conversation respectfully in *An Address to Miss Phillis Wheatly, Ethiopian Poetess, in Boston, Who Came from Africa at Eight Years of Age, and Soon Became Acquainted with the Gospel of Jesus Christ*, with "a number of his friends, who desire to join him in their best regards to Miss Wheatly." Hammon emphasized "god's tender mercy" to Wheatley, echoed some of her memorable phrases back to her, and encouraged her to "search for heaven's joys, / where we do hope to meet." Beneath the fatherly or ministerial admonition is the affirmation of a community of interest that transcends locale, underlined by Hammon's deliberate description of his "friends" in Connecticut, where the Lloyds sojourned during the war.

For Hammon, Wheatley was too secular and too political, even dangerously so. A few years later, his fellow Africans would accuse him of de-emphasizing and thus undermining efforts to secure freedom in this world (which he denied). In 1778, writing to and about

Wheatley, Hammon focused on revelation and de-emphasized race, but he was helping to build a black network in doing so. Like Wheatley, he responded to changing times, and he evolved. Four years later, he experimented with explicitly antislavery verse. Hammon shared with Wheatley an African Christian identity. Its adherents varied on strategy but did not compromise on either the wrongs of slavery or the right to belong to Christ, Britain, or America.

Ignatius Sancho thanked a Philadelphia Quaker, Jabez Fisher, whose son had visited Wheatley in Boston, for sending him a copy of Wheatley's *Poems* (along with books by Benezet or Sharp) by wishing "that every member of each house of parliament had one of these books." For Sancho, it wasn't just that "Phyllis's poems do credit to nature—and put art—merely as art—to the blush." He also thought that the framing of the volume, with the master Wheatley showing off his prize possession and the eminent Bostonians with "splendid—titled—learned names" confirming her authorship, already reeked of hypocrisy: "These good great folks—all know—and perhaps admired—nay, praised Genius in bondage—and then, like the Priests and the Levites in sacred writ, passed by—not one good Samaritan among them." What did Sancho imagine the members of Parliament doing with her book in 1778? Ending the slave trade, or even slavery itself? Or being emboldened to continue the war against American hypocrites who kept a genius in bondage?

Jefferson wrote about Wheatley and Sancho in the condescending way he did, and carefully considered his audiences, because their efforts had implications for the international image of Virginia and the United States. The ups and downs of the war—including the French alliance in 1778, attempts to recruit or blame opponents for recruiting the enslaved in military capacities, and the continued use of the slavery issue against the Americans—all explosively reinforced the dynamics of 1772 and 1773, of Somerset's and Wheatley's moment: politicization, antislavery advances, backlash. The most difficult matter of all for some white folks like Jefferson to admit or comprehend was the emergence of the free black voices who, like black soldiers in British red or Continental blue, made it harder to equate Africa or blackness with slavery alone, but for that very reason made it more politically salient than ever to do just that.

Wheatley's very public example helped call this black network into being. Like Phillis, they were concerned with the intertwined problems of slavery and race. They were determined to deal with some whites' attempts to make slavery and antiblack racism identical if not permanent features of the new nation. Wheatley's mastery of the ancients and her participation in political debates posed a challenge to the republic in the diplomatic as well as the domestic arena. Jefferson wanted to take something modern—American-style racism, supporting American-style slavery—and render it natural, requiring no further justification as ancient. Yet Jefferson could only tentatively advance his "suspicion" of black inequality for a respectable international audience. This owed something to Wheatley's persistence.

In 1777 and 1778, Wheatley was thinking of publishing another volume, though neither of her preferred printers, Isaiah Thomas and Ezekiel Russell, had returned to Boston. The table of contents she eventually placed in an advertisement in October 1779 with James White and Thomas Adams, editors of a revived *Boston Evening-Post*, suggests that she had poems and letters at the ready, some from before but most penned after her 1773 volume. Few manuscripts of these survive, but there are clues that suggest she continued to write with multiple, contingent publishing strategies in mind. She composed in several genres including elegy, ode, and panegyric. She circulated some writings in manuscript and at least a few anonymously in newspapers while withholding others from print until the right moment and the right audience. She acted the part of a mature artist with a reputation to conserve. The absence of poems under her name in print might have derived in part from wartime conditions, but it was also a deliberate choice. (See Table 1 in the appendix.)

A lengthy poem, "The Arrival," which appeared anonymously in the *Independent Chronicle*, a new paper that had already emerged as the most sympathetic to antislavery writings, bursts with enthusiasm and pathos as it turns, unusually, from panegyric to elegy. The occasion was the return of John Hancock, serving as president of the Continental Congress, to Boston, accompanied by a mounted guard and what eighteenth-century Anglo people called demonstrations of public joy (church bells, cannon fire, formal greetings, a crowd in the streets). Hancock had been a supporter of Wheatley's, signing the attestation affirming her authorship in 1772. More recently, the very wealthy merchant had triumphed over rivals to become the indispensable man of Boston politics: popular with the people, agreeable with elites, and ideologically flexible while undeniably pro-patriot. At the time of his return he had served more than two years in Congress while also retaining titular leadership of the Massachusetts militia. His importance in 1777 was more civil than military yet, at the same time, both local and national. As his showy but impressive signature on the Declaration of Independence suggests, his fame paralleled that of the figures Wheatley had recently praised in verse, Lee and Washington, who had become so important after war came to New England.

Like so many of Wheatley's praise poems, "The Arrival" begins with classical markers: the nine Muses (called "sisters of the sacred well," as in Milton's "Lycidas"), nymphs and Tritons, "rich libation," and even "music of the coral shade" for a man who, as everyone knew, derived his wealth from the sea. Hancock's return can hardly be more momentous or happy. The first, clarifying mention of the actual occasion then deliberately evokes popular hymns about the second coming of Christ: "He comes! I hear the golden sound . . .'Tis HANCOCK comes!" The author depicts the merchant as popular hero and public servant, returning home to accolades—not only "the loud paeans of th'exulting throng," but also gold-lettered tributes that hang in the street as if "Some hand immortal drop'd it from the skies." Hancock is Poseidon, his masculine strength tempered only by the homely virtues proven by the very fact of his return.

Anticipated by an emphasis on his return to "domestic walls," the poem shifts into elegy, asking, "HANCOCK, why that sudden tear?—/ O deign to tell it, and thy grief we'll share." Once again Wheatley joins subject, poet, and community in a public outpouring of emotion. In Hancock's case, the return to home and grief proves that he is about more than the wealth that, contributed to political causes, had made him so popular and powerful. The rich man has private woes. In 1777 he had lost the rock of his life, his aunt Lydia Henchman Hancock, as well as the infant daughter he and his new wife, Dorothy Quincy Hancock, had named after Aunt Lydia. The poem mentions, in a footnote, only the death of "the late Mrs. HANCOCK": she evidently didn't know about the recent loss of the baby, who had been sent home during the summer with her mother in a desperate attempt to preserve her health. (It is also quite possible that she not only knew Lydia Hancock but also knew that she had freed her slaves and left them funds in her will.) The story told here is of a devoted son who keeps the flame of an extended family, especially a benevolent mother figure who—a true Hancock— looks down benevolently on all of Boston.

With the turn to Lydia Hancock the poem not only flips genres: it flips genders. The mother figure is now one of the generous deities, the statesman a teary-eyed picker of graveyard weeds and planter of flowers. The poet ventriloquizes the mourning Hancock just as Wheatley had earlier spoken for deceased children and their parents after their ascent. Like Thomas Gray, Edward Young, and other "graveyard school" poets, Wheatley moves consciously or unconsciously away from a strictly religious resolution of death and focus on worship and toward a stress on human relationships, including the relationship between mourners and poets. It can also be read as another appeal for friendship, for patronage, and for identification, like the poems for

Washington and Lee. She shows John Hancock in the best possible light at a moment when some criticized him for extravagance and others for demagoguery. (The *Boston Gazette*, partial to the more radical faction, gave his arrival just one understated sentence.) By allying his public and private virtues, the poem justifies the celebration of Hancock. It performs the relationship between the public and the private mourning Wheatley had turned into her expertise and joins the Bostonian and American planes on which she had come to operate. The poet in the poem has the capacity to traverse heaven and earth (the poem literally begins above and ends in the ground), but also emphasizes the strong, decisive influence of women on the second most famous man of the republic, who has been taught to feel what they feel and to mourn women as well as celebrate men. As much as ever, Wheatley tried to appeal to both men and women as readers and patrons, now through the revolutionary cause.

A few weeks later, after the American victory at Saratoga, she appears to have experimented again in a more fantastical vein, extrapolating from late October reports and the ensuing festivities in Boston that singled out the victorious general. Horatio Gates had been present at the siege of Boston and "had impressed the New Englanders." Subsequently he became a favorite of theirs and in turn praised Yankee soldiers at a time when others, like Washington, expressed skepticism about militiamen and short-term Continental enlistees. Invoking "the adventurous muse" (the title of a famous poem by Isaac Watts; she had used "advent'rous strain" and "advent'rous lays" in *Poems*, but referred to her own muse increasingly often after 1773), she again begins Homerically, as in the Washington and Lee poems, by depicting the poet's task as parallel to those of the "glorious chief" who, also with "divine assistance," manages "to bound the limits of thy country's woes."

After her usual mention of the Muses, laurels, and heaven's direction, Wheatley paints a more violent picture, a more desperate victory than in earlier panegyrics. Gates "nobly stood the rage of thousands" on the battlefield to save civilians, symbolized by women and children and displaced farmers. This is the "savage," hard civil war, with "deeds infernal" and "useless waste" wholly blamed on England, that New Englanders had experienced and read about and that became controversial again during this campaign, with reports of atrocities on both sides. As in *The Iliad*, the hero responds in kind, setting and raising the level of justified "gore." Wheatley fully adopts both the pleasure and the disgust in war that characterizes the Homeric epic tradition, in which women inspire, justify, celebrate, and sometimes also limit manly battles. Having praised the hero for doing what he must do—what God directs—she projects forward, again into an elegiac mode, to Gates's "glorious god-like shade," imagining the gratitude of a future graveyard walker, who will remember his deeds "after all these horrid wars are o'er." This imagined "swain," a male figure, conjures the feminine figures of "virtue" and "liberty" who "found a bounteous patron" in Gates. Liberty rewards the great general by placing his "deeds with those of Heav'ns imperial race."

During the same months that these poems appeared, the slavery question had burst into the open again, in Massachusetts, as the state began a long and complicated effort to create a new constitution. Massachusetts is usually celebrated for its robust tradition of town meetings and for the seeming innovation of successive elected conventions that wrote and then in 1780 ratified its charter for republican government. Convention and ratification, however, evolved after the legislature's attempt to make a new constitution failed, controversially, to establish a consensus on key questions of representation, the extent of the franchise, and the seemingly minor—but impossible for the revolutionaries to disentangle—questions of emancipation and "nonracial citizenship." These entangled questions were also inflected by an urban-rural split, and related controversies over worsening economic conditions, that would plague the state in the years to come.

In December 1777, a committee formed by the elected assembly returned a draft of a new constitution that retained key executive powers, including the right to dissolve the legislature, that reminded many Massachusetts voters of the actions of former governors like Bernard, Hutchinson, and Gage. As revisions proceeded, the representatives tabled a proposed provision to end slavery in Massachusetts. While widening the franchise for elections to the lower house of the legislature to include all white men regardless of whether they owned property, they also added a clause that explicitly disenfranchised free blacks and Natives. Proceeding to act formally as a convention in January, delegates compromised on executive power to some degree, giving up the veto power, but in exchange conservatives won restrictions on suffrage and qualifications for elective office. When the terms of the debate and compromise that occurred behind closed doors leaked out, questions of democracy, race, and slavery fully entwined in the process of reform and constitution-making.

In the convention, and in the newspapers, those who were for more suffrage for white people seemed to be aligned with those who would let free people of color join them at the polls. Writers in the *Boston Gazette* and the *Independent Chronicle*, the papers where the poems to Hancock and Gates had appeared, advocated for a commitment against slavery in the state's new laws and constitutions. On January 8, William Gordon pointed to the lack of a bill of rights and called distinctions of color for voters "ridiculous, inconsistent and unjust." No other American state, he observed, had done anything of the kind.

Three weeks later, while the convention still worked over its drafts, another anonymous writer in the *Independent Chronicle* offered a rebuttal to these antislavery criticisms in the form of a poem called "The Constitution," supposedly taken "from the celebrated Captain Gulliver's travels when a proposal was made at Lilliput to admit the negroes into those assemblies." Jonathan Swift's famous novel *Gulliver's Travels* had said nothing explicit about African slavery or citizenship. It was a satire on the travel literature that made species distinctions among humans based on body sizes and supposed similarities to animals. The book was also understood by some as a critical response to colonialism in Ireland and abroad. The larger target of the writer of "The Constitution" was democracy, in which "Distinctions all, are thrown aside." Swift's imagery provided a familiar example of worlds turned upside down, where small creatures (Lilliputians) bind large ones (Gulliver), and wise and seemingly humane animals, the equine Houyhnhnms, don't question their enslavement of brutish Yahoos (humans who look like Gulliver). Far from antislavery, "The Constitution" purported to show how suffrage reform would lead, in the hands of the Constitution's critics, to "The barrier . . . tumbled down / Twixt' *Guinea Old*, and our *Young Rome*."

The next, obvious step was race mixing, "when all the senatorial band, / Will take *their Phillis* by the hand." Foolish democrats would then forbid racial discrimination of any kind. They would not even take into account the well-known objections of the "southern gentry" to the end of slavery in any part of the new union. The author admitted that the absolute, natural color line he demanded would ultimately require emancipation and the expulsion of freed Africans. He'd sacrifice slavery to save Massachusetts from equality. In the meantime, though, he appealed to women—"the fair"—to make their supposedly natural revulsion against black mates clearer. Viewed as a whole, the poem takes on the democratic revolution that would end slavery and undermine class distinctions by asking women to do their part to keep things as they are. This was the supposed reading lesson of *Gulliver's Travels*, even if Swift himself had offered a bitter attack on how seemingly enlightened Europeans invoke nature to oppress the lowly when morality and religion fail them.

Whether or not she saw the reference to "Phillis" as a direct and personal provocation, Wheatley would have understood that the future of slavery and of black citizenship could be determined in Massachusetts constitution-making. Given her familiarity with Augustan poets like Pope and Dryden, she also knew how satirical verse battles were conducted. Yet she had not replied to or engaged in satire before. She didn't risk her reputation by signing a reply, but this anonymous response in an African and feminine voice suggested just how difficult, how charged, how potentially revolutionary or counterrevolutionary this moment in history had become for her as well as for the enslaved of Massachusetts. If this poem is hers, it is a key work in her oeuvre, a culmination of her development as a politically engaged antislavery writer.

Would replying itself, an "answer to a fool," drag her down? The question occupies the first two eight-line tetrameter stanzas of "Reply to THE CONSTITUTION," though it answers itself. There is no choice when "rancour rages uncont[a]in'd . . . Promiscuous wreāk'd on friends and foes." "Rancour" and "prejudice," it needed to be pointed out, always miss their "prize." The dirt and disgust that the author would pin on Africans is really characteristic of this mode of "uncontain'd" rage.

For Wheatley, the sin of political racism far transcends the specific questions under consideration in the constitutional debate:

> Say, why this insult and disgrace—
> So freely thrown on Afric's race;
> Or shall we, wondrous author! Own,
> That insult can from thee be thrown?
> Our different hue tho' nature gave,
> Does colour constitute the slave?
> For that can man of sense despise?
> From thee can want of virtue rise?
> What barrier can that race divide,
> But in thy ignorance and pride?
> The sole distinction nature made,
> In good, and ill, alone display'd.

Having established the relativity and essential meaninglessness of race as just another of nature's colors, she then proceeds to give a lesson on slavery. This redefinition, she maintains, is from "the sacred page," but it actually derives more from the Stoic philosophers, or Horace, who explicitly questioned whether a man who is slave to his passions or self-delusions is really free:

> *The* slave *is he, whom passion sways;*
> Mean slave? *Who envy's voice obeys:—*
> *More sable far, his* mental *hue,*
> *Who bids fair virtues path adieu.*

Instead of race justifying slavery, or slavery being relativized as a metaphor, color becomes a metaphor for enslaving passions. Unthinking racists, in other words, act like stereotypical slaves. The argument parallels Swift's savage satire on savagism, in which Europeans display their barbarism in how they treat those they call barbarians.

But she is only getting started with her own satire on colonial thinking, the justifications that allow Europeans to grab overseas wealth in people and then pretend to exist apart from the colonized and enslaved. "For what you cross'd the seas profound?" she asks: "The wisdom absolute should keep, / That *barrier true*, the roaring deep." If the author of "The Constitution" wanted to fantasize racial separation, the first step should be to leave Africans alone, in Africa, where "Each Afric would well pleas'd remain, And cultivate his native plain; / Wou'd view around the rural scene, / All beauteous in eternal green." As in the exchange of poems with Lieutenant Rochfort and much French natural history writing, even the savage state has its virtues, such as Edenic innocence and peace: so far from the sexualized scandal that the author predicted under the new constitution.

Wheatley had repeatedly claimed a virtuous feminine voice and sought to make white women her natural allies. "Reply to THE CONSTITUTION" scorches her opponent for reducing their contributions to their choice of mates: "Each generous Afric's bosom burns, / . . . When in insulting strain you dare, / With scandal touch *Columbia's fair*." She finally exposes "The Constitution" for its attempt to divorce both the slavery issue and the citizenship issue from the American revolutionary struggle. Fortunately, the actual General Court (sitting as the convention) understands freedom. She again allegorizes freedom as a goddess, as kind and generous rather than "jealous" and angry:

> *Nor does the Queen disdain to hear,*
> *The suit her sable sons profer;*
> *But gracious, with a smile divine—*
> *Assents, and frees the injur'd line.*

It's his "satire," not black or white women, that is "low, [and] promiscuous." The author has earned the ultimate neoclassical insult: an anti-monument with an anti-epitaph. He'll be the one submerged "[i]n *dark oblivion's sable deep.*"

This exchange of verses over the Massachusetts Constitution, like Jefferson's exchange with Wheatley, suggests a trend that would become more and more apparent in the years to come. The Revolutionary War produced a virulent political racism as a backlash against black empowerment, even though the debates that led up to independence had provided antislavery openings. Not surprisingly given how much of the imperial conflict had started there, Massachusetts remained a battleground for what the Revolution would mean. The Revolution was still moving both for and against slavery, both for and against race, and both for and against Phillis Wheatley.

Wheatley's awareness of and participation in these developments help explain the even more antislavery effort she made in this vein five months later, in response to the death of her former correspondent General David Wooster in battle against British forces raiding coastal Connecticut. The Continental Congress proposed building a memorial, but perhaps since the raid was a relatively minor affair, and the elderly Wooster's death was not widely reported, Wheatley may not have learned of it until the summer of 1778, when she replied to a letter from the widow Mary Clap Wooster "inclosing a paper containing the Character of the truly worthy General Wooster." Had Mrs. Wooster provided the raw materials and asked for an elegy? She was the sister-in-law of the Reverend Timothy Pitkin, who had been the addressee of an earlier Wheatley elegy, a friend of Occom's, and a trustee of Dartmouth College. This was in effect an exchange, part of a patronage relationship. Wheatley responded with a particularly daring and personal poem even though she hadn't actually "been honour'd with a personal acquaintance" with Mary Wooster.

The Wooster elegy seems at once more heartfelt and more explicitly political than the earlier poems to great soldiers. She must have felt certain that the Woosters' sympathies were with her, and also possibly emboldened by her recent efforts to praise leading figures. She launches directly into verse, mid-letter to Mary, in the only surviving version: "From this the Muse rich consolation draws / He nobly perish'd in his Country's cause." Wooster is the perfect patriot: "His Country's Cause that ever fir'd his mind / Where martial flames, and Christian virtues join'd." There is no hint of flaw; he dies "inly serene."

This is not just because only good generals die in battle. It is because Wooster can be allied to the highest cause, the noblest version of the American Revolution. Picturing his dying moments and last words like one of Homer's heroes on the battlefield, Wheatley makes the most of the opportunity to memorialize by putting her most explicit and challenging antislavery statements into Wooster's mouth. If freedom is the common cause, abolition is the necessary result:

> But how, presumptuous shall we hope to find
> Divine acceptance with th' Almighty mind—
> While yet (O deed Ungenerous!) they disgrace
> And hold in bondage Afric's blameless race?
> Let Virtue reign—And thou accord our prayers
> Be victory our's, and generous freedom theirs.

What may seem rough or drafty—some vagueness of subject and object—in the rest of the poem derives from Wheatley's aims. This poem is about the construction of the revolutionary community, much as the letter that contains the poem is about Phillis's own network. The "us," or "ours," for Wooster, is the Americans, and "they" or "them" shifts between certain Americans—the enslavers—and the Africans who deserve freedom. Wheatley portrays an American hero who can divert his vision from the enslavers to the enslaved. Her Wooster chooses to identify with Africans over his mistaken fellow patriots as more godly and more deserving of freedom. It is an audacious ventriloquism that makes Phillis Wheatley's own voice the arbiter of patriotism. That she writes the story in her own name marks her as African and American as well as free.

Wheatley ends the poem with a gesture to what Mary Wooster herself might do: "Tis thine, fair partner of his life, to find / His virtuous path and follow close behind." This might seem vague and trite, if not itself "presumptuous," as an admonition to the wife of a general and daughter of a president of Yale College, were it not immediately followed, in the letter, with a more specific request for Mrs. Wooster to "do me a great favour by returning to me by the first opp[ortunit]y those books that remain unsold and remitting the money for those that are sold—I can easily dispose of them here for 12/£m.o each." She ended the letter charmingly, apologizing for its length in light of her "fondness" and "respect" for the deceased and her sincere sympathies with "the great loss you and your family Sustain."

To follow David Wooster's "virtuous path" could mean abolition, but it could also mean very real help for an emancipated Phillis Wheatley. Nowhere does she make more apparent or explicit how much the material and the political had merged with the literary and the personal than in this poem and letter. The fates of the emancipated and the enslaved were linked. Her search for friends, and kin, continued. Her poems remained a weapon, she hoped one of peace and freedom.

23

THE ENDS

During the spring of 1778 citizens of Massachusetts continued to argue, in fits and starts, about whether freedmen could be citizens. The Reverend William Gordon wrote a series of articles against the proposed constitution that included an attack on both its silence about slavery and its enfranchisement of men "except Negroes, Indians and Molattoes." This fifth article was "blacker than any African; and if not altered, will be an everlasting reproach upon the present inhabitants, and evidence to the world, that they mean their rights only, and not those of mankind, in their cry for liberty." But proponents of the anti-black clause continued to worry about what allies in the southern states would think if Massachusetts freed or enfranchised Africans, and Gordon lost his job as chaplain of the Massachusetts Assembly for speaking his mind.

Despite antislavery public opinion evident in the resolves of some of the towns, emancipation via legislation stalled again. The state also continued to go back and forth on the question of black troops. Still, the bill of rights in the actually ratified Massachusetts constitution of 1780 did include language about "all men" being "born free and equal." Enslaved people began to use that provision in court when suing for their freedom. No single decision banned slavery, though

judges seemed reluctant to enforce hereditary bondage. At the same
time, the market for young black men and women in the newspapers
remained active through 1783.

The Revolution had discredited and weakened slavery but also
sapped the attack on slavery. How and why and when slavery ended
in Massachusetts has been a historians' chestnut ever since. In one
important sense, emancipation came rather suddenly, when enslavers
stopped being able to depend on courts and markets to work for them.
In every other sense, it would be gradual, and its meanings unclear, as
if the people who increasingly called themselves white wanted to forget how long it had taken, all those accusations of hypocrisy, or even
that slavery had ever been significant in the Bay State. The ambiguities
of emancipation persisted and magnified throughout the final years of
Wheatley's life and shaped the actions she took. She tested the meaning and substance of her freedom. She experienced on a personal level
many of the triumphs and the tragedies of the first U.S. emancipation,
which might also be called the first Reconstruction.

On March 12, 1778, seventy-two-year-old John Wheatley died. Throughout his life and Phillis's, Wheatley's name and fortune had meant
both enslavement and an uncertain amount of protection and security. Now that the enslavement was over, the protection and security
dissolved as well. Though she was probably living in his house or with
his Lathrop children and grandchildren, John Wheatley's will left
all the parts of the estate to Nathaniel or to Mary Wheatley Lathrop.
There was confusion about the house and shop: Nathaniel insisted he
was coming home with his family after the war, so it would actually
be rented out, rather than sold, until Nathaniel died in Boston in 1783.
Regardless, the will made no mention of Phillis, despite her need for a
new home. To John Wheatley, she was no longer, if she ever had been,
truly considered family.

In the only surviving detailed description of the man, the *Boston*

Gazette praised John Wheatley's "quiet and universally benevolent disposition," his "industrious and thoroughly honest" business practices, and his "faith in the great Redeemer." Phillis Wheatley's own testimonies to his benevolence in the past had been brief and general, not nearly as effusive as her praise of Susanna Wheatley in a poem and a letter to Obour Tanner. Her quick response to John Wheatley's death suggests that the practicalities were far more important than personality or sentiment.

On April 1, three weeks after John died, Phillis Wheatley publicized her intention to marry a man named John Peters. On May 28 she asked Obour to send future correspondence to an address in Queen Street, where Peters had a store. Ties to what remained of the extended Wheatley family still mattered: on November 26, two months after Mary Wheatley Lathrop died of a "tedious" sickness, the Reverend John Lathrop performed the actual wedding ceremony of Phillis and John Peters. Still, when the male Wheatleys' failure or disinclination to provide for her became finally clear, or when their power over her finally ebbed, she chose, immediately, to form her own family.

Who was John Peters? He was seven years older than Phillis, had been baptized as Peter by a minister named Peters in 1751, and had formerly been known as John Francis and as Peter Frizer. Originally from Middleton, Massachusetts, a rural town closer to Salem than to Boston, he had left the farm of John Wilkins, where his parents and brothers had been enslaved, after repeated threats and incidents that suggest he expected and had reason to expect special treatment. In other words, he might have been a blood relation of Wilkins. By the time he was twenty, in 1766, he'd had the increasingly common experience of being warned out of Boston. Strapped municipalities tried to get rid of possible poor relief cases and more frequently declared black folk to be strangers rather than natives and thus owed nothing by the community. John Peters might have left another enslaver, or he had been rented out, working toward his freedom by getting Boston wages.

Wheatley, then, could have known him for many years before their engagement.

Peters became a successful grocer and supplier and forged a new understanding with his former enslavers John and Naomi Wilkins. He marketed the products of their farm and supplied goods from Boston. Later he became known for wearing a wig and carrying a cane—gentlemen's attire—and for representing other blacks as well as himself in court. Courts were "a relatively level playing field" for blacks in Massachusetts. His litigiousness on his own behalf can be considered typical of men of commerce in a volatile, cash-poor economy, and of New Englanders more generally. Hannah Mather Crocker remembered him as "a man of noteriety." To Francisco de Miranda, a Venezuelan traveling in New England, he was a "sagacious negro." Abigail Mott recalled him as a person of "considerable learning." One of Susanna Wheatley's sisters described "not only a remarkable looking man, but a man of talents and information [who] wrote with fluency and propriety, and at one period read law."

Given that some other Marshall-Wallcut-Wheatley family descendants came to dislike Peters, indulged in stereotypical descriptions of him as lazy and surly, and blamed him for how they lost touch with the famous former slave who had died young, these positive descriptions affirm that Wheatley had chosen to partner with a black man whose virtues, standing, and prospects in town approached her own. What John Peters was doing in the market and in court—making a name, representing the race—with similarly mixed success, seems analogous to what Wheatley was doing in print.

In the short run, John and Phillis Peters prospered. In the longer run, they did not. Like the white Wheatleys, Obour Tanner and her Newport friends later tut-tutted that Phillis had married down, even ruined herself. Hannah Mather Crocker, who got several other things wrong in her short account of Wheatley's life composed decades later, wrote that "he did not treat her w[e]ll," so much so that "she soon fell a prey, to disappointment and her keen sensibility proved a sudden decline and she died."

The rogue marriage that disappointed wiser friends and family was a very familiar story told by women about women. It's also hearsay. It is always easy to judge marriages by their results as measured by the later fates of a man or a woman, seasoned with the kind of gossip that the Wheatley descendants could provide about John Peters's grand ambitions and failings as a provider. They had empathetic as well as personal motives to stress Phillis's victimhood as a woman who, they said, suddenly had to keep house and raise children when she supposedly (the Wheatley descendants preferred to imagine) had experience doing neither.

They also suggested, variously at different times, that John Peters *both* did not want her to work outside the home and expressed frustration at her failure to earn money. It's impossible to tell whether the double standard that led to these judgments of the Peterses' marriage existed during the stresses of wartime or emerged later to help justify the family's failure to support the brilliant young woman they described as almost but not quite kin. The dynamics of the Peterses' marriage have dissolved in a haze of rumor and self-serving justifications that documents like tax records do all too little to clarify. What the records do establish is that they owned, for a time, a substantial house in Boston, and then later in Middleton, where he ran the Wilkins estate until a rift with the family turned the neighborhood against them. For a time, Peters's mercantile activities extended beyond Boston. Like many Bostonians, poor and genteel, during very hard years, John Peters won and lost court cases, faced arrest, and experienced incarceration at a time when prison was as much for debtors as it was for violent offenders.

These seemingly extraordinary circumstances were actually rather ordinary in eastern Massachusetts around 1780. Before we pronounce them tragic, as most accounts of Wheatley's life have done, it's better to pause, to consider first what marriage meant to her and her generation.

The hardest thing for enslaved men and women to do in eighteenth-century New England was to keep families together—because Africans' flexible and unpaid labor, available in the marketplace and subsumed into white families in a cash-poor economy, helped keep those white families afloat. When blacks had their own families, white families' needs often interfered. In the 1770s, young enslaved women continued to be advertised for sale for "no fault" except being pregnant: a state that threatened, at least temporarily, to turn a savings into a cost. The antislavery petitioners of the early 1770s, such as Felix Holbrook, summarized their own oppression as a state of having "no property. We have no Wives, no Children. We have no City. No Country." New England had tied all these things together. Marriage and family epitomized, actualized the town-based belonging, household sufficiency, and relative equality that Yankees were known for and were fighting for in 1778. The antislavery petitioning men of 1774 tried to make it clear by describing wives and children as the essence of what slavery took from them—*their* property—reminding authorities that in American slavery, that loss, that oppression, could be repeated again and again, generation after generation: "Our children are also taken from us by force."

Phillis had some property—her book—and the possibility of another volume, but it hadn't proven to be enough to support her. She would have lost the roof over her head as the Wheatley property passed to Mary and then, within months, to an absent Nathaniel Wheatley. Getting married made more than economic sense. It connoted freedom, meaningful freedom, a kind that both John and Phillis sought to create and preserve.

The privacy that Wheatley, a public figure, seems to have insisted upon, or that John Peters enforced to the great frustration of some of Phillis's former patrons and friends, had a distinct logic. One of its results is that we know little of the last six and a half years of Wheatley's life. She gave birth at least once, possibly three times. She moved, with her husband and probably one child, to Middleton in 1780, and back to Boston in 1783. There are suggestions that she worked, in and out-side the home, but also hints, in a court deposition, that her husband tried to shield her from kitchen work during their Middleton years, so much that it became a source of conflict with the other members of the household. She suffered illnesses, possibly related to the respiratory ailments she had written about to Obour earlier. She kept writing. She tried to make her marriage work.

As a trader, Peters initially caught a fortunate wave as demand for goods rose. Having roots in Boston probably worked to their advan-tage as a couple. He partnered with Josias Byles Jr., a nephew of the Reverend Mather Byles, to sell goods in Worcester County. His travel was unusual and extensive enough that someone tipped off the Mas-sachusetts Council, which ordered him to be seized and searched on suspicion of trading with the enemy. These orders made a point of mentioning that John Peters had "lately married the famous Poetess, a Negro Girl sometime past Servant to the late Mr. Wheatley of Bos-ton." By July 1780, though, Peters lost a critical court judgment. He had to pay, in hard currency, more than his assets, at a time of ram-pant inflation and controversy over price controls and the payment of debts and taxes. For some period, Peters might have left town to avoid debtors' prison, or have been intermittently incarcerated. (This was an increasingly common tactic of creditors, to have people imprisoned to try to get them or their families to give up hidden resources.) He was also traveling often back and forth from Middleton to Boston. At some point, Phillis stayed with Elizabeth Wallcut for six weeks or more, and might have assisted in her girls' school, only to be "collected"—rudely and ungratefully according to the Wheatley family lore—by her husband.

In her last surviving letter, to her "friend & Sister" Obour, carried by a "Cumberland" in May 1779, she stated that she was "well . . . tho' I have been Silent, I have not been unmindful of you but a variety of hindrances was the cause of my not writing to you.—But in time to Come I hope our correspondence will revive—and revive in better times—pray write me soon, for I long to hear from you—you may depend on constant replies." One of the hindrances was pregnancy and child care. A prayer written on June 13, sometimes attributed to her as "accidentally discovered in her bible," asks for God to "be pleased when thou bringest to the birth to give [me] strength to bring forth living & perfect a being who shall be greatly instrumental . . . a vess[el] of Honor filled for thy glory." Later in 1779, she may have taken advantage of her husband's absence to publish anonymously, in the friendly *Independent Chronicle*, a eulogy for "the young, the generous, and the gay" George Eustis. As in the prayer, the poem emphasizes "nature's universal sovereign, GOD." Death, the "cruel Monarch of the dreadful shade," has taken his body, but his immortal soul looks down, "unbodied" and "from shackles freed." More intensely than even her earlier elegies, this one plays with an ambiguity about "the darkness" that is both death and life on earth.

The next week, she published a proposal for a new, two-hundred-page volume of poems and letters. James White and Thomas Adams, the young printers who had just published John Lathrop's funeral sermon for his wife, Mary, set an inflation-driven high subscription price of £12 bound and £9 "sew'd in blue paper"—half up front, as usual. She may not have chosen a publisher luckily or well: while the proposal ran for many weeks, White and Adams, in a familiar pattern during these economically volatile years, struggled to get their newspaper out that winter and even shut it down for a time. On the other hand, it had usually been the younger, upstart printers like Isaiah Thomas and Ezekiel Russell (who were now working in Worcester and Danvers, respectively) who had been willing to test the market with a book proposal, which itself required no cash layout, only some column inches in their own paper. She used her married name, Phillis Peters. The proposal, in the voice of the publisher or third party, tried to position the volume as not only another amazing curiosity from an African author but also an inspiration to lovers of the arts and to young people especially.

While the title *A Volume of Poems and Letters on Various Subjects* links the book to its 1773 predecessor, the immediate mention of the dedication of the book "to the Right Honourable Benjamin Franklin Esq: One of the Ambassadors of the United States at the Court of France" presents the volume as timely in the wake of the French alliance that bolstered the American bid for independence. The dedication also was a distinct effort to secure Wheatley's identity as an American poet. Instead of showcasing the local content as she had proposed to do in 1772, highlighting her piety and classical learning, or foregrounding the British ties she had ultimately stressed in 1773, the selection and order of poems emphasizes engagement with the Revolutionary War, beginning with "Thoughts on the Times" and then following with the three poems to Generals Lee, Washington, and Wooster. These patriotic poems take the edge off the fact that there are subsequent poems in the volume to British officers as well, including one addressed to Rear Admiral John Montagu, who had been especially hated by patriots in Boston, and which, intriguingly, is the last poem listed. There are also elegies, friendship poems, and allegorical lyrics like "To Penelope" and "Niagara." At a time when she drew as much as ever on her own piety to deal with momentous changes in her everyday existence, as the "Prayer" suggests, she seems to reach out for a more secular audience than in 1773, less driven by the evangelical network that had supported her earlier efforts but that, with the absence of the Wheatleys and the breakdown of transatlantic missions and publishing projects, couldn't sustain her as an author.

As with the poems, the letters selected for inclusion are a deliberate reminder of her elite connections. They also signal her opposition to slavery by including a letter to Benjamin Rush, who had praised her in print as a one-woman antislavery argument in his pamphlet on the subject. The letters section leads with Lord Dartmouth—probably her introduction to the poem carried by the Wooldridges, so a letter that had presaged and helped set in motion her London trip—and ends with her sometime patron the Countess of Huntingdon, the addressee of three of the thirteen letters. Besides a letter to the Reverend Timothy Pitkin and one to "Mrs. S. W." (which could be for Susanna Wheatley, sent while in London, but also could be Susannah Wooldridge), only one other of the thirteen is addressed to a New Englander. Instead, the letters demonstrate her geographical range, beyond the American politics of the day that the first several poems seem to emphasize. A letter to "the Hon. T. H. Esq." is either Thomas Hubbard or the disgraced governor Thomas Hutchinson, now of London, possibly from her trip or before his departure to England.

Unfortunately, the Massachusetts economy took its worst turn, especially for the towns, just as the proposal appeared in the *Evening-Post*. If Phillis and John Peters hoped her poems would help pull them into continued solvency, or even help offset the looming lawsuit for £400 that went against him, they were disappointed.

The family soon left Boston for Middleton, where they spent at least the next three years, somewhat separated from Phillis's connections. John Wilkins had died, leaving a small bequest of £10 to John Peters— not as much as he gave to the enslaved maid Dinah Cubber, who was promised support for life if she remained with the widow and a sole remaining, disabled daughter. But Naomi Wilkins had already turned to Peters in 1779 as a substitute patriarch, to manage the farm and legal matters. Peters and Cubber beat back challenges to the will from John Wilkins's brother and Naomi's own family, and in early 1780 Naomi asked Peters to come live at the farm, "for he had done more for them than all their friends or relations since the time of his [her husband's] sickness." In exchange, she deeded the house and a surrounding 108 acres to him on the condition of his "comfortable support & maintenance" of the women. This was a common provision for property transfer in wills, in form like a modern reverse mortgage, in which younger men would receive the homestead if they promised to "pay" meanwhile to maintain a mother or siblings there or elsewhere. What was unusual was for a former slave to take the part of the master of the house. John Peters's talents, work, nativity, and connections had provided an innovative refuge against hard times, a possible hedge against debts. The Peters family moved in on April 27.

The white Wheatleys came to believe that Phillis wilted during this rustication. As a woman of Boston who had lived in fine houses on its central, busy streets, she may have. But then again, we don't know what landscapes she remembered from Africa, or what circumstances might have been better or worse for her own or her child's health. According to Margaretta Odell, she soon had two other babies to care for. She also could have had access to town life and printed matter in Salem, where the young printer and bookseller John Dabney later inscribed his copy of her *Poems* with his fond memories of discussing literary topics with her.

While the couple moved to the country and Peters commuted periodically to answer his Boston court dates, a striking switch occurred. The urban economy began to recover, while farming communities like Middleton suffered even more during the early 1780s, in part because of debt collections. Economic pressures probably contributed to what quickly became a stressful situation at the Wilkins-Peters farm. Like most patriarchs, John wanted things done his way, including the arrangement of furniture and labor in the house. Dinah Cubber did not want to take orders from him. His ambitions and the increase in bodies to cook and clean for must have increased her workload. A tipping point appears to have been Peters's insistence that his wife not cook—whether to preserve her health or her time as a mother or a writer, or because she lacked the skills—and his rule that only Naomi, not Dinah, could join them at table. Meanwhile, John insisted that Naomi tell Dinah not to be "saucy to him and his wife."

The house erupted with some kind of fight in August. Afterward, each side claimed to fear the other. Naomi and Dinah moved out, and neighbors intervened. The widow refused to accept any assistance or offer of mediation: clearly she had been counseled to go to court and charge Peters with breach of contract. Suits and countersuits ensued, and it became more and more difficult for Peters to make money on the farm as Wilkins and her lawyers began to sell pieces of the property out from under him, confident that the local courts would take their side. In the end, despite the legal assistance of James Sullivan, for whom Phillis Peters had once written an elegy, Peters lost the legal battle and the farm. John and Phillis and their children were evicted, right before harvest time, on September 6, 1783. The neighbors who had taken the most active interest in the case continued to buy up the Wilkins property at auction.

The Peters family suffered a common New England experience when they lost out in a property dispute over a house and farm. In another sense, they had pioneered a black American experience, in which, despite multiple reconstructions in law and politics, most whites and the legal system still sided against them, preventing them from retaining real estate or a secure household.

By June 1784, Phillis and John had returned to Boston, where they lived in a boardinghouse. Peters successfully petitioned the authorities for a liquor license. Nothing about their everyday life comes from their mouths or pens. They faced more debts deriving in part from the legal struggle for the Middleton farm and associated marketing ventures. Some said John worked as a baker and Phillis as a seamstress and cleaning lady. She did not give up her literary ambitions, nor her deep insistence on belonging to Boston.

Nor did people expect her to fade into obscurity. Captain Rufus Lincoln of Wareham, Massachusetts, captured and on parole on Long Island, copied "On Being Brought from Africa to America" and "To Captain H——D of the 65th Regiment" into his diary. Other young poets during the early 1780s cited her as an inspiration and an example of what the American Revolution meant to them. Perhaps detecting this persistent interest, her old printer Ezekiel Russell put a woodcut of her image from the *Poems* on the cover of his *Bickerstaff's Boston Almanack for the Year of Our Redemption, 1782*. Russell continued to specialize in broadsides and pamphlets, and he would publish the first of two new Wheatley poems that appeared as pamphlets during the early months of 1784. Despite Wheatley's deeply local and material concerns at this time, both these poems reassert her connection to the Revolution and the nation.

She addressed her *Elegy, Sacred to the Memory of That Great Divine, the Reverend and Learned Dr. Samuel Cooper* to his Brattle Street congregation, but immediately frames Cooper as the renowned and popular figure he had become: "For Thee the tears of various Nations flow." Cooper had been deeply involved in Boston and Massachusetts politics as a close adviser to John Hancock. Influenced by his frequent correspondent Benjamin Franklin, he had also been a vocal proponent of the French alliance, going so far as to accept payments from the French government for his advocacy. He was one of the key figures who helped the resistance in New England scale from the local to the national and international, as well as from the secular to the sacred.

After beginning with his fame, Wheatley brings Cooper home by describing his pastoral appeal to different kinds of people, from "Sons of Learning" to "th' illit'rate throng." She explains his power as "soft persuasion," as the crowds who heard him, "by rhetoric's commanding laws, / Comply'd obedient, nor conceiv'd the cause." This almost critical note winks at the skills of the man known as the "divine politician" and suggests a real, possibly deep identification with Cooper. She immediately recuperates his reputation and erases any sense of dubious motives or manipulation by reasserting the primacy of his ministerial roles. It wasn't mere rhetoric, after all: it was revelation. Wheatley's Cooper is a preacher, but quintessentially a writer, whose way with words elevates him to solar magnificence—as always her favorite trope and greatest compliment:

> *Thy every sentence was with grace inspir'd,*
> *And every period with devotion fir'd;*
> *Bright Truth they guide without a dark disguise,*
> *And penetration's all-discerning eyes.*

THY COUNTRY mourns th' afflicting HAND divine
That now forbids thy radiant lamp to shine,
Which, like the sun, resplendent source of light
Diffus'd its beams, and chear'd our gloom of night.

After establishing Cooper's loss as one to both "*Church* and *Country*," and his "death-less name" as equal to great statesmen or poets,
she affirms her personal connection: "The hapless Muse, her loss in
COOPER mourns, / And as she sits, she writes, and weeps, by turns; / A
Friend sincere, whose mild indulgent grace / Encourag'd oft, and oft
approv'd her lays." The muse is Wheatley gesturing at humility, but in
its final appearance, at the poem's conclusion, the muse is the godly
voice that sees all and communicates from above, hearing Cooper's
"latest breath" that asked all to "copy conduct such as thine."

Another elegy, "To Mr. and Mrs. ***** on the Death of Their Infant Son," appeared in the new and women-friendly *Boston Magazine*
in September 1784 as "selected from a manuscript Volume of Poems,
written by PHILLIS PETERS, formerly PHILLIS WHEATLEY . . . inserted as a Specimen of her Work: should this gain the Approbation
of the Publick, and sufficient encouragement be given, a Volume will
shortly be published, by the Printers hereof" (who this time included
her earlier magazine editor Joseph Greenleaf). The elegy itself, perhaps
because of the age of the deceased child, or because Wheatley might
have already lost one of her own children, seems darker, with the babe
in heaven scolding the earthbound parents even more severely than in
her similar earlier verses about children. It also depicts the trials of the
sick and their caretakers in more dire terms than ever: "Should heaven
restore him to your arms again, / Oppress'd with woes, a painful endless train, / How would your prayers, your ardent wishes, rise, / Safe to
repose him in his native skies." There is no loss of skill or of devotion
to composition in Wheatley's last years. Her health might have failed,
but her pen did not.

In *Liberty and Peace, a Poem*, published as a four-page pamphlet by the printers of the new *Massachusetts Centinel* with music by William Billings to celebrate a public thanksgiving, in October, for the ratification of the Treaty of Paris, "the prescient Muse" heralds Freedom, personified as a goddess who brings peace to America:

> LO! Freedom comes. Th' prescient Muse foretold,
>   All Eyes th' accomplish'd Prophecy behold:
> Her Port describ'd, "She moves divinely fair,
> Olive and Laurel bind her golden Hair."

This time Wheatley signals that *she* is the prescient muse by actually quoting *herself.* The goddess Freedom "moves divinely fair" in precisely these words in her published poem to George Washington, which she had placed so prominently in the table of contents for her proposed second book.

According to Francisco de Miranda, who spent a month in Boston when or shortly before Wheatley wrote and published "Liberty and Peace," at this very moment Phillis Peters was "dying in indigence." Possibly this was the white Wheatleys' already well-worn story: in his journal, Miranda doesn't say whether he actually met her or the husband he describes as impressive, only that she "had several children" and "suffered the same neglect that talents experience everywhere." Miranda might have been registering his skepticism about white Boston's rumor mill while still giving Wheatley credit for what she had achieved and focusing on that achievement. To Miranda, the end of her story, which he found himself telling before its actual end, should convey how she had answered "the most cruel laws" with "the most exalted pleasures." Her existence, despite her fate, said something important, something chastened but positive, about humanity.

If she was already dying, Phillis Peters chose an uplifting message as her final legacy in "Liberty and Peace," as she depicts herself, as well as America, as a successful survivor of trauma, as the blessed center of a truly new world. Freedom will "shine" in Columbia's "future Councils."

The world takes notice of the United States' distinctive promise of free trade: "To every Realm her Portals open wide, / Receives from each the full commercial Tide." This was the optimism of the immediate post-war scene, before the political and economic difficulties of the mid- to late 1780s that threatened independence anew. The peace will resolve the material problems of recent years that Wheatley knew all too well: it will spill over even to poets, putting Britain to shame. Albion must give up the "Thirst of boundless Power, that drew / . . . the Curse to tyrants due / But thou appeas'd submit to Heaven's decree, / That bids this Realm of Freedom rival thee!" In the heady post-treaty optimism of 1784, "Galia's Power"—the French alliance—is the corrective for British arrogance, enabling America to take its place: "new born Rome shall give Britannia law."

Having established the imperial as well as the pacific theme, covered by divine will, Wheatley provides, at length, her most classical, even Virgilian, ambivalent justification for the death and destruction the Revolution had wrought. As in Homer and Virgil, the soldiers take central stage in full gore and glory, "Sent from th' Enjoyment of their native Shore / Ill fated—never to behold her more!" When swords are put away, the story can be told. And who better to tell it than the poet who had often hinted, and sometimes told, of being sent from her "native Shore"? In America, Afric's muse becomes Europe's bard.

The Revolution had been a civil war. The other side had fought in a "savage" manner. The real victims, she assures her readers with the confidence of a participant, sufferer, and witness, are also the victors—the New Englanders, the Americans:

> Columbia *mourns, the haughty Foes deride,*
> *Her Treasures plunder'd, and her Towns destroy'd:*
> *Witness how* Charlestown's *curling Smoaks arise,*
> *In sable Columns to the clouded Skies!*
> *The ample Dome, high wrought with curious Toil,*
> *In one sad Hour the savage Troops despoil.*

But this is a celebration, a thanksgiving, and Wheatley ends with "ce-lestial *Peace*" on "every Tongue," a peace that, like the sun, "drives the Shades away." Peace means sailing ships. America takes its place among the nations, in a future that is a restoration of order, like the break of day, but with an emphasis, again, on "freedom," which brings "Commerce and Plenty," and is embodied by the goddess but is other-wise as undefined as the United States. The prayer Wheatley offers makes American ships agents of the Lord's peace—not of war, nor slavery. She affirms the view from Boston as any native would, in her own special language of ocean, heaven, and sun:

> *Auspicious Heaven shall fill with fav'ring Gales,*
> *Where e'er* Columbia *spreads her swelling Sails:*
> *To every Realm shall* Peace *her Charms display,*
> *And Heavenly* Freedom *spread her golden Ray.*

She had ended with a story about ships, much as she began her ca-reer as a published poet, but bathed in sunlight, instead of tossed by a storm. Phillis Wheatley Peters died on December 5, 1784. Margaretta Odell preserved a tragic tale of Phillis wasting away "in a situation of extreme misery. Two of her children were dead, and the third was sick unto death." On the other hand, she suggests that Peters deliber-ately kept the Wheatley kin in the dark about everything, including the funeral, while stating that Phillis was buried with her third child: something that is not confirmed by the obituary or any other source. As with any public figure in Boston, "friends and acquaintances" were invited to the funeral in the newspaper that most favored her. A brief death notice also appeared in two other Boston papers, in the *Con-necticut Courant*, and in several others elsewhere. The new *Boston Magazine* paid tribute with an elegy that imagined her special mean-ing for Africans and placed her where she had imagined so many who had gone before, seated with angels, a "lyre of gold," and a "crown of glory."

———

Released from debtors' prison, where he probably was when she died, a few months later, John Peters advertised for whoever had her manuscripts—a friend? a printer? Wheatley kin?—to return them. Odell later insisted that "of course" they were returned to him and that he took off for "the south," never to be seen again. That has turned out to be another canard, for John Peters made at least two subsequent efforts to publish her second book. In June 1791, Isaiah Thomas put out a detailed proposal to publish "Wheatley's *Posthumous* WORKS, Consisting of POEMS on various subjects and LETTERS to eminent Persons in Great Britain and America, with their answers &c." Thomas insisted that this was a new work that the printers had collated, with added value like George Washington's own letter to Wheatley, "several letters" from Granville Sharp, and thoughts on her poetry by Henry Hulton, now the customs commissioner in Antigua. Seven years later, Ebenezer Andrews, Thomas's partner in Boston, worked out a plan with Peters to gather subscriptions and share the profits on the volume, but it didn't happen. Peters died in Boston in 1801.

How much does the end of a life matter? Does it matter more at thirty-one? Are the *ends*—what one lived for—more important? Phillis Wheatley's end and her ends are shadowed by the absence of the book we don't have, a pile of manuscript lost somewhere in a nation's origins, a "founding" that we are told undergirds everything, so well documented, self-evident, ever more at our fingertips. The thirteen heretofore unattributed Wheatleyan poems I have found in Boston newspapers and magazines (which appear in the appendix, along with the disputed anonymous Boston massacre poem) provide clues, a taste of what her second book and postwar career might have been like. I have placed them into the story of her odyssey I have built from her acknowledged poems and many other sorts of clues. I hope I have done so unobtrusively, signaling the lack of certainty there and, indeed, about many other aspects of her life and her writings. It has seemed more responsible to present them and to let readers make up their own minds whether Wheatley wrote them and how much that matters.

But in finding what I wasn't even looking for, I also have found the historian's paradox: to remember, to discover, to revise the past is also to realize, always, how much we do not know. There is so much that she, as well as the deeply biased archive, kept hidden from view. We may know Phillis Wheatley the poet she wanted us to know, yet hardly know Phillis Peters, just as we hardly know the West African girl who became Phillis. It's a conundrum Homer embraced and she understood very well. Her odyssey makes her intimately knowable, yet still mysterious. I hope I have told her story, the parts we can know, with something of the humility with which any American ought to approach the intertwined stories of the American Revolution and the enslavement of Africans, the emancipations that happened and those that have not.

She kept writing, kept her ends in view, knowing and telling how much and how little words could do, until the end. She told us what she thought of death, the tyrant who was also a blessing. She told us what she thought of America, and slavery, and race, and freedom, at a time and place when those words mattered. She helped make those kinds of words matter. *Sometimes by simile, a victory's won.* As Homer asked of his muse, she may help us "find the beginning" and "sing for our time too."

24

THE AFTERLIVES

Her life was celebrated and brief and controversial, its end mysterious or, some have said, tragic. Her afterlives have been many and various, her disappearance from memory lamented and, in the process, prevented. She has remained and reemerged at various times as a symbol of Black achievement and antislavery, of victimization and invisibility, and most recently of resistance and true brilliance. As during her life, she has also been a site of white doubt and denial. The story of how she has been remembered is a long one, arguably with as many twists and turns and subtleties as her life and work, though far easier to track. In the twenty-first century, she has been reclaimed by Black poets who at times find enough material to imagine a different future as well as a revised sense of the past.

After 1784 the association of Wheatley with antislavery and black equality remained obvious. In a pivotal work for the transatlantic movement to abolish the international slave trade, for example, Thomas Clarkson quoted her poems prominently and summed up her meaning for the argument over race and slavery: "If the author *was designed for slavery*, (as the argument must confess) the greater part of the inhabitants of Britain must lose their claim to freedom." Little wonder that when he advertised the subscription for Wheatley's collected and

"Posthumous WORKS," Isaiah Thomas thought it strategic to state that Wheatley had not written "great poetry" but instead emphasized her letters to the abolitionist Granville Sharp and his hope that "antislavery society members will subscribe." Seven of the ten new editions of her book published between 1785 and 1837 appeared in Philadelphia or London, the hubs of antislavery activism. Even in Boston, the myth of Wheatley's decline and lonely death, amplified in 1834 by Margaretta Odell's *Memoir and Poems of Phillis Wheatley*, did not put much of a dent in the inspiration that abolitionist writers and activists took from her life. What tragic notes did appear seem as inspired by sentimental tropes about her "tender frame" as by any perception of neglect or failure.

The appearance of Thomas Jefferson's *Notes on the State of Virginia*, drafted between 1781 and 1784 but not published in English until 1787, amounted to an early pushback against this growing antislavery sentiment and its potential to make the young nation look hypocritical. While some of Jefferson's political friends and opponents did not miss his admission that slavery was fundamentally unjust, something he avoided repeating later when he served as secretary of state, vice president, and president, his direct challenge to the notion of Wheatley's genius as evidence for racial equality attracted copycats. During his presidency a critic complained that "thousands have been influenced by the condemnation of [Wheatley by] Mr. Jefferson" and as a result Wheatley's poems "are undeservedly neglected." Jefferson continued to draw prominent criticism on the matter of Wheatley's achievement, including from the transatlantic radical Gilbert Imlay and the French polymath Henri Grégoire. Samuel Stanhope Smith, the president of the College of New Jersey, took a page from both Jefferson and Clarkson when he asked pointedly in 1810, "What planter can write so well?" On the other hand, in the late 1810s and the 1820s, during a period of backlash against the antislavery movement, a series of satirical broadsides against "bobalition" mocked "Miss Phillis" and her poetry in dialect. These caricatures attempted to undo the published evidence of eloquence and literacy that had so effectively advanced claims to black citizenship.

Antislavery northerners responded by quoting her actual poems and adding them to school curricula. In Caleb Bingham's *Juvenile Letters* (1803), a writing primer, a Philadelphia boy of fourteen writes to another, "I wish much to see Phillis Wheatley's poems. Will you be so good as to procure me the volume?" By 1836, a writer in the *Antislavery Record*, a movement newspaper, could state confidently, "Many of our young readers have heard of Phillis Wheatley." *Freedom's Journal* (1827–29), the first African American newspaper, featured several of her poems. William Lloyd Garrison's *Liberator* serialized all of her poems in 1832 and helped push new editions of her book, stating in the newly militant and sensational style of antebellum abolitionism that "it would do well to have them always at hand so we might have some conception of the amount of genius that slavery is murdering." Black abolitionists like Frederick Douglass and William Cooper Nell pointed to Wheatley as an important predecessor. She helped them argue for African Americans' birthright citizenship and patriotism, even while the resurgence of political racism also made it necessary to continue to cite Wheatley to refute the increasingly biological argument against equality. Even phrenologists got into the act, making both positive and negative claims about black intelligence from what the famous frontispiece portrait from Wheatley's book supposedly revealed about her mental capabilities.

Wheatley's afterlives continued to follow political trends in both antislavery and antiblack directions. During the Civil War, at the height of the unionist alliance with African Americans, the Massachusetts Historical Society published Wheatley's letters to Tanner and some brief biographical essays that formed a partial counterpoint to Wheatley family members' well-intentioned but condescending narrative of her decline and death. Nevertheless, as Reconstruction faded into a reunionist acceptance among many American whites that slavery had been wrong but racism was not, Wheatley began to lose her small foothold in an emerging canon of American literature. The magazine editor and Jefferson biographer James Parton tried to nail the coffin of her reputation in 1878 by portraying her as displaying a "fatal facility of imitation" that proved "the justice of Jefferson's remarks." If anything, Parton magnified Jefferson's argument that "negroes" had contributed nothing to world literature. He did so to attack the argument that "antipathy to the negro" was a problem.

Richard T. Greener, a leading black scholar and activist, answered Parton at great length in another national magazine. His essay set the terms for Wheatley's reemergence as an icon in the era of Jim Crow. For African Americans after Reconstruction, Wheatley gained a significant place in an emerging pantheon of the first civil rights struggle, a gallery of heroes and heroines populated by famous "firsts" as well as political leaders. At a time of rising discrimination and segregated, underfunded public schools, her example demonstrated especially that blacks wanted education and would thrive when given equal access and resources. The sculptor Edmonia Lewis made a bust of Wheatley for the Chicago World's Fair, leading a writer for the Detroit *Plaindealer* to observe that Wheatley "is generally known by the colored people." Wheatley came to symbolize black literacy—a political as well as social and economic imperative in the wake of literacy tests for southern voters. Maybe if she had been closer to a plantation, some speculated, thinking of the new dialect poetry of Paul Laurence Dunbar, she would have sung a "deeper song." Nevertheless, precisely because she hadn't been treated like an ordinary slave, she proved what emancipation could mean.

Black Americans founded reading circles and literary societies named after Wheatley, in the South as well as the Northeast and Midwest. A Wheatley Club in St. Paul claimed to be the first "colored club" in the state. Schools, too, began to be named for Wheatley, for example in St. Louis. Made possible by segregation, these initiatives reflected African American control over visible symbols as well as curriculum. Before long, black women were writing most of the articles and leading most of the Wheatley celebrations that appeared regularly in the burgeoning black press. They defended Wheatley's poetry from criticisms of its aging style. These versions of "female benevolence" might also be called Wheatleyan in another important sense. The forty-five "educated, refined and progressive colored women" of the New Orleans Phillis Wheatley Club "read newspapers and magazines to find anything which may be printed for or against their people, and this is thoroughly discussed by the club." Within a few years the club had built a sanatorium and a training school for nurses.

In other cities Wheatley Clubs spearheaded the establishment of temporary homes for young women who came to cities looking for work but often found themselves shut out of segregated YMCA facilities. Jane Edna Hunter founded the Phillis Wheatley Association, which achieved national prominence for its fundraising success and its especially impressive 135-room home for working women in Cleveland. The pioneering back-to-Africa nationalist Edward Wilmot Blyden had attacked Wheatley during the 1880s for her self-distancing from the continent, but this didn't stop Marcus Garvey's Universal Negro Improvement Association from naming a hotel and a ship after her decades later. What's especially striking about the period from the 1880s to the 1930s is how Wheatley served as a unifying figure for Black Americans in an age of rampant discrimination. For women, she remained a "revered forerunner." In 1933, an ad for the North Carolina Mutual Life Insurance Company in the Baltimore *Afro-American* could even quote the disturbing first four lines of "On Being Brought from Africa to America" next to Wheatley's portrait in order to suggest their own position of "leadership" in the "fight against many odds."

Wheatley's status as a black female icon inspired some continued pushback from whites, who more often just ignored black history and literature. Changing tastes in poetry, however, introduced a skepticism that literary experts, especially a new generation of African American critics and teachers, found it difficult to ignore. Romantic poets still claimed popular reverence, but modernist writers often disdained neoclassical and pious poets of the eighteenth century as too distant from real feeling or real experience. By the second decade of the twentieth century, critics had begun to withhold praise from Wheatley or balance it with dismissive comments about her poems. At best she had been a "great soul," not a great writer, "of historical interest only." Chroniclers and canonizers like Benjamin Brawley and James Weldon Johnson began to describe a Wheatley who was too ethereal, "juvenile," "pathetic," and feminine for the rough-and-tumble faced by the cosmopolitan and inescapably political black writer. W. E. B. Du Bois found her verse "trite" and "halting." (He would change his mind by 1941, however.) Most damningly, proponents of the New Negro began to describe her as insufficiently race conscious. She had too much distance from the realities of slavery and the experience of most Black people. Alain Locke found her not an example to be followed because of her "painfully negative and melodramatic sense of race." She was "the Old Negro from whom one must turn away."

Meanwhile, for women of the Harlem Renaissance era, she remained an inspirational figure who showed imagination as well as courage and toughness. The NAACP cofounder Mary Church Terrell wrote and put on a pageant emphasizing Wheatley's response to George Washington and depicted her marriage to John Peters as a happy ending. This tradition persists in the dozens of children's and young adult books that have followed upon Shirley Graham's nationally broadcast radio play and fictionalized biography of 1949. Without exception, they have been written by women. Graham added drama and solved the conundrum of the white Wheatleys in Phillis's life by imagining a forbidden love between Nathaniel and Phillis. Graham truly brought Wheatley to life and managed to explode Jim Crow–era sexual mythologies at the same time, though she does seem to have elaborated, from Terrell's play, the scene of the Wheatley "trial" that remains so impervious to scholarly debunking (my own included).

During the late twentieth century, African Americans replayed the gendered drama of Wheatley love and disavowal, now rendered even more oedipal because of how it implicated the generations of black leaders who had emphasized literacy and uplift. For men in the Black Arts Movement like Amiri Baraka and Addison Gayle, Wheatley evoked pious Uncle Tom, "the celebrated house slave." The second-wave reading of Wheatley as accomodationist had even more decidedly masculinist overtones. A redoubled emphasis on blackness as culture made the assimilating poet who seemed to throw Africa under the bus into a race traitor. It hadn't helped that some of the counterevidence from Wheatley's own writings, such as her letters to Tanner and Occom, had not been widely published or even yet discovered during the 1960s. Echoes of this dismissive take on Wheatley persist into the twenty-first century among some nationalists who state as fact that she "glorified the white race" and functioned as an "intellectual whore."

During the 1970s and 1980s, archival discoveries helped set the stage for a renewed appreciation of Wheatley as a figure engaged in the controversies of her time. The reverse is just as true: surging interest in Black Studies spilled into various fields and contributed to reassessments even as militants measured themselves against Wheatley's seeming accommodationism. A modern scholarly edition of her writings appeared in 1966, with two more to come during the 1980s, widening access to parts of her oeuvre beyond the 1773 book. Critics and historians began to suggest that she had evolved significantly as a writer during her short life. The bicentennial of the American Revolution inspired more attention to Wheatley as a historical figure of the period. More and more children's books appeared, with a renewed focus on Wheatley as someone who made a mark as a teenager and thus might appeal to young people.

Most decisively, Black women writers and scholars launched an ongoing recovery effort in 1973, when Margaret Walker gathered twelve hundred people for a different bicentennial: the Phillis Wheatley Poetry Festival at Jackson State University. Feminist literary critics, librarians, and teachers came; authors who are now themselves canonized as pioneers, including Alice Walker, Nikki Giovanni, Audre Lorde, and June Jordan, read from their work on the theme of Wheatley and women as writers. Wheatley's experience became emblematic of the silencing of black female voices by men as well as by the white establishment. Their Wheatley expressed continuities and allowed them to connect imaginatively with the ancestors. "Phillis was reborn," but as an African, the property of Black women everywhere. Alice Walker wrote that it did not matter what Wheatley wrote so much as her effort to do so, even if she might be considered "pathetic" or "misunderstood." Knowingly, Walker nodded to the mothers of the preceding generations who had respected Wheatley in praising Phillis and Phillis's mother ("Perhaps she was herself a poet"), for together "you kept alive, in so many of our ancestors, the notion of song." To Margaret Walker, "it was the still, small voice of Phillis Wheatley, as constrained as she was, that enabled us to remember how important it is to write out of your own cultural and historical moment, and to tell the truth as we see it." The poet Naomi Long Madgett went further, portraying a canny Wheatley who played the loyal slave and convert while smuggling subversive Africanisms into her poems. The sculptor Elizabeth Catlett reimagined the frontispiece portrait with West African motifs.

In our time, Black poets like Kevin Young and Honorée Jeffers and dramatists like Amanda Kemp have extended and enlivened this new tradition. They give us breathtaking imaginings of what Phillis *might have* thought and said, considered in light of the newer scholarship—what we might know if we could see all the evidence, if we had all the manuscripts, if we can go a step further than prior literary criticism and biography to realize her as a black female genius who had unusual but not unimaginable or wholly foreign experiences as a racialized oppressed person, a daughter and mother as well as a prodigy. For these writers, Wheatley is too important and too intriguing to consider just as an antislavery argument or the victim of a white arraignment and a thin archive. Like Wheatley thinking about Horace and Terence and the trials of patronage, they explore "the restraints of a conditional fame." She may still be a timeless allegory for the black artist in a white society, but now she is a conscious, crafty one. They see her straddling worlds imagined and all too real. Her physical suffering becomes a central theme. Her authentic blackness, her womanist consciousness, her enslaved experience, and what she was up against to express herself and get published are no longer questioned, but rather imagined as complex and analogous to what these writers know and feel. Jeffers has written found poems and letters for her in a range of styles that call attention to her lost manuscripts and the biased archive as well as what might have been had she lived longer. Her "age," the "Age of Phillis," is no longer just her precociousness as a child genius: it's her times, and maybe ours as well. I'm looking forward to hearing this new Phillis Wheatley sing on Broadway someday.

As this project evolved over many years, I took heart from seeing others get closer to Wheatley's own consciousness and experience than the record would seem to allow. Even for worked-over histories and seemingly antiquated poets, the facts do change, because we do. "When they tell you there are no sources . . . be skeptical. Look at old sources in new ways," pioneers of history from below told us. We can miss an archive that is hiding in plain sight. Many of the materials I've used to reconstruct Wheatley's life and art were not available at all, not easily accessed, or not considered relevant by earlier scholars and readers. Whether it is her rediscovered letters, the clues and the poems in newspapers, or the forgotten writings of Homer, Horace, Lord Lyttelton, or John Lathrop, sometimes it is only the limits of our own knowledge and imaginations (and institutions) that keep us from seeing the footprints that stereotypes and time erase. Phillis Wheatley was more interested and engaged in both her "white" and her "black" worlds than we have been able to imagine or know. She read those newspapers—and those men and women who reacted to her—very, very carefully and in doing so preserved her mark in the record. This is what made her even more than the first of firsts.

Wheatley's afterlives suggest some of the difficulties of separating the historical or the literary from the political value of writers, especially those who became controversial or lived in revolutionary times. Her changing reputation, like her life story, might seem to fulfill the civil rights narrative of progress in U.S. and African American history, but it also demonstrates the repeated reinventions of racism. She shows us that culture is wild and various and refuses to stay in the neat boxes we devise for politics and identity.

Hers is an African diaspora story, a British story, a New England story, and an American story. Eighteenth-century contexts, shorn of the whitened exceptionalist gloss we have too often given the period, explain her brilliant choices. The actions of young Africans, including Wheatley, accelerated the revolutionary process. They forced issues of slavery and of race onto the table in ways that changed her and changed the nature and substance of the imperial controversy. Phillis Wheatley reveals the Revolution as a three-way affair and a war of words in which Africans were active and heard. For our understanding of history, it is a particular shame that the very historians most insistent on the role of words in the American Revolution have been so tone-deaf to her song. It has been equally limiting, and perhaps inevitable, that shifting literary tastes have made it hard for readers to appreciate just how artful and how politically engaged she was. That this can change, that people find it possible again to read her now and hear a poet and a genius, suggests that there is something of more than historical interest in what she accomplished.

Phillis Wheatley proves that the story of the American Revolution is one of black resilience and creativity, of antislavery and antiracist possibilities, and of backlash and loss, dreams dashed and deferred. That story and the political path to and from nationhood are joined not only at the hip but in the hands that wrote the printed pages that made American independence thinkable and achievable. Her American Revolution happened and is also still being fought. The odyssey of her life and her afterlives converge in her prophecy that notwithstanding the "modern Egyptians" there is a "love of freedom." It spreads by simile: its victories may yet be won.

APPENDIX

Anonymous Poems Tentatively Attributed to Phillis Wheatley

Poems with their titles in brackets were untitled.

ON THE AFFRAY IN KING-STREET,
ON THE EVENING OF THE 5TH OF MARCH

With Fire enwrapt, surcharg'd with sudden Death,
Lo, the pois'd Tube convolves its fatal breath!
The flying Ball with heaven-directed Force,
Rids the spirit of its fallen corse.
Well sated Shades! Let no unwomanly Tear
From Pity's Eye, disdain in your honour'd Bier;
Lost to their View, surviving Friends may mourn,
Yet on thy Pile shall Flames celestial burn;
Long as in Freedom's *Cause the wise contend,*
Dear to your unity shall Fame extend;
While to the World, the letter'd Stone *shall tell,*
How Caldwell, Attucks, Gray, *and* Mav'rick *fell* . . .
[*Boston Evening-Post*, March 12, 1770]

[This poem on the Boston Massacre, which appeared without a title, matches the title in Wheatley's 1772 proposal; for further reasons for attribution see pages 103–104 and 410. It is represented by *B* in Table 2, below.]

ON NIGHT AND SLEEP

Night spreads her sable Curtains round
And all's in silent Darkness drown'd.
The Moon displays her borrow'd Light,
And twinkling Stars declare the Night.
Slumber, with all her Magic Pow'rs,
Enchants the Soul, and kills the Hours;
'Till kind Aurora's gentler Ray,
Darkness dispels, and brings on Day;
While Sol with his enlivening Beams,
Arouzes Nature from her Dreams.
[*Connecticut Gazette*, Oct. 11, 1771; *Massachusetts Spy*, Jan. 7, 1773, and Dec. 19, 1777]

ON THE DEATH OF MISS INCHES, BY A FRIEND

BETSEY is gone! To Realms unknown she flies,
And soars aloft, to greet her kindred Skies,
There she'll be welcom'd to her Saviour's Arms,
And, quitting earthly, shine in heavenly Charms.
Her Conduct here should Emulation raise,
Who most can gain, who most can merit Praise;
She sev'ral Stations laudably sustain'd,
Alike belov'd as Daughter, Mistress, Friend.
Th' afflicted Father mourns his Darling lost,
His flatter'd Hopes untimely Death has cros't;
No more the Maid with Rapture shall he view,
Source of his Care, his Joy, his Comfort too.
Her Faithful Servants the sad Loss deplore,
Their lov'd young Mistress is to them no more.
The fair Companions of her tender Youth

Her fate lament with Sympathy and Truth.
   Sad Recollection! Youth nor Beauty save
This mortal Body from the silent Grave.
Alas! how weak, how frail is human Breath?
This Day we live, the next we sleep in Death;
That awful Tyrant, in our gayest Hour,
Throws his fell Shaft, and we are seen no more.
   But hold, my daring Muse :—
      'Tis impious to complain,
   That HE who gave us Life,
         Demands that Life again.
[*Boston Post-Boy*, Dec. 13, 1773]

[NEW YEAR POEM FOR 1774]

HAIL welcome dawn, Aurora doth appear,
And with a blush brings forth the new-born year;
Kind Phoebus hastens from his sea-green bed,
And doth his blessings on the Instant shed.
But my Urania too, who long hath been
To me a stranger, with the year came in;
Great was my joy to see the rising year,
Nor less to see my darling muse appear.
I bow'd, she smil'd, and of the new-year sung,
In gentler notes, and tun'd my artless tongue.
May heaven defend us from those ills we fear,
And with ten thousand blessings crown the year,
No sound of war, disturb the rural swain,
Nor human blood, the field with purple stain:
Nor war-like drums, nor trumpets wake the spring,
Nor fatal battles, the ripe autumn bring.
And let the seasons all with joy be crown'd,

Let flow'ry blessings in the field be found:
Let harvest time repay the plow-man's care,
And peace and plenty, reign thro' all the year.
    May true liberty's, thrice glorious name!
Still ride in triumph on the wings of fame:
And may Britannia, once our parent dear,
Be reconciled to her children here;
Restore their rights, and all their wrongs redress,
That each may live in love and happiness:
While that the tyrant, and the traitor's name,
Forever sink into eternal shame.
[*Essex Journal*, Jan. 12, 1774; *Massachusetts Spy*, Jan. 20, 1774]

THE TRIUMPH OF THE REDEEMER

SOME seraph teach my daring song to rise,
O! Let me catch the music of the skies;
Illume my breast, exalt, refine the whole,
And pour melodious numbers on my soul.
What glories burst on my transported sight!
What charms with more than mortal beauty bright!
What anthems ring! What melting lays inspire!
What god-like angels strike the sounding lyre!
See! Ev'ry face the softest smiles assume,
How glows each feature with celestial bloom;
A bloom untouch'd by all devouring time;
Like flow'rs that blossom in perpetual prime.
Lo! Where in sight th' angelic armies move!
See opening fair the balmy climes of love!
Blest climes, where music strikes the warbling string,
Where joy exulting spreads its airy wing,
Where shrin'd in bliss triumphant beauty reigns,

And spring's eternal blush adorns the plains.
Oh! Could my strains with ev'ry grace appear,
Each thought that fires the soul, or charms the ear,
To me did ev'ry finer art belong,
The richest fancy, and the sweetest song;
This heav'nly theme th' harmonious voice should raise,
Warm all my thoughts and warble in my lays.
For lo! He comes, a victor oe'r the grave,
In triumph mild, exalted but to save:
In crouds th' applauding throng surround their King;
They tune their harps, and touch the finest string.
Angelic concert, musically flow,
It steals more soft, than vernal breezes blow:
Then swells a sprightlier note; all heav'n replies,
And labouring echo rings it round the skies.
Now bright as heav'n, as mild Aurora fair,
(Whose balmy breath perfumes the purer air)
He rose, with mercy beaming from his sight,
Then smil'd, and looked ineffable delight;
As when the Nightingale's melodious love,
Charms the still gloom, and fills the vocal grove;
The list'ning Zephyrs, hovering while she sings,
Catch ev'ry sound, and wast it on their wings;
Th' attentive swains her moving accents hear,
That melt the heart, and harmonize the ear;
Such (while each bosom felt unbounded joys)
Such music flow'd from his transporting voice;
While warm'd with more than rapture at their doom,
Each cheek was flush'd like roses in the bloom.
[*Boston Post-Boy*, Jan. 24, 1774]

NIGHT. A POEM.

Now sable night extends her gloom around,
And spreads her shady pinions o'er the ground;
While slumb'ring chiefs of bloody battles dream,
And courtship is the sleeping virgin's theme.
The feather'd choir forget their tuneful lay,
The toiling steer, the labours of the day;
The winds are hush'd! e'en eccho's voice seems dead,
Thick darkness wraps each drowzy mountain's head;
Grey mists ascend from every smoking flood,
And awful horror fills the silent wood,

    Lo Contemplation *lifts th' attentive eye,*
To view the splendour of the spangled sky;
Where stars unnumber'd strike th' astonish'd sight,
And twinkle through the dreary gloom of night;
Where the pale moon her peerless orb displays,
Apparent queen, all-bright in borrow'd rays,

    Arise, my soul! my muse begin the song!
The theme, his power, to whom these scenes belong.
Whose word omnisic form'd the beauteous earth,
And call'd the radiant sun and moon to birth!
In mystic order plac'd yon starry roll,
And can, or chear, or change, or spoil the whole.
Who now in darkness does his pow'r display,
And soon will change this darkness into day.
[*Royal American Magazine*, April 1774]

ON NIGHT

HASTE, solemn night, to close the eye of day,
To sooth each pain, and drive each care away,

To charm the soul of labour to repose,
While breathing zephyrs lull each folding rose;
To ease the anxious heart of thrilling fear,
While flattering hope deludes each starting tear:
'Tis silence all, and husht each warbler's throat,
Save Philomela's melancholy note.
Now wild Ambition plans each airy scheme,
But blasting Envy poisons ev'ry dream:
Now conscious guilt presumes in vain to find
One beam of comfort dawning o'er his mind;
But innocence, by downy sleep carest,
Feels no contending passions in her breast.
Now contemplation wings her sober flight,
And pours her secrets in the breast of night:
The glitt'ring stars in lucid order run,
Leaving no wishes for the absent sun.
The silent moon steals on, by slow degrees,
And seems to whisper to the list'ning trees;
'Till fair Aurora reassumes her sphere,
And drops a spangle in each cowslip's ear.
[Royal American Magazine, June 1774]

THOUGHTS ON TYRANNY

In distant periods near the ancient flood,
When simple manners were best understood,
When the long train of laws cou'd find no use,
Then social love did rule without abuse.
Then did the chain of civil order find
Its strongest links by mutual friendship join'd.
Then the great black-eye'd monster ne'er appear'd,
Tyranny—whose best motto is—be fear'd;
That scourge of nations, and the pride of kings,

That scorns the greatest, doats on meanest things.

Great Greece, in freedom's cause of vast renown,
Cou'd not submit to a mere tyrants frown;
Cou'd not endure to see her subjects yield,
And in the jaws of proud usurpers held.
From her dull slumbers she at length did rise,
Clad with all pow'r, with fortitude did strive;
Expel'd the cloud, and usher'd in the light
Of liberty, which after shone so bright.

What shall I say of Rome, that parent state?
No human grandeur e'er appear'd so great;
Spread its vast wings to earth's extremest point,
And sea and land to pay low homage join'd.
Her glorious sons, cotroul'd by tender laws,
Reach'd their top'd grandeur, and renown'd applause,
By liberty, that greatest, best of words,
The pride of patriots, and the boast of crowds.
This doom'd proud Tarquin to the shades below,
And this great Caesar with his lordly show;
Scorn to rehearse that one* of modern date,
Whose love was power, whose death untimely fate.
May his black deeds with all their hideous form
Impress the wise, and treach the fool to learn.
Declare abroad, that freedom don't appear
Under the cloak of monarchy and fear.
Hail! happy day, while patriotic fire
Glows in the breast the noble mind t'inspire.
Flam'd by this spark America will shine,
And lighten distant worlds with rays benign.

    W.

[*Royal American Magazine*, Feb. 1775]

---

*Charles I

A REBUS

TAKE the fair Place where AEn'as lost his Sire,
And that of Bliss, to which we all aspire;
Next the dull Shell-Fish, which our Bays contain,
And that which sometimes soothes severest Pain;
Then the rich Coast whence Ships their wealth convey
And him round whom vast Orbs their Courses play;
Next the Disease, whose Pain distracts the Soul,
And Element of Birds dispers'd from Pole to Pole.
Then his great Name who Britain's Sceptre sways,
And that which sickens at another's Praise.

    These if connected show the good Man's Name,
Whom warlike Bands their virt'ous Chief proclaim;
Whose double-delegated Trusts demand
The prudent Conduct of a skillful Hand.
[*Boston Evening-Post*, March 13, 1775; *Connecticut Gazette*, March 24, 1775]

ACROSTICK *ANSWER TO A REBUS IN OUR LAST*

T ROY was the Place where AEneas lost his Sire,
H eaven is the Place of Bliss we all desire;
O ysters the Shell-Fish which our Bays contain,
M ed'cine sometimes will ease the sharpest Pain;
A frican Coasts there wealthy Ships abound,
S un is the Orb that other Orbs surround;

G out is that Pain that does distract the Mind,
A ir is the Element for Birds assign'd;
G eorge the great King that holds the British Throne,
E nvy perhaps would gladly pull him down.

The good Man's Name that these initials show,
Is Governor and Captain-General too:
May Heaven direct him in that happy Way,
That shall join Britain and America.
[Boston Evening-Post, March 20, 1775; Connecticut Gazette, April 7, 1775]

THE ARRIVAL

And now ye sisters of the sacred well,
Unlock your bowers and open every cell,
In every [. . .] the rich libations bear:
Ye green nymphs come with wat'ry footsteps here,
And you, ye Tritons, bring your vocal aid,
With all the music of the coral shade.
      For hark! He comes! I hear the golden sound,
And joy's full trump suffuses it around.
'Tis HANCOCK comes!—; hear the cannon roar
Then loud acclaim, and burst them shore to shore,
See yon bright messengers that upward rise
On flaming wing and sun along the skies;
The mount impatient and the Mews declare
To off'ring angels that are hov'ring there.
BOSTONIA bow, let all thy incence roll
From earth altar and parfume the pole:
The richest wraths of civic fame be paid
To him who rais'd them from th' approaching shade
Thy HANCOCK comes!—his chariot rolls along,
Mid' the loud paeans of th'exulting throng,
To fancy's view a wond'rous tablet's [raised]
TO READ:
wond'rous tablet's [raised]
High o'er his head, with golden types emblaz'd.

Some hand immortal drop'd it from the skies,
With this inscription for admiring eyes.
This, this is he who born to bless mankind,
Goodness and greatness in the same combind.
Like ocean's God amid the bursting waves,
He faces danger and the storm outbraves.
Ev'n they who bed the trident of the main,
Oppos'd the firmness of his soul in vain,
His vast, extensive soul that could command
The wide machinery of a rising land.
But now the rattling chariot onward rolls,
And bears him to his own domestic walls.
Nor let the muse who stretch's her soaring wing
To themes so high, disdain a gentler string.
She stoops with joy to paint the flow'ry road
Of private die, where heaven-born virtue trod.

Then tell us HANCOCK, *why that sudden tear?—*
O deign to tell it, and thy grief we'll share.
Sad proof, how vain is every human joy
To the warm heart of sensibility;
When one misfortune of the softer kind,
With raven pinion broods upon the mind!
Ev'n HANCOCK's *self, tho' blest with all below;*
May, when the fates so rich a* gift remove,
Thus pour the dutious strain of filial love.
Where is that honor'd form which once appeard
With grace benign, and ever'y bosom chear'd;
That crown'd the circles of domestic joy,
And led the golden hours that glided by?
O fled forever, o'er yon milky way,
She gilds the regions of caelestial day!

---

*The late Mrs. HANCOCK.

There from her sappire seat she looks below,
And pours down balm on many a human woe:
Makes intercession for her native town,
Where once her charity and virtue shone;
Where reign'd the ten-fold lustre of her mind.
The pattern, praise and glory of her kind.
Farewell! Not all that empires can bestow,
Though from the hands of honest love they show;
No giddy fortune, no alluring dream
Of lawrel crowns that shade the front of fame;
Whilst live the golden feats of memory,
Shall blot thy vision from the mental eye.
Ah no! for even as returning spring,
With dewey fingers shall her garlands bring;
With nymphs and sylvans I'll attend thy tomb,
Pluck up each weed and spread the richest bloom;
Then having paid the last kind office there,
Pour the warm tribute of a filial tear.
BOSTON, Nov. 20, 1777.
[Boston *Independent Chronicle*, Nov. 27, 1777]

ON GENERAL GATES

HAIL! glorious chief whom destiny has chose
To bound the limits of thy country's woes;
Where all, with pleased astonishment surveys,
Shall the adventurous muse presume to praise:
Justly I may divine assurance claim,
Immortal pow'rs should sing immortal fame;
For sure if immortality descends
To guard a name that virtue comprehends,
The conquering GATES demands its earliest care,

The boundless, undefac'd reward to share;
Thee then I sing—ye gracious nine inspire
Unnumber'd beauties to attend my lyre;
Be silent all—its laurel'd triumph rears
The name of GATES, which tyrants trembling, hears;
He, who by Heaven directed, nobly stood
The rage of thousands, for his country's good;
Who, fir'd by all that warms the hero's breast,
The helpless anguish of mankind distress'd;
The tender maid, with frantic grief, in vain
Attempt to call to life her murder'd swain;
The smiling babe, with prattling voice require
The first caresses of its slaughter'd sire;
The affluent farmer banish'd from his home,
Doom'd for precarious sustinance to roam,
While wretches, with a useless waste, destroy'd
What the whole labour of his life employ'd;
These deeds infernal, and unnumber'd more,
Such acts as Hell had ne'er devis'd before;
(For ordinary crimes, when held by theirs,
A garb of purity and virtue wears)
These were what called the godlike warrior's aid,
Rejoic'd he heard, and greatly brave obey'd:
The stratagems of war his mind engage
How best to execute his destin'd rage;
Teach the vast cannon, with tremendous roar,
To wound thro' paths of death unknown before;
These where the charms for which the chief resign'd
Those scenes of life where ev'ry Joy's combin'd.
In future times, when jarring tumults cease,
And Heav'n propitious lulls the soul to peace,
When after all these horrid wars are o'er,
And Liberty's immerg'd from seat of gore;

And o'er the fields, where jocund pleasures strays;
And freeborn nature all her wealth displays:
Some hoary swain, with early care shall tread
The verdant margin of th' enamel'd mead;
Then view the tomb whose sculptur'd sides invest
The grave where GATES's honour'd ashes rest,
And cry "To thee, thou glorious god-like shade,
By rescu'd liberty let thanks be paid;
Thou, whose intrepidity serene, could dare
The ghastly horrors of destroying war;
When injur'd virtue all her woes confess'd,
She found a bounteous patron in your breast;
You heard her griefs, your friendly aid apply'd,
And nobly brave, the oppressors force defi'd:
Heav'n seen your prowess, and bid fate to bless
Each generous wish with merited success.
Well pleas'd, she went with rapid speed to place
Your deeds with those of Heav'ns imperial race;
Then o'er your country's foes a victor rode,
And prov'd that virtue is the care of God.
[*Boston Gazette*, Dec. 8, 1777]

REPLY TO THE CONSTITUTION

THE wisest of mankind has said,
Let answer to a fool be made;—
Lest fancy fond oppress with weight,
Of wisdom in his own conceit:—
But yet again, "Response deny,
And pass the low-lived scandal by;
Lest semblances of his ways appear,

(By virtue seen) with greif sincere."
    Shall we inequal strains return
Thy spleen, and answer scorn with scorn?—
Thy rancour rages unconfin'd,
Thy rancour more than love is blind;
This prejudice's in favour spies,
No failing in its darling prize:—
But, that, with boundless fury grows,
Promiscuous wreak'd on friends and foes.

    Say, why this insult and disgrace—
So freely thrown on Afric's race;
Or shall we, wondrous author! Own,
That insult can from thee be thrown?
Our different hue tho' nature gave,
Does colour constitute the slave?
For that can man of sense despise?
From thee can want of virtue rise?
What barrier can that race divide,
But in thy ignorance and pride?
The sole distinction nature made,
In good, and ill, alone display'd.
To limit thy abandon'd rage,
Once more, peruse the sacred page.
The slave is he, whom passion sways;
Mean slave? Who envy's voice obeys:—
More sable far, his mental hue,
Who bids fair virtues path adieu:—
But say, since thus ingrateful sound,
For what you cross'd the seas profound?
The wisdom absolute, should keep,
That barrier true, the roaring deep.

Each Afric would well pleas'd remain,
And cultivate his native plain;
Wou'd view around the rural scene,
All beauteous in eternal green.
Each generous Afric's bosom burns,
And thy malignant sentence scorns;
When in insulting strain you dare,
With scandal touch Columbia's fair:—
Shall thy mean insolents of tongue,
Thus charge the generous C——rt with wrong?
Say, why should jealous fury rise,
And flash from thine indignant eyes;
When kindly set from bondage free,
How gives their freedom pain to thee?

When freedom Goddess-like displays
Her banner—joyful nations gaze?
And ardent throng around her feet;
The heart with gratitude replete:—
Nor does the Queen disdain to hear,
The suit her sable sons profer;
But gracious, with a smile divine—
Assents, and frees the injur'd line.
We smile contempt at thy ill-nature,
Express'd in low, promiscuous satire.

Since fearful to remain unknown,
You'd have this monumental stone.
"A while did this great Bard display,
His glow worm momentary ray;
Then sunk profound for endless sleep,
In dark oblivion's sable deep."
[Boston *Independent Chronicle*, Feb. 12, 1778]

[ON THE DEATH OF GEORGE EUSTIS]

AGAIN *thy sovereign tyranny's display'd,*
O cruel Monarch of the dreadful shade!
Wrapt in oblivion's deep impervious gloom,
Lo! EUSTIS slumbers in the silent tomb.
From life's gay scenes, unconscious snatch'd away,
EUSTIS, the young, the generous, and the gay.

While recent objects with surprise he views,
The soul bewildering in a strange amuse;
To one unalterable state confin'd,—
He questions thus his own immortal mind.
"To what new regions sudden am I brought?
Beyond the curious search of human thought;
Beyond my own, whom late the festal choir
Rais'd notes, responsive to the sounding lyre,
A choir that first their institution ow'd
To nature's universal sovereign, GOD.
Deep and mysterious tho' its nature be,
In precept open, generous, kind, and free."
From shackles freed, th' unbodied soul can tell
Heav'n's awful bright, the dreadful deep of hell?
Discover'd now to her immortal eyes,
Revolving worlds in strange procession rise!—
Not so on earth, where petty toys display
Their charms, and "lure her from her heavenly way.
Detached now, when death *his scythe extends,*
Dropt is the curtain, and the darkness ends.
[Boston *Independent Chronicle*, Oct. 21, 1779]

TABLE 1

Extant and Acknowledged Phillis Wheatley Poems in Manuscript and Print

WHEATLEY POEM TITLE	DATE	EXTANT MANUSCRIPT (NUMBER)	PUBLISHED (B=BROADSIDE, P=PAMPHLET, N=NEWSPAPER, M=MAGAZINE)	IN BOOK PROPOSAL (YEAR)	IN 1773 BOOK
[Mrs. Thacher's Son Is Gone]	1765?	1			
On the Death of the Rev. Dr. Sewall	1765/69	3		1772	x
On Virtue	1766			1772	x
To the King's Most Excellent Majesty on his Repealing the American Stamp Act	1766/68	1		1772	x
Atheism/An Address to the Atheist	1767, 1769	3		1772	
Deism/An Address to the Deist	1767	2		1772	
To the University of Cambridge	1767	1		1772	x
[On Messrs. Hussey & Coffin]	1767		N	1772	
America	1768	1		1772	
On Friendship	1768	1		1772	

On Being Brought from Africa to America	1768?				x
To Hon. Commodore Hood	1769	1		1772	
To a Lady on her Remarkable Preservation in a Hurricane	1769				x
On the Death of Mr. Snider Murder'd by Richardson	1770	1		1772	
An Elegiac Poem, On the Death of . . . George Whitefield	1770		B, P	1772	x
On the Death of a Young Lady 5 Years of Age	1770		M (1781)		x
To Mrs. Leonard, on the Death of her Husband	1771		B	1772	x
On the Death of Dr. Samuel Marshall	1771	1	N	1772	x
To Rev. Mr. Pitkin, on the Death of his Lady	1771	1	B		x
To a Gentleman and Lady on the Death of the Lady's Brother and Sister, and a Child	1771			1772	x
Recollection	1772		N, M		x
A Poem on the Death of Charles Eliot	1772	3			x
To the Right Honourable William Legge, Earl of Dartmouth	1772	1	N		x

TABLE 1   375

Ode to Neptune	1772				x
To a Lady on her Coming to North-America with her Son, for the Recovery of her Health	1772				x
To a Lady and her Children, on the Death of her Son and their Brother	1772			1772	x
To Rev. Dr. Thomas Amory on Reading his Sermons on Daily Devotion	1772				x
On Death of a Young Gentleman	1772		M (1781)	1772	x
To Mr. and Mrs.—, on the Death of their Infant Son	1772–78?		M (1784)		
To the Hon'ble Thomas Hubbard, Esq., on the Death of Mrs. Thankfull Leonard	1773		B		x
Farewell to America. To Mrs. S. W.	1773		N		x
To Maecenas	1773				x
Goliath of Gath	1773				x
Thought on the Works of Providence	1773				x
To a Lady on the Death of Three Relations	1773				x
An Hymn to the Morning	1773				x
An Hymn to the Evening	1773				x

TABLE 1

Isaiah 1.8	1773				x
On Imagination	1773		M (1784)		x
To Capt. H——D, of the 65th Regiment	1773				x
To a Gentleman on his Voyage to Great Britain, for the Recovery of his Health	1773				X
On the Death of J. C. an Infant	1773				x
Niobe in Distress for her Children Slain by Apollo	1773				x
To S. M. a Young African Painter	1773				x
To His Hon. the Lieutenant-Governor, on the Death of his Lady	1773	1			x
An Hymn to Humanity	1773	1			x
An Answer to the Rebus	1773				x
Ocean	1773	1		1779	
An Elegy to Miss Mary Moorhead	1773		B		
To a Gentleman of the Navy	1774		M	1779	
Phillis's Reply to the Answer in our last by the Gentleman of the Navy	1774		M	1779	
To His Excellency General Washington	1775		N, M	1779	
On the Capture of General Lee	1776	1		1779	

TABLE 1   377

On the Death of General Wooster	1778	1		1779	
An Elegy, Sacred to the Memory of that Great Divine, the Reverend and Learned Dr. Samuel Cooper	1784		P		
Liberty and Peace	1784		P		

TABLE 2

Usage Frequency of Common and Unusual Words in Phillis Wheatley's
Acknowledged Poems and in Tentative Attributions

B. On the Affray in King-Street
1. On Night and Sleep
2. On the Death of Miss Inches
3. [New Year Poem for 1774]
4. Triumph of the Redeemer
5. Night: A Poem
6. On Night
7. Thoughts on Tyranny
8. A Rebus
9. Acrostick Answer to a Rebus
10. The Arrival
11. On General Gates
12. Reply to THE CONSTITUTION
13. [On the Death of George Eustis]

WORD	APPEARS IN NEW ATTRIBUTION #	APPEARS IN NUMBER OF POEMS AMONG ACKNOWLEDGED POEMS (N = 56)
Afric/Africa/Africans	#9, 11, 12	10
America	#7, 9	7
Angels/angelic	#4	7
Aurora	#1, 3, 4, 6	7
Columbia	#12	4
Contemplation	#5, 6	3
Fancy/fancy's/fancy'd	#4	9
Fly/flies/flight	#2, 6	19
Free/Freedom	#7, 12, B	11
Friends/friendship	#2, 7, 9, 12, B	19
Heaven/heav'n/heavn'ly	#2, 3, 4, 8, 9, 11, 13	41
Laurel	#10, 11	6
Lay/lays	#4, 5	15
Lo!	#4, 5, B	12
Muse	#2, 3, 5, 10, 11	26
Phoebus	#3	7
Recollection	#2	3
Sable	#1, 5, 12	8
Seraph/seraphic/seraphim	#4	7
Shades/shade	#6, 7, 10, 11, 12, 13, B	9
Snatch/snatch'd	#13	6
Sol	#1	3
Song	#4, 5	15
Soul	#4, 5, 6, 8, 11, 13	30
Sun	#5, 6, 9, 10	10
Tyrant/tyranny/tyrannic	#2, 3, 7, 10, 13	12
Virtue/virtues	#10, 11, 12	15
Zephyrs	#4, 6	3

NOTES

1. THE BEGINNINGS, THE TABLE, THE TALE

3 *"on the back of Cape Cod"*: BNL, Oct. 1, 1767; BG, Aug. 27, Oct. 5, 12, 1767; BEP, Aug. 21, 1767; "From the Newport Mercury, of Dec. 21," BPB, Jan. 11, 1768.

3 *Nantucket merchants Hussey and Coffin*: This Coffin has sometimes been identified as Nathaniel Coffin, later customs officer and an Anglican, who had a store on King Street. Vincent Carretta, *Phillis Wheatley: Biography of a Genius in Bondage* (Athens, Ga., 2011), 66. But there were many Coffins and Husseys, families related by marriage. In 1764, George Hussey of Nantucket advertised for a fourteen-year-old fugitive Indian servant, to be conveyed, if caught, to Nathaniel Wheatley in Boston. BEP, Oct. 8, 1764. The Boston merchant John Rowe reported dining "at home" with "Stephen Hussey Abiah Folger junr. Richard Coffin Isaac Paddock all four from Nantucket." Rowe Diary, Oct. 7, 1767. For the plethora of Coffins and Husseys, some interrelated, see, for example, Will Gardner, *The Coffin Saga: Nantucket's Story—from Settlement to Summer Visitors* (Cambridge, Mass., 1949); Edward Byers, *The Nation of Nantucket: Society and Politics in an Early American Commercial Center* (Boston, 1987), pt. 3.

3 *John Wheatley*: BNL, Nov. 20, 1752; BEP, Nov. 23, 1743, June 13, 1757. By 1765 twenty-two-year-old Nathaniel was also a "merchant." BEP, June 10, 1765.

3 *slave ship Phillis*: Timothy Fitch gave his slaving ships Roman names that signified African slaves to contemporaries. British American masters gave names like Caesar and Pompey to their household bondsmen, mimicking Romans themselves, who gave slaves names from Greek mythology. The masters of Phillis Wheatley's world fulfilled their imperial fantasies by imagining the slaves they owned and named as akin to Greek and Roman counterparts. Yet in Virgil's third *Eclogue*, Phillis is a beautiful woman. In Ovid's *Heroides* she is a tragic, eloquent figure. In one of Horace's odes, Phillis is a slave so virtuous as well as lovely that she must have royal parentage. Like the Christian and republican traditions, these Mediterranean idioms had universalizing, as well as inegalitarian, potential. William Fitzgerald, *Slavery and the Roman Literary Imagination* (Cambridge, U.K., 2000), 5; Virgil, *The Eclogues*, trans. Guy Lee (London, 1984), 51, 53; Ovid, *Heroides*, trans. Harold Isbell, rev. ed. (New York, 2004), 10–16; Eric Ashley Hairston, "The Trojan Horse: Classics, Memory, Transformation, and Afric Ambition in *Poems on Various Subjects, Religious and Moral*," in *New Essays on Phillis Wheatley*, ed. John C. Shields and Eric D. Lamore (Knoxville, Tenn., 2011), 66–67; Christopher Smart, *The Works of Horace, Translated Literally into English Prose* (Philadelphia, 1836), 1:97; Philip Francis, ed., *A Poetical Translation of the Works of Horace: With the Original Text, and Critical Notes Collected from His Best Latin and French Commentators*, 6th ed. (London, 1756), 1:157.

The only evidence we have as to Phillis Wheatley's physical appearance is the well-known engraving that appeared as the frontispiece in *Poems on Various Subjects, Religious and Moral* (London, 1773).

3 *"endeavouring to make letters"*: MMO, 10.

3 *The poem Phillis began*: CWC, 73–74; J. A. Leo LeMay, *The Life of Benjamin Franklin* (Philadelphia, 2006), 1:59. In her 1772 proposal for a volume, in which this poem was mentioned for inclusion (it would be dropped in the actual volume a year later), she referred to it as a poem "on two friends, who were cast away." Friends here probably means Quakers. PPW, 115–16. Houston A. Baker Jr. observed that the poem establishes a "calling" for Wheatley. Houston A.

Baker Jr., *The Journey Back: Issues in Black Literature and Criticism* (Chicago, 1980), 11, 14.

4 *"Consideration," a double entendre*: For "consideration" as monetary compensation in the poem, see Eric Wertheimer, *Underwriting: The Poetics of Insurance in America, 1722–1872* (Stanford, Calif., 2006), 64.

5 *Homer's* Odyssey *and Virgil's* Aeneid: An even more direct thematic link is the beginning of John Dryden's *Aeneid*, which begins with Juno asking Aeolus, who rules the winds and the waves, to bring down the ship of the Trojans, whom she calls "a race of wand'ring slaves." He does so, with the help of Boreas, the north wind. Ultimately, Neptune calms the waves. Aeneas and his Trojans land in Libya—later described as part of "Africk," one of numerous references in the poem to North and East African peoples. *The Odyssey of Homer in the English Verse Translation by Alexander Pope* (New York, 1942), 345; *Virgil's Aeneid, Translated by John Dryden*, ed. Frederick M. Keener (New York, 1997), 6–8, 91, 101, 235, 305. Vincent Carretta notes that the beginning of Wheatley's "Niobe" echoes the beginning of Pope's translation of *The Iliad*. Carretta, *Phillis Wheatley*, 40. For Pope's Homer as the single most important influence on Wheatley's art, see Julian D. Mason, "Examples of Classical Myth in the Poems of Phillis Wheatley," in *American Women and Classical Myths*, ed. Gregory A. Staley (Waco, Tex., 2009), 31.

In Milton's "Lycidas," a mourning poem, Neptune "ask't the waves, the felon winds, / What hard mishap hath doom'd this gentle swain? / And question'd every gust of rugged wings / That blows from off each beaked promontory." John T. Shawcross, ed., *The Complete Poetry of John Milton*, rev. ed. (New York, 1971), 161. Milton here harks back to Lucretius, who saw in shipwreck the nature of the universe. The interpretation of shipwrecks could be a hinge point between sacred and secular interpretations of reality; "Lycidas" may also filter Horace, another favorite of Wheatley's, to insert providence. Sharon Achinstein, "'Shipwreck Is Everywhere': Lycidas and the Problems of the Secular," in *Milton Now*, ed. Catherine Gray and Erin Murphy (New York, 2014), 37, 41. For the underappreciated role of Milton in Wheatley, and "Lycidas" on Wheatley's 1773 volume (in which the Hussey and Coffin poem does not appear), see Paula Loscocco, *Phillis Wheatley's Miltonic Poetics* (New York, 2014), 50–52; Reginald P. Wilburn, *Preaching the Gospel of Black Revolt: Appropriating Milton in Early African American Literature* (Pittsburgh, 2014), 57–93; Tracey L. Walters, *African American Literature and the Classicist Tradition* (New York, 2007), chap. 1; Carolivia Herron, "Milton and African American Literature," in *Re-membering Milton*, ed. Mary Nyquist and Margaret W. Ferguson (New York, 1987), 282–86. For Milton as a mediator of classical texts for eighteenth-century readers, see David Hopkins and Charles Martindale, introduction to *The Oxford History of Classical Reception in English Literature* (New York, 2012), 3:22.

5 *Africans*: John K. Thornton, *Africa and Africans in the Making of the Atlantic World, 1400–1800*, 2nd ed. (New York, 1998), 236.

6 *the salvation project presumes*: New Englanders had been telling stories of shipwrecks as providence tales in this way for quite some time, so much so that they became standard plot devices in the narration of religious lives. Wheatley's providential story is also about an inspired poet's role as a mediator between God and the subject, simultaneously humbling herself and exalting her role. The poet, in Pope and Homer's version of such a scene, channels the dead, in the "shades" below. In Dryden's version of Virgil, he channels the gods, the

ultimate religious act and act of translation. In Wheatley, the poet and the audience come together in response to trauma, and a Christian supersession that is beyond the ancients.

For providence tales including shipwrecks, see James Hartman, *Providence Tales and the Birth of American Literature* (Baltimore, 1999); Amy Mitchell-Cook, *A Sea of Misadventures: Shipwreck and Survival in Early America* (Columbia, S.C., 2013), 45, 53–54; Eve Tavor Bannet, *Transatlantic Stories and the History of Reading, 1720–1830* (Cambridge, U.K., 2011), 44. In the mid-eighteenth century, reports Cook, the *BG* reported fifteen to twenty wrecks per year. Cook, *Sea of Misadventures*, 30. For trauma, see Phillip M. Richards, "Phillis Wheatley: The Consensual Blackness of Early African American Writing," in Shields and Lamore, *New Essays on Phillis Wheatley*, 262. For women, especially in reference to "grace" in this poem, see Geneva Cobb Moore, *Maternal Metaphors of Power in African American Women's Literature* (Columbia, S.C., 2017), 18–19.

6 *world she had known*: In these Greek and Roman classics, including especially the authors she mentioned as important to her—Homer, Virgil, Terence—there are slaves who are smarter than their masters, who manipulate situations to their own ends in Terence's comedies, or who may be the loyal keys to the reclaiming of the kingdom, like Eumaeus in *The Odyssey*. Eumaeus is a boy prince who was sold away, then captured. Now an old man but still the most dependable caretaker of Odysseus's estate in Ithaca, he indicates a world in which anyone might be enslaved, but also might come to love his captors, and be in some sense a member of the family. In Homer there is a close relation between travel, encounter, war, and enslavement, one that would have meant all the more to Wheatley because of the numerous mentions of Egypt and Ethiopia, the storied African nations she would later publicly identify with, in the text. Only twenty-two lines into *The Odyssey* there is a mention of the Ethiopians—who in Pope's version are both eastern and western people: "A race divided, whom with sloping rays / The rising and the setting sun surveys." *The Odyssey of Homer, in the English Verse Translation by Alexander Pope*, 2; *The Iliad of Homer, Translated by Alexander Pope*, ed. Steven Shankman (London, 1996), 26, 89, 530; M. I. Finley, *The World of Odysseus*, 2nd ed. (New York, 1965), 39, 46, 53–54, 59, 145; Gerda Lerner, *The Creation of Patriarchy* (New York, 1986), 76–100; Page DuBois, *Slaves and Other Objects* (Chicago, 2008), 102, 128, 134–35; Orlando Patterson, "Slavery in the Pre-modern World and Early Greece," in *Slave Systems Ancient and Modern*, ed. Enrico del Lago and Constantine Katseri (Cambridge, U.K., 2008), 62–63; Page DuBois, *Trojan Horses: Saving the Classics from Conservatives* (New York, 2001), 66, 114; Edith Hall, *The Return of Ulysses: A Cultural History of Homer's "Odyssey"* (Baltimore, 2008), 36, 101, 116, 120, 132, 203; William G. Thalmann, *The Swineherd and the Bow: Representations of Class in the "Odyssey"* (Ithaca, N.Y., 1998), 49–107; Emily Watson, introduction to Homer, *The Odyssey*, trans. Emily Watson (New York, 2017), 35–37, 54–57; Richard Alston, "Introduction: Reading Ancient Slavery," Patrice Rankine, "Odysseus as Slave: The Ritual of Domination and Social Death in Homeric Society," and Leanne Hunnings, "The Paradigms of Execution: Managing Slave Death from Homer to Virginia," in *Reading Ancient Slavery*, ed. Richard Alston, Edith Hall, and Laura Proffitt (London, 2011), 18–19, 26, 34–71; Alberto Manguel, *Homer's "The Iliad" and "The Odyssey": A Biography* (Vancouver, 2007), 54; Peter Levi, *The Art of Poetry* (New Haven, Conn., 1991), 10–11; Fitzgerald, *Slavery and the Ro-*

man *Literary Imagination*, 87, 90; Laurel Fulkerson, *Ovid: A Poet on the Margins* (London, 2016), 6–7, 59–87.

In later Greek and Roman literature the importance of slaves in everyday life, as "vibrant violators and exploiters of the intimacies of family life," only intensifies. So does the ubiquity of war as a cruel, enslaving leveler. Africa appears with even greater clarity and frequency as a place on the map. The very first of Virgil's *Eclogues*, often used as a teaching text for children, is a dialogue in which one interlocutor speaks of his escape from slavery while the other forecasts exile to, among other places, Africa, in the wake of the forcible transfer of land to soldiers. And Horace—as much a favorite of Wheatley's as he was for one of her English models, Alexander Pope—repeatedly makes a theme of how patronage *and* his talents made it possible for him to live a better life despite his father's low status as a former slave. That he later lost favor, suffered exile, and wrote about that too only increased his appeal. Terence, *The Comedies*, trans. Peter Brown (New York, 2006); Joseph C. Miller, *The Problem of Slavery as History* (New Haven, Conn., 2012), 67; Peter Hunt, "Slaves in Greek Literary Culture," Sandra Joshel, "Slavery and Roman Literary Culture," and Keith Bradley, "Slavery in the Roman Republic," in *The Cambridge World History of Slavery*, vol. 1, *The Ancient Mediterranean World*, ed. Keith Bradley and Paul Cartledge (New York, 2011), 22–47, 214–40, 241–64; Virgil, *Eclogues*, 22, 33; Horace, *The Complete Odes and Epodes*, trans. David West (Oxford, U.K., 1997), v, 4–5, 12; Niall Rudd, ed., *The Satires of Horace and Persius* (1973; rev. ed., New York, 1987), 18, 66–70, 118–20, 172; William W. Cook and James Tatum, *African American Writers and the Classical Tradition* (Chicago, 2010), 19–20; Thomas Habinek, *The Politics of Latin Literature* (Princeton, N.J., 1998).

Pope defended *The Odyssey* in particular against critics who could not fathom why this seeming sequel to *The Iliad*, despite Odysseus's heroic qualities, revolved around "lower parts" like family dramas and the doings of slaves. He added explicit references to "slaves" where other translators had not done so. Indeed, eighteenth-century translators of Homer and Horace seem to have been more likely to use the word "slave," and to address the issue in commentaries, than twentieth-century translators. Compare, for example, Francis, *A Poetical Translation of the Works of Horace*, with Rudd, *Satires of Horace and Persius*; Horace, *Complete Odes and Epodes*, ed. West. A change back can be seen in Emily Watson's lovely translation of and introduction to *The Odyssey*.

7 *neoclassical literature*: Those who study U.S. history and literature have tended to view neoclassicism as mere window dressing, or the playful and pragmatic use of pseudonyms: the equivalent of a toga at a frat party. Exceptions include Martha Watson, "A Classic Case: Phillis Wheatley and Her Poetry," *Early American Literature* 31 (Jan. 1996): 103–32; Eric Slauter, *The State as a Work of Art: Cultural Origins of the Constitution* (Chicago, 2009), 169–214, who see Greek and Roman classics as both a conundrum and an opportunity for Wheatley. For more optimistic renderings, see Lucy K. Hayden, "Classical Tidings from the Afric Muse: Phillis Wheatley's Use of Greek and Roman Mythology," *CLA Journal* 35 (June 1992): 432–47; John C. Shields, *The American Aeneas: Classical Origins of the American Self* (Knoxville, Tenn., 2001); Mason, "Examples of Classical Myth in the Poems of Phillis Wheatley," 23–33; John C. Shields, *Phillis Wheatley's Poetics of Liberation* (Knoxville, Tenn., 2008); Shields and Lamore, *New Essays on Phillis Wheatley*, 3–157; Eric Ashley Hairston, *The Ebony Column: Classics, Civilization, and the African American Reclamation of*

the West (Knoxville, Tenn., 2013), 25–64; R. A. P. López, *The Colorful Conservative: American Conversations with the Ancients from Wheatley to Whitman* (Lanham, Md., 2011), 91–127; Emily Greenwood, "The Politics of Classicism in the Poetry of Phillis Wheatley," in *Ancient Slavery and Abolition*, ed. Edith Hall, Richard Alston, and Justine McConnell (New York, 2011), 153–79; John Levi Barnard, *Empire of Ruin: Black Classicism and American Imperial Culture* (New York, 2018), 23–52. For classical readership in early America, see James Raven, "Classical Transports: Latin and Greek Texts in North and Central America Before 1800," in *Books Between Europe and the Americas: Connections and Communities, 1620–1860*, ed. Leslie Howsam and James Raven (New York, 2011), 157–86; Caroline Winterer, "The Female World of Classical Reading in Eighteenth-Century America," in *Reading Women: Literacy, Authorship and Culture in the Atlantic World*, ed. Heidi Brayman Hackel and Catherine E. Kelly (Philadelphia, 2008), 105–23. Among historians, Bernard Bailyn, *The Ideological Origins of the American Revolution* (Cambridge, Mass., 1967), 26, influentially downgraded the classical presence during the era as merely symbolic; contrast more appreciative contemporary assessments in Richard Gummere, *The American Colonial Mind and the Classical Tradition* (Cambridge, Mass., 1963); Gordon S. Wood, *The Creation of the American Republic, 1776–1787* (Chapel Hill, N.C., 1969), 49–53, and more recently the work of Caroline Winterer and Eran Shalev.

7 *"soul sister"*: R. Lynn Matson, "Phillis Wheatley—Soul Sister?," in *Critical Essays on Phillis Wheatley*, ed. William H. Robinson (Boston, 1982), 113–22. For more on the twentieth-century debate over Wheatley's authenticity, see chapter 24 and the literature cited in the notes to that chapter.

10 *biographical certainty*: Black feminist scholars have elaborated the "critical fabulation" that is needed to weave a history of the enslaved out of the limited materials in a biased archive that silences at every turn. Wheatley neither obviates nor resolves the dilemma of when it might be going too far, for historians at least, to use imagination to compensate for an archive full of racial and masculinist fictions. With Wheatley, though, we can allow her own critical fabulations to be our guide back into an archive to which she responded. She certainly sheds a different light on the silencing of black women that must inform our understanding of the choices she made. Saidiya Hartman, "Venus in Two Acts," *Small Axe* 26 (2008): 1–14; Alexis Okeowo, "How Saidiya Hartman Retells the History of Black Life," *New Yorker*, Oct. 28, 2020; Kristen Block, *Ordinary Lives in the Early Caribbean* (Athens, Ga., 2012); Stephanie E. Smallwood, "The Politics of the Archive and History's Accountability to the Enslaved," *History of the Present* 6 (2016): 117–32; Marisa J. Fuentes, *Dispossessed Lives: Enslaved Women, Violence, and the Archive* (Philadelphia, 2016); Jennifer L. Morgan, *Reckoning with Slavery* (Durham, N.C., 2021).

10 *A question can be a veiled statement*: "There is a relationship between questioning and freedom," writes Lewis R. Gordon in *Fear of Black Consciousness* (New York, 2022), 64.

10 *"Sometimes by simile"*: CWC, 75.

2. THE SHIP, THE TRADE, THE WARS

11 *"Middle Passage"*: Anne Bailey, *African Voices of the Atlantic Slave Trade* (Boston, 2005), 161–62; Stephanie Smallwood, *Saltwater Slavery: A Middle Passage*

from Africa to American Diaspora (Cambridge, Mass., 2007), 191, 207; Sowandé M. Mustakeem, *Slavery at Sea: Terror, Sex, and Sickness in the Middle Passage* (Urbana, Ill., 2016), 157; Marcus Rediker, *The Slave Ship: A Human History* (New York, 2007); Saidiya Hartman, *Lose Your Mother: A Journey Along the Atlantic Slave Route* (New York, 2007). Kimberley Clay Bassard urged thinking of Wheatley as a "Middle Passage survivor." Bassard, *Spiritual Interrogations: Culture, Gender, and Community in Early African American Women's Writing* (Princeton, N.J., 1999), 35.

11 *Boyrereau Brinch*: Jeffrey Brace, *The Blind African Slave: Memoirs of Boyrereau Brinch, Nicknamed Jeffrey Brace*, ed. Kari J. Winter (Madison, Wis., 2005), 152; Tara Bynum, "Phillis Wheatley on Friendship," *Legacy* 31 (2014): 42–51.

12 *firsthand testimonies*: Vincent Carretta, ed., *Unchained Voices* (Lexington, Ky., 1996); Dickson D. Bruce, *The Origins of African American Literature, 1680–1860* (Charlottesville, Va., 2001).

12 *Margaretta Odell*: MMO, 11; Robert F. Wallcut, "Memoir of Thomas Wallcut," *Proceedings of the Massachusetts Historical Society* 2 (1841): 193–208. For Odell's *Memoir* as an exculpatory narrative and its antislavery contexts, see Eileen Razzori Elrod, "Phillis Wheatley's Abolitionist Text: The 1834 Edition," in *Imagining Transatlantic Slavery*, ed. Cora Kaplan and John Oldfield (Houndsmills, U.K., 2010), esp. 101–7; Margot Minardi, *Making Slavery History: Abolitionism and the Politics of Memory in Massachusetts* (New York, 2010), 104–8; Carra Glatt, "'To Perpetuate Her Name': Appropriation and Autobiography in Margaretta Matilda Odell's Memoir of Phillis Wheatley," *Early American Literature* 55 (2020): 145–76. Bassard suggests that Wheatley's amnesia is a "stereotype." Bassard, *Spiritual Interrogations*, 23. For New England abolitionists' selective memory in this era, see Joanne Pope Melish, *Disowning Slavery: Gradual Emancipation and "Race" in New England, 1780–1860* (Ithaca, N.Y., 1998).

13 *standing in for country*: Among scholars arguing that this memory signifies sun worship and syncretism, the first was John C. Shields, "Phillis Wheatley's Struggle for Freedom in Her Poetry and Prose," in *The Collected Works of Phillis Wheatley*, ed. John C. Shields (New York, 1988), 240–42.

14 *incentivized warfare*: Vincent Brown, *The Reaper's Garden: Death and Power in Atlantic Slavery* (Cambridge, Mass., 2007); Rediker, *Slave Ship*, 98–99; Mustakeem, *Slavery at Sea*, 157, 187–88; Toby Green, *A Fistful of Shells: West Africa from the Rise of the Slave Trade to the Age of Revolution* (Chicago, 2019), 267, 292, 322; David McNally, *Blood and Money: War, Slavery, Finance and Empire* (Chicago, 2020).

14 *Timothy Fitch*: Fitch to Capt. Ellery, Jan. 14, 1759, Fitch to Gwinn, Jan. 12, Nov. 8, 1760, Sept. 4, Nov. 1, 1761, Oct. 1762, Slave Trade Letters Collection, Medford Historical Society, www.medfordhistorical.org/collections/slave-trade-letters; Charles W. Akers Jr., *The Divine Politician: Samuel Cooper and the American Revolution in Boston* (Boston, 1982), 115, 179.

15 *"Gambia's pleasing shores"*: CWC, 87.

15 *Senegambia became even more attractive*: Philip Curtin, *Economic Change in Precolonial Africa: Senegambia in the Era of the Slave Trade* (Madison, Wis., 1975); BNL, Oct. 12, 1758, in *Documents Illustrative of the History of the Slave Trade in America*, ed. Elizabeth Donnan (Washington, D.C., 1931), 2:513; "Preface," in Michel Adanson, *A Voyage to Senegal, the Isle of Goree, and the River Gambia* (London, 1759), viii; Stephen Conway, *War, State, and Society in*

Mid-Eighteenth-Century Britain and Ireland (Cambridge, U.K., 2006), 28, 105, 227; George E. Brooks, *Eurafricans in West Africa: Commerce, Social Status, Gender, and Religious Observance from the Sixteenth to the Eighteenth Century* (Athens, Ohio, 2003), 211, 245, 251.

15 *West Africans didn't usually sell*: Philip Curtin, *The Rise and Fall of the Planta-tion Complex* (New York, 1999), 116, 121; Boubacar Barry, *Senegambia and the Atlantic Slave Trade* (New York, 1998); Paul Lovejoy, *Transformations in Slavery: A History of Slavery in Africa* (Cambridge, U.K., 1983), 69–72; John K. Thornton, *Warfare in Atlantic Africa, 1500–1800* (London, 1999); Thornton, *Africa and Africans in the Making of the Atlantic World*; David Northrup, *Africa's Discovery of Europe, 1450–1850* (New York, 2002), 55–59; Charles Barker and Victor Martin, "Kayor and Baol: Senegalese Kingdoms and the Slave Trade in the Eighteenth Century," in *Forced Migration*, ed. Joseph E. Inikori (New York, 1992), 100–125; Ty M. Reese, "'Eating Luxury': Fante Middlemen, British Goods, and Changing Dependencies on the Gold Coast, 1750–1821," *William and Mary Quarterly* 66 (Oct. 2009): 852–71.

16 *a full cargo was a full cargo*: Fitch to Gwinn, Nov. 8, 1760; Walter Hawthorne, *Planting Rice and Harvesting Slaves: Transformations Along the Guinea-Bissau Coast, 1400–1900* (Portsmouth, N.H., 2003); Sean M. Kelley, *The Voyage of the Slave Ship* Hare (Chapel Hill, N.C., 2016).

16 *women and children were increasingly enslaved*: Igor Kopytoff and Suzanne Miers, "African Slavery as an Institution of Marginality," in *Slavery in Africa: Historical and Anthropological Perspectives*, ed. Igor Kopytoff and Suzanne Miers (Madison, Wis., 1977), 10, 14, 62; Donald R. Wright, *The World in a Very Small Place in Africa: A History of Globalization in Niumi, the Gambia*, 2nd ed. (Armonk, N.Y., 2003), 109, 121–22; Hawthorne, *Planting Rice and Harvesting Slaves*, 97, 121, 204–5; Joseph C. Miller, introduction to *Women and Slavery*, vol. 1, ed. Gwyn Campbell, Suzanne Miers, and Joseph C. Miller (Athens, Ohio, 2006), 17; Curtin, *Economic Change in Precolonial Africa*, 110; David Eltis, "The Volume and Structure of the Transatlantic Slave Trade," *William and Mary Quarterly*, 3rd ser. (2001): 44; Kelley, *Voyage of the Slave Ship* Hare, 75–76, 101–2; Thornton, *Warfare in Atlantic Africa*, 146–47; G. Ugo Nwokeji, "African Conceptions of Gender and the Slave Traffic," *William and Mary Quarterly* 58 (2001): 47–68; Joseph C. Miller, "The Dynamics of History in Africa and the Atlantic Age of Revolutions," in *The Age of Revolutions in Global Context, 1750–1840*, ed. David Armitage and Sanjay Subrahmanyan (New York, 2010), 101–22, esp. 118; James F. Searing, *West African Slavery and Atlantic Commerce: The Senegal River Valley, 1700–1860* (New York, 1993); Randy J. Sparks, *The Two Princes of Calabar: An Eighteenth-Century African Odyssey* (Cambridge, Mass., 2004), 48, 101; Rebecca Shumway, *The Fante and the Transatlantic Slave Trade* (Rochester, N.Y., 2011); Akousa Adoma Perbi, *A History of Indigenous Slavery in Ghana: From the 15th to the 19th Century* (Accra, Ghana, 2004), 28, 52–53, 62, 67; Jerome Handler, "Survivors of the Middle Passage: Life Histories of Enslaved Africans in British America," *Slavery and Abolition* 23 (2002): 25–56; Audra A. Diptee, "African Children in the British Slave Trade During the Late Eighteenth Century," *Slavery and Abolition* 27 (2006): 183–96; Paul Lovejoy, "The Children of Slavery—the Transatlantic Phase," *Slavery and Abolition* 27 (2006): 197–219; Jennifer Morgan, *Laboring Women: Reproduction and Gender in New World Slavery* (Philadelphia, 2004), 57–62; E. Perry Felton, "Kidnap-

ping: An Underreported Aspect of African Agency During the Slave Trade Era (1440–1886)," *Ufahamu: A Journal of African Studies* 35 (2007); Green, *Fistful of Shells*, 276–84.

There is some disagreement about the typical origin point of slaves from Senegambia. Lovejoy, Morgan, and other scholars cited above generalize that children tended to come from relatively near the coast, but David Eltis and Stephen D. Behrendt maintain that "most transatlantic slaves shipped from Senegambia" came from distant Sahel lands. Stephen D. Behrendt, "Ecology, Seasonality, and the Transatlantic Slave Trade," in *Soundings in Atlantic History*, ed. Bernard Bailyn and Patricia Denault (Cambridge, Mass., 2009), 69; David Eltis, *The Rise of African Slavery in the Americas* (New York, 1999), 169.

17 *"African" traditions*: Francis Moore, *Travels into the Interior Parts of Africa: Containing a Description of the Several Nations for the Space of Six Hundred Miles Up the River Gambia*, 2nd ed. (London, 1755?), 29–32, 111; Lovejoy, *Transformations in Slavery*, 87; Patrick Manning, *Slavery and African Life* (Cambridge, U.K., 1990), 57, 98; Thornton, *Africa and Africans in the Atlantic World*; Miller, *Problem of Slavery as History*, 69, 74; David Eltis and David Richardson, "A New Assessment of the Transatlantic Slave Trade," in *Extending the Frontiers: Essays on the New Transatlantic Slave Trade Database*, ed. David Eltis and David Richardson (New Haven, Conn., 2008), 40–41.

17 *The Diola people*: Robert M. Baum, *Shrines of the Slave Trade: Diola Religion and Society in Precolonial Senegambia* (New York, 1999).

17 *Muslim societies in West Africa*: Shumway, *Fante and the Transatlantic Slave Trade*, 141–43; Brooks, *Eurafricans in West Africa*; Sylviane Diouf, *Servants of Allah* (New York, 1998); Paul E. Lovejoy, *Jihad in West Africa During the Age of Revolutions* (Columbus, Ohio, 2016). This process, in which liberations led to the enslavement of others, was similar to how Christianity had first functioned to oppose but later newly justified slavery in the Mediterranean and then in the Americas. For early slavery and Christians, see Orlando Patterson, *Freedom in the Making of Western Culture* (New York, 1991); Kyle Harper, *Slavery in the Late Roman World, AD 275–425* (New York, 2011); Bradley and Cartledge, *Cambridge World History of Slavery*, vol. 1.

18 *preference or bargain*: Gregory O'Malley, *Final Passages: The Intercolonial Slave Trade of British America, 1619–1807* (Chapel Hill, N.C., 2014), 42, 210; Humphrey J. Fisher, *Slavery in the History of Muslim West Africa* (New York, 2001), 117; BNL, Aug. 7, 1760, in Donnan, *Documents Illustrative*, 2:67. For suggestions of Wheatley as Fula and Muslim, see, for example, M. A. Richmond, *Bid the Vassal Soar: Interpretive Essays on the Life and Poetry of Phillis Wheatley and George Moses Horton* (Washington, D.C., 1974), 12; John C. Shields, *Phillis Wheatley's Poetics of Liberation* (Knoxville, Tenn., 2008); Jared Ross Hardesty, *Unfreedom: Slavery and Dependence in Eighteenth-Century Boston* (New York, 2016), 37; Will Harris, "Phillis Wheatley: A Muslim Connection," *African American Review* 48 (2015): 1–15. In his recent synthesis, David Hackett Fischer stresses the diversity yet emphasizes the Akan or Gold Coast origins of eighteenth-century Africans in New England, as did William D. Piersen in *Black Yankees: The Development of an Afro-American Subculture in Eighteenth-Century New England* (Amherst, Mass., 1988). David Hackett Fischer, *African Founders: How Enslaved People Expanded American Freedom* (New York, 2022), 39–52.

19 *"no Duty on Slaves"*: Fitch to Gwinn, Jan. 12, Nov. 8, 1760; Jay Coughtry, *The Notorious Triangle: Rhode Island and the African Slave Trade, 1700–1807* (Philadelphia, 1981), 27.

19 *Fitch had registered this reality*: Fitch to Ellery, Jan. 14, 1759, to Gwinn, Jan. 12, 1760, Sept. 4, 1761; David Richardson, "Shipboard Revolts, African Authority, and the Atlantic Slave Trade," *William and Mary Quarterly* 58 (2001): 69–92; Michael Gomez, *Exchanging Our Country Marks* (Chapel Hill, N.C., 1998), 43–46; Alexander X. Byrd, *Captives and Voyagers: British Migrants Across the Eighteenth-Century Atlantic World* (Baton Rouge, La., 2008), 21–22; G. Ugo Nwokeji, *The Slave Trade and Culture in the Bight of Biafra: An African Society in the Atlantic World* (Cambridge, U.K., 2010), 38–39, 137; Claude Meillassoux, *The Anthropology of Slavery: The Womb of Iron and Gold*, trans. Alide Dasnois (Chicago, 1991), 67.

19 *the scolding Gwinn received*: Fitch to Gwinn, Sept. 4, Nov. 1, 1761; Trans-Atlantic Slave Trade Database, Voyage 25481, 25220, www.slavevoyages.org/voyage /database; Rediker, *Slave Ship*, 267; Mustakeem, *Slavery at Sea*, 83; Coughtry, *Notorious Triangle*, 153; *PWW*, 3–5; Anne Farrow, *The Logbooks: Connecticut's Slave Ships and Human Memory* (Middletown, Conn., 2014), 220. Seven other ships from Africa arrived in Boston in 1761. Murray G. Lawson, "The Routes of Boston's Trade, 1752–1765," *Transactions of the Colonial Society of Massachusetts* 38 (1947–51): 88.

20 *Great War for the Empire*: Lawrence Henry Gipson, *The British Empire Before the American Revolution*, 14 vols. (New York, 1937–70); Conway, *War, State, and Society*; David Hancock, *Citizens of the World: London Merchants and the Integration of the British Atlantic Community, 1715–1785* (New York, 1995), 81–82, 216, 279, 380; Eliga H. Gould, *The Persistence of Empire* (Chapel Hill, N.C., 1999); Carol Watts, *The Cultural Work of Empire: The Seven Years' War and the Imagining of the Shandean State* (Toronto, 2007); James Watt, "'What Mankind Has Lost and Gained': Johnson, *Rasselas*, and Colonialism," and Simon Davies, "Voltaire's *Candide* as a Global Text," in *Reading 1759*, ed. Shaun Regan (Lewisburg, Pa., 2013), 22, 39; Thornton, *Warfare in Atlantic Africa*, 146–47; Maria Alessandra Bollettino, "Slavery, War, and Britain's Atlantic Empire: Black Soldiers, Sailors, and Rebels in the Seven Years' War" (PhD diss., University of Texas at Austin, 2009), 20; Vincent Brown, *Tacky's Revolt: The Story of an Atlantic Slave War* (Cambridge, Mass., 2020); Fred Anderson, *Crucible of War* (New York, 2000); Jack P. Greene, *Evaluating Empire and Confronting Colonialism in Eighteenth-Century Britain* (New York, 2013); Bryan Rosenblithe, "Empire's Vital Extremities: British Africa and the Coming of the American Revolution," in *The American Revolution Reborn*, ed. Patrick Spero and Michael Zuckerman (Philadelphia, 2016), 150–67; *BEP*, Sept. 14, 1767.

21 *girl child's knowledge*: Adanson, *Voyage to Senegal, the Isle of Goree, and the River Gambia*, 109–10, 113; Ruth Flanagan, *The Oral and Beyond: Doing Things with Words in Africa* (Chicago, 2007); Roger D. Abrahams, *The Man-of-Words in the West Indies* (Baltimore, 1983); Roger D. Abrahams, *Singing the Master* (New York, 1992), 111; Brooks, *Eurafricans in West Africa*, 31; Baum, *Shrines of the Slave Trade*; Searing, *West African Slavery and Atlantic Commerce*, 10–17; Smallwood, *Saltwater Slavery*, 196–98; Rediker, *Slave Ship*, 280–84; Brown, *Reaper's Garden*; Brown, *Tacky's Revolt*. April C. F. Langley argues that we need to see Wheatley as a "displaced Senegalese griotte." April C. F. Langley,

The Black Aesthetic Unbound: Theorizing the Dilemma of Eighteenth-Century African American Literature (Columbus, Ohio, 2008), 57; for similar interpretations, see Shields, *Phillis Wheatley's Poetics of Liberation*, chap. 4; Babacar M'Baye, *The Trickster Comes West* (Jackson, Miss., 2009), chap. 1.

3. THE TOWN, THE FAMILIES, THE YOUTH

22 *She arrived "slender" and "frail"*: MMO, 9–10; CSR; PWW, 12–13.

22 *Fifteen thousand and five hundred*: Alfred F. Young, "Ebenezer Mackintosh: Boston's Captain General of the Liberty Tree," in *Revolutionary Founders: Rebels, Radicals, and Reformers in the Making of the Nation*, ed. Alfred F. Young, Gary B. Nash, and Ray Raphael (New York, 2011), 19.

23 *John Avery's house*: The pathbreaking Wheatley scholar and biographer William H. Robinson called Avery a "seasoned agent for Boston's slave ship captains," a likely role for a molasses distiller and rum merchant. He was a man "of a liberal education," according to John Adams, who got to know him as a fellow member of the original Loyal Nine, who became the Sons of Liberty. William H. Robinson, "On Phillis Wheatley and Her Boston," *PWW*, 6; *BNL*, Jan. 13, 1763; *Diary and Autobiography of John Adams*, ed. L. H. Butterfield (New York, 1964), 1:294; see also J. Patrick Mullins, "The Sermon That Didn't Start the Revolution: Jonathan Mayhew's Role in the Boston Stamp Act Riots," in *Community Without Consent: New Perspectives on the Stamp Act*, ed. Zachary Maynard Hutchins (Middletown, Conn., 2016), 26; Edmund S. Morgan and Helen M. Morgan, *The Stamp Act Crisis: Prologue to Revolution*, 2nd ed. (New York, 1962), 160–61.

For the origins of New England slavery, see Lorenzo Johnston Greene, *The Negro in Colonial New England* (1942; repr., New York, 1969); Margaret Ellen Newell, *Brethren by Nature: New England Indians, Colonists, and the Origins of American Slavery* (Ithaca, N.Y., 2012); Wendy Warren, *New England Bound* (New York, 2016).

23 *Gwinn and Fitch offered*: BG, July 13, Aug. 3, 1761, May 31, June 7, 1762; BPB, July 6, Aug. 13, 1762; BNL, March 21, 1760, July 30, Aug. 7, 20, 1762; BEP, July 13, 27, 1761.

24 *King Street*: G. B. Warden, *Boston, 1689–1776* (Boston, 1970), 25; N[athaniel] B. S[hurtleff], "Notes and Queries: Phillis Wheatley, the Negro Slave Poet," *Historical Magazine* 8, no. 1 (1864): 32; Cornelia Hughes Dayton and Sharon Salinger, *Robert Love's Warnings* (Philadelphia, 2014), 90; Phyllis Whitman Hunter, *Purchasing Identity in the Atlantic World: Massachusetts Merchants, 1690–1780* (Ithaca, N.Y., 2001), 25. The location of the Wheatley house, according to Robinson, was King Street at Mackerel Lane, now State and Kilby Streets. *PWW*, 6.

That the site of the Massachusetts government lay in between King and Queen Streets, and that King Street led to the new and improved wharfage, attested to the uneasy compromise the stiff-necked Puritans and their descendants had made with royalism and imperial governance. As many historians have suggested, in 1760 that seemed to most Bostonians to have been a bargain well worth making. Mark Peterson, *The City-State of Boston* (New Haven, Conn., 2019).

24 *this prestigious, "fashionable" address*: Carl Bridenbaugh, *Cities in Revolt: Urban Life in America, 1743–1776* (New York, 1955), 78; *BNL*, March 21, 1760;

Lorinda B. R. Goodwin, *An Archaeology of Manners: The Polite World of the Merchant Elite of Colonial Massachusetts* (New York, 1999), 151–53; *PWW*, 12–13.

25 *Then there was the carriage*: Shurtleff, "Phillis Wheatley, the Negro Slave Poet," 33; William A. Pencak, *Contested Commonwealths* (Bethlehem, Pa., 2011), 225.

25 *"At present every merchant"*: Fred Anderson, *A People's Army: Massachusetts Soldiers and Society in the Seven Years' War* (Chapel Hill, N.C., 1984); Mark Peterson, "The War in the Cities," in *Oxford Handbook of the American Revolution*, ed. Edward G. Gray and Jane Kamensky (New York, 2013), 194–215; Warden, *Boston, 1689–1776*, 149; Boyle Journal, March 20, 1760; Bernard quoted in Pencak, *War, Politics, and Revolution in Provincial Massachusetts* (Boston, 1981), 164.

25 *Historians used to debate*: Allan Kulikoff, "The Progress of Inequality in Revolutionary Boston," *William and Mary Quarterly* 28 (1971): 375–412; Gary B. Nash, *The Urban Crucible* (Cambridge, Mass., 1979); Pencak, *War, Politics, and Revolution*, 163; John W. Tyler, *Smugglers and Patriots: Boston Merchants and the Advent of the American Revolution* (Boston, 1986), 29; O'Malley, *Final Passages*; James G. Lydon, "New York and the Slave Trade, 1700 to 1770," *William and Mary Quarterly* 35 (1978): 375–94.

26 *The casual reader of one*: David Waldstreicher, "Reading the Runaways: Self-Fashioning, Print Culture, and Confidence in Slavery in the Eighteenth-Century Mid-Atlantic," *William and Mary Quarterly* 56 (April 1999): 243–72; Robert E. Desrochers Jr., "Slave-for-Sale Ads and Slavery in Massachusetts, 1704–1781," *William and Mary Quarterly* 59 (2002): 623–64; Robert E. Desrochers Jr., "Periphery as Center: Slavery, Identity, and the Commercial Press in the British Atlantic, 1704–1765," in *British North America in the Seventeenth and Eighteenth Centuries*, ed. Stephen Foster (Oxford, U.K., 2013), 170–94; *BPB*, July 6, 1761. For Prat, see T. A. Milford, *The Gardiners of Massachusetts* (Hanover, N.H., 2005), 57–59, 84–88; John Dixon, *The Enlightenment of Cadwallader Colden* (Ithaca, N.Y., 2016), 156.

26 *The ads functioned as surveillance*: Waldstreicher, "Reading the Runaways"; Jane Kamensky, *A Revolution in Color: The World of John Singleton Copley* (New York, 2015), 164–65; Desrochers, "Periphery as Center"; Hardesty, *Unfreedom*, 134.

27 *The New England town way*: Barry Levy, *Town Born: The Political Economy of New England from Its Founding to the Revolution* (Philadelphia, 2009).

27 *two young African men*: *BG*, April 20, 1760, Jan. 12, 1761, March 15, 1762, May 9, 1763; *BNL*, April 24, June 12, 1760, June 24, 1762; Kamensky, *Revolution in Color*, 167; Patricia Cleary, *Elizabeth Murray* (Amherst, Mass., 2000), 118; Levy, *Town Born*; Barry Levy, "Levellers and Fugitives: Runaway Advertisements and the Contrasting Political Economies of Mid-Eighteenth-Century Massachusetts and Pennsylvania," *Pennsylvania History* 78 (2011): 1–32.

27 *Peter Fleet printed and delivered*: Pencak, *Contested Commonwealths*, 278; Clifford K. Shipton, *New England Life in the Eighteenth Century* (1963; repr., Cambridge, Mass., 1993), 317; Isaiah Thomas, *The History of Printing in America*, 2nd ed. (1874; repr., New York, 1970), 94, 128, 252–53; J. L. Bell, "The Other Fleet Brothers," *Boston 1775*, April 4, 2014, www.boston1775.blogspot.com/2014/04/the-other-fleet-brothers-brought-up-to.html?m=0; Bridenbaugh, *Cities in Re-*

volt, 88. Samuel Cooper, later Wheatley's pastor and the subject of one of her poems, also had a male slave who was known for his wit. *Diary and Autobiography of John Adams*, 2:14. For the long-term context of labor and racial formation, see especially John Wood Sweet, *Bodies Politic: Negotiating Race in the American North, 1730–1830* (Baltimore, 2003), and Melish, *Disowning Slavery.*

28 *black population*: *Report of the Record Commissioners of the City of Boston Containing Boston Town Records, 1758–1769* (Boston, 1887), 20; *BG*, Jan. 7, 1760, Jan. 4, 1762, Jan. 31, 1763, Jan. 2, Dec. 31, 1764; *BNL*, Jan. 6, 1763. Higher mortality rates among African Americans may cause these numbers to be higher than an accurate representation of the population numbers, but recent authorities like William D. Piersen, Robert Desrochers Jr., and Jared Hardesty have also revised previous census-dependent accounts and pushed the demographic figures up to 10–20 percent by midcentury. Greene, *Negro in Colonial New England*, 81–85; Desrochers, "Slave-for-Sale Ads"; Piersen, *Black Yankees*, 15, 21–22; Hardesty, *Unfreedom*, 5, 22; Jared Hardesty, "Disappearing from Abolition's Heartland: The Legacy of Slavery and Emancipation in Boston," *International Review of Social History* 65 (2020): 145–68. I thank Susan Klepp for her insights on sources and demography.

28 *"African wave"*: For the African wave at midcentury, I am indebted to Thomas J. Davis's unpublished manuscript on Connecticut's Africans and black governors, corroborated by correspondence with Davis, June 2019; see also Thomas J. Davis, *History of African Americans: Exploring Diverse Roots* (Santa Barbara, Calif., 2016); James A. Rawley and Stephen D. Behrendt, *The Transatlantic Slave Trade: A History*, rev. ed (Lincoln, Neb., 2009), 299; Christy Clark-Pujara, *Dark Work: The Business of Slavery in Rhode Island* (New York, 2016), 21.

29 *relations with others*: *BG*, Sept. 3, 1764; *BNL*, Sept. 24, 1761; Hardesty, *Unfreedom*, 76; Piersen, *Black Yankees*, 31, 87–95.

30 *"family-like attachment"*: Winter, *Blind African Slave*, 149, 152; *Memoir of Mrs. Chloe Spear, a Native of Africa, Who Was Enslaved in Childhood, and Died in Boston, January 3, 1815* (Boston, 1832), 9–10, 17, 23, 26, 38–41, 48. For close distancing, see Robert John Ackermann, *Heterogeneities* (Amherst, Mass., 1999), 19. On the racialization of servitude, see Elisabeth Ceppi, *Invisible Masters: Gender, Race, and the Economy of Service in Early New England* (Hanover, N.H., 2018). On the laws of slavery in Massachusetts, see John N. Blanton, "This Species of Property: Slavery and the Properties of Subjecthood in Anglo-American Law and Politics, 1619–1783" (PhD diss., Graduate Center, City University of New York, 2016).

30 *Hannah Mather Crocker*: CWC, 73; MMO, 10, 12; Hannah Mather Crocker, *Reminiscences and Traditions of Boston*, ed. Eileen Hunt Botting and Sarah L. Houser (Boston, 2011), 211.

30 *"social death"*: Orlando Patterson, *Slavery and Social Death* (Cambridge, Mass., 1982). For criticisms, see Vincent Brown, "Social Death and Political Life in the Study of Slavery," *American Historical Review* 114 (2009): 1231–49; Nicholas T. Rinehart, "The Man That Was a Thing: Rethinking Human Commodification in Slavery," *Journal of Social History* (2016): 1–23; Nicholas T. Rinehart, "Reparative Semantics: On Slavery and the Language of History," *Common-Place*, Jan. 2022.

31 *especially young ones*: Levy, *Town Born*; Newell, *Brethren by Nature*; David Waldstreicher, *Runaway America: Benjamin Franklin, Slavery, and the American Revolution* (New York, 2004).

4. THE TEACHERS

33 *family project*: CWC, 7; MMO, 9, 11; CSR; Shurtleff, "Phillis Wheatley, the Negro Slave Poet," 32; *PWW*, 19. John Wheatley's burying of "the family" in a subordinate clause simultaneously understates the women's efforts and testifies to them.

Odell also wrote that Phillis "was frequently seen endeavoring to make letters upon the wall with a piece of chalk or charcoal," suggesting (though not to Odell) the possibility that she arrived with a knowledge of literacy. MMO, 10. For speculations regarding Wheatley as potentially literate in Arabic because of the Muslim presence in Senegambia, see Shields, *Phillis Wheatley's Poetics of Liberation*, 100–104; Daniel DeWispelare, *Multilingual Subjects: On Standard English, Its Speakers, and Others in the Long Eighteenth Century* (Philadelphia, 2017), 51–59; Antonio T. Bly, "'On Death's Domain Intent I Fix My Eye': Text, Context, and Subtext in the Elegies of Phillis Wheatley," *Early American Literature* 53 (2018): 318.

33 *While girls increasingly learned to write*: E. Jennifer Monaghan, *Learning to Read and Write in Colonial America* (Amherst, Mass., 2005), 6, 236, 242–45.

33 *interview with Wheatley*: "A Conversation Between a New York Gentleman & Phillis," Dr. Williams's Library, London. Vincent Carretta offers the likelihood that this was the same dialogue John Andrews referred to as having been conducted by an unknown "Mr. Murry." Probably this was the Reverend John Murray, later the founder of Unitarianism and husband of the pioneering feminist writer Judith Sargent Murray, who had recently arrived in Boston when Andrews wrote the letter. Dialogues are a notable part of his preaching and writing. Carretta, *Phillis Wheatley*, 51–52; *The Life of the Rev. John Murray, Late Minister of the Reconciliation, and Senior Pastor of the Universalists, Congregated in Boston* (Boston, 1858), 168, 194; Sheila Skemp, *First Lady of Letters: A Biography of Judith Sargent Murray* (Philadelphia, 2012).

33 *Joseph Addison's Rosamond*: Joseph Addison, *Rosamond: An Opera* (London, 1707); Brean S. Hammond, "Addison's Opera *Rosamond*: Britishness in the Early Eighteenth Century," *ELH* 73, no. 3 (2006): 601–29; Bernard Friedman, *The Ballad Revival* (Chicago, 1961). The play leads off the second volume of Tickell's edition, often reprinted during the 1740s–60s, of *The Miscellaneous Works of Joseph Addison* (London, 1765), 2:1–46, appearing before *Cato*, which Wheatley also mentions.

34 *"alternative reality"*: A. Roger Ekirch, *At Day's Close: Night in Times Past* (New York, 2005), 160, 163–64, 249, 255, 310; MMO, 15.

34 *"I'll too my plighted Vows renew"*: Addison, *Rosamond*, 33–34.

35 *"Mrs. Thacher's son"*: Jeremy Belknap diary, 1773, Jeremy Belknap Papers, MHS. The rhymes are especially evident when we recall eighteenth-century English or Yankee pronunciations of "gone" as likely to be something closer to "gun."

35 *Belknap scribbled*: Vincent Carretta, "Phillis Wheatley's First Effort," *PMLA* 125, no. 3 (May 2010): 795–97, and Carretta, *Phillis Wheatley*, 46–47; *WPW*, 3, 145–47. For Wheatley's art as intensely neighborly like other women's writing of the era, see Caroline Wigginton, *In the Neighborhood: Women's Publication in Early America* (Amherst, Mass., 2016), esp. chap. 3.

36 *The Thachers lived a few blocks*: Clifford K. Shipton, "Oxenbridge Thacher," *New England Life in the Eighteenth Century: Representative Biographies from Sibley's Harvard Graduates* (1961; repr., Cambridge, Mass., 1995), 443–48; Clifford

Putney, "Oxenbridge Thacher: Boston Lawyer, Early Patriot," *Historical Journal of Massachusetts* (Winter 2004): 90–106; Bernard Bailyn, ed., *Pamphlets of the American Revolution, 1750–1776* (Cambridge, Mass., 1965), 1:483–99.

36 *the controversy over smallpox*: BEP, July 15, 1765; Catherine Adams and Elizabeth Pleck, *Love of Freedom: Black Women in Colonial and Revolutionary New England* (New York, 2010), 44; Perry Miller, *The New England Mind: From Colony to Province* (New York, 1955), 346–66; Waldstreicher, *Runaway America*, 39–54; Margot Minardi, "The Boston Inoculation Controversy of 1721–1722: An Incident in the History of Race," *William and Mary Quarterly* 61 (2004): 47–76.

37 *Bostonians were accustomed to ballads*: Matthew P. Brown, "'BOSTON/SOB NOT': Elegiac Performance in Early New England and Materialist Studies of the Book," *American Quarterly* 50 (1998): 322; Thomas C. Leonard, "Recovering 'Wretched Stuff' and the Franklins' Synergy," *New England Quarterly* 72 (1999): 444–55.

37 *African and European deathways*: Erik Seeman, *Death in the New World: Cross-Cultural Encounters, 1492–1800* (Philadelphia, 2010), esp. 185–231. For Wheatley as making kin, I am indebted to a comment by John Bezis-Selfa.

38 *She needed to at least perform*: "In her elegies," writes Julian D. Mason Jr., "hope and love and faith triumph over death." PPW, 11. For a similar perspective on what assimilation or acculturation would have meant, see G. Michelle Collins-Sibley, "Who Can Speak? Authority and Authenticity in Olaudah Equiano and Phillis Wheatley," *Journal of Colonialism and Colonial History* 5, no. 3 (2014). For earlier appreciations of Wheatley as performer, see Frances Smith Foster, *Written by Herself: Literary Production by African American Women, 1746–1892* (Bloomington, Ind., 1992), 32–33; Russell Reising, *Loose Ends* (Durham, N.C., 1996), 109–12; Gay Gibson Cima, "Black and Unmarked: Phillis Wheatley, Mercy Otis Warren, and the Limits of Strategic Anonymity," *Theatre Journal* 52 (2000): 479–80; Astrid Franke, "Phillis Wheatley, Melancholy Muse," *New England Quarterly* (2004): 234–46.

38 *"On Virtue"*: Few critics have offered interpretations of "On Virtue," but see Richards, "Phillis Wheatley: The Consensual Blackness of Early African American Writing," 256–57, who sees in it a conversion narrative; Loscocco, *Phillis Wheatley's Miltonic Poetics*, 51–53, who finds repurposing of Milton's "Comus: A Masque" and "Lycidas"; and Michael Monescalchi, "On Virtue: Phillis Wheatley with Jonathan Edwards," *Common-Place* 17, no. 3 (Spring 2017), which argues for the direct influence of Jonathan Edwards, whose *Nature of True Virtue* had just been republished by a Boston printer.

38 *blank verse*: Isaac Watts, *Horae Lyricae: Poems, Chiefly of the Lyric Kind* (Windham, Conn., 1798), 133, 136; David Fairer, "Creating a National Poetry: The Traditions of Spenser and Milton," in *The Cambridge Companion to Eighteenth-Century Poetry*, ed. John Sitter (Cambridge, U.K., 2001), 184. For blank verse as "never more than a minority taste," see J. Paul Hunter, "Couplets and Conversation," in the same volume, 25.

39 *"invaded all forms of discourse"*: J. Paul Hunter, "Political, Satirical, Didactic, and Lyric Poetry (1): From the Restoration to the Death of Pope," in *The Cambridge History of English Literature, 1660–1780*, ed. John Richetti (New York, 2005), 161, 163.

39 *"Few of us would read poetry"*: Paula Backscheider, *Eighteenth-Century Women Poets and Their Poetry* (Baltimore, 2005), 9, 132–33.

40 *These writer-readers included servants and women*: Paula Backscheider, "Eighteenth-Century Women Poets," in Richetti, *Cambridge History*, 209–35; Moira Ferguson, *Eighteenth-Century Women Poets* (Albany, N.Y., 1995); Norma Clarke, *The Rise and Fall of the Woman of Letters* (London, 2004); Donna Landry, *The Muses of Resistance: Laboring-Class Women's Poetry in Britain, 1739–1796* (Cambridge, U.K., 1990); Carolyn Steedman, *Labours Lost: Domestic Service and the Making of Modern England* (New York, 2009), 282–84, 294–96; Carolyn Steedman, *Poetry for Historians, or, W. H. Auden and History* (Manchester, U.K., 2018), 25–52; Susan Staves, *A Literary History of Women's Writing in Britain, 1660–1789* (New York, 2006); Norma Clarke, *Brothers of the Quill: Oliver Goldsmith in Grub Street* (Cambridge, Mass., 2016); Samuel Richardson, *Pamela* (New York, 2001), 15, 138–40, 495. Landry argues explicitly that women's servant writing in Britain "legitimated Wheatley's writing and made possible its widest dissemination" (240).

41 *remarkable proliferation of reading material*: Abigail Williams, *The Social Life of Books: Reading Together in the Eighteenth-Century Home* (New Haven, Conn., 2017), 128; John Brewer, *The Pleasures of the Imagination: English Culture in the Eighteenth Century* (1997; repr., Chicago, 2000), 132, 172, 276, 575; Margaret Anne Doody, *The Daring Muse: Augustan Poetry Reconsidered* (Cambridge, U.K., 1985), 231, 263; *BG*, Nov. 30, 1761, June 28, 1762, Nov. 19, 1764; *BEP*, Sept. 10, 1764; T. H. Breen, *The Marketplace of Revolution* (New York, 2004); Patricia Cleary, *Elizabeth Murray* (Amherst, Mass., 2000); Hunter, *Purchasing Identity in the Atlantic World*.

41 *the Reverend Mather Byles*: Mather Byles, *Poems on Several Occasions* (1744; repr., New York, 1940); Arthur Wentworth Eaton Hamilton, *The Famous Mather Byles* (1912; repr., Boston, 1972), 5–6, 21–23, 29–34, 96–102; Catalogue of Mather Byles Library, MHS; Clifford K. Shipton, "Mather Byles," *Sibley's Harvard Graduates* (Boston, 1945), 7:464–93; Paul Giles, *Transatlantic Insurrections: British Culture and the Formation of American Literature, 1730–1860* (Philadelphia, 2001), 29–39; David S. Shields, *Oracles of Empire: Poetry, Politics, and Commerce in British America, 1690–1750* (Chicago, 1990), 21, 233n2; David S. Shields, *Civil Tongues and Polite Letters in British America* (Chapel Hill, N.C., 1997), 249; LeMay, *Life of Benjamin Franklin*, 1:205, 209. For the Mather family library, see Peterson, *City-State of Boston*, 217–29. The first scholar to argue for Byles's decisive influence on Wheatley was John C. Shields, "Phillis Wheatley and Mather Byles: A Study in Literary Relationship," *CLA Journal* 23 (1980): 377–90; see also and more recently Shields, *Phillis Wheatley's Poetics of Liberation*, 168–80. Byles was also the uncle of Phillis's first recorded fan, Jeremy Belknap. Carretta, *Phillis Wheatley*, 48.

42 *Mary and Catherine*: In 1767, Mary Byles recorded the English bluestocking feminist Sarah Scott's utopian novel *A Description of Millenium Hall* (1762) and *Virtue Rewarded; or, The History, in Miniature, of the Celebrated Pamela* (an abridged 1764 edition of Richardson's novel) as two of the two dozen books she read that year, some of them even more recently published and probably bought at one of Boston's several bookstores. Mather Byles Jr. to Mary Byles, Feb. 9, 1758, Dec. 23, 1761, Feb. 11 and Oct. 4, 1762, Byles Family Papers, reel 1, MHS; Mary Byles Commonplace Book, reel 2, Byles Family Papers; Eliza Leslie, "The Daughters of Dr. Byles: A Sketch of Reality," *Graham's Lady's and Gentleman's Magazine* 20 (1842): 61–65, 113–18; Edward M. Griffin, "Stubborn Loyalists,"

Common-Place no. 7.4 (July 2007); Michael J. Eamon, "'Don't Speak to Me, but Write on This': The Childhood Almanacs of Mary and Katherine Byles," *New England Quarterly* 85 (June 2012): 351–52; Dana Rose Comi, "In the Shade of Solitude: The Mind of New England Women, 1630–1805" (PhD diss., Brandeis University, 2003), 143–45.

42 *Hannah Mather*: Crocker, *Reminiscences and Traditions of Boston*, 75, 82–83, 210–12; Eileen Hunt Botting, "Theorizing Women's Political Agency from the Margins of Hannah Mather Crocker's *Reminiscences and Traditions of Boston*," *Early American Literature* 49 (2014): 149–83; Alea Henle, "The Widow's Mite: Hannah Mather Crocker and the Mather Libraries," *Information & Culture* 48 (2013): 323–43. Perhaps the best testimony to the power of poetry for this generation of women is the plotting of dozens of poems, including some of her own, throughout Crocker's manuscript history.

Crocker mentions Phillis going to school with Mary Wheatley, but this seems unlikely because Mary was about seventeen years old when Phillis arrived in 1761. Since Mary died in 1778, Crocker probably misremembered their relative ages as she wrote during the 1820s. Perhaps what she was really remembering was the companionship of this cohort of literate girls, even as she singled out Wheatley because of her subsequent fame.

43 *A surviving notebook*: MSS 296, Phillis Wheatley Collection, box 1, vols. 1 and 2, Stuart A. Rose Library, Emory University; *CWC*, 195–97.

5. THE PREACHERS

44 *daughters, and granddaughters, of ministers*: Mary and Katy Byles never married. They lived with their father through his confinement during the Revolutionary War and remained in his house for the next sixty years, famous in Boston for their antiquated ways, including unsuppressed love for the king of England. Hannah married the son of a preacher who became a commissary and commander in the Continental army. "Joseph Crocker," in *Sibley's Harvard Graduates*, ed. Conrad Edick Wright and Edward W. Hanson (Boston, 1999), 18:406–9.

44 *"various subjects, moral and religious"*: Both George Whitefield and the wildly popular hymnodist Isaac Watts published collections titled *Sermons on Various Subjects*. Isabel Rivers, *Vanity Fair and the Celestial City: Dissenting, Methodist, and Evangelical Literary Culture in England, 1720–1800* (Oxford, U.K., 2018), 76–77.

44 *"Attestation"*: *CWC*, 8. For Hutchinson and Oliver, religion and politics remained all too parallel: they would soon charge the "black regiment" with leading townspeople into illegitimate resistance to the Crown. Bernard Bailyn, *The Ordeal of Thomas Hutchinson* (Cambridge, Mass., 1974); Douglass Adair and John A. Schutz, eds., *Peter Oliver's Origin and Progress of the American Rebellion: A Tory View* (Stanford, Calif., 1961).

45 *Phillis listed poems in the order*: *CWC*, 165.

45 *"On the Death of the Rev."*: Wheatley later corrected the awkwardness of having memorialized someone not yet dead, dating her revision for the actual 1773 *Poems* to 1769. One version survives in the papers of the Reverend Jeremy Belknap, who also saved the lines on the Thachers, and another in the papers of Selina Hastings, the Countess of Huntingdon, the patron to whom she would

dedicate her book. She likely placed it first in the 1772 proposal because it was her first poem to be read in Boston and beyond. For the variants, see *CWC*, 13–14, 109–12; *PPW*, 128–31; the manuscripts are reproduced in *PWW*, 365–69.

Sewall was the son of Judge Samuel Sewall, author of *The Selling of Joseph* (1700), the first antislavery pamphlet published in the colonies, though there is no record of the son—twelve years old in 1700—later taking a stand on slavery or the slave trade. If Wheatley was already aware of Samuel Sewall's famously controversial stance, that affinity could be plausibly effaced through the son's eminence, much as her awareness of Hussey and Coffin's membership in the Society of Friends, the only sect to have denounced African slavery, could be covered by her concern for the souls of these "friends."

46 *Ordinarily, women couldn't preach*: Catherine Brekus, *Sarah Osborn's World: The Rise of Evangelical Christianity in Early America* (New Haven, Conn., 2013); Susan Juster, *Disorderly Women: Sexual Politics and Evangelicalism in Revolutionary New England* (Ithaca, N.Y., 1994).

46 *The image of Sewall's ascent*: The version in *Poems* is nine lines shorter. "Proposals for Printing by Subscription," in *CWC*, 13–15, 107–10, 165–66; *PWP*, 116–17n, 187–88n; *PWW*, 368–69. Several years later Susanna's niece Elizabeth Wallcut sent her son Thomas, who sometimes corresponded with Phillis, an engraving of Sewall along with a copy of her elegy. Elizabeth Wallcut to Thomas Wallcut, March 18, July 20, 1773, Thomas Wallcut Papers, MHS. Of the three manuscript versions of the Sewall poem extant, one went to the Reverend Jeremy Belknap, the recorder of "Mrs. Thacher's Son." For this and other reasons, Carretta considers that one the first. Robinson chooses the one at the American Antiquarian Society, though that is dated 1769.

46 *"Spirit of the Gods"*: *CWC*, 107. The plural reference may be from the book of Daniel (King James Version) 5:13–14. King Belshazzar, begging as the unconverted for an interpretation, says to Daniel, "I have even heard of thee, that the spirit of the gods *is* in thee." Thanks to Christopher Grasso for this reference.

47 *"Sewall is dead"*: *CWC*, 108–9. For the self-interruptions, and Wheatley as echoing Milton's "Lycidas," see Loscocco, *Phillis Wheatley's Miltonic Poetics*, 57–58, which she sees as indicating the inevitable failure of mourning and elegy itself. For the open-endedness of praise poetry including its ability to celebrate the creative powers of the poet, see Susan Stewart, *The Poet's Freedom* (Chicago, 2011), 35–39.

48 *culture of Congregationalism*: Edmund S. Morgan, *Visible Saints: The History of a Puritan Idea* (New York, 1963); Miller, *New England Mind*; Juster, *Disorderly Women*; Catherine Brekus, *Strangers and Pilgrims* (Chapel Hill, N.C., 1999); Brekus, *Sarah Osborn's World*; Timothy D. Hall, *Contested Boundaries* (Durham, N.C., 1994); Douglas L. Winiarski, *Darkness Falls on the Land of Light: Experiencing Religious Awakening in Eighteenth-Century New England* (Chapel Hill, N.C., 2017), 28; Sacvan Bercovitch, *The American Jeremiad* (Madison, Wis., 1975).

49 *"To the University of Cambridge"*: *CWC*, 105–6, 165; Mason, introduction to *PPW*, 16; Adams and Pleck, *Love of Freedom*, 97–98. Carretta calls the Cambridge poem a "commencement address" in *Phillis Wheatley*, 58–59. For the striking directness and the revision that tones down the emphasis on African ignorance in the 1773 version, see *CWC*, 11–12; David Grimsted, "Anglo-American Racism and Phillis Wheatley's 'Sable Veil,' 'Length'ned Chain,' and 'Knitted Heart,'" in *Women in the Age of the American Revolution*, ed. Ronald

Hoffman and Peter J. Albert (Charlottesville, Va., 1989), 356–57; Bassard, *Spiritual Interrogations*, 40–46.

50 *Along with two other poems*: For two versions of the unpublished but circulated poems on atheism and deism, see *CWC*, 67–73. Neither was ever published during Wheatley's lifetime, but their existence in two variants suggests that they were circulated in manuscript between 1767 and 1769. Manuscripts are dated 1767 and one in July 1769 in Wheatley's hand; the Quaker poet Hannah Griffitts might have had a copy in 1767 as well. Robie-Sewall Papers, MHS; Box 3, Whitwell Autograph Collection, MHS; Carretta, *Phillis Wheatley*, 54, 210n4. To one recent critic, "privileges" connotes racial domination. Alexis Pauline Gumbs, "Phillis Wheatley," in *Four Hundred Souls: A Community History of African America, 1619–2019*, ed. Ibram X. Kendi and Keisha N. Blain (New York, 2021), 131–32.

50 *secular and rakish tradition*: Robert Herrick, "To the Virgins, to Make Much of Time," poets.org/poem/virgins-make-much-time; Gay quoted in Doody, *Daring Muse*, 212.

51 *"Must Ethiopians be employ'd"*: *CWC*, 71, 72. For Ethiopianism authorizing Christian speech, see Carretta, *Phillis Wheatley*, 57. John C. Shields speculates that these poems were attempts to persuade the orthodox Reverend Sewall to baptize her and contrasts them with her later "relaxed Christianity." Shields, *Phillis Wheatley's Poetics of Liberation*, 129, 146.

51 *The revivals called the Great Awakening*: Thomas Kidd, *The Great Awakening: The Roots of Evangelical Christianity in Colonial America* (New Haven, Conn., 2007), 213; Edward Griffin, *Old Brick: Charles Chauncy of Boston, 1705–1787* (Minneapolis, 1980); Levy, *Town Born*; Newell, *Brethren by Nature*.

52 *The new evangelicals praised*: Erik Seeman, *Pious Persuasions: Laity and Clergy in Eighteenth-Century New England* (Baltimore, 1999), x, 147–48; Erik Seeman, "'Justice May Take Plase': Three African Americans Speak of Religion in Eighteenth-Century New England," *William and Mary Quarterly* 56 (April 1999): 393–414; Mark Peterson, *The Price of Redemption* (Princeton, N.J., 1999), on awakening in Boston; Frank Lambert, *Inventing the Great Awakening* (Princeton, N.J., 1999); Kidd, *Great Awakening*; Winiarski, *Darkness Falls on the Land of Light*, 181–85, 321, 326; Carretta, *Phillis Wheatley*, 33.

Scholars are divided about whether evangelical Christianity empowered African Americans (in New England or elsewhere in early America) or whether it contributed toward or against rising racial consciousness, with historians of religion and of African Americans being relatively optimistic: see, for example, Adams and Pleck, *Love of Freedom*; Piersen, *Black Yankees*; Joanna Brooks, *American Lazarus: Religion and the Rise of Native and African American Literatures* (New York, 2003); Hardesty, *Unfreedom*, 136, 152–63. For a sharp pessimistic view, see Sweet, *Bodies Politic*, chap. 3, who emphasizes an erasure of ethnic identities but an elaboration of racial ones. It is striking that optimists about religion and race tend to differentiate the revivalists and new denominations like the Methodists and Baptists from the establishment, whereas pessimists see more continuity and similarities. For a long and nuanced view focused on churches, see Richard J. Boles, *Dividing the Faith: The Rise of Segregated Churches in the Early American North* (New York, 2020).

53 *an evangelical project from the start*: Kidd, *Great Awakening*, 147; Eric Slauter, "Looking for Scipio Moorhead: An 'African Painter' in Revolutionary North America," in *Slave Portraiture in the Atlantic World*, ed. Agnes Lugo-Ortiz and

Angela Rosenthal (New York, 2013), 95–96; Wendy Raphael Roberts, "Phillis Wheatley's Sarah Moorhead: An Initial Inquiry," *Papers of the Bibliographical Society of America* 107, no. 3 (2013): 345–54; Wendy Raphael Roberts, *Awakening Verse: The Poetics of Early American Evangelicalism* (New York, 2020), chap. 2. The Moorheads and the Wheatleys became so close that when John was immobilized in 1772, his most regular visitor would be John Moorhead.

54 *Mohegan preacher and teacher Samson Occom*: W. DeLoss Love, *Samson Occom and the Christian Indians of New England* (1899; repr., Syracuse, N.Y., 2000), 92; David J. Silverman, *Red Brethren: The Brothertown and Stockbridge Indians and the Problem of Race in Early America* (Ithaca, N.Y., 2010), 48, 55, 71; Hilary Wyss, *English Letters and Indian Literacies* (Philadelphia, 2012), 11, 67–71; Linford D. Fisher, *The Indians' Great Awakening* (New York, 2012), 65; Laura J. Murray, "What Did Christianity Do for Joseph Johnson? A Mohegan Preacher and His Community," in *Possible Pasts: Becoming Colonial in Early America*, ed. Robert St. George (Ithaca, N.Y., 2000), 160–80; Sandra Gustafson, *Eloquence Is Power: Oratory and Performance in Early America* (Chapel Hill, N.C., 2000), 90–96.

55 *Occom's traveling to England*: BEP, April 29, June 17, 1765; Colin Calloway, *The Indian History of an American Institution: Native Americans and Dartmouth* (Hanover, N.H., 2010), 16; Jenny Hale Pulsipher, *Subjects unto the Same King* (Philadelphia, 2007); Coll Thrush, *Indigenous London: Native Travelers at the Heart of Empire* (New Haven, Conn., 2016), 108–14; Silverman, *Red Brethren*, 80–81; Kidd, *Great Awakening*, 210, 243; Joanna Brooks, ed., *The Collected Writings of Samson Occom* (New York, 2006), 19, 248, 265.

56 *He had represented his people*: Harold Blodgett, *Samson Occom* (Hanover, N.H., 1935), 104, 117; Love, *Samson Occom*, 135; Occom to Wheelock, June 24, 1771, in Brooks, *Collected Writings of Samson Occom*, 98; Brooks, *American Lazarus*, chap. 3; Calloway, *Indian History of an American Institution*, 22–28.

56 *"As to her WRITING"*: CWC, 7; Grimsted, "Anglo-American Racism and Phillis Wheatley's 'Sable Veil,'" 387–88; Susanna Wheatley to Occom and Nathaniel Whitaker, Dec. 31, 1765, Occom Circle Project, Dartmouth College, https://www.library.dartmouth.edu/digital/digital-collections/occom-circle.

6. THE MONARCH, THE POETS, THE SUBJECTS, THE ENSLAVED

57 *Samson Occom could play a very special role*: Love, *Samson Occom*, 140; Brooks, *Collected Writings of Samson Occom*, 63, 84, 98, 122, 267–68; Bannet, *Transatlantic Stories and the Histories of Reading*, 172, 175; Silverman, *Red Brethren*, 71–86; Wyss, *English Letters and Indian Literacies*, 65; Eric Hinderaker, "The 'Four Indian Kings' and the Imaginative Construction of the First British Empire," *William and Mary Quarterly* 53 (1996): 487–526.

58 *In 1766, the monarch of four British kingdoms*: For monarchical culture and politics, see Richard L. Bushman, *King and People in Provincial Massachusetts* (Chapel Hill, N.C., 1985); Brendan McConville, *The King's Three Faces: The Rise and Fall of Royal America, 1688–1776* (Chapel Hill, N.C., 2006); Eric Nelson, *The Royalist Revolution* (Cambridge, Mass., 2014). For political arguments generally, see Jack P. Greene, *Peripheries and Center* (Athens, Ga., 1986); Jack P. Greene, *The Constitutional Origins of the American Revolution* (New York, 2011); Craig Yirush, *Settlers, Liberty, and Empire: The Roots of Early American Political Theory, 1675–1775* (New York, 2011).

59 *"The King our Father"*: BEP, Oct. 21, 1765.

60 *Royal anniversaries had become*: BG, Sept. 20, 27, 1762, June 6, Aug. 15, 1763, June 9, 1766; BEP, Sept. 24, Oct. 29, 1764, June 10, Aug. 19, Sept. 23, Oct. 28, 1765, Sept. 22, Oct. 27, 1766.

61 *Poets took notice*: Joseph Addison, "To Mr. Dryden," "A Poem to His Majesty," in *The Works of Joseph Addison*, ed. Richard Hurd (London, 1906), 1:1–2, 3–10; Peter Smithers, *The Life of Joseph Addison*, 2nd ed. (Oxford, 1968), 21–22, 30–31, 42–43; James Anderson Winn, *John Dryden and His World* (New Haven, Conn., 1987).

61 *Harvard tutors*: Shields, *Oracles of Empire*, 163–65; Suvir Kaul, *Poems of Nation, Anthems of Empire* (Charlottesville, Va., 2000); Shields, *American Aeneas*, 89–95; Clarke, *Brothers of the Quill*, 109–10, 118–21.

61 *"A Poem on the Accession"*: BG, Feb. 14, Jan. 10, 1763; BNL, Jan. 13, 1763; Shields, *Oracles of Empire*, 10; "A Poem on the Accession of King George III," BNL, Aug. 26, 1763.

62 *formulaic neoclassicism provided some cover*: Doody, *Daring Muse*, 217, 231; James Thomson, *Poetical Works*, ed. J. Logie Robertson (1908; repr., London, 1971), 398. Doody, perhaps the foremost champion of Augustan verse, finds in the result an embrace of oxymoron, a doubleness expressed by and in the couplet form: an "Augustan poetic ideal that every utterance should speak twice at the same time" (231). For Pope, see John Sitter, "Pope's Versification and Voice," in *The Cambridge Companion to Alexander Pope*, ed. Pat Rogers (New York, 2007), 37; Patricia Meyer Spacks, *Reading Eighteenth-Century Poetry* (Oxford, 2009), 83; Howard D. Weinbrot, *Britannia's Issue: The Rise of British Literature from Dryden to Ossian* (Cambridge, U.K., 1993); Dustin Griffin, *Patriotism and Poetry in Eighteenth-Century Britain* (Cambridge, U.K., 2002), 56–63, 71–73, 293; Helen Deutsch, *Resemblance and Disgrace: Alexander Pope and the Deformation of Culture* (Cambridge, Mass., 1996); Laura Brown, *Alexander Pope* (London, 1985); Howard Erskine-Hill, "Pope and Slavery," in *Alexander Pope: World and Word*, ed. Howard Erskine-Hill (Oxford, 1998), 27–54; John A. Richardson, *Slavery and Augustan Literature: Swift, Pope, Gay* (New York 2004); Scott Hess, *Authoring the Self: Self-Representation, Authorship, and the Print Market in British Poetry from Pope Through Wordsworth* (London, 2005), 69–108.

62 *Mather Byles*: Byles to Pope, May 18, 1728, in C. Lennart Carlson, introduction to *Poems on Several Occasions*, by Byles, xxii; Shipton, "Mather Byles," in *New England Life in the Eighteenth Century*, 231–32; Shields, *Civil Tongues and Polite Letters*, 237–63. John C. Shields was first to propose Mather Byles as a mentor and major influence. For his latest accountings, see his "Phillis Wheatley's Theoretics of the Imagination," in Shields and Lamore, *New Essays on Phillis Wheatley*, 355–59, and Shields, *Phillis Wheatley's Poetics of Liberation*, 168–80.

63 *"acute self-consciousness"*: Giles, *Transatlantic Insurrections*, 18–39; Phillip M. Richards, "Phillis Wheatley, Americanization, the Sublime, and the Romance of America," *Style* 27, no. 2 (1993), 194–221; Byles, *Poems on Several Occasions*, 52–55, 78.

63 *Write for ETERNITY*: Eaton, *Famous Mather Byles*, 219, 147–52, quoted at 146; Max Cavitch, *American Elegy* (Minneapolis, 2007), 39.

65 *"fled from the Oppression"*: Merrill Jensen, *The Founding of a Nation: A History of the American Revolution, 1763–1776* (New York, 1968), 43–51, 70–97; Ian Christie and Benjamin W. Labaree, *Empire or Independence* (New York, 1976), 42–45; Waldstreicher, *Runaway America*, 175–78; Richard L. Merritt, *Sym-*

bols of American Community, 1735–1775 (New Haven, Conn., 1966); "A Few Thoughts on the Method of Improving and Securing the Advantages Which Accrue to Great Britain from the Northern Colonies," *BG*, Sept. 10, 1764.

65 *"What wise parent ever treated"*: *BEP*, May 27, July 8, 22, Aug. 12, 1765.

65 *August 14*: *BEP*, Aug. 19, 1765; Brian Deming, *Boston and the Dawn of American Independence* (Yardley, Pa., 2015), 70; Robert St. George, *Conversing by Signs: Poetics of Implication in Colonial New England Culture* (Chapel Hill, N.C., 1998), chap. 3; "To the Publisher," *BEP*, Sept. 23, 1765.

67 *Effigies proceeded to the courthouse*: *BEP*, Oct. 18, Nov. 5, 12, 1765; Molly Perry, "Buried Liberties and Hanging Effigies: Imperial Persuasion, Intimidation, and Performance During the Stamp Act Crisis," in Hutchins, *Community Without Consent*, 52–53. Joshua Fogarty Beatty notes other comparisons of colonists to "negro" slaves in Boston newspapers in 1765, in his "'Fatal Year': Slavery, Violence, and the Stamp Act of 1765" (PhD diss., College of William and Mary, 2014), 62–63.

67 *center of protests*: *BEP*, May 5, 19, 26, 1766; Pitt quoted in Robert Middlekauff, *The Glorious Cause*, rev. ed. (New York, 2005), 116–17; Beatty, "'Fatal Year,'" 186–87, 190–97; *A Report of the Record Commissioners of the City of Boston, Containing the Boston Town Records from 1758 to 1769* (Boston, 1886), 183.

68 *Bostonians would celebrate the anniversary*: "To the Publishers of the Boston Evening-Post," *BEP*, March 23, Aug. 21, 1767; David Waldstreicher, *In the Midst of Perpetual Fetes: The Making of American Nationalism, 1776–1820* (Chapel Hill, N.C., 1997), 18–30.

69 *"meanest peasants"*: "To the King's Most Excellent Majesty," Simon Gratz Autograph Collection, Historical Society of Pennsylvania, manuscript photocopy also in *PWW*, 364; *CWC*, 106. James A. Levernier argues that "meanest peasants" implies slaves in "Style as Protest in the Poetry of Phillis Wheatley," *Style* 27 (1993): 172–93.

70 *"When wars came on"*: Grimsted, "Anglo-American Racism and Phillis Wheatley's 'Sable Veil,'" 350–51.

70 *dating at 1768*: For variants, see Robert Kuncio, "Some Unpublished Poems of Phillis Wheatley," *New England Quarterly* 43 (1970): 287–97. Carretta, *Phillis Wheatley*, 69, sees the line as "a not-so-subtle reminder that not only taxed colonists should be set free." See also Grimsted, "Anglo-American Racism and Phillis Wheatley's 'Sable Veil,'" 351–52, who sees the move as intentionally and necessarily subtle, one that could be noticed or ignored by readers. For Wheatley as making the king into a "Homeric demigod" and entrapping the audience into imagining liberation, see Carla Willard, "Wheatley's Turns of Praise: Heroic Entrapment and the Paradox of Revolution," *American Literature* 67 (1995): 238–41. Barnard emphasizes the king's choice in *Empire of Ruin*, 34–35.

71 *"are not slaves"*: *CWC*, 12–13; Jonathan Mayhew, *The Snare Broken* (Boston, 1766), quoted in Beatty, "'Fatal Year,'" 214.

7. THE NATIONS

72 *King George III devolves from terrifying potentate*: Michael McKeon, *The Secret History of Domesticity* (Baltimore, 2005).

72 *"to the slavery of France"*: "To the Publishers of the Boston Evening-Post," *BEP*, March 23, 1767.

72 "Let us still be loyal": *BEP*, Oct. 28, 1765, Aug. 21, 1767; *BNL*, Aug. 20, 1767. For monarchy and paternalism as tropes, see Jay Fliegelman, *Prodigals and Pilgrims* (New York, 1982); Edwin Burrows and Michael Wallace, "The American Revolution: The Ideology and Psychology of National Liberation," *Perspectives in American History* 6 (1972).

73 *another Indies*: Ashley L. Cohen, *The Global Indies: British Imperial Culture and the Reshaping of the World, 1756–1815* (New Haven, Conn., 2020).

73 *James Otis had seen the problem*: James Otis, *The Rights of the British Colonies Asserted and Proved* (1764), in Bailyn, *Pamphlets of the American Revolution*, 1:436–37, 439–40; Mark Somos, *American States of Nature: The Origins of Independence, 1761–1775* (New York, 2019), 63–65; Alexander R. Jablonski, "'Providence Never Designed Us for Negroes': Slavery and British Subjecthood in the Stamp Act Crisis, 1764–1766," in Hutchins, *Community Without Consent*, 148–73, Adams quoted at 164.

74 *The ease with which Otis*: *BG*, May 19, 1766; *BEP*, March 3, 1766; John R. Galvin, *Three Men of Boston* (1976; repr., Washington, D.C., 1997), 15. This was not a one-off on Otis's part. According to John Adams, who saw Otis as having made the first major statement of the American Revolution, Otis already connected natural rights with antislavery in his speech against the Writs of Assistance case in 1761. William Tudor, *Life of James Otis of Massachusetts* (1823; repr., New York, 1970), 69. For the West Indies, see Andrew Jackson O'Shaughnessy, *An Empire Divided: The American Revolution in the British Caribbean* (Philadelphia, 2002); Jack P. Greene, "'Of Liberty and the Colonies': A Case Study of Constitutional Conflict in the Mid-Eighteenth-Century British American Empire," in *Liberty and American Experience in the Eighteenth Century*, ed. David Womersley (Indianapolis, 2006), 21–102. For the long-term ties of Boston and Barbados especially, see S. D. Smith, *Slavery, Family, and Gentry Capitalism in the British Atlantic: The World of the Lascelles, 1648–1844* (New York, 2006). On the problem of colonial identity in the coming of the Revolution, see T. H. Breen, "Identity and Nationalism on the Eve of the American Revolution: Revisions Once More in Need of Revising," *Journal of American History* 84 (1997): 13–39; Stephen Conway, "From Fellow Nationals to Foreigners: British Perceptions of the Americans, Circa 1739–1783," *William and Mary Quarterly* 59 (2002): 65–100; Waldstreicher, *Runaway America*, chaps. 6–7; Jack P. Greene, *Evaluating Empire and Confronting Colonialism in Eighteenth-Century Britain* (New York, 2013).

74 *Some others, especially of the younger generation*: Timothy Pickering, "Will the Printers (at Such a Time as This) Be So Good as to Publish the Following Remarks and Cautions," *BG*, May 26, 1766; *Report of the Record Commissioners . . . Containing the Boston Town Records*, 183; George H. Moore, *Notes on the History of Slavery in Massachusetts* (New York, 1866), 124, 126–28; *Journals of the House of Representatives of Massachusetts*, 50 vols. (Boston, 1973), 43:110; *BG*, Feb. 23, March 30, 1767; Nathan Appleton, *Considerations on Slavery* (1767), in *Am I Not a Man and a Brother: The Antislavery Crusade of Revolutionary America*, ed. Roger Bruns (1977; repr., New York, 1980), 128–37; Duncan J. MacLeod, *Slavery, Race, and the American Revolution* (New York, 1974), 18; Patricia Bradley, *Slavery, Propaganda, and the American Revolution* (Jackson, Miss., 1998), 99–100; Peter A. Dorsey, *Common Bondage: Slavery as Metaphor in Revolutionary America* (Knoxville, Tenn., 2009), 107; John K. Alexander,

Samuel Adams, 2nd ed (Lanham, Md., 2011), 56–57; Christopher Cameron, *To Plead Our Own Cause: African Americans in Massachusetts and the Making of the Antislavery Movement* (Kent, Ohio, 2014), 52–53.

Months earlier, Appleton's father, minister of the First Church in Cambridge, gave a sermon to mark the repeal of the Stamp Act that explicitly compared the slavery of the Jews in Egypt, and the risk of it in Mordecai and Esther's Persia, to what the Bostonians faced in 1766. "This serves to indear the King (if possible) yet more and more to us," he added. Nathaniel Appleton, *A Thanksgiving Sermon on the Total Repeal of the Stamp-Act* (Boston, 1766), 12–13, 17. Charles W. Akers was the first to note the 1766–67 antislavery upsurge among Whigs and to suggest its influence on Wheatley in "'Our Modern Egyptians': Phillis Wheatley and the Whig Campaign Against Slavery in Revolutionary Boston," *Journal of Negro History* 60 (1975): 402–3. For Appleton, see also Nicholas Wood, *Let the Oppressed Go Free: The Revolutionary Generation of American Abolitionists* (Philadelphia, forthcoming), chap. 2.

75 *New York's action*: "Britannus Americanus," "Nestor," "A Friend," "Messrs. Edes and Gill," "NORTH-AMERICA," *BG*, Sept. 7, 28, 1767, Jan. 18, July 18, Nov. 7, 1768; Jensen, *Founding of a Nation*, 244.

75 *Phillis drafted a mini-epic*: MS in Rush Family Papers, series 4, box 14, folder 27, Library Company of Philadelphia; *CWC*, 73–74, 165. The poem is listed in her 1772 proposals as "On America, 1768." The manuscript is in the papers of Julia Stockton Rush (the daughter of Annis Boudinot Stockton) and Benjamin Rush. Rush was later a promoter of Wheatley's; after Wheatley's death a rumor suggested that her second volume of poems was in the possession of the family. Thomas Fortune Fletcher found the three poems in the Benjamin Rush family papers in 1931. On a hunch, Fletcher, as part of his research for his Columbia master's thesis, had reasoned that since Wheatley had contact with Benjamin Rush and Benjamin Franklin, any extant manuscripts might be in Philadelphia. None of these poems had appeared in the 1773 volume. But since Fletcher did not publish on Wheatley aside from announcing his discovery in the *Pittsburgh Courier* in 1931 and including "America" in an article in the *Amsterdam News* in 1935 (which mentions that he was planning a biography), very few scholars incorporated these new poems into their considerations of Wheatley until their rediscovery decades later. *Bio-bibliography*, 96; "Thomas Fortune Fletcher Discovers 'America,' Poem Which Phillis Wheatley Wrote but Never Finished," *Amsterdam News*, Oct. 26, 1935.

Philadelphian Hannah Griffitts copied "Atheism" into her own commonplace book. *PPW*, 118, 125–26. For Griffitts and Stockton and women's manuscript culture, see Susan Stabile, *Memory's Daughters: The Material Culture of Remembrance in Eighteenth-Century British America* (Ithaca, N.Y., 2004); Catherine La Courreye Blecki and Karin A. Wulf, eds., *Milcah Martha Moore's Book: A Commonplace Book from Revolutionary America* (University Park, Pa., 1997); Carla Mulford, ed., *Only for the Eye of a Friend: The Poems of Annis Boudinot Stockton* (Charlottesville, Va., 1995); Susan E. Klepp and Karin Wulf, eds., *The Diary of Hannah Callender Sansom: Sense and Sensibility in the Age of the American Revolution* (Ithaca, N.Y., 2010), 237; Shields, *Civil Tongues and Polite Letters*. The manuscript of "To the King's Most Excellent Majesty" also has the flourish under the signature "Phillis."

77 *"an unexpected likeness"*: "Simile," in *The New Princeton Handbook of Poetic Terms*, ed. T. V. F. Brogan (Princeton, N.J., 1994), 271.

78 *Pope had argued, in favor*: *Iliad of Homer, Translated by Alexander Pope*, ed.
Shankman, 11–12; Pamela Poynter Schwandt, "Pope's Transformation of
Homer's Similes," *Studies in Philology* 76 (1979): 387–417. See also Pope's com-
ments in *The Odyssey of Homer, Books I–XII*, ed. Maynard Mack (New Haven,
Conn., 1967), 141n447, and *The Odyssey of Homer, Books XIII–XXIV*, ed. May-
nard Mack (New Haven, Conn., 1967), 115n238. Addison had addressed similes
and the ancients in *The Spectator*, no. 160. John Goodridge, "Stephen Duck, *The
Thresher's Labour*, and Mary Collier, *The Woman's Labour*," in *A Companion to
Eighteenth-Century Poetry*, ed. Christine Gerrard (Malden, Mass., 2014), 213.
For similes as pointing to transformation, including changing the perspective
of readers and their relationship with authors, see Lorna Hardwick, "Reception
as Simile: The Poetics of Reversal in Homer and Derek Walcott," *International
Journal of the Classical Tradition* 3 (1997): 326–38.

79 *"narrative concentration"*: McKeon, *Secret History of Domesticity*, 437.

79 *She claims maternity but seems*: Oxenbridge Thacher had explored the notion
of Britain as an unfeeling mother to her "British American" children: "We
will not here insist on the parental tenderness due from Great Britain to us
and suggest she must suffer from sympathy with her children, who have been
guilty of no undutiful behavior . . . We will suppose her for this little moment to
have forgot the bowels of a mother." Thacher, *Sentiments of a British American*
(1764), in Bailyn, *Pamphlets of the American Revolution*, 1:495.

80 *epic of growth*: John P. McWilliams, *The American Epic: Transforming a Genre,
1770–1860* (New York, 1985); Christopher N. Phillips, *Epic in American Culture:
Settlement to Reconstruction* (Baltimore, 2012), 16; Anna-Julia Zwierlein, "Milton Epic and Bucolic: Empire and Readings of *Paradise Lost*, 1667–1837," in *The
Oxford Handbook of Milton*, ed. Nicholas McDowell and Nigel Smith (Oxford,
2011), 675; Karen Edwards, "Milton's Reformed Animals: An Early Modern
Bestiary: T–Z," *Milton Quarterly* 43 (2009): 265–67. For sophisticated and balanced treatments of Wheatley's claims to American identity as both a sacred
and a secular project, see Richards, "Phillis Wheatley, Americanization, the
Sublime, and the Romance of America"; Phillip M. Richards, "Phillis Wheatley and Literary Americanization," *American Quarterly* 44 (1992): 163–69; Rafia
Zafar, *We Wear the Mask: African Americans Write American Literature, 1760–
1870* (New York, 1997), chap. 1. For Agenoria as goddess of courage and industry, Vincent Carretta cites two eighteenth-century English sources in his newest
edition, *WPW*, 151.

81 *Her cohort was growing up*: BEP, June 2, 1766 (two girls aged thirteen and nine-
teen), Sept. 1, Oct. 20, 1766, April 20, Nov. 16, 1767; *BG*, July 28, Aug. 4, 1766,
June 1, 8, 29, 1767, June 4, 11, 1770; *BNL*, April 27, May 29, 1766, July 18, Oct.
10, 1768; Peter Benes, "Slavery in Boston Households," in *Slavery/Antislavery in
New England*, ed. Peter Benes (Boston, 2003), 12–29; Gloria McCahon Whit-
ing, "Power, Patriarchy, and Provision: African Families Negotiate Gender and
Slavery in New England," *Journal of American History* 103 (2016): 583–605;
Hardesty, *Unfreedom*. For slave advertisements and their effects, see Waldstreicher, "Reading the Runaways," and Desrochers, "Slave-for-Sale Advertisements and Slavery in Massachusetts."

82 *"breeds too fast"*: *BG*, Aug. 21, Nov. 29, 1767, Oct. 10, 1768; *BNL*, July 10, 31,
1766; *BNL*, Jan. 5, 1769.

82 *"snarling set of levelers"*: "Sophistes," *BG*, July 13, 1767.

83 *form of the Hamitic curse*: "NO BEAM NO MOTE," *BG*, Jan. 18, 1768; David

M. Goldenberg, *Black and Slave: The Origins and History of the Curse of Ham* (Berlin, 2017).

83 *"On Being Brought from Africa"*: The 1772 proposals date the poem at 1768. *CWC*, 13, 165.

84 *slave trade itself may save souls*: Henry Louis Gates Jr., *The Trials of Phillis Wheatley* (New York, 2003), 71; Cedrick May, *Evangelism and Resistance in the Black Atlantic, 1760–1835* (Athens, Ga., 2008), chap. 2; Seeman, "'Justice May Take Plase.'"

84 *That others were resorting to satire*: "Messrs. Edes and Gill," *BG*, March 30, 1767.

85 *If we call it a "diabolic die"*: Philip Gould, "The Rise, Development, and Circulation of the Slave Narrative," in *The Cambridge Companion to the African American Slave Narrative*, ed. Audrey Fisch (New York, 2007), 18; Philip Gould, *Barbaric Traffic* (Cambridge, Mass., 2003), 65–66; Grimsted, "Anglo-American Racism and Phillis Wheatley's 'Sable Veil,'" 356–57; Carretta, *Phillis Wheatley*, 71; Spencer Jackson, "A Black Tory Abolitionist in Early America: Phillis Wheatley's Republican Poetics," *Postcolonial Studies* 23 (2020): 382–83; Spencer Jackson, *We Are Kings: Political Theology and the Making of a Modern Individual* (Charlottesville, Va., 2020), 79; Daniel Cottom, *Ravishing Tradition: Cultural Forces and Literary History* (Ithaca, N.Y., 1996), 96–99; William J. Scheick, "Phillis Wheatley's Appropriation of Isaiah," *Early American Literature* 27 (1992): 136; Levernier, "Style as Protest."

86 *she also questions racial thinking*: For ventriloquized whiteness, see Betsy Erkkila, "Revolutionary Women," in *Mixed Bloods and Other Crosses: Rethinking American Literature from the Revolution to the Culture Wars* (Philadelphia, 2005), 83. For Wheatley relativizing race, see Katy L. Chiles, *Transformable Race: Surprising Metamorphoses in the Literature of Early America* (New York, 2014), 31–63. For Wheatley as refuting the curse of Cain, see William J. Scheick, *Authority and Female Authorship in Colonial America* (Lexington, Ky., 1998), 121–23. For June Jordan, the poem conveys an essential message of resistance: "Once I existed on terms other than yours." June Jordan, "The Difficult Miracle of Black Poetry in America, or Something Like a Sonnet for Phillis Wheatley," *Massachusetts Review* 22 (1986): 252–62.

For readings of the poem as subversive, see also, for example, Sondra O'Neale, "A Slave's Subtle War: Phillis Wheatley's Use of Biblical Myth and Symbol," *Early American Literature* 21 (1986): 144–65; Reising, *Loose Ends*, 83–89; Cook and Tatum, *African American Writers and the Classical Tradition*, 11; Tara Bynum, "Phillis Wheatley's Pleasures," *Common-Place* 11, no. 1 (Oct. 2010); MaryCatherine Loving, "Uncovering Subversion in Phillis Wheatley's Signature Poem," *Journal of African American Studies* 20 (2016): 67–74. For the poem as a "cryptic" negation of race through religion, see Brooks, *American Lazarus*, 38, 46. For the theme of ancients and moderns and their relevance for slavery, see David Waldstreicher, "Ancients, Moderns, and Africans: Phillis Wheatley and the Politics of Empire and Slavery in the American Revolution," *Journal of the Early Republic* 37 (2017): 701–34. For Wheatley's entire oeuvre as shot through with similar sarcasm, see Antonio T. Bly, "'By Her Unveil'd Each Horrid Crime Appears': Authorship, Text, and Subtext in Phillis Wheatley's Variants Poems," *Textual Cultures* 9 (Winter 2014): 112–41.

In her 1773 *Poems*, Wheatley revised her earlier 1767 reference to her homeland as a "sable Land of error"—too racial?—to "land of errors, and Egyptian gloom." Bassard, *Spiritual Interrogations*, 43–44. Dwight McBride notes that in her writings Wheatley "does not hate Africa; she hates 'pagan' or 'Egyptian' Africa." McBride, *Impossible Witnesses* (New York, 2001), 113; see also Collins-Sibley, "Who Can Speak?" Joel Pace argues that "the descriptor 'Pagan' subtly links Africa with the pagan cultures of Greece and Rome." Joel Pace, "Journeys of the Imagination in Wheatley and Coleridge," in *Transatlantic Literary Studies, 1660–1830*, ed. Eve Tavor Bannet and Susan Manning (Cambridge, U.K., 2012), 242.

86 *"May I O eternal salute aurora"*: CWC, 70, 71, 105, 131.

87 *References to the sun as Aurora*: Samuel Garth et al., *Ovid's Metamorphosis in Fifteen Books* (New York, 1961), 439; Pope, *The Odyssey of Homer, Books XIII–XXIV*, ed. Mack, 17, 238; *Iliad of Homer, Translated by Alexander Pope*, ed. Shankman, 382.

87 *Latin poets like Horace*: Habinek, *Politics of Latin Literature*, 14; Dennis Feeney, *Beyond Greek: The Beginnings of Latin Literature* (Cambridge, Mass., 2016).

88 *"garrison'd town"*: Samuel Adams, "Vindex," in *The Boston Massacre: A History with Documents*, ed. Neil L. York (New York, 2010), 67.

8. THE OCCUPATION

89 *A thousand men, then hundreds*: BEP, Oct. 3, 1768; *Boston Chronicle*, Oct. 3, 1768; BG, Nov. 21, 1768; Eric Hinderaker, *Boston's Massacre* (Cambridge, Mass., 2017), 89, 110; Serena Zabin, *The Boston Massacre: A Family History* (Boston, 2020), 54–55; Gipson, *British Empire Before the American Revolution*, 11:164; Richard Archer, *As if an Enemy's Country: The British Occupation of Boston and the Origins of Revolution* (New York, 2010), 106–13; John W. Shy, *Toward Lexington: The Role of the British Army in the Coming of the American Revolution* (Princeton, N.J., 1965), 250, 303–4; John Gilbert McCurdy, *Quarters: The Accommodation of the British Army and the Coming of the American Revolution* (Ithaca, N.Y., 2019). The adult male population of Boston during the 1760s has been estimated as about 3,750, 1,500 of whom would have been property owners. Tyler, *Smugglers and Patriots*, 8.

90 *Boston's patriot leaders embraced the spectacle*: Boyle Journal, Oct. 3, 1768; BEP, Oct. 3, 1768; Archer, *As if an Enemy's Country*, 86–93; Jensen, *Founding of a Nation*, 247–53, 264; Neil R. Stout, *The Royal Navy in America, 1760–1775* (Annapolis, Md., 1973), 120, 122–23; Dirk Hoerder, "Boston Leaders and Boston Crowds, 1765–1776," in *The American Revolution: Explorations in the History of American Radicalism*, ed. Alfred F. Young (DeKalb, Ill., 1976), 248; Warden, *Boston, 1689–1776*, 188–90; Hiller B. Zobel, *The Boston Massacre* (New York, 1970), 71, 73.

90 *initial book proposal*: "Proposals for Printing by Subscription," in *CWC*, 166. No other poems on the arrival of the troops appeared in Boston newspapers.

90 *the arrival of the ships and soldiers*: Archer, *As if an Enemy's Country*, 129; Oliver Morton Dickerson, ed., *Boston Under Military Rule, 1768–1769, as Revealed in a Journal of the Times* (Boston, 1936), x–xi, 13; Akers, *Divine Politician*, 91; Arthur M. Schlesinger, *Prelude to Independence: The Newspaper War on Britain, 1764–1776* (1957; repr., Boston, 1980), 100–102; BEP, March 13, 20, 1769. For theater in the British Empire, see Daniel O'Quinn, *Entertaining Crisis in the Atlantic Imperium, 1770–1790* (Baltimore, 2011); Daniel O'Quinn, *Staging Governance: Theatrical Imperialism in London, 1770–1800* (Baltimore, 2020); Kathleen Wilson, "Three Theses on Performance and History," *Eighteenth-Century*

Studies 48 (2015): 375–90; Elizabeth Maddock Dillon, *New World Drama: The Performative Commons in the Atlantic World, 1640–1849* (Durham, N.C., 2014). For reassertions of propaganda's importance in the Revolution in light of internet-era sensibilities, see Russ Castronovo, *Propaganda 1776* (New York, 2014); William B. Warner, *Protocols of Liberty* (Cambridge, Mass., 2013).

93 *The soldiers both fraternized and clashed*: Tudor, *Life of James Otis*, 337; Alfred F. Young, *Liberty Tree: Ordinary People and the American Revolution* (New York, 2006), 118; Linda Colley, *Captives* (New York, 2003); Zabin, *Boston Massacre*.

93 *balance of power*: Dickerson, *Boston Under Military Rule*, 16, 21; Zobel, *Boston Massacre*, 102; Zabin, *Boston Massacre*, 61–63.

94 *The troops experienced both harassment and hospitality*: Warden, *Boston, 1689–1776*, 219–23, 227; Shy, *Toward Lexington*, 384; *BG*, Nov. 7, 1768, April 30, 1770; Stout, *Royal Navy in America*, 121–22; Christopher P. Magra, *Poseidon's Curse: British Naval Impressment and the American Revolution* (New York, 2016), 123, 138; Dickerson, *Boston Under Military Rule*, 50; Hinderaker, *Boston's Massacre*, 121, 150–54; Zabin, *Boston Massacre*, 69, 132–33; Bradley, *Slavery, Propaganda, and the American Revolution*, 51–53.

95 *the well-liked commodore*: Jensen, *Founding of a Nation*, 290; Akers, *Divine Politician*, 114.

95 *"Commodore Hood, in this act"*: Stout, *Royal Navy in America*, 139, 150–51; *BEP*, Oct. 31, 1768; *BPB*, Dec. 5, 1768; Boyle Journal, Oct. 31, 1768; Dickerson, *Boston Under Military Rule*, 30.

95 *Her praise poem*: This poem is the third of the folded page and comes after "America" and "Atheism." Rush Family Papers, series 4, box 14, folder 27. The poem is in the list of her first, February 1772 book proposal but did not appear in the 1773 volume. Another praise poem to an officer, "To Captain H—D of the 65th Regiment," did appear in her book. *CWC*, 41, 76, 184. For Hood's virtues, see Daniel A. Baugh, "Samuel Hood: Superior Subordinate," in *George Washington's Opponents*, ed. George Athan Billias (New York, 1969), 291–326. The dynamics of Wheatley's earlier and later praise poems have been addressed with particular sensitivity but with a different emphasis by Carla Willard, "Wheatley's Turns of Praise." For assimilation, see Richards, "Phillis Wheatley and Literary Americanization."

96 *In a sense it combines the themes*: *CWC*, 67–68.

97 *bloody backs*: Shy, *Toward Lexington*, 306–10; L. Kinvin Wroth and Hiller B. Zobel, eds., *Legal Papers of John Adams* (Cambridge, Mass., 1965), 3:86, 202–3, 283.

97 *The disturbing similarities cut another way*: Robert Middlekauff observes that "having to receive challenges by sentries on the streets, their own streets, affronted a people accustomed to personal liberty, fired their tempers, and gnawed away at their honor." True enough, though these are the kinds of characterizations that some prominent English people would before long make of all Americans, highlighting mastery of slaves rather than freeborn Britishness or New England or American freedom, as the cause of such personality traits. Robert Middlekauff, *The Glorious Cause: The American Revolution, 1763–1789*, rev. ed. (New York, 2005), 202; "Speech in Support of Resolutions for Conciliation with the American Colonies," *Edmund Burke on the American Revolution*, ed. Elliott R. Barkan (New York, 1966), 85. For town-based status, violence, and children, see Levy, *Town Born*.

97 *Relying on minors to police transgressors*: Neil Longley York, ed., *Henry Hulton*

and the American Revolution: An Outsider's Inside View (Boston, 2010), 142; Peter Shaw, *American Patriots and the Rituals of Revolution* (Cambridge, Mass., 1982), 193–95; J. L. Bell, "From Saucy Boys to Sons of Liberty: Politicizing Youth in Pre-revolutionary Boston," in *Children in Colonial America*, ed. James Marten (New York, 2007), 204–16; William Pencak, "Play as Prelude to Revolution: Boston, 1765–1776," in *Riot and Revelry in Early America*, ed. William Pencak, Matthew Dennis, and Simon P. Newman (University Park, Pa., 2002), 127–30; York, *Boston Massacre*, 85; Dickerson, *Boston Under Military Rule*, 50; Peter C. Messer, "'A Scene of Villainy Acted by a Dirty Banditti, as Must Astonish the Public': The Creation of the Boston Massacre," *New England Quarterly* 90 (2017): 502–39.

98 *Less than half of the soldiers*: Hinderaker, *Boston's Massacre*, 147–48; Deming, *Boston and the Dawn of American Independence*, 123, 132.

98 *"Laws I am sure I never"*: "To the Printer," *BNL*, Aug. 31, 1769; Middlekauff, *Glorious Cause*, 207; *BG*, Jan. 11, 1770; Wroth and Zobel, *Legal Papers of John Adams*, 2:397; J. L. Bell, "Theophilus Lillie: Shopkeeper, Importer, Seeker of Liberty," *Boston 1775*, Feb. 21, 2007, www.boston1775.blogspot.com/2007/02 /theophilus-lillie-shopkeeper-importer.html.

99 *On Thursday, February 22*: Young, *Liberty Tree*, 119; Zobel, *Boston Massacre*, 174; *BNL*, Feb. 22, 1770; *BEP*, Feb. 26, 1770; Wroth and Zobel, *Legal Papers of John Adams*, 2:420.

Most studies of the Boston Massacre still barely mention the earlier Richardson-Seider event, a tendency noted more than half a century ago by Jesse Lemisch, "Radical Plot in Boston (1770): A Study in the Use of Evidence," *Harvard Law Review* 84 (1970): 485–504. The important thing here is that the earlier event was clearly important to Wheatley at the time and that her Seider poem might have garnered more attention had not the subsequent, even more violent "massacre" occurred.

100 *"little hero and first martyr"*: *BEP*, Feb. 26, 1770; *BG*, Feb. 26, 1770; *BNL*, Feb. 22, March 1, 1770; Zobel, *Boston Massacre*, 65–66; York, *Boston Massacre*, 30; Wroth and Zobel, *Legal Papers of John Adams*, 2:400; Emil Baensch, *A Boston Boy: The First Martyr to American Liberty* (Manitowoc, Wis., 1924); Robert A. Ferguson, *The American Enlightenment, 1750–1820* (Cambridge, Mass., 1997), 9–14; J. L. Bell, "The Life and Death of Christopher Seider," "Christopher Seider, Shooting Victim," "Christopher Seider: Household Servant, Schoolboy?," and "Heroic Pieces Found in His Pocket," *Boston 1775*, May 24, June 26, 2006, Dec. 30, 2001, Feb. 24, 2020, www.boston1775.blogspot.com. The words "heroic" and "pieces" were both usually used for poems.

100 *Wheatley, too, couldn't look away*: Zobel, *Boston Massacre*, 158; Shy, *Toward Lexington*, 311; Hinderaker, *Boston Massacre*, 150–54. In addition to the specific phrases from newspaper reports that Wheatley uses, her rendering of "Snider" matches that of the papers as well. *CWC*, 77–78; Sidney Kaplan and Emma Nogrady Kaplan, *The Black Presence in the Era of the American Revolution*, rev. ed. (Amherst, Mass., 1987), 173. Those who appreciate Wheatley's art usually turn away from this crowd-pleasing effort: even those who praise her political savvy don't have much time for it. Carretta praises the decision not to include it in her 1773 volume, even after it appeared in her 1772 proposal. But the pioneering Wheatley scholar William H. Robinson characterized it as speaking "from the dead center of the seething, partisan crowd." It would be fair to say that this poem exemplifies much of what modern readers don't like about both *The Iliad*

and eighteenth-century panegyric. It is another significant step in her use of elegy to link her personal and political ambitions. *PWW*, 93, 153–54; see also Betsy Erkkila, "Phillis Wheatley on the Streets of Revolutionary Boston and in the Atlantic World," *Early American Literature* 56 (2021): 357–58.

102 *accounts of the Seider funeral*: *BG*, March 5, 1770. On the other hand, she had not yet appeared in a Boston newspaper or stand-alone broadside, though her poems were being circulated outside the city.

102 *market for slaves*: *BG*, Oct. 30, Nov. 6, 27, 1769; *BEP*, June 1, 19, Oct. 30, 1769; *BNL*, March 9, June 1, 15, Oct. 19, 1769; *BPB*, June 12, 1769; "An Earnest Address to the Country, upon SLAVERY," *Boston Chronicle*, March 2, 1769.

103 *Thomas Walker, one of the Afro-Caribbean drummers*: *BG*, March 12, 26, 1770; Shy, *Toward Lexington*, 317; Archer, *As if an Enemy's Country*, 183, 201; York, *Boston Massacre*, 85; Zobel, *Boston Massacre*, 182; *BNL*, March 8, 1770. One Bostonian remembered the original victim who insulted a soldier and was beaten up as "a black man" who had "a master" who beat up the soldier in turn. Tudor, *Life of James Otis*, 375.

103 *Three days later, on the fifth*: Deming, *Boston and the Dawn of American Independence*, 145–46; Mitch Kachun, *First Martyr of Liberty: Crispus Attucks in American Myth and Memory* (New York, 2017), chap. 1; Dirk Hoerder, *Crowd Action in Revolutionary Massachusetts, 1765–1780* (New York, 1977), 223; *BNL*, March 15, 1770; *BEP*, March 12, 15, 1770; *BG*, March 12, 26, 1770.

103 *Phillis wrote another poem*: *BEP*, March 12, 1770. Wheatley included the poem "On the Affray in King Street" in her 1772 proposals, as she did with the Seider poem (which survives in manuscript). In addition to the several typical Wheatley words (see Table 2 in the appendix), the *BEP* Boston Massacre poem self-identifies as a woman's poem. Finally, the use of "shades" and "corse" and heaven-directed events repeats conventions from the Seider poem. Rather different poems appeared in the extant Boston Massacre broadsides. *Massachusetts Broadsides of the American Revolution*, ed. Mason I. Lowance Jr. and Georgia B. Bumgardner (Amherst, Mass., 1976), 30–31; *A Verse, Occasioned by the Late Horrid Massacre in King-Street* (Boston, 1770); *A Monumental Inscription on the Fifth of March* (Boston, 1770), in Philip Davidson, *Propaganda and the American Revolution, 1763–1783* (Chapel Hill, N.C., 1941), facing 222; York, *Boston Massacre*, 233.

William H. Robinson was the first to identify the poem as Wheatley's or an excerpt of a longer one of hers, and to reprint it, in *PWW*, 17, 455. For an attribution based on the use of italics and classical references, see Antonio T. Bly, "Wheatley's 'On the Affray in King Street,'" *Explicator* 56, no. 4 (1998): 177–80. Carretta, Shields, and Mason did not include the poem in their editions for lack of proof.

104 *the king's men retreated*: Boyle Journal, March 27, 1770; Akers, *Divine Politician*, 103; Bailyn, *Ordeal of Thomas Hutchinson*, 161–62; Nathaniel Coffin to Charles Steuart, March 12, 1770, Charles Steuart Papers, National Library of Scotland (microfilm M-68-2, reel 2, Rockefeller Library, Colonial Williamsburg Foundation).

9. THE FRIENDS

106 *"black regiment" of clergymen*: "From a London Paper," *BNL*, June 21, 1770; "From the New Hampshire Gazette," *BEP*, March 23, 1770; *BG*, April 29, 1770;

John Lathrop Sermons, box 1, John Lathrop Papers, MHS; John Lathrop, *Innocent Blood Crying to God from the Streets of Boston. Preached on the Lord's Day Following the Bloody 5th of March 1770* (London, 1770); James McLachlan, "John Lathrop," *Princetonians: A Biographical Dictionary, 1748–1768* (Princeton, N.J., 1976), 432–33; Alice M. Baldwin, *The New England Clergy and the American Revolution* (Durham, N.C., 1928), 111–12; Gipson, *British Empire Before the American Revolution*, 11:285; Zabin, *Boston Massacre*, 170; *BG*, April 12, 1771.

106 *outcome of the soldier trials:* James Kendall Hosmer, *The Life of Thomas Hutchinson* (1896; repr., New York, 1972), 189; Bailyn, *Ordeal of Thomas Hutchinson*; Adair and Schutz, *Peter Oliver's Origin and Progress of the American Rebellion*, 29, 41, 91.

107 *black "Companies" meeting regularly:* "Messrs. FOWLE and THOMAS," *MSP*, Sept. 29, 1770; *Massachusetts Gazette*, Feb. 28, 1771; *BPB*, March 4, 1771; *Report of the Records Commissioners of the City of Boston, Containing the Selectmen's Minutes from 1769 to 1775* (Boston, 1893), 45; Akers, *Divine Politician*, 124.

107 *an increasing number of the young men:* *BEP*, June 18, 1770; *BG*, June 25, Aug. 13, Oct. 15, 22, Nov. 26, 1770; *BNL*, June 7, 1770. More fugitives, too, characterized the summer months of 1770. See the notices collected in Antonio T. Bly, ed., *Escaping Bondage: A Documentary History of Runaway Slaves in Eighteenth-Century New England, 1700–1789* (Lanham, Md., 2012).

108 *supporters of the nascent movement:* Samuel Cooke, *A Sermon Preached at Cambridge, in the Audience of His Honor Thomas Hutchinson, Esq; Lieutenant-Governor and Commander in Chief; the Honorable His Majesty's Council, and the Honorable House of Representatives, of the Province of the Massachusetts-Bay in New-England, May 30th, 1770. Being the Anniversary for the Election of His Majesty's Council for the Said Province* (Boston, 1770); Timothy Pickering, "TO THE ENGLISH NATION," *MSP*, Jan. 19, 1771; Gary B. Nash, *The Unknown American Revolution* (New York, 2005), 119–20; Jill Lepore, *The Whites of Their Eyes: The Tea Party's Revolution and the Battle over American History* (Princeton, N.J., 2010), Warren quoted at 74; Moore, *Notes of the History of Slavery in Massachusetts*, 130–32; Staughton Lynd and David Waldstreicher, "Free Trade, Sovereignty, and Slavery: Toward an Economic Interpretation of American Independence," *William and Mary Quarterly* 68 (2011): 597–630.

109 *The defense attorney John Adams:* Wroth and Zobel, *Legal Papers of John Adams*, 3:70–73, 77, 92, 202–5, 231n17, 266, 269, 281–82, 308, 311; Zobel, *Boston Massacre*, 257–58; Deming, *Boston and the Dawn of American Independence*, 174, 178, 202; Bradley, *Slavery, Propaganda, and the American Revolution*, 59–61; Arthur Scherr, *John Adams, Slavery, and Race* (Santa Barbara, Calif., 2018), 4–5; Hinderaker, *Boston's Massacre*, 195–97, 203–207. Hinderaker suggests that Andrew Wendell's testimony was solicited in part deliberately to maximize the sense of black participation in the "massacre," because John Adams wanted ultimately to exculpate both the redcoats and the white townspeople.

109 *John Adams's cousin Samuel Adams:* Wroth and Zobel, *Legal Papers of John Adams*, 3:92; [Samuel Adams], "Vindex," *BG*, Jan. 7, 1771; "Vindex," in York, *Boston Massacre*, 67; Zobel, *Boston Massacre*, 284. Writers in the new *MSP* mocked Jonathan Sewall, who while writing as "Philanthrop" had criticized Adams's earlier Vindex essays, for successfully arguing against the legality of the enslaved status of Massachusetts-born bondsmen in court. Sewall got a slave

freed in court on the grounds that there was no positive law of slavery in the colony, so all natives were automatically free. To his critic, he "earn[ed] dirty bread by washing AEthiop's fair." Another reply to Philanthrop suggested that he "might empty his vault," that is, defecate, at the resistance to his opinions, which had constituted "so very indecent a reply, [which] must have raised the resentment of any, but a negro slave who was well known to have been accustomed to that *meanest* of offices." "The Trifler," *MSP*, Jan. 10, 1771; *BEP*, Feb. 4, 1771; Shipton, "Jonathan Sewall," *New England Life in the Eighteenth Century*, 569–70; Emily Blanck, *Tyrannicide: Forging an American Law of Slavery in Revolutionary South Carolina and Massachusetts* (Athens, Ga., 2014), 35–36.

For differing views on Samuel Adams, race, and slavery, see Bradley, *Slavery, Propaganda, and the American Revolution*, 13–14, 64, 80, 82, 92, and Alexander, *Samuel Adams*, 56–57, 280, 341n12. While Bradley is not as careful with the evidence, Alexander it seems to me conflates Adams's abstract beliefs about slavery and his treatment of slaves in his family with his politics in public, where he repeatedly played the race card against Tories and distanced the patriot movement from antislavery. I thank John Alexander for our correspondence on this matter. John Adams displayed a kinder, gentler version of the same: his antislavery beliefs remained private and subordinated, but racial remarks formed a convenient public and political resource, especially during his earlier Boston years. See Scherr, *John Adams, Slavery, and Race*.

110 *Two acrostic poems*: *MSP*, Jan. 28, March 7, 1771.

111 *thinking about whether friendship*: *CWC*, 77, 165. For female poets on friendship, see Backscheider, *Eighteenth-Century Women Poets and Their Poetry*, chap. 4.

112 *she had bonded with Obour Tanner*: Charles Deane, "Phillis Wheatley," *Proceedings of the Massachusetts Historical Society* 7 (1863), 268–79; *PWW*, 55; Martha Bacon, *Puritan Promenade* (Boston, 1964), 31; Grimsted, "Anglo-American Racism and Phillis Wheatley's 'Sable Veil,'" 355, 372, 382; Frances Smith Foster, "A Narrative of the Interesting Origins and (Somewhat) Surprising Development of African American Print Culture," *American Literary History* 17 (2005): 321; PW to Obour Tanner, May 19, 1772, in *CWC*, 141–42; Brekus, *Sarah Osborn's World*, 126, 133, 174, 183, 184–85, 266, 282, 313. For the possible influence of black Christians on Osborn, see Wigginton, *In the Neighborhood*, 62–83. For a particularly sensitive and evocative rendering of the Wheatley-Tanner friendship, see Bynum, "Phillis Wheatley on Friendship."

114 *heartfelt letters*: Anna M. Lawrence, *One Family Under God: Love, Friendship, and Authority in Early Methodism* (Philadelphia, 2011); Brooks, *Collected Writings of Samson Occom*.

114 *a cue from his mentor George Whitefield*: John Wesley, *Sermons on Several Occasions* (London, 1864), 2:165; Whitefield, *Three Letters from the Reverend Mr. G. Whitefield* (Philadelphia, 1740), 5, quoted in George Boulukos, *The Grateful Slave* (New York, 2008), 185; Frank Lambert, *Inventing the Great Awakening* (Princeton, N.J., 1999); Frank Lambert, *Pedlar in Divinity* (Princeton, N.J., 1994), 219; Jessica Parr, *Inventing George Whitefield* (Jackson, Miss., 2015); *BNL*, Feb. 8, 1770; Cam Grey, "Slavery in the Late Roman World," in Bradley and Cartledge, *Cambridge World History of Slavery*, 1:482–509.

115 *a potent political simile*: Lambert, *Pedlar in Divinity*, 216–18, 222–24; Lathrop, *Innocent Blood*.

116 *"I am going"*: Boyle Journal, Aug. 15, 16, 17, 1770; *BNL*, Aug. 23, Sept. 20, Oct. 4, 1770; Cynthio, "On the Death of Reverend George Whitefield, in Elegiac Verse," *BG*, Oct. 8, 1770; *BEP*, Aug. 20, Oct. 15, 22, 1770; "Boston, October 8," *BPB*, Sept. 24, 1770; Lathrop sermon, Oct. 7, 1770, John Lathrop Sermons, box 4, Lathrop Papers; Karen Weyler, *Empowering Words: Outsiders & Authorship in Early America* (Athens, Ga., 2013), 47, 50.

116 *a commemorative elegy she produced*: *BG*, Oct. 15, 1770; *BPB*, Oct. 15, 1770; *MSP*, Oct. 13, 18, 1770; *BNL*, Oct. 11, Nov. 1, 1770; *Poem, by PHILLIS, a Negro Girl, in Boston on the Death of George Whitefield* (Boston, 1770); *Bio-bibliography*, 6–8; Carretta, *Phillis Wheatley*, 73.

117 *this was star billing*: *CWC*, 15–16, 113–17; Megan Walsh, *The Portrait and the Book: Illustration and Literary Culture in Early America* (Ames, Iowa, 2017), 70–73; Weyler, *Empowering Words*, 44–55.

117 *Editions followed from printers*: Weyler, *Empowering Words*, 53; Carretta, *Phillis Wheatley*, 78.

118 *"Elegiac Poem, on the Death"*: Robert Kendrick, "Snatching a Laurel, Wearing a Mask: Phillis Wheatley's Literary Nationalism and the Problem of Style," *Style* 27 (1993): 222–51; Moore, *Maternal Metaphors of Power*, 23–24; Arlette Freund, "Phillis Wheatley, a Public Intellectual," in *Toward an Intellectual History of Black Women*, ed. Mia Bay et al. (Chapel Hill, N.C., 2015), 41–42. Richards analyzes the poem as an extended revision of Elijah's ascent in 2 Kings 2:11–15 that makes a prophet of Wheatley herself: "Phillis Wheatley, Americanization, the Sublime, and the Romance of America." For a precedent in the Wheatleys' friend Sarah Moorhead's poems addressed at ministers during the earlier revivals, see Roberts, "Phillis Wheatley's Sarah Moorhead," and Roberts, *Awakening Verse*.

120 *revealed in the alternate version*: Franke, "Phillis Wheatley, Melancholy Muse," 233–34; John MacKilgore, *Mania for Freedom: American Literatures of Enthusiasm from Revolution to the Civil War* (Chapel Hill, N.C., 2016), 90–92; *CWC*, 114–16; Patricia C. Willis, "Phillis Wheatley, George Whitefield, and the Countess of Huntingdon in the Beinecke Library," *Yale University Library Gazette* (April 2006): 161–76. John C. Shields thought a London abolitionist changed the text, since it was not like Wheatley at that time to be so overt, and that she changed it back for her book in 1773. Shields, *Phillis Wheatley's Poetics of Liberation*, 94–95. Carretta writes most recently that Wheatley "rejects Whitefield's endorsement of passive acceptance of slavery by the enslaved." *WPW*, 188. No scholar has yet resolved the question of which version was the revision and which the original. The London edition necessarily appeared later, but it can't be assumed that it was a second rather than a first draft. The later version, in the 1773 *Poems*, was toned down even further, as Willis observes. Henry Pelham wrote that "Green" had read the poem before it was printed and "altered but one word in the whole, and that was the word Stars instead of star." Carretta suggests this was the belletrist Joseph Green, but it could also have been the printers Green and Russell. *WPW*, 156, 158.

121 *Wheatley wrote a letter*: PW to the Countess of Huntingdon, Oct. 25, 1770, in *CWC*, 139; *WPW*, 159.

121 *bid for friendship and patronage*: Weyler, *Empowering Words*, 38–39; *BPB*, March 4, 1771; *BEP*, March 18, 1771; Grimsted, "Anglo-American Racism and Phillis Wheatley's 'Sable Veil,'" 384; Susanna Wheatley to Archibald Bell[?],

March 29, 1773, in *Historical Magazine* 2 (1858): 178–79; Brooks, *American Lazarus*, 24–25. The letter to Huntingdon is the earliest of Wheatley's to have survived, but it is clear she wrote others earlier, such as one to Samson Occom. Huntingdon's papers also include two versions of Wheatley's elegy to the Reverend Sewall, which might have been sent to her earlier: there are no surviving cover letters. *PWW*, 365–69.

10. THE WOMEN

122 *Samson Occom wrote to Susanna*: Occom to Susanna Wheatley, March 5, 1771, Occom Papers, Dartmouth College, at the Occom Circle, www.library .dartmouth.edu/digital/digital-collections/occom-circle; Grimsted, "Anglo-American Racism and Phillis Wheatley's 'Sable Veil,'" 387–88; Edward E. Andrews, *Native Apostles: Black and Indian Missionaries in the British Atlantic World* (Cambridge, Mass., 2013), 204.

122 *the Reverend John Lathrop*: Boyle Journal, Jan. 31, 1771; *BEP*, Feb. 4, 1771; *Massachusetts Gazette and BNL*, March 21, 1771; Crocker, *Reminiscences and Traditions of Boston*, 123, 201; "The Boston Ministers, a Ballad," *New England Historical and Genealogical Register* 13 (1859): 131; John Howard Dean, "Boston Ministers," *New England Historical and Genealogical Register* 26 (1872): 420; John Lathrop, "Innocent Blood Crying to God from the Ground" (March 1770) and sermons of Dec. 6, 1770, and March 7, 1771, John Lathrop Sermons, boxes 1 and 4, Lathrop Papers; *BG*, March 12, April 29, 1771; Helen Thomas, *Romanticism and Slave Narratives* (New York, 2000), 204; Lesley Anne Moreschal, "'In ye Service of the Lord': Boston's Churches, Public Discourse, and the American Revolution" (PhD diss., Washington State University, 2012), 126, 152–55.

The white Wheatleys have sometimes been assumed to be Tories, mostly because of Nathaniel Wheatley's seemingly tepid embrace or backtracking on nonimportation, but there is really no evidence of their stance on the patriot movement, pro or con. Given Phillis's dialogue with both sides but ability to move in a patriot direction, it seems most likely that neither Susanna nor John Wheatley was passionately invested as either a patriot or a Tory during these years, or that if their politics changed at any point it did not exert the kind of decisive influence on Phillis that might have left a clue in her work or other records.

124 *John Wheatley advertised*: *BG*, July 22, 1771; John Lathrop to unknown recipient, Aug. 14, 1773, Gratz American Clergy Collection, Historical Society of Pennsylvania; Nathaniel Wheatley to Melatiah Bourn, June 3, 1775, Correspondence of Melatiah Bourn, Bourne Family Papers, Houghton Library, Harvard University; Nathaniel Wheatley to Eleazar Wheelock, Jan. 2, 1770, and Nathaniel Wheatley to William Channing, Nov. 12, 1770, in *PWW*, 305, 307. John and Mary Wheatley Lathrop's first son, John Lathrop Jr., born in 1771, made poetry his life's ambition. Lewis Leary, "John Lathrop Jr.: The Quiet Poet of Federalist Boston," *Proceedings of the American Antiquarian Society* 91 (1981): 39–89. A sign of Lathrop's support for Wheatley's secular as well as sacred ambition is the three-volume collection *The Beauties of the English Stage* (London, 1756) he inscribed for her on August 1, 1774. Fliegelman Library of American Association Copies, Stanford University Library, listed at www.librarything .com/catalog/PhillisWheatley/yourlibrary.

125 *joining Old South Church*: Moreschal, "'In ye Service of the Lord,'" 109–10; Winiarski, *Darkness Falls on the Land of Light*, 462; William H. Robinson, *Phillis Wheatley and the Origins of African American Literature* (Boston, 1999), 12; Carretta, *Phillis Wheatley*, 79.

126 *advertisements for their sale*: BG, Aug. 6, 1770, Jan. 7, May 27, June 3, July 1, 29, Oct. 3, Nov. 4, 1771; *BPB*, Oct. 8, 1770, April 22, 1771; *BNL*, Feb. 13, Aug. 27, 1772.

126 *Wheatley family reminiscences suggest*: CSR; MMO, 10, 11, 13, 14.

127 *"at all times accessible"*: MMO, 11, 15. For the Fitches, see Annie Thwing, *Inhabitants and Estates of the Town of Boston* (CD-ROM), MHS; Akers, *Divine Politician*, 115.

128 *"at table"*: BG, March 2, 1772; Henry Hulton to Robert Nicholson, Aug. 3, 1771, in York, *Henry Hulton and the American Revolution*, 253; Warren, *New England Bound*, 247; William H. Robinson, "On Phillis Wheatley and Her Boston" and "Phillis Wheatley," *Anti-Slavery Record* 11 (May 1836): 7–8, in *PWW*, 19, 458–59; MMO, 11, 15.

128 *Susanna compensated by emphasizing*: MMO, 12–13; Melish, *Disowning Slavery*, chap. 1; Jennifer Thorn, "Phillis Wheatley's Ghosts: The Racial Melancholy of New England Protestants," *Eighteenth Century* 50 (2009): 73–99.

129 *addressed to women and children*: For the networks of women, see Grimsted, "Anglo-American Racism and Phillis Wheatley's 'Sable Veil'"; Joanna Brooks, "Our Phillis, Ourselves," *American Literature* 82 (2010): 1–28. As Shields maintains, it is important not to see these elegies as produced on demand any more (or, perhaps, less) than Wheatley's other poems. Shields, *Phillis Wheatley's Poetics of Liberation*, 21. For similar arguments about the elegies expressing Wheatley's constraints, struggles, and maturity, see especially Bassard, *Spiritual Interrogations*, 64–70; Weyler, *Empowering Words*, chap. 1; William Huntting Howell, *Against Self-Reliance: The Arts of Dependence in the Early United States* (Philadelphia, 2015), 60–77; Roberts, *Awakening Verse*, chap. 4. For Wheatley as mediating grief, see also Cavitch, *American Elegy*, 51, 186–95; Julie Ellison, *Cato's Tears and the Making of Anglo-American Emotion* (Chicago, 1999), 184–90; Lucia Hodgson, "Infant Muse: Phillis Wheatley and the Revolutionary Rhetoric of Childhood," *Early American Literature* 49 (2014): 663–82; Wigginton, *In the Neighborhood*, chap. 3; Bly, "'On Death's Domain Intent I Fix My Eye.'"

130 *She began her elegy*: BG, Nov. 5, 1770; *BEP*, July 1, 8, 1771; PW, *To Mrs. Leonard, on the Death of Her Husband* (Boston, 1771), Historical Society of Pennsylvania; *CWC*, 117–18. For the importance of broadside elegies in Wheatley's oeuvre, see Weyler, *Empowering Words*, 25–75. Gates, *Trials of Phillis Wheatley*, 15, and Carretta, *Phillis Wheatley*, 78–79, identify Thomas Hubbard Sr. as a slave trader, but the source is unclear.

130 *broadside elegies*: Weyler, *Empowering Words*, 57–61; Roberts, *Awakening Verse*.

131 *"The sire, the friend, in him"*: "On the Death of Doctor Samuel Marshall," *BEP*, Oct. 7, 1771; *PWW*, 375n; *CWC*, 46–47, 118–20. There might have also been a family connection to the Tylers: the Lathrops named their second child, born in 1772, Jane Tyler Lathrop.

132 *"Thanks to my God"*: *CWC*, 45–46, 123–26; *PWW*, 191; Bassard, *Spiritual Interrogations*, 52–53; Wigginton, *In the Neighborhood*, 94–95; John Andrews to William Barrell, Sept. 22, 1772, Andrews-Eliot Correspondence, box 1, MHS.

Hannah Mather Crocker retained a copy of this poem, which may be the manuscript now in the Wetmore Papers, MHS. Crocker, *Reminiscences and Traditions of Boston*, 212.

133 *"Instruct thy mind"*: CWC, 43; *PWW*, 191; Rick Schwartz, *Hurricanes and the Middle Atlantic States: From Jamestown to the Present* (Alexandria, Va., 2007), 41–43. In her 1772 proposal, the poem is undated and seems to be grouped with those mostly from after 1770, in between several elegies: CWC, 166.

133 *"To a Lady on Coming to America"*: CWC, 41–42.

135 *fifty-five-line lyric "Recollection"*: CWC, 121–23. For L. as possibly John or Mary Lathrop, and Abigail May (b. 1754 and a member of Old South) as "A.M.," the dedicatee, see *PPW*, 141–42. This Abigail May's mother was also named Abigail. Samuel May, "Colonel Joseph May, 1760–1841," *New England Historical and Genealogical Register* 27 (1873): 114–15. For the suggestion of Agnes Moorhead or Abigail Mather, see Roberts, *Awakening Verse*, 269n88, 90.

The poem has not received much attention, but see especially Grimsted, "Anglo-American Racism and Phillis Wheatley's 'Sable Veil,'" 365–67. John C. Shields seems to have been the first to suggest an allusion to the Middle Passage: *American Aeneas*, 240. Later Shields argued that the poem is a key moment in Wheatley's turn toward aesthetics and proto-Romanticism, a move that he argues enhanced her ability to deal with slavery in her writing. Shields, *Phillis Wheatley's Poetics of Liberation*, 25–26; John C. Shields, *Phillis Wheatley and the Romantics* (Knoxville, Tenn., 2010), 45–47. See also Watson, "Classic Case"; Hairston, "Trojan Horse," 82–84, and Jeffrey Bilbro, "Who Are Lost and How They're Found: Redemption and Theodicy in Wheatley, Newton, and Cowper," *Early American Literature* 47 (2012): 568–69. "Every human breast" will recur in her letter to Samson Occom in 1774.

11. THE PROPOSAL

138 *"from the Afric muse"*: CWC, 44, 60–61, 123–24; *PPW*, 144–45n25; Paula Bennett, "Phillis Wheatley's Vocation and the Paradox of the 'Afric Muse,'" *PMLA* 113 (1998): 64–76.

140 *"Proposals for Printing by Subscription"*: BC, Feb. 29, March 14, 21, April 11, 18, 1772; Schlesinger, *Prelude to Independence*, 143–44; Bailyn, *Ordeal of Thomas Hutchinson*, 199; Christopher D. Felker, "'The Tongues of the Learned Are Insufficient': Phillis Wheatley, Publishing Objectives, and Personal Liberty," *Resources for American Literary Study* 20 (1994): 154–55. On Russell, see Thomas Goldstein, "Ezekiel Russell," in *Boston Printers and Booksellers, 1640–1800*, ed. Benjamin Franklin V (Boston, 1980), 438–42; J. L. Bell, "What Isaiah Thomas Wrote About Ezekiel Russell's Wife," "The Mysteries of Ezekiel Russell's Wife," "'A Comedy of Three Acts, Never Before Printed,'" *Boston 1775*, Feb. 9, 10, 2014, and Dec. 24, 2018, www.boston1775.blogspot.com.

140 *special capabilities of a rare individual*: Darrin McMahon, *Divine Fury: A History of Genius* (New York, 2013); Joyce E. Chaplin, "The Problem of Genius in the Age of Slavery," in *Genealogies of Genius*, ed. Joyce E. Chaplin and Darrin McMahon (New York, 2016), 11–28.

141 *the list showcases her ability*: CWC, 165–67; Kristin Wilcox, "The Body into Print: Marketing Phillis Wheatley," *American Literature* 71 (1998): 14.

142 *The merchant John Andrews*: Andrews to William Barrell, May 29, 1772, Feb.

24, 1773, Andrews-Eliot Correspondence, box 1; Wilcox, "Body into Print," 14–15.

142 *Russell admitted that his political weekly*: Russell did advertise, and reprint, a surer bet, Thomas Amory's *Daily Devotion Assisted and Recommended*—a small book of sermons that Wheatley would receive and give as a gift to Thomas Wallcut. The next year she even wrote a poem about Amory's collection. *CWC*, 180.

Thomas had also printed and sold Wheatley's Whitefield poem in a special pamphlet edition with Reverend Pemberton's funeral sermon. Just before giving up his *Censor*, Russell referred enviously to Thomas's refashioned anti-administration weekly as *"very popular and much admired." CWC*, 48–49; Ann Beebe, "Phillis Wheatley's To the Rev. Dr. Thomas Amory on Reading His Sermons on Daily Devotion, in Which That Duty Is Recommended and Assisted," *Explicator* 73 (2015): 229–34; Thomas, *History of Printing in America*, 1:154–55, 165; *BC*, April 25, May 2, 1772; Thomas Wallcut to PW, Nov. 17, 1774, in *WPW*, 126, 206.

142 *six newspapers in Boston*: Schlesinger, *Prelude to Independence*, 131.

143 *Allen's epic in progress*: James Allen, *The Poem, Which the Committee of the Town of Boston Had Voted Unanimously to Be Published with the Late Oration; with Observations Relating Thereto; Together with Some Very Pertinent Extracts from an Ingenious Composition, Never Yet Published* (Boston, 1772), 3, 14, 21; Kenneth Silverman, *A Cultural History of the American Revolution* (1976; repr., New York, 1987), 210–11; Lewis Leary, "The 'Friends' of James Allen, or How Partial Truth Is No Truth at All," *Early American Literature* 15 (1980): 165–71; Samuel Forman, *Dr. Joseph Warren* (Gretna, La., 2017), 161–66.

143 *In seemingly very different poems*: For later writings that display Allen's patriot bona fides, see Paul Lewis, ed., *The Citizen Poets of Boston: A Collection of Forgotten Poems, 1789–1820* (Lebanon, N.H., 2016), 25, 33–35.

143 *ironic style already had a Tory*: For irony and antislavery in black writing of this era, see Bruce, *Origins of African American Literature*, chap. 2. For Loyalist satire, see Bruce Granger, *Political Satire in the American Revolution, 1763–1783* (New York, 1971); Philip Gould, *Writing the Rebellion: Loyalists and the Literature of Politics in British America* (New York, 2013); Colin Wells, *Poetry Wars: Verse and Politics in the American Revolution and Early Republic* (Philadelphia, 2018).

144 *networks of information*: Warner, *Protocols of Liberty*; Castronovo, *Propaganda 1776*; Thomas C. Leonard, *The Power of the Press: The Birth of American Political Reporting* (New York, 1986), chap. 1.

145 *James Swan*: "Proposals," *MSP*, Nov. 7, 14, 22, 28, 1771, March 12, April 12, 19, 1772; *BG*, March 30, April 6, Nov. 30, 1772; *BEP*, Nov. 23, 1772; "This Day Published," *BPB*, Nov. 16, 1772; James Swan, *A Dissuasion to Great Britain and Its Colonies, from the Slave Trade to Africa* (Boston, 1772). For a different view of Russell's Tory reputation as helping to fix "an ongoing association between Wheatley and the Tory press" dating back to the Whitefield elegy, see Bradley, *Slavery, Propaganda, and the American Revolution*, 102–3. For the prices of James Allen's poem and Wheatley, see J. L. Bell, "Was Three Shillings Too Much to Ask?," *Boston 1775*, Oct. 27, 2011, www.boston1775.blogspot.com. Thanks to Nicholas Wood for help discerning the publication history of Swan's pamphlet.

145 *Swan introduced his argument*: Swan, *Dissuasion*, vi–viii, xii, 29–30, 39, 55–57; David L. Crosby, ed., *The Complete Antislavery Writings of Anthony Benezet* (Baton Rouge, La., 2013), 91–93. Wheatley's signed copy of Benezet, *Some Historical Account of Guinea* (Philadelphia, 1771), is in Special Collections, Swem Library, College of William and Mary, and is bound with Granville Sharp's *Extract from a Representation of the Injustice and Dangerous Tendency of Tolerating Slavery* (Philadelphia, 1771).

147 *"ignorance and barbarity of the darkest ages"*: Christopher Leslie Brown, *Moral Capital: Foundations of British Abolitionism* (Chapel Hill, N.C., 2006), 173, 179; PW to John Thornton, April 21, 1772, in *CWC*, 140; *PWW*, 187; David Brion Davis, *The Problem of Slavery in the Age of Revolution, 1770–1823* (Ithaca, N.Y., 1975), 377, 386–98, 529–37; John Coffey, *Exodus and Liberation: Deliverance Politics from John Calvin to Martin Luther King Jr.* (New York, 2014); Crosby, *Antislavery Writings of Anthony Benezet*, 148, 172; Swan, *Dissuasion*, 25, 61. Granville Sharp taught himself Hebrew, beginning a journey that led him to connect modern threats to the ancient constitution, which he traced to the Israelites, to the rising importance of African slavery in the British Empire. Davis says John Woolman thought the Gibeonites' enslavement was God's judgment (536–37).

148 *"Goliath of Gath"*: *CWC*, 19; Byles, *Poems on Several Occasions*, 18–23; James P. Byrd, *Sacred Scripture, Sacred War: The Bible and the American Revolution* (New York, 2013), 95, 209–10; Phillips, *Epic in American Culture*, 65–68; *CWC*, 19–25, 165–66; Foster, *Written by Herself*, 41–42; Scheick, *Authority and Female Authorship*, 111; Rosemary Fithian Guruswemy, "'Thou Hast the Holy Word': Jupiter Hammon's 'Regards' to Phillis Wheatley," in *Genius in Bondage*, ed. Vincent Carretta and Philip Gould (Lexington, Ky., 2001), 192–93; Keith Byerman, "Talking Back: Phillis Wheatley, Race, and Religion," *Religions* 10 (2019): 402; Homer, *The Odyssey*, trans. Robert Fagles (New York, 1996), 77; Virgil, *The Aeneid*, trans. Robert Fagles (New York, 2006), 47; Hairston, *Ebony Column*, 50–51; Barnard, *Empire of Ruin*, 48. Loscocco, *Phillis Wheatley's Miltonic Poetics*, 81–88, argues that Wheatley reads the biblical text through Milton's "Samson Agonistes"; see also Cook and Tatum, *African American Writers and the Classical Tradition*, 32–34. Paula Backscheider states that narrative poems based on biblical stories "could take daringly personal and subversive turns." Backscheider, *Eighteenth-Century Women Poets and Their Poetry*, 158.

149 *"royal daughter"*: *CWC*, 20–21; Byerman, "Talking Back," 401–2.

149 *a sermonic blast that allies*: *CWC*, 22–24; Scheick, *Authority and Female Authorship*, 113; Christine Levecq, *Slavery and Sentiment: The Politics of Feeling in Black Atlantic Antislavery Writing, 1770–1850* (Lebanon, N.H., 2008), 60; Alice M. Kracke, "Representing Themselves and Others: Black Poets as Lay-Lawyers in the Early Transatlantic" (PhD diss., Tufts University, 2009), 101.

12. THE MOVEMENT

151 *Wheatley and Somerset might seem to have*: Scholars who have suggested the impact of the *Somerset* case on Wheatley include Mukhtar Ali Isani, "The British Reception of Wheatley's Poems on Various Subjects," *Journal of Negro History* 66 (1981): 145; Wilcox, "Body into Print"; Vincent Carretta, introduction to *CWC*, xxv; Vincent Carretta, "Phillis Wheatley, the Mansfield Decision

of 1772, and the Choice of Identity," in *Early America Re-explored*, ed. Klaus H. Schmidt and Fritz Fleischman (New York, 2000), 201–23; Carretta, *Phillis Wheatley*, 119–31. My own earlier argument for their simultaneity and entanglement, rather than a one-way influence of Somerset on Wheatley, appeared in "The Wheatleyan Moment," *Early American Studies* 9 (2011): 522–51. For a similar recognition that emphasis on the Mansfield decision in *Somerset v. Steuart* tends to diminish Somerset's (and Wheatley's) role, see Srividhya Swaminathan, *Debating the Slave Trade: Rhetoric of British National Identity, 1759–1815* (Burlington, Vt., 2009), 134. For approaching slavery as a changing problem and as politics, the works of David Brion Davis remain essential. See his *Problem of Slavery in Western Culture* (Ithaca, N.Y., 1966), *Problem of Slavery in the Age of Revolution*, and *Challenging the Boundaries of Slavery* (Cambridge, Mass., 2001). My phrasing draws on his, as well as Joseph C. Miller, *The Problem of Slavery as History* (New Haven, Conn., 2012).

This was not the first time that the Anglo-American conversation about slavery had transformed because of changes in, and criticisms of, the traffic in persons between continents. For the long story, with equal attention to the seventeenth and eighteenth centuries, see what will be the next classic in the field, Gunther Peck's forthcoming study of trafficking in persons and race (Chapel Hill, N.C., 2023).

153 *Steuart's reward would be an audience*: Mary Maples and John M. Hemphill II, "Charles Steuart Papers, Department of Manuscripts, Library of Scotland" (1955) in Microfilm Catalog, Rockefeller Library, Colonial Williamsburg Foundation; Mark S. Weiner, "New Biographical Evidence on Somerset's Case," *Slavery and Abolition* 23 (2002): 121–36; Mark S. Weiner, *Black Trials: Citizenship from the Beginnings of Slavery to the End of Caste* (New York, 2004), 73–77; O'Malley, *Final Passages*, 50, 75, 233, 275–76; Historical Manuscripts Commission, *The Manuscripts of the Earl of Dartmouth*, vol. 2, *American Papers* (1895; repr., Boston, 1972), 70; Steven M. Wise, *Though the Heavens May Fall: The Landmark Trial That Led to the End of Human Slavery* (New York, 2005), 3–4; Thomas C. Barrow, *Trade and Empire: The British Customs Service in Colonial America, 1660–1775* (Cambridge, Mass., 1967), 187, 316n6; Morgan and Morgan, *Stamp Act Crisis*, 208–9; Zobel, *Boston Massacre*, 66.

154 *actions of the collectors*: Emory Washburn, *Extinction of Villenage and Slavery in England; with Somerset's Case* (Boston, 1864), 17–18; Nathaniel Coffin to Charles Steuart, Aug. 7, 1769, and Oct. 12, 1770, reel 2, Charles Steuart Papers; Colin Nicolson, "'McIntosh, Otis & Adams Are Our Demagogues': Nathaniel Coffin and the Loyalist Interpretation of the Origins of the American Revolution," *Proceedings of the Massachusetts Historical Society*, 3rd ser., 108 (1996): 72–116; Weiner, "New Biographical Evidence," 123–24 (but note transcription difference in my version versus Weiner's of Coffin's letter); Kirsten Sword, "Remembering Dinah Nevil: Strategic Deceptions and Eighteenth-Century Antislavery," *Journal of American History* (2010): 7, 9; Weiner, *Black Trials*, 77; Barrow, *Trade and Empire*, 244–45.

154 *transatlantic Rosa Parks*: For the comparison to Rosa Parks, and more important the argument regarding the importance of Somerset's North American experience, I am indebted to correspondence with Kirsten Sword and her important article, "Remembering Dinah Nevil," esp. 9, 11; see also Sword, *Wives Not Slaves: Patriarchy and Modernity in the Age of Revolutions* (Chicago, 2021), 252–53.

157 *Sharp would be citing*: Granville Sharp, *A Representation of the Dangerous Tendency* (London, 1769), 81–85, 91–93; Prince Hoare, ed., *Memoirs of Granville Sharp* (London, 1820); Benezet to Sharp, May 14, 1772, in Bruns, *Am I Not a Man and a Brother*, 195; E. P. Lascelles, *Granville Sharp and the Freedom of Slaves in England* (London, 1928), 37–38; Davis, *Problem of Slavery in the Age of Revolution*, 395–96; Weiner, *Black Trials*, 78–79; Gretchen Holbrook Gerzina, *Black London: Life Before Emancipation* (New Brunswick, N.J., 1995), 102–3; Waldstreicher, *Runaway America*, 192–99; Brown, *Moral Capital*, 94–97, 161–77; Swaminathan, *Debating the Slave Trade*, 72–73, 77; Granville Sharp, *An Essay upon Slavery, Proving from Scripture Its Inconsistency with Humanity and Religion* (Burlington, N.J., 1773), vi–x.

158 *"key ideological plank of the new Toryism"*: James M. Vaughn, "The Ideological Origins of Illiberal Imperialism: Metropolitan Politics and the Post-1763 Transformation of the British Empire," in *Envisioning Empire: The New British World from 1763 to 1773*, ed. James M. Vaughn and Robert A. Olwell (London, 2020), 43. For the implications of Mansfield and the notion of this as a significant moment in the imperial controversy, see Waldstreicher, *Runaway America*, 198–208; David Waldstreicher, *Slavery's Constitution* (New York, 2009), chap. 1; Waldstreicher, "Wheatleyan Moment"; Eliga Gould, "Zones of Law, Zones of Violence: The Legal Geography of the British Atlantic., Circa 1772," *William and Mary Quarterly* 60 (2003): 471–510; Eliga Gould, *Among the Powers of the Earth: The American Revolution and the Making of a New World Empire* (Cambridge, Mass., 2012), 55–58; Paul Halliday, *Habeas Corpus: From England to Empire* (Cambridge, Mass., 2010), 35, 101, 176; George H. Van Cleve, "*Somerset's Case* and Its Antecedents in Imperial Perspective," with responses by Daniel Hulsebosch and Ruth Paley, *Law and History Review* 24 (2006): 601–45.

159 *some kind of law was higher*: R. C. Simmons and Peter D. G. Thomas, eds., *Proceedings and Debates of the British Parliaments Respecting North America, 1754–1783* (Millwood, N.Y., 1982), 2:130; Waldstreicher, *Runaway America*, 199–204; Norman S. Poser, *Lord Mansfield: Justice in the Age of Reason* (Toronto, 2013), 301–2; Bradley, *Slavery, Propaganda, and the American Revolution*, 71; "Calisthenes," *BG*, Sept. 28, 1772; Henry N. Buehner, "Mansfieldism: Law and Politics in Anglo-America, 1700–1865" (PhD diss., Temple University, 2014); Ernest B. Lowrie, *Lord Chief Justice Mansfield: Dark Horse of the American Revolution* (Bloomington, Ind., 2016), 261–62; A. Leon Higginbotham Jr., *In the Matter of Color* (New York, 1978), 353–56.

160 *a creature only of "positive" municipal law*: Weiner, *Black Trials*, 70–88; Wise, *Though the Heavens May Fall*, 191; Brown, *Moral Capital*, 117–22.

161 *England as the first North Star*: Van Gosse, "'As a Nation, the English Are Our Friends': The Emergence of African-American Politics in the British Atlantic World, 1772–1861," *American Historical Review* 113 (2008): 1003–28; Aline Helg, *Slave No More: Self-Liberation Before Abolitionism in the Americas*, trans. Lara Vergnaud (Chapel Hill, N.C., 2019).

161 *Only Boston hosted a full-on debate*: Seymour Drescher, *Capitalism and Slavery* (New York, 1987), 40; Seymour Drescher, *Abolition: A History of Slavery and Antislavery* (New York, 2009), 100, 105; Gerzina, *Black London*, 122–24 ("media event"); Thea K. Hunter, "Publishing Freedom, Winning Arguments, and Massachusetts Freedom Cases, 1772–1836" (PhD diss., Columbia University, 2004), 54–55 ("coverage"); Simon Schama, *Rough Crossings* (New York,

2005), 20–63; Greene, *Evaluating Empire and Confronting Colonialism*, 178–79; Edward Long, *Candid Reflections upon the Judgement Lately Awarded by the Court of King's Bench in Westminster-Hall on What Is Commonly Called the Negroe-Cause* (London, 1772); Samuel Estwick, *Considerations on the Negro Cause Commonly So Called, Addressed to the Right Honourable Lord Mansfield . . . by a West Indian* (London, 1772); Estwick, *Considerations*, 2nd ed., in *Exploring the Bounds of Liberty: Political Writings of Colonial British America from the Glorious Revolution to the American Revolution*, ed. Jack P. Greene and Craig B. Yirush (Indianapolis, 2018), 3:2149–230; Boulukos, *The Grateful Slave*, 97–103. Hunter, "Publishing Freedom," 108–28, is the most detailed account of the reaction in Massachusetts. Bradley was the first to suggest the *BG*'s, and by extension the patriot movement's, silence about *Somerset*. For responses to the *Somerset* case in North America, the subject of some recent controversy, I am indebted to conversations with Matthew Mason as well as his "North American Calm, West Indian Storm: The Politics of the Somerset Decision in the British Atlantic," *Slavery and Abolition* 41 (2020): 723–47. See also Bradley, *Slavery, Propaganda, and the American Revolution*, chap. 4; Hunter, "Publishing Freedom," chap. 2; and for the Deep South and the Caribbean, see Edward B. Rugemer, *Slave Law and the Politics of Resistance in the Early Atlantic World* (Cambridge, Mass., 2018), 181–83.

162 *Who printed what, and what it might mean*: Schlesinger, *Prelude to Independence*, 131–49; *BNL*, Aug. 6, 1772; *BG*, Oct. 5, 1772; Waldstreicher, *Runaway America*, 199–200.

162 *The first descriptions of the trial*: Schlesinger, *Prelude to Independence*, 131; *BNL*, July 23, 1772; *BPB*, July 27, Aug. 3, 1772; *BEP*, July 27, 1772.

163 *"hold[ing] millions in chains"*: *BNL*, Aug. 27, 1772; *MSP*, Sept. 3, 17, 1772; *BPB*, Aug. 31, Sept. 7, 1772; *BEP*, Aug. 31, 1772.

164 *The coverage of the* Somerset *case*: *BEP*, Sept. 7, 14, 21, 28, Oct. 12, 19, 26, Nov. 30, Dec. 7, 28, 1772; *MSP*, Oct. 1, 22, 29, 1772; *BPB*, Oct. 5, 1772; "London, July 23," "The Independency of Judges Is the Finishing Stroke," *BG*, Sept. 21, Oct. 19, 1772.

13. THE MOMENT

165 *characterized by "lenient measures"*: *MSP*, Sept. 24, Nov. 19, 1772; *BG*, Sept. 28, 1772; *BPB*, Sept. 28, Oct. 12, 19, 1772; *BEP*, Oct. 12, 1772.

165 *While cabinet members served*: William Gerard De Brahm to Lord Dartmouth, Aug. 12, 1772, "Oath of Office," in *Manuscripts of the Earl of Dartmouth*, 2:87–88; B. D. Barger, *Lord Dartmouth and the American Revolution* (Columbia, S.C., 1965), 31–48; Ian Christie and Benjamin W. Labaree, *Empire or Independence* (New York, 1976), 164–65; S. Max Edelson, *The New Map of Empire: How Britain Imagined America Before Independence* (Cambridge, Mass., 2017), 313; Michael G. Kammen, *A Rope of Sand: The Colonial Agents, British Politics, and the American Revolution* (1968; repr., New York, 1974), 258–63; Pauline Maier, *From Resistance to Revolution* (New York, 1972), 229–30; Nick Bunker, *An Empire on the Edge: How Britain Came to Fight America* (New York, 2014), 94–114.

167 *St. Vincent policy*: Barger, *Lord Dartmouth*, 10, 69; Introduction to *Manuscripts of the Earl of Dartmouth*, 2:vii, xvi; Love, *Samson Occom*, 138–41; Edelson, *New Map of Empire*, 270; Grimsted, "Anglo-American Racism and Phillis Wheatley's 'Sable Veil,'" 384–85; Granville Sharp to Earl of Dartmouth, Oct. 10, 1772,

in Hoare, *Memoirs of Granville Sharp*, 163, 165, 166–67; Greene, *Evaluating Empire*, 1–19.

168 *"I have lately travelled"*: Wooldridge to Dartmouth, June 25, 1769, Nov. 17, 1771, Dec. 31, 1772, in *Manuscripts of the Earl of Dartmouth*, 2:84, 88, 189; Wooldridge to Dartmouth, Jan. 4, 1773, *Publications of the Rhode Island Historical Society* 7 (1899): 242; "London," *New York Journal*, Aug. 29, 1771; *Pennsylvania Journal*, May 9, 1771; James Bradley, *Popular Politics and the American Revolution in England* (Athens, Ga., 1986), 56; Barger, *Lord Dartmouth*, 88; Paul David Nelson, *General James Grant* (Gainesville, Fla., 1993), 70; Alfred B. Beaven, *Aldermen of the City of London: Temp. Henry III—1912* (London, 1908), 195–211; Ben Saunders, "The Swindler Detected: Embezzlement, Lies, and Merchant Adventurers in the Late 1700s," *100 Minories*, July 24, 2015, 100minories .lparchaeology.com/the-swindler-detected-embezzlement-lies-and-merchant -adventurers-in-the-late-1700s; Wooldridge to Dartmouth, Nov. 24, 1772, in *PWW*, 453; J. L. Bell, "'I Asked if She Could Write on Any Subject,'" "The Rise and Fall of Thomas Wooldridge," *Boston 1775*, Oct. 22, 2011, Aug. 20, 2015, www.boston1775.blogspot.com.

169 *"To the Right Hon."*: Wooldridge to Dartmouth, Oct. 10, 1772, in *PWW*, 385, 454. A facsimile of the manuscript, in the Dartmouth Papers, is reproduced in *PWW*, 385–87; for a transcription, see *CWC*, 128–29, which must be from a variant manuscript as it capitalizes every word and includes Dartmouth's surname, Legge, in the title. The importance of this exchange was first pointed out by James A. Rawley, "The World of Phillis Wheatley," *New England Quarterly* 50 (1977): 66–70.

172 *Instead of political restrictions seeming*: *CWC*, 128–29. Mary Nyquist concludes her study of early modern anti-tyranny with the observation that this poem of Wheatley's is the first historical example "where the injustice of interstate political slavery conveyed by antityrannicism is directly aligned with chattel slavery, which therefore appears similarly unjust." Mary Nyquist, *Arbitrary Rule: Slavery, Tyranny, and the Power of Life and Death* (Chicago, 2013), 368.

172 *explains her good citizenship*: Peter Coviello, "Agonizing Affection: Affect and Nation in Early America," *American Literature* 37 (2002): 443–45; Ellison, *Cato's Tears*, 120–22; Joseph Rezek, "The Print Atlantic: Phillis Wheatley, Ignatius Sancho, and the Cultural Significance of the Book," in *Early African American Print Culture*, ed. Lara Langer Cohen and Jordan Alexander Stein (Philadelphia, 2012), 33–38; Barnard, *Empire of Ruin*, 39. Kaplan and Kaplan identified the poem as an exemplar of the "black patriot position" in *Black Presence in the Era of the American Revolution*, 178–79.

173 *It introduces the slave persona*: For the slave persona as Wheatley's contribution, see Will Harris, "Phillis Wheatley, Diaspora Subjectivity, and the African American Canon," *MELUS* 33 (2008): 29.

174 *cover letter she gave to Wooldridge*: Wooldridge to Dartmouth, Nov. 24, 1772; PW to Dartmouth, Oct. 10, 1772, in *CWC*, 143–44.

175 *Brook Watson, a merchant*: PW to David Wooster, Oct. 18, 1773, in *CWC*, 147; Charles Royster, *The Fabulous History of the Dismal Swamp Company* (New York, 1999), 194, 198; Brian DeLay, "Watson and the Shark," in *The Familiar Made Strange: American Icons and Artifacts After the Transnational Turn*, ed. Brooke Blower and Mark Philip Bradley (Ithaca, N.Y., 2015), 9–20; Kamensky, *Revolution in Color*, 279–80.

175 *Susannah Kelly Wooldridge*: J. L. Bell, "Phillis Wheatley Day at Old South," "The Mystery of Mrs. W——," "Phillis Wheatley and Susannah Wooldridge," *Boston 1775*, Aug. 17, 18, 19, 2015; Bell calls "Ode to Neptune" a "commission piece" possibly for Susannah in New York.

178 *"serene," "mild," feminine Britannia*: CWC, 41, 179; Patrick Moseley, "Empowerment Through Classicism in Phillis Wheatley's 'Ode to Neptune,'" in Shields and Lamore, *New Essays on Phillis Wheatley*, 95–110.

14. THE CAMPAIGN

179 *attestation as her passport*: John Andrews to William Barrell, Feb. 24, 1773, Andrews-Eliot Papers, MHS; *CWC*, 8. A version of the attestation later published was dated October 28. *PWW*, 404–5; John Torpey, *The Invention of the Passport*, 2nd ed. (New York, 2018).

180 *"Judges" conjures the image*: The popular myth of Wheatley's actual "examination" or "trial" by a "Wheatley court" of learned judges seems to have originated with a pageant by Mary Church Terrell and an otherwise carefully researched radio play and children's book by Shirley Graham, *The Story of Phillis Wheatley* (New York, 1949), chap. 7. It hardened from imagined scene with invented dialogue to all-important fact and symbol for African American literature in important and widely heard and read talks and essays by Henry Louis Gates Jr. and Nellie Y. McKay. Henry Louis Gates Jr., "Writing, 'Race,' and the Difference It Makes," in *Loose Canons: Notes on the Culture Wars* (New York, 1993), 51–53; Henry Louis Gates Jr. and Nellie Y. McKay, "From Phillis Wheatley to Toni Morrison: The Flowering of African American Literature," *Journal of Blacks in Higher Education* 14 (1996–97): 97–98 (reprinted as the introduction to *The Norton Anthology of African American Literature*); Gates, *Trials of Phillis Wheatley*, 5; Nellie Y. McKay, "Naming the Problem That Led to the Question 'Who Shall Teach African American Literature?'; or, Are We Ready to Disband the Wheatley Court?," in *White Scholars/African American Texts*, ed. Lisa A. Long (New Brunswick, N.J., 2005), 18. Gates cites Graham as a source in the bibliography for *The Trials of Phillis Wheatley*, 102. Whatever its merits as a primal scene for African American literature and literary criticism (and poets and critics still find it useful), this origins story or "primal scene" (unintentionally) underestimates Wheatley's achievement and recognition by 1772. For a somewhat fuller accounting of the myth with citations to other scholars' critiques of Gates on this point, see my "Wheatleyan Moment," 528–31, and the literature cited there, including especially Phillip M. Richards, *Black Heart: The Moral Life of Recent African American Letters* (New York, 2006), 72; Brooks, "Our Wheatley, Ourselves," 1–4, 17–18; and subsequently Max Cavitch, "The Poetry of Phillis Wheatley in Slavery's Recollective Economies, 1773 to the Present," in *Race, Ethnicity, and Publishing in America*, ed. Cécile Cottenet (New York, 2014), 210–30.

180 *associations in Boston*: Hulton to Robert Nicholson, May 10, 1773, in York, *Henry Hulton and the American Revolution*, 279; CWC, 181, 192, 206.

181 *Chauncy had blamed slaving*: Akers, "'Our Modern Egyptians,'" 403; Carretta, *Phillis Wheatley*, 88; CWC, 8, 48–49; Grimsted, "Anglo-American Racism and Phillis Wheatley's 'Sable Veil,'" 388; Howell, *Against Self-Reliance*, 70–72; Griffin, *Old Brick*; John Corrigan, *The Hidden Balance: Religion and the Social The-*

ories of Charles Chauncy and Jonathan Mayhew (New York, 1987). Chauncy himself would be the subject of a laudatory poem in a style similar to Wheatley's in the *BPB*, March 1, 1773.

182 *"large emolument" from the publication*: Andrews to William Barrell, Feb. 24, 1773, in *Bio-bibliography*, 16; *PWW*, 27–28.

182 *Bell made a trip*: *BPB*, Oct. 26, 1772, for Calef's probable departure; Calef to Susanna Wheatley, Jan. 5, 1773, in Susanna Wheatley to Occom, March 29, 1773, in Mason, introduction to *PPW*, 6–8.

183 *Huntingdon was "greatly pleas'd"*: G. J. Barker-Benfield, *Phillis Wheatley Chooses Freedom: History, Poetry, and the Ideals of the American Revolution* (New York, 2018), 48; Shurtleff, "Phillis Wheatley, the Negro Slave Poet," 178–79. For Huntingdon's assistance with publication and its importance, see Grimsted, "Anglo-American Racism and Phillis Wheatley's 'Sable Veil,'" 383, 389; Christopher Felker, "The Tongues of the Learned Are Insufficient: Phillis Wheatley, Publishing Objectives, and Personal Liberty," in *Texts and Textuality*, ed. Phillip Cohen (New York, 1997), 89–99. For the Methodist language of loving fellowship, see Lawrence, *One Family Under God*.

183 *A portrait needed to be taken*: Susanna Wheatley to the Countess of Huntingdon, Feb. 20, April 30, 1773, in "Letters of Phillis Wheatley and Susanna Wheatley," ed. Sarah Dunlap Jackson, *Journal of Negro History* 57 (1972): 212–14; Occom to Samuel Buell, 1773, in *Collected Writings*, 103; MMO, 18; Slauter, "Looking for Scipio Moorhead," 89–116; Gwendolyn DuBois Shaw, *Portraits of a People* (Seattle, 2006), 32–34; Lucy Peltz, "Living Muses: Constructing and Celebrating the Professional Woman in Literature and the Arts," in *Brilliant Women: 18th-Century Bluestockings*, ed. Elizabeth Eger and Lucy Peltz (New Haven, Conn., 2008), 68–69. During the spring of 1773, when John Wheatley suffered a fall, John Moorhead visited him "almost every Day." Susanna Wheatley to Occom, March 29, 1773.

185 *her own papers*: Bacon, *Puritan Promenade*, 23; Beth Fowkes Tobin, *Picturing Imperial Power* (Durham, N.C., 1999); Barker-Benfield, *Phillis Wheatley Chooses Freedom*, 48. Wendy Raphael Roberts maintains that from the appearance of the volume it is a book of hymns—ironically, not her own likely choice, since Wheatley chose not to write the kinds of hymns that would have appeared in that format and binding. But many if not most volumes of poems were published in small formats. Roberts, *Awakening Verse*, 145–46.

185 *"To S. M."*: CWC, 59–60. For another possible praise poem, an anonymous and undated broadside, *An Ode, On the BIRTH DAY of Pompey Stockbridge*, which has been suggested inconclusively to be Wheatley's, see *PWW*, 457, and Kaplan and Kaplan, *Black Presence*, 174.

186 *romantic in two important senses*: In his own book of poems thirty years before, Mather Byles had sought to encourage American painters even while admitting that the colonies looked "barbarous" from a London perspective for not having produced painters or poets. Mather Byles, "To Pictorio," in *Poems on Several Occasions*, 89–93; Lena Hill, *Visualizing Blackness and the Creation of African American Literary Tradition* (New York, 2014), 39–41. For Wheatley on the cusp of the usually identified period of Romantic poetry, see Shields, *Phillis Wheatley and the Romantics*.

186 *African and indigenous men as published authors*: James Albert Ukawsaw Gronniosaw, *A Narrative of the Most Remarkable Particulars in the Life of James Albert Ukawsaw Gronniosaw, an African Prince* (1772), in Carretta, *Unchained*

Voices, 32–58; Barker-Benfield, *Phillis Wheatley Chooses Freedom*, 54; *BPB*, Jan. 25, 1773; Joanna Brooks, "'This Indian World': An Introduction," and Occom to Wheelock, Jan. 27, 1773, to Samuel Buell, 1773, in Brooks, *Collected Writings of Samson Occom*, 22–24, 100, 103; Brooks, *American Lazarus*, chap. 3; Bannet, *Transatlantic Stories*, 139–40, 166–80.

187 *Boston publicity campaigns*: Gipson, *British Empire in the Age of the American Revolution*, 12:35–38; Schlesinger, *Prelude to Independence*, 148–49; Warner, *Protocols of Liberty*; Deming, *Boston and the Dawn of American Independence*, 199–207.

188 *problem of slavery*: The starting point remains Davis, *Problem of Slavery in Western Culture* and *Problem of Slavery in the Age of Revolution*.

188 *a series of petitions*: "For the Massachusetts Spy," *MSP*, Jan. 28, 1773; "This Day Published, Price 7 Coppers, and SOLD by E. Russell. The Appendix," *MSP*, Feb. 4, 11, 18, 1773; Davis, *Problem of Slavery in the Age of Revolution*, 276–77; Chernoh Sesay, "The Revolutionary Black Roots of Abolition in Massachusetts," *New England Quarterly* 87 (2014): 99–131; Cameron, *To Plead Our Own Cause*, 57–60; John Allen, *An Oration on the Beauties of Liberty*, 4th ed. (Boston, 1773), in Bruns, *Am I Not a Man and a Brother*, 260–62; *BEP*, May 17, 1773; *BPB*, May 17, 1773; Kaplan and Kaplan, *Black Presence*, 11–15; Wood, *Let the Oppressed Go Free*, chap. 1. A direct link between Wheatley's strategies and those of the petitioners has been posited by Bruce, *Origins of African American Literature*, 53, and Slauter, *State as a Work of Art*, 196–203, who suggests their influence on Wheatley. Gary B. Nash speculates that Wheatley wrote one of the petitions: *Unknown American Revolution*, 127. Bradley stresses that other printers wouldn't publish Allen's more antislavery editions. But they did advertise it. Bradley, *Slavery, Propaganda, and the American Revolution*, 106–8; *BPB*, May 3, 17, 1773; *MSP*, May 13, 20, 1773; *BEP*, May 17, 1773.

189 *Benjamin Rush, inspired and pushed by*: Rush, *An Address* (Philadelphia, 1773), 2–3; Nash, *Unknown American Revolution*, 121–22; Wood, *Let the Oppressed Go Free*, chap. 3. Rush's pamphlet was swiftly made available in Boston. *BG*, March 29, 1773; *BNL*, March 25, 1773.

191 *Ruth Barrell Andrews*: Ruth Barrell Andrews Commonplace Book of Poems, MHS; Wendy Raphael Roberts, "'Slavery' and 'To Mrs. Eliot on the Death of Her Child': Two New Manuscript Poems Connected to Phillis Wheatley by the Bostonian Poet Ruth Barrell Andrews," *Early American Literature* 51 (2016): 665–81; Roberts, *Awakening Verse*, 152–55; *CWC*, 166. Ruth Andrews might not have been in a position to write or publish pamphlets, but she is likely to have inspired Wheatley's mention by Rush in Philadelphia. The timing is striking: she wrote and presumably circulated "Slavery" after Phillis's manuscript was already on its way to London and possibly after the "attestation" began to collect signatures from important men like her uncle Joseph Green, in the latest part of the prepublication saga that her husband tracked so avidly in his letters to Ruth's own brother William Barrell, merchant in Philadelphia, to whom he also sent some of Wheatley's poems. Another source for Benjamin Rush's knowledge might seem to be Julia Stockton Rush, but she was born in 1759 and they did not marry until 1776.

191 *would be received*: *CWC*, 125–27; *WPW*, 166–67; Roberts, "Slavery," 671–73, 680n13; John Andrews to William Barrell, Sept. 22, 1772, Andrews-Eliot Papers.

192 *"On Night and Sleep"*: "On Night and Sleep," *MSP*, Jan. 7, 1773; *CG*, Oct. 11, 1771;

CWC, 27, 32–33, 60. For the *CG* and slavery, see Bradley, *Slavery, Propaganda, and the American Revolution*, 116–23; *CG*, May 1, 1772. On my tentative attribution of this and other poems to Wheatley, see the appendix and my essay, "Anonymous Wheatley and the Archive in Plain Sight : A Tentative Attribution of Nine Published Poems, 1773–1775," *Early American Literature* 57 (Fall 2022).

193 *Edward Young's*: Ekirch, *At Day's Close*, 207; Edward Young, *The Poetical Works of Edward Young, with a Memoir* (Boston, n.d.), 1:4, 75, 286, 319, 344; Harry M. Solomon, *The Rise of Robert Dodsley: Creating the New Age of Print* (Carbondale, Ill., 1996), 97; Blanford Parker, *The Triumph of Augustan Poetics* (New York, 1998), 226. Boston radical shoemaker Ebenezer Mackintosh liked to "recite from memory" from *Night Thoughts*: Young, "Ebenezer Mackintosh," 19. For night and darkness as liberating to Wheatley, especially in "An Hymn to Evening," see Devona Mallory, "I Remember Mama: Honoring the Goddess-Mother While Denouncing the Slaveowner-God in Phillis Wheatley's Poetry," in Shields and Lamore, *New Essays on Phillis Wheatley*, 19–34.

193 *Thankful Leonard: To the Hon'ble Thomas Hubbard, Esq.; On the Death of Mrs. Thankfull Leonard* (Boston, 1772) is dated and signed January 2, 1773; *CWC*, 131–32; Carretta, *Phillis Wheatley*, 89.

194 *Anonymously, she could try things out*: On Wheatley's desires and her expression of them, see Tara Bynum, "Phillis Wheatley's Pleasures: Reading Good Feeling in Phillis Wheatley's Poems and Letters," *Common-Place* 11, no. 1 (2010).

194 *an elegy about Mary Sanford Oliver*: *CWC*, 60–62; *Bio-bibliography*, 105–6. In 1706 the great hymn writer Isaac Watts dubbed Elizabeth Singer Rowe a "heavenly muse." Roberts, *Awakening Verse*, 52–54. Wheatley also referred to herself as "Afric's muse" in "A Hymn to Humanity," *CWC*, 51. For a similar but much more extended personification of Death in Young's *Night Thoughts*, see Young, "Night III," in *Poetical Works*, 58–61.

195 *To raise interest in London*: "To the Author of the London Magazine," *BPB*, March 1, 1773; Susannah Wheatley to Huntingdon, Feb., 20, 1773; *BPB*, April 19, 1772; *BNL*, April 22, 1773.

195 *Boston papers*: *BPB*, April 26, March 3, 1773; *BEP*, May 3, 1773; *BPB*, May 3, 10, 1773; *BNL*, May 6, 13, 1773; *Essex Gazette*, May 4, 1773; *CG*, May 7, 1773; *Connecticut Journal*, May 7, 1773; *New Hampshire Gazette*, May 7, 1773; *Providence Gazette*, May 8, 1773; *New York Gazette*, May 17, 1773; *Pennsylvania Chronicle*, May 17, 1773; *Pennsylvania Packet*, May 24, 1773; *Connecticut Courant*, May 25, 1773.

The customs commissioner Henry Hulton repeated the rumor before he could have read the retraction; Hulton to Nicolson, May 10, 1773, in York, *Henry Hulton and the American Revolution*, 279. The printer John Boyle, in his journal, called her "the celebrated African Poet" (Boyle Journal, May 8, 1773). In these ads Robinson hears the "muted voice" of Susanna Wheatley sticking it to the Bostonians for not being more supportive. *PWW*, 32–33.

196 *"no doubt heard of Phillis"*: *BPB*, May 3, 1773. Newspapers in Connecticut, New Hampshire, and Pennsylvania also published "Farwell to America." The *New York Journal* published her Dartmouth poem and letter as well, June 3, 1773. Others picked up the announcement of her departure. *WPW*, 168–69, 171.

196 *Wheatley composed her "farewell"*: *BEP*, May 10, 1773; *CWC*, 133–35; Watts, *Horae Lyricae*. The newspaper version of the poem is different, with less enthusiasm about return (Carretta, *Phillis Wheatley*, 136). For the poem as a "reverse

Middle Passage," see Bassard, *Spiritual Interrogations*, 47. For the suggestion that the "temptation" was freedom in England under the Mansfield decision in *Somerset v. Steuart*, see Wilcox, "Body into Print," 5; Jennifer Thorn, "Phillis Wheatley's Ghosts," 86–87; Carretta, *Phillis Wheatley*, 135–36.

15. THE METROPOLIS

198 *What she called asthma*: PW to John Thornton, April 21, 1772, to Obour Tanner, July 19, 1772, in *CWC*, 140–41, 142–43; *MMO*, 9.

199 *slave trade*: *BEP*, May 3, June 21, July 26, Aug. 9, 1773; *BG*, July 19, 1773; *BNL*, June 3, 17, July 29, Aug. 17, Sept. 23, 30, 1773; *BPB*, June 28, 1773; Samuel Eliot Morison, "The Commerce of Boston on the Eve of the Revolution," *Proceedings of the American Antiquarian Society* 31 (1923): 38; Akers, "'Our Modern Egyptians,'" 409.

199 *African slavery's evils*: "Extract of a Letter from a Gentleman in Philadelphia, to His Correspondent in Boston, the 26th Ult.," "Messrs. Edes and Gill," *BG*, July 12, Aug. 23, 1773; "Boston, Friday July 23," *MSP*, July 29, 1773; Akers, "'Our Modern Egyptians,'" 403–4; *A Forensic Dispute on the Legality of Enslaving the Africans Held at the Public Commencement in Cambridge, New-England, July 21, 1773*, in Bruns, *Am I Not a Man and a Brother*, 278–90; Bruce, *Origins of African American Literature*, 48. By the time she returned, the *Gazette* was willing to join the chorus identifying Wheatley as "the extraordinary Poetical Genius." *BG*, Sept. 20, 1773.

199 *An anonymous self-identified member*: "Messrs. Edes and Gill," *BG*, Aug. 23, 1773.

200 *meaning of the journey*: PW to Huntingdon, June 27, 1773, in *CWC*, 144; Mukhtar Ali Isani, "Wheatley's Departure to London and Her Farewell to America," *South Atlantic Bulletin* 42 (1977): 123–29; *WPW*, 45–49, 88–89, 103, 171–73, 192; Julie Flavell, *When London Was Capital of America* (New Haven, Conn., 2010). Zach Petrea speculates an antislavery connection based on the later activities of other members of the Rotch family. Joseph Rotch Jr. died in Bristol in 1773 after his late 1772 voyage. Zach Petrea, "An Untangled Web: Mapping Phillis Wheatley's Network of Support in America and Great Britain," in Shields and Lamore, *New Essays on Phillis Wheatley*, 316–17.

201 *To go to London*: Josiah Quincy Jr., London Journal, Nov. 16, 1774, in *Portrait of a Patriot: The Major Political and Legal Papers of Josiah Quincy Jr.*, ed. Daniel Coquilette and Neil Longley York (Boston, 2005), 1:228; Jerry White, *A Great and Monstrous Thing: London in the Eighteenth Century* (Cambridge, Mass., 2012), 92; Greene, *Evaluating Empire*.

202 *Africans in Britain*: Flavell, *When London Was Capital of America*, 23, 34, 48–49; Gerzina, *Black London*; Richard B. Schwartz, *Daily Life in Johnson's London*, (Madison, Wis., 1983), 39; Miles Ogborn, *Global Lives: Britain and the World, 1550–1800* (New York, 2008); Emma Rothschild, *The Inner Life of Empires* (Princeton, N.J., 2011); Susan Amussen, *Caribbean Exchanges: Slavery and the Transformation of English Society, 1640–1700* (Chapel Hill, N.C., 2007); Brown, *Moral Capital*, 285n33; Catherine Molineux, *Faces of Perfect Ebony: Encountering Atlantic Slavery in Imperial England* (Cambridge, Mass., 2013), 8–9, 273n20.

202 *At the Thorntons', Phillis met*: Susanna Wheatley to Huntingdon, April 30, 1773, in Jackson, "Letters of Phillis Wheatley and Susanna Wheatley," 214;

Carretta, *Phillis Wheatley*, 86, 97; John Lathrop to unknown, Aug. 14, 1773, Gratz American Clergy Collection, Historical Society of Pennsylvania; *WPW*, 201. Wheatley sought to deliver a letter from Richard Cary to Huntingdon that praised her behavior but hoped she would become more "evangelicall." Carretta, *Phillis Wheatley*, 96.

202 *Wheatley wrote to Huntingdon*: PW to Huntingdon, June 27 and July 17, 1773, in *CWC*, 144–45; *PWW*, 36. On July 15 she met the Reverend Thomas Gibbons, whom Occom had met in 1766. He wrote of her as "A Person of fine Genius, and very becoming Behaviour." Carretta, *Phillis Wheatley*, 96–97, 116. Gibbons's own volume of poems spoke directly to the evangelical movement, and its title, *Juvenilia: Poems on Various Subjects of Devotion and Virtue* (1750), might have provided another model. Hoxie Neale Fairchild, *Religious Trends in English Poetry*, vol. 2, *1740–1780* (New York, 1942), 105–11, 379.

203 *It was almost a fantasy*: *PWW*, 34, 318n3; PW to Obour Tanner, Oct. 30, 1772, to David Wooster, Oct. 18, 1773, in *CWC*, 146–49.

204 *a kind of grand tour*: PW to Wooster, 146–47; Carretta, *Phillis Wheatley*, 114–15; Barker-Benfield, *Phillis Wheatley Chooses Freedom*, 101–2. Odell related there having been a plan for Wheatley to be presented to George III, prevented by her return home on account of Susanna's illness. MMO, 18. One of the books Dartmouth gave to Wheatley, a copy of Cervantes's *Don Quixote*, was dated "July 1773." *Bio-bibliography*, 20.

204 *Wheatley fast collected political*: Aaron C. Seymour, *Life and Times of Selina, Countess of Huntingdon* (London, 1844), 1:461; Robert J. Taylor, "Israel Mauduit," *New England Quarterly* 24 (1951): 208–30; Kammen, *Rope of Sand*, 80–81.

204 *Franklin was the most famous American*: This London visit to Wheatley is sometimes viewed simply as an antislavery act by Franklin, presuming on his premature and exaggerated reputation as an abolitionist. The following paragraphs expand on my account in *Runaway America*, esp. 197–203, and in "Wheatleyan Moment," 538–39. See also, most recently, Kevin J. Hayes, "New Light on Peter and King, the Two Slaves Benjamin Franklin Brought to England," *Notes and Queries* 60 (2013): 205–9; and more generally, Sheila Skemp, *The Making of a Patriot: Benjamin Franklin at the Cockpit* (New York, 2013).

206 *"Upon your Recommendation I went to see"*: Franklin to Jonathan Williams Sr., July 7, 1773, and Williams to Franklin, Oct. 17, 1773, in *The Papers of Benjamin Franklin*, ed. Leonard Woods Labaree et al. (New Haven, Conn., 1959–), 20: 291–92, 445. For Nathaniel Wheatley as likely jealous, see Foster, *Written by Herself*, 43. While following my earlier account of Franklin's mixed motives in *Runaway America*, Carretta is more inclined than I to take Franklin at his word about Nathaniel's rudeness: *Phillis Wheatley*, 117. Others have suggested that Nathaniel Wheatley was nervous about losing control over Wheatley because of the *Somerset* decision. Isani, "British Reception of Wheatley's Poems on Various Subjects," 144–45.

208 *Nathaniel Wheatley*: *PWW*, 14; Carretta, *Phillis Wheatley*, 17, 108; *PPW*, 209n22; Flavell, *When London Was Capital of America*, 48–49, 127–29; PW to John Thornton, Oct. 30, 1774, in *CWC*, 158; Elizabeth Wallcut to Thomas Wallcut, Sept. 9, 1773, Wallcut Papers; Julia Penn Delacroix, "Writing with an Iron Pen: Gender and Genre in Early American Elegy" (PhD diss., University of Texas at Austin, 2013), 165n45.

209 *Granville Sharp, the abolitionist*: PW to Wooster, *CWC*, 146; Liza Picard, *Dr. Johnson's London* (New York, 2000), 250; Schwartz, *Daily Life in Johnson's London*, 55–56; Carretta, *Phillis Wheatley*, 118; Carretta, introduction to *CWC*, xxv–xxvii. This was two weeks or more later than the Franklin visit, as Sharp inscribed one of his books to her on July 21. *PPW*, 197. Sharp's pamphlet with Wheatley's signature is in the Peabody-Essex Museum Library, Rowley, Mass. She might have already owned Benezet's *Some Historical Account of Guinea*, which had a lengthy appendix that was essentially an abridgment of Sharp. Her signed copy is in Special Collections, Swem Library, College of William and Mary, where it is bound with a pamphlet by Sharp published in Philadelphia. See also Wood, *Let the Oppressed Go Free*, chap. 2

210 *"I long to see my friends"*: PW to Huntingdon, July 17, 1773, in *CWC*, 145.

210 *She could not have yet heard*: MMO, 19, insisted that she immediately "re-embarked" upon hearing by letter of Susanna's terminal illness and request that she return so that she might see her one more time. This seems unlikely given the time lag of the transatlantic mails. It might have been the plan all along for her to stay just long enough to see her book in press, or until the return voyage of the Wheatley-owned *London Packet*. The more striking and better-documented development is Nathaniel's decision not to return with her, which surprised the Wallcuts.

210 *"Ocean"*: *CWC*, 78–80; Mason, "Examples of Classical Myth in the Poems of Phillis Wheatley," 31; Laura Brown, *Fables of Modernity: Literature and Culture in the English Eighteenth Century* (Ithaca, N.Y., 2001), 53–92; Suvir Kaul, "Poetry, Politics, and Empire," in Gerrard, *Companion to Eighteenth-Century Poetry*, 28.

211 *To quote becomes a performance*: *CWC*, 78–79, 185; Julian D. Mason, "'Ocean': A New Poem by Phillis Wheatley," *Early American Literature* 34 (1999): 81. On imitation in Wheatley and contemporary culture, see Slauter, *State as a Work of Art*, 186–95; Howell, *Against Self-Reliance*.

212 *Neptune and his "vengeance"*: *Iliad of Homer, Translated by Alexander Pope*, ed. Shankman, 669, 683; "Europa," *Oxford Classical Dictionary*, 3rd ed., ed. Simon Hornblower and Anthony Spawforth (New York, 1999), 574; "Europe," in *The Classical Tradition*, ed. Anthony Pagden et al. (Cambridge, Mass., 2010), 348. The *OCD* says "made love"; Carretta says "rape" in his notes, in *CWC*, 185.

212 *Captain Robert Calef prevails*: Barnard, *Empire of Ruin*, 55–56. For "Iscarius," see *WPW*, 198; Mason, "Ocean," 82.

213 *flying too high*: *CWC*, 79–80, 168; Brown, *Fables of Modernity*, 81, 87. For flight imagery in Wheatley, see Nandin Battacharya, *Slavery, Colonialism, and Connoisseurship* (Aldershot, U.K., 2008), 139–46; Andrea Brady, *Poetry and Bondage: A History and Theory of Lyric Constraint* (Cambridge, U.K., 2021), 400–404.

16. THE EMANCIPATION

215 *might soon be freed*: *CWC*, 166; Wilcox, "Body into Print," 15. For contrasting takes on consumer politics emerging in this era, see Breen, *Marketplace of Revolution*; Lawrence Glickman, *Buying Power: A History of Consumer Activism in America* (Chicago, 2009), chap. 1.

215 *Terence*: The first lines of Suetonius's *Life of Terence*, the only source, in a con-

temporary translation identify the playwright as Publius Terentius Afer and go on to say that his master "not only bestowed on him a liberal education, but gave him his freedom in the very early part of his life." "The Life of Terence. Translated from Suetonius," in George Colman, *The Comedies of Terence, Translated into Familiar Blank Verse* (London, 1841), 28.

215 *"large emolument"*: Andrews to William Barrell, Feb. 24, 1773, MHS.

216 *self-funded emancipations*: ; Greene, *Negro in Colonial New England*, 290–96; Hardesty, *Black Lives, Native Lands, White Worlds*, 123. A good contemporary example of both the process of self-funded emancipation and its risks is Venture Smith: see *A Narrative of the Life and Adventures of Venture, a Native of Africa* (New London, Conn., 1798); see also David Waldstreicher, "The Vexed Story of Human Commodification Told by Benjamin Franklin and Venture Smith," *Journal of the Early Republic* 24 (2004): 268–78; John Wood Sweet, "Venture Smith and the Law of Slavery," in *Venture Smith and the Business of Slavery and Freedom*, ed. James Brewer Stewart (Amherst, Mass., 2010), esp. 110–17. Historians of slavery emphasize the rarity of, and barriers to, self-funded emancipation in British America compared with Spanish colonies: see Helg, *Slave No More*, 64–72.

216 *"philanthropy at bargain prices"*: Robert William Fogel and Stanley Engerman, "Philanthropy at Bargain Prices: Notes on the Economics of Gradual Emancipation," *Journal of Legal Studies* 3 (1974): 377–401; for a recent rearticulation, see George William Van Cleve, *A Slaveholder's Union* (Chicago, 2011), 71–90.

217 *"It is hoped"*: Rush, *Address*, 2–3; "London, June 1 . . . June 10," *Pennsylvania Chronicle*, Aug. 23, 1773. This report has been misdated more than once, and confused scholars because it appears with reprinted material from London newspapers dated June 1 and 10, but an original London publication has not been located. The only known notice in a newspaper in June was the June 3 appearance of Wheatley's "Farewel" in *The London Chronicle*, but the timing as well as the lack of mention of her presence in London suggests the early composition. Some have surmised an American reporting from London. It could also be a Philadelphian inserting a comment. Mukhtar Ali Isani, "The Contemporaneous Reception of Phillis Wheatley: Newspaper and Magazine Notices During the Years of Fame, 1765 to 1774," *Journal of Negro History* 85 (2000): 269.

217 *"We are much concerned"*: Isani, "Contemporaneous Reception," 260–73; *CWC*, 8; Isani, "British Reception," 144–49.

218 *antislavery in England*: For the imperial political grounding of rising antislavery, see especially Brown, *Moral Capital*.

218 *a deal that freed her*: This is Carretta's judgment in *Phillis Wheatley*, 137. In the following chapter I consider the first poem in her book, "To Maecenas," as an explicit and implicit bid for the kind of patronage that might have made it possible for her to stay in London.

219 *David Wooster*: Mukhtar Ali Isani, "Phillis Wheatley in London: An Unpublished Letter to David Wooster," *American Literature* 51 (1979): 259; Wheatley to David Wooster, Oct. 18, 1773, Hugh Upham Clark Papers, MHS; *CWC*, 147. Carretta notes the shift from passive to active voice here in *Phillis Wheatley*, 137, and *WPW*, 201–202.

220 *a copyright, a property*: For copyrighted books as property in the colonial context, I am indebted to conversations with Nora Slonimsky and her forthcoming study, *This Engine of Free Expression: Copyrighting Nation in Early America*.

220 *"who seem'd to respect me"*: PW to Thornton, Oct. 30, 1774, in *CWC*, 159; Isani, "Phillis Wheatley in London," 259–60.

17. THE PATRONS

223 *spread over an entire page*: Bio-bibliography, 21–23; *London Chronicle*, Sept. 16, 1773.

224 *Lord Lyttelton*: "Lyttelton, George, First Baron Lyttelton (1709–1773)," in *Dictionary of National Biography*; *The Poetical Works of George Lord Lyttelton* (London, 1801); *The Works of George Lord Lyttelton*, 3 vols. (London, 1776); *A Collection of Poems in Six Volumes, by Several Hands*, ed. Robert Dodsley (London, 1756), 2:1–79; *Memoirs of George, Lord Lyttelton*, ed. Robert Phillimore (London, 1845), 2:567–68; Elizabeth Carter, *Poems on Several Occasions* (London, 1762); Rose Mary Davis, *The Good Lord Lyttelton* (Bethlehem, Pa., 1939), 48, 59, 65, 209, quoted at 283; Dustin Griffin, *Literary Patronage in England, 1650–1800* (Cambridge, U.K., 1996), 25, 28, 57; Fairchild, *Religious Trends in English Poetry*, 2:198; Solomon, *Rise of Robert Dodsley*, 113; Alok Yadav, *Before the Empire of the English: Literature, Provinciality, and Nationalism in Eighteenth-Century England* (New York, 2004), 155; Harriet Guest, *Small Change: Women, Learning, and Patriotism, 1750–1810* (Chicago, 2000), 101–2; Betty A. Schellenberg, *Literary Coteries and the Making of Modern Print Culture, 1740–1790* (New York, 2016), 72–76.

226 *After the death of his neighbor*: Fairchild, *Religious Trends in English Poetry*, vol. 1, *1700–1740* (New York, 1939), 396–98, 534; John Brewer, *The Pleasures of the Imagination: English Culture in the Eighteenth Century* (New York, 1997), 158–66; Landry, *Muses of Resistance*; Solomon, *Rise of Robert Dodsley*, 12–22; Christine Gerrard, "James Thomson, *The Seasons*," and Bridget Keegan, "Rural Poetry and the Self-Taught Tradition," in Gerrard, *Companion to Eighteenth-Century Poetry*, 206, 569; Steedman, *Poetry for Historians*, 25–52; Maynard Mack, *Alexander Pope: A Life* (New York, 1985), 612, 676, 772; *The Poetical Works of William Shenstone* (Edinburgh, 1784), 1:76, 2:138; James Woodhouse, *Poems on Sundry Occasions* (London, 1764); Woodhouse, *Poems on Several Occasions* (London, 1766).

Lyttelton actually edited some of Woodhouse's poems before they appeared in his second edition: Woodhouse considered this attention "encouragement," in the tradition of collaboration that Shenstone himself had initiated with his own friends' coterie. While praising the good patron, and insisting he did not "write for hire," Woodhouse also attacked a range of injustices in his poems. By this time the cobbler had secured a post as a schoolteacher and was spending as much time exchanging letters with his new well-heeled friends as writing poems. Lyttelton also shared Woodhouse with his close friend Elizabeth Montagu, who tried to solve the patronage dilemma by placing Woodhouse as head steward on one of her estates (after which he was "no longer invited to dine at her table but had to stand at attendance"). Montagu called Woodhouse's letters "masterpieces" and respected his insistence that, despite being a servant, he would not be "servile" in their relationship, but after two stormy decades she sacked him nevertheless when she found the preface to his third volume, in 1788, to be a deliberate and nasty biting of the hand that fed him. He became a London bookseller, inherited some land in his native shire, and lived long enough to write a 28,013-line verse autobiography that mocked the whole literary patronage system, including the learned critics who had insisted that one couldn't write English verse without an education in Latin. Morris R. Brownell, "The Iconography of Pope's Villa: Images of Poetic Fame," in *Alexander Pope: Tercentenary Essays*, ed. G. S. Rousseau and Pat Rogers (Cambridge, U.K., 1998), 133–36; Betty Rizzo, "The Patron as Poet Maker: The Politics of Benefaction," *Studies in Eighteenth-Century Culture* 20 (1991): 241–66; Steve Van-Hagen, "The Life, Works, and Reception of an Evangelical Radical: James Woodhouse (1735–1820), the 'Poetical Shoemaker,'" *Literature Compass* 6, no. 2 (2009): 384–406; Adam J. Bridgen, "Patronage, Punch-Ups, and Polite Correspondence: The Radical Background of James Woodhouse's Early Poetry," *Huntington Library Quarterly* 80 (2017): 99–134; Edith Hall and Henry Stead, *A People's History of Classics: Class and Greco-Roman Antiquity in Britain and Ireland, 1689 to 1939* (London, 2020), 420, 423; Griffin, *Literary Patronage*, quoted at 43; Schellenberg, *Literary Coteries*, 101–8.

227 *lasting "preferment"*: "An Elegy on the Death of Lord Lyttelton," *Gentleman's Magazine*, (Sept. 1773), 455; Staves, *Literary History of Women's Writing in Britain*, 258–62; Clarke, *Brothers of the Quill*; Lawrence Lipking, *Samuel Johnson: The Life of an Author* (Cambridge, Mass., 1998), 65, 90–102; David Spadafora, *The Idea of Progress in Eighteenth-Century Britain* (New Haven, Conn., 1990), 63–66.

228 *Lyttelton's appeal to Pope*: "The Progress of Love. In Four Eclogues," in Dodsley, *Collection of Poems in Six Volumes*, 2:1–2; *Poetical Works of George Lord Lyttelton*, 6–7.

229 *demonstrate genius*: Keith D. Leonard, *Fettered Genius: The African American Bardic Poet from Slavery to Civil Rights* (Charlottesville, Va., 2006), 30–31; Howell, *Against Self-Reliance*, 59–60; Griffin, *Literary Patronage in England*, 34–35.

For "To Maecenas" imitating the opening of Horace's *Odes* 1, see Cook and Tatum, *African American Writers and the Classical Tradition*, 8. As Carretta notes, the Creech translation of Horace's Ode 1.1 has Maecenas "underneath a myrtle shade," and probably for that reason a 1748 biography of Maecenas has him composing poems in the shade (*WPW*, 183). Myrtle applied to blameless battle victors but also sometimes to poets. Julia Blakely, "Myrtle: The Provenance and Meaning of a Plant," *Unbound*, June 28, 2018, blog.library.si.edu /blog/2018/06/28/myrtle-the-provenance-and-meaning-of-a-plant/.

The Wheatley editors Julian D. Mason Jr., John C. Shields, and Carretta have proposed Byles, Susanna Wheatley, and Huntingdon as possible addressees of the poem, but for Maecenas as a collective of mentors, and an ideal reader, see especially Cynthia J. Smith, "'To Maecenas': Phillis Wheatley's Invocation of an Idealized Reader," *Black American Literature Forum* 23 (1989): 579–92; Emily Greenwood, "The Politics of Classicism in the Poetry of Phillis Wheatley," in *Ancient Slavery and Abolition: From Hobbes to Hollywood*, ed. Edith Hall, Richard Alston, and Justine McConnell (New York, 2011), 168–73; Lopez, *Colorful Conservative*, chap. 3; Hairston, *Ebony Column*, 48, 62; Mary Louise Kete, "Phillis Wheatley and the Political Work of Ekphrasis," in *The Call of Classical Literature in the Romantic Age*, ed. K. P. Van Anglen and James Engell (Edinburgh, 2017), 53–79.

229 *Alexander Pope*: Howard D. Weinbrot, *Augustus Caesar in Augustan England* (Princeton, N.J., 1978), 120–49; Joseph Levine, *The Battle of the Books: History and Literature in the Augustan Age* (Ithaca, N.Y., 1994), chaps. 6–7; Dustin Grif-

fin, "The Social World of Authorship, 1660–1714," in Richetti, *The Cambridge History of English Literature, 1660–1780*, 58; Woodhouse, "From *The Life and Lucubrations of Crispinus Scriblerus*," in *The New Oxford Book of Eighteenth-Century Poetry*, ed. Roger Lonsdale (Oxford, 1987), 800–802; *The Poems of Alexander Pope*, ed. John Burtt (New Haven, Conn., 1966), 625, 632; Solomon, *Rise of Robert Dodsley*, 71–72; Richardson, *Slavery and Augustan Literature*.

229 *Horace became the most translated*: Francis, *Poetical Translation of the Works of Horace*, 1:4–5; D. S. Carne-Ross and Kenneth Haynes, introduction to *Horace in English* (London, 1996), 23; Donald Money, "The Reception of Horace in the Seventeenth and Eighteenth Centuries," in *The Cambridge Companion to Horace*, ed. Stephen Harrison (New York, 2007), 318–21; Philip Ayres, *Classical Culture and the Idea of Rome in Eighteenth-Century England* (New York, 1987), 31–32; Peter Levi, *Horace: A Life* (New York, 1998); Paul Veyne, *Bread and Circuses*, trans. Brian Pearce (New York, 1992); Phebe Lowell Bowditch, *Horace and the Gift Economy of Patronage* (Berkeley, Calif., 2001); Myles Lavan, *Slaves to Rome: Paradigms of Empire in Roman Culture* (Cambridge, U.K., 2013); Mary Beard, *SPQR: A History of Ancient Rome* (New York, 2015), 144, 330; Henrik Mouritsen, *The Freedman in the Roman World* (Cambridge, U.K., 2011).

230 *"Race of Slaves"*: Francis, *Poetical Translation of the Works of Horace*, 1:138–39, 144–45, 3:61, 69, 83, 4:91. I have compared Francis and Christopher Smart's eighteenth-century translations with the renderings in *Horace: Satires and Epistles and Persius*, trans. Rudd; *Complete Odes and Epodes*, trans. West; *The Odes and Epodes of Horace*, trans. Joseph P. Clancy (Chicago, 1960); *The Satires and Epistles of Horace*, trans. Smith Palmer Bovie (Chicago, 1959); *Horace: The Complete Odes and Epodes*, trans. W. G. Shepard (New York, 1983); *The Satires of Horace*, trans. William Matthews (Keene, N.Y., 2002); Smart, *Works of Horace Translated Literally into English Prose*; *Christopher Smart's Verse Translation of Horace's Odes*, ed. Arthur Sherbro (Victoria, Can., 1979).

231 *clearly a master*: Francis, *Poetical Translation*, 4:151; Stephen Harrison, "Horatian Self-Representations," in Harrison, *Cambridge Companion to Horace*, 30; Stephanie McCarter, *Horace Between Slavery and Freedom: The First Book of Epistles* (Madison, Wis., 2015). Horace is also extraordinarily self-conscious about writing itself—so much so that he is hailed as the first writer who made writing a central theme. Late in his career he invented the new form of the verse epistle, or poems in the forms of letters, to work through the problem of writing poems as gifts to friends who were actually powerful patrons. On Horatian self-consciousness about writing, and its influence in the eighteenth century, see Deutsch, *Resemblance and Disgrace*, 140–41; Doody, *Daring Muse*, 93; Hess, *Authoring the Self*, 16.

231 *language of feeling*: Waldstreicher, *In the Midst of Perpetual Fetes*, 67–85; Andrew Burstein, *Sentimental Democracy* (New York, 1999); Sarah Knott, *Sensibility and the American Revolution* (Chapel Hill, N.C., 2009); Nicole Eustace, *Passion Is the Gale: Emotion, Power, and the Coming of the American Revolution* (Chapel Hill, N.C., 2008).

231 *the ancients versus the moderns*: Manguel, Homer's *"The Iliad" and "The Odyssey,"* 128–29; Larry F. Norman, *The Shock of the Ancient: Literature and History in Early Modern France* (Chicago, 2011); Alexandra Lieneri, "The Homeric Moment? Translation, Historicity, and the Meaning of the Classics," in *Classics and the Uses of Reception*, ed. Charles Martindale and Richard F. Thomas (Malden, Mass., 2006), 141–52.

232 The Odyssey *is for everybody*: CWC, 9–10; Daniel Mendelsohn, *An Odyssey: A Father, a Son, and an Epic* (New York, 2017), 106, 121; François Hartog, *Regimes of Historicity*, trans. Saskia Brown (New York, 2015), 41–63; Andrew Dalby, *Rediscovering Homer: Inside the Origins of the Epic* (New York, 2006), 121, 127–28; Peter Levi, *Virgil: His Life and Times* (New York, 1998), 125; Pope, *The Odyssey of Homer, Books XIII–XXIV*, 105–6n70.

232 *Moving on to the great Roman poet*: Byles, *Poems on Several Occasions*, 25–34; Harold Bloom, *The Anxiety of Influence* (New York, 1975). Slaves were usually if not always depicted as lacking in or not displaying emotion, a trend that took on greater meaning as the positive associations of sensibility became central in Anglo-American culture and that contributed to antislavery writers' emphasis on the feelings. Eustace, *Passion Is the Gale*, 70–73, 102, 253–54; Jay Fliegelman, *Declaring Independence* (Stanford, Calif., 1993), 192–94.

233 *"The happier* Terence": Terence, *Comedies*, 101, 308, 316; "The Life of Terence," in Colman, *Comedies of Terence*, 28–36; Erkkila, *Mixed Bloods and Other Crosses*, 87; Smith, "'To Maecenas'"; Lopez, *Colorful Conservative*, 114–17; Hairston, *Ebony Column*, 46–47; Bennett, "Phillis Wheatley's Vocation"; Kathleen McCarthy, *Slaves, Masters, and the Art of Authority in Plautine Comedy* (Princeton, N.J., 2000).

234 *Instead of Wheatley herself being "snatched"*: Bassard, *Spiritual Interrogations*, 62–63; Byles, *Poems on Several Occasions*, 25; Franke, "Phillis Wheatley, Melancholy Muse," 241; Griffin, *Literary Patronage in England*, 205–6; Claudia N. Thomas, *Alexander Pope and His Eighteenth-Century Women Readers* (Carbondale, Ill., 1994), 6–16. Charlotte Lennox had also been given a crown of laurel at a dinner hosted by Samuel Johnson. See also Horace's Ode 3: 30 in Francis's translation, anticipating "With conscious pride, O Muse divine,/ Assume the Honours justly thine/ With Laurel Wreaths my Head surround, / Such as the God of verse have crown'd." *Poetical Translation*, 2:123.

18. THE BOOK

236 *"sable monster"*: CWC, 11–12, 105–6.

237 *Wheatley does her utmost*: CWC, 15–19, 113–19, 165–66; PWW, 185, 187. For the impact of revisions and the choices of poems, see PWW, 30; Grimsted, "Anglo-American Racism and Phillis Wheatley's 'Sable Veil,'" 338–444; Wilcox, "Body into Print," 19–24. Wilcox sees a loss of specificity and political potency in these revisions; for a different view, by which classicism "amplified" Wheatley's positions, see Hairston, *Ebony Column*, 31–33. For the Christian and classical counterpointing as enabling criticism of slavery that one or the other alone would not have, building on my earlier treatment, see especially Roberts, *Awakening Verse*, 126–69.

238 *"trace him in the night's repose"*: CWC, 26–29; Grimsted, "Anglo-American Racism and Phillis Wheatley's 'Sable Veil,'" 367–70; Katy L. Chiles, "Becoming Colored in Wheatley and Occom's Early America," PMLA 123, no. 5 (2008): 1409–10.

239 *"praise of him who gives"*: CWC, 26–34.

240 *"iron bands"*: CWC, 34–39; Hairston, *Ebony Column*, 83–84. On the "subdued and indirect" invocation of slavery, see Carretta, *Phillis Wheatley*, 105–6; Reising, *Loose Ends*, 97–99; Eric D. Lamore, "Phillis Wheatley's Use of the Georgic," in Shields and Lamore, *New Essays on Phillis Wheatley*, 131–36.

240 *"Isaiah"*: CWC, 33–34; Scheick, *Authority and Female Authorship*, 114–17; Wigginton, *In the Neighborhood*, 101–2. For Isaiah and antislavery, see especially Wood, *Let the Oppressed Go Free*, chaps. 1–5.

240 *"Captain H——D"*: CWC, 39, 76, 178; John Mack Faragher, *A Great and Noble Scheme: The Tragic Story of the French Acadians and Their Expulsion from Their American Homeland* (New York, 2005), 346–68, 391–92; William G. Godfrey, "John Handfield," *Dictionary of Canadian Biography, Vol. III (1741–1770)*, www .biographi.ca/en/bio/handfield_john_3E.html; A. Yvon Handfield, "The Handfield Family," www.handfield.ca/homeaccueil.htm. Neither Handfield appears in any of the standard histories of the Boston Massacre or the occupation.

242 *"love of* Freedom": Ellison, *Cato's Tears*, 120; CWC, 39–40, 128–31; Coviello, "Agonizing Affection," 443.

242 *"Eumaeus tending his herds"*: Pope, *Odyssey of Homer, Books XIII–XXIV*, 15, 32n, 40, 89, 95, 158, 189, 213n, 255, 270; Emily Wilson, introduction to *The Odyssey*, trans. Emily Wilson (New York, 2018), 19, 54–57; Jean Andreau and Raymond Descat, *The Slave in Greece and Rome*, trans. Marian Leopold (Madison, Wis., 2011), 20–21.

243 *Four other new poems*: CWC, 50–52, 195–97; MSS 296, Phillis Wheatley Collection, box 2, Rose Library; Roberts, *Awakening Verse*, 155–56.

244 *"Niobe in Distress"*: CWC, 53–59; WPW, 193–94; PWW, 99; Samuel Garth et al., *Ovid's Metamorphosis in Fifteen Books* (New York, 1961), 173–79; *Iliad of Homer, Translated by Alexander Pope*, ed. Shankman, 1123; *Ovid's Metamorphoses*, trans. A. S. Melville (New York, 1986), 125–30; Thorn, "Gender, Nation, and Phillis Wheatley's 'Niobe'"; Walsh, *The Portrait and the Book*, 82–88; Slauter, *State as a Work of Art*, 198–202; Levecq, *Slavery and Sentiment*, 66–67; Joseph Fichtelberg, *Risk Culture: Performance and Danger in Early America* (Ann Arbor, Mich., 2010), 95–96, 101–3; Lucy K. Hayden, "Classical Tidings from the Afric Muse: Phillis Wheatley's Use of Greek and Roman Mythology," *College Language Association Journal* 35 (1992): 432–47; Karen Lerner Dovell, "The Interaction of Classical Traditions of Literature and Politics in the Work of Phillis Wheatley," in Shields and Lamore, *New Essays on Phillis Wheatley*, 44–45; Barnard, *Empire of Ruin*, 50; Hairston, *Ebony Column*, 58–60; Langley, *Black Aesthetic Unbound*, 71; Walters, *African American Women and the Classicist Tradition*, 28, 41–46.

244 *"To S. M. a young African Painter"*: CWC, 59–60; WPW, 195; Walsh, *The Portrait and the Book*, 91–92; Ivy G. Wilson, "The Writing on the Wall: Revolutionary Aesthetics and Interior Spaces," in *American Literature's Aesthetic Dimensions*, ed. Cindy Weinstein and Christopher Looby (New York, 2012), 59–61.

245 *James Bowdoin II*: CWC, 62–65; Mason, *Poems of Phillis Wheatley*, 110–11; Nancy Glazener, *Literature in the Making: A History of U.S. Literary Culture in the Long Nineteenth Century* (New York, 2016), 235; Stout, *Royal Navy in America*, 194n6; Thomas N. Ingersoll, *The Loyalist Problem in Revolutionary New England* (New York, 2015), 164; Frank E. Manuel and Fritzie P. Manuel, *James Bowdoin and the Patriot Philosophers* (Philadelphia, 2004), 44–45, 58–59, 86.

19. THE READERS

247 *Eleven newspapers in the colonies*: Isani, "Contemporary Reception," 263; Grimsted, "Anglo-American Racism and Phillis Wheatley's 'Sable Veil,'" 438;

Bio-bibliography, 21–25; *MSP*, Sept. 16, 1773; *BPB*, Sept. 20, 1773; *BNL*, Sept. 16, 1773; *BG*, Sept. 20, 1773; *BEP*, Sept. 20, 1773; Jack Campisi and William A. Starna, eds., *A Quaker's Tour of the Colonial Northeast and Canada: The 1773 Travel Journals of Jabez Maud Fisher of Philadelphia* (Philadelphia, 2014), 65. A few years later, Fisher's father would play his part in Wheatley's expanding fame by sending a copy of her book to Ignatius Sancho, a former slave and butler to the Duke of Montagu who was friends with Laurence Sterne and whose letters appeared in print posthumously in London in 1782. Ignatius Sancho, *Letters of the Late Ignatius Sancho, an African*, ed. Vincent Carretta (New York, 1998), 111–12.

248 *The most recent British monthlies*: *Gentleman's Magazine*, Sept. 1773, 456, *Critical Review* 36 (Sept. 1773): 232–33, and *Monthly Review* 49 (Dec. 1773), 457–59, in Isani, "British Reception," 145–48; Richard Nisbet, *Slavery Not Forbidden by Scripture* (Philadelphia, 1773), 23n, in Robinson, *Critical Essays on Phillis Wheatley*, 32; Grimsted, "Anglo-American Racism and Phillis Wheatley's 'Sable Veil,'" 405, 412–13; Henry Louis Gates, "Phillis Wheatley and the Nature of the Negro," in *Figures in Black* (New York, 1987), 61–72.

248 *Bernard Romans, a surveyor*: Romans's remarks on Wheatley in what might seem to be an unrelated project, his *Concise Natural History of East and West Florida*, which was in press in early 1774, responded not only to Benjamin Rush (who had been criticized by the West Indian Richard Nisbet for citing Wheatley's genius as an antislavery argument) but also to the initially and mostly positive reviews in the British magazines that stressed the learning as well as the inspiration behind Wheatley's book. Bernard Romans, "To the Editor of the Royal American Magazine," *Royal American Magazine*, Jan. 1774, 32–34; Bernard Romans, *A Concise Natural History of East and West Florida* (New York, 1775), 1:105. In a February 1774 advertisement for the *Natural History* as a two-volume work in progress, Romans wrote that "about 159 pages are already printed," which would have included the Wheatley reference on page 105. *BNL*, Feb. 10, 1774.

248 *The reviewer John Langhorne*: Slauter identifies Langhorne based on the index to the volume in *The State as a Work of Art*, 183, 336–37n32. For imitation as positive aesthetic value in this period, with particular reference to Wheatley, see also 186–95; Howell, *Against Self-Reliance*, 46–81. John C. Shields championed Wheatley's neoclassicism and blasted the less than informed criticism of her work but also found her, in the end, to be a proto-Romantic avatar of imagination. Shields, *Phillis Wheatley's Poetics of Liberation*; Shields, *Phillis Wheatley and the Romantics*.

249 *Mercy Otis Warren*: Warren to Sarah Walter Hesilrige, Dec. 1773 or March 1774, in *Mercy Otis Warren: Selected Letters*, ed. Jeffrey H. Richards and Sharon M. Harris (Athens, Ga., 2009), 21–23; Nancy Rubin Stuart, *The Muse of the Revolution: The Secret Pen of Mercy Otis Warren and the Founding of a Nation* (Boston, 2008), 48–49, 55–58, 68–69.

250 *"Four Lines in Latin Verse"*: *BNL*, Feb. 24, 1774. Thanks to my colleague Joel Allen for the translation from the Latin.

251 *There were many readers*: Marshall Brown, "The Poet as Genius," in *The Oxford Handbook of British Poetry, 1660–1800*, ed. Jack Lynch (New York, 2016), 210–26; Chaplin, "Problem of Genius in the Age of Slavery"; Mary Scott, *The Female Advocate* (London, 1774), vii, 26–27; William Shenstone, "From Elegy XX," in *Amazing Grace: An Anthology of Poems About Slavery, 1660–1810*, ed. James G.

Basker (New Haven, Conn., 2002), 92–94; Mukhtar Ali Isani, "A Contemporary British Poem on Phillis Wheatley," *Black American Literature Forum* 24 (1990): 565–66; Ferguson, *Eighteenth-Century Women Poets*, 40; Petrea, "Untangled Web," 324–28; Carretta, *Phillis Wheatley*, 167. The 1773 Burlington, New Jersey, edition of Granville Sharp's pamphlet included Shenstone's poem: *An Essay on Slavery*, 26–28.

251 *diary of Philip Vickers Fithian: Journal and Letters of Philip Vickers Fithian: A Plantation Tutor of the Old Dominion, 1773–1774*, ed. Hunter Dickinson Farish (Charlottesville, Va., 1957), 72–73; Andrew Levy, *The First Emancipator: The Forgotten Story of Robert Carter, the Founding Father Who Freed His Slaves* (New York, 2005), 60–61, 64; John Fea, *The Way of Improvement Leads Home: Philip Vickers Fithian and the Rural Enlightenment in Early America* (Philadelphia, 2008).

252 *Meanwhile, Phillis found herself*: PW to Tanner, Oct. 30, 1773, in *CWC*, 148; Elizabeth Wallcut to Thomas Wallcut, Sept. 9, Dec. 15, 1773, Christopher Wallcut to Thomas Wallcut, March 8, 1774, Wallcut Papers. Nathaniel named a first daughter after Susanna (Oct. 31, 1774), but Mary named her subsequent daughters Jane and Mary.

252 *Phillis had a new job*: PW to David Wooster, Oct. 18, 1773, Hugh Upham Clark Papers, MHS; PW to Tanner, Oct. 30, 1773, to John Thornton, Dec. 1, 1773, in *CWC*, 149, 150; *Proceedings of the Massachusetts Historical Society* 7 (1863–64): 276n1. For a somewhat different but suggestive reading of these letters, see Joseph Rezek, "The Racialization of Print," *American Literary History* 32 (2020): 432.

　　The letter to Wooster was "favour'd by Mr. Babcock's servant." The Babcocks were a merchant family with members in Boston and Rhode Island as well as New Haven; Primus Babcock later served in the First Rhode Island Regiment during the war. Judith Van Buskirk, *Standing in Their Own Light: African American Patriots in the American Revolution* (Norman, Okla., 2017), 104.

253 *She wrote similar letters*: PW to Wooster, Oct. 18, 1773, to Tanner, Oct. 20, 1773, March 21, May 6, 1774, to Hopkins, Feb. 9, May 6, 1774, in *CWC*, 149, 151, 154, 156–58; *CG*, June 17, 1774.

254 *delayed the landing of the* Dartmouth: See the suggestions about the timing of the ship's arrival and unloading by J. L. Bell and Benjamin L. Carp quoted in Richard Kigel, *Heavenly Tidings from the Afric Muse: The Grace and Genius of Phillis Wheatley* (St. Paul, 2017), 260–63, 271–72; Warden, *Boston, 1689–1776*, 279–82; Deming, *Boston and the Dawn of American Independence*, 227–30; Benjamin L. Carp, *Defiance of the Patriots: The Boston Tea Party and the Making of America* (New Haven, Conn., 2010), 108.

254 *Wheatley penned an especially lengthy elegy*: Rowe, *Diary*, Aug. 22, Dec. 6, 1773; *BG*, Dec. 6, 1773; *BNL*, Dec. 9, 1773; *WPW*, 114–16, 156, 202–3 The broadside is "Printed from the Original Manuscript, and sold by William M'Alpine." PW, *An ELEGY, To Miss Mary Moorhead, on the DEATH of her Father, the Rev. Mr. JOHN MOORHEAD* (Boston, 1773).

254 *The obituaries and the funeral sermon*: David MacGregor, *An Israelite Indeed: A Sermon, Occasioned by the Death of Rev. Mr. John Moorhead* (Boston, 1774), 7, 27; PW to John Thornton, March 29, 1774, in *CWC*, 155–56; Occom to Eleazar Wheelock, Jan. 27 and June 1, 1773, to Samuel Buell, 1773, to John Moorhead, April 10, 1773, in Brooks, *Collected Writings of Samson Occom*, 7, 23, 102–106; Love, *Samson Occom and the Christian Indians of New England*, 169–78; Blodgett, *Samson Occom*, 121; Silverman, *Red Brethren*, 88–90.

255 *"A Son of AFRICA"*: Brooks, *Collected Writings of Samson Occom*, 59; *CG*, May 1, 1772 (with thanks to Andrew Lang for discovering the "O." letter, in the same issue, which I agree is probably by Occom); "A Son of AFRICA," *MSP*, Feb. 10, 1774.

257 *sin of slavery*: *CG*, March 11, 1774, also as PW to Occom, Feb. 11, 1774, in *CWC*, 152–53; Christopher Hill, *The English Bible and the Seventeenth-Century Revolution* (New York, 1994), 113; Coffey, *Exodus and Liberation*, 55, 97.

258 *divine chastisement*: Gipson, *British Empire Before the American Revolution*, 12:115; Jensen, *Founding of a Nation*, 431–33; Somos, *American States of Nature*, 217–73; Moore, *Notes on the History of Negro Slavery in Massachusetts*, 136–37; Cameron, *To Plead Our Own Cause*, 61–62; Sesay, "Black Revolutionary Roots of Slavery's Abolition in Massachusetts," 117–18; Bruce, *Origins of African American Literature*, 54–55; Wood, *Let the Oppressed Go Free*, chap. 2.

258 *If New England patriots were comparing*: Warren to Arthur Lee, Dec. 21, 1773, in Maier, *From Resistance to Revolution*, 228; Coffey, *Exodus and Liberation*, 87 (Benezet quoted), 95–101; Day in Brycchan Carey, "A Stronger Muse: Classical Influences in Eighteenth-Century Abolitionist Poetry," in Hall, Alston, and McConnell, *Ancient Slavery and Abolition*, 131–32; Brown, *Moral Capital*; Wood, *Let the Oppressed Go Free*, chap. 3; *Royal American Magazine*, Jan. 1774.

258 *"A Christian"*: "The Preacher," "A Christian," *MSP*, March 3, May 19, 1774. Erkkila, "Phillis Wheatley on the Streets of Revolutionary Boston," 364–65, argues that Wheatley's use of "our" with "modern Egyptians," in response to Occom, signals common cause with natives.

259 *The report of her death*: *MSP*, March 10, 24, 1774; *CG*, March 11, 18, 1774; *PWW*, 204.

260 *published anonymously*: See my "Anonymous Wheatley." The complete texts of the thirteen unsigned poems I am tentatively attributing to Wheatley appear in the appendix; see also Table 2 for a comparison of the appearance of particular words in her attributed poems and in these poems, and Table 1 for the compared publication history of her extant and heretofore attributed poems.

260 *"after so long a time"*: Andrews to William Barrell, Jan. 18, 1774, Andrews-Eliot Papers.

261 *"magazines offered [to poets]"*: Jennifer Batt, "Poems in Magazines," in Lynch, *Oxford Handbook of British Poetry, 1660–1800*, 63.

261 *By sending new poems*: New ads for Wheatley's book appeared, probably after a new shipment arrived. *Rivington's New York Gazetteer*, April 14, 1774; *CG*, June 17, July 15, 1774; *Pennsylvania Journal*, June 22, 29, July 27, Aug. 17, 1774; *BPB*, June 27, 1774.

262 *"impersonal authority"*: Peter Levi, "Anon.," in *The Art of Poetry* (New Haven, Conn., 1991), 106; John Mullan, *Anonymity: A Secret History of English Literature* (Princeton, N.J., 2007), 20, 57, 75; Robert J. Griffin, introduction to *Faces of Anonymity*, ed. Robert J. Griffin (New York, 2003), 4, 15; Mark Vareschi, *Everywhere and Nowhere: Anonymity and Mediation in Eighteenth-Century Britain* (Minneapolis, 2018).

262 *"Betsey" Inches*: "On the Death of Miss Inches, by a Friend," *BPB*, Dec. 13, 1773.

263 *Poet's Corner*: "For the Essex Journal, &c.," *Essex Journal*, Jan. 12, 1774; "Poet's Corner. From the Essex Journal, &c.," *MSP*, Jan. 20, 1774. This could be the poem "Thoughts on the Times" that was to be the first in the volume proposed in 1779. *CWC*, 167.

263 *"The Triumph of the Redeemer"*: "The Triumph of the Redeemer," *BPB*, Jan. 24, 1774; PW to Tanner, Oct. 20, 1773, to Thornton, Dec. 1, 1773, to Tanner, March 21, May 6, 1774, to Thornton, March 29, 1774, in *CWC*, 148, 149–50, 153–57.

264 *Susanna's illness and death*: PW to Thornton, Dec. 1, 1773, March 29, 1774, to Tanner, March 21, 1774, to Samuel Hopkins, Feb. 9, 1774, in *CWC*, 150, 151, 154, 155; Christopher Wallcut to Thomas Wallcut, March 8, 1774, Wallcut Papers.

265 *degree of control*: *PWW*, 45; MMO, 19.

267 *"chiefs of bloody battles"*: "Night. A Poem," *Royal American Magazine*, April 1774, 154; PW to Tanner, March 21, May 9, 1774, in *CWC*, 153, 156–57.

267 *"fair Aurora reassumes her sphere"*: "On Night," *Royal American Magazine*, June 1774, 231–32; PW to Tanner, March 21, May 9, 1774, in *CWC*, 153, 156–57.

20. THE BARBARIANS

268 *Phillis wrote as soon as she could*: PW to Tanner, to Hopkins, May 6, 1774, in *CWC*, 157; *WPW*, xvii, 205; "This Day Is Published," *BPB*, June 27, 1774; *CG*, June 17, July 15, 29, Aug. 5, 1774.

269 *power struggle in the empire*: MSP, Feb. 10, 17, March 3, 1774; "A Christian," *Royal American Magazine*, Jan. 1774, 97; Petition for Freedom, May 25, 1774, Jeremy Belknap Papers, MHS, www.masshist.org/database/viewer.php?item_id=550&pid=4&ft=%20End%20of%20Slavery; Moore, *Notes on the History of Negro Slavery in Massachusetts*, 136–44; Cameron, *To Plead Our Own Cause*, 61; Sesay "Revolutionary Black Roots of Slavery's Abolition," 117–19; Wood, *Let the Oppressed Go Free*, chap. 3.

269 *John Mein resurfaced as "Sagittarius"*: John Mein, *Sagittarius's Letters and Political Speculations Extracted from the Public Ledger* (Boston, 1775), 1, 7–8, 12, 15, 21, 38–39, 44.

269 *Coercive Acts*: Andrews to William Barrell, May 18, 1774, in "Letters of John Andrews Esq. of Boston, 1772–1776," 327; Boyle Journal, May 13, 15, 28, 1774; David Ammerman, *In the Common Cause: American Response to the Coercive Acts of 1774* (New York, 1975), 5–10; Warden, *Boston, 1689–1776*, 288–96; Deming, *Boston and the Dawn of American Independence*, 251–75; Gipson, *British Empire Before the American Revolution*, 12:127; PW to John Thornton, Oct. 30, 1774, in *CWC*, 158.

270 *The blockade of Boston*: Mary Beth Norton, *1774* (New York, 2019), 78, 85; Ingersoll, *Loyalist Problem in Revolutionary New England*, 136; Neil R. Stout, *The Perfect Crisis: The Beginnings of the Revolutionary War* (New York, 1976), 81–84.

271 *sailed for London*: Andrews to William Barrell, Aug. 16, 18, 1774, in "Letters of John Andrews," *Proceedings of the Massachusetts Historical Society* 8 (1865), 342; *Salem Gazette*, July 15, Sept. 16, 1774; John Allen, *The Watchman's Alarm to Lord N——h; or, The British Parliamentary Boston Port-Bill Unwrapped* (Salem, Mass., 1774), 25–29; John M. Bumstead and Charles E. Clark, "New England's Tom Paine: John Allen and the Spirit of Liberty," *William and Mary Quarterly* 21 (1964): 561–70; Norton, *1774*, 159, 400; William Allen, *The American Crisis: A Letter, Addressed by Permission to the Earl Gower, Lord President of the Council, on the Present Alarming Disturbances in the Colonies* (London, 1774), 13–14.

272 *Abigail Adams*: Stout, *Perfect Crisis*, 98; Woody Holton, *Abigail Adams* (New York, 2009), 70; Abigail Adams to John Adams, Sept. 22, 1774, in *Adams Family*

Correspondence, ed L. H. Butterfield (New York, 1965), 1:161–62; see also the transcription available at the website of the MHS. The editors of the published Adams Papers wrote in 1965 that "everything about this rumored 'conspiracy of the Negroes' was kept so 'private' that the editors cannot fully elucidate it" (162n3), but they seem not to have perceived the connection to the actual petitions presented to General Gage. Edward Countryman, *Enjoy the Same Liberty: Black Americans and the Revolutionary Era* (Lanham, Md., 2012), 43.

273 *Phillis told John Thornton*: PW to Thornton, Oct. 20, 1774; MMO, 18, 19.

273 *Deborah Cushing enthusiastically sent*: Robinson, *Phillis Wheatley and the Origins of African American Literature*, 21; PW to Thornton, Oct. 20, 1774, in *Complete Writings*, 159; Deborah Cushing to Thomas Cushing, Sept. 19, 1774, box 2, Cushing Family Papers, MHS; Richard S. Newman, "The Black Book: Phillis Wheatley and the Information Revolution," *OUPblog*, Feb. 2014, www.blog .oup.com/2014/02/phillis-wheatley-african-american-writing-information -revolution. John Avery Jr., son of the John Avery who held the slaves from the ship *Phillis* when they were sold in 1761, was the Cushings' son-in-law.

274 *The Beauties of the English Stage*: Wallcut to PW, Nov. 17, 1774, Wallcut Papers; *The Beauties of the English Stage*, 3 vols. (London, 1756); Cynthia Wall, "Poems on the Stage," in Lynch, *Oxford Handbook of British Poetry, 1660–1800*, 23–39. The inscription "The gift Revd Mr. J. Lathrop to Phillis Wheatley Aug. 1, 1774" is in Wheatley's hand. Fliegelman Library of American Association Copies, Stanford University Library, www.librarything.com/catalog/PhillisWheatley/ yourlibrary.

274 *Samuel Hopkins had a different idea*: Joseph Conforti, *Samuel Hopkins and the New Divinity Movement* (Grand Rapids, 1982), 126–46; Grimsted, "Anglo-American Racism and Phillis Wheatley's 'Sable Veil,'" 377–83; Andrews, *Native Apostles*, 204–6; Vincent Carretta and Ty M. Reese, eds., *The Life and Letters of Philip Quaque, the First African Anglican Missionary* (Athens, Ga., 2010); Barker-Benfield, *Phillis Wheatley Chooses Freedom*, 5–36; Michael Monescalchi, "Phillis Wheatley, Samuel Hopkins, and the Rise of Disinterested Benevolence," *Early American Literature* 54 (2019): 413–44.

276 *"Please give my love"*: PW to Samuel Hopkins, Feb. 9, 1774, in *CWC*, 150–51; *PWW*, 43–44; Barker-Benfield, *Phillis Wheatley Chooses Freedom*, 34–36, 132.

276 *He wrote her back*: PW to Hopkins, May 6, 1774, to John Thornton, Oct. 30, 1774; Barker-Benfield, *Phillis Wheatley Chooses Freedom*, 139.

278 *her "country"*: For Wheatley as among the pioneers in developing an African identity in America that was not necessarily exclusive of other national identities, see Waldstreicher, *In the Midst of Perpetual Fetes*, 308–48; James Sidbury, *Becoming African in America: Race and Nation in the Early Black Atlantic* (New York, 2007); Daniel R. Mandell, "'A Natural and Unalienable Right': New England Revolutionary Petitions and African American Identity," in *Remembering the Revolution*, ed. Michael A. McDonnell et al. (Amherst, Mass., 2013), 41–57.

278 *"generous Offer"*: PW to Thornton, Oct. 30, 1774, to Tanner, Feb. 14, 1776, in *WPW*, 131. The most developed treatment of this episode is Barker-Benfield, *Phillis Wheatley Chooses Freedom*, 132–43.

278 *who were the barbarians*: On "barbarism," see J. G. A. Pocock, *Barbarism and Religion*, vol. 3, *The First Decline and Fall* (New York, 2003), and vol. 4, *Barbarians, Savages, and Empires* (New York, 2005); Bruce, *Origins of African American Literature*, 59–61; Gould, *Barbaric Traffic*; Greene, *Evaluating Empire*, 52–64;

Stefan Wheelock, *Barbaric Culture and Black Critique: Black Antislavery Writers, Religion, and the Slaveholding Atlantic* (Charlottesville, Va., 2016); Holger Hoock, *Scars of Independence: America's Violent Birth* (New York, 2017), 76–77, 88, 90; and Peter Silver, *Our Savage Neighbors: How Indian War Transformed Early America* (New York, 2008), 227–60. Silver provides a deep analysis of anti-Indian and related anti-British rhetoric during this period, but states that "the first sign that barbarism would become an issue in the revolutionary conflict came within hours of its opening shots" (242), when it clearly was already an issue, in Boston and London at least, a year earlier.

279 *"more than savage barbarity"*: David Hackett Fischer, *Paul Revere's Ride* (New York, 1994), 31, 65–66; Rowe Diary, July 27, 1774; John Andrews to William Barrell, Sept. 28, 1774, "Letters of John Andrews," 371, 382, 386–87; *The British in Boston: The Diary of Lt. John Barker* (1924; repr., New York, 1969), 3, 5, 11, 18, 22; Ammerman, *In the Common Cause*, 127, 136–37, 145; Theodore Draper, *A Struggle for Power* (New York, 1996), 467, 474–75; Akers, *Samuel Cooper*, 192; Gipson, *British Empire Before the American Revolution*, 11:315; Schlesinger, *Prelude to Revolution*, quotation at 231.

279 *"a domesticated core of aging officers"*: John W. Shy, "Thomas Gage: Weakest Link of Empire," in Billias, *George Washington's Opponents*, 19.

280 *Admiral John Montagu*: Sarah Kinkel, *Disciplining the Empire: Politics, Governance, and the Rise of the British Navy* (Cambridge, Mass., 2018), xi, 3, 9, 167, 169–79; Stout, *Royal Navy in America*, 155–61, Adams quoted at 155.

280 *1779 proposal for a new volume*: "To the Hon. John Montague Esq. Rear Admiral of the Blue" is listed last in the proposed table of contents, but since Montagu left in July 1774, it was most likely composed earlier than the ones described later in this chapter. *CWC*, 168.

280 *"To Lieut. R——"*: *CWC*, 83; *WPW*, 206–7. "Greaves" was likely the son or nephew of Vice Admiral Samuel Graves, the new commander after Montagu; John Prime Iron Rochfort was the namesake of a famous war hero nicknamed Prime Iron. Carretta, *Phillis Wheatley*, 148–49, 224–25n13, 225n16.

282 *"in virtue's cause"*: *CWC*, 83–84; Frank Shuffleton, "On Her Own Footing: Phillis Wheatley in Freedom," in Carretta and Gould, *Genius in Bondage*, 182–85. Suvir Kaul describes the attitude here as the "contradictory desires of the colonial and slave subject." Suvir Kaul, *Eighteenth-Century British Literature and Postcolonial Studies* (Edinburgh, 2009), 139–40.

283 *"My pen, least favour'd"*: Barker-Benfield, *Phillis Wheatley Chooses Freedom*, 143–51.

284 *the notion of unspoiled Africa*: CWC, 86–87; *WPW*, 209–10; Lamore, "Phillis Wheatley's Use of the Georgic," 120–26.

284 *"Pleas'd with the theme"*: *CWC*, 87–88; Zachary McLeod Hutchins, *Inventing Eden: Primitivism, Millennialism, and the Making of New England* (New York, 2014), 225–26; Loscocco, *Phillis Wheatley's Miltonic Poetics*, 2–3.

285 *tried not to choose*: Aaron Sullivan, *The Disaffected: Britain's Occupation of Philadelphia During the American Revolution* (Philadelphia, 2019).

285 *"Thoughts on Tyranny"*: *Royal American Magazine*, Feb. 1775, 67.

286 *"A REBUS"*: BEP, March 13, 20, 1775. James Rush, son of Benjamin and Julia Stockton Rush, told Rufus Wilmot Griswold that Wheatley "excelled particularly in acrostics and in other equally difficult tricks of literary dexterity." Rufus Wilmot Griswold, *The Female Poets of America* (Philadelphia, 1849), 31.

287 *"A Man, who I fear"*: "A Rebus," BEP, April 3, 1775; CG, April 7, 1775.

21. THE AMERICANS

288 *civil war*: Jensen, *The Founding of a Nation*, 569, 603; Rowe Diary, April 19, 1775; Abigail Adams to Edward Dilly, May 22, 1775, in *Adams Family Correspondence*, 1:200; "To the Inhabitants of Bermuda," in *George Washington: Writings*, ed. John Rhodehamel (New York, 1997), 181; David Armitage, *Civil Wars: A History in Ideas* (Cambridge, Mass., 2017), 135–37, 140–41; David Armitage, "Every Great Revolution Is a Civil War," in *Scripting Revolutions*, ed. Keith Michael Baker and Dan Edelstein (Stanford, Calif., 2015), 67.

288 *American identity*: Merritt, *Symbols of American Community*; Conway, "From Fellow-Nationals to Foreigners."

289 *fears of slave revolt*: Sylvia R. Frey, *Water from the Rock: Black Resistance in a Revolutionary Age* (Princeton, N.J., 1991), 54–58, quoted at 55; Benjamin Quarles, *The Negro in the American Revolution* (Chapel Hill, N.C., 1961); Ronald Hoffman, *A Spirit of Dissension* (Baltimore, 1973); Woody Holton, *Forced Founders* (Chapel Hill, N.C., 1998); Robert A. Olwell, *Masters, Slaves, and Subjects* (Ithaca, N.Y., 1998), 221–70; Michael McDonnell, *The Politics of War* (Chapel Hill, N.C., 2006); Robert Parkinson, *The Common Cause: Creating Race and Nation in the American Revolution* (Chapel Hill, N.C., 2016), 84; Jason T. Sharples, *The World That Fear Made: Slave Revolts and Conspiracy Scares in Early America* (Philadelphia, 2020), 207–41; Jeremy Adelman, *Sovereignty and Revolution in the Iberian Atlantic* (Princeton, N.J., 2006). For the scramble for munitions precipitating civil war, see Phillips, *1775*; Peter Charles Hoffer, *Prelude to Revolution: The Salem Gunpowder Raid of 1775* (Baltimore, 2013).

289 *Rhetoric in Massachusetts reverberated*: Samuel Johnson, *Taxation No Tyranny*, 3rd ed. (London, 1775), 36, 64, 79, 85; D. J. Greene, "*The False Alarm* and *Taxation No Tyranny*: Some Further Observations," *Studies in Bibliography* 13 (1960), 225; *Resistance No Rebellion: In Answer to Doctor Johnson's "Taxation No Tyranny"* (London, 1775), 5, 28; *An Answer to a Pamphlet, Entitled "Taxation No Tyranny"* (London, 1775), 61; Lynd and Waldstreicher, "Free Trade, Sovereignty, and Slavery."

290 *"choice of identity"*: Vincent Carretta memorably named this as Wheatley's "choice" in *CWC*, xxviii–xxxii, and Carretta, "Phillis Wheatley, the Mansfield Decision, and the Choice of Identity," and de-emphasizes choice somewhat in his biography, *Phillis Wheatley*.

290 *Wheatley became a refugee*: Rowe Diary, April 27, May 5, 1775; Boyle Journal, April 30, 1775; Jacqueline Barbara Carr, *After the Siege: A Social History of Boston, 1775–1800* (Boston, 2005), 6, 22–23; Nathaniel Wheatley to Melatiah Bourn, June 3, 1775; John Andrews to William Barrell, May 6, June 1, 1775, Andrews-Eliot Correspondence.

291 *quickly settled in Providence*: "John Lathrop," in *Heralds of a Liberal Faith, I: The Prophets*, ed. Samuel A. Eliot (Boston, 1910), 93–97; Carretta, *Phillis Wheatley*, 153–54; PW to Tanner, Feb. 14, 1776, in *PWW*, 131; Carp, *Rebels Rising*, 137–38; "To the DEALERS IN SLAVES," *Providence Gazette*, Jan. 28, 1775; *Providence Gazette*, Dec. 30, 1775, Jan. 6, 1776; Charles Rappleye, *Sons of Providence: The Brown Brothers, the Slave Trade, and the American Revolution* (New York, 2006), 144–45, 163, 170–72; Arthur Zilversmit, *The First Emancipation* (Chicago, 1967), 106–7.

292 *Washington's enlistments directive*: Edward Lengel, *General George Washington: A Military Life* (New York, 2005), 314; Quarles, *Negro in the American Rev-*

olution, 16; Joyce Lee Malcolm, "Slavery in Massachusetts and the American Revolution," *Journal of the Historical Society* 10 (2010): 427; Philip D. Morgan and Andrew O'Shaughnessy, "Arming Slaves in the American Revolution," in *Arming Slaves*, ed. Christopher Leslie Brown and Philip D. Morgan (New Haven, Conn., 2006), 192; Patrick Charles, *Washington's Decision: The Story of George Washington's Decision to Reaccept Black Enlistments in the Continental Army, December 31, 1775* (n.p., 2005), 18–23; Sweet, *Bodies Politic*, 200.

293 *incitement of violence*: Robert G. Parkinson, *Thirteen Clocks: How Race United the Colonies and Made the Declaration of Independence* (Chapel Hill, N.C., 2021), 91; Morgan and O'Shaughnessy, "Arming Slaves in the American Revolution," 188; Frey, *Water from the Rock*, 60–61, 66–67.

293 *"your Excellency"*: CWC, 88–90; Lee to Benjamin Rush, Sept. 24, 1775, in *The Lee Papers*, vol. 1, *1754–1776* (New York, 1871), 207; Barker-Benfield, *Phillis Wheatley Chooses Freedom*, 154; Carretta, *Phillis Wheatley*, 155; Shuffleton, "On Her Own Footing," 186–87.

294 *Washington himself was deeply frustrated*: Washington to John Augustine Washington, to Lund Washington, July 27, Aug. 20, 1775, in Rhodehamel, *George Washington: Writings*, 179, 184–85; Robert Middlekauff, *Washington's Revolution* (New York, 2015), 86–93.

294 *bickering generals*: Middlekauff, *Washington's Revolution*, 101–3. Pasquale S. Toscano stresses the hesitation in Wheatley's praise as a deliberate warning, even criticism. Pasquale S. Toscano, "Epic Regained: Phillis Wheatley's Admonitory Poetics in the 'Little Columbiad,'" *Classical Receptions Journal* (2020): 17–18. For the poem as a "plea and a challenge," more than praise, see also Julian D. Mason Jr. in *PPW*, 164–66n38.

294 *"One century scarce perform'd"*: CWC, 89–90; Thomas J. Steele, "The Figure of Columbia: Phillis Wheatley plus George Washington," *New England Quarterly* 54 (1961): 264–66; Jenna M. Gibbs, *Performing the Temple of Liberty: Slavery, Theater, and Popular Culture in London and Philadelphia, 1760–1850* (Baltimore, 2014), 17–22.

295 *"If the Virginians are wise"*: Washington to Reed, Dec. 15, 1775, in *The Papers of George Washington, Revolutionary War Series*, vol. 2, *16 September 1775–31 December 1775*, ed. Philander D. Chase et al. (Charlottesville, Va., 1987), 551–54; Parkinson, *Common Cause*, 146–76; Lengel, *General George Washington*, 313–14; Charles, *Washington's Decision*; Henry Wiencek, *An Imperfect God* (New York, 2005), 201–5.

296 *"repeatedly pass[ing] acts"*: "To the Virginia Gazette," Nov. 24, 1775, in *The American Revolution: Writings from the War of Independence*, ed. John Rhodehamel (New York, 2003), 82, 85–86.

297 *In a long letter*: Washington to Reed, Feb. 10, 1776, in Rhodehamel, *George Washington: Writings*, 211–16.

299 *"the famous Phillis Wheatley"*: Silverman, *Cultural History of the American Revolution*, 404; Washington to PW, Feb. 28, 1776, in *The Papers of George Washington, Revolutionary War Series*, vol. 3, *1 January 1776–31 March 1776*, ed. Philander D. Chase (Charlottesville, Va., 1988), 387; Deming, *Boston and the Dawn of American Independence*, 410–15; *Virginia Gazette*, March 30, 1776; *Pennsylvania Magazine*, April 1776, 193.

There is uncertainty about whether Wheatley ever visited Washington at Cambridge. Carretta, *Phillis Wheatley*, 157, discounts the story as unlikely given Wheatley's probable residence in Providence well into 1776 and wartime restrictions on movement. But this does not take into account that precisely because they were not seen as combatants, African Americans and women were often granted freedom of movement across lines. (Cf. Judith Van Buskirk, *Generous Enemies: Patriots and Loyalists in Revolutionary New York* [Philadelphia, 2002].) The nineteenth-century historian Benson Lossing got the story of an actual visit at headquarters from the earlier historian and Washingtoniana collector Jared Sparks and/or the poet and scholar Henry Wadsworth Longfellow, both of whom lived in the house Washington used as headquarters, now known as Longfellow House. For the most thorough investigation of the legend, the sources, and the likelihood of an actual visit, see Kigel, *Heavenly Tidings from the Afric Muse*, 353–75.

Sparks and other commentators since have cited Washington's interaction with Wheatley as a reflection of his goodness or even a positive influence on Washington's attitudes about slavery. See, for example, Wiencek, *Imperfect God*, 208–14, and subsequently Ron Chernow, *Washington: A Life* (New York, 2010), 219–21. These same writers often brush over the Dunmorean context and the limited and contingent nature of Washington's concession to already enlisted free black troops, on which, see Lengel, *General George Washington*, 313–15; Charles, *Washington's Decision*; and Parkinson, *Common Cause*, 173–75.

300   *The "seemingly devoted" patriots*: PW to Tanner, Feb. 14, 1776; Parkinson, *Common Cause*, 248–49; Brown, *Moral Capital*, 169, 191n53.

300   *With her friends of color*: The manuscript reads "Zingo" rather than "Lingo" as it appears in *CWC*, 131. I thank Tara Bynum and Vincent Carretta for clarification on this point and for conversation on Wheatley's friends and acquaintances in Rhode Island, the subject of a paper Bynum gave at the Library Company of Philadelphia in 2019; see also Tara Bynum, "Caesar Lyndon's Lists, Letters, and a Pig Roast: A Sundry Account Book," *Early American Literature* 53 (2018): 839–49. Benjamin Carp pointed out the identity of Zingo Stevens (sometimes Stephens); see also his *Rebels Rising*, 137–38.

300   *John Lathrop's sermons*: "Innocent Blood Crying to God from the Ground," Undated Sermons, box 1, Undated sermon, 1768 folder, box 4; untitled Sermon, March 7, 1771, box 4; "A Summary Account of Wars in America Under the Reign of George the III," box 3, Sermon fragments [1775 or 1776], Miscellaneous Papers, box 11, "Sermon Preached on a Day of Thanksgiving and Prayer Aug. 1, 1776," "A Thanksgiving Sermon, Preached December 12, 1776," box 5, Lathrop Papers.

302   *General Charles Lee*: *Life of Jeremy Belknap, D.D.*, ed. Jane Belknap Mercou (New York, 1847), 94; David S. Lovejoy, *Rhode Island Politics and the American Revolution* (Providence, 1965), 190; *BG*, Jan. 8, 1775; John Shy, "Charles Lee: The Soldier as Radical," in *George Washington's Generals*, ed. George Athan Billias (New York, 1964), 28, 32–34; Phillip Papas, *Renegade Revolutionary: The Life of Charles Lee* (New York, 2014); Charles Royster, *A Revolutionary People at War* (New York, 1979), 40–43; John Ferling, *Almost a Miracle: The American Victory in the War of Independence* (New York, 2007), 167, 170–71; David L. Preston, "Varieties of 'Patriotism' in the Post-1763 British Empire: The Strange Case of Charles Lee," in Olwell and Vaughn, *Envisioning Empire*, 197–225; *BIC*, Jan. 2, 1778; Lengel, *George Washington*, 172; Stephen Brumwell, *George Washington: Gentleman Warrior* (London, 2015), 270; Paine, "The American Crisis, Number 1," in Rhodehamel, *American Revolution*, 238.

303   *"On the Capture of General Lee"*: *CWC*, 90–92; Toscano, "Epic Regained," 14,

18–19; Thomas, *Alexander Pope and His Eighteenth-Century Women Readers*, 239–41. Toscano, "Epic Regained," 18–20, brilliantly reads the poem, one of the least commented on in Wheatley's oeuvre, as part of her developing "admonitory poetics" in a series of military mini-epics, humiliating Lee despite voicing Lee's own "tour de force rebuttal." But Wheatley also makes Lee as interesting, complex a character as he actually was (see Shy, "Charles Lee"), while rightly emphasizing the general as a loquacious type whose triumphs and tragedies flowed from his tongue.

The only surviving copy of the Lee poem is in Bowdoin's papers, but the poem is listed in the 1779 proposal. Bowdoin was in a position to know that Lee had undermined Washington's leadership, as Carretta stresses, but he might also have responded ambivalently to the poem's deliberate ambiguities and wondered how it would be read.

304 *"the famous Phillis Wheatley"*: CWC, 88; Carretta, *Phillis Wheatley*, 158–59.

22. THE FREE

305 *Wheatley's opportunities changed*: Voltaire, *Oeuvres Completes*, ed. Louis Moland (Paris, 1882–85), 48:594–95, in Robinson, *Critical Essays on Phillis Wheatley*, 33; Gates, *Figures in Black*, 17–18; Joan DeJean, *Ancients Against Moderns* (Chicago, 1997); Norman, *Shock of the Ancient*; Louis Sala-Molins, *Dark Side of the Light: Slavery and the French Enlightenment*, trans. John Conteh-Morgan (Minneapolis, 2006), 49, 75; Christopher L. Miller, *The French Atlantic Triangle: Literature and Culture of the Slave Trade* (Durham, N.C., 2008), quoted at 76; Eugene P. Chase, ed., *Our Revolutionary Forefathers: The Letters of François, Marquis de Barbé-Marbois, During His Residency in the United States as Secretary of the French Legation* (New York, 1929), 85.

305 *Wheatley was an American curiosity*: Susan Scott Parrish, *American Curiosity: Cultures of Natural History in the Colonial British Atlantic World* (Chapel Hill, N.C., 2006); Waldstreicher, *Runaway America*, 210–24; Jonathan I. Israel, *Democratic Enlightenment: Philosophy, Revolution, and Human Rights, 1750–1790* (Princeton, N.J., 2012), 413–79.

306 Notes on the State of Virginia: Thomas Jefferson, *Notes on the State of Virginia with Related Documents*, ed. David Waldstreicher (Boston, 2002), 175–81. Jefferson kept revising the work and did not publish it until after Wheatley's death, in 1785. For the definitive scholarly edition, clarifying many matters and incorporating Jefferson's revisions, see Thomas Jefferson, *Notes on the State of Virginia: An Annotated Edition*, ed. Robert P. Forbes (New Haven, Conn., 2022).

307 *Short-guy joke*: Jefferson relished the story about a dinner party in Paris where Raynal "got on his favorite theory of the degeneracy of animals, and even of man, in America." Franklin then looked around and said, "Let us try this question by the fact before us. We are here one half Americans & one half French . . . Let both parties rise, and we will see on which side nature has degenerated." The guests stood up. All the Americans were tall, the French shorter, "and the Abbé [Raynal] himself particularly, was a mere shrimp." Jefferson to Robert Walsh Jr., Dec. 4, 1818, Library of Congress, founders.archives.gov/documents /Jefferson/03-13-02-0407.

308 *degeneration thesis*: PW, *Poems on Various Subjects, Religious and Moral* (London, 1773), v, Library of Congress copy; E. Millicent Sowerby, comp., *Cata-*

logue of the Library of Thomas Jefferson (Charlottesville, Va., 1983), 4:491;
Merrill D. Peterson, *Thomas Jefferson and the New Nation* (New York, 1970),
252–58; Miller, *French Atlantic Triangle*, 63–65, 84; David Brion Davis, *Slavery and Human Progress* (New York, 1984), 107; Caroline Winterer, *The Mirror of Antiquity: American Women and the Classical Tradition, 1750–1900* (Ithaca, N.Y., 2007), 31–35; Hannah Spahn, *Thomas Jefferson, Time, and History* (Charlottesville, Va., 2011), 252n18; Howell, *Against Self-Reliance*, 52–53; Christopher P. Iannini, *Fatal Revolutions: Natural History, West Indian Slavery, and the Routes of American Literature* (Chapel Hill, N.C., 2012), 232–34; Michel-Rolph Trouillot, *Silencing the Past* (Boston, 1995), 81–85; Srinivas Aravamudan, *Tropicopolitans* (Durham, N.C., 1999), 289–315.

308 *Jefferson clearly felt "threatened"*: Dorsey, *Common Bondage*, 174; Davis, *Problem of Slavery in the Age of Revolution*, 45; M. I. Finley, *Ancient Slavery and Modern Ideology* (New York, 1980), 96–97.

309 *formerly enslaved poet Terence*: Terence, *Comedies*, 101, 316n; Bennett, "Phillis Wheatley's Vocation"; Jenny Davidson, *Breeding: A Partial History of the Eighteenth Century* (New York, 2009), 162; Jefferson, *Notes on the State of Virginia*, 180. For Jefferson's depoliticization and domestication of classics, see Eran Shalev, "Thomas Jefferson's Classical Silence, 1774–1776: Historical Consciousness and Roman History in the Revolutionary South," and Peter S. Onuf, "Ancients, Moderns, and the Progress of Mankind: Thomas Jefferson's Classical World," in *Thomas Jefferson, the Classical World, and Early America*, ed. Peter S. Onuf and Nicholas P. Cole (Charlottesville, Va., 2011), 219–47, 35–55.

310 *Jupiter Hammon*: Stanley A. Ransom, ed., *America's First Black Poet: Jupiter Hammon of Long Island* (n.p., 2019), 19; Mary Lloyd, *Meditations on Divine Subjects: by Mrs. Mary Lloyd; To which is Prefixed, an Account of her Life and Character. By E. Pemberton* (New York, 1750); Cedrick May, *Evangelism and Resistance in the Black Atlantic, 1760–1835* (Athens, Ga., 2008), 2, 33–35; Phillip M. Richards, "Nationalist Themes in the Preaching of Jupiter Hammon," *Early American Literature* 25 (1990): 123–38; Rosemary Fithian Guruswamy, "'Thou Hast the Holy Word': Jupiter Hammon's 'Regards' to Phillis Wheatley," in Carretta and Gould, *Genius in Bondage*, 190–98; Cedrick May and Julie McCown, "'An Essay on Slavery': An Unpublished Poem by Jupiter Hammon," *Early American Literature* 48 (2013): 457–71; Frances Smith Foster, "A Narrative of the Interesting Origins and (Somewhat) Surprising Developments of African-American Print Culture," *American Literary History* 17 (2005): 721; Bruce, *Origins of African American Literature*, 32–38, 50–55, 58–61; Sidbury, *Becoming African in America*, 17–38.

311 *Ignatius Sancho thanked*: *Letters of the Late Ignatius Sancho*, 111–12.

312 *Wheatley was thinking of publishing*: BEP, Oct. 30, 1779, also in CWC, 167–69. For further reflections on Wheatley's publication strategies, see Waldstreicher, "Anonymous Wheatley."

313 *A lengthy poem, "The Arrival"*: "The Arrival," BIC, Nov. 27, 1777; William Gordon, "Letter V," BIC, Oct. 3, Nov. 14, 28, 1776; Akers, "'Our Modern Egyptians,'" 246; Akers, *Divine Politician*, 240; Harlow Giles Unger, *John Hancock: Merchant King and American Patriot* (New York, 2000), 261; Nina Sankovitch, *American Rebels: How the Hancock, Adams, and Quincy Families Fanned the Flames of Revolution* (New York, 2020), 182, 296; BG, Oct. 6, 1777.

314 *private woes*: William M. Fowler, *The Baron of Beacon Hill* (Boston, 1980), 22, 33, 49, 106, 208. Sankovitch also notes that Wheatley wrote a "panegyrick" to

Samuel Quincy, which is nonextant but appeared in her first, February 1772 book proposal. Quincy was closely associated with Hancock, and Carretta describes him as the "Wheatley family lawyer" who handled the estate transition between John and Nathaniel in 1774. Sankovitch, *American Rebels*, 161–62, 331–32; Carretta, *Phillis Wheatley*, 152–53; *PWW*, 163.

314 *Like Thomas Gray*: Suvir Kaul, "Thomas Gray, *Elegy Written in a Country Church Yard*," in Gerrard, *Companion to Eighteenth-Century Poetry*, 277–90; Austin Lane Poole, ed., *The Poems of Gray and Collins*, 4th ed. (London, 1919); *BG*, Oct. 6, 1777; Barnard, *Empire of Ruins*, 45.

315 *Horatio Gates had been present*: *BG*, Oct. 27, Nov. 10, 17, 1777; "On GENERAL GATES," *BG*, Dec. 8, 1777; George Athan Billias, "Horatio Gates: Professional Soldier," in Billias, *George Washington's Generals*, 90; Richard M. Ketchum, *Saratoga* (New York, 1997), 269–78, 405; Dean Snow, *1777: Tipping Point at Saratoga* (New York, 2016), quoted at 9; Max M. Mintz, *The Generals of Saratoga* (New Haven, Conn., 1990), 182, 225; Simone Weil and Rachel Bespaloff, *War and "The Iliad,"* trans. Mary McCarthy (New York, 2005); Manguel, *Homer's "The Iliad" and "The Odyssey,"* 224; Jacqueline Fabre-Serris and Alison Keith, eds., *Woman and War in Antiquity* (Baltimore, 2015); James Anderson Winn, *The Poetry of War* (New York, 2007).

316 *effort to create a new constitution*: Stephen E. Patterson, *Political Parties in Revolutionary Massachusetts* (Madison, Wis., 1973), 153–89; Robert J. Taylor, ed., *Massachusetts, Colony to Commonwealth: Documents on the Formation of Its Constitution, 1775–1780* (1961; repr., New York, 1972), 48, 53; Oscar Handlin and Mary F. Handlin, eds., *The Popular Sources of Political Authority: Documents on the Massachusetts Convention of 1780* (Cambridge, Mass., 1966), 22; Nash, *Unknown American Revolution*, 290–305; Van Gosse, *The First Reconstruction: Black Politics from the Revolution to the Civil War* (Chapel Hill, N.C., 2021), 169–70.

316 *In December 1777, a committee formed*: For a summary of these events, see Nash, *Unknown American Revolution*, 295–97.

317 *"ridiculous, inconsistent and unjust"*: Handlin and Handlin, *Popular Sources*, 179–81; "To the Impartial Public," *BIC*, Nov. 28, 1777; Eleutheros, "To All PRINTERS on the CONTINENT," *BG*, Dec. 22, 1777; "To the Convention of Massachusetts-Bay," *Boston Continental Journal*, Jan. 8, 1778.

318 *"The Constitution"*: *BIC*, Jan. 29, 1778. Gulliver resists but is subject to the racial criteria that distinguish Houyhnhnms from the smelly, enslaved yahoos he resembles: he is ultimately expelled because he might lead a rebellion of the yahoos. Aravamudan, *Tropicopolitans*, 137–39; Laura Brown, *Ends of Empire: Women and Ideology in Early Eighteenth-Century English Literature* (Ithaca, N.Y., 1993), 188–99.

319 *"Reply to THE CONSTITUTION"*: *BIC*, Feb. 12, 1778.

320 *metaphor for enslaving passions*: Peter Garnsey, *Ideas of Slavery from Aristotle to Augustine* (Cambridge, U.K., 1996), 128–56; Patterson, *Freedom in the Making of Western Culture*, 187–99, 264–90; Claude Rawson, *God, Gulliver, and Genocide: Barbarism and the European Imagination* (New York, 2001).

321 *It's his "satire"*: *BIC*, Feb. 12, 1778. For the author's brief and similarly racist reply supposedly quoting Gulliver again, merely asserting that the author of the reply was "A THING which needed no reply" because "the NOSE, the truth should tell," see *BIC*, Feb. 19, 1778.

321 *The Revolutionary War produced*: On the proslavery and antislavery aspects of

the Revolution, see David Waldstreicher, "The Hidden Stakes of the 1619 Controversy," *Boston Review*, Jan. 24, 2020, bostonreview.net/race-politics/david -waldstreicher-hidden-stakes-1619-controversy; David Waldstreicher, "The Changing Same of U.S. History," *Boston Review*, Nov. 10, 2021, bostonreview .net/articles/the-changing-same-of-u-s-history.

321 *in response to the death*: PW to Mary Wooster, July 15, 1778, MHS; Mukhtar Ali Isani, "'On the Death of General Wooster': An Unpublished Poem by Phillis Wheatley," *Modern Philology* 77 (1980): 306–10; "Philadelphia. In Congress, June 17, 1777," *BIC*, Aug. 14, 1777; *PPW*, 72–74, 144–45n25, 170n43; *CWC*, 92–94.

323 *hero who can divert his vision*: Toscano, "Epic Regained," 21–22.

323 *"the great loss"*: PW to Mary Wooster, July 15, 1778, Hugh Upham Clark Papers, MHS.

23. THE ENDS

324 *During the spring of 1778*: "A Constitution and Form of Government for the State of Massachusetts Bay," *BIC*, March 19, 1778; William Gordon, "Letter 1," "Letter II," *BIC*, April 2, 9, 1778; "Letters of Reverend William Gordon, Historian of the American Revolution, 1770–1799," *Proceedings of the Massachusetts Historical Society* 63 (1930), 305; Moore, *Notes on the History of Slavery in Massachusetts*, 177–79, 194–95; Blanck, *Tyrannicide*, 66–68, 125–27; Taylor, *Massachusetts, Colony to Commonwealth*, 64–65, 69, 126; Countryman, *Enjoy the Same Liberty*, 66; Blanton, "This Species of Property," 552–83; Melish, *Disowning Slavery*, 56, 66–67, 85; Adams and Pleck, *Love of Freedom*, 139; Minardi, *Making Slavery History*; Zilversmit, *First Emancipation*; Van Gosse and David Waldstreicher, introduction to *Revolutions and Reconstructions: Black Politics in the Long Nineteenth Century*, ed. Van Gosse and David Waldstreicher (Philadelphia, 2020), 20–22.

325 *John Wheatley died*: Nathaniel Wheatley to John Lathrop, March 21, 1779, box 11, Lathrop Papers; *Salem Gazette*, Sept. 11, 1783; *BEP*, Oct. 4, 1783, Jan. 1, March 25, 1784. The Wheatleys' response to Phillis's emancipation mirrored, or we might say anticipated, the post-revolutionary and post-emancipation tendency of whites in Massachusetts to disassociate themselves from black people, to render them strangers, even to forget how important the enslaved had been in their lives. Melish, *Disowning Slavery*; Minardi, *Making Slavery History*.

326 *her own family*: *BG*, March 16, 1778; Will of John Wheatley, Feb. 14, 1778, box 11, Lathrop Papers; Robinson, *Phillis Wheatley and the Origins of African American Literature*, 23; Thwing, *Inhabitants and Estates of the Town of Boston*; PW to Tanner, May 28, 1778, to Mary Wooster, July 15, 1778, in *CWC*, 161, 162; Carretta, *Phillis Wheatley*, 172–73.

326 *John Peters*: Cornelia Hughes Dayton and Sharon V. Salinger, *Robert Love's Warnings: Searching for Strangers in Colonial Boston* (Philadelphia, 2014), 129; Cornelia H. Dayton, "Lost Years Recovered: John Peters and Phillis Wheatley Peters in Middleton," *New England Quarterly* 94 (2021): 309–51. For an early review of the "contradictory rumors" around Peters, which have been recycled ever since, see Charles F. Heartman, *Phillis Wheatley (Phillis Peters): A Critical Attempt and a Bibliography of Her Writings* (New York, 1915), 23–24, and Charles Fred Heartman, ed., *Phillis Wheatley (Phillis Peters) Poems and Letters: First Collected Edition* (New York, n.d.), 12.

327 *Peters became a successful grocer*: Kunal Parker, "Making Blacks Foreigners:

The Legal Construction of Former Slaves in Post-Revolutionary Massachusetts," *Utah Law Review* 75 (2001): 75–124; Scott Hancock, "'The Law Will Make You Smart': Legal Consciousness, Rights Rhetoric, and African American Identity Formation in Massachusetts, 1641–1855" (PhD diss., University of New Hampshire, 1999), 15; Crocker, *Reminiscences and Traditions of Boston*, 82; CSR; A. Mott, "A Short Account of Phillis Wheatley," *Berks and Schuylkill Journal*, June 16, 1827; Abigail Mott, *Biographical Sketches and Interesting Anecdotes of Persons of Colour to Which Is Added a Selection of Pieces of Poetry* (New York, 1826), 12; Henri Gregoire, *Enquiry Concerning the Intellectual and Moral Faculties, and Literature of Negroes*, trans. D. B. Warden (Brooklyn, 1810), 236–37; Shurtleff, "Phillis Wheatley, the Negro Slave Poet," 33–34; Charles Deane, "Phillis Wheatley," 268–69n, 279; John S. Ezell, ed., *The New Democracy in America: Travels of Francisco de Miranda in the United States, 1783–1784*, trans. Judson P. Wood (Norman, Okla., 1963), 165; MMO, 20, 28–29; Caroline May, *The Female Poets of America* (Philadelphia, 1859), 40.

The negative reputation of Peters was challenged with new research by Carretta, *Phillis Wheatley*, 175–76, though he stresses her loss of identity and status after the marriage, and most recently by Dayton, "Lost Years Recovered," which adds much to the story; see also Minardi, *Making Slavery History*, 120–21; Honorée Fanonne Jeffers, "'The Dear Pledges of Our Love': A Defense of Phillis Wheatley's Husband," in *The Fire This Time*, ed. Jesmyn Ward (New York, 2016), 63–82, also as revised in Jeffers, "Looking for Miss Phillis," in *The Age of Phillis* (Middletown, Conn., 2020), 167–89. For earlier and similarly skeptical views of the traditional accounts deriving from the white Wheatleys, see especially Richmond, *Bid the Vassal Soar*, 43–47; Akers, "'Our Modern Egyptians,'" 399–400; PWW, 53–54, 58, 65.

328 *substantial house in Boston*: Carretta, *Phillis Wheatley*, 182; Dayton, "Lost Years Recovered."

328 *what marriage meant*: Piersen, *Black Yankees*; Melish, *Disowning Slavery*, 26–28; Levy, *Town Born*; Adams and Pleck, *Love of Freedom*, 104; Sarah M. S. Pearsall, *Polygamy: An Early American History* (New Haven, Conn., 2019), 147; Sword, *Wives Not Slaves*, 232–36.

330 *tried to make her marriage work*: Frances Smith Foster, *'Til Death or Distance Do Us Part: Love and Marriage in African America* (New York, 2010), 82–83, observes that in the records of the Free African Union Society in Newport, Rhode Island, during the 1780s and 1790s, marriage appears to be "a site of conflict between whites and blacks." See also, on marriage as a site of struggle and resistance for the enslaved and free in later periods, Brenda Stevenson, *Life in Black and White: Family and Community in the Slave South* (New York, 1996); Laura F. Edwards, *Gendered Strife and Confusion: The Political Culture of Reconstruction* (Urbana, Ill., 1997); Tera W. Hunter, *Bound in Wedlock: Slave and Free Black Marriage in the Nineteenth Century* (Cambridge, Mass., 2017).

330 *As a trader, Peters might have*: Ralph V. Harlow, "Economic Conditions in Massachusetts During the American Revolution," *Publications of the Colonial Society of Massachusetts* 20 (1918): 163–92; Carr, *After the Siege*, 98; Barbara Clark Smith, *The Freedoms We Lost: Consent and Resistance in Revolutionary America* (Boston, 2010), 183–210; Bruce H. Mann, *Republic of Debtors: Bankruptcy in the Age of American Independence* (Cambridge, Mass., 2003); Dayton, "Lost Years Recovered," 320–22; Arthur W. H. Eaton, "Old Boston Families Number Four: The Byles Family," *New England Historical and Genealogical Register*

69 (1915): 102–3; CSR; MMO, 22–23; Nathaniel B. Shurtleff, "Phillis Wheatley, the Negro-Slave Poet," *Boston Daily Advertiser*, Dec. 31, 1863; Carretta, *Phillis Wheatley*, 177–78, 182–83.

330 *In her last surviving letter*: Phillis Peters to Tanner, May 10, 1779, in *CWC*, 162; "Prayer Sabbath—June 13, 1779," in *CWC*, 96; *PWW*, 346; Carretta, *Phillis Wheatley*, 184–85, 232n40; *BIC*, Oct. 21, 1779.

331 *she published a proposal*: "PROPOSALS," *BEP*, Oct. 30, Nov. 6, 27, Dec. 4, 11, 18, 1779; *WPW*, 212. Some biographers attribute the "mistake" of a high-priced volume, and her use of her married name exclusively, to John Peters, though Carretta also suggests that Phillis might have tried to publish when John was out of town. Carretta, *Phillis Wheatley*, 178, 181; *PWW*, 349n.

332 *A Volume of Poems*: For the proposed volume as wide-ranging but more secular, see Carretta, *Phillis Wheatley*, 178; for the breakdown of religious projects, see Kate Carté, *Religion and the American Revolution* (Chapel Hill, N.C., 2021). The nonappearance of the General Gates poem in this book proposal might argue against its attribution to Wheatley, but it should be recalled that many of Wheatley's extant or published poems did not appear in her earlier proposals or her book; her first book changed significantly from the listing in the first proposal to the actual volume.

332 *the letters selected for inclusion*: Julian D. Mason Jr. proposes Thomas Hubbard, the addressee of one of her earlier elegies, but this seems less likely because of his death on July 17, 1773. *PPW*, 214n.

333 *the Massachusetts economy*: Harlow, "Economic Conditions," 188–89.

334 *Peters family moved in*: Dayton, "Lost Years Recovered," 322–27.

334 *Phillis wilted during this rustication*: Parker, "Making Blacks Foreigners"; Carretta, *Phillis Wheatley*, 183; Dayton, "Lost Years Recovered," 327–29; John Dabney's copy of *Poems on Various Subjects, Religious and Moral* in Peabody-Essex Museum Library, Rowley, Mass. For Wheatley's supposed abandonment and despair as unproven, and a striking contrast to her "upbeat" poems of 1784, see especially Robinson in *PWW*, 60–61, and in *Phillis Wheatley and the Origins of African American Literature*, 25.

334 *"saucy to him and his wife"*: This account, as in earlier paragraphs, relies on Dayton, "Lost Years Recovered," 328–45, who discovered many documents in court records, supplemented with research into Middleton and the Wilkins families.

335 *lost out in a property dispute*: For another contemporary New England example, see Gretchen Holbrook Gerzina, *Mr. and Mrs. Prince* (New York, 2008).

335 *Phillis and John had returned to Boston*: Bio-bibliography, 25; MMO, 21–23.

335 *Captain Rufus Lincoln*: *The Papers of Captain Rufus Lincoln of Wareham, Mass.* (1903; repr., New York, 1971), 65, 94 (thanks to Roberto Flores de Apodaca, via Woody Holton, for this reference); Bruce, *Origins of African American Literature*, 63; "The Choice. By the Late Heman Harris, of Wrentham," *BIC*, May 20, 1784; "The Prospect of America," in *The Literary Remains of Joseph Brown Ladd, M.D.*, ed. Elizabeth Ladd Haskins (New York, 1833), 35 (a poem probably written between 1779 and 1783 and no later than the author's death in 1786); "Wrote After Reading Some Poems Composed by Phillis Wheatley, an African Girl," *New York Morning Post*, March 17, 1785; Weyler, *Empowering Words*, 63.

335 *Ezekiel Russell put a woodcut*: *Bickerstaff's Boston Almanack for the Year of Our Redemption 1782* (Boston, 1781).

336 *"Elegy, Sacred to the Memory"*: *CWC*, 99–100; Fowler, *Baron of Beacon Hill*,

109–10; Akers, *Divine Politician*, 279–80, 329–30, 352. For the Cooper elegy as uniquely personal, see Shields, *Phillis Wheatley's Poetics of Liberation*, 146–47, 166–67. The separate stanza on beginning "Thy Country" does not appear in an extant manuscript version. *CWC*, 98.

337 *Another elegy: Boston Magazine*, Sept. 1784, 462, 488; *CWC*, 94–96; Stuart, *Muse of the Revolution*, 175; Delacroix, "Writing with an Iron Pen," 198. Carretta places this poem as written before Wheatley's marriage because it does not carry her married name, as the listing of the poem in the *Boston Magazine* did, but this could be a publisher's choice or a compositor's error, because her name is also misspelled as "Wheatly." *PWW*, 215.

337 *"Liberty and Peace": CWC*, 101–2. Carretta notes that "Liberty and Peace" might have marked either Congress's ratification of the peace treaty in January, or a thanksgiving day called for by Governor Hancock on October 28 for November 25, 1784, but the latter date seems less likely given her death on December 5. *PWW*, 214.

338 *Francisco de Miranda*: Miranda, *New Democracy in America*, 165.

340 *"celestial Peace": CWC*, 101–2. For the international focus, see Zafar, *We Wear the Mask*, 38; for the theme of Atlantic commerce reopened in the poem, see Peterson, *City-State of Boston*, 324. Barnard describes "Liberty and Peace" as Wheatley's "most Virgilian" poem in *Empire of Ruins*, 46. For classical and eighteenth-century appreciations of war's moral ambiguities, see Winn, *Poetry of War*.

340 *Phillis Wheatley Peters died: BIC*, Dec. 9, 1784; *MMO*, 23–24; Carretta, *Phillis Wheatley*, 190; *Bio-bibliography*, 33; Minardi, *Making Slavery History*, 102; Jennifer René Young, "Marketing a Sable Muse: The Cultural Circulation of Phillis Wheatley, 1767–1865" (PhD diss., Harvard University, 2004), 42; "Obituaries" and Horatio, "Elegy on the Death of a Late Celebrated Poetess," *Boston Magazine*, Dec. 1784, 619–20, 630–31; Cavitch, *American Elegy*, 191–92.

341 *Peters made at least two subsequent efforts: BIC*, Feb. 10, 1785; *MSP*, July 7, 1791; Andrews to Thomas, June 2, 1798, box 1, folder 16, Isaiah Thomas Papers, American Antiquarian Society. An essay in criticism by Hulton on Wheatley's poems, clearly written after her book was published, is in the Henry Hulton Sketches, William Clements Library. He warns her that "she must expect that what she now writes will be viewed with a severer eye than her first compositions."

In 1849, Rufus Griswold described the book manuscript as being in the possession of "an accomplished citizen of Philadelphia, whose mother was one of the patrons of the author," probably James Rush and Julia Stockton Rush. *BIC*, Feb. 10, 1785; Griswold, *Female Poets of America*, 32; *PWW*, 66; Dayton, "Lost Years Recovered," 350n98.

342 *As Homer asked of his muse*: See the first verses of *The Odyssey* in two resonant modern translations: Homer, *The Odyssey*, trans. Wilson, 105 ("tell the old story for our modern times. Find the beginning."); and Homer, *Odyssey*, trans. Fagles, 77 ("sing for our time too").

24. THE AFTERLIVES

343 *The story of how she has been remembered*: Farah Jasmine Griffin notes the "many lives" of Wheatley's "On Being Brought from Africa to America," in *Read Until You Understand: The Wisdom of Black Life and Literature* (New York, 2021), 20–31, updating Henry Louis Gates Jr.'s emphasis on its status as

"the most reviled poem in African American literature" while also highlighting Wheatley's evolution into a position of moral authority by the time of the Dartmouth poem. One might say that her reputation has had a similar evolution. Gates stated twenty years ago that Wheatley was "not a household word within the black community": this may no longer be the case, thanks in part to his own efforts. Gates, *Trials of Phillis Wheatley*, 70–71.

343 *After 1784 the association*: Thomas Clarkson, *An Essay on the Slavery and Commerce of the Human Species, Particularly the African* (London, 1786), in Robinson, *Critical Essays on Phillis Wheatley*, 43–44; *MSP*, July 7, 1791; "On Phillis Wheatley," *Massachusetts Centinel*, Nov. 25, 1789; *Bio-bibliography*, 35–57.

344 *Jefferson's political friends and opponents*: Winthrop D. Jordan, *White Over Black* (Chapel Hill, NC, 1968), 283–84, 437, 442, 446, 460n55; "The American Observer. No. III," *Baltimore Republican*, Jan. 5, 1802; *Female Advocate* (New Haven, Conn., 1801), 29; *The African Miscellanist; or, A Collection of Essays on the Subject of Negro Slavery* (Trenton, 1802), 32–33; Robinson, *Critical Essays on Phillis Wheatley*, 44; Young, "Marketing a Sable Muse," chap. 3.

344 *satirical broadsides against "bobalition"*: *Boston Commercial Gazette*, June 27, 1811; *Dreadful Riot on Negro Hill!* (Boston, 1827); *Grand Bobalition of Slavery* (Boston, 1819); Waldstreicher, *In the Midst of Perpetual Fetes*, 323–44; Sweet, *Bodies Politic*, 378–80; Minardi, *Making Slavery History*, 108–11; Weyler, *Empowering Words*, 66–73.

345 *Antislavery northerners responded*: Caleb Bingham, *Juvenile Letters; Being a Correspondence Between Children, from Eight to Fifteen Years of Age* (Boston, 1803), 57; Elizabeth McHenry, *Forgotten Readers: Recovering the Lost History of African American Literary Societies* (Durham, N.C., 2002), 97–98, 101; Young, "Marketing a Sable Muse," chap. 4; Tabitha LaShay Joy Lowery, "Early Black Poetry, Social Justice, and Black Children: Receptions of Child Activism in African American Literary History" (PhD diss., West Virginia University, 2020), 9, 30–34, 42; *Liberator*, Feb. 11, 18, 1832, March 22, 1834; Robinson, *Critical Essays on Phillis Wheatley*, 54; "Poems by Phillis Wheatley," *Frederick Douglass's Paper*, Aug. 31, 1855; William W. Banger, "Are the Blacks an Inferior Link in the Chain of Nature?," *Pottsville Miner's Journal*, Dec. 28, 1861; Rachel Walker, "Facing Race: Popular Science and Black Intellectual Thought in Antebellum America," *Early American Studies* 19 (2021): 630–35.

345 *the Massachusetts Historical Society published*: Deane, "Wheatley"; *Bio-bibliography*, 64–66.

345 *Nevertheless, as Reconstruction faded*: Gates, "Phillis Wheatley and the Nature of the Negro," in Robinson, *Critical Essays on Phillis Wheatley*, 215–32; James Parton, "Antipathy to the Negro," *North American Review* 263 (July–Aug. 1878): 69.

346 *Richard T. Greener*: Richard T. Greener, "The Intellectual Position of the Negro," *National Quarterly Review* 81 (July 1880): 164–89.

346 *Wheatley gained a significant place*: *Weekly Louisianan* (New Orleans), Feb. 7, 1880; "Xenian Doings," *Cleveland Gazette*, April 26, 1884; John R. Slattery, "Phillis Wheatley, the Life and Work of a Colored Poetess," *Catholic World*, July 26, 1884; "New London Notes," *New York Freeman*, June 12, 1886; "Local Varieties," *Boston Herald*, Feb. 4, 1887; *Detroit Plaindealer*, March 17, 1893; Charita Elaine Gainey-O'Toole, "'Strange Loomings': Phillis Wheatley and the African American Literary Imagination" (PhD diss., Harvard University, 2017), 21; Kevin K. Gaines, *Uplifting the Race* (Chapel Hill, N.C., 1996); "The Study of Character," *Illinois Record* (Springfield), July 23, 1898.

346 *Black Americans founded reading circles*: "Naming the Schools," *Cleveland Gazette*, Dec. 28, 1890; "Phillis Wheatley Club," *Indianapolis Freeman*, Aug. 20, 1892; "Morton Gleanings," *Philadelphia Tribune*, July 4, 1914; "Old Mississippi," *Chicago Defender*, Aug. 12, 1916; Anne Ruggles Gere, *Intimate Practices: Literacy and Cultural Work in U.S. Women's Clubs, 1880–1920* (Urbana, Ill., 1997), 112–13, 220; McHenry, *Forgotten Readers*, 243–44; Laurie F. Maffly-Kipp, *Setting Down the Sacred Past: African-American Race Histories* (Cambridge, Mass., 2010), 248; *Worcester Daily Spy*, Feb. 3, 1895; "The Phillis Wheatley Club," *New Orleans Times-Picayune*, April 23, 1898; "Greenville, S.C.," "In Public Schools," "Y.W.C.A.," *Baltimore Afro-American*, April 25, 1925, Nov. 6, 1926, July 2, 1927.

347 *Wheatley Clubs spearheaded the establishment*: "Phillis Wheatley Ass'n," *Pittsburgh Courier*, Feb. 14, 1931; "Phyllis Wheatley," *Chicago Defender*, Jan. 14, 1939; James C. Wade III, "Phillis Wheatley Association Celebrates 100 Years of Service," *Cleveland Call & Post*, May 25, 2011; Jane Edna Hunter, *A Nickel and a Prayer* (Cleveland, 1940); *Baltimore Afro-American*, April 15, 1933; Robinson, introduction to *Critical Essays on Phillis Wheatley*, 9; Gates, *Trials of Phillis Wheatley*, 75; Colin Grant, *Negro with a Hat: The Rise and Fall of Marcus Garvey* (New York, 2008), 187, 243, 265, 288, 352. Blyden's great-granddaughter, a historian, is more forgiving, noting that while Wheatley depicts Africa as backward, she never stopped identifying as African. Nemata Amelia Ibitayo Blyden, *African Americans and Africa: A New History* (New Haven, Conn., 2019), 6, 18–19, 74, 87, 210.

347 *Changing tastes in poetry*: "The Negro's Estimate of His Race," *State* (Columbia, S.C.), Oct. 1, 1905; Benjamin Griffin Brawley, "Phillis Wheatley, Negro Poet," *Springfield Republican*, July 3, 1910; *Bio-bibliography*, 86; Robinson, *Critical Essays on Phillis Wheatley*, 7–8, 56, 58–59, 85–87; William Stanley Braithwaite, "The Negro in Literature" (1924) and Wallace Thurman, "Negro Poets and Their Poetry" (1928), in *The New Negro: Readings on Race, Representation, and African-American Culture, 1892–1938*, ed. Henry Louis Gates Jr. and Gene Andrew Jarrett (Princeton, N.J., 2007), 186, 415–17; Gainey-O'Toole, "'Strange Loomings,'" 50–52, 65–66; W. E. B. Du Bois, "Phillis Wheatley and African American Culture," in *The Oxford W. E. B. Du Bois Reader*, ed. Eric J. Sundquist (New York, 1996), 328–42; Jeffrey C. Stewart, *The New Negro: The Life of Alain Locke* (New York, 2018), 526. The condescension persists in some sophisticated versions of the literary history, even those that depend on the insights of feminist scholars. See, for example, Robert Reid-Pharr, *Conjugal Union* (New York, 1999), 3–4; Nicholas T. Rinehart, "Lateral Reading Lyric Testimony; or, The Difficult Miracle of Black Poetry in the Americas," *American Quarterly* 73 (2021): 639–70. For the image of poets and the popularity and variety of audiences for poetry in this period, see Joan Shelley Rubin, *Songs of Ourselves: On the Uses of Poetry in America* (Cambridge, Mass., 2013).

348 *she remained an inspirational figure*: Mary White Ovington, *Phillis Wheatley: A Play* (New York, 1932); Mary Church Terrell, *Phillis Wheatley, a Pageant* (Baltimore, 1933), program in box 21, folder 2, Black Print Culture Collection, Rose Library; Lurana Donnels O'Malley, "'Why I Wrote the Phyllis Wheatley Pageant Play': Mary Church Terrell's Bicentennial Activism," *Theatre History Studies* 37 (2018): 225–55; Graham, *Story of Phillis Wheatley*; Gerald Horne, *Race Woman: The Lives of Shirley Graham Du Bois* (New York, 2000), 104; "Drama Contest to Reveal Life of Phillis Wheatley," "Phillis Wheatley Play-Writing

Contest Wins Top Enthusiasm," "Phillis Wheatley Birthday Observance," *Atlanta Daily World*, Sept. 30, 1951, Feb. 23, April 29, 1952; Marilyn Jensen, *Phillis Wheatley* (Philadelphia, 1987); Ann Rinaldi, *Hang a Thousand Trees with Ribbons* (New York, 1996); Catherine Clinton, *Phillis's Big Test* (Boston, 2008); Afua Cooper, *My Name Is Phillis Wheatley* (Toronto, 2009).

For the persistence of the image of Wheatley "summoned to appear" before the "tribunal," among thoughtful historians, critics, and poets, see for very recent examples Hardesty, *Black Lives, Native Lands, White Worlds*, 124; Jesse McCarthy, *Who Will Pay Reparations on My Soul? Essays* (New York, 2021), 92–93; Jeffers, *Age of Phillis*, 80–82 (who makes doubt about the "trial" her theme yet posits that it might as well have happened); Eve L. Ewing, "Proof [Dear Phillis]," in *The 1619 Project* (New York, 2021), 93–94.

348 *African Americans replayed the gendered drama*: Gates, *Trials of Phillis Wheatley*, 76–81; Randall Robinson, *Defending the Spirit* (New York, 1998), 66; Rajen Persaud, *Why Black Men Love White Women* (New York, 2009), 33–35, 126. For the debate as it emerged among literary critics and in the pages of the magazines like *Phylon*, compare R. Lynn Matson, "Phillis Wheatley—Soul Sister?" (1972), and Terence Collins, "Phillis Wheatley: The Dark Side of the Poetry" (1975), in Robinson, *Critical Essays on Phillis Wheatley*, 113–22, 147–58, as well as one of the first critical studies, Richmond, *Bid the Vassal Soar*, xi–78.

350 *"Phillis was reborn"*: Charlayne Hunter, "Poets Extol a Sister's Unfettered Soul," *New York Times*, Nov. 9, 1973; Luci Horton, "The Legacy of Phillis Wheatley," Margaret Walker Alexander, "A Ballad for Phillis Wheatley," and Naomi Long Madgett, "Phillis," *Ebony*, March 1974, 94–97; Dana Murphy, "Praisesong for Margaret Walker's Jubilee and the Phillis Wheatley Poetry Festival," *African American Review* 53 (2020): 299–313; Gainey-O'Toole, "'Strange Loomings,'" 128, 139; Gloria T. Hull, "Black Women Poets from Wheatley to Walker," *Negro American Literature Forum* 9 (1975): 91–92; Alice Walker, *In Search of Our Mothers' Gardens* (San Diego, 1983), 235–37, 243; Jordan, "The Difficult Miracle of Black Poetry in America"; June Jordan, "Something Like a Sonnet for Phillis Miracle Wheatley," in *The Essential June Jordan*, ed. Jan Heller Levi and Christoph Keller (Port Townsend, Wash., 2021), 168; "Oh Freedom! Elizabeth Catlett," Smithsonian American Art Museum, www.americanart.si.edu /education/oh-freedom/elizabeth-catlett.

For just a sample of feminist scholars who followed up on these insights into Wheatley as a "major black presence" and a "person of ideas," see Sondra O'Neale, "Challenge to Wheatley's Critics: There Was No Other 'Game' in Town," *Journal of Negro Education* 54 (1985): 500–511; Jennifer Bernhardt Steedman et al., "Archive Survival Guide: Practical and Theoretical Approaches for the Next Century of Women's Studies Research," *Legacy* 19 (2002): 233; Mia Bay et al., introduction to *Toward an Intellectual History of Black Women*, 9–10; and Freund, "Phillis Wheatley, a Public Intellectual," 35–52.

350 *In our time, Black poets*: Gainey-O'Toole, "'Strange Loomings,'" chap. 4; Kevin Young, "Homage to Phillis Wheatley," in *Blue Laws: Selected and Uncollected Poems, 1995–2015* (New York, 2016), 313–32; Yusef Komunyakaa, "Séance," *Callaloo* 24 (2001): 1070–71; Rowan Ricardo Phillips, "Homage to Mistress Wheatley," in *A Companion to African-American Studies*, ed. Jane Anna Gordon and Lewis Gordon (Malden, Mass., 2006), 171–79; James E. Ford III, "The Difficult Miracle: Reading Phillis Wheatley Against the Master's Discourse," *Centennial Review* 18 (2018): 181–223; Alexis Pauline Gumbs, "What She Did

Not Say," in *Spill: Scenes of Black Feminist Fugitivity* (Durham, N.C., 2018), 61–73; Jeffers, *Age of Phillis*; Alison C. Rollins, "Phillis Wheatley Takes the Turing Test," *American Poetry Review* 50 (May–June 2021): 29; David Mills, "Jupiter & Wheatley's Suite," *Boneyarn* (Ashland, Ohio, 2021), 57–68. See or hear also Charles Johnson, "Poetry and Politics," in *Soulcatcher and Other Stories* (New York, 2001), 25–32, and Amanda Kemp's wonderful plays: *Phillis Wheatley: From Africa to America and Beyond* and *To Cross an Ocean Four Centuries Long,* www.amandakemp.bandcamp.com/album/phillis-wheatley-from-africa -to-america-and-beyond.

351 *"When they tell you"*: Jesse Lemisch, "Author's Postscript," in *In Search of Early America: The William and Mary Quarterly, 1943–1993* (Williamsburg, Va., 1993), 137; Young, *Liberty Tree*, 7–19; Waldstreicher, "Anonymous Wheatley."

353 *"love of freedom"*: PW to Occom, Feb. 11, 1774, in *CWC*, 153. For slavery and freedom as "joined at the hip," see Nathan Irvin Huggins, "The Deforming Mirror of Truth," *Revelations: American History, American Myths* (New York, 1995), 275.

ACKNOWLEDGMENTS

Late in the previous century, down Route 7A from Robert Frost's house in Shaftsbury, Vermont, colleagues at Bennington College rekindled a younger man's interest in poetry. Stephen Sandy's farewell gift of his "Moving Out" resonated through several subsequent moves: "You never know to what your knowing tends / and move uncertainly to certain ends." Perhaps Anne Winters will hear echoes of "The Displaced of Capital," and Steven Cramer of his "Villanelle After a Burial." Their words and their sympathies have stayed with me. Edward Hoagland, too, with his kindness and his tolerance for eccentricity, made me want to keep thinking about New England's ironies, the lives of travelers, and their struggles to say what they're meant to say.

I wrote paragraphs about Wheatley in two previous books, but the idea for this one came out of the classroom, at Temple University, where students in "The Literature of Slavery" debated Wheatley's stance on slavery in "On Being Brought from Africa to America," inspiring me to stand up and read it aloud twice, in different voices. I don't think it would have been the same over Zoom. Joshua Stefel won a College of Liberal Arts grant to collaborate with me as a research assistant during the next semester, and his enthusiastic and conscientious work on the memory of Wheatley influenced the arc of the story here. Much later, at the CUNY Graduate Center, Israel Ben-Porat helped with Wheatley's use of the Hebrew Bible, as have our subsequent conversations about ancient texts in modern worlds. Hamilton Craig proofread and discussed with a winning combination of humility and piercing intelligence.

The late and deeply missed Alfred F. Young was a crucial early sounding board and inspiration, cheering me on, walking me around the Boston Freedom Trail, and editing my first essay on the topic. Al urged me to find Phillis on the streets of Boston. Carla L. Peterson also provided early assurance that my approach would be distinctive and valued; coming from her, this meant a great deal. Equally memorable conversations with Ronald Bailey, John Bezís-Selfa, Tara Bynum, Betsy Erkkila, François Furstenberg, Amanda Kemp, Sarah Knott, Harvey Neptune, Phillip M. Richards, Jacqueline Robinson, Andrew Schocket, Nora Slonimsky, Kariann Yokota, and as always the honorary New Yorker Shane White kept me going. My wonderful colleagues at the Graduate Center, Herman Bennett, Benjamin Carp, Cathy Davidson, Duncan Faherty, and James Oakes, also pointed out paths and provided encouragement. On reading an early essay, Duncan asked, "Where are the poems? Are you going to read the poems?" It was the right question, and the book is the answer. If it was too much poetry for you, please blame Duncan. In 2010 and then again in 2021, self-described "historian without a license" Vincent Carretta asked what I had discovered in the archives, which certainly kept me on my toes. His careful scholarship did much more, and I must thank him for his broad shoulders.

Andrew Burstein and Nancy Isenberg have been my most reliable, sympathetic, yet exacting readers of drafts, Andy on style, Nancy on interpretation, both on process: no one could ask for sharper eyes, or more loyal friends. Ben Carp, Woody Holton, Matthew Mason, Michael Meranze, Jim Oakes, Gunther Peck, David Reynolds, and Eric Slauter read and critiqued drafts of the full manuscript with great care and timeliness. At the GC, the Politics, Early America and Culture reading group of Arinn Amer, Alexander Gambaccini, Miriam Liebman, and John Winters and the student-run Early American Republic Seminar workshopped multiple chapters over the past several years: what a boon and a joy to have students, including Jessica Rose Georges, Ted Knudsen, Madeline

Lafuse, Andrew Lang, and Helena Yoo Roth, transform so quickly into colleagues. Audiences at the annual conferences of the Association for the Study of African American Life and History, the Society for Historians of the Early American Republic, the Sons of the American Revolution, Indiana University, Lehigh University, Iona College and the Institute for Thomas Paine Studies, the Columbia Early American History seminar, the Washington Area Early American seminar, the McNeil Center for Early American Studies, the Omohundro Institute of Early American History and Culture, Michael Zuckerman's salon, Steven Hahn's Interdisciplinary Workshop in the Global Nineteenth Century at New York University, Steve Pincus's British and Imperial History Workshop at the University of Chicago, and Tara Bynum's OI Coffeetable also helped with their tough, good questions. In two SHEAR biography workshops, Monica Najar, Paul Quigley, Amy Speckart, and Tamara Plakins Thornton provided rigorous writerly feedback: thanks also to Craig Thompson Friend for making those workshops happen. Individual chapters and papers also benefited from written comments by Jason Ahlenius, John Blanton, Amy Chazkel, Liz Covart, Aston Gonzalez, the late Rhys Isaac, Catherine E. Kelly, Harvey Neptune, Thomas Richards Jr., Gunja Sengupta, Nora Slonimsky, Kirsten Sword, and Nicholas Wood.

At the beginning and end I was lucky enough to have great editors at FSG. Thomas LeBien made me ambitious about this project, ironically after insisting that I be quick and concise in the previous one. We didn't know that it would set me back so many years, but I believe he was right once again. Not least because taking so long netted me Alexander Star, who lived up to his phenomenal reputation. Ian Van Wye thoughtfully shepherded me through a publication process that has advanced technologically since my last time. Ingrid Sterner proved to be the kind of copy editor authors dream of, or would if they knew.

I had many reasons to think about childhood, about family, about women, about voice, and about loss as I researched and wrote these pages. Kim Waldstreicher (1970–2011), my sister, modeled precocious wit, kindness, and generosity of spirit: we won't forget. My brother Jeff walked with me through it all, more dependable than the train lines and cell phones that connect us between Philly, the city, and the island. Without Jacqueline Robinson, I may never have dared this project, or the shape it ultimately took; I can only hope it lives up to the wisdom she showed while I was writing it. Jackie, Maya, and Moses were always there astounding me with their eloquence, depth, embrace of life, and consistent refusals of nonsense. They made what Wheatley did as a teenager seem believable and that much more important.

Blanche S. Waldstreicher (1937–2016) taught by example what poetry can do and so was the greatest influence on this work, all the way to one of the last things she wrote, for a writer's workshop at the Saddle Brooke Institute for Learning in Retirement that she and my father, Joel, helped create: "Don't ask how I died: ask how I lived." Now that I think I understand something I failed to ask her about—why the two oldest volumes in the house were the works of William Cowper and Robert Bloomfield—I wish we could talk about it, but I know that she believed that while I can still hear her voice, she is still listening.

> *As long as the river runs into the ocean*
> *As long as the shadows pass over the hollows in the mountains*
> *And the sky feeds the stars,*
> *Your charm, your name, your actions*
> *Will remain with me forever, wherever I may be.*

(From book 1 of Virgil's *Aeneid*, translation by Blanche Brussel, ca. 1954)

INDEX